PRINT AND PUBLIC POLITICS IN THE ENGLISH REVOLUTION

This is a major reassessment of the communications revolution of the seventeenth century. Using a wealth of archival evidence and the considerable output of the press, Jason Peacey demonstrates how new media – from ballads to pamphlets and newspapers – transformed the English public's ability to understand and participate in national political life. He analyses how contemporaries responded to political events as consumers of print; explores what they were able to learn about national politics; and examines how they developed the ability to appropriate a variety of print genres in order to participate in novel ways. Amid structural change and conjunctural upheaval, he argues that there occurred a dramatic re-shaping of the political nation, as citizens from all walks of life developed new habits and practices for engaging in daily political life, and for protecting and advancing their interests. This ultimately involved experience-led attempts to rethink the nature of representation and accountability.

JASON PEACEY is Senior Lecturer in British History at University College London, and is also a Fellow of the Royal Historical Society. His previous monograph, *Politicians and Pamphleteers: Propaganda During the English Civil Wars and Interregnum* (2004) was *proxime accesit* for the Royal Historical Society Whitfield Prize.

Own (?)

CAMBRIDGE STUDIES IN EARLY MODERN BRITISH HISTORY

SERIES EDITORS

JOHN MORRILL
Professor of British and Irish History, University of Cambridge,
and Fellow of Selwyn College

ETHAN SHAGAN
Professor of History, University of California, Berkeley

ALEXANDRA WALSHAM
Professor of Modern History, University of Cambridge,
and Fellow of Trinity College

This is a series of monographs and studies covering many aspects of the history of the British Isles between the late fifteenth century and the early eighteenth century. It includes the work of established scholars and pioneering work by a new generation of scholars. It includes both reviews and revisions of major topics and books which open up new historical terrain or which reveal startling new perspectives on familiar subjects. All the volumes set detailed research within broader perspectives, and the books are intended for the use of students as well as of their teachers.

For a list of titles in the series go to:
www.cambridge.org/earlymodernbritishhistory

PRINT AND PUBLIC POLITICS IN THE ENGLISH REVOLUTION

JASON PEACEY

CAMBRIDGE
UNIVERSITY PRESS

2013

CAMBRIDGE
UNIVERSITY PRESS

University Printing House, Cambridge CB2 8BS, United Kingdom

Cambridge University Press is part of the University of Cambridge.

It furthers the University's mission by disseminating knowledge in the pursuit of education, learning and research at the highest international levels of excellence.

www.cambridge.org
Information on this title: www.cambridge.org/9781107044425

© Jason Peacey 2013

First published 2013

A catalogue record for this publication is available from the British Library

ISBN 978-1-107-04442-5 Hardback

For Annette, who has waited too long for this and for much else.

'the things common to all men are more important than the things peculiar to any men. Ordinary things are more valuable than extraordinary things; nay, they are more extraordinary'.

G. K. Chesterton

Contents

Acknowledgements

This is a long book that took a long time to complete, and it is a great pleasure to be able to acknowledge the many debts that I have incurred. I would like to express profound gratitude to dozens of librarians and archivists for their assistance and tolerance, in the face of awkward enquiries and excessive ordering. I am particularly grateful to the Folger Shakespeare Library, the Huntington Library and the Beinecke Library, each of which facilitated my research with short-term fellowships, and to librarians at the Houghton Library, Duke University, the New York Public Library, Columbia University, the American Antiquarian Society, Cambridge University and Worcester College, Oxford. I would like to thank a number of private archives for granting me permission to cite their material: the Duke of Northumberland; the Duke of Norfolk; the Duke of Beaufort; the Duke of Devonshire; the Marquess of Salisbury; the Marquess of Bath; Viscount De L'Isle and Dudley; Sir Richard Carew-Pole; the Worshipful Company of Goldsmiths; the Worshipful Company of Stationers; the Lamport Hall Preservation Trust; as well as Sir Edmund Ralph Verney, Bt. I also want to express my gratitude to UCL (for research leave), and to the AHRC (for a grant which enabled me to tour English local archives). Among academic colleagues, I would like to thank my editors at Cambridge University Press for immensely constructive advice, and all those who have offered encouragement and references: Phil Baker, Andrew Barclay, Sabrina Baron, Lloyd Bowen, Mike Braddick, Manfred Brod, Bill Bulman, Norah Carlin, Ben Coates, Tom Cogswell, David Como, David Cressy, Richard Cust, Barbara Donagan, Jackie Eales, Joel Halcomb, David Hayton, Simon Healy, Andy Hopper, Ann Hughes, Peter Lake, Vivienne Larminie, Tom Leng, Patrick Little, Charles Littleton, David Magliocco, Allan Macinnes, Angela McShane, Sears McGee, Michael Mendle, John Miller, Steve Pincus, Tim Reinke-Williams, Gary Rivett, Stephen Roberts, Ian Roy, David Scott, Bill Sherman, Peter Stallybrass, Laura Stewart, Elliot Vernon and John Walter, as well as the late Peter Lindenbaum, who is sadly missed.

The three people who have done most to keep me on my intellectual toes, however, are Alex Barber, Chris Kyle and Noah Millstone. Our conversations have not always been entirely sober, but they have always been valuable, and it's hard not to think that the two things are related. Finally, I want to thank a bunch of people for keeping my feet firmly on the ground, including Martin Naylor, Duncan Peebles, Alasdair Ford, Adrian Ward and John Gibson. Like others, they have been nagging me to finish this book, but they also make sure that I realize there are more important things in life. Which obviously brings me to Annette, a much more important thing in my life, who has suffered unduly at its hands.

Abbreviations

Where footnotes contain citations to more than one manuscript from within a particular archive, these will be placed after the relevant abbreviation for the archive followed by a colon, and will be separated by semi-colons.

Add.	Additional Manuscript
AHR	*American Historical Review*
All Souls	All Souls College, Oxford
Alnwick	Alnwick Castle, Northumberland
Al. Oxon.	*Alumni Oxoniensis*, ed. J. Foster (4 vols., Oxford, 1891–2)
Andrew Hay Diary	*The Diary of Andrew Hay of Craignethan*, ed. A. Reid (Scottish History Society, 39, 1901)
Antony	Antony House, Cornwall
APC	*Acts of the Privy Council*
Arundel	Arundel Castle, Sussex
Badminton	Badminton House, Gloucestershire
Baillie	*The Letters and Journals of Robert Baillie*, ed. D. Laing (3 vols., Edinburgh, 1841–2)
Bethlem	Bethlem Royal Hospital Archives, Beckenham, Kent
Beinecke	Beinecke Library, Yale University
BIHR	*Bulletin of the Institute of Historical Research*
Birch, *Charles*	*The Court and Times of Charles the First*, ed. T. Birch (2 vols., London, 1848)
Birch, *James*	*The Court and Times of James the First*, ed. T. Birch (2 vols., London, 1848)

BJL	Brynmor Jones Library, University of Hull
BJRL	*Bulletin of the John Rylands Library*
BL	British Library, London
BLR	*Bodleian Library Record*
Bodl.	Bodleian Library, Oxford
Book of Examinations	*The Book of Examinations, 1622–1644*, ed. R. Anderson (Southampton Record Society, 1936)
Borough of Leicester	*Records of the Borough of Leicester*, ed. H. Stocks (Cambridge, 1923)
Burton Diary	*The Diary of Thomas Burton*, ed. J. Rutt (4 vols., London, 1828)
Cam. Soc.	Camden Society
Cary, *Memorials*	*Memorials of the Great Civil War*, ed. H. Cary (2 vols., London, 1842)
CCA	Canterbury Cathedral Archives, Kent
CCC	*Calendar of the Proceedings of the Committee for Compounding*, ed. M. Green (5 vols., London, 1889–92)
CCL	Canterbury Cathedral Library, Canterbury
CCSP	*Calendar of the Clarendon State Papers*, ed. W. Macray et al. (5 vols., Oxford, 1872–1970)
CD 1621	*Commons Debates 1621*, ed. W. Notestein et al. (7 vols., New Haven, 1935)
Chatsworth	Chatsworth House, Derbyshire
Chequers	Chequers Court, Buckinghamshire
CHB IV	*The Cambridge History of the Book in Britain. Volume IV*, ed. J. Barnard and D. McKenzie (Cambridge, 2002)
CHC	Coventry History Centre, Coventry
'Cheney Culpeper'	'The letters of Sir Cheney Culpeper', ed. M. Braddick and M. Greengrass', in *Seventeenth Century Political and Financial Papers* (Camden Society, 5th series, 7, 1996)
Chetham	Chetham's Library, Manchester
Chirk Accounts	*Chirk Castle Accounts, A.D. 1605–1666*, ed. W. Myddleton (St Albans, 1908)
CJ	*Commons Journal*

CKS	Centre for Kentish Studies, Maidstone
Clarendon	E. Hyde, Earl of Clarendon, *The History of the Rebellion and Civil Wars in England*, ed. W. Macray (6 vols., Oxford, 1888)
Clarendon, *Life*	*The Life of Edward, Earl of Clarendon* (3 vols., Oxford, 1827)
Claydon	Claydon House, Buckinghamshire
CLRO	Corporation of London Record Office, London
Cobbett	*Cobbett's Parliamentary History of England* (36 vols., London, 1806–20)
Columbia	Rare Book and Manuscript Library, Columbia University, New York
Cooper, *Annals*	C. Cooper, *Annals of Cambridge* (5 vols., Cambridge, 1892–1908)
CP	*The Clarke Papers*, ed. C. Firth (4 vols., Camden Society, new series, 49, 54, 61–2, 1899–1901)
Crosfield	*The Diary of Thomas Crosfield*, ed. F. Boas (London, 1935)
CSPD	*Calendar of State Papers Domestic*
CSPV	*Calendar of State Papers Venetian*
CUA	Cambridge University Archives, Cambridge
CUL	Cambridge University Library
D'Ewes Autobiography	*The Autobiography and Correspondence of Sir Simonds D'Ewes*, ed. J. Halliwell (2 vols., London, 1845)
D'Ewes, ed. Coates	*The Journal of Sir Simonds D'Ewes*, ed. W. Coates (New Haven, 1942)
D'Ewes, ed. Notestein	*The Journal of Sir Simonds D'Ewes*, ed. W. Notestein (New Haven, 1923)
Devon Accounts	*Devon Household Accounts, 1627–59*, ed. T. Gray (2 vols., Devon and Cornwall Record Society, 1995–6)
Diary of John Evelyn	*The Diary of John Evelyn*, ed. E. De Beer (6 vols., Oxford, 1955)

Diary of John Harington	*The Diary of John Harington, MP, 1645–53*, ed. M. Steig (Somerset Record Society, 74, 1977)
DRO	Derbyshire Record Office, Matlock
Duppa Corr.	*The Correspondence of Bishop Brian Duppa*, ed. G. Isham (Northamptonshire Record Society, 17, 1951)
Earwaker	*The Constables' Accounts of the Manor of Manchester*, ed. J. Earwaker (2 vols., Manchester, 1892)
EcHR	*Economic History Review*
Eg.	Egerton Manuscript, British Library
EHR	*English Historical Review*
EKRO	East Kent Record Office, Dover
Ellis, 'Letters'	H. Ellis, 'Letters from a subaltern officer', *Archaeologia*, 35 (1853)
ERO	Essex Record Office, Chelmsford
ESRO	East Sussex Record Office, Lewes
Fairfax Corr.	*The Fairfax Correspondence*, ed. G. Johnson (2 vols., London, 1848)
Flemings in Oxford	*The Flemings in Oxford*, ed. J. Magrath (Oxfordshire Historical Society, 44, 1904)
Fox, *Oral and Literate*	A. Fox, *Oral and Literate Culture in England, 1500–1700* (Oxford, 2001)
FSL	Folger Shakespeare Library, Washington DC
Gangraena	T. Edwards. *Gangraena* (London, 1646)
Giles Moore	*Journal of Giles Moore*, ed. R. Bird (Sussex Record Society, 68, 1971)
GL	Guildhall Library, London
GMRO	Greater Manchester Record Office, Manchester
Goldsmiths	The Worshipful Company of Goldsmiths, London
Greg, *Companion*	W. Greg, *A Companion to Arber* (Oxford, 1967)
Harl.	Harleian Manuscript, British Library

Harris, *London Crowds*	T. Harris, *London Crowds in the Reign of Charles II* (Cambridge, 1987)
Hatfield	Hatfield House, Hertfordshire
Hatton Corr.	*Correspondence of the Family of Hatton*, ed. E. Thompson (Camden Society, new series, 22–3, 1878)
Hayton, *Commons*	D. Hayton et al., *The House of Commons, 1690–1715* (5 vols., Cambridge, 2002)
HEH	Henry E. Huntington Library, San Marino, California
HJ	*Historical Journal*
HLQ	*Huntington Library Quarterly*
HMC	*Historical Manuscripts Commission*
Houghton	Houghton Library, Harvard University
HR	*Historical Research*
Hughes and Larkin	*Tudor Royal Proclamations*, ed. P. Hughes and J. Larkin (3 vols., New Haven, 1964–9)
HWJ	*History Workshop Journal*
IWCRO	Isle of Wight County Record Office, Newport
'James Master'	'The expense book of James Master', ed. S. Robertson, *Archaeologia Cantiana*, 15–18 (1883–9)
Jansson	*Proceedings in the Opening Session of the Long Parliament*, ed. M. Jansson (7 vols., Rochester, New York, 2000–2007)
JBS	*Journal of British Studies*
JEccH	*Journal of Ecclesiastical History*
JHI	*Journal of the History of Ideas*
JMH	*Journal of Modern History*
Josselin Diary	*The Diary of Ralph Josselin, 1616–1683*, ed. A. Macfarlane (Oxford, 1991)
JRL	John Rylands Library, Manchester
Juxon	*The Journal of Thomas Juxon*, ed. K. Lindley and D. Scott (Camden Society, 5th series, 13, 1999)
Knights, *Opinion*	M. Knights, *Politics and Opinion in Crisis* (Cambridge, 1994)

Knights, *Representation*	M. Knights, *Representation and Misrepresentation in Later Stuart Britain* (Oxford, 2004)
Knyvett	*The Knyvett Letters, 1620–1644*, ed. B. Schofield (Norfolk Record Society, 20, 1949)
Lans.	Lansdowne Manuscript, British Library
Larkin and Hughes	*Stuart Royal Proclamations*, ed. J. Larkin and P. Hughes (2 vols., Oxford, 1973–83)
Larking, *Proceedings*	*Proceedings, Principally in the County of Kent*, ed. L. Larking (Camden Society, 80, 1862)
Laud, *Works*	*The Works of the Most Reverend Father in God, William Laud* (7 vols., New York, 1975)
'Lewis Dyve'	'The Tower of London letter-book of Sir Lewis Dyve, 1646–7', ed. H. Tibbutt, in *Publications of the Bedfordshire Historical Record Society*, 38 (1958)
Life of Dugdale	*Life, Diary and Correspondence of Sir William Dugdale*, ed. Hamper (London, 1827)
LJ	*Lords Journal*
LMA	London Metropolitan Archives
Locke Corr.	*Correspondence of John Locke*, ed. E. De Beer (8 vols., Oxford, 1976)
Londino-Batavae	*Ecclesiae Londino-Batavae Archivum*, ed. J. Hessels (3 vols. in 4, Cambridge, 1887–97)
Longleat	Longleat House, Wiltshire
LPL	Lambeth Palace Library, London
Ludlow Memoirs	*Memoirs of Edmund Ludlow*, ed. C. Firth (2 vols., Oxford, 1894)
Luke Journal	*The Journal of Sir Samuel Luke*, ed. I. Phillip (Oxfordshire Record Society, 29, 31, 33, 1950–3)
Luke Letter Books	*The Letter Books of Sir Samuel Luke*, ed. H. Tibbutt (Bedfordshire Historical Record Society, 42, 1963)

Mdx County Recs	*Middlesex County Records. Volume III*, ed. J. Jeaffreson (Middlesex County Record Society, 1888)
Montereul	*The Diplomatic Correspondence of Jean de Montereul*, ed. J. Fotheringham (2 vols., Edinburgh, 1898)
MP	Main Papers (Parliamentary Archives)
Nalson	J. Nalson, *An Impartial Collection of the Great Affairs of State* (2 vols., London, 1682–3)
NLS	National Library of Scotland, Edinburgh
NLW	National Library of Wales, Aberystwyth
NP	*The Nicholas Papers*, ed. G. Warner (4 vols., Camden Society, new series, 40, 50, 57 and third series, 31, 1886–1920)
OBS	Oxford Bibliographical Society
OPH	*The Parliamentary or Constitutional History of England* (24 vols., London, 1761–3)
ORS	Oxfordshire Record Society
OUA	Oxford University Archives, Bodleian Library, Oxford
Oxinden and Peyton Letters	*The Oxinden and Peyton Letters, 1642–1670*, ed. D. Gardiner (London, 1937)
Oxinden Letters	*The Oxinden Letters, 1607–1642*, ed. D. Gardiner (London, 1933)
P&P	*Past and Present*
PA	Parliamentary Archives, Westminster
Penshurst	Penshurst Place, Kent
Pepys Diary	*The Diary of Samuel Pepys*, ed. R. Latham and W. Matthews (11 vols., London, 1970–83)
PER	*Parliaments, Estates and Representation*
PH	*Parliamentary History*
PJ	*The Private Journals of the Long Parliament*, ed. W. Coates et al. (3 vols., New Haven, 1982–92)
Proceedings 1614	*Proceedings in Parliament 1614*, ed. M. Jansson (Philadelphia, 1988)
Rawl.	Rawlinson

RO	record office
Rolls of Freemen	*The Rolls of Freemen of the City of Chester*, ed. J. Bennett (2 vols., Record Society of Lancashire and Cheshire, 1906–8)
Rous Diary	*Diary of John Rous*, ed. M. Green (Camden Society, 66, 1856)
RS	Record Society
RSLC	Record Society of Lancashire and Cheshire
Rugg	*The Diurnal of Thomas Rugg, 1659–1661*, ed. W. Sachse (Camden Society, 3rd series, 91, 1961)
Rushworth	J. Rushworth, *Historical Collections of Private Passages of State* (8 vols., London, 1721–2)
Salusbury Corr.	*Calendar of Salusbury Correspondence, 1553–c.1700*, ed. W. Smith (Cardiff, 1954)
Salt Library	William Salt Library, Stafford
SB	*Studies in Bibliography*
SHC	Surrey History Centre, Woking
SHL	Senate House Library, University of London
Spalding, *Memorialls*	J. Spalding, *Memorialls of the Troubles in Scotland and England* (2 vols., Aberdeen, 1850–1)
SR	*Statutes of the Realm*
SRO	Scottish Record Office, Edinburgh
SRS	Scottish Record Society
SS	Surtees Society
Stat. Co.	The Worshipful Company of Stationers, London
STC	A. Pollard and G. Redgrave, *A Short Title Catalogue of Books Printed in England. . . 1475–1640* (3 vols., London, 1976–1991)
SUL	Sheffield University Library
Sydney Papers	*Sydney Papers*, ed. R. Blencowe (London, 1825)
Tatton Park	Tatton Park, Knutsford, Cheshire
TCD	Trinity College Dublin

THSLC	Transactions of the Historical Society of Lancashire and Cheshire
TNA	The National Archives, Kew
TRHS	*Transactions of the Royal Historical Society*
TSANHS	Transactions of the Shropshire Archaeological and Natural History Society
TSAS	Transactions of the Shropshire Archaeological Society
TSP	*A Collection of the State Papers of John Thurloe*, ed. T. Birch (7 vols., London, 1742)
Tudor Constitutional Documents	*Tudor Constitutional Documents*, ed. J. Tanner (Cambridge, 1951)
TWAS	Tyne and Wear Archives Service, Newcastle
'Twysden narrative'	Sir Roger Twysden, 'An historical narrative', *Archaeologia Cantiana*, 1–4 (1858–61)
UCL	University College London
UL	University Library
Vaughan, *Protectorate*	*The Protectorate of Oliver Cromwell*, ed. R. Vaughan, 2 vols., London, 1839)
Verney Notes	*Verney Papers. Notes of Proceedings in the Long Parliament*, ed. J. Bruce (Camden Society, 31, 1845)
Walker Revised	A. Matthews, *Walker Revised* (Oxford, 1988)
Whitelocke Diary	*The Diary of Bulstrode Whitelocke, 1605–1675*, ed. R. Spalding (Oxford, 1990)
Whiteway	*William Whiteway of Dorchester* (Dorset Record Society, 12, 1991)
Wing	D. Wing et al., *Short-Title Catalogue of Books Printed in England. . . 1641–1700* (5 vols., New York, 1972–94)
Wood, *Life and Times*	*The Life and Times of Anthony Wood*, ed. A. Clark (5 vols., Oxford, 1891)
Worcester College	Worcester College, Oxford

WYAS	West Yorkshire Archive Service
York Depositions	*Depositions from the Castle of York*, ed. J. Raine (Surtees Society, 40, 1861)
Yorkshire Diaries	*Yorkshire Diaries and Autobiographies in the Seventeenth and Eighteenth Centuries* (2 vols., Surtees Society, 65, 77, 1877–86)

Citing pamphlets and newsbooks

In order to keep footnotes manageable, abbreviated references have been given for seventeenth-century pamphlets and newsbooks. Pamphlets are cited with a short title and author's surname (where appropriate), followed by the publication date and a standard bibliographical reference. Material that is not listed in these reference works is given a short title and is preceded by an archival reference. Newsbooks are likewise cited with short titles, and with standard bibliographical references from C. Nelson and M. Seccombe, *British Newspapers and Periodicals, 1641–1700* (New York, 1987).

Introduction

To anyone who witnessed the extraordinary events of the English Revolution, it was hard not to conclude that there were two spectres haunting public life. The first was a new intensity to public interest in parliament and its business; and the second was that this was linked to developments in print culture. It is these observations that provide the foundation for this book, and that suggest avenues of enquiry which historians have only rarely pursued. The pamphlets and newspapers of the Civil War era have obviously figured prominently in modern scholarship, but attention has tended to focus on the *nature* and *content* of such material. Historians have been preoccupied by their value as evidence about the events of Civil War and revolution, about the strengths and weaknesses of successive regimes to control and exploit the press, and about the ideas and characters of their authors and publishers. Print has tended to be seen, in other words, as providing the key to understanding the period's extraordinary creativity and experimentation, in terms of the collapse of censorship, the increasingly sophisticated use of 'propaganda' to manipulate public opinion and the emergence of a 'public sphere' of political debate.[1] What has less obviously been explored is the *impact* that such material had on political culture and the lives of ordinary citizens. This book represents an attempt to take up this challenge, and its aim is to assess how print affected political processes and practices; how it influenced the attitudes and behaviour of contemporaries; and how it helped to transform the nature and shape of the political nation. The aim of this introduction is to set out the book's methodology and arguments (section III), and to situate it historiographically (section II), but it begins by discussing the shock with which contemporary observers encountered a new political mood and novel

---

[1] J. Raymond, *Pamphlets and Pamphleteering in Early Modern England* (Cambridge, 2003); J. Raymond, *The Invention of the Newspaper* (Oxford, 1996); J. Peacey, *Politicians and Pamphleteers* (Aldershot, 2004); M. Braddick, *God's Fury, England's Fire* (London, 2008).

political texts, and the ways in which they sought to connect the two phenomena.

i Contemporary reactions to print and 'popular' politics

That political culture was taking a popular turn in the mid seventeenth century seemed clear from both extraordinary episodes and everyday life. Parliamentary elections, for example, became notably febrile and quite often disorderly. The Kent election for the Long Parliament saw an unusually large crowd, and amid the clamour to ensure that voters' preferences were recorded, the walls of the 'shire house' were 'broken down'. Elections at Maldon and Sandwich witnessed interventions by 'a rabble', with the 'commonalty' assembling 'in a tumultuous manner . . . without any authority, warrant or command'. A 'tumultuous rabble' also appeared at Newport (Isle of Wight) in 1645, where the 'scum of the town' were 'apt for a mutiny' and sought to 'awe the freeholders in their election'.[2] More generally, England's middling sort, and even its lower orders – including yeomen, husbandmen, and servants, and tradesmen from cutlers to worsted combers – were thought to have become 'bold talkers'. They were sensible of their grievances and clamorous for news, and they were willing and able to discuss political and religious affairs in an argumentative fashion, and in ways that led to high language and bitter divisions – in private houses, in drinking establishments and in the streets. All too often such scenes became 'tumultuous' and boiled over into festivities that bordered on disorder, not least as the 'multitude' demanded new and 'free' parliaments, amid bonfires, bell-ringing and shouting.[3]

Struck by this intense public engagement with parliament and current affairs, contemporaries sought to understand how it had come about, and very often they emphasized the role of cheap print. Recognizing what historians have subsequently described as the 'print revolution', in other words, their critical gaze focused on the emergence of political and religious pamphleteering and news reporting, and on the undermining of the *arcana imperii*. Although some contemporaries regarded such material as little more than 'bum fodder', many others were less sanguine and were fearful

---

[2] CKS, U47/57/O1, p. 15; FSL, W.b.600, p. 132; EKRO, Sa/AC7, fos. 366, 367v; PA, MP 24 Nov. 1645; BL, Add. 70005, fos. 174–7v; *Proceedings*, 599.250, p. 3968.

[3] Aberdeen UL, MS 2538/1, fos. 33v, 44; Birch, *Charles*, i. 130; BL: Eg. 2536, fo. 443; Add. 38855, fo. 56; Add. 70106, fo. 164; Add. 70110, fo. 74; Add. 78194, fo. 66; Add. 78221, fos. 98–v; *HMC 2nd Report*, p. 47; *Rugg*, p. 39; *Civicus*, 298.084, p. 769; Devon RO: ECA Book 63, fos. 380–v, 391; ECA Book 64, fos. 6v–7, 8v, 20v; Worcs. RO, BA1714, p. 714; Bodl. MS Tanner 65, fo. 278.

about the effect of cheap print. In some senses, of course, such fear had obviously been evident for many decades. A 1586 Star Chamber decree described the 'abuses and enormities' of an unregulated printing industry, and James I bemoaned the 'disorderly printing, uttering and dispersing' of 'seditious, schismatical and scandalous books and pamphlets'. James sought to restrict access to the 'corantos' (newsbooks) that emerged during the Thirty Years' War, and he protested about the 'great inconveniences' that were caused by 'seditious, popish and puritanical books'. He became concerned that authors of cheap literature were 'traducing . . . religion and the state', and his concerns were later echoed very clearly by his son, Charles I.[4] This hostility, moreover, was also echoed in popular discourse. A tract called *A Scourge for Paper-Persecutors* complained about 'a confused world of trumpery', and about 'infectious swarms' of 'guilty sheets' that could be observed 'walking in the streets'. It was also noted that 'each wall and public post' was 'defiled' by the 'cuckoos of our times'. However, such attacks became much more prevalent when the collapse of censorship in 1641 heralded ever larger waves of cheap print. Divines of all persuasions grumbled about 'the late overflowing of the presses', and about living in a 'scribbling age' when 'so many needless, useless, senseless pamphlets come every day sweating from the press'. They bemoaned the prevalence of 'gall and bitterness and devilish calumnies', and they likened pamphlets to 'a swarm of locusts' that had ascended from Hell, 'so grossly scurrilous, malicious, and contumelious'. Even Civil War journalists expressed wonder that more care was not taken to suppress 'dangerous books', which were 'enough to put the world into a combustion'.[5]

The foundations of such hostility were fairly clear. First, print was thought to threaten royal authority, and pamphleteers were considered to be 'state meddlers' and 'busy fellows' who 'peer into the art of our government'.[6] Secondly, cheap print was thought to have displaced scholarship with trivialities and lies, as learned works were supplanted by pamphlets that were 'new and old in six days', and by 'lascivious, idle and unprofitable books, pamphlets, playbooks and ballads'. Such material, it was claimed, led to 'the increase of all vice, and withdrawing people from studying, reading and

---

[4] *Tudor Constitutional Documents*, p. 182; Larkin and Hughes, i. 583, 599; BL, Add. 72439, fo. 2; *CSPD 1631–3*, p. 426; *CSPD 1633–4*, p. 222.

[5] *Scourge* (1625, 6340), pp. 2, 5; *Returne* (1641, G1199), sig. A8; BL, Add. 20065, fo. 123v; *Continuation* (1642, C5960) p. 5; FSL, V.a.454, p. 69.

[6] Birch, *James*, ii. 355; BL, Add. 72439, fo. 2; Lupton, *London* (1632, 16944), pp. 140–1; Nott UL, Ga/12768/618; *CSPD 1625–49*, p. 567; Northants. RO, IC 4631; Bodl. MS Eng.hist.e.184, fo. 7v.

learning the word of God'.[7] Thomas Fuller likened the press to an unruly horse that had 'cast off its bridle', such that serious books which 'dare fly abroad are hooted at by a flock of pamphlets'. Edward Browne argued that 'lying and scandalous pamphlets fly about the city in every corner, and prove vendible ware, whereas solid and learned men's works are nothing regarded'.[8] Scholars were thus usurped by 'pettifogging scribes', and writers worried about contributing to 'the riot of ... luxuriant pamphlets'. They strove not to be confused with those who 'ply their pens as plow-men do their plow, and pester posts with titles of new books', and with those who 'torment both paper, press and pen'.[9] Thirdly, and most importantly, contemporaries feared the *participatory* impact of cheap print, and they worried that print would foster unwelcome debate and division among the commonalty. They feared, in other words, the influence of 'clubs and clouted shoes', and an undermining of social distinctions by 'a sea of democracy'. They feared for the prospects of political stability when 'every man' of 'base condition' could do whatever 'seemeth good in his own eyes'. The danger, as the Earl of Dorset stated in 1647, was that 'apprentices turn privy councillors' and that 'confusion' would become 'the mother of order'.[10]

In contemporary discourse, therefore, we witness concerns about popular *participation* that were intimately connected with the print revolution. This was clear from Laud's desire to avoid 'more noise' by allowing controversies to be 'further stirred', as well as from claims about pamphlets being 'scattered' and 'dispersed abroad', geographically and socially, such that they were 'in sight of all'. These worries were generated by evidence that pamphlets could be found in 'kitchen-cobweb-nooks' and that they were being read by 'apprentices' and 'maids'. Indeed, since cheap print circulated through webs of communication that involved networks of travellers, pamphlets came to be described in the same fearful terms as the wandering poor; as 'vagabond books, which like rogues are to be whipped to the place of their births'.[11] Underpinning such concerns were fears about simple folk

[7] Lupton, *London*, pp. 140–1; Nalson, i. 666; BL, Harl. 4931, fos. 87–v; *Duppa Corr.*, p. 91; *HMC Verulam*, pp. 55–6; *Life of Dugdale*, p. 264; Davis, *Heaven* (1656, D422A), sigs. A2–v, A4v; Fuller, *Sermon* (1648, F2460), sig. A3.

[8] Fuller, *Holy State* (1642, F2443), sig.A2; Browne, *Paradox* (1642, B5103), sigs. A3–v.

[9] Lupton, *London*, pp. 141–2; *Scourge*, pp. 5, 7, 10, 17; HEH, HM 22039; Heath, *Clarastella* (1650, H1340A), pp. 36–7.

[10] BL: Add. 78233, fo. 44; Add. 33058, fo. 71; Cary, *Memorials*, i. 293; Northants. RO, IC353; CKS, U269/1/CP147; U269/C248.

[11] *CSPD 1629–31*, p. 404; TNA, SP 16/176, fo. 75; Nott. UL, Cl/C/27; BL, Sloane 1983B, fo. 47; Birch, *James*, ii. 355; *Scourge*, pp. 1, 3; CCL, U85/38/8, fos. 1, 1v, 36v; Durham UL, MSP 70, pp. vii, 129–30; HEH, EL 7908; J. Peacey, 'The paranoid prelate', in *Conspiracies and Conspiracy Theories*, ed. B. Coward and J. Swann (Aldershot, 2004), pp. 113–34; Fox, *Oral and Literate*, pp. 336–43, 348.

being 'abused' and 'seduced', and about the danger of 'awaking ... unquiet and turbulent spirits'. Some contemporaries felt that pamphlets would 'stir up sedition' and 'poison the hearts' of the part of society that had 'no voice or authority in our commonwealth', and that had no place meddling with political affairs.[12] Certain topics, in other words, were thought to be unfit for public discussion, and it was felt that ordinary subjects would become 'statesmen' and that the authorities would be 'exposed to the rancour of the rude', as well as to the 'witless multitude'.[13] This attitude had been evident in Henry VIII's complaint about scripture being 'disputed, rhymed, sung and jangled in every alehouse and tavern', and in his injunctions that the Bible was not to be read by 'women', or by 'artificers, apprentices, journeymen, serving men ... husbandmen nor labourers'.[14] It was revealed in Ben Jonson's mocking commentaries on the burgeoning culture of news, as well as in Shakespeare's tale of the disreputable Autolycus and dopey Mopsa.[15] And it was eminently clear from James I's attacks on 'lavish and licentious speech' regarding matters of state. Indeed, James repeatedly complained about 'an itching in the tongues and pens of most men', and he was appalled by the tendency for people to 'meddle with things above their capacity' and 'above their reach and calling'. To him 'matters of state' were 'no themes or fit subjects for vulgar persons'.[16]

Such concerns about participation, and about 'idle discourse' by members of the public, obviously became even more apparent during the 1640s, although it is important to recognize that they were in no sense hegemonic. Commentators complained about 'a prateing of news', about how 'the giddy tattling crowd ... talk their fancied grievances aloud' and about the 'wrangle and jangle' of tongues in taverns and alehouses, bakehouses and barbers' shops. The result, according to one observer, was 'a confusion of babbling and pro and conning'.[17] Confronted by 'talkative' subjects, of course, many contemporaries were determined to control the press and to

---

[12] TNA, SP 16/177, fos. 8–v; Laud, *Works*, vii. 317, 326–7; Hughes and Larkin, iii. 15; BL, Sloane 1983B, fo. 47; T. Smith, *De Republica Anglorum*, ed. M. Dewar (Cambridge, 1982), ch. 24.

[13] *CSPD 1629–31*, pp. 404, 411; TNA: SP 16/176, fo. 75; SP 16/176, fo. 75; SP 16/177, fos. 8–v; Nott. UL, Cl/C/27; BL, Sloane 1983B, fo. 47; *CSPD 1628–9*, p. 187; Hughes and Larkin, iii. 14–15; *Rous Diary*, p. 121; *Scourge*, p. 2.

[14] *SR*, iii. 896.

[15] B. Johnson, *Staple of News*, ed. A. Parr (Manchester, 1988); W. Shakespeare, *Winter's Tale* (Cambridge, 2007), 4.3.23–5, 4.4.249–64, 5.2.24–5.

[16] Larkin and Hughes, i. 243, 495–6, 519–21.

[17] BL, Add. 72439, fo. 6; *CSPD 1631–3*, p. 426; *Crosfield*, p. 61; HEH, HM 55603, fo. 10v; FSL, W.b.600, p. 129; Northants. RO, IL4298; Howell, *Informer* (1643, H3122), p. 30; Warmstry, *Pax Vobis* (1641, W886), p. 29; Durham UL, MSP 9, p. 215; Taylor, *St Hillaries* (1642, T508), pp. 3, 5; *Remonstrance* (1642, R991), sigs. A2–v, A4–v.

produce 'propaganda' that would 'undeceive' the public. This response was epitomized by Sir Roger L'Estrange, who famously exclaimed that 'tis the press that has made 'em mad, and the press must set 'em right again'.[18] Others, however, were more sanguine about the participatory effects of cheap print, and were even willing to embrace the print medium. During debates over church reform in the 1640s, for example, the vicar of Ashington was said to have 'solicited hedgers at the hedges and plowmen at the plough, [and] threshers in the barns', and he apparently did so with literature aimed at 'the ploughman and artisan' and intended for the 'satisfaction of the common people'. Samuel Hartlib went even further. He actually championed the impact of print on popular politics, by predicting that 'the art of printing will so spread knowledge that the common people, knowing their own rights and liberties, will not be governed by way of oppression'.[19]

In other words, evidence from the mid seventeenth century indicates that contemporaries were struck by the emergence of cheap print and anxious to connect it with the events of their troubled age. They did not necessarily agree on whether such material was welcome, but they were fairly united in trying to grapple with what it might do to political life and popular participation. And it is precisely *this* desire – to think about the impact of cheap print on everyday life – that underpins this book, and its goal is to engage with both the methodology of the 'print revolution' and the historiography of seventeenth-century political culture.

ii The historiography of the print revolution

The 'impact' of print has been hotly contested by historians of the early modern period, and the purpose of this section is to draw attention to these debates and to the methodological and conceptual issues that they raise. The aim is to argue that the 'print revolution' offers valuable ways of enhancing our understanding of seventeenth-century political culture, but that the field remains inadequately conceptualized and that new questions and approaches are required.

The first point to make is that the historiography of the print revolution – in terms of how it is studied and why it matters – has become excessively polarized. This can be seen fairly clearly in the debate between Elizabeth Eisenstein and Adrian Johns. Where Eisenstein made enormous

---

[18] *Crosfield*, p. 40; *CSPD 1639*, pp. 233–4; *CSPD 1639–40*, p. 305; TNA, SP 16/441, fos. 128–29v; Birch, *James*, ii. 276; *Observator*, 1 (13 April 1681).

[19] Antony, BC/24/2, fo. 65; *Dialogue* (1642, D1346); Hartlib, *Macaria* (1641, P2409A), p. 13.

claims for the link between printing and the Reformation, the Renaissance and the Scientific Revolution, and for its role in the development of nations, languages and individualism, Johns stressed the need to examine local situations and specific individuals. He argued that the 'print revolution' played out differently in different counties and that the 'impact' of print depended on how individuals reacted in particular circumstances. Another way of putting this is to say that where Eisenstein emphasized structural change, Johns stressed contingency and human agency, and if Eisenstein was a 'parachutist' – surveying huge swathes of historical territory from a great height – then Johns was a 'truffle-hunter', who adopted a somewhat microscopic approach to both problems and evidence.[20] More obviously, of course, this polarization can also be observed in broader debates about political and religious upheaval in Tudor and Stuart Britain, where the issue of print has rarely been far from the surface. Thus, while pamphlets and newspapers were central to the work of Marxist historians like Christopher Hill – for whom print technology was linked to social change and the emergence of new voices and radical movements – his critics considered such material to be much less relevant.[21] Such 'revisionists' refocused scholarly attention away from 'society' and the radical fringes, in favour of a narrative of 'high politics'; away from printed sources towards manuscript archives; and away from London towards the localities. The latter proved crucial to a characterization of the early seventeenth century as a period in which political and religious divisions were thought to have been unwelcome intrusions into an otherwise harmonious and orderly world. Indeed, revisionists downplayed the idea that 'provincial people were generally conscious of the political problems of the period', and they actively denied the value of printed texts as historical sources.[22]

A second and much more important point involves the ways in which historians have responded to such provocative claims, and to the sense that neither Marxists nor revisionists offer a satisfactory account of early modern political culture. Here, my aim is to suggest that, while social historians and 'post-revisionists' have dramatically enhanced our understanding of both elite and popular politics, and of *how* as well as *why* the

[20] E. Eisenstein, *Printing Press as an Agent of Change* (Cambridge, 1979); A. Johns, *Nature of the Book* (Chicago, 1998); A. Johns, 'How to acknowledge a revolution', *AHR*, 107 (2002), 106–25; E. Eisenstein, 'An unacknowledged revolution revisited', *AHR*, 107 (2002), 87–105.

[21] C. Hill, *World Turned Upside Down* (London, 1972).

[22] A. Everitt, *Community of Kent and the Great Rebellion* (Leicester, 1966), p. 121; J. Morrill, *Nature of the English Revolution* (London, 1993), p. 215.

revolution happened, significant problems remain unresolved and unaddressed, not least in terms of how the revolution unfolded and how it was experienced.

Among social historians, therefore, significant challenges have been made to the revisionist account. This has involved questioning the idea of the insular 'county community', the idea of political harmony within provincial communities and the idea that political awareness was restricted to a narrow elite. Considerable emphasis has been placed on the vitality of popular politics at a local level, on evidence of genuine beliefs among the 'hazily documented multitudes' and on the idea that social deference could be taken for granted. Attempts have been made to overcome a polarized model of 'elite' and 'popular' political cultures, and to argue that there existed a spectrum of consciousness, awareness and activity, which stretched from local elites through the gentry and the 'middling sort' and down to the humblest members of society.[23] And a wealth of research has recovered the political meanings of customary practices and disorderly episodes, which have been shown to have involved 'popular' legalism, respect for customary rights and determination to enforce justice and good governance. The upshot has been an enhanced appreciation that local communities were politicized and participatory, and that even humble citizens were able to make decisions about how to overcome grievances through tactics that ranged from petitioning to direct action.[24] In local settings, in other words, popular practices provide an insight into what the anthropologist James C. Scott calls 'weapons of the weak', and a way of connecting violent and riotous behaviour – exceptional and apparently spasmodic episodes – with less dramatic everyday interactions – from grumbling and cursing to formal interventions in political processes. Such practices enabled problems

---

[23] D. Underdown, *Revel, Riot and Rebellion* (Oxford, 1985), p. 163; D. Underdown, *A Freeborn People* (Oxford, 1996), pp. 10–11, 50; T. Harris, 'Problematising popular culture', in *Popular Culture in England*, ed. T. Harris (Basingstoke, 1995), p. 14; T. Harris, 'Introduction', in *Politics of the Excluded* (Basingstoke, 2001), pp. 21–4; M. Braddick and J. Walter, 'Grids of power', in *Negotiating Power in Early Modern Society* (Cambridge, 2001), pp. 1–42.

[24] Underdown, *Revel*, pp. 119, 123; Underdown, *Freeborn*, pp. 46–9; A. Wood, *Politics of Social Conflict* (Cambridge, 1999); A. Wood, 'Collective violence, social drama and rituals of rebellion in late medieval and early modern England', in *Cultures of Violence*, ed. S. Carroll (Basingstoke, 2007); J. Walter, 'A "rising of the people"?', *P&P*, 107 (1985), 90–143; K. Wrightson, 'Two concepts of order', and J. Walter, 'Grain riots and popular attitudes to the law', both in *An Ungovernable People?*, ed. J. Brewer and J. Styles (New Brunswick, 1980), pp. 21–46, 47–84; R. Manning, *Village Revolts* (Oxford, 1998); J. Kent, 'Folk justice and royal justice in early seventeenth century England', *Midland History*, 8 (1983), 70–85; P. Clark, 'Popular protest and disturbance in Kent', *EcHR*, 29 (1976), 365–82; K. Lindley, *Fenland Riots* (London, 1982); B. Sharp, *In Contempt of all Authority* (Berkeley, 1980).

to be resolved and policies to be negotiated, even to the point that elite power could be said to have become constrained.[25]

The challenge, however, has been to think beyond the issue of class domination, to connect local practices with participation in national politics and to address the impact of print. First, therefore, attempts have been made to challenge that idea – which remained central to the work of historians like David Underdown – that 'popular' politics was real but limited in scope. This has sometimes taken the form of scholarship regarding 'state formation', in terms of the growing reach of the state and the need to respond to the 'experience of authority', and it has also involved ideas about the 'monarchical' or 'unacknowledged' Republic. Considerable emphasis has thus been placed on the integrative and educative potential of a governmental system that involved extensive office-holding and local self-government.[26] At other times, the aim has been to demonstrate how 'micro-political' struggles in the localities interlocked with national issues and generated involvement in national institutions.[27] Here, numerous studies have argued that arenas like parliament served as 'points of contact' for members of the public, as voters, petitioners, lobbyists and libellers, and it has been demonstrated that 'little businesses' in provincial England revealed the interplay of local and national issues, as well as considerable knowledge about political proceedings and the workings of the state.[28]

---

[25] J. Walter, 'Public transcripts, popular agency and the politics of subsistence in early modern England', in *Negotiating Power*, pp. 145–7; Braddick and Walter, 'Grids of power', pp. 5–7.

[26] Underdown, *Freeborn*, p. 10; M. Goldie, 'The unacknowledged republic', and S. Hindle, 'The political culture of the middling sort', both in *Politics of the Excluded*, pp. 125–52, 153–94; P. Withington, *Politics of Commonwealth* (Cambridge, 2005); S. Hindle, *The State and Social Change in Early Modern England* (Basingstoke, 2000), pp. 16, 23–6, 89, 115; S. Hindle, 'Hierarchy and community in the Elizabethan parish', *HJ*, 42 (1999), 835–51; A. Fletcher, 'Honour, reputation and local officeholding in Elizabethan and Stuart England', in *Order and Disorder in Early Modern England*, ed. A. Fletcher and J. Stevenson (Cambridge, 1985), pp. 92–115; J. Kent, 'The rural "middling sort" in early modern England', *Rural History*, 10 (1999), pp. 27–8; P. Griffiths, 'Secrecy and authority in late sixteenth and seventeenth century London', *HJ*, 40 (1997), 925–51; K. Wrightson, 'The politics of the parish in early modern England', in *Experience of Authority in Early Modern England*, ed. P. Griffiths (Basingstoke, 1996), pp. 10–46.

[27] I. Archer, 'Popular politics in the sixteenth and early seventeenth centuries', in *Londinopolis*, ed. P. Griffiths and M. Jenner (Manchester, 2000), pp. 26–7, 41–2; P. Collinson, 'The monarchical republic of Queen Elizabeth I', *BJRL*, 69 (1987), 394–424; D. Cressy, 'Binding the nation', in *Tudor Rule and Revolution*, ed. D. Guth and J. McKenna (Cambridge, 1982), pp. 217–34; J. Walter, 'Affronts and insolencies', *EHR*, 122 (2007), 35–60.

[28] G. Elton, 'Tudor government, the points of contact: Parliament', *TRHS*, 5th series, 24 (1974), 183–200; D. Hirst, *Representative of the People* (Cambridge, 1975); D. Dean, 'Parliament and locality from the middle ages to the twentieth century', *PH*, 17 (1998), 1–11; D. Dean, 'Parliament, Privy Council and local politics in Elizabethan England', *Albion*, 22 (1990), 39–64; D. Sacks, 'The corporate town and the English state', *P&P*, 110 (1986), 69–105; J. Hart, *Justice upon Petition* (London, 1991);

Secondly, and less successfully, attempts have been made to integrate print culture into this revised picture of local politics. Underdown, for example, recognized the potential impact of pamphlets and newspapers, but found little evidence that such material penetrated into local society, especially below the level of the elite. He suggested that the evidence and analysis contained within Civil War literature 'may have been too sophisticated for the more plebeian public', and that it was 'unlikely' that pamphlets and newspapers 'made any impact on the common people'. And he thought that too little was known about patterns of readership, and that 'regular exposure to the newsbooks may have solidified the loyalties of some partisans ... but it made others totally cynical'. In other words, Underdown remained convinced that the bulk of the population would have had only a poor understanding of events that took place 'far away in Westminster, remote from the daily realities of provincial life'.[29] More recently, of course, Underdown's conclusions have been modified by ground-breaking research into the impact of print outside the political elite. This has involved examining literacy and the circulation of libels, ballads and broadsides, as well as the relationship between political literature and oral culture, all of which has revealed that print became both accessible to popular audiences and integral to the lives of humble citizens. Indeed, it has been suggested not just that provincial England witnessed a *literate environment* of libelling, rumour and news, but also that the pamphlets and newspapers of the 1640s helped to integrate local communities into national politics.[30] As yet, however, such work offers only suggestive insights into the relationship between print and local politics after 1640, and into the impact

P. Croft, 'Libels, popular literacy and public opinion in early modern England', *HR*, 68 (1995), 266–85; P. Croft, 'The reputation of Robert Cecil', *TRHS*, 6th series, 1 (1991), 43–69; R. Cust and P. Lake, 'Sir Richard Grosvenor and the rhetoric of magistracy', *BIHR*, 54 (1981), 40–53; R. Cust, 'Anti-Puritanism and urban politics', *HJ*, 35 (1992), 1–26; P. Lake, 'Puritans, popularity and petitions', in *Politics, Religion and Popularity in Early Stuart Britain*, ed. T. Cogswell et al. (Cambridge, 2002), pp. 259–89; A. Bellany, 'An "embarrassment of libels", in *Politics of the Public Sphere in Early Modern England*, ed. P. Lake and S. Pincus (Manchester, 2007), pp. 144–67.

[29] D. Underdown, 'Community and class', in *After the Reformation*, ed. B. Malament (Manchester, 1980), pp. 147–65; Underdown, *Revel*, pp. 123, 162, 168, 174, 176, 208, 223, 235, 236, 239; Underdown, *Freeborn*, pp. 10, 72, 73, 76, 110.

[30] D. Cressy, *Literacy and the Social Order* (Cambridge, 1980); Fox, *Oral and Literate*, pp. 19, 36–7; T. Cogswell, 'Underground verse and the transformation of early Stuart political culture', in *Political Culture and Cultural Politics in Early Modern England*, ed. S. Amussen and M. Kishlansky (Manchester, 1995), pp. 277–300; A. Bellany, '"Raylinge rymes and vaunting verse"', in *Culture and Politics in Early Stuart England*, ed. K. Sharpe and P. Lake (London, 1994), pp. 285–310; A. Bellany, 'Libels in action', in *Politics of the Excluded*, pp. 99–124; A. Bellany, 'Singing libel in early Stuart England', *HLQ*, 69 (2006), 177–93; J. Walter, *Understanding Popular Violence in the English Revolution* (Cambridge, 1999); Walter, 'Politicising the popular?', pp. 95–110; D. Cressy, 'The Protestation protested', *HJ*, 45 (2002), 251–79.

of print beyond London. Thus, while studies of the capital have done much to reveal the vibrancy of public politics, the impact of cheap print on humble individuals and the entanglement of the 'lower orders' in 'high politics', there remains a great deal to be done to assess how far these conclusions apply beyond Nehemiah Wallington and beyond the capital.[31]

A second means of challenging revisionism involved rethinking conflict and consensus within early Stuart England. This 'post-revisionist' turn has involved a series of argumentative strategies, which sometimes involved questioning the idea of the 'county community' and sometimes involved rethinking the nature of politics at a national level. They also involved a renewed interest in pamphlets and newspapers, and a central idea underpinning much recent scholarship has been that political texts and 'communicative practices' reveal a richer picture of political life. First, great strides have been made in recovering the vibrancy of contemporary news culture, even before the development of professional and commercial print journalism. This made it possible to challenge claims about the ignorance and isolation of local communities, at least at the level of the gentry, and to challenge claims that they were immune from debates that occurred at a national level.[32] Secondly, considerable emphasis has been placed on the determination of political grandees to communicate with a fairly wide public. Such communications strategies reflected the desire to court popular support and manipulate public perceptions, and they encouraged members of the public to contribute to political and religious debates; and by exploring how public discourse connected the elite with the world 'beyond Westminster', it has been possible to challenge revisionist claims about the pervasiveness of political and religious consensus.[33] Thirdly, 'post-revisionists' sought to recover the political content within genres like ballads, libels and murder pamphlets that had been dismissed by revisionists, in order to break down the distinctions between 'political' and

---

[31] D. Freist, *Governed by Opinion* (London, 1997); K. Lindley, *Popular Politics and Religion in Civil War London* (Aldershot, 1997); K. Lindley, 'London and popular freedom', in *Freedom and the English Revolution*, ed. R. Richardson and G. Ridden (Manchester, 1986), pp. 111–50; A. Bellany, 'The murder of John Lambe', *P&P*, 200 (2008), 37–76; P. Seaver, *Wallington's World* (London, 1985).

[32] R. Cust, 'News and politics in early seventeenth century England', *P&P*, 112 (1986), 60–90; F. Levy, 'How information spread among the gentry', *JBS*, 21 (1982), 11–34; M. Frearson, 'The distribution and readership of London corantos', in *Serials and their Readers*, ed. R. Myers and M. Harris (Winchester, 1993), p. 2; A. Bellany, *Politics of Court Scandal in Early Modern England* (Cambridge, 2002); Fox, *Oral and Literate*, ch. 7.

[33] P. Lake, 'The politics of popularity and the public sphere', in *Public Sphere*, pp. 59–94; R. Cust, 'Charles I and popularity' and T. Cogswell, 'The people's love', both in *Politics, Religion and Popularity*, pp. 211, 34, 235–58; A. Hughes, *Gangraena and the Struggle for the English Revolution* (Oxford, 2004); J. Peacey, *Politicians and Pamphleteers* (Aldershot, 2004).

'non-political' texts and between 'elite' and 'popular' politics. By finding politics and political information within even the most popular forms of contemporary literature, in other words, new ways were found of suggesting that humble readers could become fairly well informed about contemporary issues and debates.[34]

Ultimately, of course, a number of post-revisionists have also detected the emergence of a seventeenth-century 'public sphere'. It seemed plausible to argue, in other words, that private individuals who had once been merely *addressed* by monarchs as subjects could now come together in order to engage in rational and critical debate about political issues, more or less free from political interference, and in ways that fostered openness and accountability.[35] Naturally this 'public sphere' has not always been described in strictly Habermasian terms. The 'post-reformation public sphere' was not necessarily 'free', 'commercial' or 'rational', or indeed anything other than episodic. Nevertheless, it involved a process by which debates and divisions that had previously been contained spilled over into public exchanges involving new readers and perhaps a national audience, as well as new tactics relating to disputation and mobilization and much less restrained rhetoric. As such, scholars have addressed the degree to which print broadened the political nation and intensified public life; drawn attention to the growing importance of 'public opinion'; and explored the ways in which marginal groups became integrated into a national culture. Thus, while there is little agreement about how clearly the Civil Wars witnessed a 'watershed' in political culture, or about whether print was 'transformative', there is nevertheless a growing consensus that print was an increasingly important part of public life.[36]

As with 'new social history', however, 'post-revisionism' faces serious challenges, not all of which have been successfully navigated. The first is to think beyond the creators of texts – whether members of the elite or of a

---

[34] Fox, *Oral and Literate*, pp. 382–98; A. McShane and M. Jenner, 'The roasting of the Rump', *P&P*, 196 (2007), 253–72; J. Walter, 'The pooremans joy and the gentlemans plague', *P&P*, 203 (2009), 29–67; P. Lake, 'Puritanism, Arminianism and a Shropshire axe-murder', *Midland History*, 15 (1990), 37–64; P. Lake, 'Deeds against nature', in *Culture and Politics*, pp. 257–83.

[35] T. Dykstal, 'Introduction', *Prose Studies*, 18.3 (1995); C. Calhoun, 'Introduction', in *Habermas and the Public Sphere* (London, 1997); J. Raymond, 'The newspaper, public opinion and the public sphere in the seventeenth century', in *News*, ed. Raymond, pp. 109–40.

[36] T. Harris, 'Introduction', in *Politics of the Excluded*, pp. 21–2; T. Harris, 'Problematising popular culture', in *Popular Culture*, pp. 10, 23, 26–7; P. Lake, *The Boxmaker's Revenge* (Manchester, 2001); P. Lake and D. Como, '"Orthodoxy" and its discontents', *JBS*, 39 (2000), 34–70; Hughes, *Gangraena*; P. Lake and S. Pincus, 'Rethinking the public sphere in early modern England', *JBS*, 45 (2006), 270–92; D. Zaret, *Origins of Democratic Culture* (Princeton, 2000); M. Knights, 'How rational was the later Stuart public sphere?', in *Public Sphere*, pp. 252–67.

broader public – in order to analyse *readers* and the *reception* of printed material. Thus, despite attempts to model the 'communications circuit' and to undertake archival research into reading practices, only limited methodological headway has been made regarding reactions to cheap print.[37] As a result it has proved difficult to analyse responses to pamphlets and newspapers, especially among humble and provincial readers, and historians struggle to think beyond the 'implied reader' or to see beyond politicized claims that were made about the response to print in contemporary analysis.[38] A second challenge involves thinking beyond a model of participation that centres on *public* discourse. However valuable it is to follow Habermas in highlighting a shift from discourse emanating *from* political authorities to texts that were *about* power, authority and legitimacy, and however relevant it is to examine a bourgeois and commercial world of print and polemic, there is a danger of fetishizing *published* material at the expense of other vitally important dimensions of political 'discourse'. It may thus be problematic to concentrate on newspapers and pamphlets at the expense of less public genres of print, and to overlook the ways in which print was used to participate in political systems and processes.[39] In analysing the Civil Wars, in other words, it might be useful to make a methodological and conceptual shift analogous to that which was made in Ethan Shagan's work on the Reformation. By emphasizing popular 'accommodation' and 'collaboration', Shagan moved beyond disputes about whether reform was done 'to' or 'by' the people, and suggested instead that the reformation was achieved 'with' popular involvement.[40] Likewise, in the mid seventeenth century, it is important to move beyond a model of political discourse involving texts that were either produced *by* the authorities or that involved public debate *about* current affairs, and to recognize that texts were used to participate *in* political processes. In other words it is possible to remain focused on

[37] R. Darnton, *Forbidden Bestsellers of Pre-Revolutionary France* (New York, 1996), pp. 181–97, 217–31; R. Darnton, 'What is the history of books?', *Daedalus*, 111 (1982), 65–83; R. Chartier, *The Cultural Origins of the French Revolution* (Durham NC, 1990), pp. 81–2; J. Rose, 'The history of books: revised and enlarged', in *The Darnton Debate*, ed. H. Mason (Oxford, 1998), pp. 83–104; R. Darnton, *The Kiss of Lamourette* (New York, 1990), pp. 154–87; R. Darnton, 'History of reading', in *New Perspectives*, ed. P. Burke (Cambridge, 2001), pp. 157–86.

[38] D. Underdown, 'The problem of allegiance in the English civil war', *TRHS*, 5th series, 31 (1981), p. 92; Underdown, *Freeborn*, pp. 11, 72–3, 98–9, 110; Harris, 'Introduction', in *Popular Culture*, p. 7; D. Randall, *Credibility in Elizabethan and Early Stuart Military News* (London, 2008); Raymond, *Invention*, pp. 116–18, 140, 219; Harris, 'Problematising', pp. 6–7; D. Woolf, *Reading History in Early Modern England* (Cambridge, 2000).

[39] J. Habermas, *Structural Transformation of the Public Sphere* (Cambridge, 1989), pp. 65–6, 119; C. Taylor, *Modern Social Imaginaries* (London, 2004), pp. 89–90.

[40] E. Shagan, *Popular Politics and the English Reformation* (Cambridge, 2003).

Habermasian *issues* – topicality, and texts produced by members of the public – without being restricted to his *model* of the public sphere. Indeed, by thinking about print as a participatory tool, it will be possible to avoid the pitfalls of a debate about the 'role' of print that either emphasizes how it transformed popular attitudes and ideas, and thus 'caused' political change, or else questions its importance by stressing that popular consciousness and 'public opinion' existed before the print revolution. In assessing the impact of print, in other words, it is necessary to avoid exaggerating its transformative power without dismissing its role in the emergence of an increasingly participatory culture.[41]

This brief survey of the literature on print and political culture in the early modern period reveals very clearly that the issues involved are large and that the stakes are high. It also highlights the kinds of problem with which this book is concerned, as well as the hurdles that need to be overcome. My aim is to intervene in these debates about the period, about print and about how to study the past, by building on the insights of 'new social history' and by pushing further along (and perhaps beyond) 'post-revisionist' arguments. My goal is to break down dichotomies between elite and popular culture, national and local affairs, and formal and informal behaviour, and to challenge recent claims about the public sphere, albeit without resorting to the kinds of arguments that are normally deployed against Habermas's concept. This will be done by focusing on print technology during a particularly intense phase of the 'print revolution' – as both a 'parachutist' and a 'truffle-hunter', and as both a 'lumper' and a 'splitter' – by making claims about structural change as well as contingency and human agency. I want to argue that the English revolution was transformative in terms of changes in political culture that affected the entire population, and I want to suggest that print was at the heart of this transformation, even if it could not be said to have caused it.

iii Method, structure and arguments

The method for achieving these goals will involve exploring popular participation in national political life, and examining the role that print played in the lives of people beyond Westminster, and the book will focus on how ordinary citizens engaged with national affairs and how they interacted with national institutions. 'Popular' here does not necessarily mean plebeian, and the aim is not to write what might be regarded as yet another history 'from

---

[41] Harris, 'Understanding'; Darnton, *Forbidden Bestsellers*, pp. 169–80.

below'. Instead the aim is to explore the ways in which participation was undertaken by people who were not directly involved in the machinery of court and parliament, and the goal will be to explore participation at all levels of society and in all parts of the country; to assess the social depth of national politics, and to find 'citizens concealed within subjects'. As such the book will 'reunite the fractured labours of political and social historians', and examine what historians of the book describe as the 'communications circuit'.[42] This means incorporating readers as well as writers, and printers as well as publishers, and it also means exploring the nature of printed texts and the conditions in which they were conceived, produced, distributed and consumed. More particularly, it means examining a range of *everyday practices* that were associated with print culture and political participation, rather than merely concentrating on the nature of public beliefs, and on occasional and extraordinary aspects of contemporary culture.

All too often, therefore, public involvement in political affairs is reduced to topics like motivation and allegiance, and to episodes like elections and crowds, in ways that fail to do justice to the realities of contemporary life. The danger with analysis of 'motivation' is that it can sometimes generate unproductive debates about the relative importance of things called 'politics' and 'religion'. Studies of 'allegiance', meanwhile, tend to concentrate on issues of consciousness and class; on the ways that different social groups reacted to the Civil Wars; and on the possibility the outcome of the revolution reflected the shifting status and fortunes of different types of people. With elections and crowds, meanwhile, there is a danger of concluding that participation was either effective but occasional (and limited to a small section of society), or else that it was socially inclusive but essentially episodic, metropolitan and blunt. Either way, conventional approaches to participation tend to be fragmentary and limited, and they tend to overlook the things that ordinary citizens did on a day-to-day basis. What needs to be done, therefore, is to concentrate on the processes involved in political life and, in 'popular' participation, and to explore mobilization and public engagement. And this means examining a wider range of low-level actions and interventions, each of which might be regarded as insignificant, but all of which are crucial to how politics worked in the early modern period. These participatory practices, moreover, need to be explored in ways that concentrate on how they altered during the print revolution of the 1640s

---

[42] T. Judt, 'A clown in regal purple', *HWJ*, 7.1 (1979), 66–94; G. Eley and K. Nield, 'Why does social history ignore politics?', *Social History*, 5 (1980), 249–71; P. Collinson, 'De republica Anglorum', in *Elizabethans* (London, 2003), pp. 1–29.

and 1650s. My suggestion, therefore, is that quotidian practices provide the key to understanding public perceptions about both print and politics, and that they can be used to develop a composite picture of political culture, and one that reveals common habits and modes of behaviour.[43] These are the methods of microhistory, 'thick description' and *altagsgeschichte*, in terms of 'popular' history 'from below', a focus on lived experiences and the attempt to analyse how 'private' individuals negotiated processes and *presented* themselves in public arenas. They will be employed, however, not in an episodic fashion – through a rich and extraordinary case study – but rather in a systematic or synoptic manner, with a view to detecting broad changes in institutional practices, political culture and the mentalities associated with political participation.[44] Indeed, they will be employed to address the three basic issues: how people followed political affairs; how easy it was for them to understand what was going on; and how they could intervene. It is these issues that provide the book's structural rationale.

The first of these issues involves the readers of pamphlets and newspapers, and Part I examines the everyday practices associated with the consumption of cheap print. This will involve assessing what material was available to readers, what they read and what processes were employed to access printed texts. It will also mean addressing the reading process, by analysing how contemporaries responded to what they read and how cheap print was perceived. The key argument of Chapters 1–3 can be summarized thus: printed texts relating to news and current affairs became part of the everyday lives of people who lived through the Civil Wars, irrespective of whether they were grand or humble, and irrespective of whether they lived in London or in the 'dark corners of the land'. Printed texts relating to current affairs were *ubiquitous* and were avidly consumed in a variety of different ways, and they were something to which people became accustomed, not because they were straightforwardly *credible* or *authoritative*, but rather because they were considered to be *useful*. Evidence will be produced, in other words, to challenge scholarly reservations about the reach of and response to print, and to suggest that contemporary apprehension about cheap print gave way to critical engagement with a variety of genres, and

[43] J. Morrill, 'The religious context of the English civil war', *TRHS*, 5th series, 34 (1984), 155–78; Underdown, 'Allegiance', pp. 69–93; M. Braddick, 'Mobilisation, anxiety and creativity in England during the 1640s', in *Liberty, Formality, Authority*, ed. J. Morrow and J. Scott (Exeter, 2008), pp. 175–93.

[44] J. Brewer, 'Microhistory and the histories of everyday life', *Cultural and Social History*, 7 (2010), 87–109; G. Levi, 'On microhistory', in *New Perspectives*, pp. 97–119; P. De Vivo, 'Prospect or refuge?', *Cultural and Social History*, 7 (2010), 387–97; A. Lüdtke, ed., *The Experience of Everyday Life* (Princeton, 1995); B. Gregory, 'Is small beautiful?', *History and Theory*, 38 (1999), 100–10.

even to something approaching addiction to pamphlets and newspapers. None of this will involve claiming that the print revolution changed political culture, but it will nevertheless highlight important changes to the *context* in which public politics and participation took place. As such, it provides an important foundation for what will follow.

The second issue involves the 'public face' of parliament, and the practices associated with the accessibility of political proceedings, and Part II will assess newspaper and pamphlet coverage of parliamentary machinations. Here the questions revolve around what readers could learn about the nature of parliamentary politics, the extent to which it was possible to follow daily events at Westminster and the degree to which the authorities sought to maintain secrecy within the corridors of power. The central argument in Chapters 4–6 will be that the period witnessed a *democratization* or *vulgarization* of once privileged information, as print broadened access to evidence about the workings, processes and proceedings of parliament. Pamphlets and newspapers covered not just the events of the Civil Wars – the battles and the bloodshed – and the ideological dimensions of the conflict, but also political proceedings at Westminster. Indeed, they did so in ways that helped people to analyse political processes (especially corruption and factionalism), personalities (including the attitudes and performance of individual MPs and peers), and proceedings (in terms of what was happening inside parliament on a daily basis). This process was neither complete nor straightforward, but it did reflect novel attitudes towards transparency and 'access', and a degree of willingness to publicize not just how parliament operated, but also what business had been done, was being done and was going to be done. As with developments regarding the spread of print, moreover, this fairly dramatic shift in the openness of parliament – in terms of both analysis and information – did not directly change the nature of public politics. Nevertheless, the improved provision of information and analysis certainly enhanced the potential for participation, and it did so in ways that were sometimes tacit and sometimes explicit. It even made it possible to judge the performance of individual public figures in entirely new ways.

The third issue involves methods of participation, and Part III will assess a range of practices whereby members of the public *appropriated* print in order to take part in the parliamentary process. Here the goal will be to establish how easy it was to produce printed texts, how such texts could be used to make interventions in public life, and what such interventions reveal about contemporary attitudes to parliament, participation and the political system. The argument of Chapters 7–11 will be that the affordability of the print medium fostered new methods of participation and made traditional methods more widely available, thereby empowering new sections of the political nation and providing 'weapons of the weak'. The result was that 'popular' politics became much more obviously proactive and participatory, rather than reactive and defensive, and even humble individuals will be shown to have used print to engage in business at Westminster, by using various kinds of texts and a variety of tactics and strategies, not all of which were dramatic or demonstrative. These interventions will also be used to demonstrate how people responded to a situation in which parliament was regarded as a potential solution to political problems, but also as an obstacle to the resolution of grievances, and how they coped with the participatory problems that they encountered. It will reveal, in other words, how people coped with *frustrated expectations*. Central here will be evidence that contemporaries thought about the relationship between different kinds of participation, appreciated the existence of a spectrum of tactics and displayed tactical awareness. This will make it possible to analyse the circumstances in which they were willing to engage in tactical escalation, by shifting from discrete, polite and formal participatory methods – like petitioning – to those that were informal, more or less public and perhaps even forceful, including lobbying, protesting and mass politics. In other words, examining everyday political practices will reveal that the kinds of popular politics upon which historians tend to concentrate – like crowds – formed only a small part of the range of options available, and that mass activity was often the last resort rather than the first option. Indeed, such shifts in behaviour will be used to highlight two more findings.[45]

The first is that participatory tactics – and the ways in which they changed in the face of delays, obstructions and opposition – were intimately linked to the appropriation and deployment of different kinds of text, and that this affects our understanding of the relationship between political participation and public discourse. What will emerge is that print could be employed as a participatory tool without necessarily engaging with a broad public, producing commercially available texts or becoming involved in a 'public sphere'. Indeed, what will also emerge is the importance of non-commercial print genres – such as the handbill, flyer, broadside and short pamphlet – that could be used to make fairly targeted interventions through discrete and restrained distribution. In other words, analysing printed texts requires being sensitive to the 'form' and 'function' of specific genres, and being aware that such texts were often non-commercial and intended for

---

[45] M. De Certeau, *Practice of Everyday Life* (Berkeley, 1988), pp. xix, 37.

limited circulation.[46] Studying such 'ephemera', moreover, will be integral to a demonstration of how contemporaries understood the range of tactical options that were available to them, and how they shifted between interventions that were local, oral and scribal and those that were national and printed. It will also underpin analysis of the ways in which contemporaries used different genres of print within the parliamentary domain, in relation to petitioning, lobbying and protesting, as well as in relation to interactions with specific public figures. The decision to deploy print was often a sign of frustration, and this frustration could eventually lead to new tactics and more public forms of print, as people made assessments about the effectiveness of different approaches to the parliamentary process. To the extent that print was appropriated and employed, in other words, it will be shown to have been used in a variety of ways, and the book will argue that contributions to public discourse through commercial print can only be understood in the context of more circumscribed kinds of participation.

The second finding involves enhancing our appreciation of political thinking during the period, and the importance of what has been described as the 'social history of ideas'. Here the book will argue that 'contextualized' political thought requires not just the examination of pamphlets and newspapers, but also of texts that were generated in the course of political participation. This is because a key context in which intellectual thought and innovation took place involved the communicative practices associated with parliamentary affairs, and because ideas may have 'trickled up' from frustrated members of the public rather than 'trickled down' from intellectuals.[47] Historians have only just begun to explore the degree to which members of the political elite were engaged in a process of rethinking the role of 'public' men and the nature of representation, and the contention of this book will be that such thinking took place in the context of 'popular' thought.[48] Here, too, the key lies in contemporary perceptions that parliament could become a problematic obstacle to the successful resolution of grievances, rather than a potential solution to them. In other words, personal experience of the parliamentary system, together with frustrated expectations regarding its processes, can be shown to have prompted

---

[46] P. Stallybrass, 'Little jobs', in *Agent of Change*, ed. S. Baron (Amherst, 2007), pp. 315–41.

[47] R. Chartier, 'Intellectual history or sociocultural history', in *Modern European Intellectual History*, ed. D. LaCapra (Ithaca, 1982), p. 29; Darnton, *Forbidden Bestsellers*, ch. 6; D. Rollison, *Commonwealth of the People* (Cambridge, 2010), pp. 19–20, 80, 238, 313.

[48] Cust and Lake, 'Grosvenor', 40–53; R. Cust, 'The 'public man' in late Tudor and early Stuart England', in *Public Sphere*, pp. 116–43; J. Peacey, 'Sir Edward Dering, popularity and the public', *HJ*, 54 (2011), 955–83.

independent reflections upon very basic principles and concepts, as well as shifts in rhetoric about representation and accountability. This was what Gerald Aylmer called the 'ideology of disillusionment', and it can be shown to have involved a bottom-up and practice-led form of political thinking.[49] Indeed, to the extent that this involved novel and increasingly aggressive attitudes towards both representatives and the parliamentary system, it provides an important way of rethinking Civil War 'radicalism', not least in the localities and among the general public. Here, there is a real risk of overlooking radical impulses that became evident in the ideas and arguments of people who were not conventionally regarded as radicals, and even in the claims made by royalists. There is also a danger of concentrating upon a small band of activists and pamphleteers, and upon the revolutionary and transformative aspects of their thought, in ways that have made them seem fascinating but essentially marginal and extraordinary. By equating radicalism with a Leveller 'party', for example, scholars like Underdown found little support for the movement in the localities, beyond those few firebrands who represented 'a head without a body'. A neglected dimension of radical 'levellerism', however, involved respect for customary rights and a restorative approach to liberty, and a willingness to tap into local political style, and this provides new ways of thinking about both the phenomenon and its wider relevance. It provides, in other words, a way of connecting the Levellers' brand of radical thought with the complaints of any number of other people who developed their own grievances as part of the participatory process.[50]

In sum, the book will demonstrate the degree to which print became integral to the political life of the nation and to the practices associated with political culture and parliamentary affairs. These practices will be shown to have involved a spectrum of ways that print could be accessed, a spectrum of print genres that shed light on processes and proceedings, and a spectrum of tactics that could be used as a tool to aid different participatory methods. Civil War print culture, meanwhile, will be shown to have played an important part in transforming awareness about 'current affairs', methods for engaging with the political elite and ideas about the political system, and across all three sections of the book such arguments will be shown to be

---

[49] G. Aylmer, 'Collective mentalities in mid-seventeenth century England III', *TRHS*, 5th series, 38 (1988), p. 7.

[50] J. Peacey, 'Radicalism relocated', in *Varieties of Seventeenth and Early Eighteenth Century English Radicalism*, ed. A. Hessayon and D. Finnegan (Farnham, 2011), pp. 51–68; Underdown, *Revel*, pp.114–15, 213, 231–2; J. Davis, 'Afterword', in *English Radicalism, 1550–1850*, ed. G. Burgess and M. Festenstein (Cambridge, 2007), pp. 356–8.

applicable across the country and across the social spectrum. Ultimately, this analysis will highlight four larger implications for our understanding of political culture.

The first implication relates to a broadening and deepening of the political nation, as national issues and institutions became pervasive features of everyday life, as local issues more readily found expression in parliament, and as the practices associated with local politics became integrated into a much broader spectrum of participatory methods. This brought new intensity to public life, and it seems feasible to call it a *democratizing* process. It involved what Benedict Anderson called 'simultaneity' – shared and contemporaneous awareness about events that were of relevance to the entire political nation – and what Charles Taylor calls 'radical horizontality'. This democratizing process was not necessarily experienced equally by all groups in society, but it nevertheless indicates the emergence of something resembling an integrated national political culture, involving processes that were shared even if they were not experienced in a uniform way.[51] Moreover, it is also a process that only becomes evident by rethinking conventional approaches to the study of 'popular' politics. In other words, it is only by shifting attention away from popular 'allegiance' and by downplaying the significance of the 'public sphere' that it becomes possible to gain a proper understanding of just how *participatory* political life became during the English revolution.

The second implication is that the period witnessed a fairly dramatic process of what Roger Chartier calls 'typographical acculturation', in terms of familiarity with and immersion in the world of print. This acculturation needs to be understood not merely in terms of reading habits (consumption and reception), but also in terms of the appropriation and deployment of print by members of the public.[52] The third implication is that by exploring Civil War print culture through the lens of quotidian practices, it becomes possible to analyse what Charles Taylor called 'social imaginaries'. These can be defined as ideas and expectations about how public life and political institutions worked and failed to work, as well as about how they ought to work and might be made to work. Such ideas were not always well-articulated, but they can nevertheless be distilled from the political practices by which they were inspired, in terms of attitudes towards the accessibility

[51] Taylor, *Social Imaginaries*; B. Anderson, *Imagined Communities* (London, 2006).
[52] R. Chartier, *Forms and Meanings* (Philadelphia, 1995), pp. 11–18, 29, 88–95; R. Chartier, 'Culture as appropriation', in *Understanding Popular Culture*, ed. S. Kaplan (New York, 1984), pp. 234–43; De Certau, *Practice*, pp. xxi, 165–76.

and transparency of the political process, and ideas regarding parliament and representation. Parliamentary practices thus reveal a 'social imaginary' that is striking in terms of the emphasis placed upon openness and participation. They also provide a way of examining how this 'imaginary' was developed and amended in response to political experiences, as citizens began to engage in a more contemplative kind of political thinking, and strove to adapt existing political theories.[53]

A fourth and final outcome of such analysis will be a more general assessment of the 'impact' of print. Here the central claim will be that the effects of the print revolution were partly structural, partly conjunctural and partly a matter of the precise circumstances in which people found themselves, and of the particular ways in which they responded. These different strands to the print revolution will provide themes that run through the book, rather than arguments that fit within particular chapters or sections, although the need to consider this range of forces helps to justify the book's expansive nature. In other words, it is difficult to consider the impact of print without taking account of broad changes relating to literacy, the economics of the printing industry and the dynamics of the book trade, as well as contemporary attitudes towards the accessibility and transparency of political institutions. Likewise, it would be a mistake to assess such structural forces without recognizing the conjunctural impact of the Civil Wars, not least in terms of the transformation of parliament during the Civil Wars, and the ways in which individuals were both 'pushed' and 'pulled' into participating in its proceedings as they came to terms with the consequences of Civil War. Finally, while the bulk of the analysis will involve the ways in which specific individuals engaged with print as actors in *l'histoire événementielle*, these precise episodes will only make sense within a much broader context. Such interactions with print certainly reflected the particular pressures and problems that people faced, but the ways in which members of the public adapted to specific situations through improvization and experimentation were also conditioned by broader circumstances, and were indeed influenced by structural change at a deeper level. The 'liberating potential' of print thus became more or less a reality because of the circumstances of Civil War, and because of the ways in which it was deployed by particular people, in particular ways at particular moments.

---

[53] Taylor, *Social Imaginaries*, p. 25.

PART I

Consuming print

Introduction

In the summer of 1640, the English government became aware of an alarming footnote to the depressing story of the Bishops' Wars, when it discovered that copies of a Covenanter pamphlet – *Information from the Scottish Nation* – had been found hidden under a stone in Braintree churchyard. An investigation revealed a clandestine communication network centred around Edward Cole, a clothier from Barfold in Suffolk, who had apparently been employed to spread such literature, and who sought to ensure that copies were read by soldiers billeted in the area. One of these, a carpenter called John Fryer, claimed to have met Cole at the White Hart Inn, to have been invited to 'walk down the street' to the churchyard, and to have been told about the hidden books. Cole apparently declared that 'if he and the rest of the soldiers had such a book . . . they would make fine sport with it', and Fryer, despite being unable to sign his name, replied that he would 'go a mile to see such a book'. By following Cole's directions, indeed, he quickly found a copy 'lying in one of the arches of the church'.[1] This was symptomatic of a wider phenomenon, and similar stories emerged from across the country. John Castle informed the Earl of Bridgewater that Covenanters had 'cast and spread abroad into this kingdom above 10,000 printed copies' of their 'pestilent pasquil', thus 'making their cause to be common'. Any number of officials came across copies in the localities and sent them to London. In Worcestershire an Irishman was found with a copy of *The Short Declaration of the Kirk of Scotland*, while in Sussex a copy of *The Intentions of the Army of the Kingdom of Scotland* was given in to a Justice of the Peace (JP) by a Lewes draper, and in Cambridgeshire 'certain printed pamphlets and discourses' were handed over by a local chandler, having been 'sent to him from London' and delivered to his house 'by a common carrier named Powell'. Scottish pamphlets, in other words, were being 'printed, dispersed and spread' throughout England, thereby contributing

[1] *CSPD 1640*, pp. 622, 634–5, 647; TNA: SP 16/464, fos. 182, 186–v, 194v–5; SP 16/465, fos. 8, 85.

25

to complaints about 'the swarming of lascivious, idle and unprofitable books, pamphlets, playbooks and ballads'. Charles I, indeed, sent an urgent circular to deputy lieutenants across the land, denouncing 'wicked and traiterous' pamphlets which had been 'clandestinely sent into this our kingdom and spread in sundry parts thereof'.[2]

On one level, of course, the king should not have been surprised by stories about the appetite for Scottish texts and their availability in England. After all, scribal news from Scotland had been available in London since at least 1637, when stationers were prosecuted for making and selling copies. However, manuscript versions of Covenanter literature may only have circulated to those who were well-connected, or who had fairly deep pockets. The Earl of Huntingdon's bookseller, Henry Seile, charged between 2s and 2s 6d for such texts in the late 1630s, and the earl paid precisely the same sums for other items in York in September 1640. In addition, the government had grown familiar with stories about how print brought such texts into England in much larger numbers, thereby ensuring that 'seditious pamphlets' were circulating around the towns of northern England. They also became readily available in the capital, and in February 1640, John Castle discovered one such tract in London, where it was 'sold as if it were *sine privilegio*'. By March 1640 it had been discovered that the Scots planned to disperse as many as 2,000 copies of *An Information from the Estates* into England, 'to make their cause good and their grievances intolerable' on the eve of the Short Parliament.[3] What was particularly worrying about the Braintree case, however, was evidence about the *readership* of Covenanter literature, and that it could no longer be assumed that such material was destined merely for a narrow coterie of Puritan dissidents within the gentry and the clergy. It was now being read by provincial yeomen, like Henry Lawrence of Pampisford in Cambridgeshire, and circulated through all manner of networks. In Lawrence's case, this involved a lace seller from London called Mr Davy, who had brought a copy to his house on a social visit.[4]

[2] *CSPD 1640*, pp. 614, 638, 648, 653–4; TNA: SP 16/464, fo. 127; SP 16/465, fos. 25, 90, 119; SP 16/466, fo. 171; Spalding, *Memorialls*, i. 321–9; BL, Add. 26785, fo. 27; HEH: EL 7847, 7849; HA Military Box 1/30; Lancs. RO, DDN1/64, fo. 167.

[3] *CSPD 1637–8*, pp. 26–7; SUL, Hartlib 34/6/4–10; HEH: EL 7824; HAF Box 12/10; HAF Box 14/24; HM 55603, fo. 30; Beinecke, Osborn 17537; *CSPD 1638–9*, p. 473; *CSPD 1639*, p. 152; Cumbria RO, Ca/2/120/3; Spalding, *Memorialls*, i. 257–8, 260; BL, Add. 11045, fo. 108; Rushworth, iii. 1094–5; *CSPD 1640*, p. 27; TNA, SP 16/450, fo. 167.

[4] *CSPD 1639*, pp. 159, 198–9; TNA: SP 16/420, fo. 346; SP 16/421, fos. 151, 153, 155–v; Bodl. MS Bankes 65, fo. 94.

This suggests that the literature produced by the Covenanters can be used not just to explore their ideological influence on English politics, but also to highlight the broad changes in political communication that revolved around the social and geographical 'reach' of print during the mid seventeenth century. Developments in print culture seem to indicate that dramatic changes were taking place in the penetration of political news, information and opinion. Indeed, it seems undeniable that by the summer of 1640, printed texts massively outnumbered scribal versions, that they were reaching every corner of the land, and that they were being consumed across the social spectrum. Whether or not Covenanter texts were always distributed indiscriminately – by being scattered and given away – their intended audience was extremely broad, and a determined effort was clearly being made to appeal to 'weavers', 'butchers' and 'cobblers'.[5]

The first part of this book aims to demonstrate that Covenanter tactics reflected broader trends by which politics became 'common'. These involved structural changes regarding the penetration of news and opinion through the medium of cheap print (which had considerable advantages over scribal media), and they also involved public clamour for such material in the conjunctural circumstances of Civil War and revolution. The result was a significant change to the context in which public or 'popular' politics took place, which involved the growth of the political nation and an intensification of reportage and debate. These claims will be substantiated by close scrutiny of the practices associated with the consumption of print, in terms of the patterns and processes by which texts were accessed by members of the public, and the ways in which such material was read and understood. This will involve employing methodological tools that challenge conventional approaches to consumers and readers, and it will mean addressing three key issues.

Chapter 1 will assess whether obsessive collectors such as George Thomason reflected broader trends in terms of owning considerable quantities of pamphlets and newspapers. Here the approach to *ownership* of print will focus on archives rather than merely libraries, in order to recover information about items that were acquired rather than merely those which were preserved, catalogued and bequeathed, and in order to supplement evidence about *what* material readers obtained with information about *how* and *when* print was purchased. Chapter 2 will then move beyond ownership of printed material in order to scrutinize the *accessibility* of

---

[5] *CSPD 1640*, p. 660; *CSPD 1640–1*, pp. 161–6; BL, Harl. 2135, fos. 14v–15; *CSPD 1625–49*, p. 601; Northants. RO, IC 4632; Beinecke, Osborn fb.106/6.

pamphlets and newspapers, partly by focusing on factors such as price, print runs and literacy, but more importantly by addressing the social geography of print culture. This will mean examining the extent to which printed material was available across the country and across the social spectrum, to those beyond London and to those who did not necessarily have the means to purchase it. The approach here will involve analysing provincial book-selling, the public display and announcement of official literature, and the free distribution of political and religious texts, but it will also involve examining a bundle of practices relating to the circulation of ideas and information within social networks, including communal reading, the sharing of texts and the tendency for print to generate oral discussion and debate. In these opening chapters the argument will be that the consumption of printed political news and comment became not merely common but ubiquitous. This meant that avid reading of tracts, pamphlets and newspapers was not merely limited to a metropolitan or gentry elite, but rather transcended social boundaries and geographical obstacles, and that a broad cross section of the population gained regular and substantial access to both topical information and contemporary debates. In other words, the audience for Civil War print culture was less segmented and stratified than historians have assumed, and there was significant common ground in terms of the material which was read by different groups in society.

Chapter 3 will then reflect on what contemporary practices and comments reveal about *perceptions* of print culture. Here the focus will be on the ways in which contemporaries responded to what they read, and the ways in which people from across the social spectrum adapted to the print revolution. Although this will involve recognizing that different people approached such works in different ways, and took different things from them, the response to cheap print will be shown to have been more complex than has sometimes been recognized. The aim, therefore, will be to acknowledge that printed news and polemic posed challenges to readers, in terms of credibility, truth and trustworthiness, but also to suggest that these were not entirely insurmountable, and that they did not preclude avid consumption and critical reading, even among fairly humble readers. In a variety of ways, in other words, contemporaries came to terms with cheap print, acquired a fairly sophisticated understanding of how the media worked, and developed a pragmatic sense of the utility of print.

CHAPTER I

The ownership of cheap print

George Stancombe, an obscure vicar from Birchington in a remote corner of
the Isle of Thanet, was a loving husband, a capable minister and a loyal
parliamentarian. He also had a very useful habit of signing the pamphlets
that he purchased, thereby permitting the virtual reconstruction of a library
that has long since been dispersed. His bookshelf contained at least 150
pamphlets for the period between April 1641 and October 1643, and it
reveals a fascination with national affairs, parliamentary speeches and
official declarations. He followed Strafford's trial and the Army Plot, read
Henry Parker's *Observations* and Eglisham's *Forerunner of Revenge*, and
monitored the descent into conflict through dozens of news tracts. He
kept abreast of the Civil War by purchasing tracts relating to peace treaties
and the Scots, as well as reflections on the transformation of political culture
like *Sober Sadnes*.[1] At the other end of our period, meanwhile, the accounts
of another rural minister, Giles Moore of Lindfield in Sussex, record not just
the books and pamphlets that he purchased, but also the methods by which
they were acquired. He occasionally visited London's bookshops, but more
often he had material sent down to him, and particularly intriguing is
evidence regarding his consumption of news. In the summer of 1656,
Moore made an arrangement with a local carrier, John Morley, for the
delivery of newspapers on a weekly basis, for which he paid between 1s 6d
and 2s per quarter, or between 1d and 2d per copy. Moore thus received his
newsbooks on a regular basis, alongside letters, the occasional sugar loaf,
and parcels of ribbon, pease and currants.[2]

Stancombe and Moore enable our understanding of the 'print revolution'
to be significantly enhanced, by facilitating analysis of readers as well as

[1] Many of Stancombe's pamphlets survive in the Folger Shakespeare Library, at the Houghton Library
in Harvard, and at the Huntington Library, as well as at Duke University. See: *Al. Oxon.*, iv. 1406;
Larking, *Proceedings*, p. 180; *LJ*, vi. 278, 282; *Walker Revised*, 213.
[2] *Giles Moore*, pp. 180–2, 305–6.

texts, and the reach of print rather than merely its content. This is often thought to be an elusive goal, because sources tend to be 'inert' regarding consumption, particularly in terms of 'low' culture and non-elite readers in the localities.[3] The aim of this chapter is to challenge such assumptions, by investigating the response to popular political material across the country and across the social spectrum. My argument will be that the Civil Wars witnessed profound changes in the consumption of polemic and news, and that whereas scribal circulation had been unable to satisfy the demand for such material in the 1620s and 1630s (section i), new opportunities were provided once it became impossible to control pamphleteering and journal-ism in the 1640s. Amid a clamour for news and debate during the revolu-tionary upheavals, printed texts brought information and analysis within reach of a much broader political nation, and the chapter will highlight the pervasiveness of cheap print, and the evidence which suggests that contem-poraries acquired it in large quantities and on a regular basis. Such changes can only really be explored by recovering contemporary practices relating to consumption, and in the first instance this will involve focusing on the *ownership* of printed material, to develop a picture of the demand for print, its reach, and also the reasons why it was consumed. As Stancombe and Moore suggest, this will be done by looking beyond inventories and library catalogues, sources that are conventionally important for analysing book ownership, but that have only limited value for the historian of cheap print (section ii). The chapter will scrutinize other traces of long-lost libraries (section iii), and delve deeper into the practices and processes associated with the purchase of pamphlets and newspapers (section iv), not least in terms of the relationships between consumers and booksellers (section v). By being attentive to sources that reveal consumption practices as well as traces of ownership, it will uncover what people knew about print and how they went about getting it.[4] This will mean acknowledging the central importance of London's print trade, but it will also mean emphasizing that people did not actually need to be in the capital to exploit its resources, not least because of the possibilities offered by sociable networks and the business practices of individual booksellers. Ultimately, it will be possible to

---

[3] H. Hackel, *Reading Material in Early Modern England* (Cambridge, 2005), pp. 9, 17, 214; J. Fergus, *Provincial Readers in Eighteenth Century England* (Oxford, 2006), pp. 1–2, 4–5, 14–16; A. Halasz, *Marketplace of Print* (Cambridge, 1997), pp. 8–13.

[4] E. Leedham-Green and D. McKitterick, 'Ownership', in *CHB IV*, pp. 323–38; D. Woolf, *Reading History in Early Modern England* (Cambridge, 2000), ch. 3; J. Raymond, 'Irrational, impractical and unprofitable', in *Reading, Society and Politics in Early Modern England*, ed. K. Sharpe and S. Zwicker (Cambridge, 2003), pp. 189, 199–204; J. Raymond, *The Invention of the Newspaper* (Oxford, 1996), pp. 264–8.

argue that pamphlets and newspapers were treated as everyday items, but not necessarily as trivial acquisitions, and this process of shedding light on the vibrancy of print culture will demonstrate the seriousness with which political events were followed by people from different walks of life and different parts of the country, and even the emergence of something approaching a shared national culture of news and comment.

i The limitations of scribal culture

Before analysing the ownership of print it is necessary to take a step back, and to consider the scribal news culture that existed before the 1640s. Scholars are increasingly aware of the appetite for topical information and comment, and of the existence of commercial and sociable practices that went some way towards catering for such demand. Nevertheless, serious doubts remain about the capacity for such material, and even for primitive 'corantos', to satisfy demand, and about the degree to which such texts penetrated beyond London and beyond the nobility and greater gentry.

The limitations of scribal culture are immediately clear from its most well-known sub-genre: commercial scribal newsletters. Such texts – by men such as Captain Rossingham – were highly prized by their readers, and they were packed with parliamentary news and political gossip.[5] Indeed, scholars have underestimated the scale of this scribal news industry. Relatively little attention has been paid to the news services operated by men like Samuel Hartlib, to the news gathering that was undertaken for specific grandees by information brokers like William Ravenscroft, John Castle, Georg Rudolph Weckherlin and Henry Robinson, or to the involvement in such practices of men like John Dillingham and Daniel Border, who would later become prominent print journalists.[6] The danger, however, is that newsletters have made a greater impact on historians than they did at the time, in the sense that their reach would have been extremely limited. Indeed, regular access to detailed newsletters may have been fairly rare beyond a narrow elite of well-connected and powerful grandees who could afford a subscription fee of perhaps £20 per annum.[7]

[5] BL: Add. 11045; Harl. 7000, fos. 352–57v; Bodl. MS Carte 77, fos. 346–428v, 468–9v.
[6] Northants. RO, IC 231b; IC 232; SUL, Hartlib 44/2/1, 5, 7; 44/3/2; 7/27/20; 31/3/7, 9, 15; 32/2/5, 7, 13, 15, 19; ERO, D/DBa/A39/7, unfol.; BL, Sloane 3317, fos. 21–2v, 29, 30–1, 44–v; HEH, EL 6470; EL 7807–63; BL, Add. 72275–6; Warw. RO: CR2017/C5/30, 57, 65, 74; CR2017/C115; CR2017/C100/1–4; *HMC Montagu*, pp. 132–4, 138–41, 143–6, 146–54, 163–4, 166–7; BL, Add. 70112, unfol.
[7] Bodl. MS Tanner 65, fo. 78; I. Atherton, 'The itch grown a disease', in *News, Newspapers and Society*, ed. J. Raymond (London, 1999), pp. 41, 48.

Of course, it was not necessary to subscribe to such services or to employ news agents in order to gain access to topical information. For most people outside a narrow elite, a more realistic option involved *ad hoc* methods for acquiring news. Scribal 'separates' – stand-alone items that could be acquired commercially from scriveners, scribes and booksellers – were clearly more affordable, and made it possible to access a fairly wide range of political and parliamentary documents, including 'all the speeches, and all their particular proceedings'.[8] The trade in such material undoubtedly became more significant in the 1620s, and continued into the early months of the Long Parliament, when parliamentary speeches, petitions and orders, as well as reports of Strafford's trial, were acquired by gentry families across the country, and indeed collected, bound and conserved as a record of 'that great and memorable parliament'. Once again, however, it is possible to question the availability and affordability of such texts, and the degree to which they trickled down into the hands of a popular audience.[9] During the late 1630s, for example, reports of state trials were difficult to come by and extremely expensive. Writing in February 1634, for example, Ralph Verney professed himself to be one of those 'country clowns' who could not get accurate information about the censure and punishment of William Prynne, and in 1637 the Earl of Huntingdon spent 6s 8d merely to get a copy of the indictment of the Puritan 'martyrs', Burton, Bastwick and Prynne. Likewise, for those unable to attend John Hampden's Ship Money trial, there developed a lively trade in scribal copies of the key documents, but at a hefty price. Huntingdon paid 2s 6d for a copy of the judgment, while copies of Croke's speech changed hands for 10s, and Sir Thomas Pelham spent £1 on a complete collection of the arguments.[10] The same was also true in the early phase of the Long Parliament. Sir Thomas Barrington's accounts reveal that a scribal copy of the articles against Strafford cost 10s, while a speech by John Glyn cost 6s, and another by Oliver St John cost 1s. A document containing three speeches by John Pym and John Maynard cost a further 1s 4d. Likewise, the Savile family of Rufford paid 2s 6d to 'a fellow which brought speeches' in May 1640, and the same sum for a speech by Lord Digby in May 1641. These prices may explain why John Rous not only recognized the existence of a market for news, but also

[8] FSL, F.c.7. C. Kyle, *Theater of State* (Stanford, 2012), ch. 4; *Papers of Sir Richard Grosvenor*, ed. R. Cust (Stroud, 1996), pp. 43–51; J. Morrill, 'William Davenport and the "silent majority" of early Stuart England', *Journal of the Chester Archaeological Society*, 58 (1975), pp. 119–23.

[9] Beinecke, Osborn b.229.

[10] *Letters and Papers of the Verney Family*, ed. J. Bruce (Cam. Soc., 1853), pp. 157–8; HEH, HAF Box 12/10; Bodl. MS Eng.Lett.b.1, fo. 239v; BL, Add. 33145, fo. 109.

reflected on the uncertainty of 'country intelligence', and the regularity and reliability with which texts circulated was probably limited.[11] Indeed, even prominent individuals found it difficult to follow political developments. Brilliana Harley complained in 1626 about 'how ignorant we country people be', adding that she would 'be glad to hear what you do in the Parliament', and John Pory recognized that scribal news did not reach the 'ploughman and artisan'. As such, when a 1629 sermon mocked the obsession with current affairs – 'What news? Everyman asks what news?' – its author was probably drawing attention not just to people's fascination with news, but also to their frustration regarding the inadequacy of its supply.[12]

The same logic also applies to scribal versions of political and religious tracts, and particularly of texts that were controversial in nature. Some such material was readily available from stationers like John Sunbury and George Humble, or from scriveners like George Starkey, and some texts certainly reached apprentices and household servants, at least in London. Here too, however, there are grounds for questioning how widely key texts circulated, and how deeply they penetrated beyond an elite audience. Contemporaries faced serious obstacles in terms of the availability of scribal texts, even if the most well-known scriveners charged the highest prices, and even if jobbing clerks and local scribes had lower fees, and enabled texts to be copied all over the country.[13] In a few instances, of course, such material was circulated deliberately and provocatively by political grandees, and occasional evidence shows works turning up in surprising places, as with the copy of 'A Letter from the Devil to the Pope' that was found in the possession of widow Taylor in Wokingham.[14] Nevertheless, the production and distribution of seditious material was both expensive and difficult. The trade in texts like 'Tom Tell Troth', 'The Forerunner of Revenge' and 'Vox Populi', as well as the pamphlets of Sir Robert Cotton, was risky, and some of those involved got into trouble with the authorities. In addition, works that were particularly inflammatory – such as attacks on the Duke of Buckingham – quickly shot up in price and became extremely scarce. Indeed, when texts were popular, lengthy and contentious their inflated price would have put them beyond the reach of all but the wealthiest of readers. In 1630, therefore, a

---

[11] ERO, D/DBa/A2, fos. 61–3, 64v; Notts. RO, DD/SR/A4/43, unfol.; *Rous Diary*, pp. 3, 18, 19, 22, 35–6, 37–8, 39.

[12] BL, Add. 70110, fos. 12–v, 100; *Rous Diary*, p. 44.

[13] BL, Add. 22591, fos. 2, 31, 40, 54, 81, 274, 355; R. Cust, 'News and politics in early seventeeth-century England', *P&P*, 112 (1986), p. 64.

[14] HEH: EL 7902, 7908; EL 7974.

scribal copy of a notorious Puritan text like Alexander Leighton's *Sion's Plea* apparently cost as much as £1.[15]

Such evidence about the demand for, but problematic supply of, news and opinion provides the crucial context for understanding the impact of print, not least in terms of the enthusiastic response to early corantos and gazettes.[16] Contemporaries were struck by the potential reach of printed texts, and the rhetoric with which they were surrounded was markedly different to that regarding scribal culture. John Pory recommended corantos as a means of becoming familiar with 'that which the vulgar know', and those who proposed setting up an official government newspaper saw it as the best means to disperse important information 'into all the veins of the whole body of the state', and to reach the 'vulgar' rather than merely the gentry. Indeed, this was precisely why corantos were thought to be troubling, and the decision to suppress them in 1632 was explicitly seen as a means of ensuring that 'the people's heads might not be filled with idle discourse'.[17] Of course, commentators obviously recognized that this would not dampen the demand for news, and Pory argued that 'this smothering of the corantos is but a palliation, not a cure'. He also predicted that 'they will burst out again one of these days'. However, this sense that printed news was likely to reach a significantly bigger audience explains why corantos were strictly controlled when they reappeared in the late 1630s, so that news might not be obtained through 'strangers and careless persons'.[18]

What emerges from an examination of pre-1640s news culture, in other words, is a sense that there was considerable demand for news, but that scribal genres would have been prohibitively expensive for anyone beyond the gentry. Such circumstances did not necessarily preclude more widespread circulation of topical information, but they clearly had a profound impact upon contemporary ownership of such material. A much more likely way of enhancing the penetration of news involved printed texts, which proved popular when they were available, and which helped to overcome the limitations of scribal culture and to satisfy the demand for comment and information. Before 1640, however, print culture involved a limited range of texts, and overwhelmingly continental news. Indeed, the restricted nature

[15] Bodl. MS Bankes MS 63, fos. 44–v, 46; MS Bankes 19, fo. 12; LPL, MS 942/18; Birch, *Charles*, i. 149, 169, 227, 229, ii. 61; CKS, U269/1/CB137; BL, Harl. 287, fo. 261.

[16] *Rous Diary*, pp. 7, 31, 44, 63, 67, 70, 75; FSL: L.d.420; X.d.441/2–4; *Barrington Family Letters*, ed. A. Searle (Cam. Soc., 1983), pp. 201–27; SUL, Hartlib 9/1/12/1–2; BL, Harl. 389, fos. 1, 5, 56, 68, 79, 81–4, 87, 104, 106; *Crosfield*, pp. 7, 14, 57–8.

[17] TNA, SP 14/124, fos. 230–v; *CSPD 1619–23*, p. 330; BL, Add. 72439, fos. 1–6; *Crosfield*, p. 61.

[18] Birch, *Charles*, ii. 186; TNA, SP 16/280, fo. 186; *CSPD 1638–9*, p. 182; TNA, SO 3/12, fo. 8v.

of pre-Civil War news culture is apparent from the emergence of texts like 'diurnall occurrences' in the opening weeks of the Long Parliament, which catered for demand, and which can be found in many gentry archives, but which remained pricey, at around 1s 6d per week.[19] This is the context for exploring the degree to which printed pamphlets and newspapers circulated following the much discussed 'explosion' of print after 1641.

ii Pamphlet libraries

The idea that Civil War pamphlets and newspapers brought political information and ideas to a larger audience seems obvious, not least given the number and range of texts that appeared. These are famously evident in the collection of the London bookseller, George Thomason, but there is obviously a risk that he was an oddity, who was unusually interested in print and unusually able to get his hands on it. My contention, however, is that Thomason was *not* unique, but that this only becomes clear by recognizing the limitations of conventional methods for analysing the consumption of print. These tend to concentrate on library catalogues, inventories and sale catalogues, sources that only rarely offer datable and precise evidence, even if they demonstrate that an obsession with cheap print was fairly common.

Library catalogues are valuable for demonstrating that scholars and members of the elite amassed large collections of printed works, but they are problematic in any number of ways. They very often concentrate on scholarly works and sizeable volumes, and less substantial items are rarely outlined in detail.[20] Where pamphlets and newspapers are mentioned at all, they tend to be included as 'bundles', as miscellaneous volumes of bound tracts, or as 'pamphlets, letters and speeches, bound'.[21] In addition to problems about detail, there are also problems of dating, and many lists were evidently compiled long after collections were developed, such that there is little clarity about when specific works were acquired.[22] Indeed, documentary evidence that was generated within the lifetime of individual readers is often extremely vague about the content of particular libraries. Of the Earl of Conway's collection in 1643, therefore, we know only that it

---

[19] TNA, SP 16/493, fo. 166; CKS, U269/A390/1.

[20] BL: Sloane 555; Harl. 4394; Harl. 4638, fos. 148–v; D. McKitterick, *Library of Sir Thomas Knyvett* (Cambridge, 1978); *Library of Robert Burton*, ed. N. Kiessling (OBS, 22, 1988); J. Lievsay, 'A cavalier library', *SB*, 6 (1953), 141–60.

[21] FSL, Add. 984; HEH, EL 6495; NLW, MS 9065E/2092; BL: Sloane 1346, fo. 14; Harl. 813, fo. 199v.

[22] BL, Sloane 1780; Northants. RO, FH 4023.

included 46 'chests of books', while we know no more of Sir Thomas Peyton's collection in October 1644 than that it contained 73 folios, 102 quartos, 244 octavos, and 135 duodecimos, as well as 'divers unbound and stitched books'.[23] Equally enigmatic are sources pertaining to property that was seized from royalists in the 1640s. These were intended to estimate value rather than to specify contents, and many refer merely to books of 'little value', 'small parcels of pamphlets' and 'bundles' of 'old stitched books'.[24] Inventories and wills, meanwhile, offer clues about book ownership beyond the elite, but they, too, concentrate on monetary worth rather than specific items. One notable example merely referred to pamphlets that were scattered indiscriminately around a particular house, including a pile found 'behind the door'.[25]

Such problems – the need for datable and precise evidence – undermine the utility of even the most detailed catalogues. These include lists for the libraries of the Sidney, L'Estrange and Gell families, each of which offers rich detail about substantial pamphlet collections, and about the contents of bound volumes of tracts and newspapers.[26] Here the central difficulty involves whether material was purchased at or near the time of publication, and some collections can be shown to have been amassed long after the events to which their contents relate. A case in point involves Richard Smith, a London prison manager whose 1674 library catalogue itemized entire bundles of Civil War tracts, including petitions, official statements, and newspapers. These included over 1,000 acts, orders and declarations from 1642 to 1660, over 500 pieces regarding the king, the parliament and the army (1642–8), 175 parliamentary speeches from 1640 to 1642, 300 petitions, 109 works by William Prynne, and 90 works by (or relating to) John Lilburne. The collection also included a volume of 200 news pamphlets, complete runs of *Mercurius Aulicus* and the *Perfect Diurnall*, and 119 news pamphlets by Marchamont Nedham, as well as almost 300 other assorted newspapers. The problem, however, is that only some of this material was purchased at the time of its appearance, and many more

[23] BL, Add. 70105, unfol.; *Oxinden and Peyton Letters*, p. 72.
[24] TNA, SP 20/7, fos. 5v, 9, 10v, 20v, 25, 26, 27v, 30, 43v, 53v, 55, 57v, 59, 63, 116; BL: Add. 28191A-B; I. Roy, 'The libraries of Edward, 2nd Viscount Conway', *BIHR*, 41 (1968), pp. 35, 41–2.
[25] CKS, U352/F7; Beds. RO, TW1137; L. Weatherill, *Consumer Behaviour and Material Culture* (London, 1997); H. French, *Middle Sort of People* (Oxford, 2007), pp. 155–96; J. Halliwell, *Ancient Inventories* (London, 1854), p. 82.
[26] CKS, U1475/Z45/2, fos. 2v-213; Norfolk RO, LEST NE1; DRO, D258/72; BL, Harl. 4618; Chetham, Mun.A.2.67.

acquisitions were made after the Restoration, when Smith was 'constantly known every day to walk his rounds through the shops'.[27]

Very occasionally it is possible to analyse library lists that contain detailed information about cheap print and that also have more obvious provenance. In 1646, the inventory of the Earl of Essex's library contained pamphlets by John Vicars, Thomas Edwards, William Prynne, John Lilburne and Henry Parker, and before 1647 Sir Thomas Roe acquired twenty volumes of French mercuries, acts of parliament, and pamphlets by the likes of John Bastwick and Calybute Downing.[28] The library list of a Mr Preston, which was compiled in the 1650s, detailed 'seven volumes of tracts betwixt king and parliament, 1641 and 42', 'seven volumes of tracts, 1642–3', and a volume of the king's declarations from 1642. Preston also owned volumes containing 'speeches in Parliament' (1640–1), as well as a pamphlet by Bastwick 'with others', *A Paradox for these Times* 'with others', Milton's divorce tract 'and others', and Ferne's resolving of Conscience 'and others', as well as the *Grand Remonstrance* 'and others'.[29] Sir Robert and Lady Heath collected official declarations and proclamations during the 1640s, while Sir Edward Dering amassed nearly 500 items before the Civil Wars broke out, including many pamphlets from 1640 to 1642, suggesting that he immersed himself in the political and religious controversies of the period.[30] Of course, these people hardly offer a representative cross-section of the political nation, and it is obviously no coincidence that conventional sources relating to the ownership of print relate to members of the political, scholarly or clerical elite. Fortunately, however, some of the most valuable surviving lists go at least some way towards addressing this problem, by also providing evidence relating to lawyers and administrators as well as men from the mercantile elite and middling sort in provincial England, whose spheres of influence were local rather than national.

The most prominent of these was Sir Arthur Annesley, a Presbyterian MP during the 1640s who became a powerful statesman after the Restoration and whose vast collection was detailed in a 1686 sale catalogue. Although this did not itemize every pamphlet and newspaper, it appears that material from the Civil War era extended to over 7,000 items, not including eleven volumes of newspapers such as the *Kingdomes Weekly Intelligencer* and *Perfect Diurnall*, or nine volumes of *Mercurius Politicus*

---

[27] BL, Sloane 771; *Bibliotheca Smithiana* (1682); T. Birrell, 'Books and buyers', in *Under the Hammer*, ed. R. Myers (London, 2001), pp. 56–7.

[28] BL, Add. 46189, fos. 155v–8; HEH, HA Inventories Box 1/20; Badminton, FmS/D3/2/7.

[29] BL, Sloane 203, fos. 309–14v.   [30] BL, Eg. 2983, fo. 79; FSL, V.b.297, fos. 10–17v.

and *Mercurius Publicus*.[31] A much later list of both parliamentarian and royalist literature involves material that was almost certainly acquired by Daniel Fleming during his time as a law student at Gray's Inn, and many items bore his ownership signature (or that of his wife), and contained his annotations.[32] Somewhat less elevated, albeit well-connected, was John Browne, clerk of parliament during the 1640s, whose library contained 79 volumes of tracts, pamphlets and newspapers, covering the years 1641 to 1663, and a total of just under 1,900 items.[33] More intriguing still, perhaps, is the library of Samuel Jeake, merchant and town clerk of Rye, which contained at least 1,200 items, including many volumes of pamphlets and newspapers, the contents of which are outlined in remarkable detail.[34] By far the most significant catalogue, however, is the least well known. It relates to Robert Harvey, a London merchant who settled in Quainton in Buckinghamshire, and it provides a complete account of fifty-three bound volumes, almost all from the period between 1640 and 1652. What is fascinating about Harvey's collection is that it was acquired by a provincial figure who played only a minor part in the Civil Wars, but who nevertheless purchased over 2,000 items over a twelve-year period. Indeed, Harvey's collection may once have been even larger, given that the catalogue is suspiciously silent about newspapers, which may have been purchased but not preserved. The inescapable conclusion is that amassing large quantities of pamphlets was not restricted to Thomason, who emerges as being exceptional in the *scale* of his collecting, but not in the urge to devour cheap political print. Indeed, it is possible to show that, at least during the period from 1641 to 1649, Harvey acquired up to 35 per cent of the volume of non-newsbook material that was acquired by the infinitely more famous Thomason.[35]

iii Library traces

Much as they might be problematic, therefore, catalogues and inventories occasionally prove to be extremely valuable, so long as they are used with care. In order to gain a deeper understanding of ownership patterns, however, especially in terms of the appetite for print among 'less extraordinary readers', it is necessary to employ different sources about material that

[31] *Bibliotheca Angleseiana* (1686), sigs. Gg2–v.
[32] *English Books of the Sixteenth and Seventeenth Centuries* (Christies, 26–27 Feb. 1969), pp. 11–78.
[33] PA, Braye 104.
[34] *A Radical's Books*, ed. M. Hunter et al. (Woodbridge, 1999), pp. 52–3, 98–9, 142–3, 180, 212–15.
[35] FSL, M.b.29.

was amassed at the time but never catalogued. This involves examining 'traces' of former libraries, in terms of extant collections and the reconstruction of dispersed material, both of which provide a flavour of print consumption, even if not a complete picture regarding specific individuals. By trading off a comprehensive picture for a contextual one, in other words, it will be possible to enhance our appreciation of contemporary attitudes to print, not least in terms of the possibility that pamphlets and newspapers were highly prized, even if they were not treated as collectable.

On very rare occasions, therefore, early modern libraries survive more or less intact and in their original locations. Some of these involve untraceable leads, such as the eight bundles of pamphlets containing 'the occurrences of the times' that the Bodleian acquired from Richard Branthwayt of Ringwood in Hampshire in the mid 1640s.[36] This collection almost certainly remains within the library, but it cannot be traced with ease. Others can be located but are problematic. In the case of Thomas Plume, vicar of Greenwich in the late 1650s, this means some 7,000 items, including many of the most important political and religious pamphlets of the period, but another example of a collection that seems to have been acquired after the Restoration rather than during the revolution.[37] More promising is the library of Griffin Higgs (d. 1659), dean of Lichfield, which remains at Merton College Oxford, and which reflects Civil War acquisitions involving official and polemical literature, as well as parliamentary speeches, accounts of the king's trial and discussions of the army and the Levellers. Similarly, the extant library of Thomas Hall, Presbyterian master of the grammar school at King's Norton (Worcestershire) – catalogued in his own time and bequeathed to the parish and to the public library in Birmingham – includes over forty volumes of Civil War pamphlets, and well over 500 items.[38] Such collections can sometimes be reconstructed even if they have been disbound, and thus stripped of valuable contextual information. These include the pamphlets of Fabian Phillips and Walter Yonge, the library of Sir John Bramston junior, and the collection of the Earl of Bridgewater, the latter of which included over 1,800 pamphlets from 1640 to 1660.[39] At other times, 'libraries within libraries' are revealed by

---

[36] *Bodleian Library Account Book*, ed. G. Hampshire (Oxford, 1983), p. 150.
[37] *Catalogue of the Plume Library*, ed. S. Deed (Maldon, 1959).
[38] *Bibliotheca Higgsiana*, ed. P. Morrish (OBS, 1990); D. Thomas, 'Religious polemic, print culture and pastoral ministry' (University of Birmingham PhD, 2011), pp. 9, 16–85, 424–570.
[39] *A Catalogue of Books Chiefly Relating to English and American History* (1884), pp. 31–50; *Catalogue of a Collection* (London, 1901), pp. 21–104; H. Hackel, 'The countess of Bridgewater's London library', in *Books and Readers*, ed. J. Andersen and E. Sauer (Philadelphia, 2001), pp. 138–59. The Phillips and Yonge pamphlets are in UCL Special Collections.

owners' annotations, as with the army secretary, John Rushworth, and Sir Arthur Annesley. In both of these cases it is possible to supplement sale catalogues with extant, albeit incomplete, material. A similar process permits the recovery of the 'prison library' of John Squier, vicar of St Leonard's Shoreditch, which contained at least 260 Civil War pamphlets, and of at least part of the collection of Henry Oxinden. The latter includes around 450 items that survive within Elham parish library, 226 of which date from 1641–2.[40]

Beyond this, and as Stancombe demonstrated, even stray volumes of Civil War material can occasionally prove revealing, particularly if they remain in their original bindings. In many instances, therefore, it is possible to peer onto early modern bookshelves, even if only in decontextualized ways. This might mean a bound gathering of fifty-nine newspapers from February to July 1649, or the volume of forty-six proclamations and acts from the late 1650s that can be traced to John Howland.[41] It might also mean stray volumes from scattered collections, some of which supplement known library lists. These include Sir Edward Dering's copy of *The Privileges and Practice of Parliaments*, Sir Roger Twysden's copy of Naunton's *Fragmenta Regalia*, and the copy of Joshua Sprigge's *Anglia Rediviva* that belonged to Cornelius Holland. There also exist 300 pamphlets from 1641–2 that were owned by Sir Richard Grosvenor, stray items from Robert Harvey's collection, and volumes of Jeake's pamphlets that were omitted from his 'register', as well as William Dowsing's many 'fast sermons'.[42] Very occasionally, notes and annotations also provide what amount to provisional or interim library lists, and while these are often crude and cryptic, they generally relate to traceable pamphlets, and sometimes to identifiable individuals. A copy of the prayer book belonging to Christopher Parkes (minister at Bolton in Yorkshire) contains detailed lists of books that he owned in the 1640s and 1650s, as well as books that he wanted, by authors such as Prynne and Baxter, and Scottish covenanters and Smectymnuans, as well as tracts about Lilburne and James Naylor.[43]

---

[40] F. Henderson, '"Posterity to judge"', *BLR*, 15 (1996), 247–59; CUL, Syn.7.64.118; T. Connor, 'Malignant reading', *The Library*, 7th series, 7 (2006), 154–84; S. Hingley, 'The Oxindens, Warlys and Elham Parish Library' (University of Kent PhD, 2004), ch. 5, appendix 4.

[41] FSL, 150–373q; HEH, 482218.

[42] FSL, STC 7750; FSL, STC 19846 (copy 3); *Papers of Sir Richard Grosvenor*, p. xvi; HEH, HM 1554; *Radical's Books*, pp. 244–9, 327–8, 330–2; J. Morrill, 'William Dowsing the bureaucratic Puritan', in *Public Duty and Private Conscience in Seventeenth Century England*, ed. J. Morrill (Cambridge, 1992), pp. 179–82. Holland's volume is now owned by the Naseby Battlefield Trust.

[43] For example: FSL, V.a.95.

In such cases, of course, valuable and datable information that links particular books to individual readers can be obtained only at the expense of a comprehensive picture of specific collections. This trade-off is hard to avoid, and it does at least enhance our appreciation of contemporary attitudes to print, something where there is also much to be gained by means of a rather different methodology. This involves examining printed material that survives among private manuscript papers. Some such gatherings were acquired later, by family members who had antiquarian interests, but many others were contemporary creations.[44] Pamphlets and broadsides, as well as official literature and newspapers, can thus be found scattered among the papers of many prominent families, such as the Harleys and the Cokes, the Lowthers of Cumbria, the Levesons of Staffordshire and the Gells of Derbyshire, as well as the Hesilriges of Leicestershire. At Antony House, meanwhile, there survive almost 140 pamphlets and newspapers from the 1640s that have ownership signatures of William and Courtenay Pole, and other archives contain a variety of tracts that belonged to men such as Richard Brownlow of Lincolnshire and his local vicar, Charles Woodward of Alford, as well as to the London mercer, Thomas Papillon, and Captain Richard Orlebar of Hinwick House in Wellingborough.[45]

What is striking about such stray items, preserved among family papers rather than in libraries, is that they shed valuable light on contemporary attitudes towards pamphlet literature. In some cases, of course, items were filed within archives because they had effectively become manuscripts, not least the many almanacs that were annotated by gentlemen and their wives, and by humble troopers in provincial regiments. For Henry Oxinden, meanwhile, Juvenal's satires became a handy diary, and for Norton Knatchbull a pamphlet by William Prynne became a prayer book, and both men stored these books among their private papers.[46] More often, and perhaps more importantly, acts, ordinances and declarations were often kept separately from other printed material, because they were integral to the working lives and official duties of particular individuals. Thus, the Farington papers contain a royal proclamation from June 1642 regarding the commission of array, while the Lowther papers contain orders regarding

---

[44] Beds. RO, X/171/33–57; Wilts RO, MS 2057/F6/2–8; BJL, DD/HO/2/7, 17, 31, 58, 64, 70; Devon RO, 1392M/L1645/22–39.

[45] BL: Add. 70003, fos. 213v-14; Add. 70004, unfol.; Add. 70081–2; Add. 69923; Cumbria RO, D/LONS/L13/10/1; Staffs. RO, D593/V/4/1–52; DRO, D258/12, 15, 21, 30, 32, 34, 53; Leics. RO, DG21/282, 283, 287; Antony, CZ/EE/29; PZ/B2/19–25; Lincs. RO, BNLW 4/8/2/29–46; Northants. RO, P(L)142–3, 216–20; Beds. RO, OR 2093/7–22.

[46] Warw RO, CR136/A/20; WYAS (Leeds), WYL230/3590; Berks RO, D/ELs/F18; CKS, U49/F19; BL, Add. 34169–72; FSL, 222477q; CCL, Elham, 915; CKS, U951/Z44.

the 1641 Poll Tax, and instructions about compounding for delinquency, and the papers of Colonel John Moore contain ordinances of relevance to local government in Lancashire. Similar items can also be found repeatedly among the papers of those who sat on county benches and local commissions, including John Clifford of Gloucestershire, who kept Husband's collection of parliamentary orders among his official manuscripts.[47]

In fact, this treatment of print as part of 'working papers' was merely a symptom of a bigger phenomenon, and one that has profound consequences for the reliability of libraries as guides to the consumption of cheap print. This involved the way in which a variety of genres were treated like manuscripts, as part of the process of adapting to the print revolution. This applies to works that were conventionally read in scribal form, such as political verses and parliamentary speeches. It also applies to newspapers, perhaps because they, too, had evolved from newsletters and manuscript accounts of 'diurnall occurrences'. Thus, the papers of Colonel John Harington, a parliamentarian officer from Kelston in Somerset, contain 49 newspapers and pamphlets from the 1640s and 1650s, while the archives of the provincial royalist, Sir Justinian Isham, contain nearly 400 newsbooks from 1642 to 1660, including a complete run of *Mercurius Politicus* from 1652. Indeed, what Isham's newspaper collection demonstrates very clearly is that such material, like many other items found within personal papers, was treated differently because it was regarded not merely as useful but also as ephemeral. Isham sometimes preserved only certain parts of specific texts, and even made cuttings from newspapers, keeping pages that were particularly relevant rather than hoarding all of the items that he bought.[48]

iv The practices and processes of consumption

In other words, a methodology that both *reconstructs* early modern libraries and explores their traces, rather than one that relies on extant catalogues, enhances our picture of the ownership of print. It confirms that contemporaries purchased Civil War pamphlets and newspapers in large quantities, and it suggests that such practices were evident beyond a metropolitan political elite. It also opens up avenues of enquiry that relate to *perceptions* of

---

[47] Lancs. RO, DDF/2437/93; Cumbria RO, D/LONS/L13/9/Box 1; D/LONS/L13/1/9; Liverpool UL, MS 23.1.59–60.
[48] NLS, Adv.33.1.1/13; Som. RO, DD/MI, Box 18/102; CKS: U951/Z49/5; U269/O294; Cumbria RO, D/LONS/L13/10/1/16–17, 51, 52; BL: Add. 69923; Add. 46376A; Northants. RO, Catalogue of Isham newspapers.

print culture, in terms of how and why print was valued. By looking beyond the consumption of those whose libraries came to be catalogued, and to those who did not necessarily strive to collect and preserve pamphlets and newspapers, it becomes clear that a rounded appreciation of the ownership of print requires delving more deeply into the processes by which such material was acquired, and into the *practices* that were involved.

Intrinsic to this process is a shift away from libraries and printed artefacts towards archival evidence, not least in terms of commonplace books and diaries. Very often such sources offer only fragmentary evidence about book ownership, such as Drayner Massingberd's reference to 'my book of acts of parliament', now apparently lost, or Sir John Archer's notes that reveal the days he spent reading Thomas Edwards's *Gangraena*. Any number of pocketbooks, meanwhile, list pamphlets 'to be had', as with the diary of Roger Hill MP, who was naturally interested in purchasing contributions to the paper war between king and parliament in 1642.[49] These are *hints* regarding the purchase of cheap print, and they survive further down the social spectrum. The minister of Earls Colne in Essex, Ralph Josselin, reflected that 'a supply of books is necessary for me', but he also recognized that 'my means [are] but small to purchase them', and as such he resolved to 'buy but few, and those of choice and special concernment'. These 'special' books included parliamentary debates and an account of the king's trial, both of which he evidently acquired. Nehemiah Wallington, of course, mused about 'finding so many of these little pamphlets of weekly news about my house', and on how he likened them to 'so many thieves that had stole away my money before I was aware of them'.[50]

Such comments are valuable, but they are of course vague, and they need to be supplemented by more detailed evidence regarding book purchases. From the annotated almanacs of extraordinary and obsessive bibliophiles like Anthony Wood, it is possible to trace the purchase of large quantities of pamphlets and newspapers in the 1650s.[51] More generally, purchasing can be observed at least some way across the social spectrum. Lord Buckhurst's diary for the early 1650s recorded the purchase of books like Hobbes's *Leviathan*, and frequent dealing with the bookseller, Henry Seile, while John Syms of Devon, sometime parliamentarian naval chaplain, recorded specific purchases, such as three tracts by Prynne in one volume (2s 6d), several newspapers (1s 2d), and copies of the *King's Cabinet Opened* and

[49] Lincs. RO: MM10/1; MISC.Don.310; UCL, Ogden 7/45, fo. 2; HEH, HM 55603, fo. 1; BL, Add. 47787, fos. 15, 57; Bucks. RO, D/W/97/7, unfol.

[50] *Josselin Diary*, pp. 53, 155–6; BL, Add. 40883, fo. 15v.   [51] Wood, *Life and Times*, i. 211–314.

Prynne's *Popish Royal Favourite*.[52] It can also be observed by both Londoners and men in the provinces. Sir Humphrey Mildmay purchased a royal declaration in April 1640 (10d), 'pamphlet books' (10d) and *Mercurius Aulicus*, as well as various other newspapers, almanacs and pamphlets, and on one occasion he paid 1s 4d 'to a fellow for mercuries and other pamphlets'. In Yorkshire, Adam Eyre purchased controversial pamphlets by John Saltmarsh, William Dell and William Lilly, as well as the occasional newspaper. In Gloucestershire, Nathaniel Clutterbuck of Eastington purchased 'weekly news' among other books, and in the Isle of Wight, Sir John Oglander settled bills for pamphlets and newspapers that had been acquired over time from booksellers. For such material he paid 8s in February 1643 and a further 10s 6d in the following May. Finally, a Wiltshire JP called John Ridout recorded not merely the titles that he wished to acquire, and the booksellers from whom he planned to get them, but also a priced list of over 150 items that had already been purchased. It included authors likes William Prynne, William Lilly, Thomas Edwards and Ephraim Pagitt, pamphlets such as *Englands Troubles Anatomised* and various parliamentary ordinances.[53]

Ridout, in other words, provides evidence not merely of pamphlets and newspapers being desired and acquired, but also of familiarity with the process involved in consuming print. This deepens our understanding significantly, and it emerges much more clearly from private correspondence between friends and family, and between employers and servants, not least in terms of the lengths to which individuals were prepared to go to trace particular items. Abel Barker in Leicestershire thus asked Edmund Wright in London to acquire a specific book that was to be sent 'by the next return of Harrington's carrier', and John Braddill of Portfield (near Whalley in Lancashire) asked John Blackburn to do the same, depending on availability and prices. During 1659, Justinian Isham received information and assistance regarding new and forthcoming books from Theodore Grene of Clements Inn, including a reply to Harrington's *Oceana*. Indeed, this example is intriguing because the book was not yet out, and Grene promised to send a copy as soon as it appeared. Grene also exchanged books with specific booksellers, and forwarded newspapers to Northamptonshire.[54]

[52] CKS, U269/F3/1, fos. 21v, 27v–32; BL, Add. 35297, fos. 180v–82v.
[53] BL, Harl. 454, fos. 137, 138v, 145, 146v, 147, 162v; A. Eyre, 'A dyurnall', in *Yorkshire Diaries* (SS, 65, 1877), pp. 4, 10, 24, 42, 53, 57, 62, 63, 68, 93; Glos. RO, D149/F13, fos. 1, 127–8v; IWCRO, OG/AA/31, pp. 6, 9; BL, RP 678, unfol.
[54] Leics. RO, DE730/4, fo. 46v; Lancs. RO, DDB85/20, fos. 30–2; Northants. RO, IC 451; IC 459A.

Much richer detail about the practices and processes involved in the purchase of print comes from private financial papers, including personal, household, estate and even kitchen account books. This is not to say that such material is invariably useful, and erratic accountancy practices present frequent problems. Titles were not always specified, as with the accounts of Sir Edward Dering, of Sir Thomas Myddleton's librarian at Chirk Castle, and of Sir Thomas Reade's steward at Barton St Helens in Abingdon.[55] Purchases might be aggregated and summarized, as with Sir John Pelham's bill of 14s for 'little books', the Earl of Northumberland's entry of 16s 8d for books and pamphlets (1648), and Lord Lovelace's expenditure of 1s 2d on newsbooks (1654).[56] And detailed entries were often reserved for substantial items, like the collections of Prynne's pamphlets (6s) and parliamentary ordinances (16s) that William Collins purchased for his employer, the Earl of Salisbury.[57] Nevertheless, the most valuable examples are much more helpful, recording individual purchases of single pamphlets, newspapers, acts and ordinances. Lord Buckhurst and the Earl of Middlesex both paid 4s 6d for Sir Edward Dering's collection of speeches in 1642, and Middlesex paid 1d for a copy of the Protestation, 2d for a speech by viscount Saye, and 3d for a parliamentary declaration. Likewise, a detailed picture also emerges about the purchases made by the Temple family, from a 1659 account of £3 9s 8d spent on newsbooks, petitions and acts, as well as parliamentary speeches.[58] Most often such purchases were made for the male heads of substantial households, but this was not always true, and sometimes the stated recipients were also women. This could mean the captive Princess Elizabeth, for whom the Earl of Leicester provided occasional diurnals in the late 1640s, but it could also mean almanacs for Hester Temple and Lady Barrington, sermons and newsbooks for Lady Barrington and the countess of Huntingdon, and even catechisms and primers for the latter's laundry maid and almanacs for the staff of Bishop Cosin's kitchen.[59]

Scrutinizing private accounts also reveals very clearly the importance of London – 'the rendezvous for expenses' – as a marketplace for print. This naturally emerges from the accounts of individuals who were based in the capital, such as the Earl of Bath and Sir Richard Temple, both of whom

---

[55]　BL, Add. 47787, fos. 57v-8v, 60–61v, 65–v; *Chirk Accounts*, pp. 8–81; SHL, MS 26, fos. 85v–91v; Northants. RO, FH 2504.
[56]　BL, Add. 33148, fo. 143v; Alnwick, U.I.6, unfol.; BL, Add. 63465, fo. 55.
[57]　CUL, Dd.viii.33, fos. 48v, 75v.
[58]　CKS: U269/A4/1–2; U269/A390/1; CUL, Buxton 127/2, fos. 59–60v; HEH, HM 46533.
[59]　Penshurst, MS 398; HEH, STTF Box 17/21, 41; ERO, A18/2; A14, fo. 57v; HEH, HAF Box 16/39; Durham Cathedral, Sharpe 163, p. 61.

made numerous purchases of newspapers and pamphlets, including speeches and acts of parliament, either singly or in small bundles.[60] And particularly interesting in this regard are the accounts of law students. Thus, from October 1652 to September 1653 John Buller spent £2 17s 6d on newspapers, and on posting them to his father, Francis Buller of Shillingham near Saltash in Cornwall. German Pole and James Master, meanwhile, both supplemented frequent spending on newspapers and 'little books concerning the times' – on which Master spent 3s 4d between July and November 1647 – with additional purchases of official and polemical literature, including tracts by Milton, Prynne, Lilburne and Nedham, accounts of political trials, pamphlets regarding the army, and even the satirical *Parliament of Ladies*.[61] Beyond residents, however, London's bookshops also served more occasional visitors, not least servants and employees. These included Nicholas Fazakerly, who purchased parliamentary acts while visiting London for Viscount Molyneux; Paul Adams, who regularly purchased newspapers when attending to Viscount Montague's business; and William Proctor, who bought newspapers and pamphlets for Sir Peter Temple, including *Aulicus*, *Britanicus* and the *Kingdomes Case*. Hercules Commander made similar purchases for John Crew, whose acts, votes and speeches, as well as 'odd sheets of pamphlets', came from 'Mr Sharley', 'Mr Leigh' in Fleet Street, and 'the woman at Westminster'.[62] Perhaps the most striking example of this phenomenon, however, involves Lady Alice L'Estrange of Hunstanton, whose every visit to the capital involved purchases of pamphlets from Abel Roper. These included declarations and ordinances, as well as accounts of parliamentary speeches and state trials, but they also included tracts by the dissenting brethren and pamphlets about the antinomians. During the mid 1640s, indeed, L'Estrange acquired everything from Laud's scaffold sermon to a 'railing book' by Lilburne, and propaganda by London Presbyterians and Scottish covenanters as well as the *Parliament of Ladies*, not to mention newspapers like the *London Post* and the *Moderate Intelligencer*.[63]

Obviously, it would be easy to respond to a case like L'Estrange's by pointing out that very few people had the capacity to visit London regularly, or to rely upon their servants as she so obviously did. However, this would be to underestimate the importance of 'proxy shopping', in terms of the

[60] IWCRO, OG/CC/127; *Devon Accounts*, ii. 95, 114, 142–4, 146, 152; HEH, ST 54/2.
[61] Antony, BA/20/3; DRO, D5557/10/1; 'James Master', i. 160–216, ii. 241–59, iii. 321–52.
[62] Lancs. RO: DDM/1/60; DDM/1/76; HEH: BAv.6(1); STTF Box 22/4; STTF Box 26/16; Bodl. MS Eng.Misc.e.6, fos. 41v, 61v, 83v, 92, 105v, 114v; Chester RO, DAR/F/3, pp. 13–35.
[63] Norfolk RO: LEST P7, pp. 195–6, 207, 211, 219, 264–85; LEST P10, pp. 10–60.

ability to rely on friends and kinsmen, and perhaps even those we might call 'news agents'. This can be seen repeatedly in the accounts of L'Estrange herself, as well as in those of Sir John Wittewronge, while the Barrington family paid one Captain Clement for news sent down from London 'at several times'.[64] Such examples make it clear that pamphlets were despatched across the country in letters and via carriers. From Devon the Earl of Bath paid for bundles of between three and thirteen pamphlets that were sent from London in the late 1640s and early 1650s, and the accounts of the Temple family for 1642 include a payment of 1s 4d for sending 'a parcel of books of news'. In the case of Lady L'Estrange the method employed was the 'Burnham post', while for others it meant local carriers, like Goodwife Mew, to whom payments were made for delivering books both large and small to Sir Edward Nicholas at Horsley in Surrey. The steward to the Lowther family made payments to the Kendal carrier for newspapers brought from London in July 1642, and his counterpart within the household of the Savile family of Rufford made regular payments to carriers who 'brought speeches', acts and ordinances, and to those who delivered 'diurnalls and books sent into the country'.[65] Of course, this kind of evidence obviously has limitations, and it only rarely disaggregates expenditure in order to reveal delivery costs and the affordability of the practice. Indeed, fragmentary evidence suggests that sending a pamphlet through the post could be an expensive business, with Sir Thomas Myddleton paying 13d for a pamphlet of Cromwell's declaration in 1654, and Daniel Fleming paying 1s for a single newspaper in 1659. Nevertheless, these may have been exceptional examples, and in general the inland post and carrier system probably worked perfectly well as a means of conveying printed material into the localities in an efficient and affordable manner, and it even seems to have ensured that pamphlets became available in rural Scotland.[66]

By facilitating analysis of consumption practices, therefore, private accounts enhance our understanding of *how* print was acquired, rather than merely *what* was purchased. Beyond this, however, the practical dimensions of the print marketplace also bring into sharper focus contemporary attitudes to pamphlets and newspapers. Central here is the idea that pamphlets and newspapers were regarded as *incidental* expenditure. With

---

[64] Norfolk RO: LEST P7, p. 247; LEST P10, pp. 67, 123; Herts. RO, D/Elw/F18, p. 153; ERO: D/Dba/A3, fo. 60v; D/DBa/A4, fos. 2, 5, 13v, 18, 27.

[65] *Devon Accounts*, ii. 114, 143, 157–8; HEH, STTF Box 14/38; Norfolk RO, LEST P10, pp. 90, 101, 109, 134, 160; JRL, NP 14; Cumbria RO, D/LONS/L3/1/6; Notts. RO: DD/SR/A4/25, A4/43, A5/1/7–13.

[66] *Chirk Accounts*, p. 42; HMC Le Fleming, p. 367; *Andrew Hay Diary*, p. 103.

the Earl of Bath and Daniel Fleming, for example, pamphlet expenditure was set out among postal charges, perhaps because the cost of a newspaper in London was about the same as for sending a letter across the City (2–3d), and significantly less than the cost of sending a letter to Buckinghamshire or Warwickshire (3–6d).[67] Many of those visiting the capital on political business, like Sir Thomas Barrington, Sir Robert Harley and Sir Richard Temple, accounted for printed items among their quotidian expenses for travel around the city, food and drink, and lodgings. Very often, indeed, such purchases were recorded among what Thomas Thynne called 'idle expenses', and what Lord Brooke's auditor called 'trifling money'. Thus, 'a parcel of pamphlets' or 'the mercury' might be entered amid expenditure on music masters and fencing equipment, fiddlers and players, food and hair-cuts, or theatre-going. They appear alongside occasional virtues and more regular vices, from poor relief to gambling debts, but more often they can be found among the costs of everyday life. This meant ribbon, gloves, silk, lace and buttons, or perhaps wax, pens and money bags, or else tobacco, brim-stone, mouth glue, loaf sugar, and 'sweet oranges and lemons'. During the late 1640s James Master's accounts refer to 'candles and a newsbook' (1s), 'cheese, whey, and 3 newsbooks' (1s), and 'cherry tart and a newsbook' (1s 4d), as well as to expenses for 'going by water, setting up my horse, and for pamphlets' (2s 6d). Lowther's accounts contain an entry for *Englands Cry* and a pound of cherries', and 'for washing and for news'.[68]

However, if the expenses associated with cheap print were incidental and ephemeral, then they were certainly not trivial, given the quantities of print that were involved and the frequency with which items were purchased. The scale on which cheap print was acquired is evident from Sir Edward Dering's accounts for the early 1620s, with ten items acquired for 2s 3d on one occasion in 1621, and forty-one items bought on 11 July 1623, at a cost of £3 14s 7d. It is also clear from the Paris accounts of the royalist ambassador, Sir Richard Browne, which reveal hefty payments to the local 'gasetere' [gazeteer].[69] It is most striking, however, from the accounts of the Barrington family, who had been obsessed by newspapers since the 1630s,

[67] *Devon Accounts*, ii. 149; Cumbria RO (Kendal), WD/Ry/239, 243; HEH, STTF Box 26/10, 16; ERO, D/DBa/A8, fo. 4; HEH, ST 51; ST 54/1.

[68] ERO, D/DBa/A9, fos. 10, 14v; BL, Add. 70091, unfol.; HEH, ST 51; ST 54/1; Longleat, Thynne 69, fos. 77–100; Warw. RO, CR1886/Box 411/15, p.7; Cumbria RO, D/LONS/W1/10, pp. 3–27; DRO, D5557/10/1; CUL, Pell 5/17; Antony, BC/26/18/33; Houghton, MS 605, unfol.; CKS, U350/E4, unfol.; Norfolk RO, LEST/P10, pp. 10, 120, 147; BL, Add. 69880, fo. 77; Longleat, Thynne 65, fo. 22v; Herts. RO: D/Elw/F18, pp. 123, 126, 137; D/Elw/F20, p. 131; 'James Master', i. 166, 170, 175, 178, 179, 184; Cumbria RO, D/LONS/W1/10, pp. 13, 27.

[69] CKS, U350/E4, unfol.; BL: Add. 78225, fos. 14–66; Add. 78231A, unfol.

and whose accounts record payments of £5 7s 11d on 'books of news' between November 1646 and March 1657, in addition to the ninety-five newspapers that were itemized but not priced. This could have generated as many as 1,400 items, and if we also allow for the twenty-seven occasions on which the accounts record the purchase of an unspecified volume of news-books, as well as the money that was spent on six months' worth of newspapers from Captain Clement, then the family was probably averaging in excess of two newspapers per week on a regular basis.[70]

This sense of the importance of everyday expenses – and that a regular supply of news was considered 'very necessary' – can be given added weight by considering not just the *scale* of spending on cheap print, but also its *frequency*, and by demonstrating how the shopping patterns of contemporary readers altered during the 1640s. Thus, having been addicted to 'pamphlets, proclamations and pictures' since the 1620s, the 1640s saw Sir Simonds D'Ewes consume such material in much greater quantities and in a much more regular manner. In the week 22–29 May 1641, for example, he acquired seven pamphlets for 17d, while in the week 5–12 June he purchased eight pamphlets for 11d, and in the week 4–11 September he bought sixteen pamphlets, including parliamentary speeches and corantos, all for 19d. In the week 19–26 November, D'Ewes purchased no less than thirty-six pamphlets, at a cost of 3s. Such behaviour continued throughout the 1640s, and in weeks when more substantial works were acquired – including Sprigge's *Anglia Rediviva* and the final part of Edwards' *Gangraena* – D'Ewes could spend as much as 16s.[71] Similar behaviour emerges from the accounts of Sir Thomas Barrington, which reveal even more starkly the extent to which newspapers had come to be considered as *essential* purchases. Beginning in the early months of the Long Parliament, therefore, Barrington acquired speeches and pamphlets in large quantities, and as political tension mounted in 1642, such purchases became more frequent and more extensive. Having purchased two newsbooks on 18 April, therefore, he added an unspecified number of additional titles the very next day, and a further sixpence worth of newspapers the day after that. Between 17 and 23 June, meanwhile, he bought a further 2s 2d worth of pamphlets, and between 2 and 16 July, he spent a further 4s 10d. During the eight weeks between mid March and late May 1644, moreover, Barrington spent 12s 4d on newsbooks, ordinances and pamphlets, on no less than sixteen separate

[70] ERO, D/DBa/A3–A5.
[71] Chetham, A.3.90, fos. 3v–4; BL, Cotton Charter xvi.13, fos. 5v–14; *Library of Sir Simonds D'Ewes*, ed. A. Watson (London, 1966), pp. 226–47; BL, Harl. 7660, fos. 29v–30, 34v–6, 49, 60v, 67, 73v, 80v.

occasions. Such habits were sustained fairly consistently by Sir John Barrington during the later 1640s and 1650s, most obviously by purchasing eight newspapers between 1 and 15 May 1650, and sixteen newspapers between late January and early March 1651, and by June 1652 he had developed a regular pattern of buying two newspapers every week. Between January and April 1660, meanwhile, an obsessive reader like Anthony Wood spent £1 9s 3d on assorted pamphlets, on no less than thirty-seven separate occasions.[72]

Although it might be argued with some justice that D'Ewes, Wood and the Barringtons were atypical, it is important to recognize that other accounts reveal similar patterns, in terms of the frequency with which purchases were made and the acquisition of multiple newspapers every week. In the early 1640s, for example, the Earl of Bath's monthly acquisitions could involve up to six pamphlets, while by the early 1650s they included between three and nine newspapers. During the Republic, Sir John Lowther made purchases of pamphlets and newspapers every few days, while during the Protectorate Sir Richard Temple sometimes visited bookshops every other day, in order to acquire newsbooks, ordinances, speeches and proclamations, and he spent between 6d and 9d each time.[73] Such behaviour, indeed, seems to have been fairly common. In the first two weeks of November 1650, Sir Edward Dering junior made four separate visits to bookshops, spending over 16s, and in the last two weeks of July 1651 he made three visits, and spent 21s. James Master visited bookshops up to three times a week in late 1646 and early 1647, and between 8 and 19 June 1647 he bought newspapers – sometimes more than one – on five separate occasions. Sir John Wittewronge purchased 'several small books' on no less than six occasions in January and February 1641, followed by many other tracts and speeches in the months that followed, and, like the Barrington family, both he and Daniel Fleming had a habit of purchasing more than one newspaper per week.[74] Equally common, of course, was the tendency for the intensity with which print was consumed to reflect periods of particularly acute tension. For Sir Thomas Barrington this meant April to July 1642, when he acquired new material on seventeen occasions, while for his son it meant May to July 1660, when pamphlets were purchased on twenty-seven

[72] ERO: D/DBa/A2, fos. 61–3; A14, fos. 31v–43v; A18/2; A3, fos. 32–v, 53v–5v, 63, 67–v; A4, fo. 9v; Wood, *Life and Times*, i. 211, 235, 266, 275, 301–10.
[73] CKS, U269/A526; *Devon Accounts*, ii. 95, 142–3, 152–8; Cumbria RO, D/LONS/W1/10, pp. 3, 11, 13, 15, 17, 23, 25, 27; HEH, ST 51; ST 54/1.
[74] BL, Add. 22466, fos. 55v–6, 65v–6; 'James Master', i. 166–9; Herts. RO, D/Elw/F18, pp. 11–15, 25, 106, 114, 127, 129; Cumbria RO (Kendal), WD/Ry/243.

occasions. For Master it meant the second half of 1647, when 'little books concerning the times' figure much more prominently in his accounts, and for Daniel Fleming it meant the period surrounding the dissolution of the Rump in April 1653.[75]

v Relations with booksellers

This sense that pamphlets and newspapers were purchased more avidly at some times than at others does not undermine the importance of print culture. Indeed, it reinforces the impression that, by shining a light on the practices that were associated with print consumption it is apparent how much value contemporaries placed on printed texts during the trauma of Civil War and revolution. Again and again, therefore, people demonstrated a desire to keep up-to-date with developments and debates that bordered on the obsessive. This tendency was evident beyond London and beyond the political elite, even if it is harder to demonstrate for the middling sort and their inferiors, and even though it was much more pronounced among grandees and wealthy gentlemen. However, there is one further way of analysing the practices associated with print consumption, and it involves bookseller bills, which survive in surprisingly large numbers. Such bills reinforce key themes that have already been highlighted, regarding the scale and regularity with which purchases were made, and the ability to access London's bookshops. But they also reveal new facets of print culture. These revolve around the benefits associated with forging strong relationships with booksellers, and the ability of people to *navigate* the print marketplace.[76]

At the most basic level, itemized bills that were sent by stationers to their customers add weight to conclusions about booksellers and books sold. They highlight the significance of traders like Henry Seile, who supplied the Earl of Huntingdon, Lord Hatton, Viscount Mansfield, the Earl of Salisbury and Lord Buckhurst, as well as the children of Charles I, from the 1630s to the Restoration.[77] They also provide a flavour of the trade in cheap print. An intriguing bill sent to Edward Harley in March 1642 suggests that he was undertaking a crash course in military skills, in

---

[75] ERO, D/DBa/A14, fos. 34v, 38, 40v, 42–43v; A7, fos. 3–10; 'James Master', i. 167–9; *Flemings in Oxford*, pp. 32, 41, 45, 48, 54–9.

[76] M. Bohannon, 'London bookseller's bill', *The Library*, 4th series, 18 (1938), 417–46; Woolf, *Reading History*, pp. 218–19.

[77] HEH, HAF Box 11/19; Northants. RO, FH 2659, 2661; Nott. UL, Pw1/242–3, 245, 247; Hatfield, Bills 210/15, 16; CKS: U269/A4/1; U269/A4/2; FSL, X.d.95/1–3.

preparation for an impending Civil War, but many more shed light on pamphlets, speeches and official declarations.[78] John Waterson provided proclamations and books on the Sabbath, and on legislation emanating from the Scottish parliament, as well as almanacs and newsbooks from 1642. During the 1650s, Thomas Dring supplied the Temple family with religious works and almanacs, as well as with copies of the *Humble Petition and Advice*, speeches in the Cromwellian parliaments and newspapers.[79] Bills sent to Sir Valentine Pell by Daniel Pakeman itemized works like Joseph Hall's *Divine Right of Episcopacy*, Henry Parker's *Case of Shipmony*, and Thomas Favent's account of Richard II's 'merciless' Parliament of 1388. Bills that were sent to Sir Robert Harley in the 1650s detailed sermons and religious treatises, as well as Cromwell's speeches, declarations and despatches, and the *Eikon Basilike*, not to mention various books by Prynne and Baxter and assorted newspapers.[80]

Where bookseller bills prove particularly enlightening, however, is in relation to the methods by which contemporaries became knowledgeable and efficient consumers. First, they attest to the strength and duration of the relationships between specific stationers and their customers. These include the links between Alice L'Estrange and both Henry Seile and Abel Roper, and between the Harleys and Philemon Stephens, the latter of which lasted for at least three decades.[81] Secondly, they also indicate that customers became aware of the specialisms of particular stationers. It seems to have been recognized, therefore, that Richard Whitaker, Henry Seile and Francis Tyton were more reliable suppliers of political tracts and news than George Thomason, ironic though that may seem.[82] And thirdly, they reveal that the benefits of forging and maintaining such relationships were manifold. These included being able to exchange books, to operate accounts and to run lines of credit, all of which facilitated the process of securing a steady stream of pamphlets and newspapers. Lord Buckhurst ran up bills of between £1 and £2 with Seile, while Harley's credit was thought to be good for up to three years, and Wittewronge's regular acquisitions from

[78] Bodl. MS Eng.Hist.e.308, fo. 76; BL, Add. 4232, fos. 8v, 10; Longleat, Thynne 81, fos. 235, 358, 374; HEH, HAF Box 12/10.

[79] HEH: HAF Box 12/19; Box 13/38, 46; STTF Box 24/54; Box 25/19.

[80] CUL, Pell 5/1–4; Bodl. MS Eng.Hist.e.308, fos. 77-v; BL, Add. 70067, unfol.; Nott. UL, Pw2/Hy/121.

[81] Norfolk RO, LEST/P10, pp. 54, 85, 91, 96, 97, 99, 101, 121, 138, 156, 158; BL: Add. 70002, fo. 82; Add. 70007, fo. 112; Add. 70066, unfol.; Nott. UL, Pw2/Hy/20.

[82] Penshurst, MS 397; CKS: U269/A4/1; U269/A4/2; Herts. RO: D/Elw/F18, pp. 25, 122, 124, 127, 134, 135, 137, 174; D/Elw/F20, pp. 78, 80, 82, 104, 110, 120, 132, 135, 149, 151, 157, 160, 161; Northants. RO, FH 2652.

Francis Tyton could be settled at periodic intervals in the late 1650s, in instalments of between 15s and £10.[83] Equally, in a period before Term Catalogues and widespread advertising, booksellers also supplied information about new and forthcoming material; used their judgment to recommend titles to clients; and even sent pamphlets and newspapers that had not been ordered, if they were thought to be of interest. Henry Herringman, for example, informed Sir Justinian Isham that 'there are some other books come forth which are worthy your worship's reading', including some 'small books', although he refrained from sending any without a specific order. Henry Seile not only provided Viscount Mansfield with regular supplies of *Mercurius Politicus*, but also sent 'some other newsbooks', having apparently been instructed to use his judgment and his knowledge of Mansfield's taste. Similar behaviour also emerges from other cases, including one involving dozens of bills between the Earl of Lauderdale and his booksellers (John Crooke and Thomas Underhill) in the late 1650s. Indeed, any number of examples indicate that such practices were predicated on the willingness and ability of booksellers to send items 'upon trust', as with the stationer who supplied Symon Sachell, minister of Bleasby in Nottinghamshire.[84] Indeed, the ties between booksellers and clients occasionally blossomed into lasting friendships, something which is apparent from the bills that Richard Thrale sent to John Buxton of Witham in Norfolk almost every week in the late 1630s. Thrale sent many works of divinity and religious controversy 'according to your order', but he also used his appreciation of Buxton's interest in the Bishops' Wars to provide information about new and forthcoming works. These included an imminent declaration by the king, 'which will be very large in folio of the proceedings of Scotland'. To these recommendations, moreover, Thrale also added his own news reports, based upon 'credible news' circulating in London, and he also sent books 'which are come forth lately such I think as you will like of'.[85]

By far the most telling relationships, however, were developed by the Earl of Salisbury and Sir Thomas Cotton. Salisbury's bills confirm that different booksellers were used for different kinds of material (including books for children), and that newsbooks and pamphlets were generally supplied by Hugh and Katherine Perry. They evidently satisfied his fascination for

---

[83] CKS: U269/A4/1; U269/A4/2; Bodl. MS Eng.Hist.e.308, fos. 77–v; Herts. RO: D/Elw/F18, p. 174; D/Elw/F20, pp. 110, 120, 132, 135, 149, 151, 157, 160–1.

[84] CCL, Elham 915; Northants. RO, IC 3418; Nott. UL, Pw1/242, 243, 245, 247; Belvoir Castle, Tollemache MSS 959–960; Chester RO, DAR/A/59; *Flemings in Oxford*, pp. 127–8; Notts. RO, PR.SW.75/46.

[85] CUL: Buxton 44/2–5, 7–8; Buxton 59/84; Buxton 34/6.

battlefield news reports, his thirst for pamphlets by Lilburne, Wither, Prynne and Asshurst, and his curiosity for the *Agreement of the People*. They also sent regular supplies of newspapers like *Perfect Occurrences*, *Perfect Diurnall* and the *Moderate Intelligencer*, as well as *Civicus* and *Britanicus*. Indeed, the Perrys granted Salisbury a line of credit that enabled the purchase of over £3 worth of newspapers in the 1650s, and they seem to have sent him parcels of pamphlets on an almost daily basis, thereby ensuring that he was able to read two or three newspapers every week.[86] Similarly rich are the bills that were sent to Sir Thomas Cotton during the 1650s. These once again reveal that different types of material were obtained from different stationers, and that Cotton spent considerable sums of money on 'small books' and newsbooks. Between 1652 and 1658, therefore, his bills for such material amounted to £10 8s 3d, and he may have spent a further £3 to £4 in 1659 alone. This suggests that Cotton might have purchased as many as 1,300 items between 1652 and 1658, and another 400 in 1659, giving a total of perhaps 1,700 tracts and newspapers, or almost 30 per cent of the volume of material acquired by Thomason during the same period. They also indicate that new items were being acquired on almost a daily basis, and that Cotton's craving for news led him to acquire both of the official Cromwellian newspapers on a regular basis, even though the two texts were almost indistinguishable. They also reveal that, during the tense week following the reassembly of the Rump in May 1659, Cotton read no less than *six* different newspapers.[87] And what is particularly striking about Cotton is that he highlights how a culture of 'news junkies' extended even to retired and politically inactive country squires.

vi Conclusion

Booksellers like Thrale and Tyton, and customers like Salisbury and Cotton, make it clear that contemporary fascination with print led at least some people to develop practices that effectively involved *subscribing* to the latest supplies of pamphlets and newspapers. Indeed, as a law student in London during the Republic, German Pole did precisely this, by opening an account with Matthew Walbancke for the provision of newspapers. He eventually paid a bill for £1 11s 8d, and continued the arrangement when he

---

[86] Hatfield: Bills 210/5, 7, 14–16; Bills 254/1–5, 14, 16; H4, H7, H8, J5, L7, M1–2, M5, M7; *HMC Salisbury XXII*, pp. 215, 235, 383–91, 426; *HMC Salisbury XXIV*, p. 282.

[87] BL, Add. 8128, fos. 23, 34, 42–3, 46–51, 54v, 72, 75, 78, 81, 85v–6; J. Peacey, 'Sir Thomas Cotton's consumption of news', *The Library*, 7th series, 7 (2006), 3–24.

returned to Derbyshire. Similar deals also seem to have been struck by others, and there may thus have been many more people subscribing to newsbooks than to 'fast' sermons.[88] As such, our appreciation of the ownership of cheap print has developed far beyond what becomes apparent from the analysis of library catalogues and inventories. While the methodological problems with such sources can sometimes be overcome, and while they occasionally prove revealing about the volume of pamphlets and newspapers that contemporaries acquired and preserved, they can only be used to address certain aspects of the contemporary response to the print revolution. They demonstrate that Thomason was not alone in collecting huge quantities of material, and that even provincial squires were fascinated by news and pamphlet culture, but they offer few subtle insights regarding contemporary attitudes towards cheap print, or about the processes and practices that were involved in its acquisition. Broadening our archival canvas, on the other hand, makes it possible to deepen our understanding about print consumption, and makes it possible to appreciate the lengths to which contemporaries were prepared to go to obtain large and frequent supplies of news and polemic. Such material became a vital part of people's reading, and it could be acquired even by those who lived far away from London. Trivial in terms of cost, tracts and newsbooks were considered anything but inconsequential, and it is striking how much money was spent on such material over extended periods, and how much energy was involved in ensuring its regular and uninterrupted supply.

Such conclusions, of course, are based in very large part upon evidence relating to a fairly narrow socio-economic group, concentrated within the aristocracy of nobility and greater gentry, although occasionally stretching into the middling sort. Nevertheless, this fact – an inevitable consequence of archival survival – does not detract from the importance of the findings, for however much this analysis has been dominated by political grandees, some of the richest evidence has involved provincial squires who lacked political clout. Some readers were entrenched within the world of commerce rather than politics, or were minor clerics from far-flung corners of the land, and many might even be characterized as being disengaged or non-aligned members of the 'silent majority'. However, it remains apparent that much more needs to be done to demonstrate that the print revolution made a significant impact on the vast bulk of the population, within or below the 'middling sort'. This is the task of the next chapter, the aim of which is to focus attention upon the *accessibility*, rather than the *ownership*, of print.

[88] DRO, D5557/10/1–2; Antony, BA/20/3; Morrill, 'Dowsing', pp. 181–2.

CHAPTER 2

The accessibility of print

Reflecting back on the months prior to his enlistment in the parliamentarian army in 1642, Ensign John Hodgson of Coley Hall near Halifax recalled the print culture that he had witnessed. He noted how 'papers flew up and down' regarding massacres in Ireland, and how pamphlets were 'scattered amongst us', and he reflected on things 'read and heard', not least that 'the safety of the people is the supreme law'. A few years later, another Yorkshireman, Adam Eyre, who hailed from yeoman stock in Penistone, compiled a 'diurnall' that likewise recorded local political discourse. This involved oral news and the borrowing of books, including the king's answer to parliamentarian propositions, and being able to buy pamphlets by John Saltmarsh in Sheffield, newspapers in York and other works in Wakefield.[1] Both cases raise new questions regarding the reach of print, reading practices and the response to Civil War pamphlets and newspapers. These involve moving beyond the ownership of print to explore the significance of oral news, rumour and how far current affairs could be followed by people of humble status. The aim of this chapter, therefore, is to establish how, and how easily, men like Hodgson and Eyre – provincial and non-gentry – gained access to the world of print, either as customers with limited access to London's bookshops, or without purchasing print at all. This means concentrating on the *accessibility* of print, in terms of the availability of pamphlets and newspapers and the practices of readers, and it means testing the limits of the reading nation, both geographically and socially.[2]

To the extent that accessibility has been addressed by scholars, it has been done by exploring literacy, print runs and the price of texts. These are important structural factors, which obviously affected the possibility of engaging with political affairs, but each offers a problematic guide to the

---

[1] *Autobiography of Captain John Hodgson*, ed. J. Turner (Brighouse, 1882), pp. 21–3; A. Eyre, 'A Dyurnall', in *Yorkshire Diaries* (SS, 65, 1877), pp. 4, 7, 23, 35, 40, 43, 53–4, 57, 62–3, 68, 92–3, 104.
[2] Fox, *Oral and Literate*, ch. 7.

reach of print. First, strikingly high literacy levels significantly underestimate the ability to read, and overlook the fact that it was more important to
live within a literate environment, where there were 'bridges' to literacy,
than to possess specific skills.[3] Secondly, it is possible to challenge claims
that the impact of pamphlets and newspapers was limited because texts had
only limited print runs. This is not just because examples can be found of
works that sold in editions of 3,000, 4,500, 6,000 and even 12,000, but also
because print runs offer a poor guide to consumption. They mask evidence
about pamphlets that lay unsold on stationers' stalls, and which, 'like a
cittern, every comer takes it up', and they hide the possibility that individual
copies had many readers, and that some kind of multiplier needs to be
employed.[4] Thirdly, there are grounds for questioning the argument that
pamphlets and newspapers were prohibitively expensive. At between 1d and
4d for a pamphlet of up to sixty-four pages, and at 1d or 2d for a newspaper,
prices had almost certainly risen under the impact of inflation and lax
controls. It may also be true that pamphlets were sometimes expensive
outside London. Samuel Jeake once paid 3d for a newspaper, while Eyre was
charged 6d for a newsbook at York. And it is certainly true that prices rose
dramatically when works were proscribed.[5] However, printed texts were
much cheaper than scribal ones. Prices fell from 1s 6d to 1d as 'diurnalls'
came to be printed, and words literally became cheap. If affordable scribal
separates involved somewhere in the region of 1,600 *characters* for 2d, or
3,000 characters for 4d, then a penny pamphlet probably contained around
5,000 *words*. Moreover, there is little reason to doubt that at these prices
pamphlets were within easy reach of all but the most humble labourer, and
that a lot could be read for very little. More importantly, issues of price
overlook the possibility that purchase was rarely required to secure access to
printed material, even by women, artificers, husbandmen and labourers.[6]

Once again, therefore, problems with conventional methodologies make
it necessary to explore the size and shape of the audience for news and

---

[3] D. Cressy, *Literacy and the Social Order* (Cambridge, 1980); T. Laqueur, 'The cultural origins of popular literacy in England', *Oxford Review of Education*, 2 (1976), 255–75; M. Spufford. 'First steps in literacy', *Social History*, 4 (1979), 407–35; Fox, *Oral and Literate*, pp. 17–19, 36–41, 44, 47.

[4] *Elencticus*, 312.29, sig. Ff2v; *CCSP*, iv. 643; *TSP*, vii. 470–1; BL, Stowe 354, fos. 111–12; TNA, SP 16/516, fo. 20; Chequers, MS 782, fo. 93; TNA, AO 3/1276, part 2; *CSPD 1653–4*, pp. 193, 436; *Baillie*, ii. 116, 367; CKS, U350/C2/96; Chester RO, CR63/2/691/39; *Diurnall*, 504.246, p. 1984; H. Barker, *Newspapers, Politics and English Society* (Harlow, 2000), pp. 46–7.

[5] Bodl. MS Eng.Misc.c.338, fos. 19, 28v, 69; Beinecke, BZ21.5.3/8, 9, 16, 18; *HMC Salisbury XXII*, pp. 389–90; *HMC Salisbury XXIV*, p. 282; *A Radical's Books*, ed. M. Hunter (Woodbridge, 1999), p. 327; Eyre, 'Dyurnall', p. 93; *TSP*, iv. 717; *Oxinden Letters*, pp. 286–7, 292; *PJ*, i. 254–5; CKS: U269/A4/1; U269/A390/1; Claydon, Verney reel 8.

[6] TNA: ASSI/45/4/3/103; SP 16/493, fo. 166; ERO, D/DBa/A2, fos. 61–4v; CKS, U269/A390/1.

comment in different ways, through factors relating to the structures of print culture, the conjunctural circumstances of Civil War and the everyday agency of contemporaries. The central concern of this chapter is to assess the likelihood that pamphlets and newspapers played an increasingly important part in everyday life, irrespective of social status or geographical location. My argument will be that people encountered print with increasing frequency and intensity, even in remote corners of the land, and that although pamphlets and newspapers were not experienced in exactly the same ways by people from different walks of life, the print revolution nevertheless ensured that politics was experienced in unprecedented ways even by humble citizens. This reflected important changes in the infrastructure of print, and it can be explored through practices which made such material accessible even without financial outlay or ownership. In other words, the chapter will concentrate on the *supply* of print, rather than on *demand* (as revealed in purchases and ownership), and on the practices associated with the circulation and reading of printed texts. It will examine what material was available across the country, in both urban and rural settings, and to people across the social spectrum. It will analyse networks of bookselling (section i) and the stock of those who sold printed wares (section ii). This will involve utilizing inventories, adverts and legal records, as well as incorporating evidence about itinerant traders, in order to demonstrate structural developments as well as changes which accompanied the Civil Wars (section iii). In addition, the chapter will explore the methods associated with circulation of texts (section iv) and evidence about reading and note-taking (section v), as well as evidence about communal reading and free distribution (sections vi and vii). This will reveal how contemporaries accessed print without necessarily having to own it; demonstrate the intensification of established practices in the circumstances of revolutionary upheaval; and highlight the emergence of new phenomena that brought print into the lives of the 'lower orders'.

i The bookselling network

The place to start is with the networks of bookselling, to demonstrate a spectrum of availability rather than a polarized world, in which print was either present or absent from particular communities, and to rethink the nature and scale of the book trade. Here a central problem has been the tendency to concentrate on London and Westminster, in terms of St Paul's Churchyard, the Exchange and Westminster Hall. This reflects the ease with which the capital's book trade can be reconstructed, as well as contemporary appreciation of its national and even international pre-eminence, but it detracts from the vibrancy of bookselling elsewhere. This was evidently undergoing significant change, something that can be investigated with the help of imprints, civic and legal records, and both wills and inventories.[7]

Bookselling outside London was obviously dominated by the university towns and cathedral cities, which makes eminent sense, given the presence of clerical and scholarly clients. In the case of Oxford, this meant that no less than twenty-seven different booksellers were active between 1640 and 1660, and in the great centres of ecclesiastical power it is sometimes possible to demonstrate the scale and genealogy of individual outlets. When Michael Harte of Exeter died in 1615, he left a stock of over 4,500 items, worth £103, which passed to his former apprentice, John Mongwell, and then to Abisha Brocas, one of a number of booksellers in the city.[8] However, what can also be demonstrated is that bookselling probably took place in almost every town in the country, from Abingdon to Warrington. Some of these traders are fairly well known, like Hugh Audley of Hull and Stephen Bulkeley of Newcastle, the latter of whom operated one of three shops in the town by the 1650s. Others, however, are much less visible, but can be identified from trade tokens, corporation records and customers. These individuals – from William Weekely in Ipswich to William Weeks in Plymouth – probably numbered hundreds at any one time, and they suggest that the nationwide book trade was extensive and booming.[9]

There are a number of reasons why the scale of bookselling has been underestimated. First, provincial booksellers operated in much less secure and stable conditions than their London colleagues, which probably meant that numbers fluctuated wildly. A case in point involves William Ballard, who faced sequestration and repeated imprisonment during the 1640s and 1650s, and who drifted in and out of the book trade, both in Bristol and Dublin. Secondly, those involved in bookselling might easily be overlooked because they were primarily engaged in other trades. This is evident from individuals like Philip Unett of Lichfield (mercer) and Peter Ince of Chester

---

[7] Aberdeen UL, MS 2538, fos. 19–v; *Art of Living* (1642, P942), sig. A2v.

[8] J. Peacey, 'The popular print culture of Oxford, 1640–1660' (forthcoming); *Politicus*, 361.442, p. 12; BL, Add. 59785, fo. 69; *Rolls of Freemen*, pp. 70, 117, 124, 137, 138, 147, 155; Chester RO, Z/AB2, fo. 120; Devon RO: ECA/Ancient Letters 16; ECA/Orphans Court Inventories 191; ECA/Orphans Court wills 74.

[9] *STC*, iii. 207–15; *Wing*, iv, 1003–23; G. Williamson, *Trade Tokens* (3 vols, London, 1967); BL: Add. 29624, fo. 158; Add. 70052, unfol; Cumbria RO, DRC/1/4, pp. 172–3, 258; Leics. RO: PR/I/88/138; PR/I/40/290; *Whiteway*, p. 48; CHC, BA/H/3/20/2, p. 404; Worcs. RO, BA9360/A10, Box 3; Lincs. RO: W1667/ii/593; AC/AD/29, p. 60; *HMC Fifteenth Report, part 10*, p. 40; Notts. RO, PRNW; *York Depositions*, p. 46; *Rous Diary*, 54; Glos. RO, D3673.

(draper), as well as from the civic records of Coventry, where the role of local mercers only becomes clear because they tried to block the arrival of specialist booksellers. Thirdly, many provincial booksellers probably traded in more than one location. These included Peter Whalley, who operated in both Northampton and Coventry in the early 1630s, before handing over the latter of these businesses to a kinsman, John Cartwright, who quickly became the town's leading bookseller. Indeed, the complaint against interlopers by Coventry's mercers specified that a Mr Nevill 'intendeth not to inhabit or dwell in the said city ... but to place his man in that city, as he doth usually place his own servants in other cities ... thereby to engross the whole trade in the country for his own private gain'.[10]

There are thus many reasons for thinking that the scale of provincial bookselling has been underestimated, and that there were plentiful opportunities for accessing print around the country. This probably explains how, in the summer of 1641, Sir John Gell was able to purchase books in both Tetbury and Bath, neither of which had a designated bookseller.[11] What none of this evidence permits, however, is the chance to assess the nature of the stock carried by booksellers outside London, and it is to this topic – which is crucial for an assessment of the reach of pamphlets and newspapers – that attention must now turn.

ii Taking stock

Analysing the stock of provincial booksellers is vital for assessing whether their clientele extended beyond clergymen and schoolmasters, and it generally involves inventories, adverts and correspondence with suppliers, as well as lists of debtors and fragmentary ledgers. As with private libraries, however, these offer only inadequate evidence regarding pamphlets and newspapers, which makes it vital to supplement such material with legal and official records, as well as with information from individual customers. Doing so reveals that cheap print became an essential part of provincial bookselling in the 1640s and 1650s.[12]

What emerges certainly suggests that devotional and instructional literature, like Bibles and prayer books, as well as hornbooks, primers and dictionaries, formed the bedrock of many provincial businesses. These

[10] Bristol RO: 4962/2; FC/BB/2/1; *CCC*, p. 1652; TNA: SP 23/65, p. 119; SP 23/168, pp. 483–93; Bodl. MS Carte 60, fo. 288; Carte 165, fo. 129; *Rolls of Freemen*, p. 98; Chester RO, WS 1648–9; *CSPD 1637–8*, p. 73; CHC: BA/H/17/F8/4/3; BA/H/3/17/1, pp. 589, 615; BA/C/17/34/1; BA/H/3/17/2, p. 23.
[11] DRO, D258/5/1/25.　　[12] Bodl. MS Top.Oxon.c.154, fos. 161–76; Beinecke, Osborn 1524.

included the operations run by William Lambert of Preston and Joseph Howes of Nottingham, as well as those of Walter Dight and John Mongwell in Exeter, although works by Hildersham, Harsnett, Perkins and Preston were purchased by citizens and gentlemen as well as by clerics and school-masters. Nevertheless, this is a misleading and incomplete picture, because adverts focused on 'big-ticket' items with extended shelf lives, rather than on topical and ephemeral texts, and because inventories concentrated on items of particular value. Once again, therefore, ways need to be found of fleshing-out intriguing references to 'small stitched books' and to 'books of small worth and pamphlets'.[13] This can be done through the accounts of individual customers, which reveal that local booksellers traded in topical and controversial material as well as in ballads and almanacs. Both royalist and parliamentarian pamphlets were sold by booksellers in Oxford and Cambridge, and such activity appears to have become fairly common across the country. Acts, ordinances and declarations were available in Norwich and Kendal, as well as from the shop of Tobias Jordan in Gloucester, and from Thomas Thomas and William Ballard in Bristol, and any number of traders in cheap print can be identified because of their involvement in selling seditious material.[14] Abraham Attfen of Norwich was identified as a seller of Puritan pamphlets in 1640, and in the 1650s and 1660s successive mayors of Leicester drew attention to scandalous pamphlets that were being sold locally, and these illicit texts were probably only a fraction of what was available outside London. In Newcastle, William London sold pamphlets by Milton and Prynne, as well as parliamentary reports and newsbooks, and Robert Booth of Warrington stocked pamphlets by John Ley and Joshua Sprigge, and something described as a 'remonstrance', valued at a penny. At Richard Scott's shop in Carlisle it was possible to see pamphlets that responded to Hamon L'Estrange's history of Charles I, as well as tracts by James Harrington, while in York numerous contributions to the paper war between the king and parliament were available in 1642.[15] What was true in

[13] Lancs. RO, WRW/R57A/12; Notts. RO, PRNW; Devon RO, Z19/36/14, fos. 3v, 7v, 21v, 47v, 110v, 125, 139v, 143v; *Flemings in Oxford*, pp. 393, 395, 401; C. Chilton, 'Inventory of a provincial bookseller's stock of 1644', *The Library*, 6th series, 1 (1979), 133–41; A. Rodger, 'Roger Ward's Shrewsbury stock', *The Library*, 5th series, 13 (1958), 247–68; Leics. RO, PR/I/95/44; Durham UL, DPRI/1/1626/C7/1–7; Lincs. RO, INV120/72.

[14] *Bodleian Library Account Book*, ed. G. Hampshire (OBS, ns. 21, 1983), pp. 121–92; Wing, iv. 278–80; Norfolk RO: LEST P7, pp. 206, 212; LEST P10, pp. 36, 80, 86; TNA, SP 28/299, fo. 364; Bristol RO: F/Au/1/22–26; Cumbria RO (Kendal), WD/Ry/260.

[15] *York Depositions*, p. 46; TNA, SP 16/434, fo. 191v; *Borough of Leicester*, pp. 386, 397, 488–9; *Catalogue* (1658, L2850), sigs. A3, P–v, Q, V2, V3, X2, Y4; W. Rylands, 'Booksellers and stationers in Warrington', THSLC, 37 (1888), pp. 70, 72, 75–6; *Flemings in Oxford*, pp. 99, 102, 127–8; Cumbria RO, D/LONS/L13/10/1/23.

the North was also true in East Anglia. In Norwich Alice L'Estrange found copies of Thomas Edwards' *Gangraena*, and in King's Lynn she was able to acquire pamphlets by David Jenkins, while in Bury St Edmunds John Rous saw pamphlets relating military news in September 1642. Indeed, such material clearly reached all corners of the land, and common members of the trained bands at Worcester saw 'sundry printed papers' regarding royalist plundering in the early months of the Civil War.[16]

Such material was topical, but its relevance would have lasted weeks or months, and this makes its availability comprehensible. What local book-sellers may have found harder to justify stocking were newspapers, given that time needed to be allowed for delivery and that specific texts rapidly became obsolete. Nevertheless, even newsbooks were fairly readily avail-able outside London. This is implied by the frequent newspaper adverts that drew attention to local problems (lost property) and local services (fairs) in counties as far away as Derbyshire and Lincolnshire, and in places like Stow-on-the-Wold (Gloucestershire), Bishops Stortford (Hertfordshire), Burpham (Suffolk), Stone (Staffordshire) and Buckminster (Leicestershire).[17] This suggests that advertisers came from, and expected to find readers in, provincial England. Secondly, the wide-spread availability of newspapers is also evident anecdotally. In 1651, for example, the brothers Philip and Richard Unett of Lichfield were accused of selling 'divers scandalous books written against the parliament, as *Pragmaticus*, *Melancholicus* etc'. Similar texts were available at both York and Leicester in 1644, at Plymouth and Edinburgh, and at Gloucester, where Tobias Jordan was able to supply Captain Blayney with 'a parcel of newsbooks' in 1643. Indeed, it also seems clear that urban booksellers facilitated the supply of news to rural readers. Charles Howard of Naworth (Northumberland) acquired newspapers from a Newcastle shoe-maker, who was paid 11s 4d for 'diurnalls' and letters on 15 December 1648, and during the 1650s the accounts of the Hatcher family of Holywell Hall (Lincolnshire) reveal that newspapers were available at nearby Stamford. Likewise, a minor gentleman like George Norton of Dishforth in Yorkshire was able to acquire newspapers (as well as Acts of Parliament) at York in the early 1650s, accounting for them alongside toys for his

---

[16] Norfolk RO, LEST P10, pp. 24, 52, 101, 130, 147; *Rous Diary*, p. 123; Worcs. RO, BA1714, p. 289.

[17] *Politicus*: 361.382, p. 1643; 361.420, p. 600; 361.442, p. 13; 361.561, p. 348; 361.563, p. 831; 361.564, p. 397; *Proceedings*, 599.155, p. 2423.

children and bills for mending shoes.[18] Similarly, local suppliers were essential for satisfying the thirst for news that was displayed by Alice L'Estrange, Daniel Fleming and Anthony Wood. L'Estrange regularly acquired newspapers and 'other such books' from Norwich and King's Lynn, while Fleming used a succession of Kendal mercers to secure such material on account, at around 4d per issue. And Anthony Wood recognized that, among *nine* regular booksellers, Richard Davis could supply pamphlets, while Edward Forrest was better for news. In December 1656, therefore, Wood and Forrest entered into a formal 'bargain', by which Wood paid 2s per quarter to get newsbooks 'the next day they came to Oxford, being every Wednesday and Saturday'.[19]

By far the most striking evidence about provincial newspaper-selling, however, emerges from Chester, and from a dispute between a local book-seller, Richard Thropp, and his London supplier, Edward Dod. This 1651 lawsuit reveals that, during a 69-week period between July 1650 and November 1651, Dod sent no less than 102 parcels of pamphlets (including acts, declarations and tracts on the Engagement controversy), and 1,646 sheets of newspapers, the latter at 0.6d per sheet. This meant that Thropp received an average of sixteen sheets of news *per* delivery, with deliveries arriving every four or five days. Although postage costs would have been significant, even a mark-up of 100 per cent would not have pushed the price of an eight-page newspaper above 2d. Moreover, Thropp was not the only bookseller in town, and an advert by William Thorppe specifically drew attention to the fact that his customers could acquire 'news weekly'.[20] It would not be necessary to employ a particularly large multiplier, therefore, to conclude that hundreds of Chester residents would have been reading the news on a regular basis.

Given the frequency with which inhabitants of provincial England resorted to London to acquire pamphlets and newspapers, it must be assumed that bookselling in the localities was unable to satisfy the demand for such material. Perhaps supplies were sometimes irregular; perhaps the range of available material was limited. However, this ensured that contemporaries began to recognize the business opportunities that were

---

[18] TNA: SP 23/168, pp. 483, 485, 487, 491, 493; SP 21/17, p. 18; SP 28/299, fo. 364; *Aulicus*, 275.241, p. 1192; Devon RO, 1499M/Add.3/E3, fo. 79; *Andrew Hay Diary*, p. 204; *Naworth Estate and Household Accounts*, ed. C. Huddleston (SS, 168, 1953), pp. 17, 53; Lincs. RO, Holywell 82; WYAS (Leeds), WYL150/5982–4.
[19] Norfolk RO: LEST P7, p. 257; LEST P10, pp. 24–147; *Flemings in Oxford*, pp. 398–431; *Library of Anthony Wood*, ed. N. Kiessling (OBS, 3rd series, 5, 2002), p. 435; Wood, *Life and Times*, i. 211–301.
[20] TNA, CHES 15/61.

available. In 1649, therefore, the Lancashire MP Ralph Assheton argued that it would be a 'good deed' if bookshops were established in rural villages like Whalley, Clitheroe and Downham, not just because this would prevent people from being 'ignorant of the truth of passages' but also because 'there is nothing more coveted or vendible than news'. Moreover, whether or not such advice was heeded, it is clear that traders outside the capital became integral to the process by which topical and polemical material was made accessible to people across the country, beyond clerics and schoolmasters, and in ways that have not previously been appreciated. Of course, the impact of transport costs upon the price of printed texts may have ensured that the most humble readers were excluded from this facet of the provincial print trade. However, to the extent that this was true, there may have been other sources of supply that were much more affordable, if less systematic. This involved the itinerant trade in cheap print, where both the scale of the bookselling network and the accessibility of pamphlets and newspapers underwent a dramatic transformation after 1640.[21]

iii Wandering with pamphlets

The peripatetic trade in cheap print is scarcely unknown, and scholars obviously recognize that pedlars, chapmen and hawkers distributed print across England – in the streets, in alehouses and at fairs. In the early 1630s one John Vaux was even prosecuted for repeatedly selling alamanacs, libels and 'a companie of little small books' from the communion table at St Helen, Auckland. Indeed, they were central to the creation of an integrated book trade that served London and the localities, town and country, elite and poor. Many, indeed, had credit arrangements with, and acted as agents for, London stationers. However, attention has traditionally focused on 'small books and pleasant histories' – ballads, pious pamphlets and moral-izing tales – and a neglected story involves an important shift that took place in the 1640s, and that saw topical and polemical material being touted by itinerant traders, in both urban and rural settings.[22] More obviously even than the spread of provincial bookshops, this had a dramatic effect on the availability of cheap print and news.

---

[21] Chetham, A.3.90, fos. 30–v.
[22] Durham Cathedral, Hunter 17, fos. 58–v, 60v, 64v; *Occurrences*, 465.5129, p. 1115; M. Spufford, *Small Books and Pleasant Histories* (Cambridge, 1981), pp. 111–28; T. Watt, 'Publisher, pedlar, pot-poet', in *Spreading the Word*, ed. R. Myers and M. Harris (Winchester, 1990), pp. 61–81.

These developments can most obviously be observed in London, although even the capital's street trade in print remains inadequately understood. In 1639 a Scottish visitor was struck by the fact that ballads were 'sold by whole hundreds in the City', and by how 'such news as this comes out by owl-light in little books or ballads to be sold in the street'. The key word here is 'news', and it seems clear that street vendors were increasingly involved in selling topical material. This is occasionally evident from imprints and parliamentary records, as well as from commentators like Thomas Wharton, who claimed in March 1642 that 'the streets ring with crying the printed good news out of Ireland'. Another contemporary described 'walking London's street, which echo with nothing more of late, than news and newsbooks'.[23] Particularly enlightening, however, are the Bridewell records. These make frequent reference not just to ballad singers, including those who were working for publishers like Francis Grove, but also to young and poor itinerants who were found 'wandering in the streets selling pamphlets'. Occasionally, explicit reference is even made to seditious material, and to newspapers like *Mercurius Pragmaticus*.[24] Such examples attest to the scale on which pamphlets and newspapers were sold on the streets, and to the concern that such practices caused, and as early as September 1643 the problem was considered sufficiently serious to prompt an act of London's common council, against 'a multitude of vagrant persons, men, women and children, which after the manner of hawkers, do openly cry about the streets, pamphlets, and other books'. This had only a limited effect, however, and in subsequent years it became clear that *Mercurius Britanicus* was 'hawked in all the streets by the newsboys' – thus 'feeding the hatred of the vulgar' – that Henry Marten's *Resolve About the Person of the King* was sold in the streets by women like Abigail Rogers, and that the Levellers used a 'mercury woman' (Mrs Eeles) as 'a common disperser of dangerous pamphlets'.[25] Successive attempts to control such practices were equally unsuccessful, however, not least because hawkers – many of them maimed soldiers – protested about their need to make ends meet, and about the monopoly exercised by the Stationers Company. This ensured that the funeral of John Bradshaw, who had presided over Charles I's trial, descended into chaos as ballad sellers peddled a work called *Bradshaw's Ghost*, and that the dying days of the

[23] NLS, MS 2688, pp. 762, 766; *Quaeries* (1659, C6197), p. 11; *CJ*, ii. 683; Bodl. MS Carte 2, fo. 494; *Antidotum* (1644, A3500), sig. A2; *Downefall* (1641, D2088).

[24] Bethlem: BCB 8, fos. 381, 384v, 388–9; BCB 9, pp. 34, 145, 401, 439, 441–2, 606, 645, 664, 692.

[25] Stat. Co., Court Book C, fo. 191v; *Common* (1643, L2851P); *CSPV 1643–7*, pp. 207–8; *LJ*, viii. 615, 684; PA, MP 23 Jan. 1647; *LJ*, ix. 163; *CSPD 1648–9*, pp. 310, 328, 331.

commonwealth witnessed repeated scenes in which 'jeering things' against parliament were 'cried up and down in the streets', and sold by 'poor girls'.[26]

More importantly, perhaps, such developments were replicated nation-wide, so that the hawking and peddling of pamphlets and newspapers became much more widespread. This is clear from an order of the Council of State in June 1650, which instructed a stationer in Market Harborough (William Thompson) to suppress local hawkers, in response to complaints about their role in spreading 'scandalous and seditious pamphlets' throughout Leicestershire. By 1655, indeed, the problem had become sufficiently serious to prompt national legislation, and by this stage it was clear that London stationers were supplying hawkers with new kinds of material. The previous year, Hertfordshire justices had prosecuted John Winsor for bringing 300 scandalous pamphlets to Hemel Hempstead for sale, having acquired them from a London printer.[27] More obviously, this new emphasis on itinerant traders as distributors of political texts is clear from the fact that leading ballad publishers, like John Wright and Francis Coles, diversified into news and topical material after 1640. For Wright this meant official parliamentary printing, and for Coles it meant newspapers and pamphlets, and what makes such developments fascinating is the possibility that both men retained their existing networks of hawkers and pedlars. This was certainly the case with Thomas Whitaker, another pub-lisher who shifted from traditional forms of popular literature to political pamphlets, who left numerous bequests to pedlars and chapmen. It may even have been the case that Milton's polemical pamphlets were distributed in this fashion during the Republic.[28] In other words the 1650s witnessed important developments whereby publishers responded to the circumstan-ces of Civil War by making pamphlets and newspapers available across the country, and even to those who lacked the means to access bookshops, either in London or the localities.

[26] Stat. Co., Court Book C, fo. 196; CLRO, Rep. 57, fo. 59; *LJ*, ix. 457–8; *Warrant* (1649, F253), pp. 3–5; *Mdx County Recs*, pp. 104, 194; *CSPD 1649–50*, p. 400; *CSPD 1650*, p. 514; *CSPD 1654*, p. 59; *HMC Leyborne Popham*, pp. 16–17; Aberdeen UL, MS 2538/2, fo. 15*; *Rugg*, pp. 28, 74; *CSPD 1659–60*, p. 343; *CCSP*, iv. 341.

[27] Bodl. MS Tanner 62, fo. 275; *CSPD 1650*, p. 185; *Diurnall*, 504.268, p. 2158; *CSPD 1655*, pp. 300–301; *Orders* (1655, C7151), p. 112; Herts. RO, QSR 9/221.

[28] T. Watt, *Cheap Print and Popular Piety, 1550–1640* (Cambridge, 1991), pp. 75–6, 172, 234, 268, 274–6, 289–93, 302, 311, 316–18; Spufford, *Small Books*, pp. 94, 96, 98, 153n30, 265; BL, Add. 78259, fo. 107.

iv Private circulation

Thus far, the accessibility of print has been explored through a supply-side analysis of the book trade in provincial England. Sources regarding the infrastructure of bookselling shed light on the impact of pamphlets and newspapers in very different ways from evidence about ownership and purchasing patterns, and suggest that such material was *likely* to have been encountered on a much more regular basis than has been recognized hitherto. In the remaining sections of this chapter, however, such claims about contemporary *acculturation* to print will be developed in rather different ways. This will involve moving beyond the possibilities for purchase and ownership to consider contemporary practices relating to the circulation of print, in terms of the possibilities for distributing print freely and for reading texts without financial outlay. This will mean exploring private networks and individual readers, as well as public and communal practices, both of which will reveal an intensification of traditional processes in the conjunctural circumstances of upheaval and revolution. This will significantly enhance our understanding of the degree to which print became a pervasive feature of everyday life, and to which it shaped contemporary experiences of the Civil War, irrespective of geographical location or social status. In the first instance, this will be done by demonstrating how pamphlets and newspapers became integral to a culture of gift-giving, borrowing and shared consumption, within more or less restricted circles of friends, family and colleagues.

Recovering such practices relies to a large extent on gentry correspondence, which frequently reveals how contemporaries discussed what they had read and what they wanted to read. This often meant pamphlets and newspapers, like 'the *Intelligencer* and the *Scout*', which Cheney Culpeper hoped to obtain in the mid 1640s. Such comments reveal a fascination with new material – as when Philip Moreton wrote home to Cheshire about a tract containing the charge against the judges in 1641 – and with 'bitter' and seditious texts, like those by John Lilburne. They also indicate that it was common to discuss information that had been culled from newspapers. In January 1644, therefore, Julius Bedell asked Edward Montagu to supply 'two lines' by which to 'partake of your news by *Mercurius Aulicus*, *Mercurius Britanicus*, and other books', while in 1651 Viscount Conway asked Edward Harley about something he had seen in 'the Thursday book'.[29] Very often this involved the

---

[29] 'Cheney Culpeper', pp. 174–5, 197, 201, 203, 206, 231; Bodl. MS Tanner 60, fo. 156; MS Tanner 66, fo. 109; BL: Add. 33936, fo. 238; Add. 38847, fo. 38v; Add. 64923, fo. 3; Bodl. MS Carte 74, fo. 155; BL, Add. 70006, fo. 242v.

dispersal of information from individuals in London who had the best access to printed material – as Dr Richard Berrie did for Marmaduke Monckton while attending delinquency hearings – but such material could also be mentioned by people outside London. Thus, William Richardson reflected on what 'the London diurnall reports' in a letter from Milneraig in Scotland in 1653.[30] More importantly, it became increasingly common to enclose pamphlets and newspapers within letters, alongside phrases like 'I have sent you here enclosed all the printed news', and promises that correspondents would 'receive some pamphlets'. Although some people were nervous about sending controversial and proscribed literature, and were only willing to send items that 'fear no light', the reality is that a vast amount of material was circulated in this fashion, very often as an adjunct to personal newsletters.[31]

Moreover, while these comments and practices may sometimes reflect 'proxy shopping', the nature and tone of such correspondence often implies gift-giving rather than a cash nexus. Letter-writers frequently assumed that their correspondents had regular supplies of print, and that they had already seen particular items, and recipients often made humble pleas for material and expressed profound gratitude when it arrived.[32] In addition, the practice of enclosing printed texts tended to involve family members and friends, as well as servants and employees, rather than agents and factors. Philip Moreton sent newspapers to his father in Cheshire, along with contributions to the 'paper war' of 1642, while William Knight of Rowington (near Warwick) received pamphlets and newspapers from a son who was a London wine merchant, and from another who was at Clements Inn. In the winter of 1642–3, Sir Philip Musgrave's sources of pamphlets included a family friend, John Taylor of the Inner Temple. Particularly revealing in this regard are the letters of John Fitzjames of Leweston (Dorset), who repeatedly made requests for newspapers he wished to receive from his mother and one Mr Levitt, and who repeatedly expressed frustration if his supply was interrupted or delayed. In December 1648, for example, he complained that 'those *Pragmaticus* you send are antedated a week, which I desire may be sent hereafter in season', and he implored his correspondent

[30] Nott. UL, 12768/7, 10, 14, 17, 20, 28, 40, 43, 51; Warw. RO, CR136/B68e; NLW, MS 9064E/1883; Bodl. MS North.c.4, fo. 91; BL, Add. 21425, fo. 165; *Diurnall*, 503.177, pp. 2671–2.

[31] BL, Add. 70007, fo. 156v; NLW, MS 9063E/1694, 1858; Bodl. MS Tanner 66, fo. 110; Nott. UL, Cl/C/281; Leics. RO, DE730/1, fos. 58–61; Cumbria RO, D/MUS2/2; DRO, D258/34/71; BL, Add. 38847, fo. 38v; Beinecke, Osborn fb.156, fos. 130–1; CKS, U1015/C1/1; Antony: BA/24/2, fo. 173; BC/26/18/41; PC/G4/9/20; Longleat, Thynne 10, fos. 230, 240.

[32] HEH, HA 14356; Staffs. RO: D868/2/33, D868/3/22; D868/4/84; D868/2/70; BL: Add. 78223, fo. 9; Add. 70112, unfol.; Add. 78303, fo. 12; Add. 22916, fo. 55v; Add. 70106, fo. 164; Harl. 382, fos. 115, 226; CUL, Buxton 102/36; Lancs. RO, DD/HU/46/5; Longleat, Thynne 9, fos. 50, 65v.

to 'send me some news; you do not imagine how hungry we are here'. On another occasion Fitzjames explained that 'I . . . harken after a new ballad, and for anything else that is new', and recommended switching the day on which material was posted, to ensure that supplies 'come new to my hands' instead of being 'stale and worth nothing ere I read it'.[33] In all this correspondence, Fitzjames never once hinted that he paid for such services.

In observing this giving and receiving of printed texts, several important themes emerge. First, they indicate that gentry women were enthusiastic readers and distributors of topical material, who gained access to 'printed papers' even in remote parts of the country. Many wives received newspapers and pamphlets from their husbands and from household servants, and Sir Roger Twysden not only ensured that his wife received 'all the king's speeches and letters', but also relied upon her to act as librarian and archivist.[34] Secondly, pamphlets and newspapers circulated beyond their initial recipients, much more obviously than did personal letters and manuscript separates. Although Robert Hobart sent such material to friends in 1641 with the explicit recommendation that they should 'keep it or burn it', rather than to allow it to circulate, such examples are fairly rare. Writing from Preston in December 1640, Richard Kinge promised Edward Parker that he would forward 'new speeches' as he received them, and in 1641 Thomas Stockdale passed on printed pamphlets that he received to Lord Fairfax, and Sir John Gell later sent newspapers to his family in Derbyshire with the explicit recommendation that they should 'let Sir Cornelius see the *Moderates*'. When Francis Godolphin sent similar texts to Cornwall in 1646, he instructed their recipient to be 'no niggard of them to such who care to see how grossly we are led like sheep to the slaughter'.[35]

These themes become strikingly clear from the network around Henry Oxinden of Barham in Kent. Oxinden's correspondence not only includes detailed private newsletters relating to parliamentary affairs and street politics, but also reveals a fascination with libels against Archbishop Laud, and the frequency with which controversial literature was sent down from London. During the Long Parliament, Oxinden displayed an insatiable

---

[33] BL, Add. 64922, fos. 29, 31v, 57, 108; Beinecke, Osborn 8096; *Knyvett*, pp. 102–10; BL: Add. 11047, fo. 86, 87v, 100, 102, 104, 109, 111v; Add. 33936, fos. 254, 264; Birmingham City Archives, MS 1098/115, unfol.; Cumbria RO, D/MUS/5/5/Box 89/Bundles 2–3; Alnwick, MS 548, fos. 27, 40v, 44v; MS 549, fos. 38, 73v.

[34] Cornwall RO, RP/1/10/27; CKS: U269/C267/12, 15, 17–19; U269/C283; U350/C2/96; Norfolk RO, KNY 759; Staffs. RO, D868/3/40; BL: Harl. 379, fo. 79; Add. 26785, fos. 32, 60v; Add. 46500, fos. 3, 9, 11-v, 29; Add. 34161, fo. 2.

[35] Bodl. MS Tanner 65, fos. 257, 276, 278; HEH, HM 66705; BL, Add. 18979, fos. 99v, 105; DRO, D258/30/14/3; Cornwall RO, RP/1/10/23.

appetite for parliamentary speeches, which his friends and kinsmen initially struggled to satisfy, although by May 1641 James Oxinden was able to boast that 'speeches and new books I will fill a whole shelf in the study with'. During the winter of 1641–2 such texts evidently came thick and fast, and other kinsmen enclosed printed texts to 'save . . . the labour' of describing them, or assumed that Oxinden had already received the latest material. The only correspondent with whom Oxinden discussed money was Thomas Denne, who was asked to 'send me down the most material latest printed books by the Friday and Thursday posts constantly', and who was instructed 'to keep a note what you disburse for them, and it shall be repaid you with thanks'. Denne was probably a special case, because of the volume and regularity involved, and more commonly Oxinden relied on the kindness of kinsmen to secure the type of material that both he and his wife enjoyed reading and discussing. What is also clear, however, is that such material circulated beyond Oxinden's house. In January 1642, he passed one of Sir Edward Dering's parliamentary speeches to Katherine Culling, asking that she should show it in turn to one Mr Huffam, and in 1644 he forwarded 'printed papers weekly' to Thomas Denne on the Continent.[36]

Oxinden's willingness to send newspapers to mainland Europe highlights a third theme to emerge from contemporary correspondence: the geographical reach of Civil War material. Pamphlets and newspapers were sent regularly from London to Scotland – 'to spare my writing' – and Lord Grey of Warke felt confident that Colonel John Moore received regular supplies of 'our news in print' at Dundalk in Ireland in 1647. And other private networks also facilitated the distribution of print to readers as far away as Antwerp, Livorno and even Constantinople, not least to supply royalist exiles with regular supplies of evidence about the old country. Here it would be easy to focus on grandees like Sir Edward Hyde and Sir Edward Nicholas, and on Paris-based diplomats like Sir Richard Browne, but it is also noteworthy that such material was accessible outside the court and beyond the French capital. Sir Thomas Hamner acquired 'levelling books' in 1647, while Thomas Holder read English newsbooks in Heidelberg in 1654, and William Hammond felt satisfied that English newspapers provided him with adequate news in the late 1650s.[37] The most telling evidence,

---

[36] *Oxinden Letters*, pp. 142, 162–3, 172, 174–5, 186, 188–9, 198, 257, 270–1, 285; *Oxinden and Peyton Letters*, pp. 65, 96, 110, 126, 154, 208–9; BL: Add. 28000, fos. 72, 87, 218; Add. 28001, fo. 126; Add. 28002, fo. 174.

[37] *Baillie*, ii. 171; Liverpool UL, MS 23/69; Lancs. RO, DDF/411, unfol.; SUL, Hartlib 32/2/23, 34, 40; BL, Add. 78193, fos. 25, 31v, 53; TNA, SP 18/41, fo. 279; *CSPD 1653–4*, pp. 243–9; BL: Add. 70105, unfol.; Add. 15858, fo. 13; Add. 18982, fo. 242; Add. 59785, fos. 25v, 45, 84; Add. 78191, fos. 106, 133.

however, involves the Verney family. In exile in France during the 1640s, therefore, Sir Ralph Verney received the *Parliament Scout*, the *Moderate Intelligencer* and *Mercurius Pragmaticus* on a weekly basis, and friends clearly assumed that he was well supplied with such material. He placed orders for specific books, like Thomas May's *History* and Husband's collection of ordinances, often after receiving word of new publications from men like Sir Roger Burgoyne, and he was particularly fascinated by 'strange libels' and by tracts that were 'hellish' and 'infernal bitter', and that were likely to 'cost him his life'. This voracious appetite for new material, and this taste for illicit texts that 'nobody dares sell', ensured that while newspapers were sent as gifts, pamphlets needed to be paid for, and some correspondents even sent price lists, as if to secure his approval, and the result was that individual bundles sent from London could contain up to three dozen tracts.[38]

Thus, while it is difficult to generalize about how many readers are likely to have seen any particular pamphlet or newspaper, such evidence makes it perfectly clear that the reach of print was a factor not merely of print runs but also of a 'multiplier'. Such practices – involving successive recipients of specific items, and repeated onward circulation – ensured that there were many more readers than texts, and that many readers gained access to material without spending any money. Indeed, in what ought to be regarded as a fourth theme to emerge from contemporary correspondence, liberal distribution of print can be shown to have been common beyond the gentry, especially within the military. The civil servant, Robert Blackbourne, sent newspapers to parliamentarian ships at Portsmouth, and the subaltern officer Nehemiah Wharton received printed news from London in 1642. Even more striking is the behaviour of Captain Adam Baynes, who frequently despatched printed texts to acquaintances and colleagues in the country who found themselves 'in a barren corner for news', and who apparently refused offers of payment.[39] Here, too, it can be demonstrated that individual recipients ensured onward distribution. Thus, in his capacity as parliamentarian scoutmaster, Sir Samuel Luke not only sought 'printed diurnalls as they come out', but also circulated these within the ranks, which meant grandees like the Earl of Essex as well as 'servants'. Wharton likewise passed on the news that he received, to 'the captains of our regiment' and to the regimental chaplain, Obadiah Sedgwick.[40]

---

[38] Claydon, Verney reels 6–10, 14.

[39] TNA, SP 18/48, fo. 274; *CSPD 1652–3*, p. 549; Ellis, 'Letters', pp. 317, 318; BL: Add. 21417, fo. 108v; Add. 21418, fos. 185, 188, 247, 329, 403; Add. 21419, fos. 69, 74, 112, 211.

[40] *Luke Letter Books*, pp. 23, 36, 117, 239, 252, 260, 268, 322, 329, 423; *Luke Journal*, iii. 221–2; Ellis, 'Letters', p. 323.

v Distribution and note-taking

This sense that relatively free distribution of print made pamphlets and newspapers available to a fairly broad public can be further enhanced through sources wherein note-taking methods imply widespread circulation. By examining things like commonplace books, it once again becomes clear that conventional practices underwent significant modification in the circumstances of Civil War. Such material is most commonly analysed for learned reading, not least in terms of the lending and borrowing of weighty texts, but such sources can also be used to trace interest in current affairs by individuals who copied scribal texts. During the early 1640s, therefore, such material permits analysis of reading habits among MPs (Roger Hill), gentlemen far removed from London (Sir John Oglander and Henry Oxinden), and provincial members of the middling sort and lesser gentry, like Nathaniel Clutterbuck of Eastington (Gloucestershire), normally in terms of speeches, petitions and even the 'diurnall occurrences'.[41] It is logical to assume, although difficult to prove, that such items were copied because they had merely been borrowed, but what can also be demonstrated is that printed texts became an increasingly important source for commonplacing, in ways which once again reveal that print genres were promiscuous, that the reading of news and polemic became more intensive, and that the period witnessed a democratization of political note-taking.[42]

During the early phase of the Long Parliament this sense that printed texts fuelled more extensive note-taking is difficult to detect, since notebooks often contain material that was also available in scribal formats, although experienced commonplacers like John Rous, who had grown familiar with 'separates', quickly noted the possibilities offered by print.[43] Thereafter, however, it is safer to assume that copies of popular texts – like the Hertfordshire petition (1642), Laud's scaffold speech (1645), the 'heads of the proposals' (1647) and the catalogue of regicides (1649) – were being drawn from pamphlets and newspapers. Sir Simonds D'Ewes made a copy of the inflammatory broadside entitled *A Question Answered* in 1642, while William Davenport used printed pamphlets as his source for

---

[41] BL: Add. 35331, fos. 8v–81v; Add. 28640, fos. 90–136; Add. 46500, fos. 52–7v; Add. 28011, fos. 62–121; Harl. 4931, fos. 41–138; FSL: V.a.454, pp. 1–41, 46–89; V.a.275, pp. 128–69; V.a.192; Glos. RO, D7115/1; D149/F13, fos. 46–96v; CKS, U47/47/Z1–2; Beinecke: Osborn 6159; Osborn fb.200; Chester RO, DAR/I/29; CUL: Dd.xi.73, fo. 35, 67v–70, 102v; Add. 89, fos. 5–25; IWCRO, OG/AA/30.

[42] Cornwall RO, T1760; Beinecke, Osborn 5220, 1760.

[43] Beinecke, Osborn 12940, 13082; FSL, G.b.2, fo. 83; Herts. RO, D/EP/F11; BL, Add. 41844A; Lancs. RO, DDB85/20, fos. 122–9; Durham UL, MSP 9, pp. 124–281; *Rous Diary*, pp. 99–100, 104–8, 113, 121.

Strafford's scaffold speech (1641), the charge against Charles I, and the trial of the Duke of Hamilton (both 1649).[44] Indeed, the use of print was sometimes entirely explicit, in terms of named newspapers, official declarations and famous pamphlets, and copyists sometimes included page numbers from printed editions, and recorded details from title pages.[45] Very occasionally, readers took notes from material that was already owned, or indeed made cuttings from texts they had purchased, but more often they did so from material that had been borrowed. This is implied by an anonymous notebook containing references which enabled the author to compare material that had been copied with printed texts that were owned, and it is made explicit by those who made notes from texts that had been 'seen' rather than acquired, and that merely 'came to my hands'. It was probably a printed text – relating to 'several lords and other parliament men' – that was copied to order by an Exeter scrivener in August 1642, having been borrowed by a household servant from his master's lodger. Likewise, when John Rous took notes from a newspaper called *Speciall Passages* in November 1642, he did so from a copy that he had seen at 'Mr Pratte's at Hockwold'; and in the late 1650s Andrew Hay of Craighnethan frequently recorded news items that he had noted in printed texts which were owned by friends and acquaintances.[46]

Surveying such notebooks and diaries creates the impression that, in the circumstances of Civil War, the development of print culture ensured that the borrowing and lending of pamphlets and newspapers became more common, and that note-taking became more extensive. Paradoxically, such phenomena probably reflected the fact that printed texts were more affordable, less valuable and more willingly shared. It is possible that it became easier to borrow printed texts from booksellers in the 1640s than it had been for people like John Felton in the 1620s, and in 1647 Richard Lloyd of Drury Lane asked Thomas Gell to 'get me a view of the book of ordinances', which he merely sought to borrow from a stationer 'to read it over'.[47] It certainly

[44] BL: Add. 37719, fos. 153v–55v, 196–7; Add. 9327, fos. 82–91; Leics. RO, DE730/3, fos. 66, 75; Lancs. RO, DDF/4; CKS, U47/47/Z1, pp. 149–53; ERO, D/DRg3/4; Chester RO, CR63/2/19, fos. 2–112v.
[45] CUL, Add. 89, fos. 26–64; Beinecke, Osborn b.52, Vol. 2, p. 128; BL: Eg. 2194, fos. 1–9v; Add. 41202A, fo. 13v; Add. 61681, fo. 26; Add. 9327, fo. 81; Eg. 2194, fos. 3–15; Harl. 980, fos. 200–226v; Add. 61481, fos. 104–5; Add. 28011, fos. 51–v, 53, 58v, 99–101; TCD, MS 805, fo. 33v; Bodl. MS Eng. Hist.e.308; *Sydney Papers*, pp. 3–156; Staffs. RO, D260/M/F/1/6, fos. 102–108v; Cornwall RO: V/BO/5; T1608/6, T1636; Glos. RO, D7115/2; Lincs. RO: 8ANC8/60; HILL39/1; CCA, U182/4/3/2; Lancs. RO, DDB85/20, fo. 144; Durham Cathedral: Sharpe 123; Hunter 33/52; Hunter 125, pp. 142–51.
[46] BL: Harl. 1929, fo. 32; Harl. 2125, fos. 143–v; Add. 37719, fos. 19–204v; Bodl. MS Rawl.D.141, pp. 80, 133; *Rous Diary*, pp. 15–17, 63, 79, 127–9; Devon RO, ECA 64, fo. 7v; *Andrew Hay Diary*, pp. 171, 185–6, 226.
[47] TNA: SP 16/118, fo. 21; SP 16/114, fos. 53–v; SP 16/119, fos. 31–2; DRO, D258/17/31/50.

became common for pamphlets and newspapers to be lent and borrowed in a liberal fashion, and men like Henry Oxinden could be both grateful borrowers and generous lenders. In May 1642 he explained to one correspondent that 'I have sent you such news as is latest, and desire it again at my man's return, in regard I borrowed it of Mr Swan', and with the regicide John Dixwell he was prepared to share works by Lilburne and Thomas Edwards, copies of the *Eikon Basilike*, and speeches by both Laud and Strafford, as well as copies of *Pragmaticus* and other 'diurnalls'.[48] The result was the development of new kinds of notebook: news diaries that were modelled on and drawn from printed sources. One reader constructed 'A true relation of all the proceedings of the king and Parliament' (April–August 1642), which was culled from official declarations, parliamentary speeches, the 'diurnall occurrences' and printed newspapers, as well as assorted verses and pamphlets. Another example with a journalistic title – 'certain memorable accidents' – covered both Kent and the broader nation in the early 1640s, and although the local material probably came from personal observation, other passages were lifted directly from pamphlets and from newspapers like *The Kingdomes Weekly Intelligencer*.[49]

Indeed, it also seems clear that the commonplacing of news became a practice that was much more obviously shared across the social spectrum. This sometimes involved fairly obscure provincial clerics, like Thomas Wyatt of Ducklington and John Syms of Devon. Wyatt recognized as early as 1641 that 'all business and proceedings are in print ... to be seen of by any that will', and he noted that there was 'an abundance weekly of all done in Parliament and diurnalls written and printed', as well as 'many petitions'. His diary, like that of Syms, contained numerous references to a wide range of printed texts. On other occasions it meant provincial citizens like Henry Townshend of Elmley Lovett (Worcestershire) and James White of Exeter. Townshend drew on parliamentary orders and printed proclamations, as well as speeches, newspapers and satirical pamphlets, and White gradually transformed his official town chronicle into a detailed record of national affairs by gathering evidence from printed sources, from the pamphlets of 'Smectymnuus' to the speeches of Sir Edward Dering and the texts printed during the 'paper war' between king and parliament in 1642, as well as from early newspapers.[50] Much more intriguing, however, are texts

---

[48] BL, Add. 28000, fo. 189; CKS, U47/3/E2, fos. 46v–7.
[49] BL, Eg. 2654, fos. 1v–181v; Bodl. MS Rawl.D.141, pp. 1, 53, 129–30.
[50] Bodl. MS Top.Oxon.c.378, pp. 234–40, 306–410, at pp. 328, 334; BL, Add. 35297, fos. 166v–80v; Worcs. RO, BA1714, pp. 1–42, 131–5, 483, 634–8, 684; Devon RO, 73/15, pp. 101–18.

generated by individuals from more humble backgrounds. These include Jeremiah Baines, the Southwark brewer who later became a parliamentarian officer and Cromwellian MP, whose reading extended beyond a limited personal library to include a variety of religious tracts, as well as Elizabeth Jekyll of St Stephen Walbrook, the wife of an imprisoned merchant, whose notebook incorporated stories about parliamentarian 'mercies' that were drawn from contemporary newspapers.[51]

By far the most famous evidence with which to demonstrate that the print revolution enabled humble readers to commonplace news involves Nehemiah Wallington, the Eastcheap woodturner. Wallington obviously used notebooks as part of the process of reflection and contemplation, and he also had one eye on posterity, which may have led him to make extracts from the voluminous body of material that lay around his house. However, close inspection of his volumes reveals an obsession with the events of the Civil Wars, and he clearly gathered information not merely by 'the hearing of the ear' or by 'what my eyes have seen', but also by making detailed notes on an enormous volume of pamphlets and newspapers. This generated not merely 'three paper books of the weekly passages of Parliament, 1640, 1641', but also notes on Laud's diary and on the Engagement controversy, as well as substantial news diaries. Extensive though his own pamphlet collection may have been, indeed, it is hard to believe that he owned all of the hundreds of texts upon which he drew.[52] Much less famous than Wallington, but no less important, is the Covent Garden barber, Thomas Rugg, whose 'diurnall' has rarely been recognized as a compilation of, and reflection upon, contemporary print culture, even though he titled it 'Mercurius Politicus Redivivus'. Like Wallington, Rugg was fascinated by the 'marketplace of news' that made 'town talk' after the collapse of the Protectorate, and by the fact that people 'bought up' such material 'as fast as they could meet with any'. However, while he frequently referred to the 'jeering books' that appeared every day, there is little indication that he personally acquired the titles to which he referred, from which he quoted, and upon which he regularly drew.[53]

With Rugg and Wallington, therefore, as with many other contemporaries, it seems clear that tumultuous events led to heightened interest in current affairs, and that the print revolution made texts more widely

---

[51] BL, Add. 32477, fos. 8, 66, 73; TNA, PROB 11/356, fo. 236v; Beinecke, Osborn b.221, pp. 3, 7, 8, 13.
[52] GL, MS 204, pp. 16, 38, 43; BL: Add. 40883, fos. 48, 188v; Add. 21935, fos. 53–110; Sloane 1457, fos. 27-v, 72v, 76; FSL, V.a.436, pp. 5–167; Tatton Park, MS 68.20.
[53] *Rugg*, pp. 2–74; BL, Add. 10116, fos. 3–26.

available and much more visible. Accessibility was enhanced not merely in terms of material becoming cheap enough to buy and easy enough to locate in a commercial marketplace, but also in terms of individuals from all walks of life being able to gain sight of a steady flow of texts. This might involve the practices associated with gift-giving, but it also involved lending and borrowing, both of which facilitated onward distribution and the circulation of printed material. It was no longer necessary to be wealthy in order to amass large quantities of texts, and it was possible to follow political debates and developments without the need for financial expense, on the basis of access to friendly and familiar networks. Indeed, in the case of Rugg, and in a setting like London, it is tempting to suppose that the accessibility of print was a factor of its ubiquity and commonality, and its visibility to members of the general public at a much more profound level.

vi Communal practices

Thus far, the exclusive focus of attention has been on individual readers, whether as purchasers or customers, or as lenders and borrowers, and the relationships involved have almost exclusively been those between private citizens. However, early modern reading often took place in a more public environment, and as such it is possible to consider how far political news and polemical texts were read in a communal fashion, and the degree to which the relationships involved were those between citizen and community. This has received only limited scholarly attention, other than occasional references to shared spending by members of the gentry, or more obviously the early history of 'public' libraries. This tends to mean parish libraries rather than the much rarer civic institutions like Chetham's foundation in Manchester, and collections that tended to be based on donation rather than purchase from the public purse, and on the translation of private collections into quasi-public facilities. Nevertheless, there is some evidence that such libraries contained pamphlets, statutes and ordinances, rather than merely theological and devotional texts. And at least some facilities – like Chetham's – were intended to be freely accessible to the 'common people', rather than restricted to scholars and gentlemen, and were based on visions of public provision that were shared by men like Hartlib.[54] Moreover, evidence does suggest that there had always been other ways in

---

[54] Dorset RO, DOB/21/1; *Londino-Batavae*, III.ii. 2021–2, 2043–4; GL, MS 7396/6, fo. 228; C. Condren, 'More parish library', *Library History*, 7 (1987), 141–62; A. Snape, 'Seventeenth century book purchasing in Chetham's library', *BJRL*, 67 (1985), 783–96; SUL, Hartlib 29/4/28.

which printed texts were available in communal settings, and that during the 1640s and 1650s it was increasingly common for conventional practices to be modified to accommodate political and topical texts, both in London and beyond, and in both urban and rural settings, in ways that facilitated public consumption and indeed discussion of current affairs.

First, it is possible to examine the libraries of political institutions, both nationally and locally. At Westminster, for example, MPs, clerks and administrators had access to a wealth of printed material, which was often replenished at the start of each parliamentary session, and which included pamphlets and petitions as well as statutes, ordinances and assorted reference works, and these texts were sometimes bought in bulk to be distributed around the palace.[55] From within parliament, moreover, MPs frequently circulated printed material to their constituents, or at least to clerics and civic leaders in borough corporations. Sandwich was sent reports of Strafford's trial, while Hythe received 'the last news here in print', a covenanter pamphlet and the king's declaration regarding the 'five members', and pamphlets and newspapers were also sent to Hull on a fairly regular basis. Much more sustained was the stream of material sent to Norwich by Richard Harman and Thomas Atkin, to save 'the labour of writing'. This could mean 'the diurnall with six other printed papers', or news of a plot and copies of the *Kingdomes Weekly Intelligencer*, or else pamphlets 'whereby you shall see what news is at present'. It seems likely that such material circulated beyond the council chamber. When Sir Robert Harley sent packets to Ludlow containing 'proceedings in the Parliament' in 1641, he explicitly asked that they should be shown to 'the Puritan party in these parts', while Ralph Assehton sent books and pamphlets for 'the ministers and such neighbours as you think fit'.[56]

Such practices were clearly designed to ensure that printed texts were available to ordinary citizens. This is evident not merely from the zeal of Harley, but also from the tendency for corporate bodies – many of which were remarkably open and accessible – to purchase news and information. This sometimes involved scribal texts: Newcastle secured 'constant intelligence' by subscribing to a newsletter service (at a cost of £4 to £5 per year), while the churchwardens at Lambeth paid for manuscript copies of three

[55] TNA: AO 3/1088/1; SP 28/307, unfol.; SP 28/309, fo. 79; Beinecke, Osborn fb.159/40, 90.
[56] EKRO: Sa/C1, pp. 84–5, 87, 102, 128; H1257; D. Scott, 'Particular business in the Long Parliament', in *Parliament, Politics and Elections*, ed. C. Kyle (Cam. Soc., 5th series, 17, 2001), pp. 300–341; BL: Add. 22619, fos. 31–230; Add. 22620, fos. 60–182; Add. 15903, fo. 71; Add. 19399, fo. 26; Shropshire RO, 212/364/44; Chetham, A.3.90, fos. 30–v.

books 'concerning the Irish affairs'.[57] However, the practice of acquiring such information became much more common once it was made affordable by the print revolution. Any number of boroughs acquired acts and ordinances, as well as reference tools like guides for JPs and constables, and even the polyglot Bible, but many also acquired texts like a speech by Oliver St John, or a copy of Sir Hardress Waller's 1648 *Representation*, and some made fairly systematic attempts to secure supplies of newspapers.[58] The same was also true of other corporate bodies and organizations, from livery companies to the Eastern association, the latter of which spent 15d on pamphlets in November and December 1643. Particularly active in this regard were parish churchwardens and constables, who frequently purchased not merely books for days of humiliation, fasting and thanksgiving, but also acts and ordinances and texts containing parliamentary proceedings and official propaganda, to be 'published' in church.[59]

Such evidence about corporate acquisitions opens up the possibility of exploring communal *reading*, either aloud or in private. In the late 1630s, for example, *News from Ipswich* was read aloud at the house of Henry Burton's parish clerk, while in 1649 an account of the king's trial was read collectively at Tetbury, and in the late 1650s newspapers and declarations were perused by Andrew Hay and his friends in Scotland. On another occasion, a reading of William Prynne's lengthy speech on the eve of Pride's Purge was held at a local parsonage in Suffolk, in the presence of John Clopton and Sir Thomas Barnardiston.[60] Indeed, it was fairly common for printed texts to be 'published' by individuals by means of much more public readings. Sometimes this involved provocative gestures, like Thomas Cotton of Bergholt (Essex) reading news in the streets of Colchester, or John Lilburne reading *Englands New Chains* before a London crowd, but they may also have been fairly routine. Ministers like Richard Herring read pamphlets from his pulpit in Drew Stanton (Somerset), and Mr Swann

[57] TWAS: MS 543/30; MS 543/31, fo. 6v; MS 543/32, fo. 209; *Lambeth Churchwardens' Accounts*, ed. C. Drew (Surrey RS, 47, 1950), p. 167.

[58] CKS: Md/ACmi/3, fos. 3v, 96v; Md/FCai; Hants. RO, W/E6/2, unfol.; CHC: BA/H/3/20/2, p. 352; BA/H/3/20/3, p. 24; Plymouth RO, PMR 1/132, fos. 273v, 290v, 294v; Bristol RO, F/Au/1//27, p. 53; Cornwall RO: B/Bod/285–6; B/Ives/138, fos. 25, 27v, 38; B/Lis/290; Lincs. RO, L/1/1/1/6, p. 84; EKRO, Sa/C4; *Borough of Leicester*, pp. 453, 454–5, 483, 518, 534.

[59] GL: MS 11571/12, fo. 398; MS 12065/3, fo. 187; MS 6122/2, unfol.; MS 3054/2, unfol.; MS 30032/1, unfol.; TNA, SP 28/299, fo. 611; *Churchwardens' Accounts*, ed. H. Swayne (Salisbury, 1896), p. 225; Leics. RO, DE720/30, fos. 63, 79–v, 94v; *Lambeth*, p. 157; Notts. RO, PR1710, p. 49; *HMC 3rd Report*, p. 330.

[60] Bodl. MS Bankes 18, fo. 42; BL, Add. 78259, fo. 77; *Andrew Hay Diary*, pp. 171, 185–6, 226; ERO, D/DQs18, fo. 70v.

apparently engaged in 'publishing proclamations' and 'reading books' to his workmen in Kent in 1643, to 'put them . . . upon their late rebellion'.[61]

Between the private house, the church and the public street, of course, lay a range of other venues where print could circulate, not least alehouses and inns, whose importance has naturally been overshadowed by coffeehouses, and by concentration on the display of ballads. Here, too, the 1640s witnessed a transformation, with the emergence of overtly political songs – like the one about the 'five members' that was apparently performed by Mr Gollop at *The Bear* in Exeter in 1642 – but also with newspapers and pamphlets. *The Bear* also witnessed a conversation in October 1642 about George Eglisham's *Forerunner of Revenge*, involving a local gentleman, Francis Giles, and a husbandman, Thomas Hill of Bishops Nympton, while in January 1642 one lodger at nearby Coleridge Inn read a paper containing 'some passages about the parliament', and 'a copy of an act or declaration'.[62] In July 1641, newspapers apparently became a focal point for conversation among 'threshers and mowers' in a Somerset alehouse, prompting Florence Smyth to complain that they were 'wild rascals', and that parliamentary affairs kept them 'in more awe than we can'. In 1643, meanwhile, it was alleged that Robert Redcroft had been found in a Horsham alehouse, 'publishing a scandalous pamphlet against the parliament'. His copy of *A Plaine Case* had clearly been doing the rounds, and he apparently received it from 'one Butler, a papist', who in turn received it from Mr Edgely, 'a minister at Nuthurst'. Such tales mean that it was not too fanciful to attribute to Marchamont Nedham the view that 'ploughmen and shopkeepers' who 'read diurnalls over their ale' would be able to 'know the truth of things?'[63]

As accessible places of promiscuous social interaction, of course, inns and alehouses helped to ensure that pamphlets and newspapers generated conversations in shop doorways and on the streets. Following the reading of Eglisham's pamphlet at *The Bear*, therefore, one auditor promptly passed on what he had heard to a local weaver, Abe Hooper, on his way home. Similar episodes occurred on many other occasions, in other towns across the country. In 1642, a conversation took place in the doorway of Ambrose Frost's shop in Ipswich, in which 'printed papers newly come to town' prompted criticism of the king, and in January 1645 a heated exchange

---

[61] *CSPD 1634–5*, pp. 252–3; *CSPD 1649–50*, p. 59; Bodl. MS J. Walker.c.4, fo. 166; MS Tanner 62, fo. 275.

[62] Devon RO: ECA Book 64, fos. 7v, 15v; ECA Book 63, fo. 391.

[63] *Correspondence of the Smyth Family*, ed. J. Bettey (Bristol RS, 35, 1982), p. 174; Bodl. MS Nalson 16, fo. 86; *Mercurius Politicus* (1660, M1768A), p. 12.

occurred at the door of William Chandler's shop in Dover, involving a shoemaker and a victualler, the latter of whom denounced the Scots as 'rogues and thieves' after Chandler read him a new pamphlet. Over a haircut in 1648, a Norwich barber discussed stories about the city's mayor that had appeared 'in the printed news', and in Northamptonshire in 1654 a conversation about the army prompted William Prior to produce and read aloud a copy of a republican petition by the 'three colonels'.[64]

Such stories provide insights into a world in which the lives and conversations of ordinary people – weavers, shoemakers, victuallers and barbers – had been transformed through access to print, and to print that did not need to be purchased. The key to this development was not their *politicization*, but rather the acquisition of a more detailed frame of reference in terms of news and opinion. It was 'the newest news' that enabled an Exeter worsted-comber to hold an after-dinner conversation with a clergyman about 'the affairs of the present time', and it may have been print that enabled a local apprentice to tell two of his colleagues that 'Parliament's laws were not worth a turd'. In both cases ordinary Devonshire folk may have known very well of what they spoke.[65]

vii Free distribution

This transformative effect of the print revolution – a dramatic change in the ability to access pamphlets and newspapers, and to become well informed about current affairs – makes even more sense in terms of texts that were distributed freely. This could be done privately and selectively, but it could also be done in a more public and even indiscriminate fashion, and it is yet another area where traditional practices underwent significant change in the circumstances of revolution. Conventionally, therefore, free distribution tended to involve authors – like Bramhall, Baillie and Baxter – giving away copies of their books. This was particularly common among provincial clerics, who used such practices to supplement parochial and clerical duties. Such efforts mirrored those by aristocratic and gentry grandees, who sometimes ensured that specific texts reached beyond family members to servants and estate workers, and it is striking that works like the *Eikon Basilike* were bought in bulk by Sir Ralph Verney, the Earl of Bath, William Sancroft and

---

[64] Devon RO, ECA Book 64, fo. 15v; Bodl. MS Bankes 52, fo. 61; BL, Add. 29624, fo. 174; Norfolk RO, NCR 12C/1/94; *TSP*, iii. 35.
[65] Devon RO: ECA Book 63, fos. 380–v; ECA Book 64, fos. 8v, 15v, 20v.

Lady Coke for this very reason.[66] More familiar in a Civil War context, of course, is the use of such methods by radical activists, from Levellers to Quakers and Fifth Monarchists. Copies of their tracts were distributed to sympathizers, 'to be dispersed with care and speed', and 'bundles of printed papers' could be handed out at prayer meetings, spread among ministers, and thrust into the pulpit, or even scattered indiscriminately around the streets.[67] The aim of this section, however, is to suggest not only that such tactics became increasingly common, but also that they were only one aspect of a larger phenomenon, and involved the appropriation of practices relating to official literature. The latter have received little scholarly attention, even though they took place on an increasingly significant scale, and involved increasingly sophisticated mechanisms, which ensured that topical texts became a ubiquitous feature of everyday life across the country.

There can be little doubt that official literature represented the most commonly and systematically available genre of print. Paid for by the authorities, regularly and frequently, and even translated into Welsh, print runs after 1640 often exceeded 10,000 – enough to reach every parish in the land.[68] This represented a step-change in volume, at least among parliamentarians, and at times it was also possible to print additional copies in the localities. Moreover, the orders, instructions and practices that were involved prove revealing about the determination to ensure that such material had the greatest possible impact. Sir Edward Nicholas claimed that royalist literature needed to reach places like Shropshire because 'Parliament's diurnalls and pamphlets are in everybody's hands', and this explains the development of mechanisms for circulating such material to sheriffs, mayors and local committees, and even to ships of the fleet. Thus, between February and June 1642, the sheriff of Flintshire (David Pennant) received seventeen bundles of royalist texts, sometimes involving two or three different works to be distributed.[69] What is striking about both

[66] HEH, HA 15378; *Baillie*, ii. 385; CHC, BA/H/17/A79/226; BL, Add. 70007, fo. 108; H. Love, 'Preacher and publisher', *SB*, 31 (1978), p. 232; *Giles Moore*, p. 181; Claydon, Verney reel 10; *Devon Accounts*, ii. 145–6; BL, Add. 69880, fo. 77; H. Carron, 'William Sancroft', *The Library*, 7th series, 1 (2000), p. 293.

[67] *TSP*, iii. 149–51, iv. 720, v. 272–3, 297–8, 408–9, 505; *CSPD 1649–50*, pp. 291, 307, 334; CKS, Md/Acm1/3, fo. 84; BL, Add. 43724, fos. 7v, 13; *Warwick County Records IV*, ed. S. Ratcliff (Warwick, 1938), p. 143; BL, Harl. 165, fo. 145v; *Civicus*: 298.064, p. 608; 298.066, p. 626.

[68] *CJ*, v. 474; TNA: AO 3/1088/1, part 2, fos. 10–14v; SP 28/237, unfol.; SP 23/1A, pp. 5, 8, 55, 65–6, 104; Beinecke, Osborn fb.159/40; *CSPD 1645–7*, p. 579; *CSPD 1649–50*, p. 327; *CSPD 1650*, p. 312; TNA, SP 16/515, fos. 98–9v; BL, Add. 5756, fos. 142–7; HEH, EL 7060; *The Ottley Papers*, ed. W. Phillips (TSANHS, 2nd series, 6–7, 1894–5), i. 55–6.

[69] Warw. RO, CR2017/TP646; *Ottley Papers*, ii. 344–5; EKRO, Sa/C1, pp. 87, 102, 128; *CSPD 1651–2*, p. 146; TNA: SP 16/515, fos. 98–9v; SP 16/516, fo. 20; SP 16/498, fo. 83; PA, MP 24 May 1642, 6 July 1642; Worcs. RO, BA1714, p. 481; BL, Add. 71534, fo. 22; Flintshire RO, D/DE271, fos. 3–44.

royalists and parliamentarians, moreover, is that clear emphasis was placed on public display and public reading. Texts were almost invariably ordered to be 'read in all fit and public places' and 'affixed against some posts or walls' where they might be 'publicly seen', and even 'kept forever as a record' so that 'none may pretend ignorance'. Such efforts also came to be matched by a bureaucratic desire to monitor the efficiency with which distribution took place, as provincial officials were charged with returning 'a speedy account' of their work, with the warning that 'you are to fail not as you will answer the contrary to your utmost peril'.[70]

Attempts to monitor performance probably ensured that distribution became much more thorough, but a more telling guide to the effectiveness of such practices involves approaching the issue from a local perspective. This is possible because civic authorities often contributed to the cost of transporting such material, and payments to messengers are thus recorded in borough accounts from Devizes to Ludlow and from Launceston to Shrewsbury, as well as by some parish constables. The costs involved varied from 1s to 5s, and the frequency with which such material arrived ensured that the cost to boroughs like St Ives, Worcester, Coventry and Bristol could reach £1 to £2 per annum.[71] Local archives also indicate that provision was made for onward distribution, dispersal and display, thereby ensuring that texts reached even the most remote corners of the land. In June 1642, the deputy sheriff of Derbyshire instructed the bailiff of Wirksworth to publish proclamations 'through all the market towns and public places within this county', and to 'fix the same upon usual posts', and to 'fail not as you tender His Majesties service, and will answer the contrary at your peril'. Likewise, when Thomas Wilson of Dover received copies of an army declaration in April 1653 – doubtless regarding the dissolution of the Rump – he duly passed them to Richard Culmer at Minster (Isle of Thanet), so that they could be given to Major Thomas Foach, and so that he in turn could 'let them be published and made known to the honest people'.[72] The preservation of texts and instructions at their final destination thus attests to the efficiency of the process, as do the certificates produced to show that instructions had been followed. In April 1649, therefore, the deputy sheriff

---

[70] OUA: NEP/supra/Reg.Sb, pp. 1–5; SP/E/1/4; Devon RO, 1499M/4/3; *Ottley Papers*, ii. 359; *Knyvett*, p. 123; Chester RO, Z/ML/3/325, 353, 360, 380–2; *CJ*, iv. 512; BL: Add. 22619, fo. 93; Add. 22620, fo. 164; Norfolk RO, HMN 7/172/5; Beinecke, Osborn fb.67, fo. 73; TNA, SP 23/259, fos. 24–5.

[71] BL, Add. 5756, fos. 101–3; Wilts. RO, G20/1/17, fo. 143, 164, 166; Cornwall RO, B/Laus/179/2/3; Shropshire RO, LB8/1/160–2; Cumbria RO, Ca/4/2, unfol.; CCA, CC/F/A/25, fo. 190v; Cornwall RO, B/Ives/138, fos. 4, 39; Worcs. RO, BA9360/A10, Box 3; CHC, BA/A/1/26/3, pp. 76, 89, 99; Bristol RO, F/Au/1/22, pp. 27, 30.

[72] DRO, D258/34/70; Culmer, *Parish* (1657, C7482), p. 38.

of Gloucester, John Browning, detailed the towns where he had proclaimed an Act of Parliament regarding delinquents, and officials at Ludlow noted that the Act against proclaiming Charles Stuart as King had been proclaimed at noon on 5 February 1649.[73] Finally, a wealth of evidence reveals how local officials organized the distribution, proclaiming and posting of official orders, with payments to parish clerks, bell-ringers, trumpeters and drummers, and to those involved in 'calling a proclamation' and 'nailing up ten proclamations', and even for 'a frame for the king's declaration hanging in the church'.[74] The result was that, from mundane orders to portentous statements, like the declaration of 'no further addresses' (1648) and the Humble Petition and Advice (1657), printed texts were regularly and repeatedly read at mass gatherings, in scenes that probably involved solemnity and celebration. Indeed, any number of towns not only displayed and read official literature, but also provided wood for bonfires, and food and drink, and when Launceston proclaimed the new king in 1660 over £2 was spent on 'beer and cider'.[75]

The potential importance of such practices is hard to overstate. Texts reached big crowds and were even used to quell tumults, like that which occurred in opposition to taxation in Derby in May 1645. They were sometimes transcribed from the posts to which they were fixed, and they generated conversations, like that which took place between an Exeter cutler, his servant and a local gentleman, over an order to remove altar rails and images.[76] This explains why the process could generate considerable controversy. Proclamations could be torn down, and the men delivering them could be harassed and even arrested, and such rituals and ceremonies could also provoke crowds and riots. In August 1642, the 'honest men of Ware' attacked a local royalist with 'heaps of stones which flew about his ears', after he had skipped church in order to post one of the king's proclamations, while royalists in Faversham felt compelled to stand guard by a proclamation posted on a local church door, 'that none should pull it down.'[77] Such obstacles reflected concerted attempts to undermine

---

[73] TNA, SP 23/248, fo. 35; Shropshire RO, LB7/1950–1.

[74] BL, Add. 78221, fo. 31; Leics. RO, DE625/60, fo. 67v; TNA: SP 28/307, unfol.; SP 28/304, fo. 754; SP 28/300, fo. 707; CCA: CC/F/A/25, fo. 242v; CC/F/A/26, fos. 346, 480–1; Cumbria RO, Ca/4/2–3; Cornwall RO: B/Ives/138, fos. 30, 35; B/Laus/179/2/3; Earwaker, pp. 134, 137.

[75] TWAS, MD/NC/2/1, pp. 212, 227; Berks. RO, R/ACi/1/7, fos. 82–v; Cornwall RO: B/Bod/285–6; B/Ives/138, fos. 28, 35v, 36v; B/Laus/185–6.

[76] Northants. RO, IC 243; DRO, D258/12/16, p. 3; *Rous Diary*, pp. 10–11, 34, 37, 41; Devon RO, ECA Book 62, fo. 380–v.

[77] 'Lewis Dyve', p. 71; Beinecke, Osborn fb.156, fos. 1–2; PA: MP 28 June 1642; Braye 57, fo. 6; *Some Speciall and Considerable Passages*, 605.01, p. 7; *Diurnall*, 504.004, p. 29.

opponents, which sometimes emanated from the very top, thereby ensuring that pressure was exerted to ensure that texts were read. Indeed, in July 1642 a zealous royalist like Wallop Brabazon of Leominster even used force, or at least the threat of force, to ensure that royalist texts were read by the local preacher, Matthew Clarke. Brabazon thrust a paper into Clarke's hand, telling him that 'the king requires you to read this', and when the minister attempted to reach the pulpit, Brabazon called upon the 'rude people' to stop him, to cries of 'down with the roundhead'.[78] Such pressures, as well as local prejudices, could seriously affect the impact of official material in the provinces, even if the most likely result was that people were denied access to the views of one or other side, rather than deprived of official literature entirely. Thus, John Marston, preacher at St Mary Magdalene, Canterbury, was accused of reading royalist declarations in the spring of 1642, while dissuading his parishioners from hearing parliamentarian literature. He told them that he had 'a roll of books sent down to the constable to be read ... which will cost you five or six hours' time to hear them'. Another trouble-maker was Frederick Gibb, parson of Hartest and Boxted (Suffolk), who organized public readings 'in a turbulent way ... congregating people together, on troops and heaps, and shops and greens', and who only read royalist literature.[79] Moreover, while some people were blatantly unco-operative, many more were probably nervous about obeying orders. In 1641, the Earl of Bridgwater encountered messengers who were unsure about the authority by which orders were being given, and in December 1643, Sir Edward Nicholas complained to the governor of Dartmouth that 'some of our late proclamations ... have been scarce heard of in some parts of our kingdom', because people had 'either resolutely refused or else excused the doing thereof without a writ'.[80]

What is striking about such problems, however, is the frequency with which they were overcome, not least through local initiatives. These could come from local audiences, and a Colchester weaver called Stephen Lewes complained to the authorities about only hearing the proclamations of one side (in his case parliamentarian), while Frederick Gibb's flock chided him for only reading royalist texts. They could also involve the distribution of other forms of news and polemic. Copies of The King's Cabinet Opened were despatched from London by the Committee of the West and the Treasurers

---

[78] Cornwall RO, AD/324/9; OPH, x. 421; BL, Add. 70106, fos. 165–v.

[79] Bodl. MS J. Walker.c.4, fos. 231, 234v, 247; PA, MP 27 June 1642; Bodl. MS Nalson 13, fo. 178.

[80] BL, Add. 70003, fos. 204, 221; PA, MP 31 Mar. 1642; Shropshire RO, 212/364/53; Devon RO, 1392M/ L1643/46.

at War, while accounts of a victory over the Spanish fleet were sent to George Monck to pass on to Scottish ministers, and 2,000 copies of a narrative of the Battle of Worcester were sent to Ireland.[81] More significantly, national strategies were both supported and supplemented by local campaigns to communicate with the public. As was traditional, local grandees rang church bells to mark major news events, and from Lambeth to Bodmin and Leicester this drew attention to battles at Dunbar and Worcester, and to the return of a 'free' parliament and Charles Stuart in 1660. Indeed, bells were often supplemented by bonfires, as well as by wine, beer and cakes. Thus, the townsmen of Bodmin marked the Restoration in 1660 by ordering bells to be rung, and spent 4s 6d on a bonfire and 11s on gunpowder. A further £1 5s was spent on 25 dozen buns, and no less than £3 5s was blown on a pub crawl around the town. More remarkably, such practices were also used to mark parliamentary occasions like the passage of the Triennial Act (February 1641), which was celebrated across London as well as in Coventry, where citizens were evidently aware of the wild response in the capital.[82]

More intriguing still was the proactive role that local communities played in acquiring and circulating print. Towns frequently purchased additional copies of official texts, not least at London, where 100 copies of a parliamentary declaration were bought in 1642, where 150 ordinances against unauthorized preachers were acquired in 1645, and where money was found for 600 copies of an ordinance concerning deans and chapters, 'to be sent out in every parish'. In the case of the Cromwellian Major General, James Berry, such purchases were explicitly justified in terms of providing for 'dark places'.[83] Beyond this, local officials also commissioned the printing of such material. This was obviously true in London, where the civic authorities printed and dispersed their own acts, proclamations and orders, in editions of 250 to 600; marked the raising of the siege at Lyme Regis in 1645; and ensured that 2,000 copies of acts against swearing and cursing were 'set up in the streets'. The congregation at Stepney printed a breviate of legislation regarding Sabbath observance, to be displayed 'in several convenient places in and about the church', and to the end that 'idle and disorderly

[81] ERO, D/5/Sb2/7, fo. 298; Bodl. MS Nalson 13, fo. 178; TNA: SP 28/139, Part 16, fo. 1; SP 28/301, fo. 755; *CSPD 1651*, p. 456; *CSPD 1656–7*, p. 137.

[82] *Borough of Leicester*, p. 398; Cumbria RO, Ca/4/3, unfol.; *Lambeth*, pp. 158, 159, 188; CHC, BA/A/1/26/3, pp. 74–369; *Churchwardens' Accounts*, ed. Swayne, p. 225; TWAS: MS 543/27, fos. 187v, 190v; MS 543/29–32; Cornwall RO, B/Bod/285; Bodl. MS Tanner 65, fo. 278; CHC, BA/A/1/26/3, p. 88.

[83] CLRO: CCA 1/4, fo. 152; CCA 1/5, fo. 163; CCA, 1/6, fo. 266; *TSP*, iv. 287, 316.

persons ... may be timely forewarned'.[84] However, similar practices can also be seen across the country. In North Wales Sir Thomas Middleton ordered the reprinting of an ordinance in 1644, before paying four soldiers to disperse them, while in Cheshire Sir William Brereton commissioned thousands of orders and ordinances from the London press of Thomas Underhill, who also undertook similar work for the Hertfordshire militia committee. Here, too, the aim was to do more than merely circulate official texts, and Underhill was also supplying 'letters', 'propositions' and news reports. Likewise, in 1652 the corporation at Newcastle not only paid for 500 copies of texts that summarized acts against incest, swearing and drunkenness, but also ordered 100 copies of a tract called *A Cluster of Drunkards*.[85]

Reassessing the practices by which printed texts were made freely available to readers across the country has important implications. First, it highlights the degree to which local communities became familiar with national affairs and policies, and indicates that this was not merely a matter of having texts thrust upon them. It is thus interesting to note that a text like the Presbyterian *Directory* made a much greater impact than scholars have realized. Much has been made of the fact that few churchwardens purchased the book (because of ongoing attachment to the prayer book), but this overlooks evidence that copies were sent out from London by the Committee of the West, that the county committee in Herefordshire purchased 200 copies (at a cost of over £11), and that copies were also bought by local constables.[86] Secondly, the tendency for official activity to extend to the posting and reading of news and polemic, rather than merely declarations and proclamations, encouraged the more widespread adoption of such practices. 'Posting' became an increasingly common phenomenon, not just as a means of advertising new books – the title pages of which were thought to 'pester posts' – but also as a means of circulating libels.[87] The latter were traditionally handwritten, and were probably displayed in limited numbers at a restricted number of venues, but this clearly changed in the 1640s, perhaps as early as the anti-Laudian protests of 1640, and subsequent comments indicate that such material could be seen not just at the Exchange or upon the doors of parliament, but also 'up

[84] CLRO: CCA 1/1, fos. 65–v, 154v; CCA 1/2, fos. 55v, 144v, 122, 222; CCA 1/3, fos. 58, 152; CCA 1/4, fos. 56v, 152, 223v; CCA1/5, fos. 65v, 162v–3, 264; CCA 1/6, fos. 54v, 163–v, 265v–6; CCA, 1/7, fo. 65v; *Memorials of Stepney Parish*, ed. G. Hill (Guildford, 1890–1), pp. 212–13.

[85] TNA: SP 28/16, fo. 221; SP 28/139, Part 20, p. 13; SP 28/220, unfol.; SP 28/300, fo. 176; SP 28/231, unfol.; SP 28/303, fo. 177; SP 28/251; BL, Add. 70068, unfol.; TWAS, MS 543/32, fo. 187.

[86] J. Morrill, *Nature of the English Revolution* (London, 1993), pp. 153, 164–7; TNA, SP 28/139, Part 16, fo. 1; BL, Add. 70068, unfol.; Notts. RO, PR1710, p. 49.

[87] *Scourge* (1625, STC 6340), pp. 5–7; *Borough of Leicester*, p. 425; Bodl. MS Carte 77, fo. 404v; *Kingdomes Faithful and Impartial Scout*, 210.17, p. 136.

and down many places of the City of London, and chiefly about church doors'. The use of print enabled widespread distribution, and sometimes the explicit aim was to mimic official literature, with 'papers pasted up in most of the public places of the town which the ragged sorts would have pass for proclamations'.[88]

In other words, 'libelling' was transformed through the appropriation of practices associated with official literature, and this ensured that public 'noticeboards' across the country became crowded and contested spaces, and that tactics became progressively more dramatic. Disputes arose not just about the display of official literature, but also about other texts. Royalists in Exeter attempted to respond to a republican proclamation that was 'fastened in the market place upon a post', just as parliamentarians in Oxford had distributed a fake proclamation in the king's name in January 1643, which was 'cleaved upon the gibbet post' before being removed by the authorities. By the 1650s, the practice of 'posting up railing blasphemous libels' was fairly widespread, especially by sectarians and political radicals, like the republicans who actively backed the petition of the 'three colonels' in Northamptonshire in December 1654. More disturbing still was the possibility that this would lead to even more provocative gestures, like the scattering of print in the streets, suspicions about which were not unreasonable given that 'several boxes' of the colonels' petition were dispatched to Bristol, Warwick and Leicester, and that no less than 5,000 copies were sent to Scotland.[89] Indeed, contemporary evidence reveals that the term 'scattered' genuinely meant *indiscriminate* rather than merely *widespread* distribution, and although this often happened in the dead of night, it also involved texts being dispersed among crowds and even thrown into houses and coaches. As Henry Walker demonstrated with *To Your Tents O Israel* in January 1642, this could even involve inflammatory sheets being lobbed into the royal coach.[90] Such tactics were rare before 1640, but were later used by royalists and parliamentarians alike, and the most striking examples involved the Levellers and their radical associates. In London, copies of *A Declaration of the Members of Parliament Lately Dissolved* were 'scattered

---

[88] BL, Harl. 4931, fo. 8; Harl. 6424, fos. 69v-71; LPL, MS 943, p. 717; HEH, EL 7856; Aberdeen UL, MS 2538, fos. 34v, 161; *Proceedings*, 599.240, p. 3811; *CSPD 1649–50*, p. 397; *Britanicus*, 268.028B, p. 215; BL, Add. 78316, fo. 17.

[89] *Kingdomes*, 214.298, p. 1251; Wood, *Life and Times*, i. 82; BL, Add. 28930, fo. 8v; TNA, ASSI/45/4/3/108; *TSP*, iii. 35, vi. 829–32; *Ludlow Memoirs*, i. 406–7.

[90] NLS, MS 20774, fo. 89; *Perf. Proceedings*, 599.306, p. 4854; *Occurrences*, 465.4015, sig. P4v; *Kingdomes*, 214.266A, p. 990; *Diurnall*, 503.257, p. 3938; *CCSP*, iv. 119; Aberdeen UL, MS 2538, fo. 157v; BL, Eg. 2536, fo. 360v; *Weekly Intelligencer*, 689.23, p. 181; PA: MP 9 May 1642; MP 25 June 1642.

about the city' one morning in January 1655, and then picked up by passers-by, circulated and commented upon. Likewise, in 1657, John Sturgeon was caught throwing around copies of *Killing No Murder*, bundles of which were under his arm when he was arrested. However, stories about pamphlets being 'thrown abroad' were also common across the country, as in Southampton, where one Cole – 'a perfect Leveller' – was involved in scattering pamphlets about the streets.[91]

viii Conclusion

With the indiscriminate scattering of printed texts we reach the most dramatic end of a spectrum of practices that ensured a dramatic change in the accessibility of print during the revolutionary era. This was the result of structural change in the book trade, the intensification of traditional practices in the circumstances of Civil War, and the emergence of new phenomena. Indeed, everyday practices relating to both the supply of and demand for print reveal that contemporaries became extremely well-acquainted with material relating to political affairs. Cheap texts were readily available, and since there were many ways of gaining sight of them without financial expense, a remarkable picture emerges about the degree to which national affairs penetrated across the country and across the social spectrum. This meant unprecedented familiarity – and perhaps even daily encounters – with print, and the emergence of a national news and information culture.

Of course, print was not experienced with equal intensity by all readers. It cannot be doubted that members of the social and political elite retained distinct advantages, and the broadest range of options for acquiring print. Alice L'Estrange could get pamphlets and newspapers through purchase, gift or borrowing, through family and friends, and through long-distance relationships with London booksellers, as well as through visits to London and from local booksellers and pedlars. John Buxton supplemented the services of the capital's booksellers with oral, scribal and printed news from friends and family, who sent 'the books of this week' and 'the newest books'. Sir Humphrey Mildmay satisfied his fascination with news and politics as an eye- and ear-witness around Whitehall and Westminster, by 'prateing of news', and by exploiting high-powered contacts, as well as friends and

---

[91] TNA, PC 2/49, fo. 55v; Bodl. MS Bankes 13, fo. 18; MS Bankes 18, fo. 33; PA, MP 21 Dec. 1640; Bodl. MS Clarendon 46, fo. 82; *TSP*, i. 366–7; *Kingdomes*, 214.001, p. 8; *Proceedings*: 599.286, p. 4536; 599.267, p. 4236–7; 599.309, sig. 26S4v; *Politicus*, 361.403, pp. 294, 302; 361.362, sig. 32L4v; 361.363, p. 7812; Bodl. MS Rawl.A.25, pp. 17–19; MS Rawl.A.29, pp. 268–9, 574–7; *TSP*, iii. 738–40, vi. 310–11, 315–20; BL, Add. 24861, fo. 72; *TSP*, v. 287, 396–7.

servants who could send him 'many pamphlets'.[92] Further down the social spectrum and further away from London there were fewer opportunities for consuming print, and individuals were progressively less fortunate and had progressively fewer options. Thus a minor provincial gentleman like William Elyott of Busbridge claimed to have 'no other means' of obtaining newspapers than friends like Sir Simonds D'Ewes. Nevertheless, claims about living in rural ignorance, and of having 'little wind of news' – by men such as Thomas Knyvett, Brian Duppa and Viscount Conway – need to be treated with extreme caution. Their access to print may have been imperfect, but they clearly obtained supplies of pamphlets and newspapers from 'friendly factors', and were hardly ignorant. Ignorance, in other words, was relative and subjective, and even Sir Thomas Barrington – who was particularly well-supplied with news – referred to being 'retired into the country barren of news', and to his 'poor stock of present intelligence' (September 1641). This need to contextualize contemporary comments also applies to Nathaniel Tovey of Lutterworth (Leicestershire), the most commonly cited contemporary who claimed to 'live in darkness and ignorance'. This is because no sooner had such words been penned in January 1642 than Tovey received 'some books of news' from Isabell Warner.[93] Indeed, while the most humble and geographically remote citizens could do little to guarantee regular and reliable supplies of pamphlets and newspapers, their encounters with print would nevertheless have been much more frequent than before, and certainly more substantive than scholars have recognized.

The extraordinary changes that brought this situation about are best demonstrated by exploring the 'outer limits' of print circulation before and after 1640. In tracing the distribution of pamphlets by Puritan activists in the late 1630s, therefore, it is certainly striking to witness the involvement of London woodturners like Nehemiah Wallington and James Ouldham, and wax chandlers like John Bartlet, and to observe how pamphlets reached into rural Norfolk and Somerset, to be sold and also passed around from hand-to-hand, among gentlemen, clerics and weavers.[94] Contemporaries rightly sensed that this involved a transformative extension of tactics that were usually associated with ballads and libels, but it was nevertheless unusual,

---

[92] Norfolk RO, LEST P10, pp. 109, 130, 134; CUL, Buxton 102/9, 11, 13; Buxton 59/86–8, 90; FSL, W.b.600, *passim*.

[93] BL, Harl. 382, fo. 115; CUL, Buxton, 59/89; *Duppa Corr.*, pp. 8, 41, 75, 77, 147; BL, Add. 70113, unfol.; Beinecke, Osborn 61/61; TNA, SP 46/83, fos. 48, 68; D. Underdown, *Revel, Riot and Rebellion* (Oxford, 1985), p. 138.

[94] Bodl. MS Bankes 63, fo. 42; GL, MS 204, pp. 468–70; J. Peacey, 'The paranoid prelate', in *Conspiracies and Conspiracy Theory*, ed. B. Coward and J. Swann (Aldershot, 2004), pp. 113–34.

and individual pamphlets remained difficult to obtain. This was because Puritan activism necessarily involved clandestine behaviour, closed networks, and secretive channels of communication, as well as surreptitious printing, smuggling and shared reading within self-selecting communities.[95] After 1640, however, the outer limits of print circulation were qualitatively different, even if smuggling, secrecy and hand-to-hand distribution all survived.[96] By observing the activities of radical agitators and the circulation of print within the army, it becomes clear that contemporaries were rightly concerned about the promiscuity of print. A soldier like John Radman could apparently access the *Outcry of the Apprentices* with ease in 1649, and in 1647 a copy of the *New Found Stratagem* was passed from Sergeant John Eve to Captain William Styles, and on to Colonels Cooke and Ayliffe and a scout called Roger Crofts, who in turn passed it to a minister, James Willett. Indeed, bundles of such works were distributed indiscriminately within regiments, and 'scattered abroad in the army'. In early 1649, 'divers troopers' travelled to places like Hitchin and St Albans to read out Leveller pamphlets in market places, and to fix copies in prominent locations, and pamphlets even reached naval ships, to be passed around among gunners and carpenters.[97] Such practices enabled humble soldiers to become imbued with radical ideas, and even to discuss specific parliamentary votes and resolutions in the summer of 1647, to the extent that the authorities felt compelled to respond in kind, so that republican propaganda could be 'officiously dispersed and read' among ordinary soldiers.[98]

This promiscuity of print, in terms of geographical reach and social penetration, means that contemporaries were not exaggerating when they said that pamphlets 'fly abroad in such swarms', that newspapers were 'posted up and down the country', and that printed texts of all kinds were 'dispersed in every corner of the country, city and kingdom'. They may have been right to assume that such material was read by 'ploughmen and shopkeepers' and by the 'labourer that holds the plough'; by 'the simple people' and by 'the dull multitude'. And they may have been correct to claim that ''tis the constant desire of the common people to hear of news';

[95] UCL, Ogden 7/11 (in reverse), fos. 42v–42; Nott. UL, Cl/C/27, 529, 616; CKS, U269/1/CB137; *CSPD 1628–9*, p. 563; TNA, SP 16/144, fos. 12–13v.

[96] Bodl. MS Nalson 13, fo. 261; *Occurrences*, 465.2019, sig. T2v; EKRO, H1257.

[97] *CSPD 1649–50*, pp. 123–6; Chequers, MS 782, fos. 43v, 96v; BL, Add. 4156, fo. 161; *CP*, iv. 229, 230–2; BL, Add. 70005, fo. 248v; *Kingdomes*, 214.329, p. 1498; BL, Add. 70107, unfol.; *LJ*, ix. 156; Bodl. MS Clarendon 62, fos. 141–2; *TSP*, iii. 3; *Copy* (1647, C6134); *All Worthy* (1649, BL, E551/21); *Stratagem* (1647, N641); *Mod. Intelligencer*, 419.208, sig. 10A2; *Kingdomes Faithfull and Impartial Scout*, 210.07, p. 48; *Pragmaticus*, 369.246E, sig. Kkk2v; *CSPD 1657–8*, p. 244.

[98] *Kingdomes*, 214.212, p. 550; *Conference* (1653, L2089A), pp. 3–4; *Humble* (1653, T1591).

that the public had become composed of 'intelligent readers'; and that 'the meanest sort of people are not only able to write ... but to argue and discourse on matters of highest concernment'. However, in order to probe these issues further, and to test contemporary claims that the public became less 'curious or inquisitive' about print in the 1650s, it is necessary to gauge not just what people read and what they could access, but also what they made of the material that they consumed.[99]

---

[99] *Humble Petition* (1642, B87); *Exact and True Collection*, 142.2, sig. B; *Mercurius Politicus*, p. 12; *Britanicus*, 268.051, p. 399; *Elencticus*, 312.42, sig. Ss; 316.22, pp. 169–70; *Pragmaticus*, 369.112, sig. Mv; *Britanicus*, 268.051, p. 399; *Perf. Weekly Account*, 533.45, p. 358; Bodl. MS North.c.4, fo. 105.

CHAPTER 3

Readers, reception and the authority of print

During enclosure riots at Gillingham in Dorset in 1643, a disturbance took place in a local church, in response to the reading of a parliamentary order. A local linen weaver, Richard Butler, 'turned about and laughed at it, saying it was false, and that it came not from the Parliament'. Indeed, he boasted that he would 'not obey it, for if it had been an order of Parliament, it would have been printed'. In June 1646, a rather different scene took place among citizens of Worcester who gathered to decide whether or not to surrender to parliamentary forces. They, too, were met by a text, containing royal instructions to sue for peace, albeit in printed form. Die-hard royalists were represented by Fitzwilliam Coningsby, 'a gentleman of great estate', who said that 'though the king's letter was printed at Oxford ... yet who knows it to be the king's letter but a forgery, since Mr Kempson only bought it off the bookstall'. Coningsby was suspicious that it might have been 'set forth by the lords for their own security', and he recommended waiting 'until a particular order come from His Majesty'. These two incidents offer fascinating glimpses into how contemporaries were forced to confront the meaning, authority and reliability of print, as participants in the Civil Wars. Where Butler seems to have assumed that print was authoritative, Coningsby apparently thought that a text was suspicious precisely because it was printed. Such reactions demonstrate the possibility of moving beyond approaches to the 'consumption' of print that focus on the acquisition and accessibility of various genres. The latter serve as means of addressing issues about *who* read *what*, and about *where* and *when* reading took place, but they leave unresolved other issues that are vital to an assessment of print's impact, and that centre on the problem of *reception*.[1]

Given the evidential problems involved in constructing a 'bestseller' list for Civil War pamphlets and newspapers, reception is generally approached through evidence about how people responded to what they read. This

---

[1] JRL, NP 74/1; Worcs. RO, BA1714, pp. 742, 746.

offers the chance to discuss *real* rather than *implied* readers and to avoid simplistic assessments of how ideas trickled down from authors to the public. Considerable attention has thus been paid to reading practices, to assess *why* people read and *how* they went about it, not least on the basis of contemporary marginalia and annotations.[2] Although this often involves scholarly readers, it also has potential for improving our understanding about the response to cheap print. Diarists like Adam Eyre and Sir John Archer occasionally described reading practices and habits, and texts occasionally survive with underlining and scribbled comments. William Pole of Colyton (Devon) ostentatiously defaced copies of parliamentary speeches that described MPs as 'honourable', while Thomason transformed the title of *Perfect Occurrences* to express his view that it was 'imperfect', and the owner of a radical newspaper similarly changed its title from *The Moderate* into the 'im*Moderate* rogue'.[3] Such examples are obviously striking, but a balanced assessment of contemporary attitudes towards print also requires other kinds of evidence, not least comments about particular texts – such as writers being thought 'honest', 'hellish' or 'infernal bitter', and pamphlets being described as 'dangerous', 'railing', 'spurious' or 'poor stuff'.[4] Such comments reveal perceptions about the 'authority' of printed texts, in terms of the 'truth' they contained and the 'trust' that people had in them, and one of the consequences of thinking about audiences – what Adrian Johns called a shift from technology to civility – has been to question whether printing generated what Elizabeth Eisenstein described as 'fixity', and enabled texts to be considered reliable. Indeed, it has been suggested that the print revolution actually generated *uncertainty*, and that contemporaries had profound problems with the 'credit' and 'credibility' of print, and that this explains the demand for scribal texts and 'official' literature. It has

---

[2] *Practice and Representation of Reading in England*, ed. J. Raven (Cambridge, 1996); K. Sharpe, *Reading Revolutions* (New Haven, 2000); W. Sherman, *Used Books* (Philadelphia, 2008); *Reading, Society and Politics in Early Modern England*, ed. K. Sharpe and S. Zwicker (Cambridge, 2003); L. Jardine and A. Grafton, 'Studied for action', *P&P*, 129 (1990), 30–78; R. Cust, 'Reading for magistracy', in *Monarchical Republic of Early Modern England*, ed. J. McDiarmid (Aldershot, 2007), pp. 181–99; D. Woolf, *Reading History in Early Modern England* (Cambridge, 2000); L. Jardine and W. Sherman, 'Pragmatic readers', in *Religion, Culture and Society in Early Modern Britain*, ed. A. Fletcher and P. Roberts (Cambridge, 1994), pp. 102–24; S. Zwicker, 'Reading the margins', in *Refiguring Revolutions*, ed. K. Sharpe and S. Zwicker (London, 1998), pp. 101–15; A. Cambers, *Godly Reading* (Cambridge, 2011).

[3] *Yorkshire Diaries*, p. 42; Lincs. RO: Misc.Don.310; BNLW 4/8/2/29, 35; BJL, DD/HO/2/74; ERO, D/DRg3/4; BL, Harl. 6865, fos. 180–225; Devon RO, 1700M/FZ/2; Glos. RO, D149/X1; Chester RO, DAR/H/26; Northants. RO, P(L)218; Bodl. MS Eng. Misc.e.479; FSL, C7175; Cornwall RO, PZ/B2/24; BL, E565/18; FSL, M2324.5.

[4] NLS, Wodrow Folio lxvii, fo. 148; Claydon, Verney reels 7–9; Norfolk RO, LEST P10, p. 22; Cary, *Memorials*, i. 377.

even been argued that the period witnessed a 'crisis of truth-telling', not least in the realm of news and current affairs, as readers were confronted with conflicting claims about everything from specific battles to the legal and historical foundations of the constitution and the causes of the Civil Wars.[5]

The purpose of this chapter is to challenge such claims, and to suggest that contemporaries were well aware of the problems posed by print; that they worked hard to confront them; and that their attitudes also changed over time. Once again this will be done by addressing both the rhetoric of print and the reality of everyday practice. It will begin by exploring the ways in which cheap print and popular reading were portrayed in contemporary literature (section i), and by examining the comments in which readers revealed their perception of pamphlets and newspapers (section ii). Here it will be suggested that the response to print was more complex than it appears at first, not least as the shocked reaction to the collapse of censorship and the development of new genres subsided. Indeed, the response to such material will be shown to have been fairly ambivalent, and while some worried about how to behave as readers, and about the harm that print might do, others were cautiously positive about the utility of the new media, not least because of how they thought about 'truth' and 'falsity'. These conclusions will then be developed further through an exploration of reading practices (section iii), which shed important light on attitudes to print and the motives of readers, not least by revealing evidence about individual 'taste', and the careful and ecumenical approaches that people took to the selection and analysis of reading matter. Finally, these examinations of both rhetoric and practice will permit a diachronic approach to perceptions of print culture, and an exploration of the dynamic of public trust in the media (section iv). This will reinforce the overall argument of the chapter: that whatever concerns people had about print, they developed ways of dealing with the problems that they recognized, and then nuanced these 'coping strategies' as print culture developed during the 1640s and 1650s, not least when confronted by censorship and propaganda. Contemporaries were capable of adapting to changes in print culture, and these 'coping strategies' will be shown to have been as evident in relation to cheap political print as they were in relation to the 'information overload' faced by scholars. Indeed, as Butler and Coningsby suggest, this ability to respond in a critical and analytical fashion to pamphlets and newspapers will be shown to have been

[5] A. Johns, *Nature of the Book* (Chicago, 1998), pp. 28, 31, 35–6, 172, 174, 444, 458, 465; M. Braddick, *God's Fury, England's Fire* (London, 2008), pp. 303, 369, 459; Knights, *Representation*, ch. 6.

evident across the social spectrum, rather than to have been the preserve of an educated elite. As in the preceding chapters, the aim will not be to suggest that different social groups experienced print in exactly the same way, but it will be to argue that contemporaries displayed a range of responses to print culture, and that these do not map easily or straightforwardly onto distinctions of wealth and status.[6]

i Texts and readers portrayed

Contemporary commentary upon Civil War newspapers and pamphlets is the most obvious place to begin an assessment of responses to Civil War print culture, and there is certainly plentiful evidence with which to support the idea that the 'print revolution' was regarded as detrimental. This hostility involved claims about the danger posed by texts and about the infantilism of readers, and audiences were repeatedly confronted with accusations about 'the liberty of this scribbling age', and about how cheap print 'helped to kindle this fire', exacerbated the 'combustions' of the time and 'poisoned' the public.[7] Nevertheless, this rhetoric needs to be treated with considerable care, not just because of the motives of those involved, but also because of evidence that it masks a more complex reality in terms of how commentators reflected on new genres of print.

It is hard to escape the fact that readers were bombarded with claims and counter-claims regarding lies and untruths, about entrepreneurial and mercenary authors, and about 'fictitious devisings of idle and rash wits'. Rushworth would later claim that it was impossible to produce a 'true history' from Civil War texts, because of how often they contained speeches 'never spoken' and declarations 'never passed', as well as claims about battles 'never fought' and victories 'never obtained', and 'contrivances to abet a party or interest'. Royalists alleged that parliamentarian newspapers were 'full of nonsense', and referred to them as 'our weekly legend of lies', although the same term was also applied to royalist newsbooks, which were accused of 'forced fictions, calumnies and tales'. Many pamphlets bemoaned how both sides peddled lies that 'blistered the ears of all men',

---

[6] A. Blair, 'Reading strategies for coping with information overload', *JHI*, 64 (2003), 11–28; J. Raymond, 'Irrational, impractical and unprofitable', in *Reading, Society and Politics*, p. 199; D. Randall: 'Joseph Mead, novellante', *JBS*, 45 (2006), 293–312; D. Randall, *Credibility in Elizabethan and Early Stuart Military News* (London, 2008).

[7] *Prerogative* (1644, P3219), p. 1; Williams, *Discovery* (1643, W2665) p. 69; Hall, *Sermon* (1642, H446), sig. A2v; Digges, *Answer* (1642, D1455), p. 25; *Great Assizes*, ed. H. MacDonald (Oxford, 1948), p. 12; *Impartialis*, 333.1, p. 1; *Civicus*, 298.145, p. 2062; *Narrative* (1648, N166), p. 5; *True Informer* (1643, H3122), p. 30; *Whirligigge* (1647, W1675), p. 3.

who thereby lacked access to 'solid truth'. 'Facts' presented in pamphlets were rapidly denounced as fictions in newspapers, and the confusion that resulted was summed up by a satire called 'The New Interpreter', which claimed that lying pamphlets could now be defined as 'true and perfect diurnalls'.[8] More specifically, individual stories were analysed and challenged. *Aulicus* confronted *The Weekly Account* over its version of events in Chester; described *Civicus* as 'a matchless odious forger' over an episode in Leicester; and claimed that William Prynne's edition of Archbishop Laud's diary was 'interlaced' with 'fictions'. Its editor even alleged that fraudulent texts had been 'interwoven' into the printed edition of the Naseby letters. Parliamentarians, of course, made similar allegations about royalists, with *Britanicus* mocking 'malignant frippery', 'bum-fodder' and 'ale-house intelligence', and offering detailed refutations of *Aulicus*, whose editors were said to 'frame conceits and cry them up for passages in Parliament'.[9] The flip-side of such claims, of course, involved the brags and boasts about honesty and integrity that peppered pamphlets and newspapers, as authors and journalists insisted upon their credentials. The *London Post* protested that 'we do abhor to present you counterfeits for truths', while Nedham defended *Britanicus* by claiming 'call it history, or chronicle, which you please, for I scorn all lies'. Royalists made similar promises. The editor of *Elencticus* protested that 'I write nothing but truth', and added that 'I will not write fables, broach untruths, invent plots, forge letters, feign victories, create new fears and jealousies, or anything else . . . to delude the people'. Similarly, *Pragmaticus* reflected that 'as it was my care ever to write nothing but truth, in matter of design or action, so all hitherto hath proved true to a tittle'.[10]

By the mid 1640s, therefore, readers could have been forgiven for questioning the very meaning of 'truth' and 'falsity', and for doubting their chances of discerning honesty from fiction, not least as they encountered works whose sole purpose was to catalogue 'the errors of the weekly pamphlets', and the 'false information' published by journalists.[11] Indeed,

[8] *Presse* (1642, P3293), sig. A2v; *Gentle Lash* (1644, F582), sig. A2v; *Fresh Whip* (1647, F2199), p. 3; *Poets* (1642, B3581); Rushworth, i. B3–v; *Aulicus*, 275.222, p. 1006; 275.224B, p. 1033; *Moon*, 248.26, p. 217; *Melancholicus*, 344.01, p. 1; Cleveland, *Character* (1647, C4662), pp. 3, 6; *Oxford* (1645, O851), p. 2; *Great Assizes*, p. 12; *Presse*, sig. A2; *Times* (1647, F1518), sig. C5; *Discourse* (1649, L2100A); *Pacificus*, 353.2, sig. B4v; HEH, EL 7801.

[9] *Aulicus*: 275.316, pp. 1605, 1608–9; 275.302, pp. 1332–3; 275.317, p. 1665; *Britanicus*: 286.097, p. 866; 286.114, p. 1007; 286.084, p. 762.

[10] *Kingdomes*, 214.250, p. 857; *London Post*, 233.124, p. 3; *Britanicus*, 286.101, p. 897; *Elencticus*, 312.14, pp. 104–5; *Pragmaticus*, 369.220A, sig. Y.

[11] *Fresh Whip*; *Exact and True Collection*, 142.1, p. 1; 142.2, sigs. B2v–3.

this barrage of claim and counter-claim, and such rhetoric of truth and falsity, may even have become more perplexing over time, not least as contemporaries confronted duplicate and counterfeit newspapers, and the stories told about them. From as early as December 1642, therefore, readers would sometimes have encountered multiple versions of particular titles during any one week, as well as claims to authenticity from proprietors who sought to capture and retain an audience, and to dissuade people from purchasing the work of commercial rivals. This problem only got worse as the decade progressed, particularly among royalist newspapers, as economic competition was matched by personal animosity and factional division within the journalistic community. In this situation, readers repeatedly met with extended denunciations of 'a counterfeit piece of nonsense', 'a counterfeit rascal' or 'a silly fly-blown counterfeit', as well as with promises to expose the identity of rivals and imposters.[12]

Nevertheless, such rhetorical bombast dramatically oversimplifies a more complex picture, and commentators recognized that the truthfulness of pamphlets and newspapers was not entirely straightforward. Reflecting on parliamentarian news reports, therefore, royalist editors occasionally admitted that 'somewhat of the relation may be probably true', even if they 'stretcheth the victory', and journalists were sometimes candid about former errors, and were not above issuing corrections in the light of new intelligence, even if only with bad grace.[13] Indeed, selective news reporting might even be explained and justified, normally when plots were in the process of being revealed, or when political grandees 'sat very close'. This might mean saying that news was not 'fit to be communicated', or that it was improper to 'blab . . . for the present', although editors usually provided morsels with which to 'silence the vulgar jealousies', and promised more revelations 'in due time'. Such behaviour generally reflected a willingness to conform to official secrecy, or perhaps the desire to make a virtue out of a necessity. Thus, Nedham boasted about being a champion of 'truth and reason', and about his desire to make things 'public', but even he admitted that some aspects of parliamentary business were 'too transcendent . . . for every common ear'.[14] Such comments indicate that, for all of the hyperbole about print being untrustworthy, editors alerted readers to the complexity

---

[12] *Diurnall*, 513.28B, sig. Ee4v; *Britanicus*: 286.028B, p. 215; 286.028A, p. 215; *Moon*, 248.17, p. 146; J. Peacey, 'The counterfeit silly curr', *HLQ*, 67 (2004), 27–57.

[13] *Aulicus*, 274.4, p. 29; 275.228B, p. 1082; *Elencticus*, 312.36A, p. 277; *Britanicus*, 268.008, p. 64; *Perfect Summary*, 530.20, p. 200.

[14] *Continuation*, 638.47B, np; *Occurrences*: 465.3024, sig. Aa4; 465.3029, sig. Ff4v; *Kingdomes*, 214.105, p. 845, 214.107, p. 850, 214.175, p. 311, 214.232, p. 715; *Britanicus*, 208.108, p. 960.

of categories like 'truth' and 'falsity', and rather than becoming despondent, people may have reflected that pamphlets and newspapers could play at least some role in understanding the times.

Similar issues arise regarding Jonsonian claims about the public response to cheap print, particularly among the lower orders. A 1642 petition expressed concern that 'scandalous' pamphlets 'fly abroad in such swarms', and that they would 'cloud the pure air of truth' and 'present a dark ignorance' to those who lacked 'the two wings of justice and knowledge to fly above them'. Commentators of all political persuasions claimed that the 'common people' had a simplistic fascination with news, and that 'silly pamphlets' were 'credulously swallowed' by people of 'weaker judgments'. Such people were too easily 'delighted', 'deceived', 'seduced' and 'abused' by 'tittle tattle news' and outrageous ideas. This was thought to explain why authors reported 'falsities' and 'impossible things', merely to 'please credulous readers' and 'tickle the ears of the giddy multitude', and why newspapers were designed to 'infect the ears of the credulous vulgar'. Authors even revived older language by arguing that public affairs were not fit to be 'questioned by every subject', and that 'private men' were not 'competent judges' of public affairs.[15] It was beliefs like these that underpinned frustrated claims about the effectiveness of pamphlets and newspapers as propaganda. Parliamentarians complained that *Aulicus* had done 'more hurt than 2,000 of the king's soldiers', and royalists grumbled about their opponents by saying that 'lying conquers thrice as many for them as the sword'.[16]

The problem with such arguments – which resurface across the ages – is that they reflected political bias rather than detached analysis. They represented attempts to besmirch opponents by ridiculing their supporters, and nervousness about the success with which rivals were winning popular support. Once again, therefore, they ought not to obscure evidence that contemporaries did not despair about the possibility that readers might show more wisdom. Commentators sometimes conceded that the problem with the 'giddy multitude' was not outright credulity, but rather a willingness to believe things that suited 'their affections', and that 'credulity' could

---

[15] *Petition* (1642, B87); B. Jonson, *Staple of News*, ed. A. Parr (Manchester, 1988), pp. 91, 96, 152–3, 166; *Aulicus*, 275.224B, p. 1033; *Recantation* (1644, R612), p. 2; *Briefe Relation*, 27.01, p. 1; *Exact and True Collection*: 142.1, title page; 142.2, sig. B; *Politicus*, 361.277, p. 5660; *Thankes* (1642, T836); *Mastix*, 339.1, pp. 6–7; *Elencticus*, 312.49, p. 399; *Anatomy* (1649, S6290), sig. A3; *Proceedings*, 599.306, p. 4854; *No Pamphlet* (1642, N1184), sig. A2; *Elencticus*, 316.22, pp. 169–70; *Elencticus*, 312.36A, p. 279; *Pragmaticus*, 370.18, sig. S2; *Politicus*, 361.403, pp. 294, 302; *Proceedings*, 599.306, p. 4854; Howell, *Trance* (1649, H3120), p. 9; *Spie*, 609.04, p. 32; *Politique Informer*, 543.1, p. 1.

[16] *True Character* (1644, T2601); *Fresh Whip*, p. 6; *Impartialis*, 333.1, p. 2; *Moon*, 248.17, p. 143.

be found across the social spectrum. They also thought it possible to navigate a way through the maze of printed texts, and championed the idea that close readers would detect falsity and forgery. This can be seen during a debate between the editors of two rival versions of *Britanicus* in 1644, one of whom admitted that the two texts were superficially identical, but then demonstrated how readers could distinguish between them, not least by highlighting his rival's 'dullness' and linguistic 'laziness', as well as his 'ridiculous knavery and partiality'. Similar lessons encouraged royalist readers to identify fake newspapers, and to 'kick away the counterfeit silly curr'. And of course, even the 'multitude' tended to be regarded as 'silly' or 'credulous' only when it accepted claims made by opponents, and might be lauded when it spurned their propaganda.[17]

Ultimately, therefore, comments about the damaging effects of popular credulity need to be read in the context of contemporary willingness to engage with a mass audience. The parliamentarians in Kent, who demanded a public recantation from Sir Edward Dering after his brief dalliance with royalism, insisted that his text should be 'no elaborate volume, but ... a pamphlet, which will satisfy the vulgar ... being the men you have misled'. Likewise, *Pragmaticus* was clearly prepared to 'tickle and charm the more vulgar phantasies, who little regard truths in a grave and serious garb'.[18] Indeed, writers on all sides frequently boasted about their successful engagement with the general public. Robert Baillie claimed that Scottish propaganda was 'well-liked, and ... searched for', while Nedham claimed to address the nation in its 'several classes', and professed to write 'within the bounds of common capacity'. He thus bragged that 'there is not now so much as a young apprentice that keeps shop, or a labourer that holds the plough, not one from the city to the country, but he can tell you that *Aulicus* is a juggling, lying piece of paper'. One journalist even went so far as to rejoice that his countrymen were guided by 'reason and knowledge', and were no longer 'guided by the tradition of their fathers', and expressed satisfaction that 'the meanest sort of people are not only able to write ... but to argue and discourse of matters of highest concernment'.[19]

Thus, while contemporaries were bombarded with claims about truth and falsity, about their 'brazen' or 'juggling' age, and about the credulity of

[17] *Elencticus*, 316.22, p. 169–70; *Kingdomes*, 214.328, p. 1496; *Britanicus*, 286.029A, pp. 223–4; *Moon*, 248.17, p. 146; *Aulicus*, 275.241, p. 1192.

[18] BL, Stowe 184, fos. 73, 75; *Pragmaticus*, 369.201, sig. A.

[19] *Baillie*, i. 188–9, 284, 299, 300, 305, 367, 412; *Britanicus*, 286.102, p. 905; 286.051, pp. 399–400; *Melancholicus*, 334.53B, p. 156; *Politicus*, 361.198, p. 3374; *CSPD 1655–6*, p. 338; *Perfect Weekly Account*, 533.45, p. 358.

popular audiences, such comments reflected fears and biases rather than reasoned judgments. Behind this thrilling rhetoric there lurked recognition that truth might be elusive, but not entirely beyond reach, and that the rivers of cheap print could be navigated to some effect if consumers became sceptical and critical readers.[20]

ii Popular perceptions of print culture

In seeking to establish whether such aspirations were realistic, it is necessary to turn attention away from contemporary commentators and towards readers themselves, to analyse evidence about how consumers responded to the material that they encountered, and how they perceived the print revolution. Here, too, it is easy to find disparaging comments which seem to confirm that contemporaries struggled to adapt to the 'disorder' of print after 1640, and to an age 'wherein the tongue and press assume so luxurious a latitude'.[21] Here, too, however, it is necessary to look beyond such rhetoric, and to recover clues which suggest that contemporaries from across the social spectrum developed ways of coping with cheap print, and that they were capable of behaving like critical and pragmatic readers.

As with the depiction of print and readers in contemporary propaganda, members of the public very obviously expressed their dislike of print in colourful prose. Thomas Wyatt of Ducklington referred to 'infinite pasquils' and to 'base', 'abusive' and 'trifling pamphlets', that 'came forth daily . . . uncivil and inhumane'. The Earl of Bath thought that newspapers were useful merely to provide his wife with 'twatling stuff', in order that she might 'twaddle by the fireside'. Readers feared that print would worsen political divisions and hasten 'a public phlebotomy', and they expressed concerns about falsities and lies. Wyatt wrote about 'so many false reports in the diurnalls and other pamphlets', and reflected that 'so many palpable lies were never known', while John Taylor of the Inner Temple explained that 'books are such idle lies and trifles as they are not worth reading', and noted that 'many books come daily forth, but little truths'. George Radcliffe decried 'lying gazettes' by saying that 'nothing is reported on one side which is not contradicted by the others', and Margaret Cavendish worried that newspapers were intended 'to amuse and deceive the people', and that

---

[20] *Pragmaticus*, 369.252B, sig. A; *Britanicus*, 286.029A, p. 223.
[21] *Diurnall*, 504.277, p. 2229; TNA, C115/N3/8556; BL, Add. 64923, fo. 3.

they contained 'nothing but falsehoods and chimeras'.[22] In correspondence as in print, moreover, contemporaries worried about the effect of such literature on the 'silly multitude' and 'half-witted men'. John Castle wrote in 1640 about the public being 'empoisoned' by 'pestilent' texts that were 'cast in amongst them', and Sir Marmaduke Langdale claimed that 'the common people believe the first story which takes impression in their minds, and it cannot be beaten out'.[23]

In fact, contemporary perceptions of print were less obviously hostile than *conflicted*. Wyatt recognized the value of ostensibly ridiculous pamphlets, which told 'much truth in jest' and which were aimed at popular audiences, and for many the central concern was not that a popular audience was being addressed, that 'too much heat' was being stirred up, or that harm was being done. Rather, it was that the lower orders needed to be convinced by the right kinds of pamphlet. When newsbook stories convinced opponents to surrender, they were regarded as highly valuable, but the problem came when the public was deliberately misled, and Sir Edward Nicholas railed against parliamentarians who sought to 'fish in troubled waters'.[24] Others expressed anxiety about situations in which particular perspectives went unchallenged, and when Richard Baxter reflected on the 'mischief' caused among soldiers by Leveller propaganda, his main worry was that 'they had such books to read when they had none to contradict them'. Likewise, in complaining that many royalist exiles loved *Politicus* 'better than their ... prayer books', some observers were afraid because Nedham's newspaper was their only source of information.[25] And many people who bemoaned the nature of the press were only really agitated about literature produced by their opponents. Thus, Thomas Stockdale's 1642 claim that 'disputing' in print was 'like to prove dangerous' ought to be set alongside his striking determination to spread parliamentarian propaganda, while Thomas Knyvett was probably concerned less with the press *per se* than with the 'lunacies' that texts merely reflected and reported.[26] Likewise, disdainful and ideologically inflected comments about cheap print also need to be set alongside more positive views about print, along

[22] Bodl. MS Top.Oxon.C.378, p. 321; CKS, U269/C267/15, 17; CUL, Buxton 59/87; *Knyvett*, p. 105; Bodl. MS Top.Oxon.C.378, p. 345; Cumbria RO, D/MUS/5/5/Box 89/Bundle 3; Longleat, Portland 2, fo. 91; Cavendish, *Life* (1667), sig. (d).

[23] SHC, G52/2/19/10, 22, 25, 28; HEH, EL 7852; *HMC Thirteenth Report I*, p. 70; *HMC De L'Isle VI*, p. 613.

[24] Bodl. MS Top.Oxon.C.378, p.391; *TSP*, iv. 170, 189, 190, 211, 287, 316; *HMC Buccleuch III*, p. 417; *HMC Hamilton (Supp.)*, p. 63; Beinecke, Osborn fb.156, fos. 130–1; SHC, G52/2/19/18.

[25] Baxter, *Reliquiae* (1696, B1370), i. 73; BL: Eg. 2535, fo. 120v; Add. 78196, fo. 31.

[26] *Knyvett*, pp. 107–8; BL, Add. 18979, fos. 109v, 117, 135; *Fairfax Corr.*, ii. 389; CUL, Buxton 59/89.

a spectrum that ran from Covenanters, who found the press politically useful, to men like Samuel Hartlib and Gilbert Mabbott, who sought something approaching liberty of the press.[27]

Such comments suggest that hostility towards print culture was pragmatic rather than principled, probably because it was difficult to argue that there was a straightforward correlation between humble status and credulity. Wallington's notebooks certainly *suggest* an unquestioning acceptance of stories from the press, which were frequently copied into notebooks without any evidence that their veracity had been questioned. Nevertheless, Wallington was not the only reader who was happy to believe stories that confirmed providentialist beliefs, and even he recognized that pamphlets and news reports 'little edify me', and that many were 'vain books'.[28] It can also be shown that confused responses to the proliferation of truth claims affected men of all ranks. In May 1641, Henry Oxinden of Deane wrote about news being 'so various and uncertain', and a few months later Edward Partherich explained that news was 'uncertain, and hath so many changes, and that on a sudden', so that 'what was believed and published for news and truth this hour, the next is changed and utterly false'. Thomas Wyatt responded to one 'true relation' by writing that 'there is not certainty in this or any other thing', and by reflecting that 'it is hard to pick out any truth', and in August 1653 another contemporary described feeling 'racked' by pamphlets, and 'boxed with their varieties and contradictions'.[29] Moreover, it was not just humble folk who responded to printed texts in ways that might be considered naive. Copies of fraudulent texts, such as the speeches that were supposed to have been made in parliament by Lord Brooke and the Earl of Pembroke, sometimes circulated among the gentry without any obvious indication that their authenticity was questioned, and this particular pamphlet famously fooled Charles I. During the Cromwellian conquest of Ireland, meanwhile, republican news reports were apparently accepted by royalist exiles, to the chagrin of some grandees, and Joseph Jane later complained that one of the Protector's declarations not only persuaded 'people of ordinary capacity', but also made an impact on 'statesmen' who should have known better.[30]

---

[27] NLS, Wodrow Quarto xxv, fo. 89; SUL, Hartlib 30/4/68; *Diurnall*, 504.304, p. 2531.

[28] FSL, V.a.436, pp. 32–3, 39, 88, 151, 167; BL, Add. 40883, fo. 112.

[29] Cornwall RO, R(S)1/1040; Antony, BC/24/2, fo. 80; BL, Add. 28000, fo. 87; EKRO, Sa/C1, pp. 139–40; Bodl. MS Top.Oxon.C.378, p. 356; MS Tanner 52, fo. 34.

[30] HEH, Stowe Temple Parliament, Box 1/16; Cumbria RO, D/MUS/5/5/Box 89/Bundle 2/2; Clarendon, *Life*, i. 161–2; BL, Eg. 2534, fo. 14; *NP*, iii. 140–1.

More important than the fact that confusion and credulity existed across the social spectrum is evidence of contemporaries challenging the veracity of printed texts, in ways that significantly enhance our appreciation of how 'truth' and 'falsity' were conceptualized. Such challenges occurred most obviously in parliament, and although MPs scarcely represent ordinary readers, they nevertheless reveal a great deal about early modern ideas regarding what constituted authentic and trustworthy texts. Members of both Houses, therefore, highlighted editions of speeches that nobody remembered having heard, not least those that were produced by 'loose beggarly scholars . . . in alehouses'.[31] More intriguing, however, are investigations into other kinds of 'false' pamphlets, containing the 'pretended' texts of petitions, letters and diplomatic despatches, because these reveal how elastic a concept like 'falsity' had become. It might mean an inaccurate text, but more obviously it meant something that had appeared without official approval or the author's knowledge, as with illicit editions of the *Protestation*, Ussher's proposals for 'reduced' episcopacy, and Oliver St John's speech about Ship Money. Indeed, when applied to newspapers that reported parliamentary proceedings, 'falsity' meant the unauthorized infringement of secrecy, irrespective of accuracy. This is important, because defining the term so broadly makes it difficult to know whether specific complaints – like those about 'forged' papers by 'journeymen printers' in 1647 – involved genuine fraud or merely a lack of authorization.[32] However, such investigations are also important because they helped members of the public to grapple with print culture. It was almost certainly parliamentary prompts – which sometimes involved letters from MPs to constituents – that led Henry Oxinden to identify counterfeit speeches, and James White of Exeter to comment that 'so much falsehood' was printed in the newsbooks. Likewise, official investigations probably explain how Thomas Rugg discovered the truth about a petition that had looked 'as if it [had] been the truest thing in the world' until it was exposed as a fake by the Committee of Safety.[33]

On many other occasions, however, members of the reading public, from all kinds of backgrounds, proved capable of challenging the authenticity of texts without any such help. For some, of course, this could be done with relative ease on the basis of specialist knowledge, as with Thomason and

[31] BL, Harl. 163, fo. 119; *PJ*, i. 165–6, 304, 311, 326, 328–9.
[32] *PJ*, i. 165–6, 416, ii. 97–8, 100; *CJ*, ii. 441, 501, 611; BL: Harl. 163, fos. 119, 136; Add. 57929, fo. 123; *CSPV 1642–3*, p. 31; *LJ*, iv. 680–1, 699, vi. 16; PA, MP 1 Feb. 1643, 24 Apr. 1643; *Occurrences*, 465.5035, sig. Ll2.
[33] BL, Sloane 1467, fo. 38; *Oxinden Letters*, p. 273; Devon RO, 73/15, p. 112; *Rugg*, pp. 11–12.

Elias Ashmole, or by virtue of being embedded within political and military circles, as with the MPs who observed the reporting of Strafford's trial, and the parliamentarian scoutmaster who monitored war reporting.[34] For others, the ability to scrutinize specific works must have been more difficult, and is thus more impressive. A country squire like Sir John Oglander recognized that the speeches attributed to Pembroke and Brooke were forgeries, and the London merchant Thomas Barrow recommended that friends should 'believe alike' reports about the capture of Reading and Oxford, 'for both are very contrary to truth'. In 1649 a letter from Edinburgh informed the Earl of Kinkardin that the latest newsbooks were 'stuffed with nonsense or very incorrect', and in 1659 Andrew Hay of Craignethan noted that he 'doubted' everything he read in 'the Scots diurnall'.[35] The reason for highlighting such comments is not to suggest that contemporaries were *adept* at exposing falsity, and some such claims represented little more than wishful thinking. In November 1659, Edmund Windham doubted the authenticity of a royal proclamation that was being 'scattered up and down', even though he had not seen it. In other cases, even well placed individuals made mistakes. Clement Walker believed that an absolutist tract by Sir Robert Filmer was actually an anti-monarchical fiction designed 'to envenom the people against the king', and in January 1660 one royalist grandee challenged a royal proclamation that was in fact genuine.[36] The real significance of such claims lies in people's willingness to *critique* what they read, something which also occurred further down the social spectrum. Sometimes this meant rather generalized statements about the press, as when the soldier, Nehemiah Wharton, wrote of 'common relations, which commonly are fictions', or when a civil servant like Josiah Berners concluded that 'abundance of falsities are printed'. On other occasions, however, the claims had greater specificity. The Worcestershire magistrate Henry Townshend detailed a series of news stories regarding the king's movements and strategy that were 'all untruth', and in 1659 the barber Thomas Rugg identified particular faked and fraudulent pamphlets. Even humble readers could be vociferous in denouncing perceived false-hoods, as in 1643 when citizens of London were seen to 'spit their venom of unbelief' on a royal proclamation that had been 'set up upon posts almost all

---

[34] *Oxinden and Peyton Letters*, p. 195; BL: Add. 64922, fo. 31v; Add. 26785, fo. 38; Harl. 164, fo. 329b; Harl. 166, fo. 62; Eg. 2535, fo. 27; Add. 78196, fo. 31; *Luke Letter Books*, p. 23.

[35] IWCRO, OG/AA/31, unfol.; *Oxinden and Peyton Letters*, p. 17; Beinecke, Boswell Box 100/1837; *Andrew Hay Diary*, p. 219.

[36] IWCRO, OG/AA/31, p. 1; BL: Add. 78194, fo. 70; Add. 78196, fo. 94; Walker, *Relations* (1648, W334), p. 138; *CCSP*, iv. 545.

the town over'. Similarly, in 1651 James Affleck of St Martin in the Fields was indicted for saying that 'none of the news was to be seen in the books'. Moreover, whatever might be made of Wallington's reading practices, another London woodturner, Thomas Sampson of Spitalfields, was prosecuted for saying that the printed edition of the Naseby letters 'were not of the king's own hand-writing', and that 'the state did counterfeit his hand'.[37]

In other words, comments by contemporary readers need to be treated just as cautiously as those by polemicists. Worried reflections on print culture – and damning indictments of pamphlets and newspapers as 'bum fodder' – sit uneasily alongside evidence about the zealous consumption and collection of such material, and they also represent the expression of political interests, and mask the fact that people were willing to try and make sense of what they encountered. Whether they did so rationally and accurately is less significant than that they practised critical engagement, and that they rarely expressed utter despair, either about humble readers, or about their own ability to grapple with print. Thus, while the Earl of Newcastle grumbled about the 'hot fits of hopes' and 'cold fits of despair' that resulted from 'such various reports', he added that 'a little time will make us wiser'. This suggests that he, like others, was learning to cope with print culture.[38]

iii Reading practices

That contemporaries coped with print culture is evident not merely from the rhetoric of print, but also from the practices associated with its consumption and distribution. By observing patterns of acquisition, and the ways in which texts were selected for reading and onward circulation, it is possible not just to learn about an individual's taste in pamphlets and newspapers, but also to discern motives for engaging with print, and attitudes towards political literature. Ultimately, indeed, it becomes possible to examine and explain why reading was undertaken with such passion despite contemporary awareness that cheap print was a problematic medium.

What is immediately apparent from contemporary behaviour, and from the way in which political texts were circulated within correspondence, is the tendency for this to occur without any intimation of distrust, disdain or

---

[37] Ellis, 'Letters', p. 328; Bodl. MS Tanner 66, fo. 242; Worcs. RO, BA1714, p.726; *Rugg*, p. 48; *Knyvett*, 123; *Mdx County Recs*, pp. 99, 184, 205; LMA, MJ/SR/970/158.
[38] *Britanicus*, 286.097, p. 866; *Mastix*, 339.1, pp. 3–4; Nott. UL, Pw1/531.

even scepticism. The Norwich MP Richard Harman sent newsbooks and pamphlets to his constituency to 'save ... the labour of writing', and to show 'what hath passed since my last', while Sir Richard Browne's correspondents did so to provide 'all the news that is extant'. Henry Elsyng explained to Thomas Knyvett that 'I need not write you anything of our occurrences', since 'all things are so constantly and duly printed'.[39] Such comments are curious, and require an explanation, because they imply a willingness to treat topical material as unproblematic. That this is odd reflects the fact that even people who were critical of the new media – like John Taylor of the Inner Temple – nevertheless sent pamphlets and newspapers into the country with comments to the effect that 'this week affords nothing to communicate but what is in the books', or that 'I have sent you all the news [that] is stirring'.[40] One possible solution to this paradox is that substituting printed texts for private letters reflected apprehension about the post being miscarried and personal views discovered, and many certainly recognized that 'these intercepting times' would not 'admit ... friendly interchange without hazard'. Texts could be circulated, in other words, to spread information and ideas without being held personally responsible for what they contained.[41] A more intriguing possibility, however, is that those who sent printed material were actively monitoring the press and making careful selections from what was available, to weed out the trash and to supply the best and latest news. When Joseph Jackson explained to the Countess of Bath that he was sending all the news that was available in April 1644, he was referring very specifically to *Mercurius Aulicus*, and when Sir Richard Browne's father listed new material in January 1642, he did so after sifting out 'factious and frivolous pamphlets', and only provided details about texts 'of a more current alloy'. Others sent 'the *truest* copy that came forth', and although Thomas Knyvett bemoaned the uncertainties of printed news – saying that 'many things are fluttering up and down, more false than true' – he nevertheless despatched 'that which I conceive to be the truest'. Thomas Margetts, meanwhile, asked Adam Baynes to provide only those pamphlets that were 'worth reading'.[42] In some cases, indeed, contemporaries even provided assessments of specific newspaper titles. Robert

[39] BL: Add. 22619, fos. 31, 49; Add. 78197, fo. 141; Add. 78198, fos. 21, 24; Eg. 2716, fos. 447, 453, 468.

[40] Cumbria RO, D/MUS/5/5/Box 89/Bundle 3; Bodl. MS North.c.4, fo. 101; BL, Add. 28000, fos. 187, 189; Add. 28002, fo. 174.

[41] Nott. UL, Cl/C/281; *HMC Egmont I*, p. 128; *Knyvett*, pp. 100, 105, 163; BL, Add. 70006, fo. 171v; IWCRO, OG/CC/59; BL, Add. 64922, fo. 92; Chetham, A.3.90, fos. 10v, 14v.

[42] CKS, U269/C283; BL, Add. 78220, fos. 14, 38; NLS, Wodrow folio lxvi, fo. 209; BL, Add. 32093, fo. 254; *Knyvett*, pp. 103, 105–6; CUL, Buxton 59/86; BL, Add. 21418, fo. 185.

Baillie explained that 'the *Diurnall* and *Intelligencer* are true; *Aulicus* and *Britanicus* are for jests only, and not worth the reading', and Sir Arthur Hopton noted that 'for matters of fact you will have it in the *Diurnall*, which is the best intelligencer'. In the late 1640s, Dr Denton described journals like *Melancholicus* and *Pragmaticus* as 'strange libels'.[43] Of course, not all correspondents were as confident in their judgments as Sir Roger Burgoyne, who once explained that the *Moderate Intelligencer* was 'very true', and Harman merely noted that the pamphlets he sent contained the news 'most *affirmed* for truth'. Nevertheless, the picture that emerges is one in which many readers offered cautious recommendations, based upon recognition of the need to sort and select material, and to do so on the basis of their understanding that different texts offered very different things.[44]

Indeed, by exploring the ways in which people made choices about what to read and recommend, much can be gleaned about *why* people engaged with cheap print, and in what ways it was thought to be beneficial. Although some tried to identify works which reflected their political beliefs, many others sought a broad spectrum of political opinion, and tried to follow particular debates. This did not simply mean arguments between royalists and parliamentarians, but also more specific exchanges between Presbyterians, Independents and sectarians, as well as those that centred on authors like William Prynne, John Lilburne, Henry Parker and David Jenkins, and on controversies surrounding the Solemn League and Covenant, the 'Agreement of the People' and the Engagement. And it was not a habit that was restricted to the political elite, but one which can also be observed among country gentlemen, merchants and clerics, as well as students.[45] Moreover, this thoughtful and ecumenical approach also extended to newspapers, and while some people read whatever they could get their hands on, others demonstrated fairly clear preferences. Dr Walker went to some lengths to acquire a 'set' of specific titles, even if he was then prepared to donate material to his friend, the army secretary William Clarke, while Cheney Culpeper explained that 'the *Intelligencer* and *Scout* are the only journals I desire'. William Pole regularly took the *Moderate*

[43] *Baillie*, ii. 171; BL, Add. 78191, fo. 133; Claydon, Verney reel 8.
[44] Claydon, Verney reel 6; BL, Add. 22619, fo. 84.
[45] HEH, HA Inventories Box 1/20; BL, Add. 46189, fos. 155v, 156v–8; CKS, U1475/Z45/2, fos. 2v–213; Hatfield, Bills 254/1–2, 14; *HMC Salisbury XXIV*, p. 282; *HMC Salisbury XXII*, pp. 389–90, 426; *Devon Accounts*, p. 146; Claydon, Verney reels 8, 10; SUL, Hartlib 13/52–53, 301–2; BL, Add. 46376A, fos. 6–13v, 42, 90, 102, 110, 132, 140; PA, Braye 104; 'James Master', i. 152–216, ii, 241–59, iii. 321–52; Bodl. MS Top.Oxon.C.378, pp. 240–391.

Intelligencer, while Sir Ralph Verney favoured the *Parliament Scout*, and only switched to the *Intelligencer* on the basis of a friend's assessment that it was 'but the *Scout* anabaptised', and that 'it is the same man writing'. John Harington favoured *Civicus* before experimenting with, and then switching to, the *Moderate Intelligencer*, and another experimenter was Sir Thomas Cotton, who supplemented his reading of both Cromwellian newspapers with the new titles that emerged once censorship collapsed in 1659. Some he evidently liked, and continued to purchase, while others were rejected after only one issue.[46]

Such patterns reveal the motives behind consumption, and although these were not the same for every reader, clear patterns nevertheless emerge. Some sought entertainment and devoured certain works precisely because they were 'foolish' and in order to 'make sport', and one of Sir Ralph Verney's correspondents wrote that 'I know you love a libel with all your heart'. Others strove to keep in touch with what 'the vulgar' knew, which may help to explain fascination with the scandalous, the seditious and the 'hellish'.[47] In many cases, however, readers rationalized the appeal of different kinds of text while also attempting very obviously to acquire a *range* of genres and opinions. Thus, the Earl of Salisbury purchased newspapers that were serious (*Perfect Diurnall*) as well as those that were more racy (*Britanicus*), while the Earl of Bath combined a mainstream newsbook (*Perfect Diurnall*) with a radical one (*The Moderate*). The Earl of Leicester read *The Moderate* even though it was edited by 'a mischievous writer', doubtless so that he could understand dissident political voices. Others – Sir Justinian Isham, Sir Peter Temple and Thomas Wyatt – read newspapers by both royalists and parliamentarians, and titles that were relatively dry (*Civicus*, *Moderate Intelligencer*, *Several Proceedings* and *Politicus*) alongside those that were more lively (*Aulicus*, *Britanicus*, *Elencticus* and *Pragmaticus*).[48] This suggests that consumption involved more than merely the desire for frivolity and scandal, and that contemporaries sought to understand the scope and range of political debate, to feel the 'pulse of these times', and to assess 'the variety of opinions' that were circulating. Thus, when John Fitzjames asked to be supplied with both the *Moderate*

---

[46] BL, Eg. 2618, fo. 48; 'Cheney Culpeper', pp. 205–6; Anthony, PZ/B2/22–3; Claydon, Verney reels 6–7; BL, Add. 46376A, fos. 66, 70, 74, 78; J. Peacey, 'Sir Thomas Cotton's consumption of news', *The Library*, 7th series, 7 (2006), 3–24.

[47] FSL, W.b.600, p. 392; CKS, U269/C267/15, 17; *HMC Cowper II*, 310; Nott. UL, Cl/C/281; Claydon, Verney reels 7–8; *Rous Diary*, p. 109; BL, Cotton Charter xvi.13, fos. 11v, 13.

[48] *HMC Salisbury XXII*, pp. 383, 385; *HMC Salisbury XXIV*, p. 282; Hatfield, Bills 254/1, 4–5; *Devon Accounts*, ii. 144, 146; *Sydney Papers*, pp. 68–95; Anthony, PZ/B2/22–3; Bodl. MS Top.Oxon.C.378, pp. 234–409.; HEH, STTF Box 22/4; PA, Braye 104.

Intelligencer and *Mercurius Pragmaticus* in September 1648, he explained that 'tis a pastime to me to read what can be said on both sides'.[49]

However, attempts to monitor the press, and to use it for specific purposes, did not merely involve the careful selection of titles. They also reveal the ability to recognize that specific pamphlets and newspapers contained both reliable and unreliable elements, and a willingness to sort the wheat from the chaff by means of close reading. Some understood that journalists were prone to exaggeration. Thomas Wiseman believed in 1641 that newspapers stretched the truth, and that there was 'much more reported than is true', while Sir Samuel Luke admitted that parliamentarian books 'can do as much for our victories as *Aulicus* can do for his Majesty's'.[50] Others recognized that the truth could be downplayed, and a report on pro-royalist rioting in London in 1648 noted that the newspaper 'tells you what they did', while pointing out that the number of apprentices involved was 'greater than it mentions'. Certain reports, in other words, were thought to have told only part of the story, so that 'what is related is truth' while much else was 'omitted', and some stories were thought to have been buried entirely.[51] Such comments indicate the ability to approach newspapers in a sophisticated fashion, something that is evident again and again. The lawyer, John Taylor, reflected that 'what is bad is concealed, and what is good is made much better than commonly it is', while John Fitzjames argued that some news 'dares not at first (many times not at all) show itself in the pamphlets'. Both would probably have agreed that 'in diurnalls ... you have some things true, among many mistakes, and lies but probably reported'.[52]

By recognizing that contemporary responses to print were subtle rather than simplistic, that different things were read for different reasons, and that texts could be consumed even though they were problematic, it becomes clear that many readers approached such texts with very specific goals, rather than as passive consumers. Some followed news and debate for solipsistic reasons, and out of a concern for their own reputation, and they preserved texts and passages in which they were themselves mentioned, not least with a view to complaining about their treatment at the hands of journalists, and

---

[49] BL, Harl. 374, fo. 282; *Knyvett*, p. 107; BL, Add. 78198, fo. 21; Alnwick, MS 548, fo. 27.

[50] Bodl. MS Top.Oxon.C.378, p. 356; CUL, Buxton 59/90; TNA, SP 16/485, fos. 176–v; *Luke Letter Books*, p. 268.

[51] *CSPV 1647–52*, p. 279; BL: Add. 78198, fo. 67v; Add. 64922, fo. 108; NLS, Wodrow Folio lxvii, fo. 130; *Luke Letter Books*, p. 252; *Sydney Papers*, p. 110.

[52] *Oxinden and Peyton Letters*, pp. 169–70; *Knyvett*, p. 103; *CCSP*, iv. 417; BL, Eg. 2536, fo. 33; Cumbria RO, D/MUS/5/5/Box 89/Bundle 3; Alnwick, MS 548, fos. 19v–20; *Anatomy* (1649, S6290), p. 2.

in the hope of securing recompense once they became the subject of 'every man's censure'.[53] The Earl of Bath complained about a newspaper 'wherein my name was used, or rather abused', and Sir John Meldrum complained about a story that gave him insufficient credit for a recent military victory, even though he professed not to seek 'applause by popular air'. And Audley Mervyn likened pamphleteers to 'reputation plunderers', and provided evidence with which to counter things that had been published about him through 'envy, private interest and competition'. Likewise, soldiers who gathered at an army rendezvous in the summer of 1647 asked the officers 'what do you by your two-penny pamphlets to us', and the notorious criminal James Hind was apparently captured at a barber's shop 'as he was reading the books concerning him'.[54] More generally, readers sought 'copious reports' and raw factual data. This might involve issues of personal interest, from the whereabouts of friends and family to new legislation that affected their official duties, and new policies that affected the material welfare of troops. Timothy Reyner of Nantwich was interested in how decisions at Westminster affected his duties relating to the customs, and Captain Richard Wisdome alighted on a story in 'the diurnall' about moves to supply 'coats and breeches' to the army.[55] Of course, it might also mean seeking information about issues of broader significance, where the willingness to be discerning and selective could result in certain portions of newspapers being read more closely than others. One correspondent thus felt able to recommend 'the beginning of *Britanicus* and the end of the *Diurnall*', while others focused on foreign affairs, where reporting seems to have been regarded as more reliable.[56]

Moreover, in addition to reading selectively *within* particular texts, contemporaries also read the passages upon which they concentrated in a sceptical fashion. In other words, their reading involved doing more than merely identifying passages that were thought to be reliable and ignoring the rest. It also meant subjecting these extracts to careful scrutiny, and this provides the final key to understanding how readers approached printed news, and what they hoped to get out of their reading. In the end,

[53] *Correspondence of John Cosin*, ed. G. Ornsby (SS, 52, 1869), p. 138; *Diurnall*, 504.277, p 2228; DRO: D258/30/23; D258/53/40; Bodl. MS North.c.4, fo. 91.

[54] CKS, U269/C294; TNA, SP 21/17, p. 18; *CSPD 1644–5*, pp. 5–6, 24; Bodl. MS Tanner 60, fos. 1–3; MS Tanner 58, fo. 129; *Oxinden and Peyton Letters*, pp. 169–70.

[55] Northants. RO, IC 454; TWAS, MD/NC/2/1, pp. 159–60; Bodl. MS Carte 73, fo. 143; *TSP*, vi. 600; BL: Add. 32093, fo. 329; Eg. 1533, fo. 49; Add. 21425, fo. 165; Add. 21418, fo. 403.

[56] Bodl. MS North.c.4, fos. 70, 78; Northants. RO, IC 359, IC 459A; *CCSP*, iv. 118; BL: Add. 78194, fo. 73; Add. 78198, fo. 19; Add. 78195, fo. 39; DRO, D258/30/14/3, 8; Scott, 'Particular business', p. 341; NLS, Wodrow folio xxv, fo. 39; *TSP*, iv. 443; SUL, Hartlib 34/4/19–20.

newspapers and pamphlets were read more or less cautiously and purposefully, and as part of a more elaborate process of following current affairs.
This seems clear from the profusion of wary comments made when discussing newspapers, such as 'tis said in a parliament diurnall', and 'if the print
say true', as well as 'it *seems* by the books' and 'if one may *guess* by the books'.
It also seems clear from Joseph Jane's reference to 'the hard digestion of the
prints'. But it is sometimes made explicit in cases where individuals read
'against the grain', as when the Earl of Bath expressed scepticism about a
story that seemed 'too good to be true'.[57] And these intimations about how
much attention was being paid to problematic texts make sense in light of
the fact that contemporaries did not rely solely upon printed sources, but
rather engaged with print as part of a broader process of gathering and
assessing news and information. First, printed news could be supplemented
by, and checked against, personal knowledge. Thomas Knyvett read newspaper reports about affairs in Lowestoft 'with much joy', precisely because
he knew very well that they were false. Richard Baxter initially thought that
stories about 'swarms of anabaptists' operating within the army were 'a mere
lie' until he himself visited the New Model and 'found a new face of
things'.[58] Secondly, newspaper stories could also be checked with other
witnesses. When William Le Neve explained that news which reached
Norwich in 1641 'treads by the steps of the corantos', he sought personal
letters that supplemented their reports, and Sir Edward Hartopp only sent a
newspaper to Sir John Coke in 1643 once its reports had been confirmed 'by
a gentleman that came post the last night'. Similarly, a news addict like John
Fitzjames explained to one friend that 'I weekly read the pamphlets, but
have no faith in any report, but what your letters confirm', and John
Percivall hoped that people would 'suspend their faith' in news reports
until they had 'true news' from 'more sure hands' than 'fame's tittle-tattling
mouth'. Among soldiers, Captain Thomas Rokeby thanked Adam Baynes
for news by explaining that 'I do rather believe it from writing than if it
came from the press', while Captain Siddal turned to Baynes upon hearing
rumours about divisions between parliament and the army, and because
'the diurnalls mention no such thing'.[59]

[57] Bodl. MS Top.Oxon.C.378, p. 369; 'Twysden narrative', iii. 151; BL: Eg. 2534, fo. 107; Eg. 2535, fo. 118; CKS, U269/C267/19.

[58] *TSP*, i. 449–50; *Duppa Corr.*, p. 8; Arundel, C26; BL, Harl. 382, fo. 241; *Knyvett*, p. 109; Baxter, *Reliquiae*, i. 71.

[59] Beinecke, Boswell Box 100/1837; BL: Add. 78220, fo. 62; Add. 78191, fos. 41v, 79; Bodl. MS Tanner 66, fo. 181; *HMC Cowper II*, 338; Alnwick, MS 548, fo. 62; *HMC Egmont I*, p. 503; BL: Add. 21417, fo. 250; Add. 21419, fo. 69.

Print, in other words, offered only one way of following current affairs, and something that needed to be interrogated, checked and analysed. It could be used in association with everything from 'flying reports' and 'fame' to authoritative verification, based upon a very clear differentiation between 'public' or 'common' news, which appeared in print for anyone to see, and 'private' intelligence, which did not.[60] Very often, indeed, people employed different kinds of sources *sequentially*, using printed sources to build upon rumours and 'strange reports', and then supplementing print with other sources of news that had not appeared in public, and using private correspondence to verify or falsify printed accounts. Ralph Assheton was wary about a rumour regarding Thomas Harrison in September 1648 – 'all the town rings of it' – and sought verification from a friend. Joseph Jane sought 'more than the books bring', and John Fitzjames repeatedly supplemented newspapers with 'private intelligence' that was 'not in the pamphlets'. He used 'written news' to remedy 'printed defects', and wished to read 'news in writing as well as lies in print', and he craved 'all the news' that did not come 'within the lash of the mercuries'. Such comments and behaviour indicate that print was problematic because it gave an *initial* impression, which might need amending in due course, and contemporaries recognized that time might reveal a more detailed, elaborate and accurate picture.[61] They also understood that news needed to be *interpreted*. Sir Arthur Hopton explained that the *Perfect Diurnall* was 'the best intelligencer', but he found it very hard to make 'a judgment upon matter of fact', and a young John Locke differentiated between using newspapers to acquire 'the most authentic news' and the task of discerning 'what you can spell from this medley'. In 1659, meanwhile, Moses Wall explained that, having trusted *Politicus* for 'matters of fact', he then read the news 'with my own gloss' to understand 'the grounds of those actions'.[62]

In the end, therefore, while *Pragmaticus* boasted that 'he which is master of these pamphlets, needs no other comment', contemporaries assigned to print a less exalted role. Print was *valued*, but it was placed within a *hierarchy* that took account of both reliability and speed, wherein newspaper reports were considered more trustworthy than mere fame, but less reliable than private intelligence, and as things that could also be used with profit because

---

[60] *Luke Letter Books*, p. 322; *Flemings in Oxford*, pp. 139–41; *Sydney Papers*, p. 39; *Baillie*, ii. 171; HEH, HA 14356; *TSP*, vii. 541.
[61] Chetham, A.3.90, fo. 16; Nott. UL, Pw2/Hy/213; Claydon, Verney reel 8; *NP*, ii. 248–9; BL: Add. 78196, fo. 32; Add. 42063, fo. 129v; Eg. 2535, fos. 62, 350, 476v, 557v; TNA, SP 77/32, fo. 293; *TSP*, vii. 159; Alnwick: MS 548, fos. 56v, 57v; MS 549, fos. 10, 65; Northants. RO, IC 3583.
[62] BL, Add. 78191, fo. 133; *Locke Corr.*, i.137; SUL, Hartlib 34/4/19–20.

they were likely to emerge rather sooner than credible information. As Lord Grey of Warke explained to Colonel John Moore at Dundalk: 'you have our news in print before I can send it you'.[63] This sense that print was valued because it offered speedy access to news was not trivial, of course, and in a rapidly changing situation people naturally wanted to get information quickly. The 'newest books' were thus highly prized, and the correspondent who explained that events were 'better related than I am able to set them down' probably meant that printed texts offered superior relations to those that could yet be penned in private.[64] But if printed reports were speedy, they also needed to be verified, and judgment about their reliability needed to be suspended until their claims could be checked against subsequent evidence, and until it could be demonstrated to be more than just 'false fire'. In 1654, Sir Edward Walker wrote to Lady Anne Howard to correct 'that most malicious information given out by the diurnall', and in 1659 Locke asked a friend for 'authentic news' by saying that this meant doing 'more than every pamphleteer doth for a penny a sheet'. This is precisely the process that Dr Denton employed in August 1653, to conclude that 'our victory at sea [is] not altogether so famous as at first report', and very occasionally it can also be observed in copies of newspapers that have been annotated with corrections and clarifications, as well as with additional information.[65]

Newspapers were thus problematic, but useful if handled with care, and a final point to make on the basis of this exploration of reading practices is that their significance was obviously enhanced in the absence of other sources, and that contemporaries found ways of coping with them even when they had few opportunities to test them thoroughly. Men may have preferred scribal news from known and reliable suppliers, but newspapers offered an acceptable substitute for those who were 'but little acquainted' with such sources. Indeed, Knyvett explained that sending a printed newspaper could 'supply my own imbecility this week'. Thus, when people professed to know nothing 'but what the printed pamphlets contain', they probably meant that they currently had at their disposal only one of the kinds of source that they usually employed when gathering and processing information.[66] Ultimately, indeed, people learned to negotiate these

[63] *Pragmaticus*, 369.220A, sig. Y; DRO, D258/30/14/8; Liverpool UL, MS 23/69.
[64] CUL, Buxton 59/90.
[65] BL, Add. 78194, fo. 143v ; NLW, MS 9064E/1883; *Locke Corr.*, i. 125; Claydon, Verney reel 12; BL: Add. 69923, fos. 50–53v; Add. 62083, fos. 93–96v.
[66] BL, Add. 78195, fo. 99; TNA, SP 77/32, fo. 308; CKS, U269/C275; CUL, Buxton 59/86; BL, Add. 78194, fo. 44.

unfortunate situations by reading *extensively*, and by assessing newspapers *against each other*. This probably explains why Lord North and the Earl of Salisbury regularly read more than one newspaper of a kind that might be regarded as dry and reliable, and it certainly makes sense of the Earl of Leicester's behaviour, since he repeatedly compared rival newspapers to note small differences and develop something approaching a reliable picture. He was not alone, and from gentlemen like William Pole and John Harington to clerics and merchants like Thomas Wyatt and Samuel Jeake, other contemporaries likewise purchased numerous texts each week, and then compared, indexed and cross-referenced them to spot inconsistencies and make judgments about journalistic truth.[67]

Examination of reading practices thus complicates and enhances our appreciation of contemporary attitudes towards print. Such practices reveal a range of motivations for reading pamphlets and newspapers, and the ability to monitor the press, in terms of selecting from what was available and scrutinizing specific works closely. They also reveal that print was a tool as much as a frivolity, and something that people used in a more or less sophisticated fashion to help comprehend their times.[68]

iv The dynamic of public trust in the media

Thus far, the aim has been to distil contemporary mechanisms for coping with print from the rhetoric and practice of authors and readers, but this obviously runs the risk of creating a static picture that pays insufficient attention to how attitudes to print changed during the course of the Civil War and revolution. Indeed, since we are dealing with a process of adapting to change, a diachronic approach is essential, in order to explore the dynamic of public trust in the media. This final section thus examines how perceptions of print developed in response to the print revolution, and as readers confronted new developments in print culture and the impact of censorship and propaganda, especially in terms of the nature and quality of news reporting during the 1650s. It will demonstrate that, while not everyone adapted in the same way or at the same pace, the ability to accommodate rapid changes in the media landscape was fairly remarkable, and

---

[67] Beinecke, Osborn b.52, Volume II, p. 128; Bodl. MS North.c.4, fo. 70; Hatfield, Bills 254/2, 14; *HMC Salisbury XXII*, pp. 389–90; *Sydney Papers*, pp. 3–151; Antony, PZ/B2/22–3; Bodl. MS Top. Oxon.C.378, p. 329; BL, Add. 46376A, fos. 22–41v, 46–89v, 94, 106, 112, 116; ESRO, FRE 609; *A Radical's Books*, 328; FSL, 150–373q; BJL, DD/HO/2/111; *Andrew Hay Diary*, p. 204.
[68] Bodl. MS Clarendon 30, fo. 208.

involved a more or less constant process of modifying habits of consumption and reading in reaction to new obstacles and opportunities.

The first striking observation to make about responses to the print revolution is the speed with which hostility subsided and objections became more muted. It is noticeable, therefore, that the bitterest attacks on cheap print occurred in the immediate aftermath of the collapse of censorship in 1641. It was in the early 1640s, in other words, that commentators repeatedly riffed on themes about the emergence of pamphleteering and journalism, about the problem of making sense of such material and about the harm it was likely to do. It was in this period that a shocked Sir Edward Nicholas noted how pamphlets were 'too common in and about London', and that Thomas Wyatt expressed surprise that 'all business and proceedings are in print', to be seen by 'any that will'.[69] Such comments obviously did not disappear after 1642, but they were expressed much less frequently, even if animosity continued to be expressed towards Grub Street hacks – 'that malicious generation of creatures lately sprung out of the corruption of these times'.[70] The exceptions to this story involve moments of particularly acute political tension, when the presses became especially busy, and when old doubts resurfaced. The period 1647–8, therefore, witnessed a surge in complaints about print culture. One of Sir Ralph Verney's correspondents noted that 'the most bitterest books and writings' were appearing 'every day', and exclaimed that 'tis a wonder how they dare to print them', and Herbert Thorndike expressed surprise that 'all libels against the times walked freely up and down the streets'. Much the same thing happened in 1659, when Thomas Rugg noticed that Londoners bought up trifling pamphlets 'as fast as they could meet with any', and when new doubts arose for people like John Martin of Rye, who professed that 'novelties' and conflicting reports 'confound my senses'. Martin became reticent about circulating news reports because 'everything is so mutable', and because it was difficult to achieve 'lasting certainty'.[71]

A second notable demonstration of how contemporaries adapted to print culture involved the response to changes in news reporting during the 1650s, and most obviously during the Cromwellian Protectorate, when readers were quick to comment on a perceived decline in the quality of available news. John Fitzjames claimed that pamphlets had 'grown so dull of late',

---

[69] Northants. RO, FH3728; *HMC Buccleuch I*, p. 289; LPL, MS 3391, fo. 94; Bodl. MS Top. Oxon.C.378, pp. 328, 334.
[70] BL, Add. 78220, fo. 63.
[71] Claydon, Verney reel 7; Durham UL, Cosin Letterbook 1a/46; *Rugg*, p. 53; FSL, V.a.454, pp. 28, 63, 69.

and that they were 'very slender', and in late 1655 Joseph Jane referred to 'the penury of the prints', to suspicions that old news was being recycled, and to the fact that 'the omissions are more observable than the relations'.[72] These observations prompted subtle shifts in the language used to describe material that was being read and circulated. Where once commentators reflected on what they *learned* from the prints, they now used less positive phrases like 'you *see* by the London prints', or 'you will *find* by the books'. Individuals became apologetic about referring people to newspapers, and about having to 'leave you to the book', and they began to express the opinion, almost unknown in the 1640s, that newspapers were no longer worth reading or 'worth the postage'.[73] The main target for such criticism was the official journal, *Politicus*, which avowedly contained less domestic news, which was recognized as being markedly different from its predecessors and which provoked claims that news reports were 'very false of late' and that 'few believe' the press. In December 1659, the royalist William Rumbold claimed that news was highly uncertain because it was 'represented through *Politicus* his spectacles, who takes the liberty to vent his own inventions beyond all his predecessors'.[74]

Such comments, however, provide the key to a third observation about changes in public perception regarding the media: that disillusionment with the press led to changes in behaviour rather than a shunning of printed genres. Indeed, it seems likely that subtle shifts occurred in how people used the texts that were available, as well as in how they contextualized them using other sources of information. For cynical observers like Sir Edward Nicholas, therefore, Cromwellian newspapers came to be used primarily as sources for European news, and he marvelled at their ability to obtain accurate information from within the Louvre even as he grew sceptical about their reliability regarding English affairs.[75] More generally, greater emphasis came to be placed on supplementing printed journalism with scribal news, and just as newspapers took on added importance with the reduced availability of manuscript newsletters, so private intelligence assumed renewed significance when newspapers became 'low and flat'. Indeed, archives reveal a fairly clear correlation between the revival of

---

[72] Alnwick, MS 549, fos. 22v, 68; BL, Eg. 2535, fos. 88, 236, 350, 402; *NP*, iii. 100–1.

[73] BL: Add. 78194, fo. 99; Add. 78195, fos. 75, 93, 99, 103, 110; Add. 78196, fo. 42; Eg. 2535, fo. 301; Lancs. RO, DDF/411, unfol.; *Borough of Leicester*, pp. 454–5; *HMC Egmont I*, pp. 523, 598; Alnwick, MS 549, fo. 22v; Leics. RO, DE730/1, fo. 60.

[74] *Politicus*, 361.224, p. 3796; BL, Eg. 2535, fo. 118; Staffs. RO, D593/P/8/2/2; Bodl. MS Clarendon 67, fos. 246–v.

[75] *NP*, i. 225.

manuscript newsletters and moments of heightened concern regarding print culture in the late 1640s and the late 1650s. It is even possible to observe attempts to reinvent professional (if not necessarily commercial) newsletter services, and even Nedham contemplated abandoning print journalism in favour of a subscription service.[76]

The fourth and most important way in which contemporary perceptions of print changed during the 1640s and 1650s involved a growing appreciation of how print culture worked, and how it was controlled through censorship and propaganda, which led to the development of more sophisticated methods for interpreting printed texts. Here, too, it is necessary to confront both the claims that were made by polemicists as well as the reflections and the behaviour of individual readers.

In public discourse, therefore, the public was confronted by a wealth of claims and counter-claims regarding authorship and propaganda, as the culture of news and pamphleteering became inextricably linked with the identities and personalities of those involved, and with their relationship to political authorities. From the mid 1640s, therefore, repeated attempts were made to unmask journalists and editors, with claims about their names and their motivations, and with lurid tales about mercenary hacks and 'petty-foggers', who had a desire for profit and 'a desperate itch' to 'abuse the kingdom'.[77] As time went on, these turned into extended biographical sketches of impoverished scholars like John Hall – 'a mercenary slave, who will pawn his soul to the Devil, for a pipe of tobacco, and a noggin of ale'. Hall was apparently hired by William Lilly and paid in pamphlets, with which he went 'begging' to MPs, and he was said to have contrived lies in an alehouse with which to 'blind the people's eyes'. Of course, Hall was not the only author and journalist to be derided as a money-grubbing and tavern-haunting hack, and equally colourful comments were made about Marchamont Nedham and Henry Walker, both of whom became notorious for their scandalous writing as well as for their brushes with the law.[78] Beyond this, of course, readers were repeatedly confronted with allegations

---

[76] BL, Add. 39922, fo. 1; Longleat, Whitelocke 9, fos. 159–66v, 188–90; Whitelocke 10, fos. 1–3; Som. RO, DD/HI/466; Staffs. RO, D868/4/32a, 91; Antony, BC/24/2, fo. 173; Salt Library, SMS 454/6; Bodl. MS Carte 228, fos. 79–88; Glos. RO, D678/1/F21/28; BL: Add. 71448, fo. 59; Add. 15750, fos. 44, 46; *Oxinden and Peyton Letters*, p. 149.

[77] *Academicus*, 260.03, p. 30; *Anti-Mercurius* (1648, M1752), sig. Av; *Civicus*, 298.145, p. 2062; *Hue and Cry* (1645, C3808), pp. 1, 3, 6; *Kingdomes Weekly Post*, 217.5, p. 39; *Occurrences*, 465.5114, p. 896; *Pragmaticus*, 370.10B, sig. K.

[78] *Psitacus*, 375.5, p. 3; *Elencticus*: 312.34, p. 262; 312.30, p. 233; 312.29, p. 222, sig. Ff2v; 312.34, p. 264; *Last Will* (1648, L533), p. 3; *Anti-Britanicus*, 267.3, pp. 24–6; *Hue and Cry*, pp. 1, 3; *Fresh Whip*, p. 3; *Elencticus*, 316.05, pp. 34–5; *Recommendation* (1647, T502), p. 6.

about writers who were in the employ of political authorities. Those who wrote for money – the 'shameless, licentious scum', and the 'rout of writers' – were thought particularly prone to the seductions of power, and a newspaper like *Britanicus* was described as 'an illegitimate creation, to whose birth the House of Commons was the father'. *Aulicus*, meanwhile, was accused of being a court 'pensioner' and a 'patentee', and it was suggested that John Berkenhead was its 'scribe', who took information and orders from Sir Edward Nicholas ('the informer') and Lord Digby ('the contriver'), who 'whispered you ... in the ear'. Subsequently, during the Republic, Nedham was derided as a 'state scavenger', and ventriloquized as saying 'tis money I want'.[79] Naturally, the writers against whom such accusations were made often defended themselves in public, by asserting their gentle backgrounds, by denying that they wrote for 'the purse and the pocket' or in order to 'subsist', and by rejecting the idea that they received direct instructions from court or parliament. By doing so, however, they merely highlighted the need to contextualize texts by acquiring information about their authors.[80]

Indeed, such accusations were only the most colourful elements of more wide-ranging claims about the degree to which the press was controlled and exploited by the political elite, either by means of censorship or propaganda. Readers found themselves not only having to grapple with texts that displayed an official *imprimatur*, but also with evidence that such things could be forged, and with the contradictory claims that were made about licensing in contemporary propaganda. Parliamentarian and republican newspapers boasted that such signs of approval represented hallmarks of quality and reliability, while royalists insisted that licences enabled readers to identify 'lies and tame nonsense'. *Melancholicus* memorably referred to 'the paper kites that fly up and down the city with Gilbert Mabbott hanging at their arses ... squirting out lies by authority'.[81] Beyond this, readers would have become familiar with allegations that plots foiled and victories won were manipulated and invented to raise money, and with the image of the 'paper kite' that was deployed to test or soften-up an audience. They would have encountered claims about faked letters, which were said to have been intercepted 'none

---

[79] *Bellicus*, 279.19, p. 7; *Anti-Britanicus*, 267.1, pp. 3–4; *Aulicus*, 275.222, p. 1006; BL, Add. 24667, fo. 6; *Britanicus*: 286.002, p. 9; 286.003, p. 17; 286.053, pp. 416–7; 286.005, p. 35; 286.006, p. 41; 286.016, p. 121; 286.023A, pp. 176–7; 286.067, p. 527.

[80] *Moderate*, 413.2012, sig. M4v; *Elencticus*, 312.14, p. 105; *Britanicus*: 286.021, p. 161; 286.051, p. 399; 286.085, p. 771; 286.097, p. 865.

[81] *Diurnall*, 513.28B, sig. Ee4; *Diurnall*, 512.11, sig. L4; *Diurnall*: 504.226, p. 1820; 504.304, pp. 2530–1; *Politicus*, 361.582, p. 654; *Occurrences*: 465.4017, sig. R4v; 465.5039, p. 272; *Proceedings*, 599.085, p. 1295; *Pragmaticus*, 369.102A, sig. B3; *Melancholicus*, 344.53B, p. 156.

knows where', and published to 'seduce . . . the simple people' and 'buzz their brains', as well as suggestions that real stories were withheld so as not to dishearten them.[82] Eventually, they were led to believe that propaganda was being produced in a systematic fashion, with members of the Derby House Committee being portrayed as 'task-masters' of the 'weekly romances', with tales of pamphleteers being 'set on work', and with references to 'the State's weekly gazettes'. Indeed, by the early 1650s, Walter Frost was being described as Speaker Lenthall's 'newshound', while Henry Walker was styled 'the state's newsmonger' and 'parliament pimp', who wrote a 'fardle of lies . . . prepared by a committee', and who perpetrated a 'paper plot'.[83]

In other words, readers were encouraged to think about authors and how they operated, about the circumstances in which texts were published, and about how and why newspapers came and went, and it seems clear that here, too, contemporary perceptions underwent considerable change, both at the level of specific episodes and in terms of a general appreciation of the dynamics of print culture. Thomas Rugg became familiar with seditious authors and radical printers and, like many other readers, he recognized the shifting fortunes (and titles) of particular newspapers. By observing how royalist newspapers failed to appear on time in December 1643, Sir Samuel Luke felt able to conclude that '*Aulicus* lies a dying', while in April 1645 Roger Burgoyne recognized that the *Moderate Intelligencer* was 'but the *Scout* anabaptised'.[84] Others made a point of noting and remarking upon the identity of authors and journalists. Close readers of pamphlets like *Vox Plebis* detected different writing styles, and they developed theories about textual collaboration, referred to newspapers by the names of their journalists (such as 'Mr Frost's gazette'), and recognized the factional allegiances of titles like *The Moderate*, which was described as 'a friend of the Levellers, and not to Cromwell'.[85] They also demonstrated a growing sensitivity to the impact of censorship, by commenting on incidents like the silencing of *Britanicus* for 'impudency' regarding the king, the suppression of books by the royalist judge, David Jenkins, and the banning of trial reportage during the Rump, in order to prevent royalist defendants from becoming martyrs.[86] And they proved capable of observing more general trends, not least

---

[82] *Aulicus*, 275.236A, pp. 1145–6; *Pragmaticus*, 369.217, sig. R3v, 369.220B, sig. Y3; *Elencticus*: 312.30, p. 234; 312.34, p. 265; 312.42, sig. Ss; *Elencticus*, 316.22, p. 173; Howell, *Discourses* (1661, H3068), pp. 49–50; *True Informer*, p. 30.

[83] *Pragmaticus*: 369.212, sig, Mv; 369.215, sig. P3v; 369.216, sig. Q3v; 369.232, sig. Zzv.

[84] *Rugg*, pp. 66, 69; *HMC Montagu*, pp. 148–9; *Luke Journal*, iii. 221–2; Claydon, Verney reel 6.

[85] *NP*, i. 74; *HMC De Lisle VI*, p. 461; *Sydney Papers*, pp. 77–8, 88, 93, 94–5.

[86] Claydon, Verney reels 6–7; Som. RO, DD/PH/212/17.

the growing concern with secrecy under interregnum governments. Joseph Jane concluded that Cromwell was 'so wise' as to understand the impact of press freedom during the 1640s, 'and so will not leave himself open to the humours which that entertainment of the people will produce'. Others argued that censorship ensured that journalists were 'careful ... not to displease', and that they behaved 'timorously', although Sir Edward Nicholas suspected that censorship was sometimes spurious, and that the authorities sometimes only pretended to punish wayward printers.[87]

The same mixture of specific commentary and general reflections can also be observed in relation to licensing and news management. Astute observers sought to understand how licensing worked, noted which newspapers were licensed by the authorities and recognized that licensers had an effect on what was published, and they also made sure to note when the news that they discussed in letters reflected what 'the *licensed* pamphlets speak'.[88] Much more readily observable, however, is sensitivity to the overt ways in which texts were manipulated for political reasons. Sir Simonds D'Ewes noted how letters to the Speaker were carefully edited – saying that 'the very truth must not be published on either side' – and Sir John Hotham mused that 'our masters of both sides feed us ... such meat as they think fittest'. Similar claims were also made by people outside the Westminster bubble. Thomas Wyatt concluded that an anonymous tract from 1642 entitled *An Appeal to the World in these Times of Danger* was actually 'made by Pym', on the basis of similarities between its text and one of his speeches. Others dismissed stories about plots against the Republic by claiming that these were 'discovered by sanctified eyes', while 'I poor sinful mortal cannot discern them'.[89] And while readers did not always understand the precise goals of those who manipulated stories and texts, they certainly sensed that 'artifice and design' were involved, and became more adept at recognizing Cromwellian attempts to massage perceptions of European power relations, and to 'amuse the people' and 'gain credit' with the public.[90]

More than this, however, awareness gradually developed that authors and journalists were controlled by political authorities, in ways that encouraged

---

[87] Nott. UL, Ga/12768/26; Staffs. RO, D593/P/8/2/2; Alnwick, MS 549, fo. 22v; Leics. RO, DE730/1, fo. 60; BL, Eg. 2534, fo. 236; Eg. 2535, fo. 106; *NP*, ii. 243–4; SHC, G52/2/19/10.

[88] SUL, Hartlib 28/1/61; *Sydney Papers*, pp. 97, 146; BL: Add. 78194, fo. 56; Eg. 2534, fo. 236; Eg. 2536, fo. 449.

[89] BL, Harl. 166, fo. 6a; BJL, DD/HO/1/26; Bodl. MS Top.Oxon.C.378, pp.342–3; Lincs. RO, 8ANC8/66.

[90] Bodl. MS Clarendon 48, fos. 128, 258v-9; BL, Eg. 2535, fos. 88, 218; *NP*, iii. 246–7; Bodl. MS Carte 131, fo. 184; BL, Add. 78195, fo. 29.

people to adapt their reading behaviour. Thus, as observers noted how news became 'monopolised', so they came to believe that 'you must hereafter not expect it in the diurnall, but you shall have it in the letter'. However, this sense that contemporary perceptions changed as methods for controlling the press became more sophisticated can be demonstrated most clearly in relation to Marchamont Nedham, whose emergence as a well-known journalist ensured that his career and motivations were observed and analysed by readers like Richard Braham. Braham knew about his role on *Pragmaticus*, noted his surrender to parliament in July 1649, and concluded that he was 'a very knave'. Nedham's fame grew dramatically thereafter, to the point where his fluctuating fortunes and fickle allegiance attracted the attention not just of satirists and journalists, but also of men like John Evelyn and Thomas Rugg, and even of London's citizens, who petitioned against him in 1660.[91] Styled in print as an 'infamous' and 'lying court pamphleteer' – who was paid for 'contriving false intelligence', and who served the interests of 'corrupt men' – Nedham's papers were perceived by readers to be 'prophets' of the protectoral regime, and it was assumed that he had 'orders' what to publish, that he perpetrated 'state tricks', and that he was a 'base rogue'.[92] Such scrutiny of Nedham's work became particularly obvious after he was granted a journalistic monopoly in 1655, and it was accompanied by behavioural changes. Readers not only contemplated the government's motives, but also wondered whether *Politicus* was still worth reading, and even Cromwellians like James Waynwright stopped sending copies to their friends. However, in yet another demonstration of how contemporaries found ways of adapting to new circumstances, Waynwright did not shun Nedham's newspaper for long, and he renewed his acquaintance with *Politicus* during the 1656 elections. Royalists, too, continued to read Nedham's paper, although their awareness that the regime kept 'an eye on the press' to ensure that 'nothing come out to check the rascal gazetteer', together with their belief that Nedham wrote 'loud lies', probably ensured that they did so in different ways and for different reasons.[93] Many readers understood the nature of Nedham's links to the Cromwellian regime, and thus trusted his domestic news only for 'matters of fact', and also questioned

---

[91] Worcester College, Clarke MS 181, unfol.; *HMC Pepys*, p. 286; *Mercurius Politicus*, pp. 12–13; *Catalogue* (1659, T2593), p. 14; SUL, Hartlib 28/1/61; BL, Add. 78221, fo.71; *Rugg*, pp. 66–7; Staffs. RO, D868/3/30; *Politicus*, 361.567, p. 437.

[92] *Second* (1659, W1557), p. 37; *Proceedings* (1660, P3628B), p. 11; *Catalogue*, pp. 75–6; *Eighteen* (1659, E263), p. 4; BL: Eg. 2535, fo. 465; Eg. 2534, fos. 34, 236; *NP*, ii. 103–4; *HMC Egmont I*, p. 509.

[93] Staffs. RO, D868/5/8; BL, Eg. 2535, fos. 459v, 474, 478; *NP*, iii. 260–1, iv. 55; Lancs. RO, DDF/411; Bodl. MS Clarendon 67, fo. 185.

his principles, felt that he wrote 'darkly', and suggested that his meaning was difficult to discern. Nevertheless, some still found it possible to give him 'credit' for overseas news, and it is also noteworthy that provincial readers like Henry Oxinden and John Fitzjames responded to Nedham's role as a government propagandist not by spurning him, but rather by deepening their personal contacts with him, as a man 'in power and credit'.[94]

Even in Cromwellian England, in other words, contemporaries did not give up on printed news. They recognized that it remained accurate at least in certain respects, and they continued to think that it was worth reading. Rather than thinking in terms of declining trust in the media, therefore, it is more appropriate to recognize that contemporaries responded to changes in print culture by adjusting their methods for interpreting the news. This meant placing greater emphasis on scribal news, and showing greater sensitivity to the circumstances in which texts appeared, to the constraints placed upon the press, and to the motives and intentions of those involved. It also meant that, handled with care, even *Politicus* could remain useful.

v Conclusion

By surveying how print was portrayed and perceived during the Civil Wars and Interregnum, and by analysing contemporary reading practices, it becomes difficult to agree that responses to the print revolution were naive, or that the period witnessed a crisis of truth-telling. This is because contemporary polemicists appreciated that the reality was more complex, and because readers themselves show that the rhetoric of print must be treated with considerable caution. Those who lived through the upheavals and conflicts of the 1640s and 1650s were wary about print, but nevertheless used it avidly. They recognized a range of problems with pamphlets and newspapers, but found ways of dealing with them, and they adapted to new media and new phenomena by developing strategies for coping with print culture. In other words, they identified problems with printed news and polemic, but did not regard them as intractable, and so did not spurn texts because they were 'unreliable'. Individuals consumed print for a variety of reasons, and sought different things from different texts, and they did so as part of a multi-source process of interpreting their troubled age, and this process involved more or less careful selection and close reading, as well as reading that was 'extensive' in character. People did not merely read in

[94] Vaughan, *Protectorate*, ii. 126; SUL, Hartlib 34/4/19–20; *TSP*, vii. 37; *Oxinden and Peyton Letters*, pp. 143–222; Alnwick, MS 552, fos. 4–70v; Lancs. RO, DDF/411, unfol.

accordance with their own political and religious views, and their decisions about what to value were not determined by judgments about truthfulness. This is not to deny that individuals approached such issues from within specific cultural and political frameworks, or that their readings reflected passions and interests as much as rational faculties. Nevertheless, readers from the well-bred to the low-born engaged with print culture more or less seriously, rather than passively, and it was this critical engagement which ensured that they became neither resigned nor bewildered, and that they could read with enthusiasm texts that were not merely accepted or believed. Moreover, although some were obviously more astute than others, scepticism and disbelief, as well as fascination and frustration, were not restricted to a well-educated elite. Like scholars who 'read for action', in other words, readers of pamphlets and newspapers used print carefully, pragmatically, purposefully and strategically, to a far greater extent than has been recognized hitherto, and it is evidently wrong to suggest that cheap print was read 'without purpose', or for 'sub-utilitarian purposes', but merely 'through a sense of compulsion or for pleasure'.[95] Ultimately, while printed texts were not considered intrinsically dependable, they were judged not merely in terms of their trustworthiness and authority, but also in terms of their *utility* as *analytical tools*, and as tools that could be employed alongside other media, rather than treated as a better or worse alternative to them.

Returning, therefore, to the stories with which this chapter began, it seems plausible to say more than that the linen weaver was simplistic in treating print as authoritative, while the gentleman was more astute and suspicious. Reactions to Civil War print culture rarely mapped neatly onto social distinctions, and the reality is that both Butler and Coningsby were making considered decisions about specific texts. Irrespective of whether their conclusions were accurate, both men were reflecting on their experiences of print culture, and their understanding of the forces involved, and what is striking is not how difficult they found this process to be, but how confident they were in handling the texts with which they were confronted. They highlight an impressive ability to adapt to the print revolution, and the growing sophistication with which this was done by other contemporaries is clear from a letter written by Thomas Mainwaring to Richard Legh of Lyme in February 1659. Noting that a local petition had not been printed in *Mercurius Politicus*, Mainwaring confronted the possibility that the document had been rejected, but concluded instead that 'it was only Nedham's doing, because he would not disoblige my Lord Bradshaw'.[96]

---

[95] Raymond, 'Irrational', pp. 188, 192–3, 204–5.   [96] GMRO, E17/89/26/2.

PART II

Following parliament

Introduction

Sir Thomas Swinburn, sometime sheriff of Northumberland, was an avid reader of political verse, and although this did not make him particularly remarkable, the verses copied into his notebook are significant for two reasons. First, they offered detailed analysis of parliamentary processes and personalities. One verse reflected on the 'arbitrary power' exercised by leading MPs, and on how parliamentarians sought to make Charles 'a great king and give him no power' and to 'honour him much and obey him not an hour'. It revealed their treasonable intentions and their devious tactics, and, like other verses, it ruminated on the usurpation of authority by 'King Pym'. Many such texts – like the mock petition 'to the five principal members' – emphasized the central importance of a small cabal of zealots, and probably ensured that their fame spread far and wide, particularly among the gentry.[1] Others offered a much richer prosopographical analysis, such as the text that described in detail a larger group of 'Brownists' who had 'conspired' to 'betray the king's crown and posterity, to subvert the government to be merely arbitrary, to root out all true religion and bring in atheism'. In some cases, indeed, such verses made a fairly considerable splash, and a text like 'The Game at Piquet' – which contained fictionalized speeches by numerous political figures – circulated fairly widely.[2] As time went on, moreover, the genre became increasingly sophisticated, and examples like 'The Parliament's account' and 'The Scout Generall' offered detailed analysis of political corruption, from the perquisites received by MPs to the payments made for 'lies' and spies', as well as the electoral management that ensured the return of clients and 'discontented men'.[3] Secondly, Swinburn's verses can be connected with

---

[1] Durham UL, MSP 9, pp. 243, 255.
[2] BL: Sloane 1467, fos. 130–v; Stowe 185, fos. 94–5v; Add. 78316, fo. 82; Lancs. RO, DDB85/20, fos. 122–9; Longleat, Portland 2, fos. 119–20.
[3] Durham UL, MSP 9, p. 256; BL, Add. 24667, fo. 5.

contemporary print culture. One item, *The Sence of the House* (March 1644), was copied from a notorious printed broadside, and it provided pen-portraits of numerous MPs and peers, scrutinized the relationships between specific politicians and analysed how parliamentary processes had been abused. This involved revealing the motivations and machinations behind particular episodes, such as the failure to reach a peace settlement with the king, which was attributed to MPs' fear of losing lucrative offices, and to the political exploitation of the 'close committee'.[4] Other texts – not least the 'Game at Piquet' – began life as scribal texts before achieving wider circulation in print, and indeed before being collected and repackaged after the Restoration.[5]

The existence of such verses, and their circulation in print, suggests that political discourse had undergone dramatic change since the 1620s, and that detailed evidence about both processes and personalities had become much more readily available. Of course, there are doubts about whether such material was intended for, or could be comprehended by, a popular audience. There are also grounds for distinguishing between 'white letter' verses that contained detailed political commentary, and that were aimed at a knowledgeable audience, and 'black letter' ballads, which were much more popular but also much less sophisticated. It is certainly likely that specific allusions in texts like *The Sence of the House* – including a speech by Sir Henry Ludlow that referred to his father's notorious 'parliament fart' – would only have been appreciated by a few political insiders.[6] Nevertheless, the general sense of the passage from which it came – which involved opposition to peace by an outspoken firebrand, the link between parliamentarian zeal and political treason, and MPs' determination to protect known radicals – would surely have been clear to a much broader readership. As such, there may have been truth in the claim – made in another verse which Swinburn copied from a printed pamphlet – that discussion about 'the brave parliament' occurred 'about the town' and among 'the common people'. Indeed, detailed political verses of this kind probably circulated fairly widely. In 1646, the Worcestershire gentleman Henry Townshend copied a verse that reflected on those who 'make kings great by curbing crowns / that settle peace by plundering towns / that govern with

---

[4] *Sence* (1643, S2551); Durham UL, MSP 9, pp. 299–300; *Occurrences*: 465.2013, sigs. Nv–2, N3; 465.3008, sig. H3v.

[5] *Shufling* (1659, N517); *The Rump* (1662, B4851).

[6] A. McShane, 'The roasting of the rump', *P&P*, 196 (2007), 252–72; A. McShane, 'The gazet in metre', in *News and Politics in Early Modern Europe*, ed. J. Koopmans (Leuven, 2005), pp. 131–50; BL, Add. 4149, fos. 213–15.

implicit votes / that establish truth by cutting throats'.[7] More obviously, detailed political verses frequently appeared in popular newspapers like *Pragmaticus* and *Elencticus*. These involved pithy and ironic references to 'Salisbury the valiant, Pembroke the witty, Denbigh the chaste and Mulgrave the pretty', as well as lengthy diatribes regarding the legacy of financial impropriety. The latter involved analysis of the 'sweet lickings' that could be exploited by MPs, in terms of 'beneficial offices and places of trust', and 'fair and fat employments which peace would utterly destroy', all of which were outlined with specific details about individual grandees and the perks that they were reluctant to give up.[8] Finally, it can occasionally be demonstrated how verses that were rich in political detail reached a popular audience. One Mr Maxwell was prosecuted in April 1642 for 'speaking' dangerous verses against Pym in Stafford, and similar material reached the eyes and ears of common drinkers, as with the ballad that was sung about the 'five members' in an Exeter tavern in 1642. More generally, political verses appeared in the cheapest forms of print throughout the Civil War period, and were then copied into commonplace books, as happened with a verse from *Elencticus* that was transcribed by William Smith, a minor clerical official at Durham Cathedral. Sometimes they were even 'scattered about the streets', as happened with *Alas Poor Parliament* (1644), a poetic attack on the earls of Essex and Manchester. Indeed, mocking verses about specific MPs were precisely the kind of 'jeering' and 'abusey' texts that fascinated the Covent Garden barber, Thomas Rugg, whose notes from the late 1650s included lines from a printed ballad called *Rump Dock't* that were said to be 'in almost everybody's mouth'.[9]

The existence of detailed and sophisticated political verses, and the possibility that they reached a wide audience through pamphlets, broadsides and newspapers, raises important questions about Civil War print culture. These relate to how the print revolution affected the circulation of political information, analysis and understanding beyond a narrow elite, and what this revealed about attitudes towards participation by people who were traditionally excluded from the corridors of power. It is to these questions that the second part of the book is devoted, and the aim will be to build on evidence about how people read about political affairs – in terms of the

---

[7] Durham UL, MSP 9, p. 215; *Common* (1645, C5571); Lancs. RO, DDB85/20, fo. 53; BL, Harl. 164, fos. 400–1; Worcs. RO, BA1714, p. 684.

[8] *Pragmaticus*, 370.01, sig. Av; *Elencticus*, 312.47, pp. 386–7.

[9] NLS, MS 2687, p. 1115; Devon RO, ECA Book 64, fo. 7v; Durham Cathedral, Hunter 125, pp. xxii–iii; *Prentises* (1642, A3587), p. 3; *Alas* (1644, A837); *Hue and Cry* (1649, C4671A); Notts. RO, DD/HU/1, p. 247; *Rugg*, pp. 11, 23, 26, 30, 54–5.

ubiquity of print, typographical acculturation and reading practices – in order to explore how easy it was for them to follow and understand political processes, proceedings and personalities. The chapters that follow will thus explore the *public face* of parliament during the 1640s and 1650s. This will mean analysing how the institution was portrayed and how its processes were analysed (Chapter 4); the degree to which daily proceedings were made accessible, either in person or in print (Chapter 5); and the possibility for assessing the performance of individual MPs and peers (Chapter 6). The argument will be that the period witnessed a transformation in the quantity and quality of information that emerged from parliament, as well as a dramatic change in the sophistication with which the institution was analysed. These changes – which made it possible for readers of cheap print to follow the day-to-day workings of parliament, its members and its committees, as well as parliamentary elections – meant that awareness of processes, proceedings and personalities ceased to be privileged in quite the way that it once had been. They also reflected important structural and conjunctural factors – relating to secrecy and accountability – that historians have generally overlooked. My argument will be that the Westminster system was relatively open to the public, and that in the circumstances of revolution – not least when parliament was empowered and its sessions were regular and protracted – MPs and peers proved willing to tolerate accessibility, and even to encourage transparency. In a period marked by civil war, political upheaval and experimentation, members of the political elite not only became concerned about public perceptions and popular awareness, but also proved willing to re-evaluate the role of parliament and its members, to rethink the relationship between representatives and the public, and to reflect on the need to account for political performance, and even on the desirability of basing electoral politics on the characters and careers of specific MPs. In other words, by exploring quotidian practices relating to the publicizing of parliamentary affairs, it will be possible to highlight the *personalization* of political culture, and the *vulgarization* or *democratization* of political awareness and understanding. The effect of such developments was to enhance the possibility for participating in political life in an active rather than passive manner, and as agents rather than merely as observers. It was also to improve people's ability to make targeted formal interventions in day-to-day proceedings, and to interact with members of both Houses, and to hold them to account for their behaviour.

CHAPTER 4

Analysing parliament and its problems

Between July and May 1648, four remarkable pamphlets appeared from the pen of 'Amon Wilbee', to provide 'the poore oppressed, betrayed and almost destroyed commons of England' with an account of 'a generation of ambitious, imperious' MPs, and of the 'subtle practices' of 'a haughty traiterous party in the Houses'. Wilbee targeted Presbyterian grandees – such as the Earls of Manchester and Stamford, Sir Philip Stapleton, Denzil Holles and Sir Walter Earle – who had violated laws and liberties, who displayed 'boundless ambitious and insatiable avarice', and who sought to 'save their own stakes and secure their own lives'. Such men were apparently 'unable to give any good account' of the money they had received, and Wilbee argued that a political settlement was impossible so long as they stood to benefit financially. More importantly, Wilbee also analysed the 'power and subtlety' of their 'practices', their manipulation of processes and proceedings for political ends, and their ability to 'deceive and seduce' other MPs, as well as their tendency to wield patronage for political effect. This was done by means of detailed prosopography, which revealed how the Commons was filled with 'sons', 'creatures' and 'malignants', all 'punies in state matters' who were thought to 'dance after these men's pipes, and walk by their lights'. To this he added detailed case studies that revealed how the political system worked to the detriment of individual citizens. Wilbee concluded that 'the very essence and end of a Parliament' had been 'perverted', not least because of the tendency to combine legislative, judicial and administrative roles, and he argued that MPs were 'elected by us' but 'act not for us', that they had 'betrayed their trusts', and that they ought to be 'questioned' and held 'accountable'. Pointing out that MPs were 'servants not masters', Wilbee challenged their claim to political immunity, saying that this was 'a new hydra-headed prerogative' that would lead to 'arbitrary rule'.[1]

---

[1] *Plain Truth* (1647, W2112), pp. 3–5, sigs. B2–C3; *Prima Pars* (1647, W2113), pp. 3, 9–11, sigs. Cv–F3v; *Secunda Pars* (1647, W2114); *Tertia Pars* (1648, W2115), pp. 1–3, 8, 16, 19, 23, 47, 52, 55.

Wilbee was not alone in analysing parliamentary practices, procedures and proceedings in this way, and certainly not alone in alleging that corruption could be revealed, and that parliament had been 'perverted'. However, he highlights very well the kinds of issues, evidence and analysis that emerged in print during the 1640s and 1650s, as well as the kinds of conclusions that were offered about parliamentary representation and political accountability. The aim of this chapter is to explore the ways in which authors and journalists responded to a prolonged period of parliamentary government and constitutional experimentation, and to suggest that this strange conjunction witnessed a transformation of existing practices for reporting and discussing parliamentary affairs. This involved a greater sense of the need to scrutinize the Westminster system, and an enhanced willingness to do so, and to do so through the medium of cheap print. The chapter will rethink the nature of conventional 'guides' to parliament and how these became available in affordable printed editions, rather than merely in scribal formats (section i). It will then examine the ways in which pamphlets and newspapers discussed factions (section ii), processes in the Commons and Lords (section iii), and the nature of committees and councils during the 'assault' on parliamentary politics (section iv), before assessing the impact that such analysis had on public affairs (section v). The latter will involve examining how the rhetoric of factions and corruption became common parlance, as well as the growing sense that this provoked anxiety at Westminster, not least in the face of radical ideas about parliament, and growing calls for reform. The significance of this evidence lies in how it reveals a *vulgarization* of institutional analysis, which ensured that the integrity of parliament and its members became the subject of public discourse beyond a narrow elite. This did not necessarily ensure that readers of cheap print could gain precisely the same level of awareness as more privileged members of society, but it certainly involved a significant *democratization* of focused political discourse, and the chapter will pay particular attention to the awareness and response of readers, from the diarist John Evelyn to the London merchant Thomas Juxon, as well as assorted weavers, brickmakers and shoemakers. The result will be a two-pronged challenge to the existing historiography relating to parliament during the revolutionary decades. First, it will be possible to suggest that the public response to parliamentary government involved a reaction not just to the 'tyranny' of county committees – in a spirit of localism and neutralism – but also to an engagement with Westminster politics. Secondly, it will be feasible to move beyond analysis of parliament that concentrates on the *reality* of factionalism and the emergence of adversary politics, in order to explore the ways in which the institution of parliament was *portrayed* and *perceived*.[2]

i Guide books

The intensification of traditional practices relating to the discourse of parliament that occurred during the revolution can be observed most obviously in relation to the basic 'guides' that were available for those who lacked first-hand experience of Westminster affairs and knowledge about its processes. Such texts, by insiders like Henry Elsynge and William Hakewill, explained the 'course of passing bills in Parliament', and offered 'remembrances' for, and 'observations' on, rules, orders and privileges, as well as 'policies' for use by members of both Houses.[3] These works, and the text by which they were inspired – the 'Modus tenendi parliamentum' – are obviously well-known to parliamentary historians. Nevertheless, they have generally been analysed in terms of their dating and accuracy, which means that their purpose, and the reasons for reading them, have been misunderstood. Rather than being dry and factual, they were often politically charged, and they could be written (and certainly employed) to reflect on the inadequacies of the parliamentary system, and on the ways in which these could be overcome. This explains why they were exploited by Sir John Eliot and Viscount Saye in the 1620s and 1630s, and how they could be used by the gentry and nobility. In short, such texts not only provided tools for navigating and negotiating parliamentary procedures, but also played an important role in developing *perceptions* of the Westminster system. As such, they formed part of a wider and much more important discourse relating to the nature of parliament, and to visions of the kind of institution that it might or could become.[4]

However, while analysis of parliament was not invented in the 1640s, crucial texts about the Westminster system were conventionally available only to a restricted audience. Nevertheless, locating parliamentary guidebooks within a broader context of debate about parliament, and demonstrating that they circulated beyond MPs and peers, provides important

---

[2] R. Ashton, 'From cavalier to roundhead tyranny, 1642–9', in *Reactions to the English Civil War*, ed. J. Morrill (London, 1982), pp. 185–207; J. Adamson, 'Politics and the nobility in civil war England', *HJ*, 34 (1991), 231–55; M. Kishlansky, 'Saye what?', *HJ*, 33 (1990), 917–37; M. Kishlansky, 'The emergence of adversary politics in the Long Parliament', *JMH*, 49 (1977), p. 619.

[3] C. Sims, 'Policies in parliaments', *HLQ*, 15 (1951), 45–58; V. Galbraith, 'The Modus Tenendi Parliamentum', *Journal of the Warburg and Courtauld Institutes*, 16 (1953), 81–99.

[4] Bodl. MS Tanner 88*, fos. 115–v.

evidence that contemporaries were becoming increasingly concerned about national politics. More importantly, it is also clear that knowledge about parliament and its problems began to reach a much wider audience. This is evident from Sir Francis Kynaston's 'True Representation of Forepast Parliaments', which involved not just an absolutist diatribe but also a reflection of contemporary concerns about the way in which texts like 'The Privilege and Practice of Parliament' were beginning to be printed, thereby encouraging public debate.[5] In other words, while Kynaston was an unreliable guide to the constitution, he was right to sense that parliamentary guidebooks were beginning to be democratized in the 1620s, and this became much more obvious after 1640, as old treatises began to appear in pamphlet form. This began with piracy, and Hakewill explained how growing demand for such material made it impossible to restrict the circulation of his account of the legislative process. The production of illicit copies led to a pirated version in print, and this in turn necessitated an authorized version. What subsequently emerged from the attempt to pro-tect authorial integrity, however, was a burgeoning market for affordable guides to parliament and its procedures, and subsequent decades witnessed numerous editions of similar texts, many with official sanction.[6] Moreover, while these were most obviously consumed by the kind of people who might otherwise have purchased manuscript editions, they also ensured that awareness about parliamentary procedures could be obtained by country squires like Henry Townshend. Subsequently, indeed, texts that described constitutional experiments and explained political processes circulated even more widely. Printed editions of the 'Instrument of Government' (1653) were not only purchased by members of the gentry and then copied and commonplaced, but were also printed in newspapers, and by 1657 it was explicitly argued that the 'Humble Petition and Advice' should be 'printed and published, [so] that the people may know how they shall be governed'.[7]

Examining texts that outlined and discussed parliamentary procedures and constitutional arrangements thus sheds valuable light on how the political system was portrayed and perceived. It reveals an appetite – well beyond the political elite – for an understanding of Westminster institu-tions, both in terms of how they worked and how they could be criticized

---

[5] CCL, U85/38/8; BL, Lans. 213, fos. 146–76; Durham UL, MSP 70; *Privileges* (1628, STC 7749).

[6] *Orders* (1641, E2675); *Manner* (1641, H214); *Manner* (1641, H211), sig. A4; *Order* (1641, H218); *CJ*, ii. 166; *Modus* (1659–71, H215); Scobell, *Memorials* (1656, S922); Scobell, *Remembrances* (1657, S930).

[7] Cumbria RO, D/LONS/L13/10/1/11; Lincs. RO, BNLW4/6/3; *Flemings in Oxford*, p. 403; Worcs. RO, BA1714, p. 14; Norfolk RO, LEST P10, p. 156; DRO, D258/15/1/1; All Souls, MS 167, fo. 6; TCD, MS 805, fos. 32–3; *Diurnall*, 503.213, sigs. 10E–10Fv; *Burton Diary*, ii. 135; Cornwall RO, B/Bod/285.

and improved, and it demonstrates that this curiosity was met in a variety of accessible and affordable ways, both official and non-official, and both authentic and pirated. Indeed, the fact that such issues began to be addressed by Civil War newspapers indicates that it is to journalism and cheap print that attention must now turn to investigate contemporary analysis of parliament in greater depth.

ii Analysing factions

Historians are now aware that political reporting and comment changed in important ways after the opening of the Long Parliament. Analysis that was traditionally restricted to private correspondence became available in print, not least as professional newsletter-writers were usurped by scribal journals like 'diurnall occurrences', and then by printed newspapers. What has rarely been noted, however, is that print journalism, and cheap print more generally, contained a wealth of information about parliamentary affairs, alongside insights into the parliamentary process and power relations within Westminster. Teasing out these strands adds much to our understanding of how a sophisticated appreciation of parliament – in terms of processes, personalities and problems – could be acquired by the general public, and how it could be translated into common parlance. The place to begin – and the foundation on which such analysis was built – is with ideas about 'faction'. Factions were suspected of enabling oligarchic groups to exert excessive influence; to abuse, corrupt and overawe parliament; and to ensure that public welfare was sacrificed to private interests. Claims were repeatedly made about how MPs abused their privileges, indemnified themselves and failed to pay debts, thereby bringing hardship to merchants and creditors, removing the benefit of justice and replacing liberty with slavery. As such, attempts were made to understand how this situation had come about, how factions operated and how they affected policy-making, in ways that some-times involved detailed prosopographical analysis. This could be found not merely in substantial volumes by insiders (like Clement Walker), but also in pamphlets and newspapers from across the political spectrum, and even in popular verse.[8] It could then be copied into private notebooks, not merely by well-connected gentlemen like Sir Roger Twysden, but also by London

---

[8] *Letter* (1648, L1733), p. 2; Jenkins, *Discourse* (1647, J590), pp. 2, 4; *Certain* (1647, C1739), p. 7; Walker, *Relations* (1648, W329/W334A), p. 4; Chestlin, *Persecutio* (1648, C3785), p. 61; Lilburne, *Defiance* (1648, L2099), p. 2; Wither, *Letters* (1644, W3166), pp. 4, 12; Musgrave, *Fourth* (1647, M3148), pp. 7, 12; Prynne, *Machivilian* (1648, P4007A), p. 3; *Westminster* (1648, W1469), p. 2; *Anatomy* (1648, A3062), p.1; *Eight* (1647, E258), pp. 4, 6; Beinecke, Osborn b.52, Vol. 2, p. 128.

merchants like Thomas Juxon, thereby raising the tantalizing possibility of tracing how print influenced the political analysis of contemporary readers.[9]

Awareness and analysis of factionalism developed fairly quickly during the early 1640s. The process of observing specific debates, of noting when proceedings became heated and protracted, and of recording when formal 'divisions' occurred, rapidly became a feature of popular journalism, which could even offer precise details about voting figures in the Commons. As one journalist wrote of the debate on the abolition of episcopacy in June 1641, 'great opposition there was on both sides'.[10] Initially, this language of 'sides' did not extend to the identification of distinct and organized *groupings*. Nevertheless, contemporaries quickly became aware of the 'faction' of 'fiery spirits' – 'the juggling junto' who were most eager for 'further reformation', and who spearheaded the assault upon the royal prerogative – and after war broke out it proved possible to focus on what might be called 'war' and 'peace' parties, and to notice how votes became increasingly tight.[11] More obviously, however, factional labelling began in earnest from early 1644. This involved the language of 'Presbyterians' and 'Independents', as claims about the bifurcation into 'parties' and 'interests' – such as Nedham's 'gang of Scottified jockies' in the Commons – became common currency in print, and in notes by onlookers like Juxon and Thomas Wyatt of Ducklington.[12] This is not to say that the debate around factionalism was straightforward, of course, and readers were confronted by competing claims and disputed analysis. Nevertheless, it became increasingly difficult to deny the existence of more or less formal 'parties' at Westminster, and Juxon even suggested that factionalism had become the subject of 'every man's tongue'.[13]

Having identified such 'interests' and 'parties', however, contemporaries did not restrict themselves to arguing that factions sought to 'engross all power', but also deepened their analysis in a number of ways. This involved monitoring change over time, reflecting on policies and political agendas and scrutinizing the structural dynamics of specific groups. The first of these

---

[9] 'Twysden narrative', ii. 102; *Juxon*, pp. 24, 49, 70, 95, 103, 106, 113, 116, 135.

[10] For example: *Continuation*: 638.20, p. 2; 638.25A, pp. 2–3; *Certaine Informations*, 36.18, p. 139; 36.20, p. 155; *Diurnall*: 511.35A, sigs. Mm2–3v; 511.24A, sigs. Z–2, Z3v; *Diary*, 144.132, sig. D4; *Occurrences*, 465.2018, sig. S2; *Scout*, 485.43, p. 360; Durham UL, MSP 30, fos. 14v, 31, 50v.

[11] Chestlin, *Persecutio*; BL, Add. 4180, fo. 174; *Baillie*, ii. 83, 115; *Juxon*, pp. 34–5; *Scout*, 485.41, p. 343; *Kingdomes*, 214.114, p. 911.

[12] 'Cheney Culpeper', pp. 297–9; Walker, *Relations* (1648, W329, W334A) sigs. A4–A4v; *Aulicus*, 275.307, pp. 1392–3; *Pragmaticus*, 369.206, sig. Fv; *Occurrences*, 465.3046, sig. Yyv; *Juxon*, pp. 35–6, 75, 104; Bodl. MS Top.Oxon.c.378, p. 236.

[13] *Britanicus*: 286.025, pp. 193–4; 286.054, pp. 427–8; 286.060, p. 474; *Juxon*, p. 103.

involved plotting the shifting balance of power between different groups at Westminster. Thus, it was understood that Essex's peace party was 'undone' by the war party, and that the 'Independents' drifted towards a religious policy that would cause tension with their Scottish allies, and this rise of the Independents during 1645 became visible to people outside Westminster. It was recognized, for example, by Juxon, not least in response to the publication of 'secret' intelligence in the royalist press, and such onlookers also noted the resurgence of the Presbyterians in 1646, and their undermining of the Independents in the spring of 1647. Indeed, it was also noted that the subsequent impeachment of the 'principle men of the Presbyterian faction' (June 1647) would leave the Independents as 'masters of the kingdom'.[14] Although some of these well-informed observers – like Sir Lewis Dyve – probably had private sources of intelligence, it is likely that many others developed their awareness through access to pamphlets like *Westminster Projects* and newspapers like *Pragmaticus*. The result was that, even during the complex machinations of 1648, individual readers managed to navigate the shifting sands of factional politics, in terms of waning Scottish influence at Westminster, the resurgent fortunes of the Presbyterians and divisions over the Newport Treaty. They also proved capable of detecting tensions among Independents, between those who persisted in seeking a harsh settlement, and those 'court beagles' and 'babes of court' (like Viscount Saye) who saw personal advantages in a lenient settlement, and who began to speak with a 'court tongue'. Of course, the quality of such analysis was not entirely consistent, and the official grip on newspapers during the 1650s ensured that factional tensions went largely unnoticed. Nevertheless, detailed analysis reappeared with the collapse of censorship in 1659, and this explains how men like Thomas Rugg were able to analyse 'Lord Fleetwood's party' and then identify various interest groups in the restored Rump and Long Parliament.[15]

Beyond mapping the fortunes of different factions, print culture also enabled observers to enhance their understanding in a second way, by attributing specific *policies* to particular parliamentary groups. This involved analysing things like the creation of specific committees, the formulation of

[14] Prynne, *Machivilian*, p. 3; *Certaine* (1648, C1697), sig. A2; *Juxon*, pp. 75–6, 94, 104, 135; *Baillie*, ii. 83, 230, 277, 319; *Aulicus*, 275.307, pp. 1392–3; BL, Add. 21066, fo. 15; 'Cheney Culpeper', pp. 297–9; 'Lewis Dyve', p. 60; Claydon, Verney reel 8.

[15] Bodl. MS Clarendon 30, fos. 232–3; Wildman, *Putney* (1647, W2171), p. 2; *Certaine*, sig. A4v; *Westminster*, p. 2; 'Lewis Dyve', p. 61; Bodl. MS Clarendon 31, fo. 67v; Claydon, Verney reel 9; *Pragmaticus*: 396.117, sig. R2v, 369.205, sig. E, 369.206, sig. Fv; *Occurrences*, 465.5083; sig. Nnnnv; Add. 78221, fos. 20–v; *Militaris*: 346.2, p. 14; 346.3, sig. C; 346.5, sig. E2; *Rugg*, pp. 23, 43.

peace proposals and the pressure for 'recruiter' elections, as well as revealing the factional influence behind issues like the enforcement of the Solemn League and Covenant and the process of negotiating with the king. It proved possible to recognize who instigated the votes for 'no further addresses' (January 1648), and to make deductions about different attitudes towards the king and the Scots, and similar analysis enabled contemporaries to follow the subsequent machinations which led to the reversal of this policy, and the renewal of attempts to reach a negotiated settlement. Likewise, during Richard Cromwell's Parliament in 1659, observers reflected on the Harringtonian influence on Commons' debates, on the republicanism of Sir Arthur Hesilrige and his 'angels', and on the monarchism of 'the other party', and John Evelyn made similar connections between parties and policies in the restored Rump. Indeed, during the final phase of the Long Parliament (February 1660), Rugg proved capable of distinguishing between three distinct parties, one of which favoured government by 'a single person', while another favoured 'a commonwealth', and a third was 'indifferent' and 'ready to side with the stronger party'. This almost certainly reflected his substantial diet of printed pamphlets and newspapers.[16]

This ability to attribute specific policies to particular factions, in ways that informed the reactions of individual readers, is perhaps most evident during the trial of Charles I. By pigeonholing individual MPs, the most astute observers comprehended the part played by factions at Westminster as events unfolded, even if their interpretations are liable to be challenged. Marchamont Nedham, for example, employed a detailed prosopography of MPs to dismiss the possibility that Charles I faced death, and although his analysis may be regarded as questionable, it seems to have made an impact at the time. It may have informed the views of John Evelyn, who recognized that only certain Independents sought to 'crucify' the king, while others were willing to see Charles re-established, and who also contemplated the possibility that a coup by a powerful junto was more likely than a bloody revolution.[17] Indeed, there are good reasons for thinking that such arguments would have been taken seriously by members of the public. Contemporaries had grown used to the need to expose political cunning and dissimulation; to the possibility that grandees were motivated by things

[16] *Baillie*, ii. 141; *Montereul*, i. 74, 266; *Juxon*, pp. 69, 71; *Aulicus*: 275.207, p. 828; 275.141B, p. 580; *Warning* (1647, W916), p. 7; Bodl. MS Clarendon 30, fos. 256–7; MS Clarendon 31, fo. 64; Claydon, Verney reels 8–9; *Pragmaticus*: 369.117, sig. R3; 369.219A, sigs. Tv, T3v, 369.221A, sigs. Aav–2; Northants. RO, IC 451; BL, Add. 78221, fos. 5, 98v; *Rugg*, pp. 48–9.
[17] *Pragmaticus*, 369.219A, sigs. Tv, T3v, 369.221A, sigs. Aav–2, 369.239, sig. Eeev, 369.240B, sigs. Fffv, Fff3; Bodl. MS Clarendon 34, fos. 17r–v; BL, Add. 78221, fos. 24v–5, 28.

other than ideology and conviction; and to the likelihood that specific policies – particularly regarding the king – involved political expediency, factional manoeuvring and the desire for popular support. As one commentator argued, politicians 'shift resolutions and friends oftener than shirts'. Attempts to expose such scheming by political factions are evident even in the cheapest genres of print, and such texts can be found within contemporary collections, just as their message about the need to analyse political strategies struck a chord with onlookers like Juxon.[18]

The third way in which contemporaries improved their appreciation of factionalism involved proto-sociological analysis of factional 'structures', and of the relationships on which they were based. Journalists and polemicists argued that factions were loose associations – coalitions or 'confederacies' with more or less serious internal divisions – and recognized that this affected political developments, insofar as compromise proved necessary to maintain unity. In early 1649, therefore, Nedham stressed that the planned proceedings against Charles I reflected the Independents' need to retain the support of radicals ('fantastic John Leydons'), and such ideas about Machiavellian politics were replicated in comments by contemporary onlookers.[19] Writers were also aware that such interest groups were bicameral, and although journalists occasionally detected tension *between* the two Houses, fault lines at Westminster were more often seen as being *vertical* rather than *horizontal*. This was certainly how Juxon understood parliament in the mid 1640s.[20] Moreover, while individual peers were obviously credited with significant power, the leadership of factions was not thought to rest exclusively in the upper House. It was certainly suggested in December 1647 that the Independents sought 'a very great lord to be their head', and that Cromwell served a 'lordly interest', but relations between grandees were generally portrayed in terms of collusion rather than clientage. In mid 1648, indeed, Nedham suggested that the influence of peers was more apparent than real, and that 'the lower is the upper House', and this idea found some support beyond the world of print.[21]

---

[18] Wildman, *Putney*, pp. 8–9; *Militaris*, 346.4, sig. D2v; Bodl. MS Clarendon 34, fos. 17r–v; *Pragmaticus*: 369.207A, sig. Gv; 369.210, sig. K, K2; 369.214, sig. O3v; 369.111A, sigs. L–Lv; DRO, D258/21/1; 'Lewis Dyve', pp. 73, 77; BL, Add. 78221, fo. 10; *Juxon*, pp. 116, 120, 147.

[19] Prynne, *Machivilian*, p. 3; Bodl. MS Clarendon 34, fos. 17, 72v; *Pragmaticus*, 369.239, sig. Eee4; 369.118B, sig. S2; 369.204, sig. D4v; *Juxon*, pp. 34–5; *Montereul*, ii. 109; Claydon, Verney reel 8.

[20] *Aulicus*, 275.229, pp. 1088–9; *Certaine Informations*: 36.18, p. 138; 36.25, p.198; *Scout*: 485.47, pp. 393–4, 396; 485.80, p. 640; 485.82, pp. 653, 656; *Britanicus*, 286.130, pp. 1111, 1117; 286.065, p.514; *Kingdomes*, 214.007, p. 49; 211.088, p. 705; *Juxon*, pp. 34–5.

[21] Bodl. MS Clarendon 30, fo. 233; Lilburne, *Two* (1647, L2193), pp. 4–5; Lilburne, *Additional* (1647, L2112A), pp. 17–23; *Cromwell's Last* (1648, L1979), pp. 2, 5; *Pragmaticus*: 369.217, sig. R4v; 369.218, sig. S; *Pyms Juncto* (1643, P4306); *Letter*, p. 9; BL, Add. 78221, fo. 5; *Baillie*, ii. 344; 'Twysden narrative', iii. 175; Warw. RO, CR136/B68e.

This understanding of party structure made it possible to identify small groups of leaders and grandees. In reflecting on the 'fiery spirits' in the early months of the Long Parliament, therefore, the names of Viscount Saye, Lord Brooke and John Pym – 'the great Parliament man' – cropped up regularly in parliamentary reporting, and in the case of the latter two their deaths were also widely reported.[22] Recognition of their power and importance spread far and wide with amazing speed, and although this was to be expected among those who haunted Westminster Hall, it can also be observed much further afield. Sir Humphrey Mildmay regularly referred to Pym (or 'Pimp') *and his company*, and described him as 'a fine deviser' of 'treasons', but more remarkable are men like George Preston, vicar of Rothersthorpe (Northamptonshire), who in December 1640 named his livestock after 'ten of the active parliament men'. Thomas Wyatt, meanwhile, recognized that this group formed 'the sticklers in Parliament'.[23] Following the attempted arrest of the 'five members' in January 1642, an Irish soldier called Francis Edmunds was overheard at a Covent Garden tavern, saying that 'if he knew where Mr Pym, Mr Hampden and Mr Strode were to be found he would ease the king of further trouble by them'. At another drinking den a Cambridge medic called Thomas Shawberry was heard referring to 'King Pym' as a 'rascal' whom he wished to assassinate. During the summer of 1642 similar reports flooded in from across the country. A Sussex pewterer, James Chapman, was overheard claiming that Pym 'was a traitor and a knave', while William Tucke of Exeter – who was described as a servant to Edward Wood – was accused of getting a local scrivener to copy a 'scandalous song . . . concerning several lords and other parliament men', and confessed to having heard a musician singing about the 'five members'.[24]

Such comments reveal an ability to engage in prosopographical analysis, and this became much more sophisticated after Pym's death in 1643. By this stage the leading enthusiasts for war were thought to include Saye ('a star in the firmament') and Oliver St John ('Pym's successor', or 'our second Pym'), as well as Sir Henry Vane and Lord Wharton, while their rivals were said to be led by the Earl of Essex, and later by Denzil Holles, Sir Philip Stapleton and Sir John Clotworthy. Here, too, it is striking that such men

---

[22] *Sence* (1643, S2551); *Pyms Juncto*; *New Orders* (1642, N693), p. 4; Chestlin, *Persecutio*, p. 53; *Letter from Mercurius* (1643, L1489B), pp. 3, 9; *Britanicus*, 286.016, p.128; Durham UL, MSP 30, fo. 3v, *Diurnall*, 504.021, p. 165.

[23] FSL, W.b.600, p. 192; BL, Add. 11045, fo. 146v; Jansson, ii. 246; *Walker Revised*, p. 283; Bodl. MS Top.Oxon.C.378, p. 346.

[24] *PJ*, ii. 8, 9, 39, 42, 43; *Book of Examinations*, p. 39; Devon RO, ECA Book 64, fo. 7v.

were recognizable to members of the public, rather than merely to political commentators. Thus, in January 1644, Sarah Dennis of St Giles in the Fields was indicted for describing Saye as a 'roundhead rogue', and for saying 'a pox take him'.[25] This indicates that the ability to identify factional leaders was not limited to men from the political elite, and as factional divisions hardened, a broader range of observers appreciated the oligarchic nature of such groups, agreed on the identity of their leaders and concurred regarding the emergence of new power-brokers. Onlookers thus noted the rise of Oliver Cromwell, who by May 1648 had even been labelled 'King Oliver', and newspapers frequently referred to Cromwell and Saye ('that pestilent Machiavellian') as 'the two fathers of the faction'. John Lisle was described as 'a grandee of the faction', while Lord Wharton and Nathaniel Fiennes were described as the 'two twins of valour', and attempts were even made to connect such groups with administrators like Gabriel Becke and journalists like John Dillingham.[26] Moreover, this 'cabinet council' of 'junto-men' – who 'steer the affairs of the whole kingdom' – was also fairly widely known outside parliament. Their role in initiating policies and legislation came to be widely understood, and astute analysts recognized that what mattered was not the number of these grandees, but their quality and zeal. Viscount Saye was described as someone who 'with a twine thread leads about our wise nobility', and grandees thus came to be styled 'hocas-pocasses' and 'jugglers', terminology that spread fairly quickly through the world of pamphleteers and journalists.[27]

Identifying grandees was only part of the story, however, and the process of analysing parliamentary factions also involved scrutinizing the *internal dynamic* of such groups, and the relationships between leaders and their supporters. These explanations went beyond merely describing Sir Thomas Wroth as the 'fool' or 'monkey' of Edmund Prideaux, portraying John Swinfen as Prideaux's 'spaniel', and deriding Cornelius Holland as 'Sir Henry Vane's zanie', and they also went beyond identifying kinship ties

[25] *Britanicus*: 286.025, pp. 193–4; 286.021, pp. 163–4; 286.020, p. 154; *Baillie*, ii. 133, 136, 141–2; *Juxon*, pp. 34, 52, 53, 75–6, 84, 104, 131, 154; LMA, MJ/SR/939/34.

[26] *Juxon*, p. 157; Bodl. MS Clarendon 30, fo. 233; *Pragmaticus*: 369.111A, sig. L3; 369.203, sig. C2v; 369.227, sig. Oo; 369.207B, sig. Gv; 369.208, sig. H3; 369.106, sig. F2v; 369.217, sig. R4v; Prynne, *Machivilian*, p. 3; *Passes* (1648, P659), pp. 3–5; *Tricks* (T2272), p. 3; *Letter*, p. 4; *Cuckoos-nest* (1648, C7459), p. 6; *Perfect Summary*, 528.03, p. 23; *Bellicus*, 279.19, p. 7; *Elencticus*, 312.06, p. 46.

[27] *Baillie*, ii. 141, 216, 335, 401; *CCSP*, iii. 267; 'Lewis Dyve', pp. 57, 60, 68, 84, 89; Claydon, Verney reel 8; Bodl. MS Clarendon 30, fo. 233; *Pragmaticus*: 369.119, sig. T2v; 369.219A, sig. Tv; 369.228, sig. Pp3; 369.221A, sig. Bb2; *Melancholicus*, 344.49A, pp. 295–6; Walker, *Relations*, p. 23; Lilburne, *Additional Plea*, pp. 17–23; Prynne, *Machivilian*, p. 7.

between men like Anthony Nicoll and John Pym.[28] Moreover, while it was
sometimes recognized that individual MPs were 'servants and tenants' of
peers, and while the aristocratic connections of men like Michael
Oldisworth and Robert Scawen were occasionally outlined, members
were rarely characterized as being 'clients' or 'men of business' in a straightforward way. Observers recognized that grandees relied on the support of
others, and that MPs gravitated around them, and Nedham argued that
Lord Wharton 'thrusts his nose into every man's breech, to under feel all
humours in zeal to the cause', just as Vane did in the Commons.[29] Such
comments suggest that the hierarchies within factions involved not just
power, but also charisma and political views, and in developing these ideas
observers offered interpretations of factional allegiance that were both
complex and challenging. In essence, most MPs who could be connected
with particular factions were categorized as being either 'politicks' and
'confederates' or 'mechanicks' and 'creatures'. Collectively such individuals
represent 'puppets', upon whom the grandees worked by 'gulling and
deluding', but it was also possible to make important distinctions between
different types of people.[30] The 'politicks', therefore, were active and
aligned 'backbenchers' – the 'zanyes', 'jack-puddings' and 'agitators' –
who were regarded as 'the common vote-drivers of the faction', or as the
'journeymen' who served the interests of grandees. Such men could dom-
inate committees and intimidate lesser MPs, and these 'bilbo-worthies' were
thought to 'keep all the rest in awe, and . . . wind up their fellow members
like Jacks to provide roast meat for their myrmidions' and to 'carry the votes
which way they please, and set the House upon wheels'. Their number
included Herbert Morley (one of the 'firemen of Independency'), John
Swinfen (who had his 'wages' paid by Denzil Holles's 'tribe') and Walter
Long, who was characterized as the Presbyterian 'parliament driver', and
who was accused of rallying support for particular votes with 'tamperings
and violence'. Nedham referred to such men as 'the blind harpies of
Presbytery, who have screwed their voting instruments to the highest
peg', and such 'tame patriots' ensured that no 'juggling' could be affected
'but by consent of the Hocus-Pocusses'. What is interesting about such

---

[28] *Pragmaticus*: 369.238A, Ddd2v; 369.239, sig. Eee3; 369.214, sigs. O2, O3; *Moderate*, 413.2012, sig. M3v;
   Baillie, iii. 16; *Second Centurie* (1648, E317D), p. 4; *Letter*, p. 7.
[29] *Troublers* (1648, E3067), p. 2; *Anti-Projector* (1646, A3504), p. 4; *Newes from Pembroke* (1648, B2968);
   Pembroke's Speech (1647, E80A); *Lord of Pembrokes* (1648, M3169A); Walker, *Relations*, pp. 1–3;
   Pragmaticus, 369.111A, sig. L3.
[30] *Westminster Projects*, 710.5, p. 4; *Elencticus*, 312.55, sig. Hhh4v; *Pragmaticus*, 369.238A, sig. Ddd;
   Prynne, *Machivilian*, p. 7; Walker, *Relations*, sigs. A4–A4v.

analysis, however, is not only that assessments about the composition and strength of different groups became common in newspapers and pamphlets from 1647 onwards, but also that it filtered into wider society, at least in terms of private correspondence among the gentry.[31] The 'mechanicks', meanwhile, were a far larger group, who tended to sit in 'tame silence', as 'timerous, self-seeking or time-serving warping members'. Either through fear, self-interest or the desire to 'please a prevailing party', such men were said to 'care not what they pass or vote'. Although their identity remained much more obscure, they probably included those whom Clement Walker called the '*vulgar* Independents', who were 'but the props and properties to the grandees', and those whom Nedham called 'the Brazen heads', who were 'taught to speak Aye or No, which they deliver at certain hours by direction, just like Cheapside clock-strikers'. They were, in other words, lobby-fodder and 'voting instruments', and Nedham derided them as 'state-catamites', who were 'packed' into parliament 'to carry and vote', and as men 'upon whom any votes whatsoever may be begotten'.[32]

What makes such analysis particularly striking is that it offers a challenge to simplistic assumptions about 'patrons' and 'clients'. This is because it was 'mechanicks' who were most often regarded as clients of the grandees, while the 'politicks' were thought to be excluded from inner circles, and even kept in the dark on key issues. Indeed, the latter were also considered to be much more ideological than the grandees, who were thought to be interested in power rather than in political principles or religious purity. Walker suggested that the 'politicks' pursued factional goals 'with more seriousness' than their leaders, and he considered them to be ideologically naive in 'not perceiving anything of design' in the positions taken by grandees, and of failing to recognize cynicism and power politics. Contemporaries also suggested that factions were divided between 'pure' and 'mixed' strands, and between 'royal' and 'real' wings.[33] Some even suggested that there was greater unity *between* grandees than *within* specific factions, Walker suggesting that in private the 'grandees of each party . . . close together for their own advancement'. They competed, on this account, not over substantive issues, but over 'who shall sit nearest to the throne', and Independents like

---

[31] Walker, *Relations*, p. 23; *Pragmaticus*: 369.221A, sigs. Aa-v, Bb2; 369.119, sigs. T2-v; 369.117, sig. Rv; 369.205, sigs. E, E2; Chestlin, *Persecutio*, p. 53; *Melancholicus*, 342.2, p. 16; *Moon*, 248.06, p. 56; *Militaris*, 346.4, sig. D4v; *OPH*, xvi. 91, 156; Claydon, Verney reel 8; *Elencticus*, 312.55, sig. Hhh4v; *Cuckoos-nest*, p. 6.

[32] *Aulicus*, 275.302, p. 1333; *New Presbyterian* (1647, P4021), pp. 10–11; Walker, *Relations*, p. 143; *Pragmaticus*: 369.238A, sig. Ddd; 369.119, sig. T2; 369.205, sig. E; Chestlin, *Persecutio*, p. 33.

[33] *Pragmaticus*, 369.221A, sig. Bb2; *Baillie*, iii. 16; Walker, *Relations*, pp. 1–3, 77, 112–13; *Royall* (1648, H861), p. 5; *Letter* (1645, L1447), sig. A2.

Saye were perceived to be cunning as well as oligarchic, in terms of having 'a footing in every junto'. The natural corollary of this, of course, was that 'royal' Independents had betrayed 'real' Independents, and that this increased the need to dissimulate. In other words, it was argued that Independent grandees needed to deceive and delude their supporters, in order to 'seem as real in their reciprocal oppositions as those silly ones who are in earnest', and also to purchase their loyalty with financial rewards.[34]

By exploring what people understood by the term 'faction', as well as how this concept was applied to parliamentary politics – in terms of personalities and policies, the shifting balance of power and the structure of different groups – it thus becomes clear that contemporary analysis both complements and contrasts with modern scholarship. Although few went as far as Nedham in embracing a balance of 'interests', many perceived that adversarial politics emerged in the early 1640s, that factions were driven by ideology as well as by the desire for power, and that MPs were driven by clientage as well as principles.[35] More importantly, this sophisticated analysis was made accessible to the public through pamphlets and newspapers, and came to be echoed in the observations of readers, at least to some degree, and at least among the gentry and the middling sort.

iii Analysing processes

In addition to analysing the nature and structure of parliamentarian factions, contemporaries also studied the means by which 'parties' exploited the political process, in terms of the drift towards secrecy and clandestine behaviour, the attempt to control membership of either House, and the determination to manipulate proceedings for political ends. This involved developing the rhetoric of an 'assault' on parliamentary politics, and here, too, claims regarding 'underhand dealing' and 'artificial practices' made a significant impression upon political discourse, in the sense that political commentary and print journalism seem to have informed the public perception of parliament.[36]

---

[34] Walker, *Relations*, pp. 1–3; *Pragmaticus*: 369.105, p. 37; 369.119, sig. T2v; *Westminster Projects*, 710.5, pp. 3–4; *Tell Tale* (1648, T623A); *Juxon*, p. 116; Bodl. MS Clarendon 34, fo. 17; Wildman, *Putney*, pp. 10–11, 32; *Royall Quarrell*, p. 5.

[35] Adamson, 'Parliamentary management', pp. 42, 45; Kishlansky, 'Saye what?', pp. 919–20; B. Worden, '"Wit in a Roundhead"', in *Political Culture and Cultural Politics in Early Modern England*, ed. S. Amussen and M. Kishlansky (Manchester, 1995), pp. 317–19.

[36] *Reasons* (1647, R589), p. 6; Buchanan, *Explanation* (1645, B5272), p. 56; *Aulicus*, 275.132, pp. 424–5.

The first thing to note about perceptions of parliamentary processes is that secrecy was more often noticed than considered problematic. The tendency to sit 'close', and for debates to be undertaken behind locked doors, clearly struck observers, but it could be deemed justifiable in relation to highly sensitive issues, and it was recognized that some things were 'not thought fit (as yet) to be divulged'.[37] Nevertheless, there gradually developed a sense that parliament was rather too willing to impose secrecy without good cause, that there were too many surreptitious meetings, and that matters were too often transacted 'hugger-mugger, to the prejudice of the public service'. Thus, while complaints inevitably emerged about the secretive nature of the House of Lords, more worrying was the propensity for the Commons to be run like a closed committee rather than as an open court of judicature.[38] Opposition to such secrecy would eventually be led by radicals like John Lilburne, who repeatedly called for parliament's doors to be flung open, 'that the people might have free and uninterrupted access', and to 'hear, see and consider' what was being done. However, Royalists, too, regarded secrecy as a challenge, and repeatedly promised to reveal parliamentary proceedings, with the assistance of 'a pretty nimble familiar' that 'haunts the Houses and every committee'. More importantly, such practices and comments fed into public discourse, and they help to explain why men like Juxon and Evelyn noted that 'transactions of state are with little noise', and that matters were 'clandestinely transacted'.[39]

By looking more closely at contemporary analysis, moreover, it becomes clear that commentators also developed a subtle understanding about the nature and timing of the challenge to conventional practices, in terms of attempts to control membership and manipulate proceedings. From the treatment of courtiers and monopolists in the opening weeks of the Long Parliament to the readmission of members who had defected to the king after 1642, critics repeatedly detected biased decisions regarding the composition of parliament. The Self Denying Ordinance, for example, was described as little more than a 'deceit', since MPs with military interests would still wield power over decisions regarding war and peace. More importantly, onlookers analysed electoral influence, in terms of 'underhand' proceedings, organized electioneering and ineffective vetting, and the

---

[37] For example: *Certaine Informations*, 36.20, p. 158; *Diurnall*, 513.52B, p. 3; *Kingdomes*, 214.105, p. 845; *Occurrences*, 465.3029, sig. Ff4v.

[38] *Pragmaticus*, 369.111A, sig. L2v; Buchanan, *Short* (1645, B5273), p. 59; Bodl. MS Clarendon 30, fo. 286; Harris, *Antipodes* (1647, H42), sig. B.

[39] *Occurrences*, 465.5006, p.45; ST, iv. 1273–4; *Pragmaticus*: 369.114, sog. Ov; 369.221A, sigs. Aa–v; 370.06B, sig. F3v; *Juxon*, p. 48; BL, Add. 78221, fo. 11.

Committee for Elections was dubbed the Committee of 'Affection' for pursuing 'undue courses' in specific cases.[40] Although such grievances first emerged in the early months of the Long Parliament, they became increasingly acute as years passed, not least during the 'recruiter' elections. These were perceived to have been instigated and managed for factional purposes, in order to return kinsmen, servants and tenants, and contemporaries became extremely familiar with the idea of a 'packed' parliament. Amid talk of new elections in 1650, one royalist newspaper expected that steps would be taken to ensure that no 'honest' man would be chosen, 'least he discover the knavery of the rest', and such cynicism was widespread by 1654, when Andrew Huddleston of Hutton criticized 'a coarse parliament' that Cromwell had 'chosen'.[41] The reason for scrutinizing electoral practices so closely was because these were thought to have been done very purposefully, and influence over membership became intimately linked to ideas about the politicization of parliamentary processes. Allegations began to circulate that letters, petitions, motions and bills were blocked or promoted according to factional interests, and as with so many other allegations regarding the 'corruption' of parliament, these were duly noted by readers and onlookers like Juxon and Sir Lewis Dyve.[42]

What this attested to, contemporaries believed, was very deliberate planning of parliamentary business by factional grandees. Nedham exposed meetings between prominent figures like Lord Wharton and Nathaniel Fiennes, and such organization was thought to have ensured that the timing of petitions was carefully arranged; that speeches were 'elaborately composed' and 'read out of a hat'; and that it was possible to 'drive every vote to their own ends'.[43] Once again, such claims emerged fairly quickly but became more frequent and forceful over time, not least as war drew MPs out of the House. Poor attendance was frequently noted by journalists, who even provided readers with the precise number of members who were present, especially when the Commons came close to being inquorate, and when only three or four peers sat in the Lords. Likewise, they pointed

---

[40] *Diurnall:* 511.20B, p. 8; 511.15B, sig. Q2v; *Complaint* (1643, C5620), pp. 11–12; *Kingdomes*, 214.85, pp. 681–2; *Letter from a Scholler* (1642, L1436), p. 15; Chestlin, *Persecutio*, pp. 57, 59.

[41] *Appeale* (1647, E2944), sigs. A3r–v; *Darkness* (1647, W3585), p. 8; *Key* (1648, K387), p. 2; *List of the Names* (1648, E317B), p. 8; Musgrave, *Fourth*, pp. 2, 8, 18; *Pragmaticus*, 369.211, sigs. Lv–L3; *Moon*, 248.37, p.299; *York Depositions*, p. 66.

[42] Musgrave, *Another* (1646, M3144); Musgrave, *Fourth*, p. 18; *Moderate*, 413.2036, sig. Nn3; *Certain Queries* (1647, C1739), p. 3; *Windsor Projects*, 710.3, p. 4; Buchanan, *Explanation*, p. 54; *Alarum* (1646, O618), p. 10; *Anti-Projector*, p. 4; *Juxon*, p. 125; 'Lewis Dyve', p. 92.

[43] *Complaint*, p. 14; *Pragmaticus*, 369.106, sig. F2v; *Warning*, pp. 8–9; Buchanan, *Explanation*, p. 46; *Letter from an Ejected* (1648, S26), p. 3; *Reasons*, p. 7.

out when numbers rose dramatically because of a 'call' of either House, and drew particular attention to the suspicious absence of notable figures like the Earl of Northumberland, whose movements were monitored by astute readers.[44] More importantly, commentators recognized that this thinning process enabled grandees to predict voting behaviour and manipulate votes, and 'vote-drivers' allegedly mastered the art of influencing attendance to win crucial divisions. Thus, grandees apparently ensured that 'emissaries' stood by the door of the Commons, to 'call in' members of their faction 'to vote what they pleased', and to 'advance their design upon notice of a small appearance in the House'. On other occasions, meanwhile, factions were thought to have delayed debates and votes when the composition of the House was unpropitious, and even to have stifled debate entirely. As early as 1643, it was suggested that the prevailing tactic was not to win debates by 'reason and strength of argument', but rather by 'putting it to the question and carrying it by most voices', not least because most MPs were thought to be incapable of understanding policy issues, and to prefer following their leaders by 'implicit faith'.[45] And from the early 1640s commentators also became aware that measures could be pushed through a 'thin' House, while MPs were 'in bed or at play, or some worse employment', most famously in order to pass controversial resolutions such as the 'Declaration of Dislike' (March 1647) and the votes of 'no further addresses' (January 1648). The prevalence of such allegations ensured that these tactics were widely understood. Juxon recognized that the first of these decisions – a response to agitation within the army – was promoted by Presbyterians late at night, when the Commons was sparsely populated, and royalists later argued that measures to block an inquiry into MPs who had been excluded from the 1656 parliament were 'surreptitiously gained' in the absence of most members.[46]

On other occasions, of course, techniques for stifling debate were perceived to have been more forceful in nature. Prynne referred to 'menacing speeches', and other commentators outlined methods for silencing inconvenient speakers, and the threat of physical force was seen as a device with which grandees terrified members into acquiescence or absence. This

[44] *Diurnall*: 504.027, p. 209; 504.248, p. 1993; 504.272, p. 2186; *Elencticus*, 312.56, sig. Iii3; *Pragmaticus*: 369.239, sigs. Eee2–v, Eee4; 369.238A, sig. Ddd3; Cumbria RO, D/MUS/5/5/Box 89/Bundle 1/16; *Letter from a Scholler*, p. 15.

[45] *Letter from a Scholler*, p. 15; Chestlin, *Persecutio*, p. 60; *OPH*, xvi. 91, 156; *Brief* (1647, P3908), p. 10; *Complaint*, p. 12.

[46] *Complaint*, p. 14; *OPH*, xvi. 77–8; Walker, *Relations*, pp. 73–4; *Pragmaticus*: 369.230, sigs. Ttv–Tt2v; 369.227, sig. Nn4v; Chestlin, *Persecutio*, pp. 59, 60; *Juxon*, p. 155; Bodl. MS Clarendon 52, fos. 287–8.

formed part of the charge against the 'eleven members' in June 1647, but it was also suggested that the votes regarding the militia on 22 July 1647 – which precipitated the tumultuous 'forcing of the Houses' – resulted from the Commons being 'very thin' once many members had been 'driven away by menaces'. Royalists claimed that Sir Henry Vane 'openly threatened' to use the army to persuade Presbyterians to withdraw from the Commons, thereby enabling Independents to exploit a numerical advantage.[47] Ultimately, of course, contemporaries became aware that it was possible to affect the balance of power in parliament permanently, by means of the mob, impeachment or 'purge'. It was understood that crowds ensured the departure of royalists in 1641 and 1642, that MPs purged 'rotten members' to enable new elections, and that the Solemn League and Covenant was enforced to prevent Independents from taking their seats. More famously, the attempt to 'sift and winnow' parliament in June 1647 – with the impeachment of eleven Presbyterian MPs – was widely discussed in print, where it was portrayed as an 'act of terror' to 'fright' colleagues and strengthen Independents' grip on parliament. An equally furious public debate accompanied 'Pride's Purge' in December 1648, when readers were provided with the number and names of MPs who were forcibly excluded from the Commons.[48] Yet again, reports and allegations in print generated comments and speculation among readers, who evidently picked up and passed on subsequent analysis of the various groups that could be discerned within the Rump, the parliamentary purges and exclusions in the 1650s, and the disputes over membership of the House in 1659.[49]

Once again, therefore, pamphlets and newspapers serve a range of useful purposes. They signal sophisticated attempts to assess the impact of factions at Westminster, reveal a perception that the 'assault' on traditional practices began in the earliest phase of the Long Parliament, and highlight how such ideas and arguments filtered down into the kinds of cheap print that were consumed across the country and across the social spectrum. This helps to explain why members of the public discussed the fate of parliament within their sociable networks, and why they echoed the sentiments of polemicists and journalists.

---

[47] Prynne, *Machivilian*, pp. 5–6; Chestlin, *Persecutio*, p. 62; *Baillie*, ii. 99; *Aulicus*, 275.302, np; *OPH*, xvi. 75; Walker, *Relations*, pp. 40, 50.

[48] *Cabinet* (1660, D1225), p. 4; Chestlin, *Persecutio*, p. 62; *Warning*, pp. 2, 3; Walker, *Relations*, sigs. A4–A4v, pp. 36–7, 48–9, 60, 98; Prynne, *Machivilian*, p. 27; *Pragmaticus*: 369.101, p. 5; 369.238A; *Diurnall*: 504.008, p. 57; 504.029, p. 225; 504.280, pp. 2252–4.

[49] DRO, D258/21/1; *Juxon*, p. 162; 'Lewis Dyve', p. 68; Claydon, Verney reel 8; BL, Add. 78221, fos. 5, 24–v, 26, 27, 30–v; *Pragmaticus*, 369.239, sigs. Eee3v–4; *Presentment* (1660, C6219); *Rugg*, pp. 23, 42.

iv Analysing committees and cash

More worrying even than 'management' of the two Houses was the danger that they would be sidelined entirely. This was the third key area in which pamphlets and newspapers offered readers detailed and challenging accounts of factional behaviour, and in which they influenced the perceptions of readers. These claims centred on committees as arena for factional politics, and as the mechanisms by which business was controlled, and by which the functions of court and state were hijacked, and the result was a rhetoric about the usurpation of parliament, about financial corruption and ultimately about tyranny.[50]

The 'illegality' of committees and 'committee law' became a pervasive strand within Civil War analysis. It united writers from across the political spectrum, and is evident in commentators as diverse as John Lilburne and William Prynne, and once again it began with allegations about how political influence was brought to bear on membership of key bodies. David Buchanan suggested that Independents 'screwed themselves in employment' and got 'a main hand in all businesses', while Clement Walker claimed that 'active speaking men' named one another to 'every committee', and that 'friends' and factions ensured that members of committees were 'birds of a feather'. Others suggested that the Speaker 'diligently' watched 'the eye of Pym' when committees were being created, and that factions planted 'their instruments' as chairmen in 'all places of action'. As such, commentators analysed particular committees, demonstrated how individuals were intruded and 'cashiered', and even claimed that grandees responded to situations in which specific committees could no longer be controlled by creating new ones or forming secretive sub-committees.[51] By thus controlling membership, factions were thought to be capable of controlling proceedings. Observers recognized 'notable friending' on specific issues, and 'much siding and engaging one another in their committees', and they highlighted cases where 'packed' committees proceeded in a blatantly biased fashion. Committees were thought to provide another means by which to smother particular business and favour specific interests, and one former MP suggested that such bodies served 'the revenge, envy, avarice, or the corrupt humours and passions of the authors'. As a result it was argued that 'the remaining part

---

[50] *Letter* (1643, L1757), p. 4; *Letter from a Scholler*, p. 6; *Engagements* (1647, D664), p. 63.

[51] Lilburne, *Defiance*; Prynne, *Magna* (1648, P4020), p. 3; Buchanan, *Explanation*, p. 52; Walker, *Relations*, pp. 4–5, 53; *Pragmaticus*: 369.222A, sig. Dd; 369.103, sig. C2; 369.238A, sig. Ddd3; BL, Add. 31954, fo. 182; Chestlin, *Persecutio*, p. 61; *Anti-Projector*, p. 4; *New Charge* (1647, N594), p. 5.

of the House are but cyphers ... to ratify what is forejudged by the said committees'. It was also alleged that committee reports were susceptible to factional manipulation, so that parliament was 'abused and misled', and that political manoeuvring resulted in either excessive secrecy or overt publicity, to the extent that a 'rabble' could be permitted to attend specific meetings to harangue opponents.[52] Well-connected observers like John Evelyn heard about 'clandestine committees' and biased machinations from powerful friends, but Sir Roger Twysden gained similar insights by reading newspapers. Indeed, given that the figure of the corrupt committee-man even appeared in broadside verses, it is possible that cheap print informed Mary Moore's claim that the Committee of the Navy included 'the basest rogues in Christendom'. Printed texts may also have provoked the statement that 'committees sat to cosen and cheat the people', for which Mary Davis, the wife of a Clerkenwell brewer, was indicted in 1645.[53]

While all committees were regarded as being susceptible to factional manipulation, particular concern was obviously expressed regarding 'standing' committees. Complaints were made that such bodies operated secretively and clandestinely, and one observer explained that the Committee of Revenue 'meets but seldom, sometimes not full, and most times ... full of great causes', and that it generally sat only between 8am and 9am.[54] Especially suspicious were executive bodies such as the Committee of Safety (1642), the importance of which would not have been lost on readers. It was widely derided as a factional tool, and became the model for grumbling about 'close' committees, even in popular verse, and Juxon referred to it scathingly as 'the committee of destruction'. Its successor, the Committee of Both Kingdoms (1644), was likewise recognized as being a factional creation and as an Independent cabal, not merely by Westminster insiders like Robert Baillie, but also by Londoners like Juxon, doubtless because machinations regarding its inception, powers and performance were widely reported.[55] Once again, the rhetorical heat surrounding such bodies

---

[52] *Key*, p. 5; *Westminster Projects*, 710.5, p. 1; *Complaint*, pp. 10, 14; *Anti-Projector*, p. 4; *Letter from an Ejected*, p. 10; *OPH*, xvi. 75–80; Walker, *Relations*, pp. 4–5; *Gangraena*, iii. 189–90; Chestlin, *Persecutio*, pp. 21–2, 26, 60–1; *Aulicus*, 275.302, p. 1332; *Diurnall*, 504.227, p. 1826; *Pearle* (1646, O632A), p. 3; Harris, *Antipodes*, sig. B.

[53] BL, Add. 78221, fos. 9–10; 'Twysden narrative', ii. 60–1, iii. 125; *Committee-Mans* (1647, C5565); *HMC Tenth Report IV*, p. 97; LMA, MJ/SR/970/158.

[54] Walker, *Relations*, pp. 54, 55–8, 65; *Oxinden and Peyton Letters*, p. 80; BL: Add. 28001, fo. 43; Add. 22619, fo. 208; Chestlin, *Persecutio*, p. 60.

[55] *Certaine Informations*, 36.06, p.48; 36.57, p. 450; *Letter from a Scholler*, p. 18; Chestlin, *Persecutio*, p. 60; *Aulicus*, 275.113, pp. 166–7; *Letter from Mercurius*, p. 2; Beinecke, Osborn b.52, Volume 2, p.128; *Juxon*, pp. 27, 47; *Baillie*, ii. 178, 187; *Diurnall*, 504.032, p. 250; *Britanicus*, 286.027A, pp. 207–8; Buchanan, *Short*, pp. 51–3, 57; Buchanan, *Explanation*, p. 13.

increased dramatically as time passed, reaching a peak in the late 1640s and early 1650s. The Derby House Committee (1648) was labelled as the 'packed committee of juglers', the 'cabinet junto' of 'hirelings', and 'the fraternity of Hocus Pocus', and it was said to be home to the 'new princes' and to the 'states'. Such language persisted after the establishment of the Republic. The Council of State – 'this jugglers Hall' – was seen as being equally secretive and dangerous, which prompted concerted efforts to expose its proceedings and dealings.[56] In these cases, as with all committees, allegations centred on composition, processes and power, and writers and readers alike appreciated factional struggle over membership, engaged in detailed and entertaining prosopographical analysis, and observed the creation of sub-committees, most famously to exclude the Scots from negotiations with the king in 1645. Indeed, such habits remained evident throughout the 1650s, when men like Evelyn dissected subsequent incarnations of the Council.[57] More important still was the feeling that executive committees provided the supreme demonstration of how factions sidelined parliament, and of the separation of power and interests between grandees and 'real Independents'. The 'cabinet' at Derby House was thought to epitomize the structure of factional politics, with a tiny core of Independents being privy to planning, strategy and information, and knowing 'more of affairs abroad than the common vote-drivers', and with MPs being reduced to little more than 'journeymen'. Similarly, the Council of State was accused of being 'made on purpose ... to gull the Commons and cramp the petty toes of the republic in the dark', and it was said to play 'hocus pocus tricks with the deluded Commons', who thus became little more than 'puppets' or 'state pocasses'. Once more, such criticisms were echoed by onlookers like Juxon, who responded to the Committee of Both Kingdoms by arguing that 'there wants nothing now but a dictator'. Evelyn, meanwhile, claimed that the Derby House Committee sought to 'govern the kingdom'.[58]

Where this led, of course, was to an appreciation that factions – especially the Independents – had hijacked key functions of both court and state. This

---

[56] For example: *Pragmaticus:* 369.118B, sig. Sv; 369.223, sigs. Eev, Ee4v; 369.219A, sigs. Tv, T2v; 369.210, sigs. K2, K4; 369.227, sig. Nn4v; 370.01, sig. Av; *Considerations* (1648, C1697), sig. A2; *Westminster Projects,* 710.1, p. 3; *Elencticus,* 312.18, p.134; *Moon,* 248.01, p. 3.

[57] *Juxon,* p. 46; *Pragmaticus,* 369.118B, sig. Sv; Add. 78221, fos. 88–v.

[58] Walker, *Relations,* pp. 45, 77, 115–17, 141, 143, 152; *Considerations,* sig. A2; *Pragmaticus:* 369.221A, sig. Bb2; 369.213, sig. N; 369.212, sig. Mv; 369.245, sig. Lll2; 370.01, sig. Av, A2v; 370.09B, sigs. I2v–3; 370.04B, sigs. D3, D4; *Juxon,* pp. 46–7; BL, Add. 78221, fo. 5.

was implicit in rhetoric about a 'cabinet council', which was evident in press and public commentary about the emergence of a new 'court' at Whitehall (as early as January 1648), and about the resemblance between the Derby House Committee and a 'state'. It was also evident, of course, in the language of 'King Pym' and 'King Oliver', which was common in prose, verse and speech, as well as in discussions of the Cromwellian council.[59] Much more significantly, however, the usurpation of executive authority was thought to involve the seizure and deployment of the kingdom's resources, notably in relation to patronage and the public purse. People understood that finances were the 'sinews of war', and a source of power, and like all good investigators, they knew to 'follow the money'. Much effort thus went into understanding the 'cunnings' and 'crafts' used to 'catch moneys'. Indeed, by alleging that parliament had 'milked' over £40 million from the people, there emerged apocalyptic language regarding 'state pick-pockets', and about 'locusts, caterpillars, and horse-leeches', not least in terms of how money was accounted for and managed.[60]

Contemporary attempts to interpret the politics of parliamentarian finances began early in the war. In 1644, *Aulicus* recognized that factionalism and oligarchy were predicated upon monetary control, and observers not only monitored how unprecedented sums of money were raised, but also explored the mechanisms and structures through which this was managed and distributed. This meant identifying the chief 'millers' of money, scrutinizing the executive committees that 'engross all the profits', and critiquing those who administered the system. These were the men that Clement Walker styled the 'excoriating rabble of pestiferous vermin'. Commentators drew attention to 'the multiplicity of money committees' (especially the Committee of Revenue), in order to demonstrate that the Independents were 'the nimblest to harken after moneys', and that they 'thrust themselves' into positions where 'fingering of money' took place. Critics also recognized that 'he that commands the money commands the men', and as a result attempts were made to analyse how money was used to 'over-awe and over-power' MPs.[61] It thus became clear that money was used to reward friends while being withheld from rivals. Buchanan claimed that Independents would 'pleasure some

---

[59] 'Lewis Dyve', p. 84; BL, Add. 78221, fos. 5, 61–2; *Letter*, p. 12.
[60] *Eye-Salve* (1647, E3936), sigs. Av, A3v ; Buchanan, *Explanation*, p. 56; *OPH*, xvi. 122; Prynne, *Magna*, p. 3; Walker, *Relations*, p. 8; *Grand Account* (1647, G1486); *London's Account* (1647, L2915); *Mod. Intelligencer*, 419.100, p. 890; *Pragmaticus*: 369.205, sig. E3v; 369.245, sig. Lll2; 369.101, p. 7; 369.111A, sigs. L–Lv; *Moon*, 248.29, p. 229.
[61] *Turn Apace* (1648, T3264), pp. 3–4; *Aulicus*: 275.207, pp. 827–8; 275.205B, p. 814; *Eye-Salve*, sig. A3v ; Walker, *Relations*, pp. 5, 141, 145; *Pragmaticus*: 369.109A, sig. I4; 369.2167, sig. Q4; *Letter*, p. 11; Buchanan, *Explanation*, pp. 53, 55–6; *OPH*, xvi. 122.

whom they do affect, and put nack upon others whom they do dislike', and that they distributed money 'for the most part among themselves', with some MPs making small fortunes. Such 'corruption' was thought to date from the earliest phase of the Civil War – not least with financial payments to the Speaker – and to have become progressively more severe, to the point where money and offices were showered on kinsmen and allies, and where the promise of financial rewards provided an incentive for 'undone merchants and decayed bankrupts' to seek election.[62]

Connected to such criticisms, of course, were complaints about the absence of mechanisms by which to monitor places of trust and account for public money. Although committees were appointed to deal with the danger that 'standing waters did gather filth', these were dismissed as attempts to 'blind the eyes of the world', and complaints mounted about financial malfeasance. Thus, while financial corruption was considered inevitable during a long parliament, specific criticisms were levelled at parliamentarian practices and procedures, and at the 'unmeasureable deceits' and 'fraudulent dealings' that emerged.[63] The focal point for such grievances were the accounts committees, chaired by men like William Prynne, which were perceived as being factional in their creation, biased in their operation and ineffectual in their outcome. Indeed, accusations regarding financial mismanagement – and about 'sharking committee men' – became a central plank in contemporary political analysis, as both Presbyterians and Independents were accused of biased accounting. Accountancy mechanisms were regarded as being structurally inadequate, since those in receipt of money had appointed the accountants, and it proved possible to highlight 'the interwoven dependencies of the account- ants one upon another', and to conclude that the upshot would be 'hocus- pocus', 'sleight of hand' and the 'secret conveyance of the public treasure into private pockets'. The result was inflammatory rhetoric about the need to 'squeeze' those who had, 'like sponges, sucked and drunk up the substance of the people', and commentators regularly reminded readers that what was at stake was 'the sweat of your own brows and the proper reward of your bleeding labours', as well as 'the milk of babes'.[64] Ultimately,

---

[62] *Occurrences*, 465.3017, sigs. R–v; Buchanan, *Explanation*, pp. 53, 56; *Letter from a Scholler*, p. 19; *Complaint*, pp. 17–18; Walker, *Relations*, pp. 67, 83, 87–8, 98, 141; BL, Harl. 166, fo. 67; *Pragmaticus*, 369.220B, sig. Z; Musgrave, *Another*, *Aulicus*, 275.207, pp. 827–8.

[63] *Oxinden and Peyton Letters*, p. 100; BL, Add. 28001, fo. 213; *CJ*, iv. 362, 477; Walker, *Relations*, pp. 5– 6, 17; *Juxon*, p. 96; *Eye-Salve*, sig. A2.

[64] *Aulicus*: 275.113, pp. 162–3; 275.132, pp. 424–5; 275.313, p. 1556; *Engagements*, p. 32; *Pragmaticus*: 369.121, sig. X4; 369.118A, sigs. S2–v; *Anatomy*, p. 8; Walker, *Relations*, sigs. A4v, Bv, pp. 9–10, 145;

as even the readers of popular verse discovered, the factional control of offices and money was thought to provide a disincentive for grandees to seek peace. Nedham argued that such men 'will never leave greasing one another in the fist, with that which the poor people ... earn with the sweat of their brows', and *Elencticus* concluded that there remained 'sweet lickings' in 'fair and fat employments which peace would utterly destroy'. In other words, since 'peace' was the enemy of 'profit', so there would be 'no such thing'.[65]

Much as with the allegations about factional corruption of parliament, therefore, suggestions that the two Houses had been sidelined, and that Westminster had been usurped by Whitehall, were powerful and sustained. They spread from substantial pamphlets and treatises into popular literature and the weekly press, thereby making a significant impression beyond Westminster. Twysden reflected on how 'ambitious appetites' had led to 'new unheard of paths to draw money from the subject', and he was appalled that MPs granted themselves special financial privileges. John Evelyn feared that financial interests would militate against a political settlement. However, the fact that similar comments were also made by people who lacked personal contacts in parliament probably provides further evidence about the impact of cheap print. These included Thomas Juxon, who perceived that financial irregularity was rife in the 1650s, and a Colchester weaver called Stephen Lewes, who exclaimed that 'the Parliament had done no good ... but sat for their own ends to enrich themselves'.[66]

v Perceptions of parliament and the transformation of public politics

The relevance of these observations and arguments lies in their potency and impact, rather than in their accuracy, and the final aim of this chapter is to explore the uses to which they were put in contemporary discourse and public life. In other words, while it is easy to argue that claims about the 'corruption' of parliament were biased, and that they sometimes lacked conceptual clarity, they nevertheless have value to the extent that they

Buchanan, *Explanation*, p. 56; Musgrave, *Another*; *London's Account*, p. 7; *Dove*, 594.124, pp. 581–2; *Letter*, p. 8; Lilburne, *Innocency* (1645, L2118), pp. 44–6, 68–72; *Reasons*, sig. B4; *Vindication* (1647, P4127), p. 4.

[65] *Second Part* (1648, P4074A), p.3; *Dove*, 594.124, p. 583; Musgrave, *Another*; *Pragmaticus*, 369.216, sig. Q4; 369.106, sig. F4v; *Reasons*, sig. B2v; *Elencticus*, 312.47, pp. 386–7.

[66] *Eye-Salve*, sig. A4; *Appeale*, sigs. A3r–v; *Windsor Projects*, 710.3, p. 5; Musgrave, *Another*; Howldin, *Lawes*, p. 4; *Alarum*, p. 10; *Troublers*, pp. 2–3; *Westminster Projects*, 710.1, p. 7; *Pragmaticus*: 369.106, sig. F4v; 369.102A, sig. B3; 369.224, sig. Gg2v; *List of the Names*; *Tell Tale*, sig. A3; *Second Centurie*; *Reasons*, sig. B2v; *Alethes* (1653, M1750), pp. 1–3; 'Twysden narrative', ii. 82–3; 214–15; BL, Add. 78221, fo. 5v; *Juxon*, p. 96; ERO, D/5/Sb2/7, fo. 298.

affected the reputation of parliament, and that they informed the assumptions and behaviour of people who interacted with the two Houses. What follows, therefore, represents an attempt to develop something that has been a minor theme throughout the chapter: assessing how far the analysis and views of disgruntled MPs and dyspeptic commentators came to be shared by a broader public, and the degree to which it underpinned their political attitudes. We know that Clement Walker's works were purchased by members of the gentry of all political persuasions, and that cheap print and newspapers were valued tools for interpreting current affairs, and it thus makes sense to explore the degree to which people picked up new ideas, rhetoric and language from the press. It also makes sense to assess whether perceptions of parliament affected ideas about political representation, and whether this underpinned calls for more or less radical reform, in ways that provoked anxiety within the political elite.[67]

Common talk about parliament was obviously plentiful, even if it generally lacked sophistication, and tended to be more or less scatological. In 1643, a London brick maker called John Parker claimed that 'the parliament were all rogues and rascals', and this sentiment was echoed the following year by a gardener called William Harmon, while Mary Hugget was accused of saying that parliament 'murdered the king's good subjects'. Many others were prosecuted for similarly 'dangerous' and 'base' utterances. Beyond London, a Norwich citizen reportedly exclaimed 'a turd for the Parliament' in 1640, while in 1642 an Exeter tailor called Nicholas Jagoe was questioned for 'dangerous words' against parliament, and two Devonshire worsted combers reported a local apprentice for saying 'that the parliament's laws were not worth a turd'. Such comments perhaps reflect only a rudimentary knowledge of parliament's workings and record, and may indicate no more than exposure to songs in taverns and alehouses which 'jeered' and 'scoffed' at parliament, and which demonstrably led to the 'scorn', 'contempt' and 'affronts' which MPs faced in public.[68] Some comments, however, were much more detailed and sophisticated. In April 1642 a Worcestershire shoemaker claimed that parliamentary ordinances had no binding force without the king's consent, and that a 'company of asses' had sat in parliament for over a year and 'done nothing but set division between the king and his people'. A decade later a Yorkshire yeoman

---

[67] CKS: U269/E2/1; U1475/Z45/2, fo. 121v; Norfolk RO, LEST NE1; 'James Master', i. 174; Longleat, Thynne 69.

[68] LMA: MJ/SR/927/3, 952/109, 947/43, 925/98, 911/27; MJ/SBB/15; Norfolk RO, NCR/16a/20, fo. 297v; Devon RO, ECA Book 64, fo. 20v; Bodl. MS Tanner 63, fo. 40; TNA, CHES/126/3; 'Lewis Dyve', p. 71; BL, Add. 78221, fos. 61–2.

alluded to financial corruption by describing MPs not merely as 'traitors' but also as 'bloodsuckers', and in 1659 Rugg highlighted the belief among 'common people' that Charles Fleetwood was merely a 'cypher' for more powerful men. In other words, contemporary onlookers, like some journalists, credited ordinary citizens with the ability to recognize and challenge the 'corruption' of parliament.[69]

Such comments beg interesting questions about how far popular opinion was informed by print culture. Some of the most sophisticated observers of procedural controversies – like Twysden and Justinian Isham – probably relied on personal experience and information from friends and family, and it is inevitably true that those who were likely to have been most reliant on print in order to understand parliament are the most difficult to bring into historical focus.[70] Nevertheless, there are ways of detecting traces of the press in popular discourse, not least linguistically. The idea of a 'mungrel Parliament', which was reported in the press after the capture of the Naseby letters, came to be applied to other imperfect bodies, like the so-called 'Pelham Parliament' of 1647, and men like Thomas Knyvett, Edward Massey and Robert Boyle referred to 'babes of grace', 'hocus pocus juggling' and 'butter boxes' in ways that suggest an engagement with Nedham's journalism. Similarly, Thomas Wyatt read a pamphlet called *Complaint to the House of Commons* (1643) as being an attack on 'the evil members of both Houses', and John Evelyn believed that popular animosity towards MPs in April 1653 sprang from a black-letter ballad entitled *The Parliament Routed*. He did so because the latter likened MPs to 'caterpillars' who had consumed the nation's treasure, alleged that members 'voted [and] unvoted as fancy did guide', and argued that 'twelve parliament men shall be sold for a penny'. Likewise, Thomas Rugg claimed that the opening verse of *The Rump Dockt* – which made detailed reference to specific MPs and to a corrupted parliament – was 'in almost everybody's mouth'.[71]

Such comments make it feasible to argue that comments and analysis in print underpinned the dynamic of political life in the 1640s and 1650s, in terms of both anxiety about the public mood and the emergence of 'radicalism'. First, therefore, it is possible to demonstrate how concern on the part

---

[69] *PJ*, ii. 178; *York Depositions*, p. 53; *Moon*, 248.02, p. 11; *Rugg*, p. 8; *Militaris*, 346.3, sig. C3v; *Parl. Intelligencer*, 486.101, p. 3.

[70] 'Twysden narrative', ii. 78, iii. 147–8; Northants. RO, IC 455.

[71] Claydon, Verney reel 8; *Occurrences*, 465.3029, sig. Ff3; Cary, *Memorials*, p. 377; BL, Add. 70005, fo. 66; Liverpool UL, MS 23/107; R. Boyle, *Works*, ed. T. Birch (6 vols, 1772), vi. 45; Bodl. MS Top. Oxon.c.378, p. 368; BL, Add. 78221, fos. 61–2; *Routed* (1653, S148A); *Rugg*, pp. 23, 30, 66–7; *Dockt* (1660, R2272).

of the elite about how parliament was portrayed and perceived affected behaviour at Westminster. It generated attempts to reassure the public, to remove grievances and to manage expectations, and it was recognized that committees that were charged with accounting for public money should not include MPs, or anyone with any 'dependance on the army'. Likewise, the Self Denying Ordinance was said to have been intended to remove the 'clamour' that members were 'all for themselves', and that they secured for themselves 'all the places of trust, preferment and profit'. Similarly, as Juxon noted, the end of the Civil War also brought pressure to end the payment of parliamentary wages.[72] Beyond this, newspapers also noted how MPs sought to demonstrate that they prioritized the public good over private interests, not least by creating mechanisms for airing grievances about bribery, office-holding and abuse of privilege. They thus noted plans to publish financial accounts, to clear 'jealousies and calumnies' and to remove 'the heavy imputation' that members had 'received many millions ... for which they could give no account'. This highlights awareness that MPs were perceived to be a burdensome grievance, and some insiders even contemplated dissolving parliament in the spring of 1649, 'to stop the mouths' of critics.[73] In other words, members demonstrated anxiety about public perceptions, and this became steadily more apparent as time passed, most obviously during the protectoral parliaments. Bernard Church noted that people were 'amazed' at 'our slow motion' in dealing with Quakers, while Lambard Godfrey feared what would be said 'abroad' about the delay in banning Christmas, and Sir William Boteler worried what would be said 'without doors' about prolonged debates over taxation. Another speaker was concerned about reports that 'we are but a rag of a parliament', made up of 'soldiers and courtiers', while Thomas Bampfield feared that a poll tax would cause 'uproar', make parliament 'stink in the nostrils of the nation', and make MPs 'odious'. Such comments reflected explicit anxiety about popular 'distrust' in relation to financial matters, on the basis of awareness that the people would 'study to have their necks from under the yoke', as well as of the memory that voting one another 'large awards' had been 'the blame of the Long Parliament'.[74]

---

[72] *Diurnall*: 504.016, p. 128; 504.027, p. 213; 504.160, p. 1283; *Scout*, 485.77, p. 617; *Occurrences*, 465.4034, sig. Ii4v; *Juxon*, p. 133.

[73] *Occurrences*: 465.3050, sig. Dd2v; 465.5023, sig. Y4v; *Diurnall*: 504.016, p. 128; 504.224, p. 1801; 504.232, pp. 1866–7; 504.255, p. 2053; 504.298, p. 2433; *Moderate*, 413.2040, sig. (rr3v); *Civicus*, 298.132, p. 1155; *Perfect Passages*, 524.1001, p. 4; BL, Add. 78221, fos. 41–v. See: *CJ*, iv. 477, v. 196, 220.

[74] *Burton Diary*, i. 128, 192–3, 230, 237, 293, ii. 24, 27, 106, 197, 199, 322.

Of course, concerns about the popular mood provoked not just willingness to reform, but also a campaign to 'manage' public attitudes, and to control how parliamentary affairs were discussed. It was alleged that attempts to restrain reporting – to cut off the 'conduit pipe of intelligence from Westminster' – represented the desire to prevent anyone from making MPs 'odious in the eyes of the world', by revealing 'the knavery of the faction'. It was also clear that insiders were frustrated by Clement Walker's willingness to expose the 'insolent usurpations' of parliament, and by the widespread availability of 'Rump ballads', which were intended to 'disgrace' MPs. Attempts were also made to manipulate public opinion. Journalists close to parliament sometimes emphasized how responsive MPs were to the criticisms levelled against them, and information about proceedings and tactics was almost certainly 'leaked' to writers like Buchanan, Nedham and Prynne to serve factional interests, even if this generally meant discrediting rivals and defending reputations more obviously than fostering positive perceptions of the institution. Prynne's pamphlets relating to financial administration and the 'eleven members' certainly demonstrate how 'secret' information could be deployed to discredit opponents, and how political motives could lead to light being shed on aspects of parliamentary practice that were otherwise shrouded in mystery.[75]

There is, however, a second and much more striking way of exploring the impact of the publicity that was given to the 'assault' on parliamentary politics. This involves the idea that it was changing perceptions of the Westminster *system* – rather than merely parliamentarian *policies* – that fostered a re-evaluation of the role of parliament and its members, and of the relationship between representatives and represented. Indeed, for commentators across the political spectrum, it can be demonstrated that grievances sprang from close observation of political processes as much as from the substantial business that was being conducted, and for both 'conservative' parliamentarians and 'radical' critics this meant awareness of 'subtle practices' and financial mismanagement.[76] It was a Leveller, John Wildman, who asked why 'the strength of the ploughman' should be 'spent in sowing the field', only for his 'tender fruit' to be 'blasted in the blossom', and who inquired why people should 'trifle away their precious time in tedious

[75] *Pragmaticus*: 369.221A, sig. Aa4v; 369.234, sigs. Bb4–v; *Melancholicus*, 344.29, p. 169; *Aulicus*, 277.2, sig. B–Bv; *Rugg*, p. 28; *Baillie*, ii. 190, 202, 215, 252, 278–9, 281–2, 352, 358–9, 367; *Juxon*, p. 117.
[76] *Eye-Salve*, sigs. Av, A4; Walker, *Relations*, sig. B, pp. 4, 6–7, 9, 12, 16, 17, 50, 58, 115–16; *Publike* (1648, P4044), p. 5; Lilburne, *Whip* (1648, L2198); *Alarum*, p. 9; Lilburne, *Birthright* (1645, L2102), p. 33; *Juxon*, p. 104. Cf Ashton, *Counter-Revolution*, pp. 44–125; M. Kishlansky, 'Ideology and politics in the parliamentary armies, 1645–9', in *Reactions*, pp. 163–83.

toilsome journeys to elections, to send the worthies of their country?' Nevertheless, there was support right across the political spectrum for the idea that 'the people . . . expect a more exact account and ample satisfaction than they have yet had, for their profuse expense of wealth and blood'. Moreover, rather than being restricted to polemicists, such grievances also provoked animosity from members of the public. General Massey's disbanded troops, who threatened tumults at Westminster in January 1647, expressed anger at 'the liberal gifts of the Parliament to their own members', adding that these were 'much spoken of among the people', who apparently said that 'surely the Parliament is dying in that they distribute their legacies so fast'. In other words, popular hostility to MPs – so that 'every man's tongue is against them', and so that 'they durst hardly appear in the streets' – sprang in no small part from genuine awareness of their behaviour at Westminster.[77]

More importantly, this disillusionment with practices and procedures also prompted thoughts about more or less 'radical' solutions, right across the political spectrum. In part this meant calls for the removal of underperforming and inadequate MPs. Cheney Culpeper sought a 'purging of our great committees', and polemicists like George Wither and John Musgrave defended the public's right to accuse members, as a bulwark against arbitrary government. Nedham, too, advocated 'impeachments and accusations', as a means by which the public could indemnify 'good members' while punishing 'ambition, avarice, pride, cruelty and oppression', and in order to protect liberty and property, and keep the commonwealth 'in good order'.[78] Equally dramatic proposals were also made by royalists and crypto-royalists, who argued that MPs who went beyond their trust, or who abused the power with which they had been invested, could be held accountable, recalled and punished, even to the point of death. Sir Roger Twysden – who argued that the 'liberty of the subject' was 'much talked of' but 'little practised' – even looked to Holland as a model of how MPs were 'strictly tied' to voters' 'instructions', and made 'subject to their censure'.[79] Beyond this, however, commentators also began to call for more widespread purges, and even for the dissolution of parliament, in order to punish those who had 'given the public treasure to themselves', and who

---

[77] Wildman, *Putney*, p. 32; *Warning*, pp. 4–5; Bodl. MS Clarendon 29, fos. 72r–v; *Juxon*, pp. 103, 149; *Certain Queries*, p. 7.

[78] 'Cheney Culpeper', p. 231; Wither, *Justitiarius* (1646, W3165), p. 14; Musgrave, *Another*; Musgrave, *Fourth*, p. 8; *Juxon*, pp. 104–5; *Reasons*, p. 4; *Vox Plebis* (1646, O636A), pp. 59–61.

[79] *Certain Queries*, p. 2; *Melancholicus*, 344.29, pp. 169–70; *Pragmaticus*, 369.245, sigs. Lll–v; 'Twysden narrative', ii. 188, 192.

had 'falsified their trust', so that power that had been delegated to MPs might be reclaimed. Such arguments were rehearsed most fully during debates about the 'eleven members' (1647). Here, supporters of the army argued that it was legitimate to 'impeach' and 'call to an account' anyone who was known to be 'guilty of gross crimes', or who advanced private or factional interests, and that it was not necessary to wait until 'accidental chance shall produce an account'. Needless to say, such ideas were vigorously challenged by Presbyterians, who were nervous about the idea (and the practicalities) of trial by press and the public, and who feared opening the door to further purges. They suggested that an MP's 'demeanour within those walls' ought not to be questioned, that people lacked the ability to judge their representatives, and that existing mechanisms offered an adequate way of punishing malefactors. Nevertheless, the language of accountability can be shown to have been used across the political spectrum. Some Presbyterians defended their impeached colleagues by making counter-claims against Independent MPs, and in May 1648 the crypto-royalist Surrey petitioners demanded 'a new Parliament', and 'an account of all the monies that we have paid'.[80]

Even more striking than these claims about MPs being accountable to the public was the tendency for disillusionment with parliamentary practice to prompt calls for root and branch reform. This involved ideas about annual (or biannual) parliaments and about electoral reform, and a perception that it was necessary to do more than merely censure individual malefactors. The aim, indeed, was to prevent 'faction' and 'oppression', as well as 'partiality and injustice' and 'court craft ... avarice and ambition', and to ensure that MPs were 'in a capacity to taste subjection as well as rule'. As such, proposals emerged to create mechanisms for ensuring good behaviour and accountability, including rigorous qualifications for membership, oath-taking and certification of wealth, as well as frequent elections. Some commentators even supported the idea that there should be strict rules governing the power of MPs, as well as the relations 'between their people and their representatives'. This tended to involve the idea of providing MPs with 'instructions' – or even a 'solemn contract' – on election day, so that they

---

[80] Wildman, *Putney*, sig. F4v; *Lamentable* (1645, W681C), pp. 6–7; *Warning*, pp. 4, 8, 10; Harbye, *Nations* (1650, H684), pp. 17–20; *Answer* (1647, A3283), p. 3; *Parliament* (1648, P508), p. 7; *Remonstrance* (1648, R961), pp. 4–8; *Engagements*, p. 47; Lilburne, *Birthright*, p. 33; SHC, G85/5/2/10a; *OPH*, xvi. 70–92, 116–59; *Moderate* (1647, M2323), p. 4; *Juxon*, pp. 157–8; *Reasons*, pp. 1, 4, 6, sig. B; *Full Vindication* (1647, P3968), pp. 4, 10–13; *Kingdomes*, 214.214, p. 572; *IX Queries* (1647, P4023), pp. 3, 6, 12; *Lawfulnes* (1647, L647), pp. 5, 7, 11, 12, 13; *Case* (1647, C1013), p. 5; Wither, *Respublica* (1650, W30A), p. 34; *Surrey* (1648, T3013), p. 2.

would 'know their trust', and once again such ideas were not restricted to the army and the Levellers. Nedham claimed that it was 'high time' that steps were taken 'for stating the privileges of Parliament into certain limits', so that people need 'no longer wander' in the 'invisible labyrinth of parliamentary privilege'. Indeed, support for parliamentary reform found support across a fairly broad political spectrum. Proposals included a sizeable and strictly enforced quorum in the Commons, greater freedom to report parliamentary proceedings, and even a public registry of members' votes, so that 'each county, corporation or any particular man may see how they behave themselves upon all occasions'.[81] What this implied, of course, was a greater role for print as a means of ensuring effective accountability, and one pamphlet explicitly argued that the people ought to 'know in print . . . which way all public monies are disposed'.[82]

vi Conclusion

During the 1640s and 1650s, print culture provided readers with a chance to explore the workings of the Westminster parliamentary system, in ways that had previously been severely restricted. Information that had once been the preserve of elite correspondence and scribal guidebooks became available in penny pamphlets, and even in political verses and black-letter ballads, and many authors and journalists joined Amon Wilbee in reporting and commenting on parliamentary practice. They presented readers with sophisticated (if contentious) analysis of a parliamentary system that had been transformed by war and factionalism, and they looked behind the scenes and beyond the two Houses, in order to explore financial and administrative management, and in order to expose those responsible for 'corrupting' the Westminster system. They suggested to readers what Sir William Waller would later opine: that the Long Parliament was 'betrayed by the insidious practices of its own members', beginning in the early 1640s, and continuing more dramatically as years passed.[83] Because such texts were widely read, their ideas and arguments helped to inform contemporary perceptions of

---

[81] *Diurnall*, 504.268, pp. 2153–5; Musgrave, *Fourth*, pp. 11–12; Lilburne, *Birthright*, p. 33; *Independency* (1648, I145), p. 14; Harbye, *Nations*, p. 71; *Kingdomes*: 214.290, pp. 1188–90; 214.285, pp. 1146–7; *Democratica* (1659, I32), sig. A2, pp. 2–3; *Engagements*, pp. 40, 42–3; *Many Thousands* (1649, R995), pp. 5–6; *New Remonstrance* (1648, N741), pp. 5–6; Jubbes, *Several* (1648, S2799), pp. 5, 7; *Officers* (1652, T1748B); *Agreement* (1649, A783A), pp. 16, 22; *Agreement* (1649, L2079), p. 3; *Foundations* (1648, L2110A), p. 10; Jubbes, *Apology* (1649, J1163), p. 16; *Standard* (1659, E3054), p. 4; *Agreement* (1647, A780), pp. 7–8; Nedham, *Lawyer* (1647, N393), p. 2; Bodl. MS Clarendon 30, fo. 286; *Certain Queries*, p. 3; *Defiance* (1646, O626), p. 2; Walker, *Relations*, p. 139.
[82] *New Remonstrance*, p. 2. [83] W. Waller, *Vindication* (1793), pp. 152, 190.

parliament and to foster reflections on national institutions across the social spectrum. Not all contemporary responses to parliament were very sophisticated, but even those at the lower reaches of the social scale demonstrated some degree of awareness about parliamentary affairs, policies and machinations. Indeed, as many within Westminster recognized, such perceptions influenced political ideas and political actions, and it is plausible to make fairly direct connections between print culture and the dynamic of public debate and popular discourse. As the following chapters will demonstrate, however, this was only one dimension of the transformation that took place regarding the public face of parliament during the 1640s and 1650s. To this picture of how pamphlets and newspapers subjected political *processes* to hostile scrutiny, it is also possible to add evidence about how journalists and commentators shed light upon daily life at Westminster, in terms of the business that was being done and in terms of who was doing what in the corridors of power. It might even be argued that the determination to report on proceedings emerged from (and fed off) the desire to understand the institution and the perception that MPs needed to be subjected to very close scrutiny. In what follows, therefore, the aim will be to supplement an appreciation of how contemporaries *analysed* parliament with insights about their ability to *report* quotidian occurrences. This will require a re-evaluation of attitudes towards the secrecy of parliamentary proceedings, but it will make it possible to argue that cheap print encouraged and enabled direct participation at Westminster, and that it fostered unprecedented awareness about the performance of individual MPs.

CHAPTER 5

Access to parliament

Judging by his notebooks, Henry Townshend of Elmly Lovett in Worcestershire was fascinated by day-to-day proceedings in parliament. He followed local as well as national elections, made brief notes on county MPs like Edmund Giles – 'a young lawyer' – and observed which members had been excluded by Cromwell in 1656. In 1653, he recorded the composition of the Council of State, and identified the most important standing committees, the names of those who had been appointed, and the times and places of their meetings. He took notes on the explanation given for the dissolution of the Rump, and made a copy of the letter sent to the 'saints' who formed Barebone's Parliament, and when the session opened he recorded the names not merely of the new Council, but also of those appointed to all of the main committees. At other times he was also able to follow proceedings in the Commons, to record the gist of key speeches and even to make a note of forthcoming business, such as the trial of the bishops in mid January 1641.[1] This suggests that Townshend benefited from both scribal news and print culture, and some of his information almost certainly came from pamphlets and newspapers. As such, he demonstrates a second way in which the public face of parliament was transformed by the print revolution. Where the previous chapter demonstrated that the media revolutionized public understanding about how the Westminster system was supposed to work, how it operated in reality and how it might be improved, Townshend's notes highlight a transformation in the amount of evidence that was available about quotidian proceedings. He provides another way of exploring the democratization of what had traditionally been privileged information, and restricted to those with powerful friends and deep pockets. He suggests that such material became readily accessible to ordinary citizens, even if not exactly commonplace. And he raises the

[1] Worcs. RO, BA1714, pp. 1–21, 187, 634–9.

tantalizing possibility that members of the public could exploit such information in order to participate in parliamentary affairs.

The aim of this chapter is to pursue the leads provided by Townshend,
and to explore how the print revolution changed the traditional culture of
secrecy surrounding parliamentary proceedings. This will mean examining
the reporting of business in both Houses, and the kinds of information that
were available to readers of cheap print, and it will also mean assessing
official attitudes towards publicity, transparency and public participation.
The goal is to challenge the idea that MPs and peers were determined to
shield their business from the public gaze by clinging to the principle of
secrecy, and to question scholarship that concentrates on attempts to
restrain reporting and restrict public access to parliament.[2] While recognizing the very real limits to openness, it will nevertheless demonstrate that
contemporaries were *conflicted* over secrecy, that divisions over accessibility
did not occur along predictable 'party' lines, and that views were anything
but static. It will describe a political elite that was willing to tolerate some
degree of transparency, that was pragmatic about when to allow press
coverage and that was more than happy to allow public participation so
long as it was *polite* and *restrained*. It will also argue that attempts to exert
control over public access and printed publicity were only partially successful; that secrecy was both a less pervasive aspiration and a less realistic goal.
Once again, this will be shown to have reflected changes to traditional
practices that occurred in the circumstances of civil war and revolution, as
pamphlets and newspapers catered for unprecedented demand for news of
parliament by vulgarizing the information that emanated from
Westminster. This involved providing readers with detailed evidence
about who sat in the Commons (section ii), as well as about key aspects
of daily proceedings, in terms of the business that had been done and would
be done, in both the Houses and their committees (section iii). In both
cases, care will be taken to recognize that, whatever could be known about
parliament in theory, this may not have been easily gleaned by individual
readers, in addition to which some information remained hidden or privileged, and some people continued to know a great deal more than others.
Similarly, doing justice to the complex reality of accessibility and transparency will also involve acknowledging instability, and demonstrating that
practices for making proceedings visible were liable to change. The chapter

---

[2] A. Aspinall, 'The reporting and publishing of the House of Commons Debates', in *Essays Presented to
Sir Lewis Namier*, ed. R. Pares (London, 1956), p. 228; H. Hale Bellot, 'Parliamentary printing', *BIHR*,
11 (1933–4), p. 86.

will thus treat evidence about secrecy and openness in a diachronic fashion (section iv), to suggest that changing attitudes and practices were indicative of attempts to *formalize* access to the corridors of power, and even to encourage public involvement in proceedings. Indeed, the picture that will emerge will be one in which direct public participation in parliamentary affairs was a more prevalent aspiration, a more realistic possibility, and a largely acceptable political reality. However, before attending to the unprecedented light which the media shed upon day-to-day activity in both Houses, the chapter will begin with an examination of public access to the Palace of Westminster.

i The public and the palace

The Palace of Westminster was anything but a serene and stately place. Its law courts attracted countless litigants, witnesses and onlookers, and it was also a significant commercial centre, with shops, stalls and more than one tavern. It was an ideal place for socializing, womanizing and drinking, and it was not always very safe. Any number of incidents reveal that tempers became frayed, that arguments took place and that fights broke out, as gloves were slapped across faces, as punches were thrown and as swords were drawn. There were murders, both attempted and real, and the famous Hall proved irresistible to many dubious characters of questionable sanity, like the woman who proclaimed herself the queen of Heaven, and who sometimes sat 'majestically . . . in the highest place in the Courts of Justice'. Such disorder obviously troubled the authorities, and in April 1645 attempts were made to calm the Hall's quarrelsome atmosphere. Nevertheless, the threat of violent disturbance was generally considered a risk worth taking, and the potential downside of a participatory culture which was highly prized.[3] Contemporaries valued the Hall as a place to gather news, either orally, scribally or in print, and what might easily have been lost were the meetings and discussions that occurred every day. These frequently involved MPs, many of whom dined at its infamous watering-holes, called 'Heaven' and 'Hell', which suggests that MPs were prepared to take the risk of being accosted by strangers. One of these was a young man who entered the Hall in December 1652, enquired if the Commons was sitting, and asked to speak

---

[3] FSL, W.b.600, pp. 13–31, 42; Birch, *Charles*, i. 74, 130, 292, ii. 99; *CSPD 1641–3*, pp. 48, 217; BL: Add. 11045, fo. 117v; Harl. 163, fo. 105; *Politicus*, 361.224, p. 3796; Bodl. MS Clarendon 46, fo. 33; *Diurnall*, 504.092, p. 728. See: C. Kyle and J. Peacey, '"Under cover of so much coming and going"', in *Parliament at Work* (Woodbridge, 2002), pp. 1–23; J. Peacey, 'To every individual member', *Court Historian*, 13 (2008), 127–47.

to Attorney General Edmund Prideaux, MP for Lyme Regis. That he was promptly apprehended by the guards reflected not his effrontery in demanding to see a specific MP, but rather the fact that he had ridden into the Hall on horseback, clad in armour and carrying an arrow.[4] Such evidence indicates that the Hall was a popular place in which to engage with political life, and it suggests not just that MPs were incapable of insulating themselves from the public, but also that they had little mind to do so. It indicates not only that the palace was an accessible place, but also that this openness had political implications with which contemporaries were more or less comfortable. The aim of this section, therefore, is to address evidence about the physical accessibility of parliament, and to suggest that official attitudes towards the public were fairly tolerant, that access was extensive (if not unlimited), and that official policy revealed something other than a straightforward determination to maintain secrecy.

The first thing to note about the tendency to accommodate citizens more or less willingly is that it extended beyond the Hall and into the political heart of the palace. Not only was it was difficult to prevent members of the public from wandering into the environs of parliament, but it also seems clear that official concern about the presence of 'strangers' only emerged in certain circumstances. The only unequivocal evidence of a desire to prevent citizens from gaining physical access to those in power relates to the Privy Council, the royalist Council of War and the republican Council of State, where attempts were consistently made to prevent the 'sauciness' of 'unknown' or 'mean' persons who showed too much interest in proceedings. In these cases, corridors and lobbies were kept clear, and meeting room doors were closely guarded, so that proceedings could be kept strictly secret. In most other settings, however, attempts to restrict public access cannot simply be attributed to concerns about the privacy of deliberations. While it is certainly true that attempts were made to preserve decorum, the mere presence of citizens tended to be regarded as problematic only at moments of heightened political tension, during outbreaks of plague and in relation to political *debates* within the two Houses. Occasional attempts to restrict public access were considered newsworthy precisely because they were exceptional, rather than because they were standard practice, and they generally resulted only in a short-term tightening of procedures. Secrecy, in other words, could be enforced fairly rigidly, but it was not maintained as

---

[4] FSL, W.b.600, pp. 137, 192; *Oxinden Letters*, p. 286; BL: Add. 78220, fo. 3; Eg. 2715, fo. 288; Stowe 185, fo. 30; FSL: V.b.161; L.b.685; Northants. RO, IC 454; F. Henderson, 'New material from the Clarke manuscripts' (Oxford University DPhil, 1998), pp. 114–15.

a matter of course, and given the memory of the Gunpowder Plot and the ongoing fear of a 'terrorist' attack, it is actually fairly remarkable that the palace complex remained so open.[5]

These suggestions are supported by evidence about the tolerant official response to the popularity of parliamentary committees. These remained largely accessible, even though they could be attended by fairly large crowds, and even though such crowds attracted the unwelcome attention of pickpockets, like the man who was ejected at the point of an MP's sword in 1657.[6] Indeed, it is fairly striking that official policy was rarely driven by a desire for secrecy. First, steps to restrict public access to committees tended to be taken only when there was a risk of mass attendance, when MPs found themselves crowded out, and when order and decency were threatened. Complaints were thus made about committee rooms being so full of 'strangers' that MPs were unable to get in, and parliamentary officers were repeatedly asked to prevent 'disorderly multitudes', and to ensure that committee rooms were not 'thronged and pestered' unnecessarily.[7] On other occasions the problem was deemed to involve the *behaviour* of the public, rather than their mere attendance. When Edward Nicholas complained about soldiers who attended committees 'in troops', to demand money and complain about their officers, he did so because they were 'in their cups' and 'insolent', and because they threatened 'to pull down the Parliament house'.[8]

Secondly, public access was a closely guarded privilege. While peers openly hoped that their committees would only admit 'parties, counsel or witnesses', attempts to restrict access to Commons committees tended to be resisted. A conservative MP like Sir Simonds D'Ewes agreed that disorder needed to be prevented, but he also highlighted an occasion when a 'stander-by' had been a valuable witness at a recent committee 'in a material point', and therefore resisted any move which would mean that 'no strangers might come'.[9] Indeed, while some business was considered sufficiently sensitive to justify the exclusion of strangers, MPs ensured that this justification was used sparingly. In February 1642, for example, D'Ewes witnessed strangers being ejected from a joint committee that was discussing 'certain letters of the Lord George Digby's', but his assumption was that secret sessions should be the exception rather than the rule. Indeed, some

---

[5] *CSPD 1637*, p. 70; BL, Add. 15750, fos. 16–v; *CSPD 1651–2*, pp. 157, 378; TNA, PRO 31/17/33, p. 232; *CSPD 1652–3*, p. 14; *CJ*, ii. 371.

[6] *Diary of John Evelyn*, ii. 547; *Burton Diary*, i. 336.

[7] BL, Harl. 164, fo. 172v; *D'Ewes*, ed. Notestein, pp. 293, 370; *CJ*, ii. 65, 88.

[8] SHC: G52/2/19/16; G85/5/2/10.   [9] *LJ*, iv. 172; *D'Ewes*, ed. Notestein, p. 164.

witnesses – like the Presbyterian ministers James Cranford and William Jenkins – valued the ability to bring 'a company of starched faces' with them, 'to hum up themselves and hiss down the honourable committee'.[10] Moreover, while 'close committees' clearly became more common in the 1640s, the contemporary notice taken of them indicates their novelty and newsworthiness, rather than their prevalence, and observers from across the political spectrum were quick to complain if committee hearings were conducted 'privately and in the dark'. Thus, when the MP John Maynard was examined before peers in early 1648, he asked that 'all the doors might be left open, for every man to hear what he said'.[11]

Similar themes emerge regarding the presence of strangers in the lobbies of either House. Thus, while MPs and peers sometimes attempted to clear the lobbies, and the staircases that led to them, their concerns tended to involve the 'clamour' caused by large crowds, rather than principles regarding public access. In January 1641, for example, measures were taken to prevent excessive numbers of footmen and servants from entering the lobbies or standing on the stairs, while in February 1642 Philip Skippon informed the House that there were 'a great many women about the doors of both Houses', and that there would be five times as many the following day. On 29 September 1646, meanwhile, the Commons ordered guards to stand at the foot of the stairs to prevent access to the lobby, 'by reason of much people flocking about the House of Commons door', who threatened to 'hinder the members passing in and out'.[12] Nevertheless, MPs saw nothing intrinsically wrong with granting public access to the lobby, or with being contacted by constituents and messengers while they were in the chamber. It certainly seems clear that members of the public saw the lobbies as places 'to hear news' and observe proceedings, and recognized that the easiest way of getting letters to MPs was to send them to 'the door of the House'.[13]

What MPs were not prepared to tolerate was the intrusion of strangers into the Commons, although here, too, their actions need to be interpreted with care. It is perfectly apparent, therefore, that unwelcome visitors tended to be identified, called to the bar and removed, either with a reprimand or a

---

[10] *PJ*, i. 367, 453–4; *Politicus*, 361.004, p. 50.

[11] *D'Ewes*, ed. Coates, p. 16; *D'Ewes*, ed. Notestein, pp. 370, 158, 164; *Pearle* (1646, O632A), p. 3; Walker, *Relations* (1648, W329/W334A), pp. 4–5; Bodl. MS Clarendon 30, fo. 286.

[12] *LJ*, iv. 396–7; *CJ*, ii. 400; *PJ*, i. 207, 247; *Die Martis* (1648, E2669A); *Orders of the House of Commons* (1756), pp. 5–6; *Occurrences*, 465.4040, sig. Pp3.

[13] BL, Harl. 165, fo. 224; GMRO: E17/89/26/2, 22/4, 29/2; JRL, Legh of Lyme Corr., Box 2/15–16; SBT, DR98; *Pepys Diary*, i. 17, 50.

fine. Nevertheless, responses to such episodes are fairly striking. 'Strangers' tended to be treated leniently, and attention often focused on keeping people out of the chambers when parliament was *not* sitting, and genuine anxiety also seems to have been reserved for those who were mentally deranged. These included the man who, upon being spotted in the House in November 1647, gave his name as 'Jehojadah the high priest, king of kings and lord of lords'. Another was Captain Andrew Windsor, who tried to claim a seat in the upper House as Lord Windsor in December 1641, and who struck an attendant when he was apprehended. Despite such violence, he was merely removed with a 'rebuke', on the grounds that he was 'distracted'.[14] Moreover, the real problem with strangers was not their presence during formal proceedings (motions, bill readings, petitions, etc.), but rather their attendance during debates. It was when debating commenced that efforts were made to eject strangers, and even then the people who had 'hearkened to the debate' were only sworn to secrecy, rather than punished more severely. There was nothing to stop them, however, from simply retreating to the lobby, to see what could be seen, and hear what could be heard, from outside the House.[15]

Such evidence indicates that there were limits to what the public was supposed to witness, and that these centred upon *debates*, during which the doors of the House were theoretically closed. However, given that it was still possible to overhear speeches from the lobby, there are grounds for caution regarding the effectiveness of secrecy, and for reconsidering whether even debates were truly sacrosanct. The overhearing of debates worried peers much more than MPs, and the Lords occasionally passed orders that 'none may come to harken at the doors'. Only in exceptional circumstances, however, did the Commons consider their debates to be sufficiently sensitive to warrant a news blackout. This required clearing the lobbies and closing the doors that stood at the top of the stairs leading up from Westminster Hall, all of which was fairly laborious. There were certainly occasions where 'we shut up our doors, and though some went in and out, yet kept private what we were about', but these were fairly rare. Finding the outer door closed one day in June 1643, for example, D'Ewes 'conceived that the House was about some great business of weight and secrecy', and the same thing happened the following August, when John Pym indicated that 'he had a matter of some moment to communicate to the House, and

---

[14] *Diurnall*, 504.281, p. 2264; *D'Ewes*, ed. Notestein, p. 296; *LJ*, iv. 319, 396–7; TNA, SP 16/451, fo. 41; *Occurrences*, 465.5046, p. 317; Bodl. MS Rawl. D.141, p. 17.

[15] *PJ*, i. 385, 391; *Journal of James Yonge*, ed. F. Poynter (London, 1963), p. 157.

desired that the outward door might be shut'. On this occasion Pym related sensitive news about high-level defections to the royalist cause, which was ordered to be kept highly secret, at least temporarily.[16] Such behaviour was considered unusual and newsworthy, and in January 1648 one journalist explained that secrecy had temporarily been tightened because MPs were discussing 'high and weighty matters', and noted that 'none were suffered to come near to disturb the House'. Moreover, it is also worth recognizing the existence of a more prosaic motive for preventing access to debates: fear that onlookers would be shocked by MPs' behaviour. On 3 May 1641, therefore, when D'Ewes expressed concern that 'many strangers' were near the door, he did so in response to disorderly shouting by MPs, and because strangers 'might interpret worse of it than it indeed deserves'.[17]

MPs thus demonstrated particular and half-hearted reasons for protecting secrecy, but more intriguing is the possibility that the issues that really governed their behaviour involved disease, disorder and decorum. At times, therefore, the decision to clear the lobbies almost certainly reflected a concern to insulate MPs from the plague, an outbreak of which in late 1641 provoked peers to exclude from their precincts anyone who did not have official business. Similarly, widespread sickness in 1647 explains an order that the doors and passages of the palace should not be 'troubled' by 'clamorous or troublesome people, upon any pretence or demand whatsoever'.[18] More commonly, however, decisions to remove the public stemmed from fear of large crowds and of disorder. One such occasion was the opening week of the Long Parliament, when intense public interest resulted in an order to remove from the lobby anyone who did not have business depending before the Commons. Subsequently, at moments of heightened importance and tension, MPs placed armed soldiers 'near the stairs coming out of Westminster Hall', and took steps to prevent 'extraordinary concourse of people'. In October 1647, for example, members expressed concern about a 'clamour' outside the doors, where people spoke 'scandalous words against the Parliament', and in January 1648 a committee was empowered to arrest anyone who caused a tumult in the lobby. Even peers sought decorum more obviously than they did seclusion, and although they sometimes sought the ability to 'retire' into the lobby without the risk of encountering strangers, it is interesting to note that such orders

[16] HEH, HA Parliament Box 2, no. 17; *LJ*, iv. 95, ix. 531; *Pragmaticus*, 369.111A, sig. L2v; *D'Ewes Autobiography*, ii. 268; BL, Harl. 165, fos. 100, 156–7.
[17] BL, Harl. 166, fos. 114, 243; *Weekly Account*, 671.501, sigs A3v–4; BL, Harl. 163, fo. 124.
[18] *CJ*, ii. 35, iv. 677, v. 285; *LJ*, iv. 396–7; *Kingdomes*, 214.201, p. 467.

were displayed in the lobby itself. Rather than removing the public entirely, in other words, the intention was to ensure that anyone who wanted to speak to peers should wait in the Painted Chamber, while servants were sent to wait in the Court of Requests.[19]

Another reason for doubting that policies and practices were driven merely by a desire for secrecy is that decisions to shut the doors and clear the lobbies were often made in tandem with orders forbidding MPs to leave the chamber. The aim, in other words, was to keep members *in*, as much as it was to keep the public *out*. This does not preclude the possibility that secrecy was the goal, but it reinforces the suggestion that concerted attempts to prevent information leaking out of the chamber involved extraordinary measures rather than everyday practices. Thus, the decision to prevent MPs from leaving on 18 November 1640 reflected a desire to stop news spreading about the impeachment of Strafford until the charge had been finalized, while a similar order on 3 May 1641 was combined with an explicit request that members should refrain from speaking to messengers.[20] These were moments of acute political tension, and such measures were genuinely exceptional. They could also be controversial, and another attempt by Pym to both clear the lobby and prevent MPs from departing was successfully opposed (30 December 1641). D'Ewes feared that such restrictions would deter MPs from attending, especially during hot and sticky weather, although it was eventually agreed that MPs could only leave their seats so long as they did not speak to anyone at the windows, or throw out messages to people below.[21] On other occasions, however, rather different concerns were evident. One was security, as on 5 January 1642, when the lobby was cleared and MPs were prevented from leaving in advance of the attempted arrest of the 'five members'. Another was procedural propriety, which was evident in orders to remove strangers from the vicinity of the House during formal votes (divisions), in order to avoid the possibility that strangers might be counted by the 'tellers'.[22] More generally, of course, the decision to close the doors reflected controversial attempts to maintain and bolster numbers, not least when there was a risk that the House would become inquorate, or when there was an opportunity to manipulate attendance for factional purposes.[23]

---

[19] *CJ*, ii. 26, v. 334, 421; *PJ*, i. 155, 286–7; *LJ*, iv. 101, 148, 172, 354.

[20] *CJ*, ii. 118, iii. 116, v. 194, 415, vii. 644, 785; *Baillie*, i. 272; BL, Harl. 164, fo. 195v.

[21] *D'Ewes*, ed. Coates, pp. 365–6; BL, Harl. 163, fo. 170v; *D'Ewes*, ed. Notestein, p. 453.

[22] *CJ*, ii. 368; BL: Harl. 164, fo. 162; Add. 6521, fo. 109; Harl. 4262, fo. 131; *CJ*, vii. 511.

[23] *CJ*, ii. 63, 217, 233, vi. 158, 431, 453, vii. 1; *D'Ewes*, ed. Coates, p. 183; *Burton Diary*, ii. 122; BL: Harl. 478, fo. 673; Harl. 164, fos. 812v, 827, 835, 837v, 843, 884v; Harl. 165, fo. 161.

Restricting public access to the Palace of Westminster, to the environs of both Houses and to parliamentary proceedings was thus anything but systematic. The presence of citizens was considered problematic only in relation to certain aspects of parliamentary business, and on other occasions it could be highly valued. Effective steps to reduce accessibility were generally only taken at moments of heightened political tension, or when MPs had good cause to fear for their safety, security and well-being, and to worry about a breakdown of decorum. Such episodes were relatively rare, generally temporary and invariably newsworthy, and they related to secrecy only in part. What this suggests is that members recognized both the inevitability and desirability of parliamentary proceedings being broadly accessible, because parliament was a focal point for public interest and private business. Indeed, it is possible to extend this argument much further, by highlighting contemporary tolerance of, and support for, public participation. This is revealed by the kinds of information that emerged from parliament, and that were allowed to appear in print.

ii Identifying MPs

One vital but largely overlooked aspect of the print revolution was the availability of new kinds of 'public information'. This meant information of a factual and utilitarian kind, which helped people to navigate public life, and which had previously been exclusive and expensive to obtain. It included evidence about the identity of officeholders, like sheriffs, lord lieutenants, army officers and lawyers, and about the composition of national and local commissions. Such material has been ignored by historians, even though it became a key feature of print culture, shaded into political commentary on specific individuals, and fascinated contemporaries. More particularly, it deserves attention because it familiarized people with the everyday world of parliament, and because its circulation was an essential pre-requisite for participation at Westminster.[24]

The most significant kind of public information to become available during the print revolution involved lists of MPs, either in quarto

---

[24] For example: *True and Exact* (1641, E2745); *Catalogue* (1642, C1393); *A List* (1642, L2442); *A List* (1648, L2470); *Diurnall*: 504.092, p. 727; 504.284, p. 2282; *Kingdomes*, 214.251, p. 866; *Politicus*: 361.082, p. 1318; 361.179, pp. 2864–6; 361.210, p. 3558; 361.387, pp. 62–3; *Proceedings*, 599.121, p. 1883; 599.226, p. 3569; *Civicus*: 298.022, p. 173; 298.097, pp. 876–7; *Occurrences*, 465.5049, p. 335; *Continuation*, 638.35, np; *Pragmaticus*, 369.102A, sig. B2v; 370.08B, sig. Hv; 370.09B, sig. Iv; *Rugg*, p. 40.

pamphlets or on broadsides. These first emerged in the 1620s, and quickly became a recognizable and popular genre and an obvious sign of the democratizing effect of print.[25] As commercial ventures, such lists highlight public demand for this kind of information, and men like William Whiteway were clearly keen to record the names of MPs in commonplace books when new parliaments assembled. This had always been possible, of course, and manuscript lists – described as 'a parliament table', as 'mapps of the Howse of Commons' and as 'libri parliamenti' – had long been purchased by members of the gentry.[26] The problem, however, was that scribal lists were fairly expensive. In the late sixteenth century they could cost anything between 7s 6d and 17s 6d, and although prices fell to between 1s 6d and 5s in the 1620s, and to as low as 1s in the early 1640s, this would still have restricted their audience considerably.[27] Printed lists were considerably cheaper, retailing at 8d in 1624, and at a mere 6d in 1640, and by 1654 Sir Richard Temple needed to pay only 1d to acquire a 'list of the parliament men'.[28] Of course, some people remained willing to pay a premium if they could get information before it appeared in print. Gilbert Walbanke sent German Pole a scribal 'list of the new representative' in June 1653, even though the printed edition appeared the following day, and Philip Jones despatched a list of Cromwell's 'other House' the evening that it was finalized in December 1657. Most people, however, seem to have converted to print versions fairly happily.[29]

That printed lists of MPs proved popular reflects the fact that many contemporaries were not merely fascinated by the outcome of elections, but also determined to acquire *useful* information. It would, of course, be foolish to assume that material *owned* was always *read*, and the pages of some such pamphlets acquired by the Gell family remain uncut to this day.

---

[25] *Order and Manner* (1624–8, 7742–6); *Names of the Knights* (1625, 7743.5); *Catalogue* (1628, 7746.4); *Most Exact* (1628, 7746.2–3); *Order of Sitting* (1628, 7744.5); *Names of the Knights* (1628, 7745.7); *Manner of the Sitting* (1628, 7745.5); *Catalogue* (1640, 7746.6, 7746.9, 7746.13, C1395).

[26] Whiteway, pp. 71, 95; *Household Books of the Lord William Howard* (SS, 68, 1877), p. 221; BL, Harl. 7660, fo. 40; DRO, D258/10/29/4; Som. RO, DD/PH/245; HEH: EL 6927; Hastings Parliament Box 2/9, 22; Hastings Parliament Box 3/10; Bodl. MS Rawl. A78, fos. 223–4; BL, Add. 38139, fos. 89–100; Beinecke, Osborn fb.161, fo. 184.

[27] C. Blair, 'The Armourers bill of 1581', *Journal of the Arms and Armour Society*, 12 (1986), p. 43; D. Dean, 'Public or private?', *HJ*, 31 (1988), pp. 537, 542n; *Lord William Howard*, p. 221; CKS, U350/E4, unfol.; BL, Harl. 7660, fo. 40; ERO, D/DBa/A38.

[28] BL: Cotton Charter xvi. 13, fo. 14; Harl. 7660, fos. 24v, 29; HEH, ST 54/1, unfol.; FSL, M.b.29, fos. 213–14.

[29] DRO: D5557/2/189; D258/15/2/1; D258/72; D258/34/29/1, 3; *Catalogue* (1653, C1401); Bodl. MS Carte 73, fo. 174; BL, Eg. 2715, fo. 431; Claydon, Verney reel 8; Leics. RO, DG21/282.

Nevertheless many people found them immensely valuable.[30] Their practical utility was certainly highlighted by early editors like Edward Grimston
(serjeant at arms), who encouraged readers to 'keep this collection by you' to
'inform your knowledge'. He expected that people would·use the lists to
assess the turnover of MPs in successive parliaments, and that they would
use the wide margins to make annotations and corrections.[31] This was
precisely what happened, and some readers acquired printed lists with the
express purpose of facilitating interactions with MPs. D'Ewes, who pasted a
printed list of local MPs into a notebook in 1625, made corrections by hand,
and other lists were similarly amended as double returns were resolved, as
factual errors could be corrected and as MPs died or were expelled. Certain
copies were revisited and revised over extended periods, and included more
or less acerbic comments. One owner of a list of peers, for example, inserted
reflections on ejected bishops, noting that William Laud was 'beheaded,
God knows why'; that John Williams was 'a traitor'; that William Juxon was
'a most learned man'; and that Brian Duppa was 'brave'.[32] More importantly, such lists came to be employed as tools for lobbying, which probably
explains why one reader added family names to a printed list of peers, and
why others devised more or less cryptic methods of categorizing MPs.[33]

More important even than pamphlets in popularizing MP lists were
newspapers, which became the most common way of accessing such information, and which better catered to readers who sought to keep abreast of
current affairs.[34] Obviously, pamphlet lists could be updated on an occasional basis. New versions during the 1640s informed readers about members who had deserted parliament (marked with an asterisk), those who had
joined the royalist parliament at Oxford, and those who had died (marked
with a 'd'), as well as those who had joined the Commons as 'recruiter' MPs.
Newspapers, however, were much more efficient in this regard, and as such
they played an increasingly important role.[35] During the Long Parliament,
therefore, journalists reported the fate of William Taylor, who was

[30] HMC Egmont I, p. 546; Duppa Corr., p. 93; CCSP, iv. 656; DRO: D258/34/29/2, 4; HEH, HM 1554;
Bibliotheca Higgsiana, ed. P. Morrish (OBS, 1990), p. 22; Library of Robert Burton, ed. N. Kiessling
(OBS, 22, 1988), p. 101.
[31] Order and Manner (1624, 7742–3), sig. A; Names of the Knights (1625, 7743.5), sig. A2; Order and
Manner (1628, 7746).
[32] Bodl. MS Rawl.A.78, fos. 224–7v; TNA, SP 28/252i, fo. 91; BL, Harl. 158, fos. 236–9; FSL, STC 7746.13,
sigs. A4, B, B3v; FSL, STC 7746.3, p. 8; BL, 1607/519, pp. 10, 12; HEH, 321031, p. 1; HEH, 55364, pp. 57–
8, 114–15; HEH, 55365; BL, 13/1(2); FSL, STC 7746.9, p. 7; Durham UL, Routh 67.g.11/4.
[33] FSL, W460, sig. Av; FSL, STC 7746.3, sig. B; HEH, 51814–5.
[34] Rous Diary, p. 40; Whiteway, p. 107.
[35] Catalogue (1642, C1410A); New Catalogue (1644, W463, N591, W465A); Names of the Knights (1648,
N134).

imprisoned in May 1641 for describing the execution of Strafford as 'murder with the sword of justice'. They also noted the ejection of Robert Trelawny in March 1642, for calling the decision to appoint a parliamentary guard 'treason'. The *Perfect Diurnall* provided detailed lists of MPs who had deserted parliament for the king's side during 1642, of those who were summoned to attend and of those who were removed from the Commons. Indeed, in many cases specific details were given of the activities – from petitioning to plundering – for which individuals had been expelled. Likewise, *Britanicus* informed readers about the 'running' or 'rotten' lords who deserted parliament in 1643, and about MPs whose loyalty was at least suspected. The latter were described as 'valiant men so long as the Parliament forces are victorious, but cowardly and effeminate if they receive a loss on any occasion'. Other newspapers identified members of the royalist parliament at Oxford, promised to give 'their names, and of some of them a character', and described the fate of those who subsequently sought to recover their places at Westminster.[36] They also helped readers to make sense of the increasingly tense political situation in the late 1640s, by naming the MPs who were impeached by the army, who fled from the Commons after the 'forcing of the houses' and who were purged by the army. This involved a wealth of information, either in terms of reports about individual MPs, or in terms of comprehensive lists.[37] Conversely, newspaper readers could also identify MPs who joined (or re-joined) the Commons, from men readmitted after periods of absence to members who were returned in bi-elections and as 'recruiters'. This might mean straightforward reporting on election results, but it could also mean discussing election disputes and the decisions made by the Committee for Privileges.[38] Moreover, such information seems to have been targeted at those who were inclined to follow proceedings more closely and to interact with the Commons. Beginning with John Venn in June 1641, therefore, newspapers recorded when new MPs actually arrived at Westminster, and provided at least sketchy biographical information about those who joined the Commons. These included William Oldfield, who inherited his father's

---

[36] Durham UL, MSP 30, fos. 44–v; *True Diurnall*, 623.09A, sig. I2v; *Diurnall*: 504.048, p. 383; 504.046, p. 365; 511.08, sig. I3; 513.23B, sig. A3; 513.24B, sigs. Aa3v–4; 513.25A, sigs. Bb, Bb4v; *Speciall Passages*, 605.06A, p. 46; *Britanicus*: 286.001, pp. 5–7; 286.003, p. 24; *Kingdomes*, 214.042, pp. 324–6; *Scout*, 485.54, p. 430.

[37] BL, Add. 46931B, fos. 150–v; *HMC Egmont I*, p. 440–1; Chester RO, CR63/2/696, pp. 126–9; *Kingdomes*, 214.226, pp. 662–3, 665; *Perfect Summary*, 528.08, pp. 63–4; *Moderate*, 413.2022, sig. (y).

[38] *Diurnall*: 504.028, p.221; 504.088, p. 702; 504.115, p. 916; 504.155, p. 1244; 504.209, p. 1677; *Occurrences*: 465.3048, sigs. Bb4–v; 465.5030, pp. 196–7.

seat at Gatton in 1645, and whose return was described as 'a good honour to the family to have such succeeding worthies'.[39]

Although the available evidence about MPs and peers was almost certainly imperfect, it seems clear that even those with limited means could gather reasonably accurate information about the composition of both Houses. The publication of such details was not just permitted but actually encouraged, and this lends further credence to the idea that public interaction with parliament was actively facilitated. This will become even clearer by analysing remarkable but neglected evidence that parliament was sufficiently 'open' to permit readers to follow *proceedings* rather than merely to become acquainted with its *personnel*.

iii Reading the parliamentary timetable

During the Gillingham enclosure riots of the mid 1640s, the troublesome Richard Butler defended his actions by boasting about his familiarity with Westminster affairs. In shops and churches he pronounced that he knew more about 'what is done in the Parliament' than did his opponents, and this may not have been mere hyperbole. This is because it proved possible for people like Butler to obtain a wealth of information about parliamentary proceedings from printed sources, in terms of business past, present and future. This would have been extremely useful to people who were interested in following current affairs, and its publication once again reveals conjunctural change and a vulgarization of traditional practices, and it was sometimes explicitly designed to foster participation.[40]

At the most basic level, therefore, newspapers offered readers a rudimentary guide to the parliamentary timetable. This meant informing people about the days and times when the Houses sat, as well as the periods when mornings were spent in the Commons while afternoons were reserved for committees.[41] It also meant providing evidence about what kinds of business were being discussed. This is one obvious area where information was selective and incomplete, and on occasions when the House 'sat very close', readers only learned about debates on issues such as peace propositions and plots after they had taken place. Nevertheless, newspapers certainly helped readers and lobbyists by reporting the regular days of the week when

[39] For example: Durham UL, MSP 30, fo. 46v; *Occurrences*, 465.5024, sig. Z2; *Perfect Passages*, 523.48, p. 381.

[40] JRL: NP 72/8; NP 74/1.

[41] *Diurnall* 504.018, pp. 139, 142; 504.030, p. 236; 504.048, p. 383; 513.49B, p. 2; *Certaine Informations*, 36.44, p. 342; *Kingdomes*, 214.051, p. 411.

'private' grievances would be addressed, and by noting the periods when *no* private business would be taken into consideration.[42] Beyond this, newspapers regularly alerted readers to upcoming debates, even if this sometimes involved editors announcing as 'forthcoming' discussions that had already happened by the time that texts went to press. In other words, readers could be given advance warning about forthcoming business, and although this practice was not adopted by every journalist, astute readers may quickly have recognized which newspapers provided such coverage.[43] It appeared fairly regularly in the *Perfect Diurnall* and the *Kingdomes Weekly Intelligencer*, readers of which may have come to expect this kind of reporting. They may thus have exploited information that the Commons planned to debate peace proposals on 19 April 1644, having read stories to this effect three days earlier. They may also have gathered information about forthcoming debates in the 'grand committee', on issues like recruiter elections and the Court of Wards. Of course, the utility of such information depended on parliament sticking to its timetable, which did not always happen. Readers of the *Parliament Scout* who hoped to exploit knowledge that the Commons would consider peace propositions on 26 April 1644 would thus have been disappointed to discover that MPs subsequently postponed their debate.[44]

Although reports regarding the parliamentary timetable were far from perfect, the appearance of such evidence in the press reveals awareness about its value to the public, and occasions when newspapers provided *useless* rather than *useful* information for potential lobbyists were almost certainly accidental. This seems clear from instances where individual editions of newspapers like the *Diurnall* announced 'forthcoming' debates that had already taken place *alongside* reports about future sessions for which people genuinely had a chance to prepare. Moreover, the frequency with which people could read about forthcoming business precludes the possibility that members objected to its publication. This was clearly true in relation to deliberations over private and public petitions, where there was obvious public interest. In September 1645, therefore, it was reported that private business would be considered every Wednesday afternoon, and in October

---

[42] *Civicus*, 298.121, p. 1068; *Occurrences*: 465.2008, sig. H4v; 465.3032, sig. Ii3v; *Diurnall*: 504.191, p. 1532; 504.269, p. 2167; 513.52B, p. 3.

[43] For misleading references, see: *Diurnall Occurrences*, 181.206, sig. A3; *Diurnall*: 504.058, p. 460; *Kingdomes*: 214.088, pp. 705–6; *Civicus*, 298.141, p. 2026; *Occurrences*: 465.4015, sig. P3v; *Diary*: 144.126, sig. Ccc; *Scout*, 485.82, pp. 653, 656, 657. For more helpful references, see: *Diurnall*: 504.196, p. 1574; *Kingdomes*: 214.121, p. 969; *Civicus*, 298.157, sig. 7L4v.

[44] *Kingdomes*: 214.050, p. 404; 214.113, p. 906; 214.146, p. 84; *Scout*: 485.043, pp. 360–1; 485.045, pp. 377–9.

1646 it was announced that every Tuesday and Friday would be set aside to hear reports from the Committee for Compounding. But it was also true in terms of debates of much broader interest. In January 1647, therefore, the *Diurnall* trailed a session on MPs' office-holding and perquisites, which was scheduled to take place in a fortnight's time, and in April 1648 readers were given almost three weeks' notice of a debate over 'securing and settling' the kingdom. Similarly, on some issues of national policy, editors flagged ongoing debates that were scheduled to take place on regular days. In June 1645, for example, it was announced that the Commons would debate church reform every Wednesday and Friday, while in December 1645 readers learned that the House would consider peace propositions on a daily basis 'till they be fully finished'.[45] The availability of such information represented at least tacit encouragement of public participation. This was only occasionally advocated explicitly, as with the call for petitions against delinquent ministers in the opening weeks of the Long Parliament. However, it is not implausible to suggest that this would have been the message that ordinary readers took from the steady flow of information from Westminster.[46]

Indeed, the apparent willingness to foster public involvement in parliamentary business became even more explicit to the extent that members permitted the appearance of information regarding the composition of its committees, and the times and places of their meetings. Here, too, Civil War print culture democratized useful but privileged information, and reflected broader cultural changes. First, therefore, it is possible to explore contemporary attitudes to information about parliamentary committees. Gentry archives reveal the circulation and discussion of scribal committee lists, as well as advice about who to lobby and which lawyers to hire, and such evidence indicates the expense which some were prepared to incur to obtain 'perfect knowledge'.[47] Personal and corporate accounts reveal payments of between 1s and 10s for lists of specific committees, while longer orders and reports could be much more expensive. Some even obtained extended extracts from the official journal, or even entire volumes, albeit at a price of £1 per quire.[48] The very fact that political information of this kind

---

[45] *Kingdomes*, 214.254, p. 890; *Diurnall* 504.263, p. 2117; 504.111, p. 881; 504.170, p. 1362; 504.241, p. 1941; 504.242, p. 1645; 504.196, p. 1574; 504.190, p. 1526; 504.180, p. 1444; 504.100, p. 793; 504.125, p. 1005.

[46] BL, Add. 24863, fo. 43; University College Oxford, MS 83, fo. 35; *An Order* (1640, 7747).

[47] BL, Add. 70007, fos. 5, 8; Claydon, Verney reel 8; *HMC Egmont I*, p. 534.

[48] Beinecke: Osborn fb.159/86; Osborn fb.169–70; Osborn fb.93; GL: MS 2883/3, p. 311; MS 12065/3, fo. 195; Cheshire RO, DAR/F/3, pp. 15–17; Bodl. MS Eng.Misc.e.118, fo. 87; EKRO, CP/Bp/123, p. 5; ERO, Q/Sba 7/1–5; Cumbria RO, D/LONS/L2/128; Lincs. RO, MM 12/2/7; *HMC De L'Isle VI*, pp. 247, 346, 377; PA, MP 7 Feb. 1642; *Burton Diary*, i. 320.

was traditionally so pricey provides the key to explaining its purpose, and to demonstrating that it represented purposeful rather than idle expenditure. Certified copies of committee lists – detailing membership, remits, and the times and places of meetings – abound in private archives, and that they were acquired with a view to influencing proceedings seems evident from the frequency with which specific names were marked by readers, even if the meaning of such annotations remains mysterious. This was true not merely for *ad hoc* committees relating to private business, but also for key standing committees – for elections, for privileges and for 'examinations'.[49]

Secondly, it is this utility of evidence regarding committees that explains its appearance in print. As with other aspects of parliamentary affairs, therefore, information about committees became much more widely available, in both official and non-official publications. This can only partly be explained by the way in which 'agents' like Adam Baynes circulated such material to members of the army, or by an extension of 'ancient' practices whereby details regarding specific committees were displayed outside the Commons, so that 'persons may take notice where they sit'.[50] Much more obviously, it can be connected to an innovative and pervasive approach to publicizing public bodies. From the Excise Office to the Statute Office, and from the Hale Commission to the commissioners for buildings, information began to be printed about individual officers (including their private addresses), and about the precise times and places where meetings were held, including notices and adverts that announced specific hearings.[51] The official who took securities on behalf of Cromwell's Major Generals was reported as holding meetings at the Cock in Fleet Street, between 9am and 11am, and again between 2pm and 4pm, while the commissioners for 'discoveries' were observed to hold meetings on Tuesdays, Thursdays and Fridays at Worcester House, where their registrar attended daily from 8am to 8pm. Such information was clearly provided to facilitate interaction with such bodies, and although in some cases this reflected the need to engage

[49] Bodl. MS Tanner 66, fos. 134, 288; BL: Add. 4155, fos. 211, 231, 245, 249; Add. 57929, fos. 69–v; Add. 71534, fo. 92; Harl. 4931, fo. 100; Add. 70108; Add. 4191, fo. 23; Add. 5497, fo. 14; Add. 24863, fo. 43; Add. 46931B, fo. 4; Add. 11044, fos. 185–6; CKS, U455/O4; Alnwick, Letters and Papers 18, fos. 3–9; SHC, G85/5/2/1; HEH: EL 7688; HA 14933; Leics. RO, DG7/P.P.6; DRO: D258/33/37/3; D1232 M/O 68–9; D258/32/35; CKS: U269/A156/2; U269/O294; Bodl. MS Tanner 65, fos. 212–13v; BL, Harl. 6806, fos. 268, 270–6; Beinecke, Osborn fb.200, fos. 417–v.

[50] BL, Add. 21427, fo. 145; *Proceedings 1614*, p. 101; *Orders of the House of Commons* (1756), pp. 75–6; *CD 1621*, p. 32; *Politicus*, 361.400, p. 262; *CJ*, vii. 587; *Lawfulnes* (1647, L647), p. 12.

[51] For example: *Strange Newes* (1642, S5894), sigs. A2v–3; *CSPD 1652–3*, p. 369; *Diurnall*: 503.210, p. 3200; 504.010, p. 73; *Politicus*: 361.182, pp. 3011–12; 361.184, pp. 3049–50; 361.243, p. 5112; 361.247, pp. 5171–2; 361.371, p. 7924; 361.384, p. 12; *Proceedings*: 599.006, p. 52; 599.011, p. 138; 599.121, p. 1883.

with interested parties, in others an attempt was being made to attract a wider audience of concerned citizens. Examples of the former include the Committee of Accounts, the hearings and procedures of which were publicized by *Politicus* in the 1650s, and the Commissioners for Irish affairs, who encouraged individual soldiers to attend their meetings, submit their accounts and lay claim to confiscated land. The same was also true of proceedings regarding delinquents' estates, where advance notice was given about hearings into particular cases.[52] More intriguing, however, are the occasions when print was used to promote public enquiries. The commissioners who oversaw the relief of Irish Protestants promoted their meetings 'so that such as have propositions to offer . . . may know to whom and to what place to repair with the same'. Similarly, the committee for improving customs and excise revenue announced a meeting in the Court of Wards, to 'receive all such proposals as shall be presented to them . . . and treat with such persons as shall there propound for the same'.[53]

Publicizing parliamentary committees thus reflected the demand for practical information, and a new attitude to transparency and participation. Indeed, it would be a mistake to assume that publicizing committees was frowned upon by the authorities. It is true that when the stationer, Henry Overton, produced a list of the committee regarding scandalous ministers (December 1640), he found enthusiastic readers but a hostile response from the Commons. The problem, however, was that his list was *unauthorized*, that he had mis-transcribed MPs' names and that he had embellished the committee's instructions.[54] Indeed, it subsequently became increasingly common for details about parliamentary committees – in terms of both membership and meetings – to appear with impunity, and even with an official imprint. This began with the 'recess committee' (September 1641) and the committee that sat at Guildhall after the attempted arrest of the 'five members' (January 1642), and many parliamentary committees garnered publicity with the express purpose of encouraging participation. Only very rarely did this elicit a negative response, and when a parliamentary delegation in Edinburgh complained about the publication of their instructions in 1648, they did so merely because this had occurred before they even reached Scotland.[55]

[52] *Politicus*: 361.294, p. 5927; 316.317, p. 7092; 361.180, pp. 2878–9; 361.182, p. 3011; *Contractors* (1650, C5975); *Diurnall*, 503.215, sig. 10G4v.
[53] BL, Add. 71534, fo. 178: *At the Committee* (1645); BL, Add. 5497, fo. 34: *Die Martii 25 April* (1643); *CSPD 1645–7*, p. 1; *Diurnall*, 504.025, p. 199; *Politicus*, 361.381, p. 1623.
[54] *An Order* (1640, 7747); *Rous Diary*, pp. 111–12; *CJ*, ii. 65; *D'Ewes*, ed. Notestein, pp. 234–6.
[55] *Names* (1641, N130); *Declaration* (1642, E2548); *Order* (1642, E2654); *Order* (1648, E1695), p. 7; *Humble Petition* (1648, H3456), sig. A4v; *Committee* (1647, E2539); DRO, D258/53/26; *Die Jovis, 20*

This last example demonstrates not merely that complaints about publicizing committees need to be contextualized carefully, but also that what began with official initiatives came to be dominated by newspapers. In other words, the complaint made by the MPs in Edinburgh centred on the behaviour of journalists, who had become the most important conduit for publicizing parliamentary committees, and who did much more than merely provide evidence about the activity of MPs *outside* the chamber.[56] Newspapers, in other words, shone a light onto parliament, even if coverage was sometimes vague, incomplete and restricted to certain journals. It is true that some committees received little publicity, and that readers were sometimes provided with information that was less than entirely helpful, such as when journalists drew attention to the venues where committees met but not to their membership.[57] Nevertheless, it remains striking how often readers could learn a great deal about what was happening in the backrooms of Westminster Palace. It was possible to become well informed, for example, about the names of the most important members of individual committees and about the identities of their chairmen. Regular newshounds may thus have recognized that Giles Greene chaired the Navy Committee and that Robert Scawen chaired the Army Committee, and information was also available about any number of other *ad hoc* and standing committees, including those relating to private bills and sectional interests. Equally common were occasions where full lists were reproduced, for committees that were arcane and specialized, as well as for major standing committees and executive bodies, such as the Committee of Revenue and the Committee for Both Kingdoms. Indeed, readers were also given the opportunity to follow changes in the composition of such bodies, and to observe how some committees were eventually wound down or replaced, having been found to be of 'little use'.[58]

What should be recognized about the tendency to publish incomplete or imperfect information is that it reflected decisions made by journalists, rather than policy made at Westminster. It probably reflected limitations

---

Julii 1648 (1648, E2624AC); *Order* (1648, E2658); *Die Lunae, 3 April* (1643, H2906); *Ordinance* (1645, E1798); Bodl. MS Tanner 58, fo. 742; BL, Add. 69923, fos. 85–6v.

[56] *Diurnall*, 504.298, p. 2420; *Occurrences*, 465.5047, p. 323; *Moderate*, 413.2039, sig. (qq2v); *Moon*, 248.01, p. 5; *Kingdomes*, 214.009, p. 65; *Civicus*, 298.112, p. 995; *Continuation*, 638.18, p. 4; *Diary*, 144.135, sig. Gg3v; *Scout*, 485.82, p. 658; *Occurrences*, 465.5050, p. 345; *Speciall Passages*, 605.13, p. 108.

[57] For example: *Diurnall*: 511.16C, sig. R2; 511.35A, sig. Mm; *Kingdomes*, 214.221, p. 628.

[58] For example: *Diurnall*: 504.003, p.24; 504.029, p. 228; 504.091, p. 720; *Civicus*, 298.137, p. 1193; *Kingdomes*, 214.263, p. 962; *Court Mercurie*, 81.02, sig. B4v; *Occurrences*: 465.5051, sig. Ddd2; 465.4028, sigs. Ee3v–4; *Pragmaticus*, 369.109A, sig. I4; *Britanicus*, 286.023A, p. 180; *Aulicus*, 275.205B, p. 814. See: Warw. RO, CR136/B68e.

of space rather than official reluctance to publicize proceedings, and it was both common and permissible to draw attention to forthcoming committee meetings in ways that facilitated participation. As with parliamentary debates, of course, such information was sometimes redundant by the time that newspapers appeared. Readers were thus given no chance of attending the committee to discuss the County Palatine of Durham (17 August 1647), the committee regarding tithes (16 September 1647) or the committee for universities (26 February 1642).[59] Nevertheless, newspapers were much more helpful about committees that met on a daily basis, or on regular occasions over an extended period. These included the committee to discuss proposals for a settlement with the king, which met in the Prince's Chamber on a daily basis in November 1647, as well as the committee for grievances, which was overseen by Alexander Rigby and Thomas Scot. They also included powerful executive committees like the Committee of Safety, which was advertised as meeting in the Court of Wards. In turn, anyone familiar with the Committee of Safety was likely to have known where to attend the Committee for Irish Affairs, which was said to meet in the same venue every Tuesday, Thursday and Saturday. Ultimately, indeed, readers were sometimes given every single piece of information that was necessary to lobby efficiently. In November 1647, for example, one of the newspapers that did most to publicize proceedings, *Perfect Occurrences*, not only printed the names of the MPs on a committee to consider the king's escape from Hampton Court, but also identified its chairman and gave the time and place of its daily meetings.[60]

The pervasive nature of such journalistic tactics indicates official tolerance of a practice that served to foster or at least facilitate participation. Contemporary readers could thus have been forgiven for thinking that their input was welcome unless it was explicitly prohibited, as when the *Diurnall* announced in December 1647 that a meeting to discuss radical agitation would involve a 'close committee'. This would surely have been the conclusion that contemporaries reached upon encountering an official pamphlet that appeared in January 1648, and that provided a list of the new committee for grievances, complete with the committee's remit, the times and places of its regular meetings, and the names of its chairmen.[61] Just occasionally, indeed, members of the public were explicitly encouraged to

---

[59] *Occurrences*: 465.5033, p. 220; 465.5037, pp. 255–6; *Continuation*, 623.07A, sig. G3v.

[60] *Diurnall*: 504.191, p. 1532; 504.245, p. 1974; 511.12A, sig. N2v; *Heads*, 180.01, pp. 1–2; *Kingdomes*: 214.205, p. 497; 214.107, p. 850; *Occurrences*: 465.5041, p. 283; 465.5044, p. 310; 465.5046, p. 315.

[61] *Diurnall*, 504.227, p. 1826; *Committee* (1647, E2539), pp. 3–6; DRO, D258/53/26.

take part in parliamentary proceedings. When a crowd of soldiers demanded arrears of pay outside the House in April 1648, the Commons insisted that they should 'repair to the knights and burgesses of the ... counties and towns, upon whose entertainments they ... were employed', in order to get their claims certified. It is even possible that efforts by the committee for the relief of Ireland to publicize its proceedings extended to the insertion of notices into newspapers, which announced their thrice-weekly meetings at the Queen's Court in Westminster, and which invited suggestions and propositions from the public.[62]

In assessing the implications of such evidence, of course, there are obvious grounds for caution. It is clear that the information available to contemporaries was incomplete, and that the ability to interact with parliament continued to be affected by wealth and status. Similarly, it is vital to remember that the picture that people could develop about proceedings was likely to be much less detailed than that which can be recovered by historians. Nevertheless, contemporaries would not have needed to engage in particularly 'extensive' reading to develop a fairly impressive awareness of parliamentary affairs, and given what is known about contemporary habits and tastes, it is not implausible to assume that those who were interested in what was being done at Westminster would have recognized which newspapers best served their needs. Moreover, what is certain is that the 1640s witnessed a profound vulgarization of the kinds of information that facilitated effective participation, and that an institution which was physically accessible also tolerated, and at times encouraged, efforts to publicize proceedings. While recognizing that accessibility and openness sometimes created problems, in other words, MPs and peers also appreciated that public interest needed to be managed rather than stifled, and that it may even have been beneficial.

iv Secrecy and formality during the Interregnum

In the light of evidence about the degree to which parliamentary secrecy was forsaken during the 1640s, it is obviously important to map the dynamic of accessibility over time. In other words, it is necessary to track the official response to public interest and print practices across the revolutionary decades, not least because of evidence which seems to suggest that parliament became more secretive during the Interregnum. The aim of this section, therefore, is to explore such evidence, and to suggest that, while

---

[62] *Diurnall*, 504.245, p. 1970; *Civicus*, 298.III, pp. 984–5.

change did indeed occur in relation to political transparency, this was not simply a matter of rolling back the developments of the 1640s. Instead, it will be argued that the aim was to *police* and *formalize* procedures and practices that facilitated participation, while also ensuring decorum.

First, therefore, it is impossible to ignore evidence of a new mood after January 1649. Contemporaries certainly detected a difference in the way in which parliamentary affairs were reported. In June 1650 Richard Berrie complained that 'everything is carried so secret', while in February 1652 George Radcliffe bemoaned the fact that 'the diurnalls of late tell us very little of what they do'. In June 1653 John Langley explained that there was 'little news stirring at this time, all passages being kept more private'. Such comments were replicated during the protectoral parliaments, when observers noted that MPs were 'very private', that 'none of their passages' were 'made public' until legislation was finalized and that 'there is very little speech of parliamentary affairs'.[63] It also seems to have become more common to voice opposition to the publication of votes 'without leave', and the conservatism of men like Sir Arthur Annesley might be thought to have informed decision-making. Thus, from the order to erect a screen at the window of the Commons in 1650, to the resolution to clamp down on the activities of journalists in 1653, it appears that MPs wanted to prevent papers from being thrown out of the chamber, and to contain the reporting of proceedings. Finally, it is also possible to highlight comments by journalists like Nedham, who explained his decision to 'omit the passages of Parliament' in September 1654.[64]

Persuasive as this evidence might seem, there are grounds for interpreting it with great care. Apart from the fact that the 'screen' may have been intended to block out the sunlight from an oppressively stuffy chamber, measures to clamp down on reporting primarily reflected concerns about accuracy, and about securing an authoritative record. Supporting Annesley's motion in April 1659, therefore, Speaker Bampfield complained that votes were 'misprinted', and that this made proceedings 'too cheap'. The same also applies to measures taken in 1653, which sprang from anxiety about the printing of 'falsities', and which reflected a determination that parliamentary reporting should be officially licensed, as Nedham, too, believed.[65] Indeed, close scrutiny of the evidence regarding accessibility

---

[63] Nott. UL, Ga/12768/26; Longleat, Portland 2, fo. 95; Staffs. RO, D593/P/8/2/2; Lancs. RO, DDF/411; Bodl. MS North.c.4, fo. 105.

[64] *Burton Diary*, iv. 415, 453; *CJ*, vi. 432, vii. 288, 296; *Politicus*, 361.224, p. 3796.

[65] *Burton Diary*, iv. 415; *CJ*, vii. 288; *Proceedings*, 599.200, p. 3157; *Politicus*, 361.224, p. 3796.

and publicity actually suggests that MPs sought to *refine* reporting procedures, rather than to re-impose 'secrecy'.

In terms of physical access to the palace, therefore, members demonstrated an ongoing concern with 'clamours' and with 'disorderly' and 'uncivil' behaviour. One commentator in 1653 reflected that 'they are more strict than ever in keeping all disorderly idle persons out of the lobby . . . for fear of disturbance'. This helps to explain why the Commons more regularly passed orders to keep the doors shut, particularly during morning sessions, although it is also likely that this reflected a determination to preserve the secrecy of debates and council elections, to ensure efficient divisions, and to deter MPs from leaving the chamber. It did not, in other words, simply reflect a desire to keep the public out and to impose secrecy.[66] Occasions when the Commons made concerted attempts to clear 'strangers' from the lobby, and when observers noted that MPs sat 'close' and 'shut themselves in', remained fairly rare, and they continued to be restricted to moments of extraordinary tension, like the dying days of the 1659 Parliament. Moreover, while Pepys suggested that the 'strictness' with which Cromwellians limited the 'free passage of strangers' reflected a new courtliness, parliament may actually have become *more* open in response to growing public interest. In December 1651, for example, it was at least proposed to make a 'fit passage' from Westminster Hall to the lobby, which would have had the effect of facilitating public access. Indeed, judging by evidence from the proceedings against Lilburne in 1651, many MPs were happy for the doors to remain open when reports were delivered to the House. Although a motion to this effect was narrowly defeated, it remained extremely difficult to prevent strangers from witnessing proceedings, or indeed from taking seats in the Commons.[67]

This sense that attempts were made to promote settled and formal practices also applies to the information that emanated from Westminster. Pamphlets listing MPs continued to be produced at the start of each parliament, sometimes in ways that enabled readers to observe how the make-up of the House had changed since 1640. A list produced at the restoration of the Rump in 1659 thus detailed who had been sitting in April 1653, and who had not yet returned, and comparative analysis was

---

[66] Bodl. MS Clarendon 46, fos. 70–2v; *Burton Diary*, i. 148, ii. 224; *CJ*, vi. 110, 146, 151, 158, 348, 367, 453, 455, 464–5, 467–8, vii. 1–2, 9, 19, 20, 41, 134, 220, 511, 543, 611, 641, 644, 784–5.

[67] *CJ*, vi. 512, 515, 560, vii. 641; *Burton Diary*, iv. 482; BL, Lans. 823, fo. 299; *TSP*, vii. 618, 662; Bodl. MS Carte 73, fos. 187–v; *CJ*, vii. 46, 71.

clearly undertaken by at least some onlookers.[68] As with earlier examples, these pamphlets were then annotated by readers, who made corrections and comments, and who also recorded the fate of the regicides after 1660.[69] Even more obviously than before, however, newspapers were now the most popular and effective way of obtaining such information, and journalists boasted about offering a more reliable and accurate service, not least because of their ability to correct errors and record the outcome of election disputes.[70] Indeed, this was precisely why newspapers were recommended to people by Secretary Thurloe, and why they were read avidly by members of the public, some of whom made notes from published lists and referred to them in correspondence.[71]

The willingness to provide readers with detailed and up-to-date information about parliament thus seems to have been undiminished in the 1650s, and it was apparent in almost every aspect of parliamentary journalism. It may even be possible to argue that editors became even more focused on the task of reporting formal proceedings, even to the extent that some newspapers resembled little more than digests of the official journals. Indeed, rather than being seen as evidence of how dull newspapers became during the Interregnum, this development probably reflected the value that contemporaries attached to useful information. First, newspapers provided increasing amounts of detail about changes to the personnel of the Commons, in terms of bi-elections that returned men like the Earl of Pembroke, in terms of 'absent' members who were readmitted to the Rump, and in terms of the ejection of corrupt characters like Lord Howard of Escrick.[72] Attempts were also made to report occasions when the House was purged more thoroughly, even if these were much less obviously sanctioned by the authorities. In 1656, therefore, lists of the men who were excluded from the first protectoral parliament circulated widely, alongside texts that contained their 'protestation', and these can be shown to have been discussed in correspondence. The subsequent

---

[68] *Maner of Siting* (1653, M461); *Catalogue* (1653, C1401); *List* (1653, L2463); *New List* (1653, N653); *Perfect List* (1654, P1497); *Names of the Members* (1654, N142); *Names of all the Knights* (1654, N125); *Perfect List* (1656, P1499); *Catalogue* (1658, C1405); *Perfect List* (1659, P1496); *List of Knights* (1654, L2399); *Catalogue* (1656, C1394); *Catalogue* (1659, C1403). See: Bodl. MS Rawl.A.78, fos. 224–7v.

[69] BL, 669.f.17/14; Bodl. MS Clarendon, 45, fos. 498–99v; HEH, 124109, p. 2.

[70] For example: *Proceedings*, 599.194, p. 3070; *Diurnall*, 503.191, pp. 2894–6; *Politicus*: 361.164, pp. 2619–21; 361.214, pp. 3632–6; 361.215, pp. 3650–1; 361.216, p. 3668. For criticism of the printed lists, see: *Politicus*, 361.555, p. 251.

[71] Bodl. MS Carte 73, fos. 26, 174; MS Rawl.A.78, fo. 223; MS North.c.4, fos. 78, 91; TNA, SP 18/74, fo. 166; Lancs. RO, DDF/411; Northants. RO, IC 437, 454; *Politicus*, 361.394, p. 165.

[72] For example: *Kingdomes*, 214.318, p. 1415; *Diurnall*: 504.299, pp. 2435–6; 504.300, p. 2374; *Politicus*, 361.055, sig. 5S4v.

bi-elections were also covered in some detail, and newspapers continued to provide biographical sketches of particular candidates. Readers were thus informed that John Whalley, who was returned at New Shoreham in 1659, was the son of Lord Whalley, sometime Cromwellian Major General and current member of the 'other House'.[73]

Secondly, journalists showed much greater zeal than before in reporting formal proceedings, in terms of matters that were being discussed and the timetable of business. Throughout the 1650s, therefore, readers were provided with regular and detailed lists of bills that were being considered, and with information about the committees to which these had been referred, in ways that informed the correspondence of onlookers as far away as Dublin.[74] In addition, reports about the days on which MPs met involved greater precision about the timing of particular sessions, whether in the Commons, in council or in committee, and although the House devoted much less time to 'private' business, it was nevertheless possible to follow the passage of specific petitions. Indeed, every effort was made to ensure that people knew when the Commons would concentrate on public business, not merely by ensuring that such information was 'posted up at the door', so that 'suitors may take notice of it', but also by allowing journalists to publicize it more widely.[75]

Thirdly, it became a great deal more common to find evidence about forthcoming debates. Although the weekly newspaper format continued to ensure that journalists sometimes published obsolete information, more strenuous efforts appear to have been made to overcome this problem, and the chances of using such evidence to make effective interventions probably increased significantly.[76] This would have served the interests of merchants, as with the bill regarding Carmen and Woodmongers and machinations regarding the Norfolk textile industry, and it would also have benefited private individuals, in terms of matters like the sale of delinquents' estates, the accounts of army officers and cases at the Committee for Petitions. It would also have assisted various radicals, who had good reason for following the progress of bills regarding blasphemy, incest and adultery, and moves to

---

[73] *TSP*, v. 456, 490–1; DRO, D258/7/18; *HMC Egmont I*, p. 579; *Politicus*: 361.337, p. 7405; 361.343, p. 7493; *Intelligencer*, 575.158, p. 135.

[74] *Proceedings*, 599.028, sig. Dddv; 599.089, p. 1353; *Diurnall*, 503.197, p. 2993; *Politicus*: 361.086, p. 1380; 361.178, p. 2847; 361.331, pp. 7304; 361.333, p. 7350; 361.368, pp. 7866–7, 7874–6.

[75] For example: *CJ*, vi. 318; *Occurrences*, 465.5114, p. 896; *Kingdomes*, 214.303, p. 1295; *Proceedings*: 599.006, p. 54; 599.017, p. 229; 599.210, pp. 3322–5; 599.269, sig. 2314; *Diurnall*, 504.293, p. 2359; *Politicus*: 361.343, p. 7492; 361.365, p. 7836; 361.569, p. 479.

[76] *Proceedings*: 599.003, p. 18; 599.008, p. 77; 599.018, p. 231; 599.029, sig. Ggg4v; 599.030, sig. Hhh; *Diurnall*, 503.032, sig. Ii4v.

conduct legal proceedings in English.[77] On some of these bigger issues, of course, debates became protracted and contentious, but this merely increased the likelihood that readers would have become aware of what was being done. For example, editors alerted people to the fact that regular sessions were being held regarding law reform (every Wednesday during January 1653, and every Friday in the following November), and regarding the propagation of the gospel (every Friday in February 1650).[78] Journalists thus had something to offer to almost anyone who planned to petition or lobby MPs, and if newspapers became less racy after 1649, then they also became much more useful.

Finally, journalists shed unprecedented light on parliamentary committees. This is not to deny that there were obstacles to 'perfect knowledge': the pressure of space meant that some committees were reported very sketchily; and the decision to rotate committee chairmen every month probably made the lobbyist's job significantly harder, even if it ensured probity.[79] Nevertheless, journalists proved much more willing to provide evidence about the membership of committees, about the remit of specific bodies, and about the times and places of their meetings. Indeed, the relaxed attitude of the authorities to the circulation of such information also ensured that it could be peddled by activists. These included the people who promoted a petition on behalf of 'the poor of this nation', who felt able to name the MPs to whom the matter was referred in March 1649, so that interested parties would know to whom they should 'make their address'.[80] Indeed, on some occasions, readers were deliberately encouraged to contribute to deliberations, and the Hale commission explicitly invited readers to submit evidence to individual members.[81]

This last trend reached a peak during the Nominated Assembly in 1653, when readers were given evidence about all of the key standing committees. This was included in the published lists of MPs, and then recycled (and supplemented) by newspapers, and what is extraordinary is that journalists and publishers were prepared to publicize committees in a systematic rather

---

[77] *Proceedings*: 599.031, sig. Kkk2; 599.032, sig. Mmmv; 599.042, p. 612; 599.050, p. 731; 599.059, p. 885; 599.098, p. 1501; 599.082, sig. 7V4v; 599.158, p. 2471; *Politicus*: 361.179, p. 2864; 361.182, p. 3018.

[78] *Diurnall*: 503.162, p. 2431; 503.204, sig. 9V3v; *Proceedings*: 599.018, p. 242; 599.172, p. 2701; 599.214, p. 3390.

[79] *Proceedings*: 599.012, sig. T2; 599.007, p. 62; *Diurnall*, 503.189, p. 2869; *Politicus*, 316.077, p. 1236.

[80] For example: *Occurrences*: 465.5115, pp. 889, 893, 896; *Diurnall*: 504.307, p. 2576; 503.143, p. 2141; *Proceedings*, 599.119, pp. 1839–40; *Perfect Summary*, 530.20, p. 195; *Impartiall Intelligencer*. 194.12, p.89; 194.14, p. 106; *Politicus*, 361.107, p. 1688; *Humble Petition* (1648, H3456), p. 8. See: All Souls, MS 167, fos. 8–9v.

[81] *Politicus*, 361.087, p. 1392; *Diurnall*, 503.113, p. 1654.

than a piecemeal fashion. Indeed, they included not merely the times and places of meetings, but also the number of MPs that was required to make each body quorate and the names of their chairmen.[82] In the case of the Committee for Petitions, moreover, readers were given practical advice about how to submit their claims and complaints, and newspapers not only noted that petitions would be received on Thursdays, and that Mondays and Tuesdays would be devoted to hearings, but also explained that petitions needed to be endorsed by at least one MP. Further directions specified that anyone who wanted to petition about trade, the poor or public debts should 'make their addresses' to the specialized committees that had been appointed to offer 'relief and satisfaction' on such matters. It was also noted that petitioners needed to specify the topics that merited scrutiny, and that they should 'set down' the names of witnesses 'in the margin of each particular, upon which they desire to have them examined'.[83]

The remarkably precise advice that was given to members of the public in 1653 represented the culmination of a trend which had been emerging steadily since 1649. It can be observed not merely in relation to local affairs and private business, but also on matters of wider interest and national importance, from the future of the excise to the relief of 'tender consciences', and from law reform to the propagation of the gospel.[84] Moreover, such evidence did not disappear from public view during the Protectorate, notwithstanding claims about the secrecy of Cromwell's government. During the 1654 Parliament, for example, readers were informed that the grand committee for religion met every Tuesday morning, and that another grand committee on the constitution sat on Thursdays, Fridays and Saturdays, and eventually that the latter was meeting on a daily basis. Likewise, during both the 1656 and 1659 Parliaments, *Politicus* drew attention to the meeting times and places of all of the major standing committees, as well as of some *ad hoc* committees. Meanwhile, amid vibrant pamphlet debates about the nature of government during the restored Rump, Nedham's journal repeatedly drew attention to forthcoming committee meetings and debates regarding the constitutional settlement.[85] On

---

[82] *Maner* (1653, M461); *List of the Names* (1653, L2463); *New List* (1653, N653); *Proceedings*, 599.204, pp. 3228–31; *Diurnall*, 503.189, p. 2861; *Politicus*, 361.164, pp. 2614, 2621.

[83] *Proceedings*, 599.200, p. 3164; *Diurnall*: 503.190, p. 2881; 503.195, p. 2965.

[84] For example: *Perfect Summary*, 530.20, p. 197; *Proceedings*: 599.051, p. 748; 599.106, p. 1641; *Diurnall*: 503.163, p. 2448; 503.096, p. 1362; 503.097, sig. 5E; *Occurrences*, 465.5122, p. 1005.

[85] *Proceedings*, 599.269, sig. 2314; *Politicus*: 361.221, p. 3748; 361.222, p. 3752; 361.223, pp. 3779–80; 361.328, p. 7256; 361.552, p. 208; 361.555, p. 247; 361.556, p. 261; 361.557, p. 288; 361.580, p. 620; 361.582, p. 655–6; 361.583, p. 672; 361.584A, p. 677.

some occasions, journalists even reported the dates on which committee reports were expected to be delivered and debated, and the continuation of such practices into the early weeks of 1660 enabled men like Thomas Rugg to record the composition of key committees in some detail.[86]

In other words, rather than witnessing a return to secrecy, the Interregnum saw the emergence of more *settled* and *durable* practices regarding political transparency. It can even be demonstrated that this extended to the processes, personnel and proceedings of the republican and protectoral councils, which were ostensibly the most secretive branches of government. The names of councillors were thus public knowledge, and details about elections appeared in all of the major newspapers, whose editors occasionally spelled out which members had been re-elected and who were the newcomers.[87] As with so many kinds of political information, moreover, this evidence was devoured by contemporaries. Some men, like Sir Ralph Verney, were impatient, and went to considerable lengths to identify councillors – and even the number of votes that they received – at the earliest possible opportunity. However, many others – including Rugg and Adam Baynes – found newspapers to be perfectly adequate as guides to the political landscape.[88] And what such public interest meant was that newspapers recognized the value of informing readers about the dates of forthcoming council elections, and even that they felt inclined to provide evidence about the composition of its committees, and about upcoming business.[89]

Parliamentary reporting can thus be shown to have been a key element of print culture during the Interregnum, in ways that have been overlooked by scholars. It was not, of course, without its limitations, and it is worth highlighting both the strengths and the weaknesses of this particular aspect of the print revolution. This can be done through two brief examples, which go some way towards challenging the apparently sensible assumption that public participation would have been facilitated most obviously in relation to matters of 'private' concern. The first concerns legislation for the relief of creditors, which was a matter of immense concern to many individuals, but which was not always covered very helpfully by journalists. Thus, while it is

[86] *Diurnall*, 503.252, p. 3866; *Proceedings*: 599.264, p. 4180; 599.271, p. 4297; *Politicus*: 361.336, p. 7389; 361.337, p. 7406; 361.400, p. 262; 361.605; Chester RO, CR63/2/696; *Rugg*, pp. 24, 25, 33, 44.

[87] For example: *Kingdomes*, 214.299, p. 1261; *Proceedings*, 599.072, pp. 1094–5; *Diurnall*, 503.010, sig. K2v; *Politicus*, 361.036, pp. 586–7. For analysis of membership, see: *Politicus*, 361.077, p. 1236; *Diurnall*, 503.204, sigs. 9V3–v.

[88] Claydon, Verney reel 16; Nott. UL, Pw2/Hy/159; *Rugg*, pp. 24, 25, 44; Chester RO, DAR/I/29; BL, Add. 21420, fo. 279.

[89] *Proceedings*, 599.071, p. 1080; *Politicus*: 361.128, p. 2024; 361.315, p. 7059; 361.307, pp. 6925–6.

true that the progress of a bill through the Commons was monitored during November 1649, the 'forthcoming' debates to which attention was drawn in the months that followed would only sometimes have facilitated participation, given the vagaries of publishing schedules.[90]

A rather different picture emerges, however, in relation to the controversial and abortive bill for a 'new representative', a matter of much greater constitutional importance and one that was considered by MPs over a protracted period. This has generally been studied to shed light on the unhappy fate of the Rump Parliament, but it also highlights just how much practical information was available to those citizens who were inclined to contribute to its success or failure. From its earliest stages in the spring of 1649, therefore, it was possible to find evidence about, and commentary upon, the names of the MPs to whom it had been referred, and to learn that they would meet every Monday and Friday at 2pm in the Exchequer Chamber. In October 1649 it was reported that the committee would convene on a daily basis, and that it would report to the Commons in a fortnight's time, and those who had grown accustomed to slippage in the parliamentary timetable may have taken heart from an announcement that the matter would be considered without fail on 9 January 1650. The matter dragged on, of course, and astute observers perhaps realized that the debates in grand committee were regularly adjourned for a week at a time, and from late 1650 readers of journals like *Severall Proceedings* could fairly easily follow the string of regular meetings, and the equally regular adjournments, until a renewed sense of urgency led to the revival of daily deliberations in October 1651.[91] During such bursts of activity, journalists were unable to trail every single meeting and debate, but coverage remained fairly consistent until the spring of 1653. Readers would have recognized that the grand committee was chaired by Erasmus Earle and William Say, and journalists regularly observed that 'all that come [are] to have voices'. This may have convinced onlookers to believe that their presence and participation was being actively encouraged.[92]

Such an inference would not have been groundless. Readers had frequently been informed that details about committees were provided so that

---

[90] *Proceedings*: 599.006, p. 52; 599.007, p. 65; 599.035, sig. Rrr; 599.037, sig. Xxx.

[91] *Kingdomes*, 214.310 p. 1347; *Impartiall Intelligencer*, 194.12, p. 89; *Moon*, 248.06, p. 56; *Proceedings*: 599.002, p. 10; 599.014, p. 182; 599.015, p. 194; 599.017, pp. 227, 229; 599.018, p. 246; 599.019, sig. Kk4v; 599.020, sig. Mm4v; 599.021, sig. Nn4v; 599.022, sig. Qq4; 599.023, sig. Ss; 599.056, p. 840; 599.081, p. 1238; 599.083, p. 1270; 599.097, p. 1499; 599.103, sig. 9O2v; 599.105, p. 1612; *Politicus*: 361.070, p. 1124; 361.071, p. 1127; 361.072, p. 1156; *Diurnall*, 503.097, p. 1361.

[92] *Politicus*: 361.075, p. 1204; 361.076, pp. 1207, 1220; 361.119, p. 1180; *Proceedings*: 599.111, sigs. 10F2–3; 599.112, p. 1725; 599.137, np; 599.177, p. 2790.

'subjects may have general notice of it'; that committees would accept 'any information' from 'any person'; and that citizens ought to know the procedures by which submissions should be made. In 1652 one journalist explained the decision to publish membership lists of ten standing committees, along with 'the places where they sit', by saying that it was done for 'the better information of such as have occasion to apply themselves unto those committees'. Such phraseology was not uncommon, indeed, and it merely replicated announcements by bodies like the committee for tithes, which appeared in more than one newspaper. These indicated that 'persons who have any thing to offer for asserting the propriety of incumbents in tithes may apply themselves to the said committee, and deliver the same in writing any Friday or Wednesday within a month'.[93] Consciously or not, such comments effectively facilitated participation by anyone who picked up a penny newspaper.

v Conclusion

In assessing the significance of parliamentary reporting in the 1640s and 1650s, it is vital to address two significant grounds for caution, relating to both readers and the authorities. With readers, therefore, there is a risk of making unrealistic assumptions about the ease with which people could follow proceedings, and there is certainly a sense in which the transparency of parliament is more obvious to historians than it would have been to contemporaries. Nevertheless, it is not clear that people would have needed to read in a particularly extensive fashion to be able to follow proceedings in some way. It may have been necessary to read certain kinds of newspaper, but it has already been shown that people were fairly astute at recognizing which titles provided which kinds of information. Moreover, it can also be demonstrated that readers like Rugg and Townshend managed to glean fairly precise evidence about parliament's business, its agenda and its committees. That they did so indicates a fascination with daily political life, and some capacity for developing the skills that would be required to participate in its affairs. This is not to say that they achieved 'perfect knowledge'. This was elusive even for the most well-informed readers, and there is a very real sense that some information remained privileged, and that those with power and money stood the best chance of gaining a comprehensive picture of what was being done at Westminster. However,

[93] *Kingdomes*, 214.242, p. 799; *Politicus*: 361.087, p. 1392; 361.164, p. 2614; 361.166, pp. 2652–3; *Diurnall*: 503.177, p. 2684; 503.193, pp. 2930–2; *Faithful Scout*, 150.126, p. 2029; *Proceedings*, 599.201, p. 3175.

while knowledge was unequal, it is abundantly clear that cheap print provided the public with unprecedented access to parliament's proceedings, and it is highly likely that members of the public came to expect extensive media coverage of its business.

The second caution relates to official attitudes to secrecy and transparency, and it is important to recognize that openness and accessibility were *contested*. Viscount Saye was uncomfortable with the possibility that people would 'take notice of the proceedings of Parliament', and at the probability that this would encourage thoughts about resisting parliamentary authority and revoking the trust placed in MPs. Sir Thomas Wroth complained about a bill that 'bred much talk abroad', and Adam Baynes bemoaned how everything done in the House was 'told abroad'.[94] MPs and peers thus reserved the right to restrict access when necessary, and to impose secrecy when they saw fit. However, this did not mean that openness was considered undesirable. Rather, it indicates that a balance needed to be struck between accessibility and secrecy, not least in order to preserve decorum and prevent disorder. Indeed, the key observation to make about official policy towards the publicity of parliament was that it recognized the reality of public interest, the need to preserve the physical accessibility of the palace, and even the utility of popular participation. MPs were nervous about publicizing proceedings, rather than intrinsically hostile to transparency, and even MPs came to rely on newspapers to follow what was being done at Westminster. Indeed, there is a genuinely ambiguous tone to the comments that members made about public scrutiny of their activity, about 'what will be said without doors', and about what would be 'noised' across the land.[95]

In other words, public knowledge about parliamentary proceedings was imperfect but impressive, while official attitudes towards transparency were complex but accommodating. Both inside and outside Westminster, contemporaries were adapting to the political realities of their times, in terms of the enhanced power of parliament and the heightened public awareness and curiosity that this inevitably generated. For all concerned this process of adaptation revolved around the media, which had the potential to vulgarize political information, to offer unprecedented opportunities for shining a light into the arcane world of Westminster politics, and to cause unease among MPs and peers. What transpired was an intimate connection between practices in the media and practices in parliament, both of which

---

[94] *Vindiciae Veritatis* (1654, F884), p. 22; *Burton Diary*, ii. 156, 237.
[95] *Burton Diary*, i. 128, 230, 237, 293, 322, ii. 24, 199, iv. 254.

reveal novelty and innovation and a striking willingness and ability to expose quotidian proceedings to the public gaze. Just how piercing this gaze could become, in terms of analysing the behaviour and performance of *individual members*, is the issue to which attention will turn in the next chapter.

CHAPTER 6

Monitoring personalities and performance

In the decades after 1660, the identities and actions of many MPs from the revolutionary era remained well known. *The Devils Cabinet-Councell* recycled what had become familiar accusations about scores of individuals, from Okey 'the drayman' to Heveningham the 'slabbering epicure', and from Marten the 'whoremaster' to Downes the 'cipher'. For numerous Independents and Cromwellians, details were provided about radical views and financial profiteering, and the author outlined their abuse of parliamentary proceedings and quoted their most famous speeches.[1] This striking text thus provides dramatic evidence of a new media culture, which brought the actions of key political figures to public attention in unprecedented ways, and which provides a third key way of exploring how the public face of parliament was transformed by print culture. This involved enabling members of the public not merely to appreciate the nature of the institution, or to monitor its proceedings, but also to gather information about the activities and attitudes of specific members. Evidence of this kind was important because it enhanced the possibility of making judgments about MPs' behaviour as *individuals*, rather than merely as part of a collectivity, and of holding them to account. Its publication in print raised further questions about the degree to which secrecy was, or could be, enforced, about how far parliament tolerated public inquisitiveness and journalistic intrusions, and about the relationship between members of the public and their representatives.

The aim of this chapter is to explore such issues, and to suggest that historians have been unduly sceptical about the possibilities for scrutinizing MPs' performance, and about the degree to which this became a live political issue. This is because they have concentrated on only one of the methods that contemporaries could use to monitor political activity, and focused on the period before the outbreak of Civil War. This has prompted

---

[1] *Devils Cabinet* (1660, D1225), pp. 1, 4, 9, 11–13, 24–5, 33–5, 42–5; *Secret History* (1709).

the suggestion that there was a rapid breakdown of secrecy in 1640, involving the appearance in print of parliamentary speeches, followed by an equally swift re-imposition of official control.[2] It is this rather simplistic picture that will be challenged here, on the basis not just of a thorough re-examination of evidence regarding members' speeches (section iii), but also of a much broader approach to the publicity that was given to MPs' activity. This involved evidence that became available before, during and after parliamentary sessions, and a mixture of publicity, propaganda and muck-raking. Of central importance will be election literature (section i), a genre that has been almost entirely ignored by historians of the Civil Wars, on the assumption that it only became significant during the late seventeenth century.[3] This is to overlook a wealth of material that emerged in the wake of George Wither's *Letters of Advice Touching the Choice of Knights and Burgesses*, which first appeared in the autumn of 1644 – when a copy was purchased for 2d by the Earl of Salisbury – and which proved highly controversial.[4] The value of Wither's work lies in creating opportunities for studying elections from the perspective of voters rather than candidates, and for arguing that electoral competition reflected not merely the enhanced power of parliament, or the prestige of sitting at Westminster, but also greater popular participation. Historians now agree that elections became increasingly politicized during the seventeenth century, and that candidates' views were thus significant, but it is also possible to argue that developments in print culture changed the terms on which elections were contested, by encouraging ordinary voters to make informed assessments about an individual's character, views and behaviour.[5] Part of the purpose of examining election literature will thus be to suggest that it reflected novel ideas about the importance of monitoring MPs, and about the legitimacy of holding them to account, but it will also be to suggest that electioneering was logical in an age that witnessed new practices for reporting parliamentary proceedings (section ii). Yet again, in other words, it will be possible to highlight the vulgarization of information that had once been privileged, and fairly deliberate attempts to break down official secrecy. These involved

---

[2] A. Cromartie, 'The printing of parliamentary speeches', *HJ*, 33 (1990), 23–44.

[3] G. Davies, 'The general election of 1660', *HLQ*, 15 (1952), pp. 212–14; Harris, *London Crowds*, pp. 106–29, 153–5; Knights, *Opinion*, pp. 208–3, 282–91; Knights, *Representation*, pp. 163–205; H. Horwitz, 'The general election of 1690', *JBS*, 11 (1971), pp. 81–3; M. George, 'Elections and electioneering', *EHR*, 45 (1930).

[4] Wither, *Letters* (1644, W3166); Hatfield, Bills 254/5; *HMC Salisbury XXII*, p. 383; *Occurrences*, 465.3040, sig. Rr2; *Kingdomes*, 214.114, pp. 911–14; *Letter Sent* (1646, L1617); SHC, BR/OC/5/21.

[5] M. Kishlansky, *Parliamentary Selection* (Cambridge, 1986), pp. 199–200, 227; *Wentworth Papers*, ed. J. Cooper (Cam. Soc. 4th series, 12, 1973), p. 153; BL, Add. 11045, fo. 97.

conscious efforts to foster public engagement, and overt attempts to scrutinize the activities of individual MPs and peers. Here, as in the previous chapter, the goal will be to demonstrate that attitudes and practices were complex and changeable, and to recognize that the information that appeared in print was imperfect in any number of ways. At the same time, however, the aim will be to challenge the assumption that there was consensus about the desirability of maintaining secrecy, and to suggest instead that policies towards publicizing parliamentary affairs involved pragmatism as well as principles. Once again, in other words, the argument will be that print culture offered powerful tools for enhancing political transparency, and for facilitating new kinds of participation.

i Informing the electorate

The obvious place to begin assessing how contemporaries judged their politicians is where voters would have begun: at elections. This section will demonstrate that, beginning in the 1640s, printed texts played an increasingly significant role in the electoral process, by advising voters how to assess the credentials of individual candidates and by facilitating overt campaigning. This will shed further light on the link between political practice and intellectual innovation, and reveal the emergence of novel ideas regarding representation and accountability; but before this can be done it is necessary to focus on the rather more mundane ways in which journalists facilitated participation, by publicizing electoral contests and controversies.[6]

The role of newspapers in parliamentary elections centred on the provision of information that enabled members of the public to take part at various stages of the electoral process, by keeping them abreast of the latest developments. This involved reporting decisions to issue new writs, for specific bi-elections as well as general elections, and publishing evidence about the dates of individual contests. Both became standard practice after 1641, and evidently proved popular with readers.[7] Editors also reminded people about the qualifications for both voting and being elected, and even provided lists of candidates.[8] Such evidence facilitated

---

[6] *HMC Salisbury XXII*, pp. 429, 431.

[7] For example: Durham UL, MSP 30, fo. 45; *Diurnall*: 504.108, p. 869; 504.240, p. 1935; 503.238, pp. 3644–5; *Occurrences*, 465.4044, sig. Tt2v; *Politicus*: 361.547, p. 118; 361.554, pp. 228, 240; 361.608, pp. 1114–15; *Proceedings*, 599.263, p. 4164. For readership: BL, Eg. 2648, fo. 276v; Lancs. RO, DDF/411.

[8] *Proceedings*: 599.246, pp. 3903–5; 599.254, pp. 4029–30; *Politicus*, 361.548, p. 135.

involvement, and its effect may have been considerable. It is worth considering, therefore, not just the importance of being warned about contests that would provoke 'some stir', but also the possibility that enhanced awareness about forthcoming elections contributed to the chaos which sometimes ensued. In late 1645, for example, the Derbyshire election witnessed a notable 'disturbance', and disorder also occurred at Westminster in July 1654, when the attendance of a 'multitude' forced the adjournment of proceedings from Westminster Hall to Tuthill Fields.[9] Much more significant, however, were journalistic tactics in the wake of elections. Beginning in the mid 1640s, therefore, newspapers reported double returns and contested elections *while they were under consideration*, in ways that facilitated interventions in the *parliamentary* process. Readers were thus informed about the disputed election at Newcastle in early April 1647, even though it was not resolved until late July, and one journalist explicitly encouraged petitioning and lobbying by suggesting that people who had witnessed electoral malpractice should 'address themselves unto the Parliament', in order to 'have their grievances redressed'. In September 1654 newspapers and public announcements notified readers that the committee for privileges would consider petitions against particular elections over a three-week period, and in January 1658 *Politicus* reported that the same body would sit every afternoon for two months, to receive petitions concerning 'undue elections'.[10]

Such evidence reveals both tacit and explicit encouragement of public participation in electoral processes, and it can usefully be set alongside the growth of electoral campaigning. This was almost unknown before the 1640s, even when contests occurred, and electioneering was traditionally restricted to correspondence involving the nobility, gentry and civic leaders, as well as occasional canvassing and perhaps even speeches by candidates.[11] Thereafter, however, tactics began to change, and conventional practices became increasingly politicized. This can be seen, for example, in relation to election sermons, which were regularly used for 'exhortation and prayer' in civic and commercial life, but which increasingly came to be used as partial

[9] *Britanicus*, 286.104, pp. 924–5; *Civicus*, 298.133, p. 1165; *Proceedings*, 599.250, p. 3968.
[10] For example: *Occurrences*: 465.4026, sig. Ccv; 465.3052, sig. Gg4; 465.4001, sig. A; 465.5030, pp. 195–7; *Diurnall*: 504.206, p. 1637; 504.193, p. 1545; 504.248, p. 3808; *Kingdomes*: 214.204, pp. 485–6; 214.219, p. 610; *Tuesday the Fifth* (1654, E2256C); *Politicus*, 361.400, p. 269.
[11] Som. RO: DD/PH 224/8–9; DD/PH 216/80–108; J. Peacey, 'Tactical organisation in a contested election', in *Parliament, Politics and Elections*, ed. C. Kyle (Cam. Soc., 5th series, 17, 2001); *Manner of the Election* (1649, M467), p. 3.

and controversial propaganda.[12] The Puritan minister, Stephen Marshall, was accused not merely of political preaching but also of overt campaigning, and in the mid 1640s Hugh Peter was described as a 'solicitor and stickler', and as 'that ubiquitary perturber of . . . our late elections'. He was berated for advancing 'the designs of his party', and for ensuring the return of 'infants' and 'unworthy members'. During the Wiltshire election of 1654, meanwhile, prominent Presbyterian preachers were attacked for distributing lists of men to be elected, and for besmirching their enemies, although they protested that such activity was entirely legitimate.[13]

Although very few election sermons survive, those that are available certainly permit such accusations to be substantiated, and indicate very clearly that ministers offered political counsel rather than merely moral guidance. At first glance, of course, they seem innocuous and platitudinous, with calls for the return of wise, courageous and public-spirited men, and for wariness regarding 'fair promises' and 'snares' that might 'entangle the ignorant'. However, they were often much more pointed. In 1660, Samuel Kem advised the voters of Gloucester to return men with 'grandeur' and 'good education', those who were 'experienced in authority', and those who came from 'the head and not the tail of the people', and such comments were highly loaded in the context of a world turned upside down. Indeed, in exhorting people to reject anyone who had sought to 'pull down the hedge of magistracy and ministry', and anyone who was 'profane' and 'perfidious', and who preferred 'policy' over 'piety', he was referring fairly explicitly to William Lenthall, sometime Speaker of the Long Parliament. Earlier, his sermon at Bristol in 1646 would almost certainly have been recognized as offering support for the New Model Army. Indeed, his call for 'a Moses and a Nathaniel, for a self-denying man, and a man without guile' represented fairly explicit backing for Richard Aldworth and Luke Hodges, who were duly returned. The printed edition was dedicated to Philip Skippon and the local committee of safety, and it was praised in the press as being 'fit for the use of all . . . places where new members are to be chosen'.[14]

---

[12] GL: MS 4326/7, fo. 340; MS 11571/12, fo. 303; MS 6440/2, fo. 545v; MS 5606/3, fo. 375v; MS 5198, unfol.; MS 5606/3, fo. 381v; MS 16988/5, pp. 217, 248; MS 16988/6, pp. 23, 61, 97, 111, 156, 179; Sedgwick, *Best and Worst* (1648, S2365); Berks. RO, R/ACi/1/7, fo. 47; *CJ*, i. 694–5; *Persecutio* (1648, C3785), pp. 56–7.

[13] *CSPD 1639–40*, pp. 580–82, 609; TNA, SP 16/449, fo. 93v; BL, Add. 11045, fo. 146v; Prynne, *Minors* (1646, P4008), p. 16; Edwards, *Gangraena*, i. 40; *Copy of a Letter* (1654, C6155); *Ludlow Memoirs*, i. 545–8; *Apology* (1654, C1914).

[14] Nye, *Sermon* (1661, N1500), pp. 15, 22–4; Gurnall, *Magistrates* (1656, G2259); Sedgwick, *Best and Worst*; Kem, *King of Kings* (1646, K250), pp. 14, 15, 17, 30, 32–3; Kem, *Solomon's* (1660, K251), pp. 2, 3, 4–5, 9, 11; *Occurrences*, 465.4008, sig. [H2v].

A similar mixture of general and specific advice, and of the drift towards overt campaigning, can also be seen within the broader culture of election literature. This, too, was frequently banal, and many pamphlets that appeared ahead of elections made no reference to specific candidates or constituencies. Such targeted campaigning was often restricted to manuscript libels produced in local contexts.[15] Pamphlets, in contrast, tended to offer generic advice. This meant discussions of the character traits that made men worthy or unworthy of election, and of the types of people who ought and ought not to be returned, as well as warnings that voters should be 'cautious and circumspect'. Very often, indeed, the purpose was polemical, rather than psephological. Demands were made for 'free' elections without external influence, for an end to costly 'feasting' of voters, and even for a system of trial by lot from a list of 'worthy' candidates. Wither responded to the 'corruption' and 'insufficiency' of many MPs by warning voters against the overtures of superficially impressive candidates. He cautioned people against accepting 'a good huntsman, a good falconer, a good gamester, or a good fellow'. He pleaded with voters to be 'wary' about who they elected, and he urged them not to listen to 'insinuations' by 'unworthy persons', who would flatter and importune in order to secure election, but who would 'never afterward regard your persons, your cause, your miseries, or your petitions'. Such ideas were echoed in other literature, and one author even claimed that 'it concerns you next to the eternal state of your souls, to make a prudent election'.[16]

Although literature of this kind lacked specificity, the emphasis on the need for caution and care suggests that its importance ought not to be underestimated. This is because the need to insure against 'abuse of trust' led commentators to argue that voters should make 'a more diligent examination . . . of those we elect'. In other words, such texts were significant less as pieces of campaign literature than as incitements to scrutinize candidates very closely, and as guides to voting tactics. Readers were advised to reject those who, through 'fear' or 'interest', would 'sacrifice the public good to passion or benefit', as well as those who 'press fastest' for election. One radical pamphlet from late 1658 thus claimed that 'the unfittest and unworthiest men are commonly the most forward to sue for places'.[17] Candidates to be avoided, therefore, included lavish talkers, men who

---

[15] *Kingdomes*, 214.204, pp. 485–6; BL: Harl. 4931, fo. 8v; Add. 11045, fo. 99v; *CSPV 1655–6*, p. 252.

[16] *Certain Considerations* (1660, C1691), pp. 4–6; *Memento* (1654, M1660); Prynne, *Minors*, p. 16; Wither, *Letters of Advice* (1645, W3167), pp. 2, 4–5, 9–10.

[17] *Necessary* (1660, L1277A); Wither, *Letters of Advice*, p. 7; North, *Looking-Glass* (1654, N1288), p. 2; *Grave and Weighty* (1658, S4510), p. 3.

were ambitious, covetous, wanton and proud, and those who were 'immoderately addicted to popularity'. Much more worthy of voters' trust were 'men of judgment and wisdom', of 'courage and fortitude' and of 'uprightness and integrity'. Moreover, such advice would surely have taken on particular significance in specific contexts. Voters were frequently advised not to elect members of a propertied elite, and those 'whom fools admire for their wealth', including landlords, usurers, debtors, gamesters and hunters, as well as courtiers and noble clients.[18] More obvious still was the animus against lawyers. These were described as a 'corrupt interest', and explicit criticism was made of the tendency for boroughs to return their recorders rather than 'statesmen', merely to have a 'mouthpiece' in parliament. Such men were said to be 'bold and talkative', and they were thought likely to 'intrude themselves into the chairs in all committees'. As men who were 'accustomed to take fees', moreover, it was alleged that lawyers would act in an 'underhand' fashion, in order to 'protect delinquents . . . with tricks and devices'. Of course, lawyers defended their relevance and utility against such 'ignoramusses', not least as part of a wider strategy of recommending that people should elect 'men of interest . . . by place and estate', and return 'notable knights' rather than 'yeomen or persons inferior'.[19]

More specific still were recommendations about assessing the public role and performance of individual candidates. Ahead of the 1644 Common Council elections, therefore, Londoners were advised to reject anyone who had refused to take the Solemn League and Covenant. Similarly, the author who anticipated fresh parliamentary elections in 1652 recommended candidates who were in fellowship with the national church, and in 1656 William Gurnall stressed the need to elect people who were friendly towards the ministry. In 1660 some tracts advocated the return of men who would protect tender consciences and support 'comprehension', while others advised the rejection of anyone who had been a lay preacher.[20] As time passed, indeed, pamphleteers expressed growing opposition to those who had received public salaries, on the grounds that private interests would affect members' judgments on issues like taxation, and because such men tended to 'put in a penny and take out a pound'. Readers were thus advised

---

[18] *Remembrancers* (1656, E3037), pp. 6–7; *Letter from a Lover* (1660, O2), p. 5; *Advertisements* (1645, S4472), p. 1; North, *Looking-Glass*, pp. 3–4; Wither, *Letters of Advice*, pp. 5–7.

[19] North, *Looking-Glass*, pp. 3–4; *Memento*; *Grave and Weighty*, p. 5; *Advertisements*, pp. 2, 6; Cook, *Vindication* (1646, C6029), p. 12; Prynne, *Minors*, p. 2; Gurnall, *Magistrates*, p. 35; *Certain Considerations*, p. 6.

[20] *Memorandums* (1644, M1679); *Right Improvement* (1652, C7448), p. 9; Gurnall, *Magistrates*, p. 36; *Letter from a Lover*, p. 6; *Necessary*.

to spurn 'excessive gainers by the times'; those 'made fat by the blood and ruins of the people', and those responsible for overseeing burdensome taxation. Explicit mention was made of excise farmers and assessment commissioners, of 'improvers' of common land and monopolists, and of military commanders, and even of JPs who had enforced government policy. This last recommendation, which obviously had draconian implications, reflected both a suspicion of 'committeemen' and a determination to separate legislative and executive power.[21]

In addition to reinforcing arguments about the corruption of parliamentary culture, such comments also indicate a willingness to engage in partisan campaigning. Gurnall's support for 'men of interest . . . by place and estate', and for a national church, would thus have marked him out as a conservative Cromwellian.[22] Others, however, were radical activists, and a 1652 pamphlet recommended bestowing votes on those who had opposed the Scots in the late 1640s, and advocated a scheme whereby prospective MPs would require the approval of local congregations. Similarly, in 1654 more than one commentator encouraged popular participation and a broader franchise, as part of a campaign against Cromwellian courtiers, while another tract from 1659 reflected the interests of civilian republicans. It not only proposed biannual parliaments, but also expressed opposition to ambitious lawyers and 'excessive gainers by the times', to 'green heads' and 'mercenary soldiers', and to those who were 'enslaved to a party or faction' and who were 'entangled' and 'engaged'. What parliament needed instead were characters with experience, and who were 'least engaged', and those who had 'least dependance' on 'great men', either for offices or 'places of preferment'.[23]

By the end of the 1650s, however, the bulk of election literature was openly 'royalist'. Voters were warned to 'meddle not' with candidates who had been 'given to such changes as have crumbled the nation into . . . parties and factions', and to avoid anyone who had shifted 'from party to party'. They were advised not just to support members of the traditional elite, but also to reflect on the activities of recent MPs, and to consider whether such men should ever be 'trusted with power' or allowed to 'sit within those walls'. Explicit reference was made to people who had shown 'malice

---

[21] *Grave and Weighty*, pp. 4, 6; *Memento; Certain Considerations*, pp. 4–6; North, *Looking-Glass*, pp. 3–4; *Admonition* (1659, A595); *Letter from a Lover; Qualifications* (1660, Q38); Wither, *Letters of Advice*, p. 7; *Necessary; Memento.*

[22] Gurnall, *Magistrates*, pp. 35–6.

[23] *Right Improvement*, pp. 9–10; *Memento*; North, *Looking-Glass*, pp. 3–4; *Grave and Weighty*, pp. 1, 3–6, 8–9, 12–13.

towards the late king', and who were enemies of monarchy, and to people who had reformed the church and tolerated sectaries. Indeed, voters were urged to reject all those who had been 'purchasers or sellers of the public revenues', and who had acquired property confiscated from the Crown, the Church and delinquents. One satire even offered mock advice about the need to elect sabbath-breakers, adulterers and regicides, as well as the bastard sons of MPs, and about the desirability of granting the vote to prisoners in Newgate, Bridewell and Bedlam.[24] Of course, late-1650s 'royalism' often had a distinctly Presbyterian tone, and this, too, found its voice in election literature. This involved explicit advice about avoiding old cavaliers who might 'lead us back to Egypt', and clear guidance on the need to return men who would protect 'our dear-bought liberties and reformation begun'. Such men were needed, it was said, to guard against a vindictive restoration settlement, and to secure religious comprehension as well as an act of indemnity. The *Admonition* of December 1659 thus opposed regicides, officeholders and the purchasers of forfeited estates, but also argued that the Covenant should be 'the touchstone or shibboleth of every person to be elected', and its author was willing to distinguish between those who had fought for parliament in the 1640s and those who were members of 'the present army'. Another tract warned voters that republicans were 'earnestly at work in all counties . . . to procure themselves to be elected again', and that people should instead return men of solid Presbyterian credentials, and those whose role models were the Earls of Essex and Manchester, as well as Sir Thomas Fairfax, Sir William Waller and Denzil Holles, or indeed any of the other 'oppressed and secluded members'.[25]

In other words, while election propaganda was usually produced for a general audience, rather than on behalf of specific candidates, its advice was not merely banal. Comments were both politicized and partisan, and their meaning would almost certainly have been clear to readers. However, two other significant aspects of such literature also require attention, in terms of tone and intended audience. First, such electioneering was sometimes aggressive and inflammatory. A good example is *Englands Remembrancers*, a republican and anti-Cromwellian pamphlet that appeared during elections for the 1656 Parliament. This used the language of 'free-born

---

[24] *Certain Considerations*, pp. 4–6; *Necessary; Qualifications; Qualifications of Persons* (1660, Q37), pp. 4–6, 10–12, 13.

[25] *Seasonable and Sober* (1659, S2216A); *Letter from a Lover*, pp. 2–3, 4, 5–6; *Admonition; Certain Considerations*, pp. 4–6.

Englishmen' and the 'good old cause', and encouraged voters to retain 'impartial judgments' in the face of 'power' and 'pomp', 'threats' and 'terror', and 'the clashing of the soldiers' arms'.[26] It represented a blatant attempt to mobilize ordinary voters and to reach the widest possible audience, and copies were thus distributed across the country by 'discontented men'. These included one Mr Cole of Southampton, who sought to unseat the local MP, John Lisle, and who 'scattered' copies around the county and 'about the streets' of Lisle's constituency, to 'dispose of them for their choice'. Copies also reached Yorkshire, where they were distributed by a Leeds schoolmaster, as well as Lincolnshire, where they were discovered in remote villages such as Kirkby, Revesby, Scrivesby, Dalderby, Hameringham and Bolingbroke. There they were distributed by Francis Fidling, who received a sizeable bundle from Peregrine Goodrick of London, and then stored them at the shop of John Chapman of Horncastle. Fidling assumed that they were produced by Sir Henry Vane, although the government eventually prosecuted a London haberdasher called Edward Wroughton, who was accused of dispersing copies at a Fifth Monarchist meeting, where three agitators arrived with 'bundles of printed papers in their arms'. Although some observers suggested that this campaign did 'little hurt' to the regime, and even that it stiffened opposition to radical candidates like William Kiffin, the importance of the episode is clear. It demonstrated how print made it possible to orchestrate an electoral campaign across the country, and it caused considerable concern about 'new broils'. It may also have ensured that the 1656 elections witnessed 'the greatest striving' that people had ever seen, in which 'all sorts of discontented people' were 'incessant in their endeavours'.[27]

Secondly, election literature involved rethinking the relationship between electors and the elected, by people from across the political spectrum. This was partly about proposing ways in which MPs could be compelled to serve their constituents. In 1660, William Prynne advised voters to supply successful candidates with explicit 'instructions', while John North wrote about the need for binding contracts between members and voters.[28] For men like Wither, on the other hand, the aim was to encourage citizens to maintain a watchful eye on individual representatives after they had been elected:

[26] *Remembrancers*, pp. 2–4, 6–7.

[27] *TSP*, v. 272, 287, 297, 303, 342–3, 349; *CSPD 1656–7*, pp. 114, 159; BL, Add. 21424, fos. 65, 85, 88; *Mdx County Records*, p. 253; Vaughan, *Protectorate*, ii. 18–19; Lancs. RO, DDF/411.

[28] Prynne, *Seasonable* (1660, P4061); North, *Looking-Glass*, pp. 1–3.

you must observe their associates, with whom they most converse, you must observe to whom they are most kind, of whose affairs they are most zealous, in whose defence they oftenest and most readily appear, to whom they have nearest relations, or strictest obligements. You must observe likewise what fame reports of their affection or disaffection, to those courses or propositions which concern the commonalty, least you lose a trustee before you be aware. Moreover, you must take notice of their diligence, prudence, faithfulness or stoutness in your service, to cherish it by due thankfulness and acknowledgements, and of their apparent negligence or failings, that ... they might be awakened and lovingly admonished ... by discreet and respective expresses, remembering them lovingly ... that though they are above you, being joined to our whole representative body, yet ... they are servants and inferiors to their respective counties and boroughs and that by them they may be called to account.[29]

Most commonly of all, commentators suggested that electoral judgments should be grounded in analysis of past behaviour. They thus advised voters to elect men whose 'faithfulness' had been put to 'some tryall', and not to trust anyone who had 'broken their faith or falsified their trust'.[30]

Thus, whether or not election literature served the interests of particular candidates directly and overtly, its importance was certainly not lost on contemporaries, and it had profound implications for the conduct of political life and for the role of the public. Either implicitly or explicitly, it advocated public scrutiny of candidates and sitting MPs, so that wise decisions could be made and so that representatives could be held to account. What this required, of course, was *information* regarding the activity of politicians, something for which there appears to have been growing demand. In 1641, for example, Thomas Stockdale advocated publishing a list of those who had voted against publishing the *Grand Remonstrance*, so that 'the county may take notice of their friends, and know how to elect better patriots hereafter'. Similarly, advice to Londoners ahead of civic elections in 1644 recommended that voters should 'get as good intelligence as you can who did best of the last year's common-councilmen, and who worst'. By 1656 voters were being encouraged to 'meet and advise together', in order to 'find out men so qualified, and then acquaint each other with your knowledge ... of them', and in 1659 it was suggested that 'there should be much exactness and curiosity in elections, as inspection, circumspection, inquisition, information, serious consideration

---

[29] Wither, *Letters of Advice*, pp. 13–14.
[30] *Remembrancers*, p. 7; *Certain Considerations*, pp. 4–6; *A Memento*; *Necessary.*

and deliberation'.[31] Such ideas raise important questions about the degree to which it was feasible to monitor the performance of MPs, and about whether this became easier during the print revolution, and it is these issues to which attention must now turn.

ii Monitoring MPs' performance

On 10 October 1646 the House of Commons debated introducing a ballot box, to replace public divisions with private voting. The idea was narrowly rejected, on the grounds that 'truth needs no corners, nor to use any such privacy', which suggests that MPs were prepared to countenance a degree of openness regarding political opinions, actions and decisions.[32] This, together with investigative journalism and the willingness of politicians to expose their opponents, explains how the media helped to satisfy Wither's demand for publicity, information and accountability. The aim of this section, therefore, is to explore the publication of evidence that made it possible to judge public figures on their political record. It returns, in other words, to the nature and limits of political transparency, and to the 'corruption' of parliamentary culture, and it suggests that a combination of official openness, factionalism and muckraking ensured that individual MPs became subject to unprecedented public scrutiny.

Political transparency during the Civil Wars took a variety of forms. These did not always concern MPs, or indeed relate to activity at Westminster, but they generally involved official and non-official publicity, professions of loyalty by public figures and the desire to expose opponents. Lists began to appear containing details about people who had compounded for delinquency, both in pamphlets and in newspapers, and these were consumed fairly avidly.[33] Statements that signalled support for either the king or parliament were likewise published in pamphlet form, providing the names of local signatories who were prepared to stand up and be counted.[34] And considerable effort was expended in whistleblowing. This was the spirit of Thomas Stockdale's idea for producing lists of people who had rejected the Protestation, 'that so the strength of the adverse faction might appear', and it also underpinned the publication of 'blacklists' regarding the

---

[31] *Eight Antiquaries* (1647, E258), p. 6; BL, Add. 18979, fo. 99v; *Memorandums*; *Remembrancers*, p. 8; *Grave and Weighty*, pp. 7–8.

[32] *Diary of John Harington*, p. 42; *Occurrences*, 465.4042, sigs. Rr2–v; *CJ*, iv. 690.

[33] *Catalogue* (1655, D2187); *Proceedings*, 599.146, pp. 2282–3; 'James Master', ii. 244; Cumbria RO, D/LONS/W1/10, p. 27; TNA, SP 23/259, fos. 13, 24–5; 159, 161, 162; *CCC*, pp. 638–9.

[34] *Ingagement* (1642, E734).

behaviour of people from various branches of public life. Such catalogues reflected factional divisions, both in religious and political affairs, and they were used to stigmatize 'delinquent' ministers of all shades, sometimes with official backing, and to expose civic leaders who opposed George Monck's march towards London a decade later.[35] Inevitably, some such information touched upon MPs, even if this generally meant extra-parliamentary activity in support of the war effort. The reading public could thus gain a fairly comprehensive picture about the behaviour of zealous royalists who had been removed from the Commons, as well as about enthusiastic parliamentarians and Interregnum republicans. In February 1660, for example, newspapers reported Monck's meetings with a clutch of MPs, and such information was read with enthusiasm by men like Thomas Rugg, who duly copied it into his notebook.[36]

None of this enabled people to assess an MP's *parliamentary* performance, of course, but it nevertheless signals broad cultural trends regarding transparency and public scrutiny. It also provides further evidence about the vulgarization of once privileged information, especially that which involved the activities and attitudes of specific individuals. This made it possible to identify which MPs had taken the parliamentary covenant and the Solemn League and Covenant, and to monitor which MPs attended committee meetings, managed conferences and delivered reports.[37] Readers may thus have gleaned that Sir Robert Harley was an *assiduous* chairman of the Committee for Elections, and that John Swinfen was a *busy* MP who was involved in discussing the Westminster Assembly's confession of faith, in preparing proposals to be sent to the king in 1647 and in promoting army disbandment. They may also have recognized that Sir Thomas Dacres was *active* in relation to matters that were relevant to his constituents.[38] Beyond this, indeed, much could also be discovered about the *opinions* of numerous members. Pym emerged as the sponsor of controversial motions – like the idea to impeach Henrietta Maria – and inflammatory declarations,

---

[35] *Fairfax Corr.*, ii. 105–7; White, *Century* (1641, W1771E); *Be it Known* (1649, B1553–4); *List* (1654, L2406); *Narrative* (1659, N215).

[36] *Symon Rodes* (1642, R1330); *Speciall Passages*, 605.02A, pp. 9–10; *Diurnall*: 511.21A, sig. V4; 513.24B, np; 504.187, p. 1499; *Occurrences*: 465.2006, sig. F4; 465.4015, sig. P; *Parl. Intelligencer*, 486.102, p. 13; 486.103, p. 32; *Politicus*, 361.608, p. 1117; *Rugg*, p. 43.

[37] *Diurnall*: 511.54, sigs. Fff2–v; 504.035, p. 276; 504.014, p. 106; *Occurrences*, 465.3005, sig. E4; *Britanicus*, 286.008, pp. 63–4.

[38] *True Copy* (1641, N1236), p. 5; *Conspiracie* (1641, C5932); *By the Committee* (1642, E1265); *At the Committee* (1642, E1240); *Die Lunae* (1645, E1239); *Glyns Report* (1641, G893); *Occurrences*: 465.5030, pp. 196–7; 465.5042, p. 293; 465.5043, sig. Ww4; *Foure Reasons* (1641, C6211); *Kingdomes*, 214.253, p. 884; *Diurnall*: 504.274, 12Z; 511.14A, sig. P2v.

including those penned during the 'paper war' of 1642. John Selden and
John Wilde were identified as having drafted controversial legislation, from
the 'Four Bills' that were presented to the king in December 1647 to the act
for punishing incest.[39] It could be deduced that John Glyn favoured a bill to
seize the estates of impeached bishops in 1642, and that MPs like Edward
Bagshaw, Sir John Evelyn and Denzil Holles supported a peace treaty in the
winter of 1642–3. It became clear that Francis Rous backed the controversial
'Directory' for public worship, that John Boys favoured a church system
based on 'classes', and that Giles Greene was lenient towards the eleven
impeached members in 1647. It was also apparent that William Ellis
supported the Self Denying Ordinance in 1645, that Miles Corbet opposed
the 'forcing of the Houses' in July 1647, and that Sir Henry Mildmay
supported the impeachment of the 'seven peers' in September 1647.[40] In
other words, journalists created the opportunity for putting identifiable
flesh on the bones of parliamentary factions.

Beyond this, readers were also bombarded with more or less credible, and
more or less inflammatory, evidence in libels and newspapers. This accusatory culture became central to Civil War politics, and it was sanctioned by
the elite, not least in terms of the charges against the 'five members', which
were printed repeatedly during 1642. Indeed it became endemic in public
discourse, in ways that brought claims about individual MPs within reach of
ordinary readers. Libels about the 'junto' often contained precise claims
about a wealth of MPs and peers, and throughout the period these 'jeering
books' proved as troublesome to the authorities as they were fascinating to
men like Rugg.[41] Equally vicious, if slightly more elevated, were pamphlets
like *Persecutio Undecima*, which railed against those named MPs who had
undermined the church, or the *Remonstrance and Declaration of Severall
Counties*, which listed the MPs who were responsible for the king's forthcoming trial in January 1649.[42] As was so often the case, however, it was
newspapers that provided the most consistent stream of accusations, and
readers who were attracted by the dirt that would be dished on MPs

---

[39] *Continuation*, 623.07A, sig. Gv; *Occurrences*, 465.5049, p. 330; *Kingdomes*: 214.021, p. 162; 214.248,
pp. 847; 214.211, p. 544.

[40] *Diurnall*: 513.21B, sig. X; 513.32B, sig. Ii3v; 504.075, p. 593; 504.213, p. 1712; 507.01, p. 8; 507.05, p. 3;
Perfect Summary, 528.09, p. 71; *Occurrences*: 465.5083, sig. Nnnnv; 465.5029, sig. Ff2v; *Proceedings*,
599.074, pp. 1115, 1122; *Continuation*, 638.18, p. 4; *Kingdomes*, 214.088, pp. 705–6.

[41] *CSPD 1641–3*, pp. 146–7; *Mode* (1647, M2311); *England* (1648, B1904A); SHC, G52/2/19/22; BL, Harl.
4931, fo. 140; Sloane 1467, fos. 130–v; HEH, HM 951; PA, MP 9 Dec. 1644; MP 13 Dec. 1644; *LJ*, vii.
97; Aberdeen UL, MS 2538/1, fos. 34–v; *CSPD 1655–6*, p. 365; DRO, D258/30/23; *Rugg*, pp. 11, 13, 23,
26, 28, 54–5, 60.

[42] *Persecutio*, pp. 21–2; *Remonstrance and Declaration* (1648, R961), pp. 4–8.

probably knew to which editors they needed to turn. The most important of these was undoubtedly Nedham, whose *Britanicus* boasted that it would 'tell you who are honest, who are faithful, [and] who are parliamentarian'. Nedham claimed to have 'universal knowledge of men', and considered that the 'best service' he could perform involved setting out 'the virtues and deserts of the best, the treachery, malignity, cavalierism of the worst', and he thus promised to take off 'all hoods, habits, cloaks, periwigs, gloves, gowns, cassocks, and everything that hides and covers the subjects, either at Oxford or London'. As editor of *Pragmaticus*, meanwhile, Nedham repeatedly offered biting depictions of MPs. John Blakiston was mocked as Thomas Scot's lackey 'upon all knavish occasions', while Sir Henry Mildmay was described as having 'a wolf in his breast, and a cormorant in his conscience'. Sir John Wollaston was derided as 'that once white-livered dog of Presbytery', who had become 'a proselyte in Independency', and who had 'a good nose' to 'hunt out bishops' lands'. Nedham boasted that he knew MPs 'so well' that he could 'truss them up in one single sheet of paper, and anatomize them in all their principles, humours, and designs'. Frequent targets included Miles Corbet, 'that grand inquisitor, and the state's cony-catcher', and Thomas Chaloner, 'that zealous man, who though he be no papist, yet could find in his heart to dispense so far with religion as to turn his king into a crucifix'.[43]

Very occasionally such attempts to expose MPs' attitudes and behaviour involved not just scrappy reportage but also systematic coverage of particular votes and episodes. Here, too, it is possible to observe a mixture of official publicity and political mudslinging, from the printing of formal dissents by minority groups of peers to the list of MPs who voted against the Earl of Strafford's attainder. Evidence about these 'Straffordians' circulated not merely among MPs, but also across the country, and it was famously 'posted at the corner . . . of Sir William Brunkard's house in Old Palace Yard', and then displayed at the Royal Exchange, under the heading 'the betrayers of their country'. In other words, however restricted the readership of contemporary newspapers may have been, it would have been hard to avoid learning the identities of Strafford's supporters in the Commons, which explains why the episode provoked complaints that MPs could no longer act freely, for fear of being 'posted' and 'traduced', and why it was widely reported that those concerned 'went in fear for their lives'.[44] Of

---

[43] *Britanicus*, 286.028A, p. 215; *Pragmaticus*: 369.109A, sig. I4v; 370.08B, sig. H3; 369.111A, sig. L2; 370.05A, sig. Ev; 369.112, sig. Mv.

[44] *After Debate* (1641, E2787A); SHC, G52/2/19/12; *Verney Notes*, pp. 57–9; Lancs. RO., DDB85/20, fos. 30–2, 35, 42; HEH, HM 66707; Glos. RO, D7115/1; *CSPD 1640–1*, p. 560; Staffs. RO, D661/20/2,

course, such intense exposure only occurred very rarely, but it could nevertheless be observed at other moments of acute political tension. Similar lists
thus circulated about the MPs who fled to the army in response to the
'forcing of the Houses' in 1647, and about those who remained at
Westminster. The lists of regicides that circulated following the king's
trial repeatedly found their way into commonplace books, before being
reprinted on the eve of the Restoration, in time to find new readers like John
Lowther and Thomas Rugg.[45]

Rare though such inflammatory lists may have been, they nevertheless
formed part of a more prevalent culture, which involved publicizing both
information and accusations, and which proved particularly striking in
relation to MPs' financial affairs. This began innocuously enough, as
members strove to publicize their donations to the parliamentarian war
effort, but it also involved leaking evidence about those who had given
money to the king. This clearly catered to a popular appetite for such
evidence, which ensured that newspapers soon got in on the act as well.[46]
Much more sensitive, however, was evidence about the money *received* by
MPs, in relation to military service or civilian office. Such information was
not necessarily secret, and many of the payments made in lieu of lost
earnings and damaged property, and in reward for 'great pains and good
service', were public knowledge. So, too, were the salaries of MPs who
served as commissioners of the great seal, which were published with
impunity alongside evidence regarding the perquisites accrued by men
like Francis Rous, John Glyn, Sir Walter Erle and Walter Long.[47] The
problem, of course, was that such benefits were not always thought to be
justified, or to have been made in a fair and transparent fashion. As such,
print culture facilitated attempts to expose financial irregularities on a case-
by-case basis. Nedham, for example, mocked the award of honorary degrees
to MPs in 1649, naming 'Sir Dumpling Waller, the fatted calf, Ingoldsby

p. 95; BL: Add. 28011, fo. 122; Add. 44848, fo. 287; Lans. 1232, fo. 163; Harl. 4931, fo. 126; Sloane 1467,
fos. 72–v; Durham UL, MSP 30, fos. 46–v.
[45] BL: Add. 46931B, fos. 150–v; Add. 37719, fos. 196–7; Eg. 2542, fo. 465; DRO, D258/10/29/5–7;
Chester RO, CR63/2/696, pp. 131–2, 152–3; *Transcript* (1649, T2028A); *Black Book* (1660, B3041);
Catalogue (1660, C1388); *Grand Memorandum* (1660, G1503); *High Court* (1660, H1960aA); *Great
Memorial* (1660, G1709); *Black Remembrancer* (1660, R1448); *Lucifers* (1660, L3440); Cumbria RO,
D/LONS/W1/10, p. 27; *Rugg*, pp. 56–7.
[46] *Names of Such Members* (1642, N128); BL, Add. 70081, unfol.; *Sundrie Knights* (1642, C1367); *Lords
that Subscribed* (1642, C1397–8); *Moneys, Men and Horse* (1642, C1385); Som. RO, DD/HI/466;
Durham UL, MSP 9, p. 257; *Diurnall*, 513.18A, p. 3.
[47] For example: *Kingdomes*: 214.182, p. 387; 214.164, p. 230; 214.168, p. 262; *Britanicus*, 286.110, p. 975;
Civicus, 298.134, p. 1172; 504.028, p. 224; 504.117, p. 931; 504.200, pp. 1604–5; 504.026, p. 208.

that Tercel of a gentleman, [and] Harrison the pert attorney's clerk', as well as 'Okey the tailor and Hewson the cobbler'. This could easily be dismissed as harmless fun, but scrutiny of financial rewards was clearly undertaken in a much more serious fashion. *Pragmaticus* decried the preferential treatment afforded to grandees like Viscount Saye, and alleged that the brothers, Henry and Richard Darley, 'procured' friends to make 'a begging motion' for money from the public purse, 'in consideration of their unknown losses'. This was said to have involved careful timing and the 'wheels of state-clockwork being oiled', and repeated attempts were made to connect improper payments with corrupt procedures. In other words, investigative journalism provided readers with hard evidence with which to substantiate the general claims about political corruption that were being bandied about in the media.[48]

Such muckraking is significant not merely in terms of how it affected public discourse, but also in terms of the light it sheds on official attitudes to the press and the public, as well as on MPs' behaviour. First, it created a vibrant culture in which the track record of individual members became *contested*, and made a pantomime out of parliament. Battles were thus fought over the reputations of men like Cornelius Holland, who was defended by *Britanicus* after having been criticized by *Aulicus* for his 'many offices'. In other cases, claims about bribery and corruption were embroidered and exaggerated, to the point where they became almost farcical. These included Daniel Blagrave, a 'decayed tradesman' who was involved in a contested election at Reading, and who allegedly sought to 'hire' MPs with gifts of sugar loaves, so that they would support him in both the Commons and the Committee of Elections. Similar claims were made against George Starkey, a 'mechanick rascal' and a 'great gamester', who had apparently lost £200 in one night 'at dice', and who allegedly procured 'country bumpkins to vote for him, and to cry him up a burgess, for 2s. a day'. In Starkey's case the accusations proved to be true, but Blagrave seems to have been treated unfairly. Although his 'bribe' was said to have been rejected 'with scorn' and then reported to the House, this was eventually revealed to have involved little more than malicious gossip, or at best a serious misunderstanding.[49]

---

[48] *Pragmaticus*: 370.06A, sig. F2v; 360.107, sig. G3; 369.224, sig. Gg2v; 369.227, sig. Nn4v; 369.106, sig. F4v; *Honest Letter* (1642, R84), sigs. A2–3.

[49] *Britanicus*, 286.024, p. 186; *Pragmaticvs*, 369.220B, sig. Z; *Occurrences*: 465.5083, sig. Nnnn2v; 465.5084, sig. Ooo02; 465.5086, sig. Qqqq3.

Secondly, the response at Westminster proved to be ambiguous and unclear, in ways that sometimes made matters worse, but that occasionally involved responding in a constructive and accommodating manner. Uncertainty about the accusatory culture that now surrounded parliament thus revealed tensions that persisted throughout the period, and while some MPs were willing to launch investigations and even to publish public accounts, 'to inform the people' and remove 'jealousies and calumnies', others defiantly resisted greater transparency. The inevitable result was that rumours and suspicions multiplied, not merely about financial abuse, but also about the chances of corruption being exposed, and about the lengths to which MPs like Viscount Lisle would go to avoid 'the dreadful doomsday of account'.[50] Newspapers followed such cases with enthusiasm, identifying the MPs who were vindicated as well as those who were found guilty of misappropriating funds. The latter included Sir Ralph Assheton, who was imprisoned for letting public money stick to his fingers and linger in his pocket-book.[51] From the mid 1640s, however, it was also possible to demonstrate that parliament at least appeared to be taking the problem seriously, and journalists consistently reported when committees were appointed to consider complaints regarding bribery and malfeasance. MPs probably welcomed the chance to secure positive publicity, and even ensured that details about such committees – including the names of their chairmen and the times and places of their meetings – were publicized officially. Indeed, these appeared alongside statements that encouraged members of the public to come forward with evidence, and were probably read with concerned interest by MPs like Thomas Gell, who would himself be accused of financial impropriety.[52]

This nervousness on the part of MPs was probably justified, given their experience with one such investigative committee, which exposed the limitations of official openness and which lay at the heart of one of the period's most striking attempts to expose financial malpractice. This body was appointed in March 1646 to examine the issue of office-holding, and it generated a detailed dossier of information about MPs who held places of profit and advantage. The aim was to 'give the kingdom full satisfaction in this great grievance', and to remove 'scandalous aspersions', and as such it was apparently considered permissible for journalists to report its regular

---

[50] CSPV 1643–7, p. 9; Diurnall: 504.016, p.128; 504.182, p. 1459; HMC Egmont I, p. 382; Kingdomes, 214.276, p. 1076; Pragmaticus, 369.212, sigs. Mv–2.
[51] Mod. Intelligencer, 419.222, sig. 10P4v; Diurnall: 504.188, p. 1508; 504.031, p. 244.
[52] CJ, iv. 362, v. 196; Occurrences: 465.3050, sig. Dd2v; 465.5023, sig. Y4v; Weekly Account, 671.332, sig. Ii; Several Orders (1647, E2729); DRO, D258/33/37/1–2, 4; Kingdomes, 214.314, p. 1382.

meetings, under the chairmanship of Thomas Sandes. However, while the issue generated public interest, there is no evidence that MPs were willing to publicize the committee's findings. This probably fuelled suspicions that they had something to hide, and ensured that the evidence was soon leaked and published in royalist blacklists. These provided chapter and verse about MPs who had remained in the army after the Self Denying Ordinance, and about the money, offices and lands that they had acquired.[53] As a result, journalists and pamphleteers were once again forced to issue lengthy defences of MPs like Cornelius Holland; denying allegations about financial profiteering and dismissing the characterization of him as Sir Henry Vane's 'zany'.[54]

Thirdly, what is striking about the mudslinging that surrounded MPs is that it resulted from factional competition rather than from the rise of radicalism. Paradoxical as it may seem, in other words, it was the emergence of party politics that promoted *individual* accountability. Indeed, the publication of accusatory literature, and the nervousness that it caused, continued throughout the period, not least with criticisms of the protectoral court and parliaments. One narrative offered an account of the 'places of profit, salaries and advantages' that Cromwell's cronies held 'under the present power', and this was published 'for information of the people'. This was, in effect, a precursor of what we would now call the register of members' interests, and by cataloguing those MPs who were related to Cromwell, or beholden to him, including the 'kinglings' who offered him the crown in 1657, it also offered a proto-Namierite analysis. But it was also a rallying cry, and it prompted readers to question whether such men were 'fit to be legislators, lawmakers, framers of governments … and leviers of money', and whether private interests would trump the public service that they were 'hired to serve'. Indeed, the author pleaded for a 'lively spirit' among the public, and implored readers to collect further such information, 'for the discovery of wickedness'.[55] These works quickly found an audience, and inspired further satirical attacks, which probably reinforced public perceptions about dubious finances and dodgy MPs. These included mock accounts of the Committee of Safety – including £243 for gowns to

[53] *CJ*, iv. 477, v. 599; Bodl. MS Nalson 14, fos. 215–24v, 327–50, 401; *Diurnall*: 504.224, p. 1801; 504.255, p. 2053; BL, Add. 28001, fo. 213; *Oxinden and Peyton Letters*, p. 100; *A List* (1648, E317A-B); *Second Centurie* (1648, E317C–D); *Second List* (1648, S2290); Walker, *Independency* (1648, W329), pp. 166–74.

[54] *Moderate*, 413.2012, sigs. M3–v; Lilly, *Astrologicall* (1648, L2211), pp. 60–71; Wither, *Respublica* (1650, W30A), pp. 18–22.

[55] *Narrative* (1657, N194), pp. 1, 7, 9–18, 19, 22–3, 32; *Second Narrative* (1658, W1556–7), pp. 13–33.

cover members' 'knavery', and £5,000 to buy pictures of Moses, Mohammed, Romulus and Remus, 'and all those that were ... founders of large empires'.[56]

In other words, while there is some evidence that MPs condoned and connived at the publication of evidence about the conduct and careers of individual members, this often involved Machiavellian tendencies rather than a spirit of transparency. It was also something about which many of those who found themselves in the public eye had cause to feel uncomfortable, although the response at Westminster involved a genuine mixture of disquiet and accommodation, and not a little soul-searching. Some MPs began to question how offices and salaries were distributed, and advised against giving 'such large rewards to one another'. They called such behaviour 'the blame of the Long Parliament', and they feared 'censure abroad', because MPs could not 'cloister up' such decisions 'within these walls'.[57] However, this kind of evidence, and the public response to its publication, were not the only things about which members needed to worry, and the final section of this chapter deals with yet another threat to official secrecy: reporting of the very words uttered in parliament.

iii   Reporting parliamentary speech

The reporting of MPs speeches requires much closer scrutiny than it has yet received, in terms of the theory and practice of secrecy. Debates represent the acid-test of parliamentary accessibility, since they were theoretically 'arcana sacra', and were 'like the Sibilline oracles anciently kept in Rome ... not to be divulged'. Whatever else the public may have been allowed to witness, in other words, discussions in both Houses were supposed to be private, and theoretically took place behind closed doors. In reality, of course, they had traditionally been treated as *privileged*, and to the extent that evidence could be acquired – at a price and by those in the know – parliamentary principles were honoured as much in the breach as in the observance.[58] As has already been demonstrated, however, the Civil Wars witnessed a significant vulgarization of information that had once been accessible to only a narrow elite, and the aim of this section is to demonstrate that the same was also true of speeches and debates. Here,

---

[56] Cheshire RO, DAR/F/3, pp. 30, 32; *Exact Accompt* (1660, R44), pp. 4–5, 7.

[57] *Burton Diary*, ii. 161–2, 197, 199.

[58] J. Redlich, *Procedure of the House of Commons* (3 vols, London, 1903), ii. 28, 36; V. Snow, *Parliament in Elizabethan England* (London, 1977), p. 187; *D'Ewes*, ed. Notestein, p. 332; *Presse* (1642, P3293), sig. A2v.

while scholars have recognized that the months preceding the outbreak of Civil War witnessed a profusion of printed speeches in pamphlet form, they have probably been too quick to argue that this trend was quickly reversed, and that this represented official displeasure regarding the violation of parliamentary secrecy.[59] The argument here will be that attitudes towards publicity were complex, that attempts to prevent the printing of such information were selective and that secrecy was never an entirely realistic goal. This was because journalists and pamphleteers ensured that readers continued to have access to at least some evidence about speeches, even if steps were eventually taken to make debates privileged once more. As such, this will provide significant evidence with which to substantiate the broader argument of this chapter, in terms of the degree to which the public was presented with evidence with which to judge the performance of MPs, and to hold them to account.

During the early seventeenth century, access to parliamentary debates was evidently fairly straightforward, at least for members of the gentry, and particularly for those who had personal contacts at Westminster. There was little concern about MPs writing letters that reported proceedings, as some did 'from my knee' in the chamber. Similar material could also be circulated by well-informed onlookers, whose services were invaluable to those whose 'ears stand wide open' for news, and newsletter-writers frequently reported debates, gave precise details about divisions and painted a vivid picture of tension within the Commons.[60] Beyond letters, of course, contemporaries also had access to scribal 'separates', the trade in which thrived during the opening months of the Long Parliament, even to the extent that they were thought to have become the most reliable source of intelligence.[61] This ability to report debates with impunity, in ways that contravened rules regarding secrecy, almost certainly reflected the fact that such material achieved only limited circulation beyond a gentry elite. It was probably tolerated, in other words, because it made little impact on the population at large. There is certainly evidence that separates could be copied by

---

[59] Cromartie, 'Parliamentary speeches', pp. 23–44.
[60] Bucks. RO, D192/8/1; BL, Add. 70122, unfol. See: BL, Add. 28000, fos. 2, 14, 148v; Add. 64922, passim; Add. 70007, fos. 5, 8; Add. 11045, fos. 114–16; Harl. 382, fo. 106; Sloane 1467, fos. 14–153v; Harl. 2111, fos. 164–v; Northants. RO: IL 3503; IC 236; Beds. RO, J1382–6, J1410; CKS, U951/C261/37; Cornwall RO, RP/1/10/2, 11–13; Beinecke, Osborn fb.94/7; Devon RO, 1700M/CP19, 20, 24; NLS: Adv.33.1.1/13, items 7, 40, 41, 57, 60, 66, 71; Wodrow quarto xxv, fos. 23–165v.
[61] BL, Harl. 390, fos. 392, 394, 414; Add. 28000, fos. 2, 60; Eg. 2651, fos. 93–106; Add. 57929, fos. 36v–119v; Harl. 4931, fos. 50–138; Sloane 1467, fos. 4–66v; Add. 46931B, fos. 62, 78–100, 153, 189; FSL, L.b.685; Bodl. MS Tanner 65, fos. 179, 193, 236, 242, 257, 280; Beinecke, Osborn b.299; All Souls, MS 181, fos. 233–345; *HMC De L'Isle VI*, p. 345; BL, Add. 11045, fo. 105.

provincial readers, and that they reached the localities fairly quickly, where even minor gentry figures could file them away with lists of MPs and notes on proceedings. By January 1642, therefore, Thomas Stockdale reflected on his ability to follow proceedings 'every day by continual advertisement', even though he and his friends were 'spectators' who lived 'at a great distance'. Nevertheless, scribal copies of individual speeches remained expensive – at 1s or more – and it is noteworthy that at least some recipients strove to restrict their onward circulation.[62]

There can be little doubt that pressure to contain the reporting of debates increased along with political tension during 1641–2, and that this related in some way to the trend for publishing such information in print. As John Ogle explained to the Earl of Ormond in February 1641, 'if all employments fail I think I must set up trade ... to sell one of Mr Pym's twopenny speeches according to the manner of the new trumpet'. This threatened to undermine the privileged status of parliamentary intelligence, and to ensure that news about proceedings reached a much wider audience. Pamphlet versions of key speeches can be shown to have been consumed avidly, and to have been circulated zealously, before being filed away or pasted into note-books.[63] The response by MPs at least *appears* to have been swift and decisive, and steps were quickly taken to limit the recording of debates. Clerks were to 'suffer no copies to go forth of any arguments or speech', while MPs were to refrain from broadcasting anything that was 'pro-pounded or agitated' in the House, and orders were passed against the irregular printing of proceedings. Indeed, action was frequently taken against those responsible for the publication of speeches, with specific pamphlets being referred to the Committee for Printing, and with concern also being expressed about the prospect of a printed compilation of such texts.[64] This apparent clampdown on reporting culminated in the expulsion of Sir Edward Dering from the Commons in February 1642, for having printed his own speeches, and he suffered the indignity of being imprisoned in the Tower and of having his books burnt by the hangman. Dering's fate was much commented upon by onlookers, who certainly sensed that

[62] Glos. RO, D7115/1; Lancs. RO, DDB85/20, fos. 1–19, 33, 82; CKS, U269/O294; Durham UL, MSP 9, pp. 172–212; *Rous Diary*, pp. 99–113; HEH, HM 1554; *Fairfax Corr.*, ii. 202, 225; Herts. RO, D/Elw/F18, pp. 13–15; BL, Add. 27395, fo. 131.

[63] Bodl. MS Carte 2, fo. 328; MS Tanner 66, fos. 66–8, 183–6v; MS Clarendon 19, fos. 110, 154; MS Top. Oxon.C.378, p. 334; Cumbria RO, D/LONS/L13/10/1/16–17; BL: Add. 78220, fo. 14; Add. 28000, fo. 158.

[64] *CJ*, ii. 12, 42, 118, 139, 148, 159, 190, 208–9, 220; *OPH*, xi. 398–9; BL, Harl. 163, fos. 28, 228, 270; Durham UL, MSP 30, fos. 48–9; Jansson, iv. 737, 744; Stat. Co., Liber A, fo. 132; *LJ*, iv. 396–7; PA, MP, 21 Sept. 1641.

parliament was becoming more secretive. William Hawkins explained that 'things are not known abroad, as they were wont to be', while Robert Hobart observed that 'the parliament house do begin to restrain copies of their proceedings, and use more secrecy than they did'.[65]

Nevertheless, it would be a mistake simply to conclude that MPs were determined to enforce secrecy, and such comments and measures require careful contextualization. Some MPs who advocated restraint did so to prevent sensitive information from reaching the king's ears before decisions were made, or to prevent diplomatic incidents, and Sir Thomas Roe was fearful that print would 'expose all our consultations . . . to the censure and exposition of the whole world'.[66] More intriguing, however, is evidence that some of those who complained about the printing of speeches did so because their fellow MPs were at fault. Thus, when Sir Simonds D'Ewes grumbled that such practices were more common 'than in any former Parliament', he was responding to formal proposals to publish speeches by Oliver St John. Sometimes, in other words, the printing of speeches was official policy, and since other pamphlets were commissioned in a similar fashion, it seems clear that many members approached the issue of secrecy in a pragmatic fashion, rather than on the basis of firm principles.[67] In other cases, moreover, the hostility to printing reflected concerns about imperfect, fraudulent and unauthorized texts. Some pamphlets were investigated because they contained words that had not been spoken in the House, or that nobody could remember having heard. This might mean unwelcome commentary upon genuine speeches, as in the case of Dering's infamous book, or texts that were entirely fraudulent, such as those which were contrived by royalist propagandists and Grub Street hacks. In February 1642, for example, D'Ewes complained about a speech that appeared under his name, but that had been composed by a poor poet and sold to a stationer for 2s 6d, and Sir Edward Hales likewise fell victim to 'a busy prating newsmonger', who attributed a speech to him to make it marketable.[68] More often still, MPs demonstrated concerns about *authority*, and in many cases the aim appears to have been to ensure that texts were licensed, rather

[65] *PJ*, i. 120, 216, 222, 261–3, 268, 283; *Diurnall Occurrences*, 181.206, sig. A3; Devon RO, 73/15, p. 110; *HMC De Lisle VI*, p. 345; Bodl. MS Tanner 65, fo. 234.

[66] *PJ*, i. 512; TNA, SP 16/483, fo. 7.

[67] BL: Harl. 163, fo. 119; Add. 57929, fos. 122v–3; *CJ*, ii. 142, 631; Stat. Co., Liber A, fo. 131; *CSPD 1641–3*, p. 224; TNA, SP 16/487, fos. 34–v; *Substance* (1641, E2316).

[68] J. Peacey, 'Sir Edward Dering, popularity and the public', *HJ*, 54 (2011), 955–83; *PJ*, i. 304, 311, 326, 328–9; *CJ*, ii. 80, 116, 472, 925; BL, Harl. 163, fo. 119; Stat. Co., Liber A, fo. 130v; *Worthie Speech* (1642, B5120); *Two Speeches* (1642, P1125); *Pembroke's Farewell* (1648, E77A); *Sir Edward Hales* (1641, T1540); Nalson, ii, p. x.

than to prevent reporting. This certainly explains the action taken against William Gaye in the spring of 1642, given that his published account of a meeting between MPs and the king was authentic (having been leaked by a clerk), and given that it also reappeared in an official text.[69] Finally, some occasions when printed speeches were suppressed involved nothing other than political bias. This certainly applied to Lord Digby, who published an accurate version of one of his speeches so that his name would not be 'fixed upon posts', and so that he would not be 'torn to pieces by the people', but whose pamphlets were then burnt in July 1641. This decision was taken simply because they contained an unacceptable speech in defence of the Earl of Strafford, rather than because the text had been made public.[70]

Close scrutiny of the response to printed speeches thus makes it clear that the desire for secrecy, or to ensure that debates remained privileged, was not the primary goal. This is important because it helps to explain why the reporting of such evidence continued into the 1640s. This is not to deny that parliamentary pressure made an impact, and the publication of speeches *in pamphlet form* all but ceased in 1642. But it is to suggest that appearances can be deceptive, and that historians have overlooked the degree to which the reporting of debates became a feature of Civil War *newspapers*. Surprisingly little attention has been paid to the weight of evidence about debates that appeared in the kinds of diurnalls and newsbooks that consumers began to read with such enthusiasm, and to the possibility that this actually offered a picture of parliamentary affairs that was richer than ever. In fact, what is striking about texts like the 'Diurnall Occurrences' is that they were able to report debates in summary form, and to discuss a much broader range of MPs than occurred in manuscript separates and pamphlets, which concentrated on a fairly narrow range of *keynote* speeches. With the rise of journalism, therefore, readers gained unprecedented access to evidence about reports delivered and motions made, such as Falkland's move to reject the London petition, Hyde's speech against the judges and Sir Thomas Widdrington's 'long speech' against Bishop Wren. They got a better flavour of the occasions when acrimonious exchanges continued into the small hours, and a more vivid sense of who lined up on either side in debates about the abolition of episcopacy and the fate of Strafford. Indeed, it even became possible to picture the chaotic

---

[69] BL, Harl. 163, fo. 9; Durham UL, MSP 30, fos. 48–v; *Some Passages* (1642, S4552); *His Majesties Speech* (1641, C2801); *PJ*, ii. 55, 57; *LJ*, iv. 653, 660, 652–3; PA, MP 22 Mar. 1642.

[70] *CJ*, ii. 208–9; BL, Harl. 163, fos. 136, 190, 250, 396v–7v; Harl. 164, fo. 200; Durham UL, MSP 30, fos. 31–v, 65; *CSPD 1641–3*, p. 6; *HMC Montague*, p. 130; *Digbies Apologie* (1643, B4762), p. 5.

scenes during a 'great debate' on the Army Plot, when controversial interventions by Lord Digby, Sir William Widdrington and Herbert Price threatened to produce 'distemper', and 'the spilling of much blood'.[71]

This kind of reporting was not merely a feature of scribal diurnals, but also remained a feature of printed newspapers. This certainly caused consternation at Westminster, where MPs even tried to proscribe the new genre entirely in November 1641, but while journalists sometimes honoured specific requests not to 'pry into their debates', little could be done to stop the appearance of material that had been garnered from the Commons, or to prevent it from being read by the public.[72] In November 1642 editors drew attention to 'many speeches' that were made regarding possible peace talks, and went to some lengths to outline the 'weighty arguments' and objections made by Pym and Sir John Evelyn. In late 1644 readers were given 'heads' of a speech in which Cromwell defended the Independents from claims that they would become 'troublesome' once a Presbyterian church settlement was introduced, and of another in which he denied that the Self Denying Ordinance would hinder the war effort. In June 1647 newspapers summarized, and selectively quoted, speeches by the 'eleven members' who had been impeached by the army, and following the 'forcing of the Houses' the following month, and the army's subsequent march on London, journalists reported the defiant speeches by peers like the Earl of Pembroke and Viscount Saye.[73] On some occasions, indeed, controversial speeches by MPs like Thomas Chaloner – who attacked the Scots over the 'disposal' of the king in November 1646 – appeared in both pamphlets and the press, thereby generating controversy not just about the ideas expressed, but also about the reporting of speeches 'without doors'.[74]

That such reporting went largely unpunished reflects the difficulties faced by MPs. Parliament probably came to believe that its best strategy for controlling the coverage of debates involved using the licensing system as leverage and punishing journalists who overstepped the mark. This proved

---

[71] Bodl. MS Tanner 65, fos. 285–8v; Tanner 66, fos. 61–2v; Glos. RO, D7115/1; *HMC Egmont I*, p. 133; *CSPD 1641–3*, pp. 104, 281; FSL, X.c.23; BL, Add. 70081, unfol.; Durham UL, MSP 30, fos. 1–v, 3–6v, 9, 12–v, 14v–15, 31, 41, 43, 49v, 50v, 69v.

[72] *CJ*, ii. 319, 501; *Heads*, 181.101, p. 5; *PJ*, ii. 97–8, 100; *LJ*, vi. 16; *Diurnall Occurrences*, 181.206, sig. A3v; *Kingdomes*: 214.107, p. 850; 214.175, p. 311; *CJ*, iv. 725; Devon RO, 73/15, p. 111.

[73] *Diurnall*, 511.24A, sigs. Z–v, Z3v; *Speciall Passages*, 605.14, pp. 115–16; *Occurrences*: 465.2016, sigs. Qv–2; 465.2018, sig. S2; 465.5024, sig. Z4; 465.5026, sig. Ccv; 465.5031, p. 202; *Kingdomes*: 214.214, pp. 569–70; 214.226, p. 662; 214.221, p. 627; *Perfect Summary*, 528.03, p. 23.

[74] Chaloner, *Answer* (1646, C1802); *Civicus*, 298.181, pp. 2447–9; *Answer* (1646, A3351A); *Moderator* (1646, M2334); *Reply* (1646, G21); *Answer* (1646, A3377); *Speech Without Doores* (1646, B2972; *Corrector* (1646, M818); *Justification* (1646, J1256).

to be a fairly effective way of dealing with Nedham's *Britanicus*, for example, but it was useless in relation to the royalist press, which reported speeches fairly freely.[75] During 1643, therefore, *Aulicus* proved remarkably adept at quoting and glossing debates, on issues from peace to Presbyterianism, and from procedural cunning to financial impropriety, and MPs and peers were shocked to discover that news leaked out from even their most private meetings.[76] Pleas were made that people should neither 'report ... nor reveal any private thing done or said in this House, to any person or persons whatsoever out of the walls of this House, upon pain of exemplary punishment', and commentators clearly feared that leaks reflected factional struggles at Westminster. The finger of blame pointed towards clerics like Daniel Featley, and attempts were made to close the 'windows and wickets and keyholes', which enabled *Aulicus* to 'see into a debate at the close committee' and to hear 'every whisper' in the Commons. However, even the punishment of royalist spies – including Captain Ogle, who could regularly be seen 'intruding himself into the company of Parliament men' – had little effect, and the reporting of debates ultimately served to fuel fears that parliamentary practices were being manipulated and perverted by conniving politicians.[77]

Once again, therefore, the publication of detailed evidence about day-to-day business in parliament resulted from investigative journalism and factionalism. This ensured that while renewed attempts were made to regulate reporting in the late 1640s, these met with little success. Royalists, indeed, remained defiant and troublesome, confident about their ability to reveal the *arcana parliamentarii*. Like others, Nedham boasted about having 'a familiar that creeps into all ... conventicles and counsels', and he promised that 'not a wigeon shall wag his beard, but I will give the results of all in either House, and the world shall have a copy of every man's conscience'.[78] The fruits of such efforts were never clearer than in relation to debates surrounding the vote to make 'no further addresses' to the king (4 January 1648). Here, parliament probably recognized that it could do no more than ensure a temporary news blackout, and while

---

[75] *LJ*, viii. 321; J. Peacey, 'The struggle for *Mercurius Britanicus*', *HLQ*, 68 (2005), 517–44.

[76] *Aulicus*: 275.116, p. 197; 275.122, p. 289; 275.123, p. 296–7; 275.132, pp. 423–5, 428; 275.137B, pp. 504–5; 275.139B, p. 548; 275.138B, pp. 523, 533.

[77] *LJ*, vi. 233, 255; *Britanicus*: 286.001, p. 7; 286.003, p. 18; 286.004, p. 27; 286.005, p. 34; 286.006, pp. 43, 45, 47; 286.012, pp. 90, 93; 286.013, p. 100; 286.024, p. 188; 286.026, p. 206; 286.027A, p. 208; *Continuation*, 638.22, p. 5; *Diurnall*: 513.26B, sig. Cc3v; 504.037, pp. 291, 293; *Kingdomes*: 214.009, pp. 71–2; 214.050, p. 401; *Aulicus*, 275.229, pp. 1088–9; 275.302, p. 1333.

[78] *CJ*, v. 292; *Tell Tale* (1648, T623A), p. 3; *Persecutio*, pp. 17, 22, 34, 35; *Pragmaticus*, 369.114, sig. Ov; 369.112, sig. Mv.

parliamentarian journalists generally refrained from offering detailed coverage, royalists showed no such restraint.[79] Indeed, they offered readers accounts that were remarkable in terms of both information and analysis. This meant reflecting on the tactics of the Independent grandees, by connecting the episode with the reform of the Committee of Both Kingdoms (the composition of which was studied in detail), and by explaining how they manipulated procedures. This involved exploiting a late night sitting and a thin House, in order to make 'the main stroke'. It was suggested that 'all things being thus prepared' – when 'mortar pieces' were 'levelled', and the 'engineers' held 'match to the ... touch-hole' – the 'principal fire-men set to work'. These included Herbert Morley, Henry Ireton and Oliver Cromwell, the latter of whom 'spat fire' in response to a speech by John Maynard, with 'the glow worm glistening in his beak'. Cromwell was said to have quoted scripture to the effect that 'thou shalt not suffer an hypocrite to reign', and to have emphasized his zeal by laying his hand 'upon the hilt of his sword'. Subsequently, these debates were quoted at even greater length by Clement Walker, who emphasized the underhand tactics and the radicalism of the speeches. Sir Thomas Wroth was said to have been used to 'feel the pulse of the House', by arguing that 'our kings of late ... were fit for no place but Bedlam', by advocating the arrest and impeachment of the king, and by proposing to 'lay him by, and settle the kingdom without him'. Cromwell, meanwhile, apparently called Charles 'an obstinate man, whose heart God had hardened', in a speech that had 'something of menace in it'.[80]

Even reporting of this kind did not lead to effective action, however, and although the spring of 1648 heralded yet another attempt to restrain press coverage of proceedings, royalist zeal and factional division ensured that leaks remained inevitable, even from the 'cabinet junto and closest committee'. Evidence continued to emerge about speeches and motions by both Independents and Presbyterians, and analysis continued to be undertaken about members' attitudes, not least on issues like the 'personal treaty' with the king. Thus when John Bulkeley reported back from the negotiations in August 1648, newspapers quoted the hostile response from Herbert Morley, Thomas Chaloner and Thomas Scot, who 'delivered the sense of the whole enraged faction', and they also quoted a speech in which John Lisle dismissed negotiations as a ruse to 'entrap' the House. On the eve of

[79] *CJ*, v. 415–6; *Montereul*, ii. 371; *Kingdomes*, 214.241, p. 791; 214.242, p. 793.
[80] *Elencticus*, 312.06, p. 48; 312.07, p. 47; 312.08, pp. 56–7; *Pragmaticus*, 369.117, sigs. R2, R4; 369.118B, sig. Sv ; Walker, *Relations* (1648, W329/W334A), pp. 71–4.

Pride's Purge, royalists reported 'notable' speeches by those Presbyterians who sought to broker a settlement, including William Prynne, Sir Robert Harley and Sir Benjamin Rudyerd, as well as a defence of the army by Richard Norton.[81] Once again, Nedham bragged about his 'nimble familiar', who 'walks among the damned spirits of Derby House, and all the other conclaves of the brethren', but it seems clear that his efforts were also facilitated by laxity on the part of MPs. During these months, therefore, even parliamentarian journalists proved willing to quote speeches, including attacks on peace negotiations by John Swinfen and John Gurdon, the latter of whom described people who were willing to accept the king's concessions as 'court beagles'.[82] More importantly, factional tensions within the parliamentarian coalition led to attempts to expose and contest particular speakers and speeches. Radical journalists, for example, exposed the new 'brats of the court', including Nathaniel Fiennes, Viscount Saye and Lionel Copley. Indeed, while Presbyterians promoted their ideas through pamphlet versions of their speeches, including one by Prynne that John Clopton and his friends spent four hours reading in Essex, the editor of *The Moderate* damned such 'simple' men out of their own mouths. He thus quoted such speeches in order to decry their 'inveterate language' and to mock their claims to learning.[83]

In the end, therefore, it was not until the autumn of 1649 that parliament managed to control such reporting, in another sign of how attitudes and practices relating to secrecy changed during the Interregnum. This followed yet more colourful coverage of the 'deep conspiracies' and 'closest debates' during the weeks and months surrounding the king's trial. Royalists thus fingered the 'implacable devils' who were most hostile to the king, and analysed shades of opinion among the secluded Presbyterians, with Nedham putting names to groups that were styled 'prudential' men, 'asserters' and 'middle men', as well as the 'forlorn hope' who were 'pillars of the Scottish interest'. Attempts were also made to identify those responsible for preparing the king's trial, those who withdrew from the House in protest and those who returned to the Commons once proceedings were

[81] *CJ*, v. 493; *LJ*, x. 111, 130; PA, MP 22 Mar. 1648; *Elencticus*, 312.18, p. 134; *Pragmaticus*: 369.214, sigs. O2–3v; 369.216, sig. Q4; 369.219A, sig. [T3v]; 369.220A, sig. X2v; 369.221A, sigs. Aav–2; 369.227, sig. Oo; 369.235, sig. Bbbv–2.

[82] *Pragmaticus*: 369.221A, sigs. Aa–v, Aa4v; 369.234, sigs. Bb4–v; *Occurrences*, 465.5082, sigs. Mmmm3v; *Militaris*, 346.2, pp. 14–15.

[83] *Militaris*, 346.3, sigs. C3v–4; 346.5, sig. E2; Maynard, *Speech* (1648, M1458–9); Prynne, *Speech* (1648, P4027); ERO, D/DQs18, fo. 70v; *Moderate*: 413.2019, sig. (t2v); 413.2022, sig. (y).

over.[84] Such exposure only came to a halt with new press legislation in September 1649, which killed off radical and royalist newspapers alike, and thereafter a remarkable degree of secrecy was achieved. This was in direct contrast to the trend regarding other aspects of the parliamentary process, and it was clearly central to the government's attempt to *formalize* parliamentary reporting, rather than to wipe it out. Thus, while early issues of *Politicus* summarized certain speeches in 1650, Nedham declined to name the MPs responsible and soon stopped mentioning debates altogether. What took their place was an older pattern of reporting, in which the only speeches to appear were those delivered by the head of state and the Speaker at the opening of new parliamentary sessions.[85] However, while the pattern of parliamentary reporting became somewhat old-fashioned, the arguments used to justify it were relatively novel, and plainly revealed anxiety about being held individually accountable. MPs expressed concern that speeches would be 'told abroad', that they would spread 'without doors', and that this would lead to elections being based on 'all we have done in this Parliament'. Moves were therefore made to impose an oath of secrecy on all parliamentary clerks, to restrict debates to 'close' committees and to dissuade members from circulating any notes about proceedings.[86]

The net result, however, was that debates reverted to being privileged information. They were almost entirely absent from print during the 1650s, and one pamphlet that purported to contain a speech by Robert Shapcote, and that was 'scattered abroad', turned out to be a 'mere libel' and was quickly suppressed. Nevertheless, speeches remained available to those with friends in high places, like Richard Leveson, who had 'daily conversation' with an 'intimate friend' in the Commons, and who hoped to 'hear constantly what will be done'. Royalists had used private correspondence to circulate evidence about debates since the late 1640s, and during the Protectorate such information was circulated by any number of MPs and clerks, and began to fill private letters once again.[87] However, this situation did not last, and such material soon reappeared in the media

---

[84] *Pragmaticus*: 370.06B, sig. F3v; 369.239, sigs. Eee2–4; 369.240B, sig. Fff3v; *Diurnall*, 504.284, p. 2284; *Moon*, 248.01, p. 3; *Elencticus*: 312.55, sig. Hhh4v; 312.57, pp. 544–5; 312.58, p. 554; 312.59, p. 558; *Melancholicus*, 342.2, p. 16; *Moderate*: 413.2026, sig. (cc); 413.2028, sig. (ee).

[85] *Politicus*: 361.004, pp. 51–2; 361.067, p. 1076; 361.221, pp. 3744–8; 361.222, pp. 3762–4; 361.224, p. 3796; 361.400, pp. 259–61; *Proceedings*, 599.197, p. 3117; *Speech* (1659, C7191); *Speech* (1657, F881); Cheshire RO, DAR/F/3, pp. 30, 32.

[86] *Burton Diary*, i. 296, 341–2, ii. 24, 199, 237, 281, 316, 336, iii. 233, 455, iv. 415.

[87] *Speech* (1654, S2967); *CJ*, vii. 383; Vaughan, *Protectorate*, i. 85–6; *Proceedings*, 599.267, pp. 4236–7; *Diurnall*, 503.257, p. 3938; Staffs. RO, D868/4/32a; *TSP*, vii. 609; Bodl. MS North.c.4, fo. 93; BL, Stowe 185, fo. 123; Bodl. MS Carte 228, fos. 79–88; MS Carte 80, fos. 751–3; MS Carte 73, fo. 166; MS

following the collapse of the Protectorate. During the weeks and months before the Restoration, therefore, readers like Thomas Rugg and John Lowther were confronted by a plethora of texts that contained supposititious and satirical speeches, and that promised more than they delivered, but they also had access to at least some authentic material from the restored Rump.[88]

iv Conclusion

The story of parliamentary reporting, as it related to the performance of individual MPs, can thus be shown to have involved not just pamphlet versions of speeches, but also other forms of information and other genres of print, from newspapers to electoral propaganda. It involved citizens who were curious for news from within the two Houses, investigative journalists who sought to shine a light into the Palace of Westminster, and public figures who recognized reasons for secrecy as well as justifications for transparency, and who were aware that granting access to sensitive information could be useful as well as dangerous. Although 'secrecy' on matters like debates was theoretically sacrosanct, it was not always easy to preserve, and MPs, peers and officials were sometimes deeply implicated in efforts to publicize proceedings, not least for pragmatic and political reasons. What this meant, of course, was that there was no straightforward revolution in the public face of parliamentary affairs, but rather a complex, fluid and sometimes paradoxical process, in which transparency was sometimes enhanced and sometimes undermined, and in which few people adopted an entirely consistent position. Some of those who proved willing to compromise secrecy, by publishing evidence about the attitudes and activities of individual members, adamantly rejected the idea that MPs could be 'called to account' for their actions, 'by every unknown person'. Indeed, even outspoken commentators like Wither sometimes defended 'sacred' secrecy, and opposed those who would 'accuse members for what they did in the House'. Nevertheless, whether they did so consciously and overtly, or merely pragmatically and practically, a great many people both inside and outside parliament can be shown to have engaged in a process of rethinking

---

Clarendon 45, fos. 140–3; MS Clarendon 46, fo. 32; *CCSP*, ii. 206, 217, 233, 236–7, 241–3, 378–80, iv. 593, 603, 606, 615–16; BL: Add. 78196, fos. 17–v, 69; Add. 78221, fos. 24–v, 27; Lans. 823, fos. 180, 195, 212, 245–6, 247, 231–2; Add. 22919, fos. 11v, 14, 78.

[88] *Politicus*: 361.606, pp. 1081–3; 361.608, pp. 1121–2; TNA, SP 18/219, fos. 93–96v; *CSPD 1659–60*, p. 375; *Faithfull Scout*, 151.008, pp. 48–9; *Brief Narrative* (1660, P3912); *Rugg*, pp. 36–7; Cumbria RO, D/LONS/L13/10/1/51. For an example of a misleading text, see: *Lord Henry* (1659, L3047A).

the relationship between politicians and the public, and of reconceptualizing the nature of representation and accountability.[89]

Once again, in other words, the circumstances of revolution helped to transform traditional public culture, in ways that involved a dynamic interplay between the practices of political life and the habits and tactics of authors, journalists and readers. This involved not merely the publicizing of processes and formal proceedings, but also a willingness to reveal evidence about speeches and votes, as well as public finances and private interests, and it not only fed into intellectual debates regarding the nature of representation, but also had implications for political participation. This was because it became much easier to make informed judgments about the performance of specific public figures, and because it was increasingly likely that the track records of specific candidates would affect parliamentary elections.

First, therefore, the possibility of gathering considerable evidence about particular characters can be demonstrated with the example of Henry Marten, whose public profile offers a useful way of exploring the nature and limits of parliamentary transparency. Although none of Marten's speeches appeared in pamphlet form, newspapers nevertheless revealed him to be an *active* and increasingly controversial MP, who served his local community, undertook committee work and made fiery contributions to proceedings. These included clashing with moderate peers like the Earl of Northumberland, as well as making the republican outbursts for which he was expelled from the House in 1643. Such coverage resumed following Marten's readmission in 1646, when it was possible to follow his behaviour in support of John Lilburne, his opposition to Presbyterians and his financial impropriety, and occasionally to read printed versions of reports that he delivered to the House. It was also possible to catch glimpses of speeches that revealed his radical populism, his tolerance of sectarians and his antipathy towards monarchy, as well as his troubled relationship with the republican regime. This reflected his ongoing support for radical activists – one report involved the intemperate exchange when Cromwell accused him of colluding with the Levellers – as well as his lax personal morality, and discussions of his activity were laden with sexual innuendos and with allegations about whore-mongering.[90] Of course, while this

---

[89] *Justification*, p. 2; Wither, *Respublica*, p. 17.
[90] *Diurnall*: 511.21A, sig. V3v; 513.45A, sig. Yy2; 504.213, p. 1714; *Aulicus*: 275.129, p. 375; 275.133, p. 452; *Continuation*, 638.52, p. 8; *Scout*, 485.08, p. 62; *Civicus*, 298.137, p. 1197; *Kingdomes*, 214.134, p. 1010; *Occurrences*, 465.4041, sig. Qqv; *Perfect Summary*, 528.08, p. 63; *New Presbyterian* (1647, P4021), p. 8;

picture seems fairly detailed, there are obvious grounds for caution regarding what Marten's treatment reveals. He was, after all, a fairly high-profile MP, and although similar information could be gathered about any number of his contemporaries, it could certainly not be replicated for every member. In addition, it must be recognized that few people were likely to have had the breadth of reading that was necessary to acquire such a rich understanding of his attitudes and activities. The public face of Marten's career that has just been described is drawn from over a dozen different newspaper titles, as well as various pamphlets, and few contemporaries probably read all of these texts. Nevertheless, people probably knew which journalists were most likely to peddle this kind of information, and the fact that Marten was a ubiquitous figure in the press suggests that it would not have been difficult for people to get some sense of his politics whatever they were reading. As such it is plausible to argue that the print revolution enhanced the possibility of following an individual MP's career, even if only in a *mediated* and *imperfect* fashion. Indeed, very occasionally it is possible to find concrete evidence of people following the careers of public figures in the pages of newspapers, and evidence that such stories could 'incense the common people'.[91]

Secondly, the plausibility of linking such publicity with electoral fortunes can be highlighted by returning briefly to election literature and to texts that explicitly referred to the performance of individual candidates. From the mid 1640s onwards, therefore, voters would fairly frequently have encountered evidence relating to the activity of sitting and former MPs, in ways that may further have enhanced their ability to make informed decisions at the polls. These were obviously published for political effect; they evidently found an audience and it may even be possible to gauge their impact. One striking example is the list, published ahead of the 1654 election, in which members of the Nominated Assembly who had supported a 'godly learned ministry' were marked with an asterisk, while sectarians were highlighted with an ominous dagger. Here it is tempting to conclude that the availability of such evidence affected the electoral fortunes of individual MPs. Thus, while 57 per cent of the former were returned to the first protectoral parliament, only 5 per cent of the latter were chosen, and this perhaps explains why the same information also appeared in 1656 and 1659,

---

Elencticus: 312.03, pp. 20–1; 312.10, pp. 71–2; 312.23, p. 174; 312.25, p. 189; *Melancholicus*, 344.49A, pp. 295–6; *Henry Marten* (1648, M2267A); *Moderate*, 413.2026, sig. (cc); *Moon*: 248.02, p. 11; 248.23, p. 194; *Pragmaticus*: 369.246B, sig. Ggg2; 370.04A, sig. D3; 370.10A, sig. K3; *Friday* (1652, M824).
[91] TWAS, MD/NC/2/1, pp. 159–60.

alongside lists of recruiter MPs and of those who had joined the royalist cause.[92] Of course, it is extremely difficult to assess the impact of such texts with much certainty, and yet evidence from 1660 suggests fairly unambiguously that sitting MPs recognized the value of drawing attention to their performance, and that some defeated candidates rued the failure to make their track records clear to voters.[93]

Thus, while there are obvious grounds for caution, such evidence suggests that during the 1640s and 1650s political information could be harvested in ways that qualitatively transformed the understanding that citizens had about specific members, and that contemporaries made a conscious connection between political openness and parliamentary elections. This suggests that the transparency that print fostered had not just a *potential* impact but also a *perceived* effect on political participation, before, during and after particular parliaments. What happened as a result is the subject of the next and final section of the book.

---

[92] *Diurnall*, 504.029, p.225; *Perfect Journall* (1656, P1489B); *Names* (1654, N142); Cumbria RO, D/LONS/L13/10/1/43; *Catalogue* (1654, C1399); *TSP*, iii. 132–3; BL, Harl. 6810, fos. 164–5; *Catalogue* (1656, C1394); *List* (1659, L2475).

[93] *Oxinden Letters*, pp. 244–5; BL, Add. 28004, fo. 203; EKRO, Sa/C4.

PART III

Taking part

Introduction

In July 1654 voters in Brecon submitted a petition to parliament against the election of Edmund Jones, accusing him of being one of the 'vipers in your bosom'. He was, they said, an example of how ex-royalists 'creep into places of trust and power, doing that by the fox which they could not perform by the lion'. What made the incident striking, however, is that the petition was supported by a printed text, which was sent to Henry Scobell, clerk of parliament, and which consisted of a three-page folio pamphlet entitled *The Humble Address, Narrative and Information*. This contained detailed allegations against Jones, and it was followed by another printed text containing *The Complaint of the County of Brecon*.[1] Such texts were used to expand on demands, to ensure that arguments were circulated around Westminster and to improve the chances of achieving success, and the case was far from unique. Indeed, having closed the previous section of the book by raising the possibility that the print revolution helped to transform electoral politics, it is now possible to demonstrate that this was precisely what happened in practice. The 1650s witnessed a slew of similar protests and petitions in printed form, both by defeated candidates and disgruntled voters, which were submitted to the Commons and the Council of State in response to specific contests, and which involved complaints not merely about the processes involved, but also about the qualities and qualifications of individual candidates. Indeed, so common did such tactics become that MPs became worried about being overwhelmed by printed texts, and in 1654 the chairman of the Committee for Elections, Sir Arthur Hesilrige, was forced to impose a time limit upon the submission of such claims and such material.[2]

---

[1] *CSPD 1654*, pp. 270–2; TNA, SP 18/73, fos. 150, 152, 163–4v; *Humble Address* (1654); *Complaint* (1654, C5615).

[2] *Politicus*: 361.218, p. 3700; 361.219, pp. 3709–10, 3716; *Diurnall*: 503.246, pp. 3771–2; 503.248, p. 3808.

When examined closely, texts relating to contested elections prove highly revealing about the nature and uses of print, and what we witness is evidence of more than one strategy and more than one genre. In some cases printed petitions were used to draw attention to grievances, while in others such texts were deployed to intervene in the parliamentary process once cases had been taken up, and involved the lobbying of MPs and officials. In 1654, for example, Nathaniel Barton issued a *Representation and Defence*, in response to claims that had been made against him by Sir Samuel Sleigh, not least that his status as an ordained minister made him ineligible to sit in parliament. In January 1659 procedural irregularities during the Gloucester election led to the production of a printed broadside by one of the candidates, Thomas Pury, which contained *Reasons* for supporting his petition as well as a certificate by his supporters. Other texts outlined *The State of the Case* between Rowland Dawkins and David Morgan, both of whom were returned at Carmarthen; *The State of the Case* regarding Henry Nevill, relating to electoral malpractice in Berkshire; and *The Case* of William Duckett and Edward Bayntun, which appeared in response to a petition against their election at Calne. On these occasions printed texts were produced by successful or unsuccessful candidates, but other interventions were made by voters. The Ely election of 1654, for example, provoked opponents of George Glapthorne to produce *A Briefe Relation* of his failings, and testimonials that he was 'a common swearer, a common curser, a frequenter of alehouses, and ... a companion of lewd women'.[3]

The importance of such texts is threefold. They indicate that print could be used as a tool with which to take part in parliamentary business; that such participation could be based on knowledge about processes, proceedings and personalities; and that printed interventions could be more or less discrete. In other words, they suggest not just that print culture provided enhanced awareness about current affairs and political institutions, but also that it facilitated participation, and they indicate that printed texts were not always part of *public* discourse. The items just mentioned were intended for limited and targeted circulation, and were intended to influence the deliberations of MPs and committee members, to whom some of them were addressed directly. They tended to be short and they were often anonymous, and those that appeared as pamphlets generally lacked imprints and

---

[3] *Representation* (1654, B989A); *Reasons* (1659, R570); BL, 1865.c.16/116: *State of the Case* (1659); *Nevill versus Strood* (1659, N508A); Beinecke, Osborn fb.16/11–14, 17: *The Case of Mr Bayntun*; *Brief Relation* (1654, B4631), pp. 1–2.

title pages. None of them appear to have been designed for commercial publication. This is not to say that elections were incapable of generating public disputation, but it is to suggest that print could be used in a variety of ways, and that it is necessary to be sensitive to issues of form and function in relation to print genres, and in relation to the methods involved in political participation. This means distinguishing between interventions that involved polite and formal engagement with a restricted audience, and those that were more confrontational and that were likely to foster public debate. It is certainly the case that elections sometimes provoked dialogue and argumentation, and that specific disputes generated pamphlet exchanges. Following the Pembroke election of 1656, for example, one side produced *The State of the Election of a Burgess* (now lost), while the other responded with an unadorned broadside entitled *Truth Manifest*. In this case, both texts were probably only intended for the eyes of MPs and clerks, but in others this was emphatically not the case, as parliamentary business spilled over into the public domain. Sometimes this involved election petitions being published *after* they had been submitted, perhaps even with official backing, in order to draw public attention to the claims and demands that they made.[4] More obviously, however, it meant polemical pamphleteering. Here, the most famous example involves William Prynne's *Minors No Senators*, written on behalf of Edward King following his electoral defeat at the hands of William Wray, the latter of whom was not only under-age but also overseas. Prynne's pamphlet came in the wake of a petition to parliament and of attempts to take action against King, and it was clearly intended to make a dramatic intervention in a controversial case, and in support of a friend and ally.[5] Other similar examples are less well known but no less important. In July 1654, for example, inhabitants of Reading who opposed the election of Robert Hammond, and who supported Captain Castle, produced a pamphlet in response to secretive and underhand behaviour by the mayor and aldermen, and in reaction to alehouse electioneering. They also complained about a local cleric who had mocked Castle's humble status, and who had intimated that his election would produce social levelling and the return of 'Goodman Parliament-man'. Likewise, in November 1656 the Berkshire election provoked not just a petition to parliament in support of Henry Neville, but also a published

---

[4] *Truth Manifest* (1656, T3156); *To the Right Honourable* (1659, T1716).
[5] Prynne, *Minors* (1646, P4008), pp. 12, 13, 16; BL: Add. 70087, unfol.; Add. 28716, fo. 30; *CJ*, iv. 233, 272, 296; *Edward King* (1646, K493); King, *Discovery* (1647, K492).

pamphlet, which complained about irregular polling and about how secretive 'cabals' had returned the sheriff's favoured candidates.[6]

Ultimately, some of the public statements that were made in response to specific elections reflected broader concerns and engaged with bigger issues. In the summer of 1654, for example, grievances relating to the Wiltshire election resulted in the publication of a pamphlet by the radical bookseller, Livewell Chapman, which set the dispute in the context of factional politics and Presbyterian agitation. The pamphlet targeted William Stone of Salisbury, who was accused of aggressive electioneering on behalf of a 'list' of candidates, and of besmirching Edmund Ludlow and Colonel Eyre as Levellers and Anabaptists. Stone, however, was regarded as nothing more than the 'factor' and 'vassal' of local clerics, who were furthering the interests of a 'Scottish faction' and promoting an agenda that included maintaining 'the oppression of tithes'. This pamphlet then elicited a forceful and public response, which defended the ministers' activities, and which intimated that Chapman was himself serving the interests of a more general campaign 'for all England'. In another case, in 1659, various inhabitants of Brecon produced *An Alarum to Corporations*, in response to their experience in civic elections and at Westminster. They complained about 'barbarous, inhumane, [and] trayterous practices' on the part of 'the giddy sort of heretics', who had used clerics and soldiers to influence elections, and they were explicitly responding to the difficulties they had faced in petitioning against a decision by the Committee of Safety. Thus frustrated, the townsmen resorted to a public denunciation of the processes and proceedings they had witnessed, and of the expense involved in making 'humble addresses and applications'. Indeed they then broadened their attack by criticizing 'merciless soldiers', the implementation of the Act for Propagating the Gospel and the abuse of tithe money, and they concluded that such problems were likely to spread across the nation.[7]

The printed texts that emerged in the wake of parliamentary elections set the scene for the third and final section of this book. This moves beyond examining reading practices and the public face of parliament, in order to explore the relationship between print culture and the methods used to take part in political life. It will begin by analysing how and why members of the public engaged in the production of printed texts (Chapter 7), before turning to the different ways in which print enhanced the capacity of

[6] *Admirable* (1654, F2200), pp. 2–3, 5, 6; *True and Perfect* (1656, T2560), pp. 2, 3, 5, 9.
[7] *Copy of a Letter* (1654, C6155), pp. 1–6; Chambers, *Apology* (1654, C1914), pp. 1–3, 10; *Alarum* (1659, A827), pp. 2, 5–7.

ordinary citizens to make targeted interventions in parliamentary proceedings, as petitioners (Chapter 8), as lobbyists (Chapter 9), and as contributors to the politics of mass agitation and street protests (Chapter 10). The section will then conclude by examining the ways in which members of the public interacted with specific MPs and peers, and with those who represented them in parliament (Chapter 11). As in previous sections, the aim will be to use everyday practices as a means of recovering attitudes towards participation and ideas regarding representation, and to explore not just the structural factors that affected the ability to express grievances and demands, but also the conjunctural forces that drew people into the world of parliamentary affairs, as well as the behaviour of particular individuals in specific circumstances. This will reveal that contemporaries developed a subtle appreciation of how to influence their representatives and a variety of ways of appropriating print. It will highlight a spectrum of participatory methods and a spectrum of print genres, and it will demonstrate the ways in which people developed tactical awareness. My aim is to suggest that contemporaries recognized when to use print discretely, when to go public and when to act in a confrontational and aggressive manner, and to show that people appreciated not just which kinds of intervention were possible, desirable and necessary, but also which kinds of printed texts were useful at different points along the participatory spectrum. Beyond this, my purpose is also to suggest that the ability to calibrate print genres with political contexts was evident across the country and across the social spectrum, and that citizens of all kinds were capable of making tactical escalations in response to the frustrations they experienced at Westminster. Finally, my goal is to suggest that these escalations involved dramatic and previously neglected processes of political thought and radicalization, not least with regard to the relationship between MPs and their constituents.

CHAPTER 7

Authors, printing and participation

As Britain slid towards war in October 1642, Edward Browne bemoaned his loss of money and reputation as a result of publishing and 'bookmaking'. He grumbled that serious and substantial books were 'not likely to sell in this age', and that publishers favoured 'a lying and scandalous pamphlet . . . or some reviling terms against monarchy and hierarchy, to uphold an anarchy'. This was what proved 'vendible ware', especially if it was possible to 'obtain an order or a vote upon it' and have it declared scandalous or obnoxious. Such claims were scarcely original, but what makes them intriguing is that they were made in a short pamphlet by someone who was ambitious to become an author, and who wrote a string of political tracts in the early 1640s. Almost two decades later, at the moment of Restoration, Sir Edmund Peirce provided another authorial testimony, justifying his ambition to become Master of Requests by explaining that he had written and published 'many things very serviceable to king and church', and that he had done so 'at much danger and expense'.[1] If Browne was a pamphleteer in spite of himself, then Peirce was unapologetic, and the comparison between them seems to reflect changing attitudes towards public debate and discourse during the revolutionary decades. Although it is true that traditional concerns about the appearance of 'dangerous books' by 'state meddlers' did not disappear, it was recognized that the 1640s witnessed unprecedented popular participation through pamphleteering. Writing from London in 1640, the Scots commissioners commented upon the remarkable 'liberty of speech' that they encountered regarding 'the most weighty affairs of this kingdom', and towards the end of the interregnum another Scottish visitor expressed amazement that the English were not just 'great readers', and 'the most knowing people in the world', but also that they were 'addicted to writing'. He explained that 'there have been of late more . . . bad books printed and published in the English tongue than in all

---

[1] Browne, *James Cambels* (1642, B5107), pp. 3, 4, 7–8; *CSPD 1660–1*, pp. 11–12, 106.

the vulgar languages', and in this he found support from Thomas Rugg, who noted that 'almost every day men writ their minds and printed it'.[2] Others suggested that anyone who wanted to write could now find 'a man to print it', whatever their 'book learning', and such rhetoric occasionally became fevered, with claims about 'a rout of writers' and a 'rabble' of authors, who constituted 'a bold, shameless, licentious scum'. Such people were said to have 'a desperate itch' to 'vomit up all the filth of thought and language'. Thus, while Samuel Hartlib and John Lilburne liked the idea that 'all men' could 'print their thoughts freely', concerns about living in a 'scribbling age' could be found across the political spectrum. The 'itch to quarrel' and the tendency for pamphlets to 'fly abroad' led to cheap print being decried as 'dangerous', and by 1660 commentators already recognized that the combination of coffeehouses and cheap print generated a threatening participatory culture, which produced dangerous ideas and 'chimeras of state government'.[3]

This chapter begins a process of testing such claims about the participatory possibilities that were available to people who *appropriated* print. Historiographically this might be considered a well-tilled field of enquiry, since considerable attention has been paid to the democratization of authorship, and to the emergence of new voices and new modes of discourse, as traditional patronage declined and as professional authors emerged, even to the point that scholars have posited the emergence of a 'public sphere'.[4] The risk, however, is that too heavy a reliance upon Habermas generates a preoccupation with political and religious polemic, in ways that provide a misleading picture of 'public' discourse; and the aim of this chapter is to deepen our understanding of the 'new voices' that emerged in print during the mid seventeenth century. This will involve broadening our appreciation of the reasons why print was appropriated and of the ways in which it was used, and it will involve doing three things. First, the chapter will explore the mechanics and costs of book production, in comparison with the expense involved in scribal publication (section i). Secondly, it will examine the ways in which individuals entered into print, and the changes that took place in the processes of authorship (Section ii). Thirdly, it will

---

[2] Birch, *James*, ii. 355; *Crosfield*, p. 4; BL, Add. 57929, fo. 36; Aberdeen UL, MS 2538/1, fo. 44; *Rugg*, p. 48.

[3] BL, Add. 19863, fos. 5–6; *Anti-Britanicus*, 267.1, p. 3; *Britanicus*, 286.086, pp. 781, 783; *Civicus*, 298.145, p. 2062; SUL, Hartlib 30/4/68; *Occurrences*, 465.5113, sig. Aaaaa; *Duppa Corr.*, p. 91; *Life of Dugdale*, p. 264; *Prerogative* (1644, P3219), p. 1; Davis, *Heaven* (1656, D422A), sig. A4v; *Burton Diary*, iv. 480; *Publique* (1648, P4149a), p. 1; *Fairfax Corr.*, p. 389; BL: Add. 78198, fo. 65; Add. 78298, fo. 103.

[4] P. Lake, *Boxmaker's Revenge* (Manchester, 2001); A. Hunt, *Art of Hearing* (Cambridge, 2010), ch. 3.

supplement this analysis of the *conditions* of authorship with a discussion of the *practices* involved, in terms of how print was deployed, and this will involve focusing on the different motives for engaging with print (section iii), and considering the ways in which newspapers became an interactive medium (section iv).

The aim of the chapter will once again be to offer a blend of structural and conjunctural analysis, and to consider the ways in which specific individuals behaved in the circumstances in which they found themselves. My argument will be that scribal culture involved significant barriers to participation; that the print medium was significantly cheaper; and that this, combined with the political and religious turmoil of the period, fostered authorship by individuals who had previously been excluded from contemporary debates. This means that the circumstances of war created both the necessity and the opportunity for exploiting print, and the chapter will demonstrate that the possibilities offered by the media were seized by public figures and private individuals alike, and by people across the country and across the social spectrum. However, this will be shown to have involved a variety of reasons, a variety of methods and a variety of genres, and by highlighting that printed interventions could involve discussions of local and personal matters, as well as fiery publications relating to national debates, the chapter will make it possible to connect polemical pamphleteering with less dramatic activities, which involved advertising, self-promotion and self-defence. Indeed, the aim will be to show how discrete printed interventions could escalate into polemical exchanges and debates, such that even the most innocuous uses of print were prone to develop political implications. Ultimately, what will emerge is a sense that interventions in 'public' life often involved something other than a desire to discuss significant matters of state, but that even practices that involved mundane and 'private' issues could sometimes generate political attitudes and ideas of a more general and indeed radical nature.[5]

i Scribal authorship and printing costs

In August 1642, a household servant from Exeter, William Tucke, employed a local scrivener to make copies of a libellous song regarding several MPs, having acquired it from one of his master's lodgers. The local trade in such material seems to have thrived, and another local penman

---

[5] D. Harkness, *Jewel House* (New Haven, 2007); T. O'Malley, 'Defying the powers and tempering the spirit', *JEccH*, 33 (1982), 72–88; D. Hall, *Ways of Writing* (Philadelphia, 2008).

confessed to being involved in the circulation of a verse entitled 'The commonwealths irreparable loss in the untimely departure of the Lady Grenville's well-affected monkey'. These examples highlight the ongoing significance of scribal methods for copying political texts, but what is less clear is how affordable the process was, and meaningful research into the costs of scribal documents has been hampered by poor and dispersed archival evidence.[6] Nevertheless, piecing together the surviving evidence about both scriveners and printers makes it possible to demonstrate that scribal publication was possible but pretty expensive, and that the financial benefits of employing stationers were particularly striking for anyone who sought to produce multiple copies of specific texts, for distribution, circulation and publication.

Most commonly the economics of scribal production can be explored in relation to legal and parliamentary documents. Private archives offer a rich seam of evidence about the expenses involved in waging, making and clarifying law, sometimes in forms that permit legal fees to be distinguished from the cost of *preparing* and *copying* legal texts. It is possible to demonstrate, therefore, that standardized court orders and writs, prepared by legal clerks, generally cost a few shillings, as did the engrossing of petitions, and that costs rose fairly quickly for any document longer than a few pages. In 1639, for example, an order from the Court of Wards cost the Gell family 18s, while individual legal 'bills' cost Alice L'Estrange anything from a few shillings to well over £1. Similar costs were incurred in relation to new parliamentary orders. During the 1640s, therefore, accounts for the Earls of Leicester and Bath reveal that these cost between 7s and £1 each, figures that are in line with the tables of fees drawn up by clerks like Robert Bowyer and John Browne.[7] In these cases, of course, we are dealing with texts whose composition required legal and clerical expertise, but evidence also indicates that the mere copying of official documents could also prove expensive. Here, too, legal account books reveal that even simple documents like orders and petitions could cost between 1s and £1 to reproduce. In 1646, for example, Coventry corporation was charged £1 10s for a copy of London's charter, and in 1656 Sir Thomas Myddleton spent no less than £5 on copies of legal judgments for a legal case in which he took an interest.[8] Copies of depositions that were generated as part of legal cases could be

---

[6] Devon RO, ECA Book 64, fos. 7v, 281; H. Love, *Culture and Commerce of Texts* (Amherst, 1998), pp. 126–7, 129, 133.

[7] DRO, D258/10/54/1; Norfolk RO, LEST P7, pp. 195, 199; Penshurst, MS 398; *Devon Accounts*, p. 114; Beinecke, Osborn fb.158/5; fb.159, fo. 86.

[8] CHC, BA/H/3/20/2, p. 408; *Chirk Accounts*, p. 62.

equally expensive, and those who needed to acquire them could easily rack up sizeable bills. Viscount Molyneux's agent paid £5 10s for copies of examinations relating to one particular case in 1656, and one of the parties to a suit involving ecclesiastical and civic authorities in Norfolk was able to secure copies of 'voluminous' witness depositions, but only at a cost of £17.[9]

Similar evidence about the costliness of official documents also emerges in relation to the copying of material at Whitehall and Westminster. During 1635, for example, the Poulters Company paid the clerk of the privy council 10s for copying a letter from the mayor of London, while the Tylers and Bricklayers spent the same amount on a petition from the Plasterers' Company, and 16s on four copies of orders issued by the council. During the 1640s and 1650s, meanwhile, copies of parliamentary votes rarely cost less than 1s, and sometimes cost much more. In 1642, the corporation of Dover paid 7s 6d to obtain a copy of an order relating to the king's servants, and in the same year the Earl of Bath paid 6s 8d for a text of a similar nature. The accounts of Alice L'Estrange and the Temple family reveal that such documents could cost as much as 15s apiece, while on more than one occasion in the late 1640s the Marquess of Ormond paid even more for copies of individual orders.[10] Similar charges also applied to anyone wanting to acquire copies of petitions that had been submitted to parliament. Livery companies paid up to a few shillings for documents that touched upon their business interests, and accounts for the Coventry corporation, and for individuals like L'Estrange and Sir Thomas Barrington, reveal payments of as much as 13s for certified copies of such texts. Once again, such prices are corroborated by the fees quoted by parliamentary clerks, which reveal charges in excess of 2s 6d for copying orders and votes, and of well over £1 for petitions, reports and ordinances.[11]

Such evidence is rich, but it is also problematic, and in order to get a better sense of how expensive scribal documents could be, it is necessary to establish in greater detail what people could expect to get for their money. First, it is necessary to address the issue of the cost *per page*, and here surviving evidence indicates that, beyond a minimum charge, the fees charged by reputable scriveners were fairly consistent, and broadly in line with Thomas Powell's *Direction for the Search of Records* (1622). This indicated that legal clerks would charge 8d per sheet, with an additional flat fee for

[9] Lancs. RO, DDM/1/66; BL, Add. 69885, fo. 109.
[10] GL: MS 2150/1, fo. 48; MS 3054/2; EKRO, Do/FCa/5, fo. 328v; *Devon Accounts*, p. 114; HEH, STT Personal, Box 11/2; Norfolk RO, LEST P7, p. 282; Bodl. MS Carte 30, fos. 342v, 344, 346v.
[11] GL: MS 3054/2; MS 11571/13; CHC, BA/H/3/20/2, p. 397; ERO, D/DBa/A43/8; Norfolk RO: LEST P10, p. 120; LEST P7, pp. 216, 268; PA: MP 1641; MP 7 Feb. 1642.

certification, and this was precisely the sum that people like William Pleydell paid for copying legal documents.[12] This is not to say that costs were stable, and fees evidently fluctuated around this baseline, perhaps in line with the scale of the task and the creditworthiness of the customer. When Richard Ferriman purchased copies of fifty-seven sheets of legal depositions, for example, his bill of just over £1 8s involved a fee of 6d per sheet, while a copy of Sir Thomas Swinburn's shrieval accounts cost 5d per sheet (for sixty-eight sheets), and by the 1650s Chancery clerks were charging as little as 4d per sheet. At other times, however, prices could be higher, with the Hastings family sometimes being forced to pay 1s per sheet for copying breviates and letters.[13] This same variability also applied to parliamentary documents. Thus, while the cost of copying bills and acts was 8d per sheet in 1658, some clerks were able to command much higher fees. In the early 1640s, therefore, people who went through the official channels could expect to pay 10d or even 1s per sheet for copying petitions and bills. This meant that a 1641 petition from Dover cost £1 13s 4d, while a draft bill by the Weavers company cost £1 2s 6d and the 'Grand Remonstrance' cost £1. At these prices it is hard to avoid the conclusion that the cost of political participation was extremely high.[14]

This impression can be modified, however, by confronting a second problem with the surviving evidence. This is that the most obvious sources regarding the cost of scribal copying relate to 'civil servants' and professional scriveners, who probably charged much more than jobbing clerks and scribes. As such it is important to recognize that the expenses involved in creating scribal texts, and thus of participating as 'authors', may have been much less daunting. Contemporaries clearly considered that fees were sometimes excessive, and the controversial republican ordinance for regulating Chancery proposed reducing 'official' charges to 4d per sheet. What is interesting about this proposal is that it represented a *concession* to the clerks, who initially faced the prospect of being able to charge no more than 2d per sheet, and their response is highly instructive. They claimed, therefore, that 2d was 'very moderate', on the grounds that their quasi-legal duties prevented them from completing more than ten sheets per day, and they suggested that 1d per sheet would represent 'good wages' for anyone who 'sat close at his writing . . . all the day', and that 'the meanest scrivener's boy'

[12] Powell, *Direction* (1622, 20166), pp. 14–15, 19, 36–7, 53, 58, 63, 66; Worcs. RO, BA9360/A10, Box 3; HEH: STTF Box 55/68; ST 54/2; HAF Box 16/53; BL, Add. 27411, fo. 108; Norfolk RO, LEST P7, p. 207.

[13] TNA, SP 24/30; Durham UL, MSP 9, p. 251; HEH, HAF Box 16/53; HAF Box 15/22.

[14] PA, MP 7 Feb. 1642; TNA, SP 28/309, fo. 110; Beinecke, Osborn fb.158/5; fb.159, fo. 86.

would not work for less than 2d per sheet. Such claims may have been provocative, but they certainly indicate that scribal texts could be copied at a much lower rate than was charged by legal and parliamentary clerks.[15] Indeed, such suggestions are borne out by surviving evidence. This indicates that making copies of pre-existing texts could be fairly cheap. The constables of Thorpe in Nottinghamshire paid 1s for making two copies of the Protestation in 1641, and in 1645 the constables of Branston spent the same amount on copying 'articles and ordinances of Parliament', in addition to spending 1s on 'drawing' a petition'.[16] This last reference, moreover, indicates that creating new documents need not have been prohibitively expensive, so long as the right workman was chosen. Standardized and straightforward bonds and recognizances might thus cost between 6d and 1s, while in 1648 the county committee in Kent paid a mere 2d for writing every warrant that it issued, not including the cost of delivering or 'dispersing' them. In other words, while cost still depended upon length, so that long texts could become extremely expensive, it does seem to have been possible to find relatively affordable ways of creating basic political texts.[17] Preparing and writing petitions, therefore, need only have cost a shilling or more, depending on length. Christopher Acreman spent 1s 6d on 'drawing and writing' a petition to the Committee of Indemnity, while the Poulters Company spent 2s 6d on preparing a petition to parliament about the excise, and Valentine Pell spent 3s on 'writing a petition to be exhibited to the Parliament'. Such charges were evidently not unusual.[18] This meant that it was sometimes possible to make multiple copies of documents for distribution and 'publication'. This can be observed fairly frequently during legal proceedings, and some people evidently found it possible to make multiple copies of 'breviates' for lawyers. On one occasion, therefore, the New England company paid 10s for 'four or five copies' of one of their 'bills', which they called 'the state of the case', and similar texts could apparently be created for as little as 3d or 4d per sheet.[19]

The importance of such evidence is that it would be a mistake to overstate the costs of scribal 'publication', but equally it would be unwise to

[15] *Ordinance. . . Chancery* (1654, E1064/31) pp. 525–6; *Reasons* (1654, R585A), pp. 2–4; Love, *Culture*, p. 131.
[16] Notts. RO, PR5767; Leics. RO, DE720/30, fos. 63, 65.
[17] Penshurst, MS 325; BL, Add. 27411, fo. 78; CKS, U350/E4, unfol.; HEH, STT Personal, Box 11/2; ST 54/2; *Devon Accounts*, p. 114; TNA, SP 28/304, fo. 754; GL: MS 11571/12, fo. 396v; MS 3054/2; DRO, D258/10/54/1.
[18] TNA, SP 24/30; GL, MS 2150/1, fo. 75; CUL, Pell 5/10.
[19] BL, Add. 27411, fo. 108; GL, MS 3054/2; MS 7945, unfol.; Longleat, Thynne 81, fos. 360, 361, 368, 408–9; TNA, SP 28/309, fo. 110; HEH, STTF Box 55/95.

underestimate the resources needed to participate in public life effectively. As critics pointed out, clerks and scriveners not only charged by the page, but also ensured that individual sheets contained very few words, by adopting a method that involved 'eight fair lines per sheet, and the trick of the large dash'. This meant that even the cheapest scribe might charge as much as 3d *per line*. Here, too, calls for change met stiff resistance, and those who opposed Chancery reform in the 1650s balked at the idea that a standard page should consist of 150 words (15 lines each of ten words), suggesting that even a requirement for seven or eight words per line would put them at a significant disadvantage.[20] However, even if some scriveners were willing to fit more words than this onto the page, costs would still have remained prohibitively high for those who sought to produce multiple copies of specific texts, in order to facilitate their distribution. In other words, while individual petitions and breviates could be produced fairly cheaply, significant quantities could not, and making even a few copies of short texts could result in substantial charges.[21]

This is in marked contrast to printing, where the costs can be shown to have been considerably lower, such that the possibilities for becoming an 'author' and for participating in public life were significantly enhanced. This is another area – the economics of print – where there is sometimes thought to be a paucity of evidence regarding the seventeenth century, but where dispersed and neglected sources offer valuable and striking insights. When the Council of State paid for the production of Samuel Morland's *History* of the Protestant sufferings in Piedmont in 1657, the bill came to £700, which seems like a vast amount until it is recognized that they produced 2,000 copies of a work involving over 700 folio pages, not to mention various maps. This meant that each sheet of printer's paper – enough for four folio pages – cost marginally less than a halfpenny to print, and this low rate can be shown to have been fairly typical. As a consequence, print offered distinct advantages for anyone who sought to produce and distribute multiple copies of particular texts.[22] What follows, therefore, represents analysis of this rich but overlooked evidence, the value of which lies in the fact that it often relates to the production of cheap print – such as official literature and polemical pamphlets – rather than sizeable works of scholarship.

[20] *Anti-Britanicus*, 267.3, p. 25; *CJ*, i. 565; *Ordinance... Chancery*, pp. 525–6; *Reasons*, p. 4.
[21] HEH, STTF Box 55/95; Lancs. RO, DDM/1/60, 66, 79; Cheshire RO: DAR/C/24; DAR/F/3, p. 21; GL, MS 3054/2; HEH: HAF Box 11/26; HAF Box 15/22; ST 54/2; EKRO, CP/Bp/73.
[22] *CSPD 1656–7*, p. 376; BL, Add. 32471, fo. 8; OUA, SEP.P.17b(1); D. McKenzie, 'Two bills for printing', *The Library*, 5th series, 15 (1960), 129–32.

The most substantial surviving accounts from the Civil War period relate to printing undertaken by Evan Tyler for the covenanting regime in Scotland (1642–7). This itemized 104 different jobs, ranging from 100 copies of a single-sheet bond to 1,000 copies of a 21-sheet account of 'proceedings betwixt king & Parlt', and it involved over 130,000 sheets of paper. For this work Tyler sought a flat fee of two shillings (Scots) or 2d (sterling) per sheet, but this was clearly regarded as excessive, and he was forced to accept 1d per sheet, in line with other official printers of the time.[23] Such rates certainly applied to the work done by City of London printers like Robert Young and Richard Cotes, the latter of whom also charged the same amount for work that was undertaken for the parliamentary authorities during the 1640s. They also applied to work completed by the royal printers in 1642, in terms of acts, proclamations and orders, as well as petitions and declarations between the king and parliament, whether this meant editions as small as 50 or as large as 10,000, as with one of the ordinances for a day of thanksgiving and for parliament's 'Protestation' (May 1641).[24] The picture that very quickly emerges, in other words, is one in which print was a much more affordable medium, and this conclusion can be emphasized by probing more deeply into archives relating to parliament and its army, and by scrutinizing fragmentary but voluminous evidence regarding payments made to a range of printers during the 1640s and 1650s. For their work on ordinances, orders and receipts, therefore, Richard Cotes and Edward Husband regularly charged 0.48d per sheet, while John Wright charged 0.66d for two small printing jobs in 1647, and Joseph Hunscott charged the City 0.84d per sheet for 100 copies of a short 8-page pamphlet in 1642.[25] However, the most valuable evidence relating to official printing involves the detailed and numerous warrants for payments to Edward Husband, the single most important official printer during the 1640s, which reveals that costs were generally much lower. On 28 July 1642, for example, he was paid for two declarations, each in editions of 9,000 and each involving 18 reams (9,000 sheets) of paper, for which he charged 13s 4d per ream to cover the cost of both paper and presswork. This worked out at only 0.32d per sheet, and the same rate was also charged by Lawrance Blaicklock in November 1643, by John Field in October 1644, and by the

[23] SRO, PA15/2.
[24] CLRO: CCA 1/1, fos. 65–v, 154v, 246v; CCA 1/2, fos. 55v, 144, 222; CCA 1/3, fos. 58, 152; CCA 1/4, fos. 56v, 152; CCA 1/4, fos. 223–v; CCA 1/5, fos. 65v, 162v–3, 264; CCA 1/6, fos. 54v, 163, 265v–6; CCA 1/7, fos. 65v–6, 150v; TNA: SP 28/301, fo. 72; SP 28/303, fo. 331; AO 3/1088/1, part 2, fos. 1–2, 10–v, 18; AO 3/1276, Part II, unfol.
[25] TNA, SP 28/301, fo. 72; SP 28/303, fo. 331; SP 28/49, fo.33; SP 28/237, unfol.

partnership of Husband and Field during the late 1640s and early 1650s, as well as by John Field when he succeeded Husband as official printer during the Rump. For all of these stationers, moreover, this appears to have been a flat rate, irrespective of the print run, even though composition charges would have been proportionally higher for works for which only a few copies were required.[26]

Charges of between 0.3d and 1d per sheet seem remarkably cheap compared to the cost of scribal production, and yet they were actually fairly expensive for the time. Both Crown and parliament paid a substantial premium for their official printing, no doubt because they needed work of a high quality, in large quantities and at fairly short notice. That other printers charged a great deal less is evident from a revealing legal dispute between the bookseller John Partridge and his printer, Thomas Brudenell. Brudenell's charges evidently varied according to the nature and complexity of the work being undertaken, and work on successive volumes of Lilly's almanac, *Merlinus Anglicus*, was charged at 6s 8d per ream, doubtless because it was difficult to typeset. This seems to have been his top rate, however, and other books by Lilly were produced for only 5s per ream, while 2,500 copies of a single sheet newspaper cost £1 5s, or a little over a tenth of a penny per copy. Other works were even cheaper still, and Brudenell charged only 4s per ream for John Booker's *Bloudy Irish Almanack* in 1646, and for a work entitled 'Military Discipline'. These figures, moreover, are broadly comparable with evidence from a parliamentary investigation in June 1642, when publishers who were questioned over the appearance of two short news pamphlets revealed that their printer, Robert White, had produced 1,500 sheets at a cost of only 18s, or 6s per ream. Likewise, they are also consistent with the fee that Henry Hills charged the army in 1649, at least for producing 5,000 copies of the officers' *Agreement of the People*.[27]

Such evidence makes it possible to reach fairly striking conclusions about the cost of producing short political texts during the 1640s and 1650s. Thus, 500 copies of a single-sided folio sheet would have cost between 10s and £1 10s, at a unit cost of between a farthing (0.25d) and a halfpenny. A thousand copies of an eight-page quarto pamphlet was likely to cost as little as 8s (Brudenell), and as much as £1 10s (Field), at a unit cost of between 0.1d and 0.36d. For small pamphlets like these, of course, no stitching was required,

[26] PA, MP 28 July 1642; TNA: SP 23/1A, pp. 5, 8; SP 28/19, fo. 125; SP 28/66, fos. 678; SP 28/68, fo. 243; SP 28/74, fo. 809; SP 28/81, fo. 441; SP 28/84, fo. 431; SP 28/98, fo. 231; E 101/67/11B, fos. 129v–30v.

[27] H. Plomer, 'A printer's bill in the seventeenth century', *The Library*, 7 (1906), p. 35; *CJ*, ii. 612–3, 615; Chequers, MS 782, fo. 93.

but for longer works where this became necessary it is also possible to calculate the costs involved, at least for pamphlets produced by Husband and Field. Here, the cost of stitching ranged from 6d per hundred, for single-sheet (eight-page) pamphlets, to 8d per hundred for works of two sheets, and 2s 6d for works where each copy comprised between fourteen and nineteen sheets of paper. Thus, while stitching was an important additional expense, it did not have a significant effect in terms of inflating the total or unit cost of producing short works like pamphlets and newspapers. For someone like Edward Husband, therefore, the total cost of an eight-page stitched pamphlet would be £1 11s 8d (unit cost 0.38d), while a sixteen-page pamphlet would cost £3 (unit cost 0.48d).[28]

This comparison of the costs involved in different methods of copying and publication confirms that scribal texts remained important, and that they provided a viable means of accessing information and participating in political affairs, while also indicating very clearly that print was not only significantly cheaper, but also that it was the only realistic way of reproducing texts in more than a handful of copies. Whereas a cheap clerk or scrivener might charge 2d for writing out 1,600 *characters*, a cheap printer might produce eight-page pamphlets – of around 5,000 *words* – at a unit cost of between a tenth of a penny and a groat (four pence). As such, for anyone seeking to produce multiple copies of short texts like these, the incentive to switch from scribal to print publication was very real, and the savings became apparent even with only a few copies. These findings make it possible to explore how the structural difference between scribal and print cultures facilitated a radical transformation in the nature of authorship in the mid seventeenth century, in the circumstances of political and religious controversy, as well as of constitutional experimentation. The place to begin is with developments in the available methods for entering into print, and for making texts public.

ii Towards Grub Street

In order to explore the circumstances in which individuals engaged in writing and publication – in terms of their reasons and their tactics – it is necessary to understand the conditions in which printing occurred. This means recognizing the role of patrons and employers, but it also means appreciating the atmosphere which was conducive to authorship, in terms

[28] TNA: SP 23/1A, p. 66; SP 28/60, fo. 111; SP 28/66, fo. 678; SP 28/68, fo. 243; SP 28/74, fo. 809; SP 28/81, fo. 439; SP 28/84, fo. 431.

of the finances and logistics of the print trade. Here it is possible to argue that while traditional methods had ongoing relevance, the period witnessed important modifications to conventional practices. These ensured that individuals had a wider range of options for funding and arranging printing and publication, all of which suggest the development of 'professional' authorship and the opening up of print culture to new kinds of writer.[29]

The first area of change related to the standard ways in which authors secured financial support, whether informally or formally, and whether privately or publicly. Here, the key developments involved the emergence of subscription funding and publishing agreements, which removed the necessity of relying on personal contacts and private networks in order to finance publications. Such things did not die out overnight, of course, although they perhaps became the preserve of scholars and academics and of those who could solicit donations from wealthy patrons in return for little more than a grateful dedication.[30] What is noticeable, however, is the tendency for subscription publication – involving public appeals for finance from a broader range of people – to become a method that was used for things other than substantial scholarly volumes.[31] More important still, however, was the emergence of publishing agreements between authors and stationers. These tended to involve the outright sale of manuscripts, even if the author's fee might only involve modest sums of money or small quantities of the finished volumes. William Prynne apparently received thirty-five copies of *Histriomastix*, and similar arrangements seem to have been made by clerics such as Oliver Heywood, whose copies could be dispersed as they saw fit.[32] However, there were also minor variations to this model. One was employed by the Oxford scholar, Nathaniel Carpenter, for his *Geography*. Carpenter agreed to pay the university printers almost £100 to print 1,250 copies, at a rate of 0.22d per sheet, or 9s 3d per ream, before selling them to a local bookseller, Henry Cripps, for 3s 4d each, a profit of 1s 10d per copy. On other occasions authors agreed to purchase a certain proportion of the print run, a practice that was adopted by the Dutch congregation in London in their negotiations with the publisher, Ralph Smith. Such deals were not universally popular – Hartlib regarded

[29] P. Lindenbaum, 'John Milton and the republican mode of literary production', *Yearbook of English Studies*, 21 (1991), 121–36.
[30] *Crosfield*, pp. 25, 60; FSL, L.d.259; Dillingham, *Commentaries* (1657, V240), sig. A3; Northants. RO, IC 343; BL, Add. 78316, fo. 126.
[31] Northants. RO, IC 398, 475, 477, 486; BL, Eg. 2984, fo. 11v; Herts. RO: D/Elw/F17; D/Elw/F18, p. 130; *Life of Dugdale*, pp. 358–60; Cornwall RO, CN 3536; Taylor, *Travailes* (1654, T438).
[32] *Remonstrance* (1643, P425), sig. A4; Greg, *Companion*, p. 278; H. Love, 'Preacher and publisher', *SB*, 31 (1978), p. 230; Bodl. MS Tanner 65, fos. 80, 118; LPL, MS 943, pp. 735–7.

them as a means by which authors fell prey to the 'villainies' of stationers – but they were certainly increasingly common.[33]

To the extent that authors could sell copies of their own books, of course, it was unclear whether this was best done privately or through booksellers. Presentation copies that were given in the hope of financial gifts offered only uncertain rewards, which were at the discretion of individual patrons, although it is clear that substantial sums could be involved. In 1640, James Howell received £3 for a copy of *Dodona's Grove*, while Sir John Wittewronge gave £1 to Robert Ward for his *Animadversions of Warre* and Sir Thomas Barrington gave £5 to a Mr Codrington. In 1645 the Corporation of London paid Ephraim Pagitt £10 for his heresiography, and in the mid 1650s the Grocers Company gave over £6 to John Ogilby for a bound copy of his Virgil translation.[34] Other authors, however, received considerably less for their efforts. These included the 'poor scholar' who received 5s for a work presented to Sir John Wittewronge in 1640, and the 'poor minister' who was given 2s 6d for a book in 1659.[35] These were almost certainly small works rather than substantial tomes, and as such they probably merited smaller rewards. The salient point, however, is that for authors who were neither scholars nor clerics it probably made sense to strike deals with booksellers. Herein lay the foundations of 'Grub Street', which flourished during the political and religious upheaval of the early 1640s, not least as the official grip on the press loosened.

'Grub Street' was a spectre that came to haunt the authorities. As publishers and booksellers became attracted to topical and controversial literature, rather than merely to learned and pious treatises, fears emerged about how readily print could be appropriated. In part this was a matter of uncontrolled presses, in terms of both the uses to which existing presses were being put and the possibility of secretive presses being set up 'in holes and corners'. Printers frequently claimed that their equipment had been used without their knowledge, and at least some radical stationers proved willing to work with radical interest groups and at the margins of legality.[36] More important, however, were suspicions that texts were being produced along professional lines. Here the problem was not so much men like

---

[33] I. Philip, 'A seventeenth century agreement between author and printer', *BLR*, 10 (1978), 69–73; *Life of Dugdale*, p. 104; *About* (1657, A99); *Londino-Batavae*, III.iii.1996–7; GL, MS 7428/18; SUL, Hartlib 30/4/70-71, 73, 76; BL, Add. 78316, fos. 126, 136.

[34] Durham UL, Cosin Letterbook 1a/27; Chatsworth, Bolton Abbey MS 179, fo. 37; Herts. RO, D/Elw/F18, p. 1; ERO, D/DBa/A39/7; CLRO, CCA 1/5, fo. 155; GL, MS 11571/14, unfol.

[35] Herts. RO, D/Elw/F18, p. 3; BL, Eg. 2984, fo. 23; Warw. RO, CR1886, Box 411/12.

[36] Chequers, MS 782, fos. 4, 43v, 44v; *CSPD 1655*, pp. 108–9; *CP*, iv. 229, 231–2; *LJ*, iv. 42, 180, 232, 398, 708, viii. 244–5, 247, 250, 253, 257, 451, 463, 684, 688; PA, MP 4 Mar. 1641, 9 Apr. 1642, 4 Oct. 1642,

William Dugdale, who once sold his services to the fen drainers for £150, as the possibility that mercenary authors would contrive and sell topical and polemical material.[37] Concern was expressed, for example, that hacks like Samuel Pecke, and publishers like Francis Coles and Francis Leach, were literally *inventing* the news, and that impecunious writers like John Bond were creating fictitious texts. Bond was pilloried and imprisoned as a 'contriver of false and scandalous libels', while Martin Eldred and Thomas Herbert were convicted of contriving a false Hertfordshire petition, which was sold to the stationer, John Greensmith, for half a crown. A poor poet from Shoe Lane called John Bennet was accused of inventing a parliamentary speech, which he then sold to Thomas Peball for the same sum. It was episodes like these that prompted Sir Simonds D'Ewes to exclaim that 'there were now abiding in and about London certain loose beggarly scholars who did in alehouses invent ... speeches of members in the House, and of other passages supposed to be handed in or presented unto this House'.[38] There was a very real sense, in other words, that the conditions of political and religious turmoil fostered the emergence of professional authors from unusual socio-economic backgrounds. A classic example is Alexander Aspinwall, a 'very poor' ex-soldier who had 'nothing but my pen to subsist upon', and who felt compelled to accept commissions for controversial pamphlets in the summer of 1659, at £1 or £2 a time.[39]

Grub Street was thus a reality rather than merely a rhetorical construct, but what was really novel about the print trade after 1640 was the possibility of commissioning stationers to produce pamphlets of a topical and controversial nature. This could be done, for example, by officials beyond London, who frequently exploited the opportunity to produce political and administrative material in large quantities for little money. Specific texts, in editions of between 200 and 1,000, evidently cost between 10s and £1 10s per ream, or between 0.24d and 0.72d per sheet.[40] In 1646, the corporation at Bristol spent 13s 6s on printing an unknown quantity of broadsides called *A Whip for a Drunkard*, which summarized legislation against sabbath-breaking, drunkenness and unlawful gaming, and which was intended for public display around the city. In 1654, meanwhile, the

29 Nov. 1642, 7 Jan. 1643, 14 Feb. 1643, 10 Feb. 1645, 13 Aug. 1646; *HMC 4th Report*, pp. 102, 111; *CSPD 1625–49*, p. 394; *CSPD 1659–60*, p. 344; Bodl. MS Rawl. A.34, p.145; *TSP*, iv. 379; BL, Add. 78262, fo. 150.
[37] Cambs. RO, R.59.31/19A, second pagination, p. 1; *Life of Dugdale*, pp. 104–5.
[38] *LJ*, iv. 660, 674, 680–1, 699, 721–2, v. 533, 547; PA, MP 1 Feb. 1643; *PJ*, i. 165–6, 326, 328–9.
[39] *CSPD 1659–60*, p. 14; *CCSP*, iv. 271–2, 282; Bodl. MS Clarendon 62, fos. 76, 141.
[40] BL, Add. 70068, unfol.; TNA, SP 28/220; SP 28/231, unfol.; SP 28/303, fo. 177; SP 28/16, fo. 221; SP 28/139, Part 20, p. 13.

organizers of fen drainage schemes printed 500 copies of *News from the Fens*, at a cost of £3 1s, which was equivalent to 17s 1d per ream, or 0.41d per sheet. Each 28-page pamphlet thus cost just under 1s 5d, compared with the £1 that was spent writing out just two handwritten copies.[41] And similar practices were also adopted by the New England Company, a chartered body that sought to convert native Americans to Christianity. In May 1659, for example, they paid Mary Simmonds £7 10s 6d to print 3,000 copies of one of their books, at a rate of only 3s 6d per ream, or less than a tenth of a penny per sheet, as well as £3 for stitching, at a rate of 2s per hundred. This meant that each copy cost less than 1d to produce. In September 1660, meanwhile, they paid John Macock £8 5s for printing 1,500 copies of *A Further Account of the Progress of the Gospel*, an 86-page quarto pamphlet, at a rate of 5s per ream (0.12d per sheet). Even if these figures did not include the paper, and even if the need to provide paper doubled the cost, the book would only have cost around one-fifth of a penny per sheet (around 8s per ream), or less than 3d each, with the cost of cutting and stitching (at a rate of 5s 8d per hundred) adding 0.68d to the cost of each copy.[42]

More importantly, the services of printers were also engaged by individuals. This was certainly true for scholars, and during the 1620s costs ranged from 8s per ream for 1,500 copies of a 20-sheet book (0.2d per sheet, and almost 4d per copy), to 15s per ream for 400 copies of an octavo work containing 2 sheets (around 0.4d per sheet, and 0.7d per copy). But it can also be observed for pamphleteers. When Samuel Hartlib paid for the printing of five pamphlets by Theophraste Renaudot in 1640, he was charged a shade over 0.1d per sheet (4s 2d per ream) for books of 12 and 16 pages, and for print runs of 1,000. Each copy thus cost around 0.2d, although other charges were also incurred, such as 1s to a woman for carriage of the books, 6d to the 'printers' chapel', and 6s for licensing and entry into the Stationers' Register, as well as 6d for advertising each work by 'setting up titles' (or 'titling') in public places.[43] The accounts of Alice L'Estrange reveal that Henry Seile was paid £5 6s for printing her husband's *Americans No Jews*, while a Mr Wilson was paid £2 for producing another pamphlet in his defence. When she published her husband's edition of Peter Du Moulin's *Heraclitus*, moreover, L'Estrange used a printer even though she required only 40 copies, and paid a mere 13s 4d, a shade over 1d per sheet, or 4d per copy.[44]

---

[41] Bristol RO, F/Au/1/23, p. 95; *Whip* (1646, W1668); Cambs. RO, R.59.31/19A, p. 7.

[42] GL, 7944/1, unfol.

[43] *Crosfield*, pp. 12, 29; SUL, Hartlib 21/15/1A-2B; Renaudot, *Questions* (1640, 20884).

[44] Norfolk RO, LEST P10, pp. 60, 79, 121, 138; L'Estrange, *Americans* (1652, L1186); Du Moulin, *Heraclitus* (1652, D2584).

Most intriguing of all, however, is evidence about the use of private printing to publish controversial texts that were unlikely to receive an official licence, and that were likely to be considered scandalous. This had obviously been done before 1640, in relation to works by Puritan activists, but examples from later decades can be explored in some detail. In 1644, Hezekiah Woodward paid 55s for printing *Inquiries into the Causes of our Miseries*, because it had been rejected by a licenser, and in February 1655, 1,000 copies of an 8-page Fifth Monarchist tract called *Queries for His Highness to Answer* cost 50s to produce, at a rate of o.6d per copy. Later in the same year, moreover, Richard Moone confessed that he had been approached by John Sturgeon to print 1,000 copies of a scandalous tract called *A Short Discovery* 'very privately', adding that a deal was struck in a local alehouse for a price of 40s, or a shade under a halfpenny per copy. Finally the two 8-page pamphlets that were written by Aspinwall in 1659 – the deal for which was also struck in an alehouse – were each printed in editions of 400 by Thomas Grimes, at a cost of £1, and at a rate of £1 5s per ream, and in each case the work took less than 24 hours.[45]

Such evidence suggests that the possibilities for producing and publishing political literature were significantly enhanced after 1640, and that Grub Street practices extended beyond those 'professional' writers who lived by their pens to those who made occasional interventions in public discourse. This was a product of the intrinsic affordability of the print medium, of the collapse of censorship and of the debates that were generated by political and religious turmoil. Printing cost a few shillings per ream of paper, and the unit cost of broadsides and pamphlets was generally only a fraction of a penny and a fraction of the cost of producing scribal texts. This meant that the production of multiple copies could be undertaken rapidly, and by those with only limited means, and costs were so low that print could be appropriated by people within and beneath the 'middling sort'. This explains why 1642 saw the appearance of a tract by the cook at Hell tavern in Westminster, and of verses by a trooper from the Earl of Bedford's regiment, and it certainly meant that printing fell within the reach of those who could pool their resources to finance pamphleteering collectively.[46] This began with 'seasonable' Puritan treatises in the 1630s, and it became much more common thereafter. In 1640, Laud expressed concern

---

[45] Longleat, Whitelocke 7, fos. 86–7, 89–92; *CSPD 1636–7*, pp. 427, 487; TNA: SP 16/346, fo. 132; SP 16/349, fos. 99r–v; PA, MP 31 Dec. 1644; Woodward, *Inquiries* (1644, W3491); *TSP*, iii. 149–51, 738; Bodl. MS Rawl. A.29, pp. 574–7, 268–9; MS Rawl. A.24, pp. 401–8; *Short Discovery* (1655, S3591); Bodl. MS Clarendon 62, fo. 142.

[46] Duke, *Fulnesse* (1642, D2501); *Encouragement* (1642, W776).

that a group of activists in London had 'joined together to maintain a private press', with which to 'print seditious and libellous books', and it was later reported that 'several clubs' existed for similar purposes. It is also well known, of course, that a key aim of Leveller and Quaker fundraising was the financing of printing and pamphleteering in a collaborative fashion.[47]

iii Reasons for deploying print

Having demonstrated the accessibility and affordability of the print medium, it is now possible to analyse the ways in which printed texts were deployed in specific circumstances, and to explore the impact that novel forms of authorship had on public debate and political practice. My aim here is to concentrate on a neglected aspect of Civil War and Interregnum pamphleteering, which looks beyond the hacks and the ideologues with whom scholars are now so familiar, and which concentrates instead on the emergence of new genres and new voices. It is largely unconcerned with unprincipled writers who eked out a living in Grub Street, with mercenary propagandists like John Jones of Nanteos, who offered his services to the highest bidder, and with committed polemicists like William Prynne and Henry Parker.[48] Instead, it examines what might be called the democratization of authorship, and the emergence into print of people who might otherwise have remained unheard, and whose aims did not necessarily involve entering the commercial marketplace of print and ideas. This includes people who wrote primarily for discrete audiences, as well as ambitious polemicists like Samuel Hunton, some of whose works were self-published, and it also includes assorted radicals, from the Leveller sympathizer William Thompson to the Quaker activists who forged links with publishers like Giles Calvert. And, perhaps most importantly of all, it also includes those whose primary goal was to address private interests and grievances.[49] In drawing attention to this new breed of pamphleteer, the aim will be to explore the circumstances in which individuals felt compelled to make one or more tactical shift, in terms of

---

[47] J. Peacey, 'Seasonable Treatises', *EHR*, 113 (1998), 667–79; *CSPD 1640–1*, p. 40; SP 16/467, fo. 16; *Civicus*, 298.084, p. 769; Chidley, *Dissembling* (1652, C3839), pp. 7, 9; N. Carlin, 'Leveller organisation in London', *HJ*, 27 (1984), pp. 957–8; T. O'Malley, 'The press and Quakerism', *Journal of the Friends Historical Association*, 54 (1979), p. 172.

[48] BL, Add. 33374, fos. 2–20; PA, MP 1647.

[49] Reynolds, *Questions* (1648, R1273); Baker, *Preparation* (1645, B497); Hunton, *Army* (1653, H3786); Hunton, *Highnesse* (1654, H3787); Hunton, *King* (1655, H3787A); SUL, Hartlib 28/1/49; Bodl. MS Tanner 65, fos. 61, 83; *Faithfull* (1647, S2826); *Modest Narrative*, 433.06, pp. 47–8; *Impartiall Intelligencer*, 194.11, pp. 84–6; *TSP*, iii. 116.

abandoning scribal texts for printed ones, substituting printed exchanges for oral disputation, and participating in increasingly acrimonious disputation. Indeed, a conscious attempt will be made to build upon recent scholarship that highlights how discourses that were traditionally discrete, private and contained not only found expression in print, but also demonstrated a tendency to escalate into vigorous and even bitter exchanges. Indeed, the aim will be to suggest that this occurred not merely in relation to issues of obvious ideological significance – as with the protracted debate involving Peter Chamberlen, James Cranford and William Kiffin – but also in any number of other contexts where it became necessary to promote local and private interests and defend individual reputations in the face of unjust allegations, 'slanders' and 'lies'.[50] The argument of this section will be that it became much more common for private business to be expressed in print, progressively more difficult to prevent debates and disagreements from spilling into print, and increasingly likely that arguments and animosities would be played out in the public domain, and in more or less intemperate fashion. This argument will be developed in five stages, involving different aspects of the revolution in 'authorship' and different reasons for appropriating print, as well as the broader significance in terms of a greater willingness to engage in political reflection and comment.[51]

First, therefore, Civil War print culture made it possible for people to reach a broad audience at fairly minimal expense, and even to bypass the commercial marketplace, and it is likely that many anonymous tracts – particularly those lacking imprints and even title pages – were privately financed and printed 'for the author'. Some of these were sold privately, and copies of the Fifth Monarchist *Queries for His Highness* were made available discretely, at 2d each, having been stored by a sympathetic bookseller.[52] However, printing costs were low enough to permit free distribution at least occasionally, and the public posting of scandalous material became possible on a much more ambitious scale, thereby making it feasible to reach a large and dispersed audience. This did not necessarily mean *indiscriminate* dispersal, of course, and efforts could be concentrated on prominent political spaces, and upon the display rather than the scattering of texts. Thus, in

---

[50] Lake, *Boxmaker's Revenge*; Chamberlen, *Letter* (1650, C1897); Chamberlen, *Bakewells* (1650, C1898); Chamberlen, *Beloved* (1650, C1907); Chamberlen, *Discourse* (1654, K424); *Disputes* (1652, C6822); *Answer* (1649, A3357); Bakewell, *Dippers* (1650, B531); Bakewell, *Chamberlain* (1650, B532); Perry, *Some Short* (1654, P1650).

[51] *CSPD 1644–5*, p. 88; *CSPD 1650*, p. 518; *HMC Egmont I*, pp. 353, 356; BL, Add. 26785, fo. 63; NLW, 11440D, fos. 137–9; *Slanders* (1655, S3956); *Declaration* (1659, D619); Ives, *Stop* (1656, I1106); Potter, *Truths* (1649, P3037); Baillie, ii. 384–6.

[52] *Hypocrisie* (1655, H3887); *Humble* (1655, H3637A); *TSP*, iii. 149–51.

1659 *The Orphans Petition* was 'pasted upon many posts of the city', as well as 'thrown into the houses of divers merchants and aldermen', while in 1654 a Quaker tract entitled *A Warning* was 'stuck up and down [in] many places of the city of London, and chiefly about church doors'. Likewise, a Leveller called Marston responded to the charge that he had murdered an agent of the Council of State by posting a printed statement around London, not least on Whitehall gate.[53] However, the literal *scattering* of texts did become increasingly common, following the examples set by John Lilburne and Henry Walker. It could occur both within and beyond London, and by the 1650s it is possible to make direct connections between private printing and indiscriminate distribution, as with the 1,000 copies of the tract that John Sturgeon produced against Cromwell. By this stage, indeed, Nehemiah Wallington may have been somewhat unusual in undertaking campaigning by means of a carefully circulated scribal text, and in avoiding print out of distaste for a situation in which 'every man broaches his own fancies', and in order not to heighten the 'many divisions that are now among us'.[54]

Secondly, the utility of print for promoting causes and fostering public debate was not restricted to ideological struggles, and our appreciation of authorial practices can be enhanced significantly by scrutinizing 'projecting'. At one extreme this meant commercial advertising by both individuals and corporate bodies, in terms of flyers and pamphlets that promoted everything from bear-baitings, plays and lectures to quack remedies, newspapers and books, as well as the investment opportunities offered by the East India and Levant companies.[55] Although generated for commercial reasons, such literature has much broader significance. This is because it shaded into the kind of material that was produced for political and religious projects of various kinds, and because it demonstrates other ways in which print fostered public debate and disputation. Projecting texts included printed 'briefs' and testimonials, which enabled targeted fundraising for specific individuals and communities, as well as the 500 printed 'tickets' that John Evelyn produced to recover lost property, but they also involved more

---

[53] *CSPD 1628–9*, pp. 30, 519; *Weekly Account*, 671.452, sig. Zzz4v; *Orphans* (1659, P497a); *Weekly Intelligencer*, 689.23, p. 181; *Proceedings*, 599.240, p. 3811; BL, Add. 78316, fo. 17; Claydon, Verney reel 10.

[54] *CSPD 1639–40*, p. 2; PA, MP 21 Dec. 1640; Rushworth, iv. 479; *Stratagem* (1647, N641); *Short Discovery* (1655, S3591); *TSP*, iii. 738–40; Bodl. MS Rawl.A.29, pp. 268–9, 574–7; CCSP, iii. 310; Vaughan, *Protectorate*, ii. 184–5; FSL, V.a.436, preface, and pp. 375–6, 387–8.

[55] *Quod* (1642, O535a); *Sir* (1647, R316); *Advertisement* (1650, B4998); *All Gentlemen* (1656, F2055); *Occurrences*: 465.5040, sig. Qq4; 465.5057, p. 402; *Diurnall*, 513.29A, sig. Ff2; *Rare Drink* (1649, H75); *Nothing* (1647, W3087aA); *These* (1644, T879); *East India* (1641, E102); *Corporations* (1657, E99D); *List* (1657, L2459B); TNA, SP 105/150, fo. 17; SUL, Hartlib 26/54, 62.

substantial projects, which were endorsed by public figures, and which were infused with political and religious meaning.[56] These included prospectuses for projects such as the polyglot Bible, and notices issued in relation to aspects of public administration, some of which had the potential to generate controversy. A particularly good example here involves conflicting claims regarding the office of first fruits in the mid 1650s, which generated more than one printed text.[57]

More obviously, projecting involved the kinds of reforms and innovations that were associated with Samuel Hartlib, and about which his papers offer rich evidence. These blended personal advancement and public spirit, and many were promoted through privately produced pamphlets and posters, not least in relation to issues like reform of the poor law.[58] With any number of such schemes – such as Edmund Felton's mechanical engine, George Dalgarno's universal language and Balthazar Gerbier's academy – printed literature was used to raise funds and secure patrons, more obviously than it was intended to raise public awareness.[59] However, many such schemes were capable of generating rivalry and competition, and of creating political waves, and as such, print also provided a means of responding to rivals and critics. This is clear from the many schemes for creating an office of intelligence in the late 1640s and 1650s, as well as from the tactics of the commissioners for New England.[60] During the early 1650s, therefore, 'books and papers', as well as 'printed letters', were sent across the country as part of fundraising drives, and in places like Falmouth and Winterborne Dantsey locals were encouraged to 'stir up others to be liberal in contributing', apparently to some good effect. In the face of allegations about the misappropriation of funds, however, pamphlets also served to defend the venture and its activists against 'false surmises and aspersions', and to indicate where and when the commissioners' accounts could be

[56] *Whereas* (1652, W1629dA); *Londino-Batavae*, III.iii.2213–4; BL, Add. 70007, fo. 213; *To Men* (1647, T1381); *To All* (1653, T1326c); *To all* (1649, T1334a); *To all* (1649, T1326a–b); *Deare* (1647, S6246); *Diary of John Evelyn*, iii. 70–1.

[57] *Propositions* (1653, P3777A); *Brief* (1653, B4567); *There* (1651, T865); *Whereas* (1643, R1416); *Whereas* (1655, W1611); *Having Seen* (1656, R1803A).

[58] SUL, Hartlib 57/4/6–7, 10–15; *Provision* (1649, P3876); Barrow, *Relief* (1656, B924A); *Charity* (1650, H993); *Pitty* (1650, L687A); *Stanleyes* (1646, S5250); *Parliaments* (1646, H995A).

[59] SUL, Hartlib 67/16/1–3; 8/40/6, 8, 11, 13, 14; 49/1/1, 3; 42/7/1; Felton, *Engins* (1644, F660); *Possibilitie* (1658, D129C); *Omnibus* (1660, D129B); *News* (1657, D129A); *Character* (1657, D128A); BL, Add. 4377, fos. 139–57; J. Peacey, 'Print, publicity and popularity', *JBS*, 51 (2012), 284–307.

[60] SUL, Hartlib 57/3/2, 3, 8, 10; Hartlib 57/3/9: *Place of Encounters*; Hartlib 57/3/3: Williams, *Office* (1657); *Generall* (1650, S4877A); *Office* (1657, E15A); *Further* (1648, H987); *Office* (1657, O148); *Weekly Information*, 684.1, pp. 1–2.

scrutinized.[61] This multi-purpose deployment of print – as both a promotional device and an aggressive political tool – is also evident on other occasions, not least in relation to competition over the Post Office during the commonwealth. In response to a flyer that was 'cast about upon the Exchange' by the operators of the 'old post' in April 1653, their rivals among the 'new undertakers' issued a sheet in which they denied allegations about the quality of their service, and complained about how 'printed papers have been scattered up and down the cities of London and Westminster, and in many considerable towns and places in England and Scotland'.[62]

A third aspect of 'authorship' that became much more striking during the Civil Wars and Interregnum, and a third reason why print became an increasingly attractive medium, involved individuals engaging in self-promotion and self-defence, as private grievances and personal battles spilled over into the public domain, and into the realm of political debate. This might involve authors distancing themselves from works that were attributed to them, and from 'bastard' copies of their books, or else defending the authenticity of texts that had been questioned.[63] More interesting, however, was the tendency for public figures to employ print to defend their reputations, which offers a useful way of demonstrating how contemporaries gradually adapted to the print revolution. In 1642, therefore, the Earl of Bath clearly became disturbed to find his behaviour attacked in a newspaper, but he responded with personal complaints to other grandees rather than with a printed defence, thereby revealing a preoccupation with his standing within only a small group of powerful individuals. Others, however, ventured into print, more or less reluctantly and out of a recognition that it was increasingly important to consider their public reputation. Prince Rupert did just this in November 1642, even though he hated the idea of living in a 'scribbling age', because he saw no other way of refuting the 'malicious lying vanities' that had been printed against him. Viscount Inchiquin, meanwhile, was somewhat less nervous about dabbling in print, and he recognized the need to cultivate writers so that he might be portrayed as 'a brave servitor in one kingdom, though I remained whoring and playing the knave in another'. In 1647, therefore, his secretary organized the printing of a pamphlet that was explicitly aimed at his critics.[64]

[61] *Reverend* (1649, T1383A); GL, 7938, fos. 22, 67, 72; Whitfield, *Light* (1651, W1999), sigs. A2–3; *Strength* (1652, W2003), sigs. A2, A3v, B2v, p. 34.
[62] *All Gentlemen* (1653, A933); *To All* (1653, T1323).
[63] *Modest* (1642, W377); Prynne, *Cheaters* (1659, P4015); Bond, *Exon* (1643); *Having* (1655, S5988).
[64] CKS, U269/C294; HEH, EL 7767; *HMC Egmont I*, p. 317; BL, Add. 46931B, fo. 169; *Articles* (1647, A3824).

Over time, moreover, reticence about using print faded markedly, and by the late 1640s its utility as a personal tool seems to have been taken for granted. John Birch justified publicizing his views as a means of forestalling abuse from 'base and unworthy fellows', and John Pyne not only denied allegations about the misuse of public money, but also proposed that public accounts should be 'printed to the public view of all the world'. In his capacity as chairman of the Navy Committee, meanwhile, Giles Green issued a *Declaration* to vindicate its financial management from 'traducers', and explicitly noted that this was necessary because 'the tongues and pens of many men, and the press, have in these latter times been so loose and disordered, as that they have been applied too frequently to the scandalising of proceedings in Parliament, and the several committees, and members by them employed'. Edward Massey, on the other hand, seems to have responded to being vilified in print by producing a whole series of declarations that defended his activity and reputation.[65] In the late 1650s, meanwhile, disgraced and derided individuals fairly regularly deployed printed texts of one kind or another to repair their reputations and rehabilitate themselves. A former MP like Sir Thomas Soame used print to publicize the repeal of votes which had expelled him from the Commons in 1649, while William Lenthall orchestrated at least two tracts to 'undeceive' readers regarding claims about his financial impropriety as Speaker and Master of the Rolls. Likewise, Philip Skippon issued a 'vindication' in the face of 'false and scandalous aspersions' regarding his role in the king's trial, which had appeared in 'several books and pamphlets'.[66]

In all of these cases, print was being used by figures from within the political elite at Westminster, but a fourth aspect of the transformation of authorship involved the use of similar practices by people outside parliament and beyond London. In part, this meant military commanders and officials who were involved in the war effort, where it is once again possible to detect concern about unauthorized texts, and a determination to defend reputations that was occasionally tempered by the fear of fuelling divisions. Major John Bernard was thus anxious to defend himself from accusations of Levellerism in 1650, but explained that 'I could not vindicate my repute without printing and publishing' and that 'such a publication would have divided the army within itself'.[67] Such fears were well founded, and several

---

[65] BL, Add. 70005, fo. 202; TNA, SP 23/254, fo. 19; Grene, *Declaration* (1647, G1817), p. 1; *Speedy Hue* (1647, S4911); *Masseys* (1647, G502); M1032–6, M1038.

[66] *Soame* (1660, S3890); *True* (1660, L1093); *Account* (1660, N20A); *Skippons* (1660, S3953A).

[67] *Declaration* (1642, E1467); *Ludlow Memoirs*, i. 72; *CSPD 1648–9*, p. 184; BL, Add. 78258, fo. 42.

local commanders who played an active role in publicizing their activities discovered that this could lead to replies and printed exchanges regarding the conduct of military affairs. Thus, Commissary General Hans Behre's printed defence against 'slanders and lies' in 1644 merely provoked a printed reply by his critics, and the fall of Leicester to royalists in 1645 led to notable score-settling.[68] On this occasion, criticism of local parliamentarians led to the publication of *A Narration of the Siege*, an *Examination* of the story by Major James Innes, and then a further response called *An Examination Examined*. The latter sought to defend the county committee from what was perceived to be an 'abusive pamphlet', but when this tract was spotted by George Booth, he felt compelled to issue yet another printed statement as a response to the way in which his role had been portrayed.[69]

What such cases reveal is the ease with which events beyond London generated pamphlets and disputations, and such uses of print became a common way of pursuing local issues. Here, too, there is evidence of occasional restraint, and although a local dispute between two preachers in Hull resulted in a printed tract by John Canne, his rival John Shaw refused to respond in kind, lest he should draw undue attention to 'a lying idle pamphlet'. Others who thought that they had been slighted in print, like Captain Wingate and George Rawleigh, merely complained to parliament about their treatment.[70] Yet again, however, such restraint became increasingly rare, as print became a weapon in every kind of dispute and battle. Sometimes these involved squabbles among professionals. On one occasion, therefore, Hugh Audley issued an 'advertisement' to denounce his sometime employee, the scrivener John Rea, and on another, officials at Merchant Taylors school sought to 'undeceive readers' about a colleague whose reaction to being sacked for drunkenness had involved producing a 'scurrilous paper ... printed and scattered abroad'.[71] Other disputes involved feuding families. Robert Burman printed a 'remonstrance' in response to the 'false scandalous libels maliciously scattered' by his wife regarding a proposed 'conjugal separation', while the Marquess of Dorchester waged war on his troublesome son-in-law, John Manners, Lord Roos. In this case, printed texts followed an acrimonious exchange

[68] *Declaration* (1644, B1780); *There Hath* (1644, T862); *CSPD 1644*, pp. 149, 155, 162.

[69] Lilly, *Starry* (1645, L2245), sig. A4-v; *Narration* (1645, N162), pp. 8–10; *More Exact* (1645, P4255); Innes, *Examination* (1645, I193); *Examination* (1645, E3713), sig. A4v; *Reply* (1645, D872A), sig. A2.

[70] Wilts. RO, A1/110/Mich/1653/114; *Yorkshire Diaries*, pp. 144–5; BL, Harl. 165, fo. 136; *CJ*, iii. 194; PA, MP 5 May 1648; *LJ*, x. 245, 251, 285, 339.

[71] DRO, D258/15/1/2; *To All* (1652, W2755).

of letters, and the row was eventually 'cried in the streets of London with ballads on the Rump', in an attempt to provoke a duel.[72]

More importantly, of course, such texts reflected political and religious tension at local levels. These most commonly involved clerics, as with the tract that defended the controversial Kentish minister, Richard Culmer; the pamphlet that was issued by Joseph Poujade, minister of the French church in Canterbury; and the pamphlet exchange that took place between the shoemakers of St Martin Le Grand and a local minister over the legitimacy of tithes. Such episodes reveal very clearly the propensity for local difficulties to generate polemical exchanges, and in the case of the Herefordshire congregationalist, Richard Delemain, a printed defence of his character and activity only appeared after a pamphlet by his local enemy, Silas Taylor, was seen circulating in London.[73] However, similar patterns can also be observed in relation to tensions within civic communities. These included the dispute over electoral rules in Norwich in 1648, when the mayor's printed analysis of the city's constitution provoked the publication of legal advice that contradicted him. On some occasions, indeed, these exchanges became strangely protracted, as with the arguments between Philip Francis and Charles Vaughan regarding local affairs in Plymouth. The same was also true in the dispute between Edward Hayward and George Kendall, two minor naval officials in Kent, which was rooted in arcane technicalities regarding ships' rigging, but which also extended to allegations about corruption, political and religious views, and the frequenting of alehouses.[74]

This last case highlights a fifth striking feature of the new kind of 'authorship' that can be observed in the Civil Wars and Interregnum, and perhaps its most important legacy. Very frequently, therefore, the use of print by individuals who sought to promote and defend their reputations resulted in authors making broader reflections on public life and topical issues. This is particularly clear, for example, in cases where individuals felt compelled to recount their experiences of authority and sought to vent their frustration over the legal and political processes that they had encountered. For some this involved grievances regarding local committees, as with

---

[72] *Remonstrance* (1645, B5748); TNA, SP 18/219, fos. 79, 92; *True and Perfect* (1660, D1920); *True and Perfect* (1660, R2400); *Lord Marquesse* (1660, D1918); *Reasons* (1660, D1919).
[73] Culmer, *Parish* (1657, C7482), sig. A2; *Apologie* (1649, P3037A); *Londino-Batavae*, III.iii.2156; *Routers* (1653, R2052a); *Hypocrite* (1654, N16A), pp. 3, 5; *Impostor* (1654, T553A).
[74] TNA, SP 16/516, fos. 59–v; *CSPD 1648–9*, pp. 53–4; Vaughan, *Misdemeanours* (1644, V119); Francis, *Misdemeanors* (1644, F2059); *Most True* (1645, V118); Hayward, *Sizes* (1655, H1229); Kendall, *Clerk* (1656, K282); Hayward, *Answer* (1656, H1228); Kendall, *Reply* (1656, K282A).

Andrew Wyke's detailed account of his sufferings at the hands of parliamentarians in Bury St Edmunds, and William Pryor's pamphlet relating to the Hertfordshire county committee, both of which shed valuable light on the mechanisms of state power by reproducing official letters, warrants and accounts. For others it meant complaints about local justice, which provoked pamphlets by the Kentish congregationalist, Thomas Belke, following his prosecution at the Kent quarter sessions, and by John Griffith in relation to his treatment by the grand jury in Cheshire. What is intriguing about the latter is that it involved a rudimentary attempt to explain the reason behind his grievance, and Griffith alleged that the jury was 'packt by the means of that pocky, rotten, lying, cowardly and most perfidious knave, Sir Hugh Calveley'.[75] Needless to say, such attacks sometimes provoked responses from local governors, although these, too, could promote political transparency. The Norfolk royalist, Sir Hamon L'Estrange, sought to 'wipe off' the 'unjust and malign spatter' of local enemies, in a pamphlet that was privately printed by his wife, and Sir John Gell's attempt to refute the 'malice' of those who provided documentary evidence that he tyrannized over Derbyshire involved making public his financial accounts.[76] More interesting still are the pamphlets that discussed the workings of national bodies. These included the court of Chancery, against which the London salter and soldier Nathaniel Burt railed in the 1650s, as well as parliamentarian commissions, and here, too, the grievances that provoked the deployment of print sometimes resulted in bitter exchanges between interested parties, not least over 'scandalous aspersions' that were 'spread abroad'. Ultimately, indeed, the authorship that resulted from personal grievances was even used to critique elements of the Westminster system, not least in terms of irregular behaviour within the Committee of Accounts, the 'packing' of the Committee of Examinations and the 'illegal' proceedings against Leveller activists.[77]

In other words, it was not uncommon for local disputes and individual grievances to find their way into print, to reach a larger audience and to be connected with broader issues, and on at least some occasions this resulted in more general reflections about politics and government. In January 1660,

---

[75] *Innocent* (1646, I207A); *Country-Mans* (1649, P4131); *Declaration* (1644, D1751), pp. 1, 2, 5; Belke, *Paire* (1646, B1792); Griffith, *Vindication* (1648, G2008).

[76] *Charge* (1649, C2062A), sig. A3; *Theeves* (1643, H1740); *Severall Accompts* (1644, S2745), p. 2.

[77] Burt, *Advice* (1655, B6140); Burt, *Appeal* (1653, B6141), p. 26; *Charitable* (1647, I28A); *Brief Vindication* (1653, J683), p. 1; Ufflet, *Caution* (1653, U18); *Diurnall*, 503.200, p. 3050; *Proceedings*, 599.211, pp. 3343–4; *Politicus*, 361.174, p. 2792; Weldon, *Declaration* (1649, W1277AD), pp. 12–13, C3v; Larnar, *Relation* (1646, T2899).

for example, Thames watermen found themselves sucked into a constitutional debate as a result of a dispute with Hackney coachmen. This reflected the fact that their appeal for support from an MP, Nathaniel Whetham, resulted in a printed statement that made them sound like hardline republicans. The watermen were appalled at the way in which their case was exploited in this way, but they responded by turning to the Presbyterian lawyer and activist, William Prynne, with the result that their revised response merely spoke to a different political agenda, and was then printed, 'given up and down' and sold in public.[78] More intriguing still is Edmund Felton's *Out-Cry for Justice* (1653), which recounted his treatment at the hands of the Excise Commissioners. This tract is interesting not just because he felt 'necessitated . . . to write and publish his oppressions to the world', but also because he located the incident within a broader political context. This involved parliamentary injustice and partiality, not least in terms of the favouritism shown to his rival (Sir Henry Spiller), but it also involved allegations about how men were 'made poor by oppression, and then despised because poor'. Most of all, of course, Felton is fascinating because he was pursuing a struggle for justice that had been initiated by his father decades earlier, and because, like his brother – Buckingham's assassin John Felton – he recognized how to connect personal grievances with national issues, even if he planned to secure satisfaction through pen and printing press rather than at the point of a dagger.[79]

iv Interactive newspapers

There is one final aspect of 'authorship' that still needs to be considered, however, which highlights once again how newspapers became an increasingly important part of daily political life. This involves the *interactive* nature of Civil War newsbooks, and the possibility that they could be exploited as a tool for political participation, and even that they became the most potent way of engaging with a national audience. This has generally been overlooked, other than by research into the rise of commercial advertising, from the marketing of new books to the promotion of local fairs, and it remains an area where logistics and practices remain poorly understood.[80] Too little attention has thus been paid to the importance of

---

[78] *Rugg*, pp. 32–3; *CJ*, vii. 828; *Address* (1659, T1744); *Declaration* (1659, D604A); *CCSP*, iv. 543.

[79] Felton, *Out-cry* (1653, F661), pp. 3, 5–6, 7; T. Cogswell, 'Destroyed for doing my duty', in *Religious Politics in Post-Reformation England*, ed. K. Fincham and P. Lake (Woodbridge, 2006), pp. 177–92.

[80] R. Walker, 'Advertising in London newsbooks', *Business History*, 15 (1973), 112–30.

newspapers as a means by which readers could learn about new publications, even though new and forthcoming books by authors like William
Prynne were not merely advertised but also promoted more subtly by means
of précis and published extracts.[81] And almost no analysis has been undertaken into journalists being 'desired' and 'instructed' to include portions of
text. In fact, this is another area where ordinary citizens had considerable
scope for making themselves heard, for around 12d per line, or perhaps 2s 6d
for a small advert, safe in the knowledge that newspaper adverts were read
fairly avidly by their contemporaries.[82]

The most obvious way in which individuals influenced the content of
newspapers was by means of personal notices, and although these might
seem innocuous, they could actually become dialogic and controversial, not
least when they touched on issues of general public concern. The vast bulk
of such notices drew attention to property that had been lost and horses that
had been rustled, in even the most remote corners of the land, as well as to
art thefts and jewel heists from the London residences of noble families.
These sat alongside adverts relating to imposters, conmen and missing
persons, from rebellious apprentices and thieving servants to wayward
wives, which sometimes involved elaborate tales rather than merely terse
notices. Indeed, since divorces could be secured only with difficulty, adverts
provided a means of waging marital warfare, as husbands notified tradesmen
that they would no longer honour the debts amassed by estranged spouses.[83]
On some occasions, however, both commercial adverts and private notices
provoked rapid replies and counter-claims, thereby emphasizing the care
with which newspapers were read and their perceived power as a means of
influencing audiences. For example, the fire-ravaged town of Ransbury in
Wiltshire used a newspaper advert to expose fraudsters who had used a
printed brief to misappropriate charitable donations, while opponents of
Oliver Williams's 'office of public advice' used a similar tactic to challenge
the legality of his operation.[84] Indeed, newspapers also became a key tool for
both promoting and challenging the work of 'projectors', even if the process
was not always straightforward. This is clear from the experience of the
commissioners for New England, who were able to arrange for the

---

[81] *Proceedings*, 599.231, sig. 20F4v; *Kingdomes*: 214.071, pp. 568–70; 214.120, p. 966; *Civicus*: 298.012,
    p. 93; 298.023, pp. 183–4.
[82] *Politicus* (1660, M1768A), p. 3; *Proceedings*, 599.239, sig. 20X4v; *Occurrences*: 465.5130, p. 1089;
    465.5127, p. 1051. For evidence of adverts being read, see: SUL, Hartlib 53/35/5–6.
[83] *Proceedings*: 599.231, sig. 20F3v; 599.181, p. 2852; *Diurnall*: 503.147, p. 2200; 503.216, p. 3296; 503.219,
    sig.10L4v; *Occurrences*, 465.5040, p. 277; 361.306, p. 6922; 361.317, p. 7090; 361.391, p. 124; 361.381,
    p. 1629; 361.441, p.160; 361.442, p. 13.
[84] *Politicus*: 361.303, p. 6073; 361.304, p. 6091; 361.365, p. 7840; *Diurnall*, 504.306, p. 2561.

publication of letters that reported on the progress of their work, but who did not always like the way in which these were glossed. As a result, they found themselves having to send complaints to specific editors and to find other journalists who were more accommodating.[85]

Such evidence indicates not merely how contemporaries experimented with print culture, but also how the weekly press provided additional ways of discussing issues that generated political heat. Very often, therefore, newspapers were used to respond to criticisms and to defend reputations. As we might expect, this was most obviously done by MPs, military commanders and those associated with publishing and the book trade. Edward Massey 'commanded' one editor to publish a riposte to 'malicious scandals', while William Lenthall used journalists as a vehicle with which to respond to accusations by a merchant called Edmund Child, and George Monck used the *Parliamentary Intelligencer* to counter allegations that had been 'basely and false represented ... by the pamphleteers'. In the weeks following the Restoration, moreover, newspapers repeatedly bowed to the wishes of public figures who had cause to fear retribution, by inserting statements in which they challenged the accuracy of stories that were being peddled about them in print, not least in relation to supposed involvement in the king's trial and execution.[86] Authors like William Lilly, meanwhile, repeatedly protested about false reports of his astrological predictions, and about counterfeit editions of his works, while licensers of the press could be observed explaining their decisions, and pointing out when their powers had been usurped, whether by unscrupulous printers or Grub Street journalists.[87]

As with other genres, however, newspapers were also capable of being exploited by people outside Westminster and outside the political elite. Having been 'falsely accused', 'defamed' and 'scandalised', for example, the London merchant Josiah Ricraft published a recantation by the men responsible. Similarly, Sir John Gell's reply to his critics in Derbyshire was inserted into *Mercurius Civicus*, while members of the parliamentarian committee in Worcestershire corrected reports that had been 'set forth in several printed papers' and 'published in one of the weekly sheets'. Likewise, the authorities in Berkshire complained about an 'infamous and scandalous

---

[85] *Politicus*, 361.068, pp. 1091–2; GL, MS 7938, fos. 9–11v; *Proceedings*, 599.105, pp. 1615–20.
[86] *Occurrences*: 465.3051, sig. Ee4v; 465.5130, p. 1089; *Proceedings*, 599.216, pp. 3417–8; *Parl. Intelligencer*, 486.127, p. 430; *Exact Accompt*, 491.103, pp. 1005–6; *Publicus*, 378.121, p. 332.
[87] *Life of Dugdale*, p. 103; *Diurnall*: 504.319, p. 2513; 503.279, p. 4288; 504.304, p. 2534; *Proceedings*: 599.115, p. 1788; 599.217, p. 3438; *Civicus*, 298.179, pp. 2427–8; *Kingdomes Faithful*, 210.19, p. 146; *Occurrences*: 465.5127, p. 1051; 465.5129, p. 1128.

libel' called *The Case of the Town of Reading*, and denounced its 'notorious lies and malicious untruths'.[88] Such tactics were also employed by members of the Woodmongers company, and by those involved in wrangling over the management of the Post Office, the 'new undertakers' for which complained that their opponents' printed papers had been inserted in *Severall Proceedings*. Indeed, when the commissioners for New England published a response to allegations about financial impropriety in 'one of the weekly occurrences', they explicitly acknowledged that this particular journal would 'go through many hands'.[89]

Ultimately, newspapers could also be used much more proactively, in order to publicize grievances, promote ideas and engage in political agitation. This might mean publishing announcements regarding contested administrative arrangements, such as the workings of the First Fruits office, which spilled over from flyers and into newspapers. But it could also mean the insertion of texts that supported propaganda campaigns and political agitation. In December 1647, therefore, a prophetical text was inserted into the *Perfect Diurnall*, and in December 1648 one of the many addresses that were inspired by army radicals, and that demanded justice for 'capital offenders', was inserted into the *Moderate Intelligencer* 'at the desire of some of the authors'.[90] Similarly, in 1649 the protracted dispute between the Earl of Rutland and the Derbyshire lead miners saw both sides inserting texts into different newspapers, while the Quakers made a habit of lobbying journalists about how they were being treated.[91] In other words, for their affordability and for their geographical and social reach, Civil War newspapers offered ordinary citizens the perfect vehicle for making themselves heard, and such texts were regularly exploited not just for commercial advertising and private notices, but also for pursuing other interests, including public issues and political campaigns.

vi Conclusion

During the 1640s and 1650s the printing press was susceptible to appropriation as never before. This reflected not just the collapse of censorship, but also the structures of the print trade, which made print eminently affordable, and the

---

[88] *Civicus*, 298.096, pp. 865–6; *Diurnall*, 504.240, 1931; *Politicus*: 361.332, p. 7330; 361.290, pp. 5864–5.

[89] *Politicus*, 361.380, p. 1613; *To All* (1653, T1323); *Proceedings*, 599.185, p. 2927; GL, MS 7938, fo. 26v.

[90] For example: *Politicus*: 361.294, p. 5927; 361.259, p. 5367; *Proceedings*, 599.291, pp. 4617–9; *Diurnall*: 503.219, 10L4v; 503.216, pp. 3296–7; 504.228, p. 1833; *Mod. Intelligencer*, 419.197, sig. 9n.

[91] *Modest Narrative*, 433.22, pp. 171–3; *Moderate*, 413.2061, sigs. Ppp2v–4; *Proceedings*, 599.290, p. 4604; *Declaration* (1655, D588), p. 1; *Something* (1655, S5707), p. 8.

circumstances of Civil War and revolution. In this situation there emerged not merely new debates and new ideas, but also new voices, which found expression through new methods for participating in public life. This involved a great deal more than the efforts of Grub Street hacks and committed ideologues, interesting though these are, and what is striking is how often print was deployed to advance and protect a range of interests, whether personal or public, commercial or corporate. Central to this democratization of writing, printing and 'authorship' was the ability to bring discrete issues to the attention of a wider public, to engage in tactical escalation by becoming involved in more or less heated exchanges and debates, and to make political observations of an increasingly detailed and general kind.

Such developments constituted a profound shift in political culture, although one that has not been properly appreciated because of a failure to thoroughly evaluate the motives and methods which underpinned authorship and printing. The benefits of such an approach can usefully be illustrated through the activity of Samuel Chidley, a London haberdasher, Leveller and religious radical, who is well known as an activist and pamphleteer, but one whose tactics have not been adequately understood. First, in 1652, Chidley undertook the private printing of *A Cry against a Crying Sinne*, in protest against the use of the death penalty for crimes of theft. This represented a response to frustrated attempts to effect reform through the political process, and a determination to reach as large an audience as possible, and the tract was distributed freely and displayed publicly and provocatively at Tyburn. Secondly, later in the same year he produced a printed flyer that outlined his strategy for making parliament pay its debts to soldiers and creditors, and that was intended for widespread distribution. Not satisfied with this, however, Chidley also adopted a third innovative tactic, by securing the insertion of this same text into prominent newspapers. This provoked an angry response from Thomas Pride, who ensured that his own notice denying any association with Chidley's campaign appeared in *Severall Proceedings*. Finally, Chidley went even further by producing a short-lived newspaper of his own, with which to respond to Pride's protest and further promote the creditors' cause. In it he likened himself to 'an eagle stirring up my nest and fluttering over my young', and invited poor and distressed citizens to 'come unto me'. Chidley asked people to 'put me in mind of your misery', and he promised to 'deliver your message swiftly, and to be a swift witness against your bloody prosecutors'.[92]

---

[92] Chidley, *Cry* (1652, C3838), pp. 2, 14, C4v; *Diurnall*, 503.143, p. 2141; *Proceedings*, 599.167, p. 2628; *Eagle*, 154.1, pp. 2–3; 154.2, pp. 15–16.

Chidley, in other words, was a new kind of author. He appropriated print as a means of promoting ideas and launching campaigns, and he recognized the utility of various genres, various methods and various tactics. What also emerges, however, is that pamphlets, posters and newspapers represented only part of Chidley's plan, and that his print campaigns were intimately linked to political petitioning and parliamentary lobbying.[93] As such, he provides not merely the perfect conclusion to a chapter about the changing nature of printed authorship, but also the ideal introduction to chapters that will analyse the relationship between print culture and much more targeted kinds of political participation.

---

[93] *Eagle*, 154.1, pp. 2–3; Chidley, *Cry*, p. 14.

CHAPTER 8

Print and petitioning

One of the least well-known facts about the poet and pamphleteer George Wither is that he was an inveterate petitioner, who frequently printed his petitions in order to present them to MPs. In 1647 he produced a single sheet regarding his financial claim against parliament, which had been verified by the Committee of Accounts, and in 1648 he appeared in person at Westminster and 'laid down a petition for arrears upon the ground'. This was taken in by 'a gentleman of the House', although 'nothing was done in it', and in 1655 and 1656 other printed petitions received help from MPs like Nathaniel Whetham. By 1659, however, Wither felt compelled to print yet another petition, which elaborated on his long suffering for want of money, offered a detailed history of his troubles and outlined the many occasions when he had experienced delays as a suitor for justice. By this stage, Wither's frustration was so great that he was even prepared to criticize a specific MP, John Fielder, whom he accused of defrauding the state. Indeed, these texts probably represent only a fraction of Wither's printed petitioning, and yet another undated plea from the 1650s only survives because a bundle that was left lying around a Whitehall office was later recycled as scrap paper.[1]

More interesting still is Wither's tendency to comment on the petitioning process, sometimes at length, sometimes by taking his cause into a more public arena and sometimes in verses that were attached to his petitions.[2] In a work submitted to MPs in 1648, therefore, Wither complained about waiting 'unheard' and 'unheeded' at parliament, and wrote about

> Petitions he hath oft conveyed,
> into your hands yet finds no aid.
> These therefore at your feet are laid,

---

[1] Wither, *November* (1646, BL, E362/2); Wither, *Humble* (1646, W3200A); *Occurrences*, 465.5086, sig. Qqqq4v; Wither, *Humble Petition* (1655, W3201); *Burton Diary*, i. 207; Wither, *Petition and Narrative* (1659, W3178), pp. 2–6; LPL, MS 938/29.

[2] Bodl. MS Rawl.A.56, fo. 333; *Burton Diary*, i. 207; Nott. UL, Ne.C.15406, p. 158; Wither, *Petition and Narrative*, p. 1.

> where let them not neglected lie,
> nor unregarded throw them by,
> but view them with a gracious eye.

In another text, similarly distributed, Wither grumbled about the 'cost, troubles and mischances' of the petitioning process, and protested that 'though the public cause should be preferred / some hours for private cause must be spared'. He even hinted that frustration with the political process could provoke radicalization, by concluding 'that he, to whom the state doth nothing owe / should rich, by three of four employments grow / whilst they pine, who thereon did all bestow'. Such ideas were then crystallized in Wither's account of *The Tired Petitioner*, a poetic address to 'noble friends' in parliament which was printed in the hope that his petition might 'obtain your answer without more delay', lest 'with my estate I lose my patience too'. Wither recognized that his failure could be explained by a lack of powerful friends and kinsmen, by a failure to bestow gifts on decision-makers and by naive faith 'that justice should be neither sold nor bought'. He reflected that such delays could be tolerated with 'uncrazed patience' so long as parliament was preoccupied by important public business, but then warned that if petitions were 'crossed for private ends' he would 'outroar the cries of all the women at your door'. He even demonstrated awareness that 'in me, although my sufferings are despised / the common grievances is epitomised'.[3]

Wither raises important questions about parliamentary petitioning, a crucial dimension of popular politics, and one where scholars like David Zaret have made connections between the use of print and the emergence of a 'public sphere'. My aim here is to build on such work, but also to suggest that Zaret has both exaggerated and underestimated the importance of printed petitions. There is certainly scope for connecting petitioning with 'Grub Street', and for arguing that such texts could be used to 'constitute' and 'invoke' public opinion, as well as to propagandize and persuade. It is also apparent that petitions came to represent the views of larger groups within society, such that authority came to be attached to texts that had the most signatures. And it is clearly true that printed petitions sometimes fostered a dialogic culture by provoking responses and cross-petitions.[4] Nevertheless, such claims make most sense in terms of mass mobilization

---

[3] Wither, *Single* (1648, W3191a), pp. 1–2, 3; Wither, *Carmen* (1648, W3150), sig. Av; Wither, *Tired* (1648, W3200), sig. A, pp. 2–3, 5, 7.
[4] D. Zaret, *Origins of Democratic Culture* (Princeton, 2000), pp. 32, 220–57; Knights, *Representation*, ch. 3; J. Hart, *Justice upon Petition* (London, 1991).

(which will be considered in Chapter 10), and they fail to do justice to the vast bulk of printed petitions, which were produced by individuals or small groups and which performed rather different functions. As Wither demonstrates, in fact, these petitions were printed *in order to be presented*, and not necessarily to publicize a case in the public sphere. They represent a less dramatic kind of politics, and reflect rather different practices and ideas, and they can be used to show that political life during the English Revolution became more participatory than ever before.

It is these discrete and everyday texts that provide the focus for this chapter. The aim is to examine how printed petitions were employed as a participatory device; to make direct interventions in the parliamentary process, exert direct influence over MPs and peers, and achieve more or less specific goals. Although petitioning is difficult to distinguish very precisely from lobbying – the subject of Chapter 9 – it is here defined as the attempt to raise in parliament an issue or grievance, involving a fairly straightforward demand rather than any detailed policy proposal. This was done in the hope that demands might be taken into consideration, or else to hasten the process whereby such issues were considered, committed, reported and resolved. The chapter will thus use the petitioning process as a means of reinforcing the argument of the previous chapter, by demonstrating that there were many different kinds of print, which served many different purposes. It will begin by exploring the growth of printed petitioning as a response to the structural and conjunctural problems associated with parliament, in terms of its processes and workload, and as a response to the opportunities offered by the print medium (section i). Thereafter, the chapter will demonstrate that printed petitions were often intended for discrete circulation to MPs and peers, rather than for general publication and distribution (section ii), and it will then explore how, when and why printed petitions were deployed as devices for participating at Westminster (section iii). This will all provide the context for understanding the relationship between targeted interventions in the parliamentary process and public political discourse (section iv), and the key argument of the chapter will be that, by recognizing the importance of non-commercial and restrained petitioning, participation can be shown to have been a multi-phasal process involving different genres of print. The key to understanding such participation is the idea that contemporaries developed perceptions about parliament by intervening in its proceedings, and that by understanding its processes and problems they became more adept at negotiating the obstacles and delays that they encountered. This involved making tactical escalations in the face of frustrated expectations, and deploying different genres of print in different circumstances, both of which demonstrate how everyday participatory practices could lead to public criticism of the parliamentary system, and to political thinking.[5]

i Navigating the petitioning process

'Popular' petitioning was obviously not invented in the mid seventeenth century, and my argument here is certainly not that it only became possible in the age of print. Rather, it is that printing helped contemporaries to overcome the very real obstacles that stood in the way of anyone who attempted to intervene in parliamentary proceedings.

In the circumstances of mounting political tension, and after eleven years of 'personal rule', petitioning was undertaken on an unprecedented scale, and contemporaries were struck by the number of petitions that greeted the Long Parliament from across the country and across the social spectrum. In the space of a couple of days in late May 1641, for example, petitions arrived at Westminster from a group of footmen, from a 'poor oppressed widow', from a soap-boiler and from the 'poor hammermen' of the Pewterers' Company.[6] The papers of individual MPs reveal just how many petitions were submitted, but they also suggest that our knowledge about them is fragmentary and fortuitous, and that many texts only survive because they were recycled as scrap paper.[7] It also seems clear that participatory expectations increased fairly dramatically during the 1640s. This reflected MPs' willingness to encourage petitioning, as well as the enhanced availability of parliamentary news in print. Specific petitions can be shown to have emerged in response to particular debates, and some petitioners clearly knew to whom they wanted their demands to be referred, and by whom they ought to be dealt.[8]

Petitioning was thus feasible, but it could also be difficult and more or less controversial, and the problems involved were both structural and conjunctural. Structurally, it seems clear that the financial hurdles involved could be ominous, in terms of consulting with lawyers, paying fees to clerks, and finding and copying relevant documents. Equally daunting was the task of negotiating the parliamentary process, and since the costs involved meant that it paid to get petitioning right, it was obviously important to receive advice

[5] D. Hirst, 'Making contact', *JBS*, 45 (2006), p. 40; Hart, *Justice*.
[6] *Salusbury Corr.*, p. 113; PA, MP 27–28 May 1641.   [7] BL: Add. 26785, fos. 127–69; Harl. 378.
[8] *Rous Diary*, pp. 111–12; BL, Add. 70105, unfol.; Add. 6682, fo. 33; Sloane 1467, fo. 70v; CKS: U951/C261/19; U55/37; *Politicus*, 361.164, p. 2614; PA, MP 19 June 1646; DRO, D258/12/16, p. 6; Devon RO, 1148M Add/18/3.

and assistance on everything from the wording of petitions to the timing of their submission.[9] More troubling still were the conjunctural problems associated with parliament's workload during the 1640s and 1650s, which made it increasingly likely that MPs and peers would respond to a flood of petitions in a less than constructive fashion. The weight of private business frequently prompted attempts to make the process more efficient, by providing petitioners with advice about when and how petitions should be submitted, and by demanding additional information to assist officials and MPs. At other times, however, it also provoked decisions to ignore private business altogether, even for months at a time. Such decisions could be justified by a desire to reduce the costs that petitioners incurred in fruitless attendance at Westminster, and by fear that petitions would interrupt more important business; but they could also be inspired by concern that the 'monstrous easy receipt of petitions' undermined authority, gave too much power to ordinary citizens and encouraged an 'inundation' of 'lewd persons'. In November 1645 Nedham suggested that excessive recourse to petitioning was 'a new humour', which was 'not usual for the subjects of this or any other kingdom', and he argued that such practices were 'not always in season'. He also suggested that petitioners should not press 'too hard upon particulars', lest they should 'distrust the judgement and care of those whom we do acknowledge the wisest and supreme council'.[10]

The danger, in other words, was that there would emerge a disparity between the theory and reality of participation, and that parliament would fail to live up to people's expectations as a forum for resolving their grievances. Whether as a result of genuine reasons (workload) or spurious excuses (partiality), many petitioners faced lengthy delays and great expense, as time was spent lodging in London and attending at parliament. The accounts of civic officials and livery companies frequently reveal the 'care', 'pains' and 'charges' involved in 'several days attendance', and how quickly costs could escalate. In prosecuting their petition against a local minister in early 1641, for example, the corporation at New Romney paid over £52 to their mayor and another servant, Mr Weevil, for the expenses involved in frequent trips to London, some of which involved staying in the

---

[9] Worcs. RO, BA9360/A10, Box 3; GL: MS 5606/3, fos. 429v, 434v; MS 4326/7, fo. 369; TNA, SP 24/30; Longleat, Thynne 64, fos. 305–v; CUL, Pell 5/10; Pell 9/34; Beinecke, Osborn fb.158/5; Osborn fb.159, fo. 86; HEH, HAF Box 15/22; BL, Add. 70003, fos. 234–5; Stowe 184, fos. 25, 33; Add. 64921, fos. 122–v; Glos. RO, D2510/16; CKS, U350/C2/90; Cheshire RO, DCC/14/74; FSL, X.d.483/129; Chetham, A.3.90, fos. 3v–4.

[10] *Proceedings*: 599.200, p. 3164; 599.202, p. 3186; 599.205, p. 3247; *Diurnall*: 504.241, p. 1941; 503.195, p. 2965; 503.191, p. 2906; *CJ*, vii. 427; BL, Stowe 184, fo. 31; *Britanicus*: 286.106, p. 937; 286.107, pp. 945–6.

capital for up to two weeks at a time. In February 1646, meanwhile, the parish of Manchester spent no less than £20 on the expenses of the delegation that attended their petition to parliament regarding a visitation of the plague.[11] The same was also true for private individuals, for whom the cost of 'drawing and engrossing' petitions could pale in comparison with the expenses involved in lodging in London, and in repeatedly travelling to Westminster, and for humble suitors the process was 'very chargeable'.[12]

Such delays and costs suggest that the key to undertaking successful petitioning without the prospect of financial ruin lay in finding *sponsors* within parliament. This was a great deal easier for some people than for others. Borough corporations tended to rely on local MPs, from whom they secured advice about the quality of draft petitions, about delays that were likely to be encountered at Westminster, and even about the gifts that needed to be bestowed upon MPs. In August 1649 Lord Howard of Escrick explained to constituents in Carlisle that he had presented their petition, while adding that 'the delay was no forgetfulness in me, but rather a timely waiting to get it freelier passed'.[13] For individuals, of course, sponsorship often depended on the ability to exploit ties of patronage, kinship and friendship. Sir Thomas Fairfax, for example, used his influence with MPs like John Moore and William Lenthall, who were able to smooth the passage of petitions from individuals such as the Countess of Kildare and Colonel Doily. This was probably helpful for cases that had been 'long depending in the House', and where the delays caused by 'weighty affairs' had resulted in 'very great expense'. Bulstrode Whitelocke admitted that the 'forwardness' of friends could prove decisive in ensuring 'a quick hearing' and a successful outcome, and such patronage and sponsorship extended from the floor of the House into committee chambers, in terms of ensuring that petitions were not only read and referred but also pursued. On more than one occasion, therefore, the Earl of Warwick asked friends like Sir Robert Harley and Sir Simonds D'Ewes to lend a hand with specific petitions, by attending committee meetings and doing 'what lawful favour you can'.[14]

---

[11] CLRO, JOR 41x, fo. 3v; GL: MS 5606/3, fos. 370v–1v, 398v–9; MS 3054/2; MS 11571/12, fos. 349v, 396; Worcs. RO, BA9360/A10, Box 3; Wilts. RO, G23/1/4, fo. 10; EKRO: Do/FCa/5, fos. 327, 328v; NR/AC/2, pp. 289–305; CHC, BA/H/3/20/2, pp. 396–7; Earwaker, p. 127; *CJ*, iv. 371.

[12] HEH, HAF 16/53; Leeds UL, ML, Political and Miscellaneous 1, fo. 70.

[13] Wilts. RO, G23/1/4, fos. 21, 49v, 51, 54–v; Berwick RO, B1/11, fo. 76v; BL, Eg. 2096, fo. 149; Add. 22619, fos. 146, 149, 164, 215, 217, 230, 235, 236; Add. 22620, fos. 20, 22; EKRO: Do/AAm2, fos. 167–v; NR/AC/2, p. 302; H1257, unfol.; Norfolk RO, Y/C 19/6, fo. 470v; Worcs. RO, BA9360/A10, Box 3; Cumbria RO, Ca/2/123.

[14] Bodl. MS Eng.Hist.e.308, fo. 105; Liverpool RO, 920/MOO/1543; *HMC Cowper II*, p. 315; Leeds UL, ML, Political and Miscellaneous 1, fo. 70; CKS, U350/C2/92; HEH, STT 2225; BL: Stowe 744, fo. 10; Add. 26785, fos. 107, 120, 125; Add. 21420, fo. 230; Add. 21425, fo. 57; Add. 70006, fo. 7; Add. 37343, fo. 210; Add. 70003, fos. 59, 232; Harl. 160, fo. 154.

Personal connections were not infallible, of course, as men like Sir Roger Twysden found to their cost. Twysden reflected on long and fruitless attendance in pursuit of innumerable petitions, some of which went unread for years, and he noted that he 'omitted nothing ... either in soliciting friends, [or] advising with counsel, sparing neither cost nor pains all that while'. However, while he secured advice, introductions and even direct influence, he also explained that 'good I could do none'. Such evidence begs serious questions about how difficult petitioning would have been for those who lacked money or friends, or both, and about how humble individuals were likely to fare.[15] Such problems may have been mitigated to some degree by the possibilities for soliciting and entertaining individual MPs, not least once it was decided that submissions to the Committee for Petitions required sponsorship by at least one local MP. In March 1650, therefore, Henry Marten was approached by Fabian Hickes of the Inner Temple, on behalf of one Mrs Gipps, who 'attends at the Parliament door to present her petition to you to get read in the House'. However, the least wealthy petitioners were likely to have the weakest leverage with MPs, and it seems clear that county MPs like Sir Robert Harley and Sir Edward Dering were unable to cope with the number of people who sought their help.[16] Another way of overcoming such problems involved employing the services of 'agents', who probably became an increasingly common sight at Westminster, and whose value lay in their expertise in dealing with parliament. On one occasion Colonel John Gell offered to pay John Bowring £400 for the successful pursuit of his case, but there may also have been cheaper options for people from humbler backgrounds. This seems clear from the work undertaken on behalf of northern soldiers and citizens by Adam Baynes, who was frequently asked to promote parliamentary petitions in the early 1650s, long before he became an MP. Nevertheless, contemporaries clearly recognized that many petitioners would struggle for want of sponsors, and in 1641 Sir John Coke ridiculed the chances of petitioners from Ashborne in Derbyshire. He explained that no MP would be foolish enough to 'prefer such a petition', and added that 'the common people do mightily mistake Parliaments'.[17]

---

[15] 'Twysden narrative', iii. 155–76, iv. 131–84; *LJ*, iv. 257, 270, 296, ix. 189, 309; *HMC 6th Report*, p. 175.

[16] GL, MS 3054/2; *Proceedings*, 599.200, p. 3164; Leeds UL, ML, Political and Miscellaneous 1, fo. 55; BL: Add. 70105, unfol.; Stowe 184, fo. 51; Add. 26785, fo. 84; CKS, U350/C2/89.

[17] DRO, D258/10/9/66; BL: Add. 21420, fos. 64, 207, 282; Add. 21426, fos. 168, 209, 345; Add. 21427, fos. 203, 213; Add. 69871, fo. 98.

The result, of course, was frustration and suspicion. In 1647, civic officials in Hereford recognized that petitions had been sidelined because time had been taken up with 'affairs of a more general concernment', but they were clearly frustrated that 'we have a long time and with much patience attended the good pleasure and resolutions of that honourable house'. Men like Twysden perceived that the tendency to attribute delays to 'the greatness of public affairs' masked unfairness and political machinations, and having heard MPs excuse 'partiality' on behalf of their friends, he chose to refer to the Committee for Privileges and Elections as 'the committee of affections'. More importantly, Twysden also used such evidence to reflect upon the parliamentary process and the constitution, in terms of the difficulties involved in petitioning, 'the justice of committees' and 'the power and privileges of the two Houses'. He even began to question 'how far they might legally require obedience from the subject'. In other words, perceptions that the petitioning process was dogged by partiality and favouritism were not merely a feature of the popular press, but also a product of personal experience.[18]

The most obvious solution to the problems associated with delays and sponsorship was to distribute multiple copies of petitions. These could be given to potential patrons and put 'into somebody else's hand', until all possibilities had been exhausted. In 1651 the borough of Berwick planned to approach a coterie of potential 'friends' in parliament and in the same year Richard Lobb envisaged reaching out to a range of MPs. Such practices are also evident from the correspondence of MPs and petitioners, from borough records and private accounts and from petitions that survive in public and private archives.[19] In 1656 Twysden recorded spending days on end at 'the Parliament door' putting copies of petitions 'into the hands of all my friends', and similar tactics can occasionally be shown to have resulted in matters being raised in the House. In April 1657, therefore, the Speaker drew attention to a paper 'which a young man gave me at the door, touching the saltmakers at Shields', who were said to be 'undone', although it is not clear that the matter went any further.[20] The problem, of course, was that making multiple copies of even the simplest texts could prove very costly. In

---

[18] Claydon, Verney reel 14; BL, Add. 70005, fo. 209; 'Twysden narrative', iii. 159–73; iv. 137–48, 166–73; R. Twysden, *Certaine Considerations*, ed. J. Kemble (Cam. Soc., 1849), p. 171; *Moon*, 248.18, p. 150; *Moderate*, 413.2036, sig. Nn3.

[19] Claydon, Verney reel 8; Berwick RO: B1/10, fo. 186v; B1/11, fo. 6; FSL, X.d.483/124; BL, Add. 70123; Add. 70125; Add. 70109; Add. 70108; Add. 70035; Leeds UL, ML, Political and Miscellaneous 2, fo. 49; Worcs. RO, BA9360/A10, Box 3; Wilts. RO, G20/1/17, fo. 164; EKRO, CP/Bp/73; Cumbria RO, WD/Ry/239; HEH, HAF Box 15/22; GL, MS 4326/7, unfol.

[20] 'Twysden narrative', iv. 179, 180; *CJ*, i. 157; *Burton Diary*, ii. 57.

1641, the Butchers paid 9s 4d for making six copies of a parliamentary petition, and 7s 4d for four copies of a petition to the Lords, and similar costs were involved in the submission of texts by the Worcester corporation in the same year (5s 6d for two copies), and by the Tylers and Bricklayers in 1656 (3s 6d for five copies). In 1647 the constable of Manchester spent 13s on 'writing diverse petitions'. The accounts of the Ducket family, meanwhile, record a fee of 14s to a scrivener 'for writing out seven cases of our petition relating to the election'. Thus, for humble suitors – like the inhabitants of Wootton in Northamptonshire, the poor fishermen of Burnham Norton in Norfolk, and the poor prisoners in King's Bench – petitions could easily involve between three and eleven manuscript sheets, and as a result extensive courting of MPs and peers would have been prohibitively expensive.[21]

It is this picture – in which parliamentary petitioning involved both heightened expectations and mounting difficulties – that provides the context for the appropriation of print, and the remaining sections of this chapter will show not just that print offered a means of overcoming the problems faced by supplicants, but also that it provided a way of expressing frustration with parliamentary processes.

ii Discrete petitioning in print

The connection between print and petitioning has clearly not been lost on scholars, and indeed it has become central to recent historiography. Whether or not this has involved claims about the emergence of a public sphere, a new consensus seems to be emerging that printed petitions reveal 'a growing readiness to go public' in relation to 'private, local or sectional causes'.[22] The aim of this section is not to deny that some petitions did indeed take particular business into the public domain, but rather to suggest that such developments can only be understood by examining much more discrete interventions, which were targeted at representatives in parliament rather than at a general audience.

The petitions that have attracted most attention, therefore, are those that were printed *after* they had been presented to parliament. These were generally produced on a commercial basis and for public sale, with the aim of drawing attention to the official response, eliciting public support and promoting particular causes. A petition from the 'postmasters of the

---

[21] GL, MS 6440/2, fo. 557v; MS 3054/2; Worcs. RO, BA9360/A10, Box 3; Earwaker, p. 135; Beinecke, Osborn fb.16/3; PA, MP 3 May 1641, 1 June 1641, 11 June 1641, 16 June 1641, 1641, 7 Feb. 1642.

[22] Hirst, 'Making contact', p. 39.

several roads of England' was thus printed in March 1653, following its favourable reception by the Commons, and then 'pasted upon the posts' around London. Petitions that were submitted against the University of Oxford in April 1649 were made available by Giles Calvert, and may even have facilitated participation by providing readers with the names of the committee to which they had been referred, complete with details about its remit and its chairman.[23] On these occasions publication was almost certainly arranged by the petitioners themselves, but from the Jacobean parliaments onwards many other petitions were exploited for political reasons by those to whom they had been presented. During the early 1640s, for example, these included everything from complaints about scandalous ministers to the grievances of silkthrowers, the latter of whom blamed the country's woes on prelates and 'popish' lords and called for the abolition of episcopacy. A particularly colourful example involved a petition by the old soldier and composer, Tobias Hume, which made dramatic claims about his poverty, his enthusiasm for military service and his promise to 'ruin the rebels all within three months, or else lose his head'. For parliamentarians, such zeal was political gold dust in July 1642, especially since Hume named the peers who had offered him financial support, as well as those by whom he had been spurned.[24] Petitioners and politicians alike, in other words, recognized the value of publicizing even the most trivial grievances and the most parochial demands, and a great many texts appeared with either tacit or overt authorization.[25]

What also seems clear, however, is that from the 1620s onwards it was just as common for petitions to be printed *before* they were presented, with a view to reaching a much smaller audience, and with the aim of influencing opinion *within* Westminster. Such texts, in other words, had a different purpose, and this explains why they were visually distinctive. They were almost invariably printed on one side of a single sheet, and they generally lacked decorative devices, bold titles or imprints, and their tendency to be ignored by historians reflects the significant archival problems that surround their study.[26] Some rare examples were preserved only once they had been

---

[23] *Apprentices* (1641, T1527A); *Cinque Ports* (1641, T1476); *Prisoners* (1655, T1365a); *Post-Masters* (1653, T1619); *Humble Representation* (1649, H3631), sig. Av; *City of Oxon* (1649, H3558), sig. Av.

[24] Longleat, Portland 2, fos. 20–28v; *Narrative* (1647, N231); TNA, SP 16/493, fos. 114–16v; *Very Considerable* (1641, V275); *Articles* (1641, A3822); *Leonard Shoreditch* (1642, H3481); *Petition and Articles* (1641, E2154–7); *Colonel Hume* (1642, H3664), sigs. A2, A3.

[25] PA, MP 21 Mar. 1643; TNA, AO3/1088/1, Part 2, fos. 1–v; *William Booth* (1642, B3740); *Holdernes* (1642, H3505); *Committee of Kent* (1646, P1788A); BL, Add. 6677, fo. 47: *Poore Distressed Miners* (1642).

[26] *Joane Thomas* (1624, 24000.7); BL: Harl. 7614, fo. 94; Add. 69917, fo. 74; *CJ*, i. 713, 797.

recycled for note-taking or financial calculations, as with the 1655 petition by merchants trading with Spain, or the petition from a plundered parliamentarian, Richard Stamper of Arundel, which was used as a receipt and made its way into the Exchequer papers. Others were recovered by antiquarians, having been left in a 'privy house' or else used to wrap tobacco. Many others exist only in the official archives of political authorities and their clerks, including a petition from Robert Vivers and Henry Benson (1648), and another on behalf of six poor almsmen in East Ham (1641). A great many more only survive in the private papers of contemporary public figures, such as the 1649 petition by the minister, Enoch Grey, which can be found among the papers of his nemesis, Sir John Bramston, or the only known copy of the petition that Sir John Gell produced from the Tower in the early 1650s, which is preserved within the family archives.[27] Finally, and perhaps most importantly, significant concentrations of printed petitions survive among the papers of the MPs to whom they were originally given, including those of Gell and Bulstrode Whitelocke. Such texts, in other words, are difficult to find and less than straightforward to identify, but by piecing together surviving evidence, it becomes clear just how frequently petitions were printed in order to be presented at Westminster, and contemporaries like George Thomason were clearly struck by how common they became, particularly during the 1650s.[28]

The reason why printed petitions were so numerous is because the ability to reproduce specific texts at minimal cost was empowering, and when contextualized properly such material proves to be revealing in a number of ways. First, print was employed not just by aristocrats and wealthy merchants, but also by citizens from across the social spectrum. Early examples involve minor officials, 'poor freemen' and 'distressed prisoners', as well as humble tradesmen like wharfingers and 'hot-pressers', as well as a group of the 'poorest sort of tobacco-pipe makers', and the reality is that print was useful to anyone who lacked alternative methods for influencing the parliamentary process.[29] Secondly, the case of someone like George Morgan, a disgruntled factor to the Alum farmers, demonstrates that printed petitions could be re-submitted on different occasions, just as it was possible to

---

[27] *Marchants* (1655?, T1560a; BL, 190.g.12/33); TNA: SP 28/295, fos. 133–4; SP 28/24, fo. 1; SP 46/99, fo. 126; SP 18/205, fo. 80; SP 18/100, fo. 41; Wood, *Life and Times*, p. 159; PA, MP 5 May 1648; 3 March 1641; Norfolk RO, COL/13/92/9; LPL, MS 3391, fo. 103; DRO: D258/30/9/1–9; D258/56/5/10/67; D258/34/10; D258/30/10/1–2; D258/30/37.

[28] DRO, D258/10/32/10; D258/15/1/2; Longleat, Whitelocke Parcel 7; *Richard Tuttell* (1654, T3388, BL, 669.f.19/10).

[29] BL, Harl. 7608, fos. 143v–6, 214–15; Harl. 7614, fos. 114–26; Add. 69917, fo. 76; *Masters and Workmen* (1642, T1650a); *Earl of Rutland* (1649, R2399a); *Tobacco-pipe* (1643, T1445B).

produce a succession of amended texts relating to ongoing grievances. Thus the London merchant, Richard Chambers, whose troubles dated back well into the 1630s, produced a series of different printed petitions in the decades that followed, in 1646, 1652 and 1654.[30] Thirdly, and most obviously, printing made it possible to produce hundreds of copies of individual texts, for distribution among MPs and peers. Contemporaries commonly referred to the printing of 'several bundles' of petitions, and in 1646 Edmund Felton was able to pre-empt the submission of a petition by his enemy, Sir Henry Spiller, by attending 'that morning at the door of the House of Commons', where he delivered copies 'to most or many of the members of the said House'. Spiller claimed that such tactics were 'slighted and disliked' by MPs, but attempts to prevent such tactics – most obviously with the imprisonment of William Bray in March 1649 – suggest that animosity sprang from the aggressive behaviour and intemperate tone of particular supplicants, rather than from principled hostility to participation through print. As such, the distribution of petitions continued largely uninterrupted. Sir Roger Twysden recalled being approached outside the Commons in 1647 by 'a person who stood in the lobby ... with several petitions in his hands to present them each member', and having been mistaken for an MP he was given a copy, read it and engaged in conversation with the petitioner.[31] Indeed, this tendency to distribute petitions to a host of MPs, rather than merely to the clerks, eventually resulted in further refinements of the genre. Some printed texts were explicitly addressed to 'every individual member of Parliament', and others added printed endorsements on the reverse of printed appeals, so that they could easily be located once they had been folded and stored away. Moreover, contemporaries clearly recognized that such tactics were essential to successful petitioning, and that printing was an invaluable tool. Charles Hotham, for example, explained that to fight his case without printing was 'near impossible, his bodily strength not sufficing to transcribe so many copies himself ... [while] to have done it by others would have been too vast a charge'.[32]

---

[30] PA, MP 21 Jan. 1641, 3 June 1641; *Chambers* (1646 and 1652, C1920-A); *Remonstrance* (1654, C1919).

[31] *HMC 5th Report*, p. 10; LPL, MS 3391, fos. 79, 82; *Felton* (1642, F662); Felton, *Out-Cry* (1653, F661), pp. 5–6, 7; *CJ*, vi. 167–8; *Occurrences*, 465.5116, p. 911; *Diurnall*, 504.295, p. 2373; *William Bray* (1659, B4311); *Petition and Address* (1659, B4310); *HMC 7th Report*, p. 47; *CSPD 1653–4*, p. 294; *Anthony Weldon* (1649, W1277AD), pp. 35–6; *CSPD 1652–3*, pp. 305, 453; TNA, SP 18/37, fos. 381–v; *Burton Diary*, iv. 440–1; Fox, *High and Lofty* (1655, F1956a); 'Twysden narrative', ii. 213.

[32] *To Every* (1659, T1340aA); *Unto Every* (1653, U99); Fox, *This for Each* (1656, F1933); BL, 190.g.12/17: *Elizabeth Salmon* (S4111a); TNA, SP 28/295, fos. 133–4: *Richard Stamper*, Hotham, *To Every* (1653, H2899).

This picture of how and why printed petitions were used can be further enhanced, however, in ways which suggest that the genre became *authoritative*. This involves demonstrating not just that the new format was an economical and acceptable way of drawing attention to petitions, but also that it came to be regarded as an *appropriate* means of submitting the formal copy for the official files. Initially this seems not to have been the case, and convention dictated that, whether or not print was employed to bring petitions to the attention of MPs, formal submission required a scribal text. When such procedural rules were honoured, as tended to be the case during the 1640s, parliamentary papers sometimes contain both scribal and printed versions of particular texts, but as time passed new tactics began to emerge.[33] This sometimes meant submitting a long scribal petition with a printed 'brief', which contained its essence in summary form, but it could also mean submitting a very brief scribal petition alongside a much longer supporting text in print. When John Thompson of Bingley outlined his losses and grievances as a result of parliamentarian service, therefore, he did so by means of a cursory petition that was written on the outside of a 21-page printed pamphlet, which he merely invited MPs to read. Eventually, the authorities came to accept that scribal copies were no longer necessary, and that printed copies could constitute official documents.[34] More than this, however, petitioners seem to have felt that print *conferred* authority. This seems clear from the tendency to use print even when petitioning smaller bodies like councils, committees and commissions, where few copies were likely to be required, and where there was much less money to be saved by switching from scribal genres. When printed petitions first began to appear, therefore, it was common to find different genres being used in tandem, with manuscript copies being submitted to committees even when printed versions were circulated to members of both Houses, but this was another area where tactics began to change in the 1650s.[35] This meant not just a growing tendency for manuscript petitions to mimic the printed page, and for *pro forma* printed petitions to be used, but also for petitions to be printed even when they were intended for specific parliamentary committees, or for London's Court of Aldermen. In such situations it is hard to avoid the conclusion that printed texts were thought to be more likely to attract attention and consideration.[36]

[33] BL, Sloane 1467, fo. 40; PA, MP 19 Aug. 1648, 27 Mar. 1648, 26 Aug. 1648, 4 Feb. 1648; *LJ*, x. 460.

[34] *CSPD 1654*, pp. 270–2; TNA, SP 18/73, fos. 150, 152, 163–4v; Worcester College, AA.s.4/9: *A Briefe*; Beinecke, Brit. Tracts 1652+T37: Thompson, *Glass* (1652, T1001); *CSPD 1650*, pp. 44–5; *CJ*, vii. 597; *Burton Diary*, iii. 45.

[35] *CSPD 1650*, pp. 44–5; TNA, SP 23/109, pp. 357–69; SP 23/108, pp. 809–25; Herts. RO, D/Elw/Z2.

[36] BL, Stowe 185, fo. 76; FSL, Add. 1086; Longleat, Whitelocke Parcel 7/94; *David Cunningham* (1653, C7584A); *John Osmond* (1657, O531a).

In other words, whether it was because they were cheap or because they were thought more likely to be read, printed petitions became an increasingly common part of the political process. This may or may not have increased the volume of petitions that were submitted to parliament, and it may or may not have permitted the participation of individuals who had previously been excluded from parliamentary affairs, but it was certainly perceived to make participation more efficient, and it is certainly possible to observe contemporaries experimenting with print as a participatory tool. As such, it is necessary to explore how printed petitions were deployed, and to analyse what they reveal about perceptions of parliament and political tactics.

iii Deploying printed petitions

Printed petitions were an embodiment of tactical thinking, and by examining the circumstances in which they were used it becomes possible to appreciate the subtlety with which even ordinary citizens approached the task of participating at Westminster. This will mean observing how they dealt with a range of problems, obstacles and frustrations, how they handled issues like sponsorship and stewardship, and how they engaged in tactical and rhetorical escalation.

At the most basic level, printed petitions were intended to overcome the problem of finding people who would act as sponsors, and as such they represented a more constructive response than that demonstrated by the Ranter, Thomas Tany. After spending hours in the lobby attempting to find someone who would promote a petition, Tany expressed his frustration by launching a frenzied attack on the doorkeeper, and a fruitless assault upon the doors of the Commons. What he had not appreciated was what hundreds of his contemporaries had learned: petitions could be printed and dispersed in the hope of finding a supportive MP, not least by humble suitors for money and arrears. These included poor widows with many children, and junior officers who sought to avoid imprisonment after returning to civilian life, and any number of others who lacked powerful contacts. Not the least of these was a Dutch cleric called Jacob Lucman, who sought help to return home in 1647 after years ministering in England.[37] For others, however, print provided a device for the *stewardship* of existing sponsors, and print was used even by those who had already secured help from patrons and

---

[37] J. Peacey, 'To every individual member', *Court Historian*, 13 (2008), 127–47; PA, MP 1 July 1645; *Francis Freeman* (1649, F2130); PA, MP 1647: *Jacob Lucman*.

'eminent friends', and by those who must already have been fairly well known at Westminster. Such people recognized that a 'printed factum' could ensure that MPs were 'well prepared' with information. William Ryley, clerk of the records in the Tower, produced a printed note asking MPs 'to assist him in his petition', and even the crippled soldier Robert Pechell laced his petition with claims that he had friends – including Cromwell – in high places. Indeed, MPs themselves sometimes dispersed printed petitions to rally support and 'gain votes', although this was regarded as 'a pretty artifice' and 'an ill-precedent'.[38]

At a deeper level, however, printed petitions shed light on contemporary perceptions of the political process, the place of parliament within it and the obstacles that needed to be overcome. Some reveal awareness of the circumstances in which it was necessary to appeal to national rather than local authorities, not least to ensure the proper enforcement of statutes, and petitions were submitted regarding the regulation of brickmaking and cloth working, the prevention of illicit building work, and the control of alehouses, tobacco shops and bawdy houses. In 1659 a printed petition was even produced by a group of Somerset beer-sellers, who complained that local excise commissioners were failing to abide by recent legislation.[39] Other petitions demonstrate attempts to appeal to higher authorities against decisions by local officials, by the courts and by bodies that answered to parliament, and this was done because injustice had been done, because jurisdictional boundaries had been encountered and because individuals had reached the end of their tether. In such cases, involving humble parishioners in Muggleswick (Durham), poor prisoners in the Fleet or Newgate and individuals who were struggling to compound for their estates, explicit recognition was shown that parliament was the highest authority in the land, and that it was the citizen's 'last refuge'. In the case of Anthony Ovington's tussles with the commissioners for compounding, one printed petition expressed frustration over a vain year-long attempt to secure a referral of the matter to parliament.[40]

Much more intriguing, however, are petitions that highlight perceptions about the parliamentary process, and about how to navigate its processes

---

[38] *Ryley* (1648, R2421a); BL, Add. 78197, fo. 4; *Pechell* (1648, P1017a); *Bushell* (1659, B6250); *Burton Diary*, ii. 224–7.

[39] TNA, SP 16/479, fo. 84; *Clothworkers* (1642, T1422A); *Lincolns-Inne* (1645, T1480e); *Sommerset* (1659, T1705bA).

[40] *Muggleswick* (1642, M2902); *Chetwind* (1650, C3799); *Rayment* (1650, R411a); *Gateshead* (1657, J1225); Longleat, Whitelocke Parcel 7/82; *For Every* (1649, B6142); *Hedworth* (1651, H1353B); TNA, SP 23/108, pp. 811–13.

and obstacles. Such interventions often reflected strained patience in the face of delays, either when urgent public business had caused private business to be set aside, or when cases were ignored or neglected. Printed petitions thus served as a means of grumbling about deferred justice, rehearsing grievances and reciting the history of failed petitioning campaigns. Edmund Felton's decision to use printed petitions in the early 1640s came after years of legal and parliamentary proceedings in relation to his dispute with Sir Henry Spiller, and the reduced officers of Colonel Sanderson's regiment used a printed petition after having waited patiently for a response to their petition for arrears, and to complain that they were 'plunged into the depth of necessity, the fiercest enemy they ever yet encountered'.[41] In any number of other cases, such as those relating to 'poor distressed widows' or impoverished soldiers, this decision to resort to print seems to have been taken apologetically, but it almost invariably involved explicit reference to fruitless attendance in pursuit of earlier petitions. In May 1649, for example, a printed paper was produced in response to the fact that earlier petitions remained unread 'in the clerk's hands', and it was this delay that was said to have 'occasioned and induced me to present my petition and case in print unto every individual member', in the hope that a petition might be 'read this day'.[42] The use of print, in other words, involved an expression of frustration with the parliamentary process, and with the fact that there were no clear rules governing the speed with which individual cases should be dealt. It also represented an escalation of tactics, albeit one that targeted a restricted audience and that fell some way short of taking matters into the public domain. Printed petitioning, in short, entailed a restrained intensification of pressure upon MPs and peers.[43]

This sense that there was an intimate connection between the deployment of print and the escalation of tactics involved more than merely the decision to deploy print as frustration grew. The multi-phasal nature of the petitioning process also meant that print could be employed in a variety of different ways. Most obviously, printed interventions could be made not just when other kinds of petitioning had failed, but also when printed petitions were ignored. In 1653, therefore, the Duchess of Hamilton

---

[41] Longleat, Whitelocke Parcel 7/85, 91, 110; *Felton*; Felton, *Out-Cry*, pp. 5–6, 7; *APC 1629–30*, p. 265; *CJ*, i. 925, 930, 932; *HMC 4th Report*, pp. 8, 29, 30, 37; *CCC*, pp. 125–6; TNA, SP 23/247, fo. 219: *Sandersons*.

[42] *Distressed* (1650, T1710a); *Pitson* (1647, P2300b); *Occurrences*, 465.125, p. 1054.

[43] PA, MP 19 Aug. 1648: *My Lord*; *Many Thousands* (1648, T1412a); *Jersey* (1650, T1737b); *Preparative* (1654, P2126).

produced a brief printed statement regarding her attempts to get a petition read, which mentioned that she had 'divers times attended in person at the door, and presented printed copies thereof unto all or more of the particular members'. Her aim was not to reproduce the text of her petition, but merely to complain that 'her said petition and case being for above these six months not read (remaining now in the clerks hands), her wants are increased to that extremity, that she and her four daughters live merely upon charity'.[44] Indeed, print could be used at *any* subsequent stage in the petitioning process, especially to draw attention to petitions that had been read and referred, but that had then become lost in the system. When faced with being blocked or forgotten, therefore, petitioners could use print to reiterate claims, overcome mishaps and misunderstandings, and rehearse cases ahead of appointed hearings and reports. In 1652 Colonel Charles Doilie explained that his petition had 'lain in the House ... these four years', and that it was 'twice ordered to be taken into consideration, but was not'. His phlegmatic response expressed hope that this 'was but a disappointment into a better opportunity'.[45] Others, however, showed signs of thinning patience. In February 1642 a printed petition from Lancashire complained that two former petitions, presented in November 1640 and January 1641, had been 'imprisoned' in a committee ever since, and although the petitioners were reluctant to 'interrupt the course of greater affairs' they felt compelled to act, because 'the condition of no other county can be of more consideration', and they thus implored the House 'that these and other grievances ... may not be perpetually forgotten'. Similar sentiments were expressed by petitioners whose cases had been considered but not reported, including the Norwich worsted weavers who claimed that many local families were being 'daily ruined' as a result.[46] Yet another kind of printed petition emerged when business stalled at the final parliamentary hurdle, when reports had been made, and when orders and ordinances had been drafted. The inhabitants of Leighton Buzzard, who had waited almost two years for a response to their petition for a 'charitable benevolence', resorted to print to complain that an ordinance 'hath ever since remained with the clerk of this honourable House'.[47]

[44] Longleat, Whitelocke Parcel 7/102: *Duchess of Hamilton* (1653); *Hamilton* (1652, H477a).
[45] *Hampson* (1647, H632aA); *Pechell* (1648, P1017a); *Sir John Scot* (1655, S2076a), sigs. A, A2; Longleat, Whitelocke Parcel 7/84, 87, 114: *Charles Doilie* (1652).
[46] PA, MP 26 Feb. 1642: *Lancaster*; Longleat, Whitelocke Parcel 7/93; *Merchants* (1650, T1738); *Remonstrance* (1653, R999); *Worsted-Weavers* (1655, G447a).
[47] Longleat, Whitelocke Parcel 7/108: *Leighton Buzzard* (1650).

What becomes clear from such expressions of impatience is that petitioners were able to diagnose the consequences and the causes of their
frustration. Most often this involved complaints about the amount of
time, money and effort expended waiting for parliament to take action.
Robert Vivers and Henry Benson wrote of 'their constant attendance and
great expenses', while the Norwich worsted weavers referred to 'their great
expenses', and Charles Doilie complained of 'his long and often waiting
here', which 'hath been of very great detriment to him'. These problems
were more serious for some than for others, of course, and although wealthy
merchants could navigate the log-jam of parliamentary business by employing agents to pursue their claims through the corridors of Westminster, such
options were rarely available to individual petitioners, whose mounting
frustration can occasionally be tracked over time.[48] A case in point is
Richard Chambers, whose 1646 printed petition referred to the patience
with which he had waited since submitting a petition in November 1641,
'out of a deep sense of your great and weighty affairs in these distracted
times'. His mood had changed considerably by 1652, however, because he
faced ongoing delays despite apparent support from Oliver Cromwell and
Oliver St John, and by this stage he claimed to be 'wearied out and
consumed by expenses and fruitless attendings'.[49] Ultimately, of course,
frustration could turn to anger, as with the printed petition 'presented at the
Parliament door' by Thomas Philpot in October 1654. This complained
that although no petitioners were supposed to wait more than forty days for
a response, MPs had ignored his case 'again and again', and such bitterness
was particularly clear with petitioners like Major Hercules Langrish, who
suspected that delays were caused by political factionalism.[50]

This suggests that there was a real danger that frustrated petitioners would
reflect on the performance of MPs, on the abuse of parliamentary processes
and on political corruption. In cases like those of Edmund Felton (1642) and
Robert Vivers and Henry Benson (1648), printed petitions complained about
how opponents had manipulated the Westminster system by using 'feigned
and false pretences' to delay hearings, con members and co-opt either House.
Similarly, this sense that the system was open to abuse emerges very clearly
from a petition by members of the Weavers' Company, who alleged that
delays and adjournments were exploited by rivals, who surreptitiously

[48] PA, MP 5 May 1648; *Worsted-Weavers* (1655, G447a); Longleat, Whitelocke Parcel 7/114: *Charles Doilie* (1652); Whitelocke Parcel 7/93: *Merchants* (1650, T1738); *Real Lenders* (1657, T1706E).
[49] *Chambers* (1646 and 1652, C1920-A); Longleat, Whitelocke Parcel 7/107; *Remonstrance* (1654, C1919).
[50] *Preparative* (1654, P2126); *Langrish* (1644, L409).

procured an order 'on an unusual day for motions, and contrary to the known rules'.[51] Between the lines of such petitions, moreover, there lurked suspicions regarding the purity and impartiality of individual members. A 1657 petition by East Anglian clothiers reflected on a campaign that stretched back thirteen years and that involved 'fifteen weeks attending during this present session', and it bemoaned having received nothing more than 'promises', none of which had come to 'a birth of performance'. In their dealings with parliament and its committees the clothiers complained that they had found 'honour abroad and self-denial not at home, and love to the public thereby . . . so cold and feeble'. On this occasion they refrained from identifying who was at fault, but others showed no such reticence, and the escalation of both tactics and rhetoric that blockages and delays provoked are clear from the petitions of Walter Elford and the Middle Temple lawyer, Robert Cole. Both men accused Augustine Garland of sitting on reports into their cases, and while Elford claimed to have spent 'many years' attending 'several committees', Cole bemoaned the fact that 'there is not held forth to the free people of this nation any relief'. The civil servant Walter Frost went one step further, and in addition to circulating a printed petition to MPs, he also printed copies of the draft report into his case, in order to pressurize its author, Lord Lisle, into delivering it to the Commons. In doing so he expressed frustration at being 'left without mercy to the vexation and charge of law proceedings'.[52]

Printed petitions thus performed a variety of functions in relation to the parliamentary process. They were deployed as part of a broader tactical armoury, and reflected determination to overcome the obstacles that petitioners faced, and they revealed mounting frustration, anger and cynicism. Indeed, it is only by understanding such restrained tactical escalations, and the gradual process by which the pressure on members intensified, that it becomes possible to analyse more aggressive ways of participating, and the additional steps by which petitioners bridged the gap between Westminster and the wider world.

iv Going public

The recent scholarly interest in printed petitions has centred in no small part on the ways in which issues were taken into the public domain through

---

[51] *Felton*, sig. B; *CSPD 1652–3*, p. 305; PA, MP 5 May 1648: *Robert Vivers* (1648), pp. 3–5, 6–15; Longleat, Whitelocke Parcel 7/101: *Weavers* (1649).

[52] *Real Lenders* (1657, T1706E); *Elford* (1659, E498B); Longleat, Whitelocke Parcel 7/83; *CSPD 1652–3*, p. 453; TNA, SP 18/37, fos. 381–v.

commercial texts, and on the tendency for debates to be generated. It has
been suggested, in other words, that exchanges between rival groups of
parishioners, between competing factions within the Vintners company,
and between retail merchants and chapmen, betoken the emergence of a
dialogic culture.[53] What is less readily appreciated, however, is that this was
merely an extension of discrete and non-commercial printed petitioning,
which makes it necessary to look much more closely at the relationship
between restrained participation and public discourse.

In some ways, therefore, a dialogic culture existed *within* Westminster, as
pre-submission printed petitions generated replies and cross-petitions, with
rival texts sometimes being distributed to MPs within days of each other.
This not only involved agile campaigners like John Lilburne, and controversial issues like the management of the Post Office, but also campaigns of
a local and a personal nature.[54] A particularly dramatic example involved a
dispute that was grounded in factionalism within County Durham, and
that centred on the personalities of George Lilburne and Thomas
Shadforth, and on their respective roles in the Civil Wars. Having festered
since the mid 1640s, this row spilled over from local committees into
parliament in 1649, and although Shadforth's printed history of the case
was intended for discrete circulation, it quickly generated a printed response
by Lilburne, who felt 'necessitated to take this course to manifest my
integrity, and blow off that dust which hath lately been cast upon me'. In
doing so with a petition directed 'to every individual member', however,
Lilburne merely provoked Shadforth to respond to what he called 'false and
cunning insinuations', even though he recognized that the two men were
being 'uncouth' in 'inveagling all the several members'.[55]

Beyond this there are a number of ways in which the circumscribed world
of printed petitions interacted with more public forms of print discourse.
First, printed petitions that were produced for limited circulation were
sometimes distributed more widely, albeit non-commercially, not least as
an expression of political frustration. This was true of Edmund Felton,
some of whose printed statements in the early 1640s were scattered around
London and Westminster 'in the night time', and it was also true of women

---

[53] *Answer* (1641, S5101); *Vintners* (1641, P1832); *Retayling* (1641, R1180); *Farthing Tokens* (1642, H3439A);
Country Chap-men (1644, H3438).

[54] Lilburne, *To Every* (1651, L2186); PA MP 24 Dec. 1642: *Posts* (1642, 7753); *Full and Cleare* (1642,
F2276); DRO, D258/10/32/10: *Katharine Stone* (1654); *To Every* (1659, T1340aA); Longleat,
Whitelocke Parcel 7/103, 106.

[55] *Shadforth* (1649?, S2833a); Lilburne, *To Every* (1649, L2077a); Shadforth, *Innocency* (1649, S2833), p. 1;
Records of the Committees for Compounding (SS, 111, 1905), pp. 275–77.

Levellers in May 1649, who were 'frustrated of their expectations', and who were said to have 'ran up and down like a company of gossips, and showed their petitions to every one'. And it was also true of the printed petition by the Shoemakers, which the cordwayner Hugh Wagstaffe was prosecuted for 'dispersing' in 1656.[56] Secondly, discrete texts sometimes responded to, provoked and shadowed public pamphlets. A discrete petition by Thomas Ellyson of Easington prompted Francis Howgill to reply with a published statement, while both Hercules Langrish and the embattled sequestrators of Cambridgeshire favoured printed texts rather than scribal petitions because they faced 'scandalous aspersions, both in print and otherwise'. They spurned traditional scribal texts, in other words, because their opponents had produced printed libels that were 'set upon posts in the market places'. On other occasions, however, restraint was deemed inappropriate, and Richard Baxter's Worcestershire petition was defended in a public tract after it had been criticized by a Quaker pamphlet from the press of Giles Calvert. Very occasionally, discrete petitions were also deployed *alongside* commercial pamphlets. In July 1649, for example, a printed petition by the Essex minister, Enoch Grey, which was produced in response to frustration with the parliamentary process, appeared at precisely the same time as his more substantial public tract, which was obviously designed to take his case into the court of public opinion.[57]

By far the most striking aspect of this public side to petitioning, however, is that it sometimes represented an additional dimension of the process whereby the pressure that was placed on parliament gradually intensified. With characters like Edmund Felton, William Bray and John Roseworm, therefore, it is possible to observe that when conventional petitions failed, and when printed petitions proved no more successful, dissatisfaction with the fact that business remained 'dead in your hands' led to case-histories being rehearsed for a much wider audience. These took the form of *An Out-Cry for Justice*, and a public appeal for 'freedom' from 'oppressive and illegal imprisonment', as well as 'an angry paper' and 'a sad complaint'.[58] Even more dramatic is the case of Charles Hotham, sometime fellow of Peterhouse in Cambridge, whose frustrated attempts to petition the

---

[56] LPL, MS 3391, fos. 79, 82; Felton, *Out-Cry*, pp. 5–6, 7; *Brittanicus*, 285.2, p. 16; *Mdx County Recs*, p. 246; *Shoo Makers* (1656, T1369B).

[57] *Ellyson* (1654, E633a); Howgill, *Answer* (1654, H3154); *Sope-Patentees* (1646, W2216); Langrish (1644, L409); *Sequestration* (1644, T1670a), sigs. A2–v, A3–v; R. Baxter, *Reliquiae* (1696), i. 69–70; Baxter, *Worcester-shire* (1653, B1455); Buttivant, *Discovery* (1653, B6339B); LPL, MS 3391, fo. 103: *Enoch Grey* (1649); Grey, *Vox Coeli* (1649, G1968), sigs. A2–A4v.

[58] Felton, sig. A4; Felton, *Out-Cry*, pp. 5, 6, 7; Bray, *Heaven* (1649, B4303), pp. 1, 2, 4; Rosworme, *Good Service* (1649, R1996); *Rosworme* (1651, R1997).

committee for reforming universities led to a series of printed texts, including a tract that was produced and sold by Giles Calvert. *The Petition and Argument of Mr Hotham* reprinted the texts of earlier petitions, and was dispersed among committee members, but it received a hostile response because it revealed the identities and actions of the MPs involved, and the upshot was that Hotham was removed from his fellowship. His response, however, was to publish the tract commercially, and then to defend his decision to go public in *A True State of the Case of Mr Hotham*, which provided a detailed account of both his case and the committee's proceedings. Although Hotham soon returned to more conventional petitioning, his frustration over long and fruitless attendance eventually resulted in the printing of a broadside petition for limited circulation, which complained about a wasted year 'at the Parliament door'.[59]

Such evidence reveals that, while there was no necessary connection between printed petitioning and 'publicity', the boundary between circumscribed print communities and the broader public was extremely fluid, and could be breached in any number of ways. This means that a thorough understanding of how print was used to participate at Westminster must recognize *interactions* between different genres, tactics and phenomena. This emerges very clearly from the case of the Derbyshire miners in 1649, which reveals frustration regarding the petitioning process, the circulation of printed petitions among MPs and the use of counter-petitions, as well as the use of print in a public fashion. Indeed, the miners' critics chose to respond by means of printed texts because they had seen copies of a tract called *The Liberties and Customes of the Myners*, because printed petitions had been 'dispersed' and 'published' by the miners' agent, Thomas Bushell, and because texts had even been 'posted up' across Derbyshire, to 'raise differences and tumults between the freeholders, owners and miners'.[60] Here, in other words, both discrete and public texts emerged as part of political campaigning, and it is clear not just that different genres fed off each other, but also that this involved tactical escalation, as tensions and frustrations led to fractious exchanges in the public domain.

What is also apparent, however, is that the experience of political participation could provoke rhetorical escalation rather than merely changes

---

[59] *Petition and Argument* (1651, H2897), pp. 1–5, 7–29, 33; *True State* (1651, H2901), pp. 2–4, 6, 13–14; *Petition and Argument* (1651, H2898); *Corporations* (1651, H2895); *CJ*, vii. 141; Hotham, *To Every* (1653, H2899).

[60] *CJ*, vi. 175; Worcester College: AA.s.4/13; AA.s.4/14: *The Case* (1649, C872A); BL: Add. 6677, fo. 51; Add. 6682, fos. 43, 46, 48; *Liberties and Customes* (1649, L1959); A. Wood, *Politics of Social Conflict* (Cambridge, 1999), pp. 270–80.

in tactics. Again and again it can be demonstrated how interactions with parliament that began with local and private issues could generate heightened political awareness, and that frustration and disillusionment prompted much more systematic thinking about the parliamentary system. In the case of the miners, this meant a fairly traditional and imprecise populism. One printed petition complained that 'prerogative hath many proctors, by whose power and policy justice is either denied or delayed', and that their 'oppressors' were 'cherished' because they were 'rich and powerful', while the oppressed were 'ready to perish for bread, because poor'.[61] Other critiques of the Westminster system were more complex, however, and involved sentiments that both fed *into* and fed *off* radical Levellerism. The poor orphans and widows of St Bartholomew's hospital in Chatham railed against 'court parasites', while poor shoemakers in London sought to 'bridle the baseness of ... covetous self-ended caterpillars, and commonwealth destroyers'. Nathaniel Burt adopted the language of 'freeborn Englishmen', and displayed a willingness to join Lilburne in using key parliamentary declarations as sticks with which to beat parliament.[62] More generally, anger that was born out of personal experience and direct participation focused on the performance of politicians, and on ideas about reforming the representative process, even to the point where frustrated petitioners questioned the legitimacy of parliamentary taxation in situations where their demands were not met.[63]

First, therefore, radicalism involved visceral criticism of individual MPs, and a willingness to make allegations about their behaviour in public. In some cases – like Robert Ramsey's attack upon Sir Thomas Walsingham – such breaches of privilege related to a member's activity outside parliament, but much more striking were claims about political corruption *inside* Westminster, especially when they involved the printing and publication of documentary evidence regarding wrongdoing. George Wood, for example, went public in 1649 with claims about the 'indirect practices' of Sir John Clotworthy, while John Musgrave accused Sir Arthur Hesilrige of a 'breach of faith and trust' after 'long and chargeable attendance' trying to get his grievances heard, which led not just to an appearance before the Council of State but also to a brief exchange of pamphlets.[64] This is another area where

[61] BL, Add. 6677, fo. 49: *Serious Representation* (1649); Add. 6682, fo. 43.
[62] TNA, SP 18/203, fo. 55: *Sea-men; Shoo Makers* (1655, T1369B); Burt, *For Every* (1649, B6142), pp.1, 8; Burt, *New-Yeers* (1653, B6145), p. 12.
[63] *Windsor Projects*, 710.3, pp. 4–5; *Moon*, 248.29, p. 229; 'A lybell' (BL, E302/19).
[64] PA, MP 30 Mar. 1648, 20 Apr. 1648; Burt, *To Every*; Burt, *New-Yeers*, p. 12; *George Wood* (1649, W3392); Columbia, Seligman 1649E/W85; Musgrave, *True and Exact* (1650, M3153), pp. 1–9, sigs. B–C2, p. 37; *Musgrave Muzl'd* (1651, M3156); *Musgrav Muzl'd* (1651, M3157); *Musgraves Musle* (1651, M3152); BL, Add. 78262, fo. 122.

the petitions of Thomas Shadforth and George Lilburne prove illuminating, because their dispute made a political football out of the reputation of the MP for Newcastle-upon-Tyne, John Blakiston. Shadforth suggested that Blakiston held damning evidence about Lilburne's activity during the Civil Wars, but Lilburne responded by dismissing Blakiston as 'a supposed member', and accused him of having abused his 'power and interest'. This not only involved Blakiston using Shadforth – his brother-in-law – to fight personal battles, but also his willingness to promote the appointment of malignant ministers and to manipulate parliamentary committees. Shadforth, in turn, defended Blakiston's integrity, suggesting that a full inquiry would enable the MP to 'appear in his splendour'.[65]

Much more serious were the detailed petitions and pamphlets by Colonel George Gill and Josiah Primatt in the late 1640s and early 1650s, in which they accused named MPs of abusing the parliamentary system and obstructing justice. At first sight, Gill's case revealed a familiar pattern, in which the long-running pursuit of a financial claim generated frustration about the 'long attendance' of a 'constant sufferer', a fruitless printed petition and then a more substantial reiteration of his demand for justice. More unusual, however, was Gill's willingness to analyse the reasons for his failure. His anger focused on Sir William Allenson ('so sharp and so eager an enemy'), and involved the progress of a case from local committee to parliament, and the blocking of his petition by an MP with whom he had been in dispute since the mid 1640s. Gill said that 'solicitation and attendance' – as well as support from Cromwell – had resulted in his petition being referred to the Army Committee, but he complained that their report remained undelivered in the hands of John Downes for nine months, 'every day almost whereof, I have attended at the door . . . at great expenses'. Gill blamed this delay upon MPs like Henry Darley and Sir John Bourchier, the latter of whom had apparently prioritized 'a particular business of his own' on a day 'purposely appointed for mine', and he added that his case 'could never be heard' even though it 'had often been called for' by members like Luke Robinson.[66]

The case of Josiah Primatt offers even clearer evidence of how local issues and parliamentary participation could result in radical anger. Like Gill's, it centred on political tension in the north-east of England, in terms of the sequestration of collieries in County Durham, and like Gill's it began in a

---

[65] *Shadforth*; Lilburne, *To Every* (1649, L2077a), pp. 1, 4–5; Shadforth, *Innocency*, p. 4.
[66] *Gill's Case* (1649, G742); Gill, *Innocency* (1651, I196), sigs. A2–v, pp. 8, 10–14.

fairly conventional fashion. This meant that frustration over delays and 'long attendance' led to the printing of petitions, in which Primatt made detailed allegations about his experience. He claimed, therefore, to have been obstructed by a local MP, Sir Arthur Hesilrige, who was accused of benefiting from the sequestered property, of using dubious tactics to prevent Primatt's witnesses being heard, and of using his influence to overrule sympathetic MPs. He also ensured that such claims reappeared in a series of printed broadsides, and the aggression with which he complained about 'oppression and tyranny' ensured a swift response from the Commons, in the form of an investigation into the 'undue printing of petitions and papers'. However, such severity almost certainly reflected a concern that Primatt's frustration had driven him into the arms of political radicals, and it is notable that his final printed petition was distributed by John Wildman and John Lilburne, the latter of whom obviously relished the opportunity to undermine one of his own enemies.[67]

Since petitioners sometimes recognized that their predicaments and frustrations mirrored those of other contemporaries, and were willing to make common cause with known radicals, it is probably no surprise that some of them used their experience to make more general claims about the inadequacies of the Westminster system. This kind of radicalism was evident in the 'very high language' of the printed petition that was handed to Twysden in 1647, and it was also clear in a 1652 printed petition by Samuel Chidley. The latter came in the wake of earlier texts that had questioned the use of the death penalty, and it demanded the delivery of an overdue report and a draft bill; and having observed how earlier petitions had 'lain dead' for six months, Chidley demanded regular committee meetings, and evidently felt entitled to 'save the committee a labour, and report it myself, that it may not lie all the year long in hand'. As such, he printed the report that he *wanted* to see produced. Subsequently, Chidley produced a more substantial tract that not only explained how frustration with conventional forms of participation had led him to engage in printed petitioning and then public campaigning, but also critiqued the record of elected officials. He thus 'put them in mind of their duty', by pointing out that this escalation of tactics would have been unnecessary if elected representatives had 'done but their duties'.[68] In these cases, of course, we are dealing

---

[67] *Compounding* (1651, P3456a); Longleat, Whitelocke Parcel 7/95: *Josiah Primat* (1651); *Petition and Appeal* (1651, P3457); *True State* (1651, T3112); *CJ*, vii. 55, 65, 71–3.

[68] 'Twysden narrative', ii. 213–14; *Samuel Chidley* (1652, C3845); Chidley, *Cry* (1652, C3838), pp. 2, 3–6, 9–24.

with petitioners who were already known radicals, but other cases suggest that the petitioning process could genuinely *foster* radical ideas. A case in point is Charles Hotham, whose frustrations and tactical escalations have already been noted, and whose texts also reveal dramatic language. Hotham became intensely critical of the performance of MPs, and having initially thought that the members dealing with his case were 'intentionally good', he came to regard them as being susceptible to the 'evil designs' of his opponents, who had intruded themselves into committee meetings and ensured 'prolongation and perplexity'. By 1653, indeed, a weary Hotham was willing not just to accuse specific MPs of having 'grossly abused the trust committed to them', but also to criticize parliament in a much more wide-ranging way. He defended the decision to publish his grievances, rather than to make private appeal to MPs, and he claimed to be 'ashamed' about having to 'beg their favour . . . as a courtesy'. He expressed outrage over 'that laquey employment of officious attendances, and tedious trotting from place to place', and over the 'daily penance' of those who were forced to do business with 'men of great place'. And he denied that the publication of committee proceedings infringed parliamentary secrecy, and demanded that such privileges should be clarified and 'published to the whole nation, [so] that other men might not be thus split . . . upon rocks under water'. Finally, Hotham concluded that, by making the process of petitioning 'impossibly difficult' and 'intolerably tedious', parliament effectively made the 'arbitrary and illegal judgments' of its committees final and irrevocable, and turned 'sufferers' into 'plain vassals'.[69]

Even more intriguing than Hotham's case, however, are those involving William Sykes and James Freize. Sykes was a London merchant who used a printed petition to call for free trade, who presented copies 'to most members of both Houses', and who became frustrated when it was 'not so much as publicly read . . . far less debated and answered'. He responded by dispersing his petition 'into several counties' and by printing another 'remonstrance', and by this stage his aim was to secure the appointment of a committee *of his own choosing*, involving Alexander Rigby and Henry Marten. He also demanded that MPs should not 'delay the discharge of their trust', so that 'the people may the better know for what end and purpose they have adventured their lives and estates in these present wars', and then reminded them that they were trustees with a duty to pursue 'the commonwealth's right, and people's privilege'. Finally, he demanded a

---

[69] Longleat, Whitelocke Parcel 7/92; *True State* (1651, H2901), pp. 2–4, 5; Hotham, *To Every* (1653, H2899); *Corporations* (1651, H2895), pp. 43–5.

purge of 'patentees, monopolisers, trade engrossers, sellers of people's right, and destroyers of free trade', and the removal of MPs 'out of all other places of public trust'.[70] Freize, meanwhile, was a poor prisoner in the Fleet who became involved in fruitless petitioning after growing frustrated with his gaoler, Sir John Lenthall, and with the Committee for Examinations. This led to complaints about buried reports, and eventually to printed pamphlets, which reproduced petitions and letters, and which demonstrated that Freize knew a great deal about parliament and its MPs. He thus claimed to have approached Henry Marten having 'seen your worth in print', but having then observed partiality the pamphlets he began producing in late 1645 used proto-Leveller titles – *A Declaration and Appeale to all the Freeborne People* (1645), *Every Mans Right* (1646) – and revealed Levelleresque tactics. Freize repeatedly blended autobiographical information with detailed evidence and inflammatory prose. He made specific allegations against the MP Lawrence Whitaker, intimated that Sir John Lenthall had been protected by his brother, the Speaker of the Commons, and appealed to Magna Carta in response to the political 'juggling' that brought favours for 'creatures', 'papists' and 'delinquents'. Finally, he demanded a 'strict account' from those who were 'intrusted' with public money, the removal of 'mercenary lawyers' from parliament, and the summoning of a new representative.[71]

In cases like these the 'radicalism' that emerged from the experience of participation was perhaps implicit, but in two other cases it was extraordinarily clear. The first involved Cornet Christopher Cheesman, sometime agent for sequestrations in Berkshire, who provides an interesting and neglected perspective on the story of hostility to local parliamentarian administration. Having witnessed financial corruption by colleagues, Cheesman took his complaints to Westminster, only to face delays – his petition remained unread in the hands of the Speaker – as well as obstruction and abuse of power. This involved his enemies using a protracted investigation – involving 'expensive, long and vexatious journeys' between Berkshire and Westminster – as a 'trick to tire out and discourage him'. Cheesman also claimed to have encountered difficulties in committees, where 'the lawyers for their fees, and the commissioners for affection, did weigh so heavy on the side of the offenders, that there could not be one dram of justice allowed the commonwealth and your petitioner'. It was

---

[70] *Humble Remonstrance* (1645, S6324B); *William Sykes* (1645, S6324A).

[71] *Declaration and Appeale* (1645, F2197bA); *Every Mans Right* (1646, F2197A), pp. 1–4; *Times Present Mercy* (1647, F2197F), pp. 1–12, 14–17.

frustrations such as these that prompted him to petition 'every individual member', and he referred to 'continual importunity, and industrious petitioning, writing and printing'. What is particularly interesting about such texts, however, is Cheesman's fiery language. He claimed that 'impartial justice and righteousness' were 'the pretended principles of all men in the world', but he recognized that 'very few ... really intend the same, otherwise than only as engines by which they may climb to the top of their ambitious affections and desires'. He had observed how men 'insinuate themselves into the very bowels of the good patriots of this honourable council and commonwealth', in order to 'possess themselves of great places of honour and profit', and he had seen how they used 'Machiavellian devices and satanical stratagems'. Cheesman, in other words, blended populist bile with radical politics, and he gave his tract a striking title: *The Oppressed Man's Out-Cry for Justice*. Indeed, having failed to get his petition read, he responded not merely by printing a commercially available account of his colleagues' 'unfaithful actings', but also by repeating his plea to MPs, in *The Oppressed Mans Second Outcry for Justice*. This was notably Lilburnian, and Cheesman cited parliament's 'book of declarations' against the regime, and bemoaned how the 'whole nation' had become filled with 'bribery, extortion, partiality, perjury and all manner of oppression and cruelty'. He also hinted at the existence of 'a grand confederacy between the commissioners and sub-commissioners', which 'must needs render the Parliament ... as a mere cypher'.[72]

Most dramatic of all was the case of John Poyntz, whose long-running property dispute ended with his being imprisoned for making an unauthorized copy of an act of parliament (1647). After over a year in prison, Poyntz printed a petition to the Lords, copies of which were dispersed at Westminster by William Pendred, and then a petition to the Commons that secured him a sponsor, and another that was addressed to 'every individual member', and that asked them to make their 'cheerful appearance *this day* for the reading of the said petition'. Further discrete texts followed after his case was referred to a committee, doubtless in expectation of a report to the House, thereby demonstrating Poyntz's willingness to deploy print at every stage of the petitioning process.[73] Much more remarkable, however, were the conclusions that he reached. Poyntz blamed his

---

[72] Cheesman, *Oppressed* (1649, C3773B), pp. 1, 4, 5; Cheesman, *Berk-shires* (1651, L3772); Cheesman, *Second Outcry* (1652, C3773C), pp. 2–5, 6–7.

[73] *LJ*, x. 460; *HMC 7th Report*, p. 48; PA, MP 26 Aug. 1648, 28 Aug. 1648: *John Poyntz, Petition and Appeal* (1648, P3131e); PA, MP 25 Nov. 1648: *To Every, Appeal* (1648, P3131C); *Case and Vindication* (1648, P3131D); *CJ*, vi. 86.

troubles on the 'power and prevalency' of John Browne, clerk of the House of Lords, and he attacked 'the slighting or laying aside [of] petitions', and claimed that 'delay of justice is the greatest injustice, and the not redressing of oppression the greatest oppression'. Beyond this he cited Lilburne to challenge the jurisdiction of the Lords over a commoner, and then reminded MPs that they had been 'entrusted', that they were obliged to 'hear, receive and redress the grievances of the people whom you represent', and that they were required to 'punish their oppressors, be they high or low, rich or poor, friend or foe, without respect to anything but pure justice'. More important still was Poyntz's suggestion that, by experiencing partiality and corruption, petitioners were becoming disillusioned with MPs. As such he issued an extremely radical threat, by telling MPs that, 'if you resolve to stop your ears against the cries of the people, let us know, that we might fly to some other refuge for protection against those who employ all their power and might to destroy us'. In other words, Poyntz suggested that 'the people of England' might be forced not just to *appeal to* their representatives, but also to '*appeal from* a Parliament of England'. Perhaps unsurprisingly, this prolonged campaign for justice saw Poyntz being drawn into the orbit of parliament's radical critics, and in November 1650 this became explicit with his request to have John Lilburne and John Wildman assigned as his legal counsel.[74]

v Conclusion

By drawing attention to the prevalence of printed petitions it would be tempting to suggest that this increasingly popular genre democratized the participatory process. In the opening weeks of the 1656 Parliament the deluge of printed texts provoked orders that no private petitions were to be 'printed before the same be read in the House', and that the serjeant-at-arms should 'seize upon such printed petitions in the hand of any such person that shall deliver or disperse the same'. One MP complained that 'they will overwhelm us', and asked whether petitioners 'mean to drown us with business', and on one occasion the House apparently descended into confusion as 'five or six constantly [stood] up at a time to offer petitions'. Satirists, too, sensed that it was now possible for 'all sorts of people, high and low, rich and poor, tagg, ragg and longtaile' to petition parliament about their grievances, and for them to do so on the basis of increased knowledge

---

[74] *Petition and Appeal*; PA, MP 25 Nov. 1648: *To Every*; *Case and Vindication*, p. 7; *John Poyntz* (1650, P3132); PA, MP 19 Mar. 1649.

about what was happening in parliament.[75] However, rather than suggesting that more people were drawn into the parliamentary system, it might make sense to argue that print gave people the hope of becoming more *effective* petitioners. This seems clear because print was rarely the first genre to which petitioners turned, because it was something to which they resorted in the face of obstacles and delays, and because printed petitions took a variety of forms, and were used in different ways at different stages of the parliamentary process. The role of print, in other words, was not to facilitate petitioning that would not otherwise have taken place, but rather to assist in the process of finding sponsors, securing support and persuading MPs. The result was probably to prolong and intensify particular petitioning campaigns, and by observing how printed texts were deployed it seems clear that contemporaries from all walks of life became more attuned to the ways and means of participating in parliamentary affairs, and more astute about how to change their tactics when faced with political hurdles. What this means, of course, is that it would be naive to claim that print was a more powerful participatory tool than wealth and influence. Nevertheless, printed petitions and pamphlets could achieve meaningful results, and parliament not only proved willing to pay attention to printed texts, but even forgave the inflammatory prose of men like George Gill, so long as their cause was considered to be just.[76] As such it is plausible to suggest that the deployment of print was a weapon for the weak, a response to participatory failure and an attempt to overcome the limitations of the politics of intimacy.

Moreover, analysis of the ways in which citizens appropriated print in revolutionary England has two significant implications for our understanding of contemporary political culture. First, it is difficult to equate printing with commercial publication, and to assume that printed petitions sought to invoke and appeal to public opinion. Instead, the deployment of print as a tool for intervening in parliament highlights contemporary awareness of a *spectrum* of textual genres, which stretched from scribal petitions to commercial pamphlets, and of a *spectrum* of audiences, from select coteries to national communities. This chapter has shown how the printed petitions that were aimed at MPs and peers have tended to be misunderstood, and that they need to be approached with great care. This is particularly clear from a text that appeared in the name of Praisegod Barebone, which was

[75] *CJ*, vii. 427, 462; *Politicus*: 361.332, p. 7334; 361.338, p. 7422; *Burton Diary*, i. 207, 269, 291–2; HEH, EL 7979.
[76] *CJ*, vii. 22, 26, 78, 93, 97–8.

submitted to parliament on 9 February 1660, and which exists in at least four versions, even leaving aside the satires that purported to contain his petitions. One version was almost certainly produced for discrete circulation among MPs, while another was published commercially after the petition had been submitted, and involved Barebone and his supporters drawing wider public attention to his views. Yet another version was produced by the official parliamentary printers, doubtless to highlight the response from the Commons, while a fourth version was issued by Barebone's enemies, who added hostile marginal commentary.[77] 'Printed petitions', in other words, took many forms, had different purposes and were intended for very different audiences.

Secondly, printed petitions shed valuable light on contemporary thinking about parliament. Petitioning seems to have been based on enhanced awareness of political affairs and parliamentary processes, and petitioners evidently understood that there were different ways of participating. Indeed, their behaviour betrayed awareness of a *spectrum* of tactics, which ran from the discrete and polite to the public and aggressive, and which individuals progressed along in a fairly predictable fashion. The use of print represented a response to frustrations, and involved addressing progressively larger audiences, and in this context it makes sense to recognize the importance of commercial pamphleteering in the public sphere while also recognizing that it was often a last resort rather than an automatic choice. What also emerges from the escalation of tactics, however, is that printed texts demonstrate how the practices involved in parliamentary participation sometimes led people to generalize about the political process, and to develop 'radical' ideas about the Westminster system. In at least some instances, therefore, Civil War radicalism was a bottom-up and experience-led phenomenon, beginning with private grievances, involving interventions in the daily life of the two Houses, and resulting in frustration, anger and political thinking. This brings us back to Wither's 'tired petitioner', who reflected that:

> . . . I have waited and endured so long,
> that no result can do me greater wrong,
> than lingering hopes. And were I quite undone,
> I possibly another course might run,
> to be repaired again, ere I obtain,
> that benefit, which I, had hope to gain,

---

[77] *Petition* (1660, B754); *Mr Praise-God* (1660, B752); *Praise God Barbones* (1660, B752A); *Petition of Mr Praise God Barebone* (1660, B753); DRO, D258/10/29/3.

> or else might find some other likely way,
> to fit me for the part I have to play.[78]

The 'other likely way' to which Wither referred generally involved attempts to rally support from a broader constituency, and Chapter 10 will explore the role of print in 'mass' politics, but before then it is necessary to explore the evolution of lobbying, a slightly different form of political participation, in the age of print and revolution.

[78] Wither, *Tired*, p. 1.

CHAPTER 9

Print and lobbying

In March 1641, an unwell Thomas Knyvett complained to his friend John Buxton that he had been under the 'tyrannical government' of his physicians, saying that 'they would make me guilty of more diseases than the commonwealth is troubled with'. He suggested that he was minded 'to exhibit a bill in Parliament against them for false imprisonment'. Knyvett's comment was obviously written in jest, but it is nevertheless revealing about parliamentary culture in the mid seventeenth century, and it reflects the possibilities that were open to contemporaries for participating in Westminster business, by submitting substantive proposals in the hope of influencing policy. In other words, Knyvett's comment suggests that the spectrum of political participation extended beyond petitioning to parliamentary lobbying, reflecting the growing importance of parliament as an institution, enhanced familiarity with its processes and proceedings, and the development of print culture. Indeed the printed lobby document became something of a literary trope. In 1659, for example, there appeared a broadside entitled *A Proposition in Order to the Proposing of a Commonwealth or Democracie*, the conceit of which was to demand the appointment of a committee to consider the ideas of James Harrington, which would meet regularly with 'the doors being open, and the room well fitted for all-comers'. More importantly, such comments also reflected the reality of parliamentary politics in the mid seventeenth century, and in 1652 the merchant and pamphleteer Henry Robinson explicitly justified the presentation of *Certain Proposalls* – as he had done before 'either in print or manuscript' – by saying that similar documents were often 'pressed upon several members of Parliament'. He also observed that MPs 'receive every morning ... as they pass into the House, other men's papers, petitions, [and] books', and although he reflected that such texts were commonly 'put into their pockets without so much as examining the title, much less perusing them afterwards', he provides clear evidence of a powerful link between the print revolution and the development of parliamentary lobbying.[1]

The aim of this chapter is to trace the emergence of the kind of lobbying that Knyvett threatened, that Harrington caricatured and that Robinson both observed and practised. Although lobbying can be distinguished from petitioning only with difficulty, and although the boundary between petitions and lobby documents was often blurred, different practices can nevertheless be identified. This chapter will focus on texts that did more than merely draw attention to grievances, and that instead involved substantive contributions to policy discussions. Lobbying, in other words, involved the provision of evidence and arguments in order to influence deliberations, decisions and policy-making, and even the legislative process. The importance of such activities has obviously been recognized by historians, particularly those who have sought to challenge outdated conceptualizations of Tudor and early Stuart parliaments. This has involved questioning the preoccupation with both constitutional conflict and consensual law-making, emphasizing the increasingly sophisticated techniques that were employed to make use of parliament and highlighting institutional responsiveness to 'pressure from below'. Nevertheless, such scholarship makes it perfectly clear that, in the period before the Civil Wars, successful lobbying was almost certainly the preserve of those with wealth and power in civic corporations and livery companies. The purpose of this chapter is to suggest that lobbying only became widespread after 1640, because of the circumstances of Civil War and the possibilities offered by print.[2]

The structure of the chapter will mirror the analysis of petitioning fairly closely. This will mean examining the problems associated with the traditional approach to lobbying, in terms of the time, effort and expense that was involved (section i). It will also mean discussing the advantages offered by the print medium for those who wanted to intervene in the parliamentary process, and developing a methodology with which to identify texts that were distributed discretely (section ii). Thereafter, the chapter will use both textual and contextual evidence to analyse the proactive and reactive methods that were involved in printed lobbying, in terms of the production and deployment of a range of different texts, which served different purposes, and which could be used at different stages of lobbying campaigns

---

[1] CUL, Buxton 59/87; *Proposition* (1659, P3775); Robinson, *Certain* (London, 1652), sig. A2.
[2] I. Archer, 'The London lobbies in the later sixteenth century', *HJ*, 31 (1988), 17–44; D. Dean, 'London lobbies and Parliament', *PH*, 8 (1989), 341–65; C. Kyle, 'Parliament and the politics of carting in early Stuart London', *London Journal*, 27 (2002), 1–11; C. Kyle, *Theater of State* (Stanford, 2012), ch. 5.

that were often multi-phasal, protracted and difficult (section iii). Beyond this the aim will once again be to use such evidence to explore the wider ramifications of participation through print. This will involve exploring substantial attempts to engage in 'projecting' and legislating, and the effectiveness of the print medium (section iv), and demonstrating the connection between discrete lobbying and public discourse, and between polite lobbying and Civil War radicalism (section v). In other words, the chapter will recover and scrutinize a significant and neglected body of printed lobby texts, and analyse the ways in which they were used, and it will argue that print became integral to the lobbying process, and that even though printed interventions were not always effective, they were perceived to offer ways of overcoming the structural and conjunctural problems associated with the participatory process. As such, print will once again be shown to have facilitated participation on the part of people who had previously been excluded from the Westminster process, or whose chances of influencing proceedings were extremely limited. As in the previous chapter, moreover, analysis of quotidian practices will be used to reveal widespread awareness about parliamentary processes and procedures, about a spectrum of participatory tactics, and about how to engage in tactical and rhetorical escalation in the face of frustrated expectations about the parliamentary process.

i Lobbying before the print revolution

As with other forms of participation in the period before the English Revolution, lobbying was an expensive, time-consuming and frustrating business, and it was not for the faint-hearted or for those who lacked deep pockets. This section will demonstrate that the problems involved were similar to, but more severe than, those encountered by petitioners, in terms of gathering 'intelligence' about processes, personnel and the parliamentary timetable, and in terms of undertaking lobbying campaigns. The latter required spending time at Westminster, paying 'ancient and accustomed fees' to doorkeepers, clerks and lawyers, and it also meant providing dinners and gifts for MPs, in the hope that they would massage the legislative process. And such campaigns also required fairly significant expenditure on documentation, from committee lists to bills and breviates.[3] By outlining the obstacles facing prospective lobbyists, it will be possible to show how corporations, companies and individuals began to experiment with

---

[3] Beinecke, Osborn fb.158/5; Osborn fb159, fo. 86; PA, MP 13 Dec. 1644.

new ways of coping with the task of influencing proceedings, and how this eventually led to the appropriation of print.

The challenges posed by the lobbying process can be demonstrated time and again through the records of mercantile companies and civic corporations.[4] In London the authorities spent hundreds of pounds every year on their 'solicitor' and 'remembrancer', who were paid a daily allowance for attending at Westminster, and whose expenses involved preparing legislation and providing gratuities for the clerks, serjeants and Speaker.[5] Such activity can also be documented for corporations outside London, albeit such organizations faced problems that were more significant and costs that were more burdensome. Many boroughs relied upon local MPs to make motions and attend committees, and to lobby those 'friends' who could be 'seasoned with our business', but the experiences of Richard Harman and Thomas Atkin – burgesses for Norwich – indicate how often the Commons became preoccupied by 'the greater affairs of the kingdom', so that little could be achieved, even 'with much ado' on a daily basis.[6] Many other towns despatched town clerks and recorders to 'solicit the Parliament', by hastening reports, answering accusations and procuring ordinances, but the obstacles they encountered often made it necessary to stay in London for weeks on end, which meant that costs could easily spiral out of control. They also discovered that the most effective lobbying methods – lavish gifts to MPs – were the most expensive of all.[7]

The task for individuals was even more daunting, of course, and meaningful lobbying was only possible for those with considerable wealth and powerful connections. 'Show your pedigree' was the advice given to Sir Ralph Verney when he sought to influence parliament, and he, like others, sought to 'fetch in' help, liaise with 'friends' and 'great men' and 'mollify' opponents. Peers like the Earl of Northumberland and Viscount Inchiquin asked for 'justice and civility' from MPs and clients, and they asked kinsmen to 'engage' powerful allies, just as clients secured similar services from patrons and employers. John Selden was lobbied by friends and academic

---

[4] Goldsmiths, Court Books V–Z; GL: MS 4326/7, fos. 369–70; MS 4326/9, unfol.; MS 5606/3, fos. 380–90v; MS 6122/2, unfol.; MS 2150/1, fo. 99v; MS 6440/2, fos. 557v, 580v; MS 11571/12, fo. 396.

[5] CLRO: CCA 1/3, fo. 147v; CCA 1/4, fos. 50v–1, 148–9, 220v–1; CCA 1/5, fos. 59–60, 155–59v, 260v–1; CCA 1/6, fos. 51v–2, 157v–8, 262–v; CCA 1/7, fos. 62v–3, 148v.

[6] BL: Add. 22619, fos. 31–208; Add. 22620, fos. 60–176; Norfolk RO, HMN 7/172//6.

[7] *Minutes of the Corporation of Boston III*, ed. J. Bailey (Boston, 1983), pp. 102, 204, 277; Cumbria RO, Ca/4/3, unfol.; Wilts. RO, G23/1/4, fo. 8; King's Lynn RO, KL/C7/10, fo. 206; CCA, CC/F/A.25, fos. 241–2, 314; *Borough of Leicester*, pp. 329, 433–7, 446–7; Worcs. RO, BA9360/A10, Box 3; CHC, BA/H/3/20/2, pp. 396–7; Plymouth RO: 1/132, fos. 258, 282v, 296v, 302; 1/133, fo. 2v; OUA: Wbα/10/11; WPβ/21/4, fo. 159.

associates like Gerard Langbaine and William Laud, who explicitly sought to exploit their 'credit' in order to enlist his support. Other aspiring lobbyists – including the controversial astrologer William Lilly – asked 'assured friends' in parliament to keep a watchful eye on proceedings, to 'speak with some of the committee' and to 'write two or three words . . . to some of your acquaintances'. They implored MPs to 'season' colleagues, attend hearings and 'say something' in the House, sometimes to very good effect. They also approached secretaries, clerks and civil servants, who might be asked to 'interpose' in committees, and it seems clear that even the most remote connections could prove useful.[8] However, even with powerful friends on board, lobbying involved significant expenditure on accommo- dation, travel and fees, as well as on wining and dining powerful individuals, 'thereby to possess them with the case . . . and make them for us'. Such costs also escalated very quickly when delays occurred, as lawyers were paid for doing nothing and as other bills accumulated. John Dury identified the lobbyist's greatest obstacle as the 'natural slowness' of parliament, and lobbyists repeatedly reflected that cases had been 'put off' in favour of important public business, that the key to success was 'happy timing', and that the most likely scenario involved both expense and uncertainty. A typical grumble was that of Henry Oxinden, who wrote in 1645 that the Committee of Revenue 'meets but seldom, sometimes not full, and most times when they have met, full of great causes, and the time of their sitting being but from eight in the morning till nine'.[9]

Such problems and frustrations were particularly onerous for people who lived far away from Westminster and who had few friends in parliament, not least those who struggled to overcome sequestration or compound for delinquency. Edmund Bradford discovered that dealing with the authorities at Westminster consumed 'time, patience and money', and he suffered serious delays despite the efforts of his lawyer, and even though he had exploited a vague acquaintance with the Earl of Pembroke, 'one of the chiefest lords that sits at this committee'. Thomas Knyvett also received

[8] Claydon, Verney reel 8; Alnwick, O.I.2f, unfol.; HEH, EL 7687; BL, Add. 46931B, fo. 55; Add. 32093, fo. 234v; Eg. 2646, fo. 265; Harl. 382, fo. 108; Add. 21424, fo. 260; Add. 70105, unfol.; Add. 70106, fos. 28, 84, 223; Add. 70113, unfol.; Add. 70003, fo. 114; Add. 28001, fo. 243; Add. 11047, fos. 87, 106–7; Add. 78222, fos. 118–35; Liverpool RO, 920/MOO/1520; Norfolk RO, KNY/591; Beinecke, Osborn 16809; Cornwall RO, R(S)/1/674; CUL, Buxton 102/11; SUL, Hartlib 46/5/5; Bodl. MS Selden Supra 108/118, 137; *Lives of those Eminent Antiquaries*, ed. Burman (1774), pp. 68–72, 81, 86, 101–3, 106; *Whitelocke Diary*, pp. 280, 499; Antony, BC/26/18.
[9] Chester RO: DAR/I/49, unfol.; DAR/F/3, pp. 20, 24; *Chirk Accounts*, pp. 144–7; Lancs. RO, DDM/1/ 60, 66; Lincs. RO, MON7/17/6; SUL, Hartlib, 1/2/9; Northants. RO, IC 455; HEH, EL 7557–9; *Fairfax Corr.*, ii. 180; BL: Add. 5494, fo. 277; Add. 28001, fo. 43.

promises of support from Pembroke, as well as from Lord Howard of Escrick and Lord Grey of Warke, but he quickly discovered that they had failed to 'declare at the committee', and that prolonged 'soliciting' was fruitless. He reflected that 'this tedious attending puts me to the greatest trial of my patience' and that 'I must not commit to paper my thoughts of these carriages'. Having secured advice from experienced lobbyists, meanwhile, John Langley practised 'private and daily soliciting of some members'. He 'sweetened' the clerks, to 'dispose them' towards his business, and he softened-up Howard of Escrick with 'much civil artifice', as well as with 'a swan pie'. Nevertheless, he still found the process 'extreme tedious and difficult', because MPs made empty promises, because it was difficult to time parliamentary interventions successfully and because he encountered 'stubborn adversaries'; and many others who found themselves in similar positions bemoaned having to deal with 'such slippery men' and became angry about the politicization of committees.[10]

Not the least significant problem for lobbyists was the cost of vital documentation, and the expense involved in producing 'several copies' of arguments and ordinances was particularly significant because such texts tended to be considerably longer than petitions. In 1642, at rates of 1s per sheet, copies of bills could cost anything between 14s and £1 7s to reproduce, and this meant that parliamentary breviates were unlikely to be affordable in anything other than tiny quantities.[11] This was true for 'corporate' lobbyists, like the Carpenters' Company, who once paid 20s for two copies of the statement that they gave to a parliamentary committee, just as it was true for the Tylers and Bricklayers, whose expenses in the early 1650s included 11s for nine breviates relating to their business at Westminster. In 1649 the corporation of Trinity House spent £2 on 'several copies' of a bill that they wanted to submit, which involved 100 sheets of paper, and they then shelled out £1 10s 1d on 'several copies' and breviates of the charter that they hoped to obtain, which involved 250 sheets. And in 1659 the University of Oxford spent £2 on a mere four copies of their reasons against the creation of a university at Durham.[12] Similar expenditure can also be observed in the accounts of provincial boroughs and private citizens, for whom the financial problems associated with lobbying were particularly acute. Remaining up to

---

[10] NLW, MS 9064 E1681; Cornwall RO, AD1239/1; Norfolk RO, JER/315, 323, 327; *Knyvett*, pp. 155, 159, 161–3; Staffs. RO, D868/5/19, 21–3, 25–7, 30–4, 39; HEH, HA 14355; Nott. UL, Ga12768; Notts. RO, DD2B/2/20–22; Herts. RO, D/Elw/Z22/7.

[11] TNA, SP 28/268, fos. 481–v; *Burton Diary*, i. 89; PA: MP 26 Aug. 1641, 7 Feb. 1642.

[12] GL: MS 4326/7, fos. 369, 371; MS 4326/9, unfol.; MS 3054/2, unfol.; MS 30032/1, unfol.; OUA, WPβ/21/4, fo. 159.

date with committee proceedings required regular supplies of information –
in terms of what had happened, what was likely to happen and who was in
charge – and in cases where such information was not available in print
individuals sometimes paid up to 5s for scribal committee lists, which could
then be marked, annotated and used to lobby specific MPs.[13] More problematic still were texts that were submitted to committee members, which
were aimed at 'furthering of the business' and at making MPs 'better
informed'. When John Dury lobbied on behalf of a scheme devised by
Benjamin Worsley in 1649, he solicited clerks, civil servants and MPs, and
also recognized that 'something must be given in writing' by way of a
'memorial'. Similar memorials included a text that offered 'Reasons' for
passing an ordinance regarding a new breach-loading gun, which was
presented to the MP John Moore by its inventor, Captain Cannon.
Another was called 'Seasonable observations', which advocated the adoption of Dutch banking practices, and which was presented to Cromwell by
Samuel Lambe.[14] At rates of around 2s per sheet, however, such texts did not
come cheap, and the cost of producing even a few copies could run to
anything between a few shillings and a few pounds.[15]

Parliamentary lobbying thus involved 'time and charge', and both fair
and foul means were used to overcome such problems. Some resorted to
intimidation, by bringing 'a rude company' to committee hearings 'in a
tumultuous manner', and Marchamont Nedham accused the Presbyterian
minister James Cranford of attending one committee with 'a company of
starched faces', who proceeded to 'hum' and 'hiss' in order to intimidate
MPs.[16] More commonly, lobbyists employed the services of professional
agents. These were used by the corporations at Berwick and Newcastle to
'agitate the town's occasions', and to 'solicit Parliament men', and they
could be armed with breviates and could act as 'daily remembrancers at
the Parliament door'. The 'adventurers' for fen drainage schemes not only
identified which MPs to target, and then wined and dined them

[13] ERO, Q/Sba 7/1–5; HEH, EL7609, 7692–7710, 7875–7; Lincs. RO: MON7/17/6; MM10/1; Chester
RO: DAR/F/3, pp. 15–17; DAR/D/98; Bodl. MS Walker.c.4, fos. 294–8; MS Eng.Misc.e.118, fo. 87;
MS Tanner 65, fos. 212–13v; Longleat: Whitelocke 8, fo. 205; Whitelocke Parcel 1/17; BL: Add. 11044,
fos. 185–6; Add. 71534, fo. 92; Cornwall RO, V/EC/3/23, 25; CKS, U269/O294; Leics. RO, 26/D/53/
1885.

[14] Bodl. MS Tanner 456, fos. 3, 5; SUL, Hartlib 1/2/9–14, 4/1/24, 61/8–9; PA: MP 7 June 1641, 11 June
1641; 55 June 1641; HEH, EL7539; FSL, X.d.443/2; Lancs. RO, DDHU53/29; BL, Add. 26785, fos.
170–82; Liverpool UL, MS 23/41; SHL, MS 201.

[15] Longleat: Thynne 81, fos. 358–61, 408–9; Thynne 64, fos. 305–v; TNA, SP 24/30; HEH, HAF Box 13/
34; HAF Box 15/22; OUA, Wbα/10/11.

[16] Norfolk RO, JER/325; *Diurnall*, 504.319, pp. 2688, 2722; *Politicus*, 361.004, p. 50.

assiduously, but also employed agents whose task was to lobby 'friends in the House' and to ensure that they were 'better informed'. The agents for the clothworkers gathered signatures for petitions, introduced legislation into parliament, and secured specific MPs as 'friends', and they boasted about their 'vigilant attendance' and 'constant endeavours', and about the time they spent 'at the House of Commons door'.[17] Very occasionally such agents also served private citizens. Jonathan Rashleigh sought to locate 'a little red-bearded man that sold books between the Devil tavern door and Temple Bar', because he was known to have expertise relating to the committee at Haberdashers' Hall. More obviously, Adam Baynes provided invaluable services for individual soldiers who lacked the opportunity to attend parliament in order to pursue their financial claims against the state. He attended committee hearings on their behalf, presented their papers and procured official orders.[18]

Unfortunately, this new breed of agents did not always make effective lobbyists, and they also came to be regarded with a degree of suspicion. Baynes had only limited success on behalf of the fen drainers, and some other agents were more or less mercenary and only more or less assiduous. Berwick certainly balked at the fee demanded by Basil Sprigge, whose salary was reduced from £20 to £10, and whose successor received only £8, while Nathaniel Bedle, the agent for the clothiers, was accused of working for 'his own praise, and for your purses'. Bedle's case is striking, however, for highlighting how the print media offered a rather different solution to the challenges faced by lobbyists. On this occasion critics suggested that he had deployed pamphlets in a 'blind' and 'frivolous' manner, but they did not question the intrinsic utility of such material. Indeed, the clothiers' case reveals how the link between print and lobbying, which had first been evident in the 1620s, became firmly established during the 1640s, to the extent that printed breviates were used by humble individuals as well as powerful corporations, and in such profusion that it becomes possible to assess both the sophistication and the dynamic of the lobbyist's art.[19]

---

[17] TWAS, MD/NC/2/1, p. 10; Berwick RO: B1/10, fos. 108v, 136v, 146v–7, 150v, 155, 156, 184v; B1/11, fos. 20v–21, 56v, 84, 100v; B9/1, fo. 45v; King's Lynn RO, KL/C7/10, fo. 494; BL, Add. 22620, fos. 113, 117, 131, 154; Arundel, A90, p. 74; Cambs. RO, R.59.31/9/5, fos. 163v, 165; BL, Add. 21422, fos. 40, 80, 106, 125, 146; Add. 21426, fo. 168; *Generall Clothiers* (1647, T1395A), sigs. A2–3; Talbott, *Briefe Answer* (1647, T127bA), p. 4; *Burton Diary*, i. 115–17, 174–5, 221.

[18] Cornwall RO, R(S)/1/33, 673; BL: Add. 21417, fos. 108v, 113, 120, 128, 204, 213, 217; Add. 21419, fos. 125, 139; Add. 21420, fos. 64, 230; Add. 21421, fos. 122, 196; Add. 21422, fo. 93.

[19] BL: Add. 21422, fos. 40, 80, 106, 125; Add. 21426, fo. 168; Add. 21423, fo. 193; Berwick RO, B1/10, fos. 155–6, 164v, 170v; B1/11, fo. 21; B9/1, fo. 46; *Generall Clothiers*, sigs. A2v–3; Talbott, *Briefe Answer*, p. 3.

ii Detecting print lobbying

The rationale for lobbying with printed texts is fairly clear, in terms of the possibility for saving both time and money. Printed texts could be produced and distributed at speed, which meant that it was easier and cheaper to find sponsors and to 'season' them with information and arguments. However, this does not mean that it is a phenomenon that can be observed easily, and assessing the impact of print on the lobbying process is necessarily perilous. This is partly clear from the business of acquiring 'intelligence', and although many contemporaries valued printed sources that provided the kind of material needed for effective participation – like committee lists – others were willing to pay a premium for privileged information. In 1652, for example, Viscount Conway paid £20 to see a draft of the Act of Oblivion, even though he knew that the information would soon be published.[20] Much more difficult, however, is the process of *identifying* texts that involved the *appropriation* of print as part of the lobbying process. The aim of this section, therefore, is to demonstrate that it was not just petitions that could be circulated discretely among MPs, and that such practices can also be observed in relation to a wealth of other material, through close scrutiny of textual, paratextual and contextual evidence.

First, the process of distinguishing between different genres of text that were associated with the parliamentary process involves non-petition material that was submitted to MPs. This was highlighted by the Presbyterian minister, Thomas Edwards, who complained not just about the appearance in print of 'abominable errors', and about the fact that dangerous books were 'sold up and down . . . and dispersed in all places', but also about works that were 'given into the hands of Parliament men . . . at the Parliament doors'.[21] Many of the books to which Edwards referred, however, were not exclusively available to MPs, and a great many of the texts that were distributed in this way were also available much more widely. These include numerous works that were commercially available, like *Jus Divinum* by the London Provincial Assembly (1654) and the *True Representation* of the Edinburgh ministers (1657), as well as more radical pamphlets by Independents and Socinians, which were known to have been given 'to diverse members . . . as they went into the House'. They may also include works by the royalist divine, Lawrence Womock, who commented to

---

[20] Nott. UL, Ga/12768/20; Cambs. RO, R.59.31/9/6, fo. 112; BL, Add. 21427, fo. 145; HEH, HA 14352.
[21] Edwards, *Gangraena*, i. 149.

friends that the presentation of published books to MPs might prevent allegations that he was fuelling acrimonious religious debates.[22] And they certainly include a number of occasions when the targeting of MPs by political and religious dissidents was accompanied by the indiscriminate scattering of books and pamphlets. One such tract was Mary Pope's *Treatise of Magistracy*, which was 'looked upon . . . as a malignant piece'.[23] In other words, texts that were distributed to MPs cannot straightforwardly be regarded as lobby documents.

Secondly, a great many pamphlets that were addressed to parliament were used to do something other than contribute to deliberations in a discrete fashion. Very often, therefore, they were published commercially, and represented public addresses on issues that deserved to be considered, or else involved texts that were printed *after* they had been presented formally and scribally. These included Leonard Lee's *Remonstrance* regarding the 'miseries of the poore', Edmund Felton's *Proposals* regarding trade and *Certain Assayes* that were 'propounded' to a committee for regulating the law, as well as a work called *The Poor Mans Friend*, which contained the text of a proposed ordinance.[24] Something similar can be demonstrated with an inveterate lobbyist like Thomas Violet, a portion of whose manuscript position papers later appeared in commercial pamphlets in the early 1650s, sometimes with official approval. This can be explained in part by the government's desire to draw attention to a former royalist who was prepared to embrace the Republic, although one such pamphlet – *Mysteries and Secrets of Trade* – was printed officially and then given to MPs, in what amounted to a lobbying campaign undertaken by the Council of State.[25] For Violet, on the other hand, such texts could be used for self-promotion, not least because they blended policy proposals with autobiographical details, and such material was later recycled when his relationship with the government became strained, to defend his reputation, draw attention

---

[22] *Weekly Account*, 671.452, Sig. Zzz4v; BL, Add. 4159, fo. 113; *Registers of the Consultations*, ed. W. Stephens (2 vols, SRS, 1921–30), i. 368, ii. 23, 30–34; *CSPD 1640–1*, p. 40; TNA, SP 16/467, fo. 16; *CJ*, vii. 405; *Proceedings*, 599.274, p. 4335; *Burton Diary*, iii. 78; *CCSP*, iv. 147; Durham UL, VMP I, pp. 85–7.

[23] *CJ*, iv. 420–1; v. 416; *Occurrences*, 465.4005, sig. E4v; 465.5053, p. 369; 465.5036, p. 247; Barber, *Answer* (1648, B691); Pope, *Heare* (1648, H1306), p. 38; *Heads*, 180.01, p. 3.

[24] *Sundry* (1646, S38); Lee, *Remonstrance* (1644, L844); Felton, *Proposals* (1653, F663); *Assayes* (1652, D85B); *Poor Mans* (1649, B6231A).

[25] *CSPD 1650*, pp. 178–82, 292, 431, 454–5, 473, 480; *CSPD 1651*, pp. 231–4, 460–2; *CSPD 1651–2*, pp. 23–5, 156, 441; *CSPD 1652–3*, pp. 15, 23, 47, 75, 233, 241, 398; *CSPD 1653–4*, pp. 123, 152, 162, 178, 199; *Politicus*, 361.029, p. 479; *True Discovery* (1650, V589); *Advancement* (1651, V578), sig. A2, pp. 127–56; *Mysteries* (1653, V583); *True Narrative* (1653, V593); *CSPD 1650*, p. 281.

to good service and seek employment.[26] In other words, many printed pamphlets that *contained* the texts of lobbying documents were not actually *used* to lobby parliament, and Violet is not the only contemporary figure for whom it is hard to disentangle printed lobbying from activity that was designed to find supporters and sponsors in a more public fashion. The engineering entrepreneur, Thomas Bushell, submitted proposals to MPs – especially those from mining areas – but also used print to raise his public profile in the hope of attracting clients and investors. The same was also true of Peter Chamberlen, whose ideas about public health and midwifery were aimed at his critics as much as at MPs, and whose many printed texts sought to attract public subscribers rather than merely to lobby parliament.[27]

Such complexities make the identification of genuine lobby documents a tricky business, but it is nevertheless possible to recover a wealth of printed material that was circulated in a discrete fashion, with the aim of influencing policy decisions. As with printed petitions, these 'pure' lobby documents tend to involve stripped-down texts that lacked title pages, ornamentation and imprints, and typical examples include a sixteen-page quarto entitled *The East-India Trade* (1641), and a single sheet containing *Some Proposals* by a 'well-wisher' to parliament (1653).[28] Of course, since such characteristics were often shared by surreptitious and scandalous pamphlets, it is also necessary to look beyond the physical appearance of specific texts, and to employ archival, textual and contextual evidence. This might mean texts – some of which are unique and previously unknown – that survive among the papers of clerks and MPs, or those that contain internal evidence of discrete circulation, like the tract on press regulation called *Scintilla* (1641). It might also mean texts that were *reported* to have been used as lobby documents, as with a subsequent contribution to the same debate called the *Second Beacon Fired* (1654), or those where annotations identify the MPs and committee chairmen to whom they were presented. These include a copy of Carew Raleigh's *Brief Relation*, which was 'presented' to Lord President Bradshaw in March 1649.[29] Very often, however, the identification of lobby documents relies entirely upon archival evidence. It is only from the correspondence of Peter Smart, therefore, that lobbying in 1648

---

[26] *Proposals* (1656, V585); *True Narrative* (1659, V594).

[27] For Bushell: SUL, Hartlib 28/1/19; 29/5/1/26, 30; BL, Add. 6677, fo. 46; DRO, D258/7/20/11; *Just and True* (1642, B6246); *Case* (1649, B6242); *Table* (1656, B6248A); *Abridgment* (1659, B304). For Chamberlen: *Voice* (1647, C1910); *Paper* (1648, C1900); *Vindication* (1648, C1909); *Humble Petition* (1649, C1908); *Publique Bathes* (1648, P4149A); SUL, Hartlib 53/18: *Atonement* (1659); *Declaration* (1659, C1894), p. 7; *Scourge* (1659, C1903).

[28] *East-India* (1641, E102); *Some Proposals* (1653, J22).

[29] Longleat, Whitelocke Parcel 7/80: *Certain Merchants*; *Scintilla* (1641, S4818B); *Second* (1654,

can be shown to have involved the use of printed papers, none of which now survive. And it is only by consulting the papers of the Commissioners for New England that it becomes clear that their printed reports of missionary work were circulated to Cromwell's councillors in 1655. Likewise, evidence about a 'printed discourse' that was submitted to MPs like John Pym only survives within the papers of the man responsible, Samuel Hartlib.[30]

Uncovering printed lobbying thus requires a multi-dimensional approach to pamphlets and broadsides, but what emerges very clearly is how frequently texts were intended for discrete distribution in order to inform the discussions of policy-makers. Such practices were not in any way confined to Westminster. There is evidence of 'printed tickets' being circulated among London's carpenters to demand new elections within their company, and printing was also used to lobby the civic authorities in London and the General Council of the army, as well as judges and juries. In 1652, therefore, Robert Norwood's *Brief Discourse* was explicitly directed towards members of the Upper Bench who were sitting in judgment on his case.[31] Printed sheets were also submitted to the authorities at Oxford University, in order to lobby the Chancellors Court and seek academic preferment. George Dalgarno used pamphlets to draw attention to his scheme for a universal language, while in 1658 the Savilian professor of mathematics, John Wallis, controversially used printed 'tickets' to lobby dons in the hope of being elected as university archivist. He then covered his tracks by 'leaving none to be publicly sold or seen', and by leaving 'not so much as . . . one foul proof at the printing house', only to have his activities exposed by Henry Stubbe.[32] However, the overwhelming bulk of surviving evidence indicates that lobbyists focused their attention on parliament, and although specific texts can rarely be dated with confidence or contextualized with certainty, it is nevertheless possible to piece together particular campaigns. One very good example involves the lobbying orchestrated by the Cinque Ports in the early 1640s.

The central aim of the Cinque Ports was to secure exemption from the subsidy bill, and they not only prompted MPs to make speeches in the Commons, but also despatched the town clerk of Sandwich, Robert Jager,

---

S4818BA); *Proceedings*, 599.263, p. 4172; 599.267, p. 4230; *We doubt* (1649, BL, E568/11); *John Elliot* (1650, E548D); *Books and Readers in Early Modern Britain III* (Maggs catalogue 1324, 2002), pp. 170–73.

[30] Durham Cathedral, Hunter 11/58; *LJ*, x. 22; GL, MS 7952, unfol.; SUL, Hartlib 7/27/29.

[31] GL, MS 4329/5, fos. 9–v; *Motives* (1647, M2942); SUL, Hartlib 47/20/1/1–8; *President* (1652, O139aA); *Weekly Intelligencer*, 689.01, p. 2; BL, Add. 69919, fo. 100; *Brief Discourse* (1652, N1380).

[32] *William Powell* (1656, P3098A); Dalgarno, *Possibilitie* (1658, D129C); SUL, Hartlib 49/1/3; BL, Add. 4377, fos. 139–57; Wallis, *Reasons* (1657, W601); Stubbe, *Savilian* (1658, S6065), p. 6.

to assist them at Westminster, at a cost of over £12. Jager oversaw attempts
to lobby MPs by means of scribal 'briefs', which were circulating by
Christmas 1640, but this fairly restrained campaign proved to be unsuccessful, and in late February 1641 Jager moaned about being 'tied every day
to attend at Westminster', waiting for the matter to be discussed. It was this
combination of frustration and mounting costs that prompted a new tactic,
and in early March Jager prepared 'an abstract' of their breviates and 'put it
forth in print', so that 'every member of the House may have one'. This was
the four-page pamphlet entitled *The Services of the Cinque Ports*, a discrete
lobby document containing their petition and their reasons for being
granted special treatment, which Jager conceived would 'be a good cause
to free the ports from this great subsidy'.[33] In this instance, Jager's confidence was misplaced, but the way in which the ports responded to their
failed intervention in parliamentary affairs is highly instructive. This is
because they recognized that printed breviates could be circulated as and
when required over protracted periods, and when another opportunity was
spotted to lobby MPs in February 1642, the pamphlets were quickly
recycled and dispersed once again by local MPs. Moreover, when parliament discussed the issue of free trade in 1642, in response to a petition from
the Merchant Adventurers, the ports made another attempt to make their
views heard before any decision was made, and thus lobbied the relevant
committee not just by wining and dining its members, but also by producing another printed breviate. This four-page pamphlet – which survives
only among the state papers and the records of the Cinque Ports – was
explicitly described as a 'breviate, which they humbly offer to the honourable knights and burgesses of the House of Commons of Parliament
concerning their grievances'.[34]

It is unclear whether the Cinque Ports continued to use printed texts
during subsequent parliamentary campaigns. They certainly continued to
spend a great deal of money on lobbying, and such 'solicitation' – which
involved a daily fee of 6s 8d, gifts for MPs, and the preparation of petitions
and breviates – explicitly mentioned attempts to 'prepare' MPs and 'gain
their favour'. They clearly recognized the need to ensure that 'when the
business was reported . . . the ports might be heard before anything [is] done

---

[33] EKRO: Do/AAm2, fo. 164v; Sa/Fat39, p. 32; Sa/AC7, fos. 383v, 384v–86v, 389v; H1209, fo. 249v; Sa/
C1, pp. 64–9; Sa/C4; BL: Stowe 744, fos. 2–v; Add. 44846, fo. 6v; *Services* (1641, S2646sA).
[34] BL: Add. 44846, fos. 5v, 8, 11; Add. 29623, fo. 133; EKRO: Sa/C1, pp. 82–7; Sa/C4/1, 3; H1257, unfol ;
Do/FCa/5, fos. 329–30; TNA: SP 16/489, fos. 196–7v: *Barons of the Cinque Ports* (1642); SP 16/539, fos.
154–55v; EKRO, CP/Z13.

to their prejudice'.[35] Moreover, their activity had already demonstrated that print was regarded as a valuable tool not just for the promotion of ideas and personalities in the public domain, but also for targeted and discrete lobbying of MPs during policy discussions. Print was perceived to offer the chance of winning friends and securing influence, and of doing so in ways that overcame the problems involved in lobbying parliament. As such, it becomes possible to explore the various ways in which such texts were deployed.

iii Tactics for lobbying with print

Printed lobbying involved contributing to the deliberative process within parliament and its committees, and the aim of this section is to recover the range of participatory tactics involved. The most obvious way of character-izing lobby documents is as *remembrancers* or *memorials*, which could be produced both proactively and reactively, and which offered brief guides to ideas, proposals and arguments, so that MPs could prepare for debates and hearings. They thus fulfilled different roles from petitions, and were usually much more substantial, and when properly contextualized it becomes clear that they served a variety of purposes. Indeed, it will even be possible to identify a range of subtly different genres, each of which related to different kinds of lobbying and different phases of the political process.

Most obviously, lobbying was undertaken *proactively*, in order to follow up, supplement and support petitions. Such texts can be difficult to spot, however, because their titles are often misleading, because they sometimes lack titles altogether and because they have escaped the notice of bibliogra-phers. Some lobby documents resembled petitions, since they opened with, and were named after, earlier texts that sought to initiate parliamentary business. In 1644, for example, a pamphlet called the *Humble Petition of Commissary Lyonell Copley* contained not just his initial complaint but also a subsequent text in which he explained his grievance to the MPs who were considering the case.[36] Other lobby documents lacked explicit titles or the names of those who produced them, as well as obvious evidence that they were intended for circulation within Westminster. These include a broad-side about the printing of Croke's law reports, a printed genealogy regarding

---

[35] EKRO: H1257, unfol.; NR/FVc/2; CP/Bp/85; Do/AAmI, fo. 247; H1211, pp. 12, 31; CP/Bp/123, pp. 1–13; BL, Add. 29623, fo. 155v.

[36] *Lyonell Copley* (1644, C6085A), pp. 1, 2, 3–7; TNA, SP 28/255, unfol.; Bodl. MS Tanner 61, fo. 98–101; BL, Add. 31116, pp. 363, 416.

a peerage dispute, and a set of detailed financial accounts from 1641, all of which seem to relate to parliamentary business. Others contained the texts of parliamentary orders and reports, and were evidently intended to refresh the memories of MPs and peers, not least during the tussle for control of the Post Office in 1642.[37] Most commonly, however, lobby documents took the form of *The Case* of an individual lobbyist, or *The State of the Case* that was being pursued, and involved a genre that can be traced back to the legal and parliamentary culture of the 1620s, and that can often only be observed through official archives and private papers.[38] Some were produced collectively, by parishioners in Covent Garden, by citizens in Southwark and by those whose interests were bound up with fen drainage schemes, and very occasionally it is possible to uncover evidence about their print runs, costs and distribution.[39] Very frequently, however, they were also produced by individuals whose business awaited resolution, including people who lacked wealth and privilege and who came from outside the nobility and greater gentry. These included the pamphleteer Henry Parker, whose *Memoriall* was presented to a committee in May 1647, but they also included any number of less well-connected individuals, such as the impoverished London bricklayer, Thomas Elwood. A fairly notable case involves a Worcestershire clothier called Clement Writer, whose *Sad Case* of 1653 reprinted earlier petitions alongside undelivered parliamentary reports, and was addressed to a Commons committee. This evidently did him little good, but a similar text was produced a little later and secured the attention of Cromwell's councillors, and in both cases Writer not only complained about the tendency to ignore his petitions, but also provided information with which to influence deliberations.[40]

These were not the only kind of lobby documents to be printed in significant quantities, however, and others were used in a *reactive* and much more obviously defensive fashion. This tended to involve texts of a somewhat different kind, which contained *Reasons* or *Considerations* relating to individuals who faced threats to their interests, not least from other

---

[37] *About* (1657, A99); *Godfrey* (1647, G927A); PA, MP 14 July 1647; Beinecke, Osborn fb.157/116; PA, MP 21 Jan. 1641, 4 Feb. 1648: *Die Jovis*; Bodl. MS Carte 74, fo. 140: *Ellis Reports*.

[38] BL, Harl. 7607, fos. 415v-6; Harl. 7614, fo. 119; Add. 70108, unfol.; Add. 70109, unfol.; *CSPD 1619–23*, p. 323; TNA, SP 14/124, fos. 136v–7; Lincs. RO, MON7/1726; PA, MP 5 May 1648.

[39] *Covent* (C944); Bodl. MS Rawl.A.33, p. 636; *Southwark* (1645, C1023a); TNA, SP 46/96, fo. 51: *Axholm*; *King* (1641, K551d); *Epworth* (1651, L2086); BL, Add. 21427, fos. 139v–40: *Fenns* (1652); *Whereas* (1650, K472); *Breviate* (1655, B4412); *State* (1650?, S5305A); Cambs. RO: R.59.31/9/1, fos. 26, 30, 31; R.59.31/19A, pp. 7, 11; R.59.31/9/6, fo. 161; *Rioters* (1655, K467).

[40] FSL, X.d.483/203; TNA, SP 18/67, fo. 146; SP 18/95, fo. 6; *CSPD 1655*, p. 63; Bodl. MS Carte 74, fo. 476; Parker, *Memoriall* (1647, M1689); *Elwood* (1659, E656); TNA, SP 18/129, fos. 161–7v.

petitioners, as well as to issues that had been addressed by other lobbyists. This was another genre that first emerged in the early Stuart period, and one that became increasingly familiar thereafter, and that was used by individuals from all walks of life. Sometimes this meant public figures like the MP John Hutchinson, who responded to allegations about financial impropriety, or powerful institutions like the University of Oxford. The latter, faced with printed petitioning by local citizens who challenged their authority, felt compelled to respond in 1649 by producing a substantial printed lobby document. They produced 200 copies, at a cost of £3 12s 6d (a rate of 0.5d per sheet), the bulk of which were given to the vice chancellor and Gerard Langbaine, 'to be bestowed abroad to our counsel and friends', not least on an expensive trip to Westminster.[41] In some cases, therefore, reactive lobbying was undertaken by prominent individuals and powerful organizations, as well as by people who had become adept at exploiting the print medium. George Wither produced *Reasons* against an ordinance that would have hampered his chance of recouping the financial losses he had incurred in the parliamentarian cause, while Thomas Violet submitted a text to the Committee of Trade that defended the 'poor women spinners of gold and silver thread'. On other occasions, however, similar texts were also deployed by obscure individuals from across the country, whose lobbying related to arcane local issues like the preservation of lighthouses at Orfordness, the sale of bishops lands in Durham or the leasing of a room to a group of London Baptists.[42] Such texts sometimes made explicit reference to the fact that they were intended to supplement other printed documents, which had been 'given in to several members of the House', and some of them even bear evidence of having been perused and annotated by MPs.[43]

The attraction of both proactive and reactive lobby documents lay in their *flexibility*, and their capacity to be used in more than one situation. They could be deployed to inform and influence committee members as they deliberated, to lobby MPs ahead of committee reports and to draw attention to cases that had been blocked or delayed, and it even seems clear that specific texts could be deployed repeatedly. However, individual lobbyists can also be shown to have devised more specialized variations on these two genres, which served precise purposes at different stages of the

[41] *Reasons* (1621, STC 23918.5); BL, Harl. 7608, fos. 383–7, 421; TNA, SP 46/64, fos. 196–200; *Hutchinson* (1649, S5312); *Answer* (1649, L363); OUA: WPβ/21/4, fos. 140, 145v; NEP/Supra/Reg.T, pp. 47, 73, 78; Wbα/10/11.
[42] *Wither* (1643, R544A); *Poor Women* (1650, T1435); Bodl. MS Carte 74, fo. 443: *Light-houses*; *Durham* (1654, R564); *Justification* (1642, R545).
[43] *Scotland* (1655, R546); Harvard Law Library: *Fines* (1650, R512F).

parliamentary process. Thomas Shadwell's *Case* made clear that his business had already been taken up by a committee, while the *True State* of Sir Robert Mansell's business explicitly asked readers for help when committee hearings were held. With the *Brief* of Walter Elford's complaint, on the other hand, it was clear that the matter was about to be 'reported to the Parliament', and many other texts that were circulated to 'every individual member' were likewise produced in anticipation of reports that were due to be delivered to one or other House.[44] In 1650, meanwhile, former tenants of the Dean and Chapter of Durham produced a printed *Case* because their business had been considered by MPs but then buried, and ultimately a specialist genre of lobbying text was devised for the purpose of *reviving* cases and *reminding* MPs about their back-story. These retraced the steps of specific lobbying campaigns, some of which had been instigated many years earlier, and they tended to involve the reproduction of a significant corpus of reports, orders and breviates, in order to provide readers with potted histories of particular cases. Sometimes, of course, it is tempting to suggest that such texts were intended for an audience wider than that of MPs, especially when they related to controversial characters that were desperate to repair their reputations, like Sir Sackvile Crow, Sir Thomas Bendish and Jerome Alexander. Nevertheless, most were submitted discretely at the start of new parliamentary sessions, as men like Charles Hotham, William Ball and Charles Webb attempted to kick-start proceedings that had stalled following earlier dissolutions. A particularly striking example, by William Beech, complained about the neglect of his business, and was designed so that the title of each copy left a blank space, into which could be inserted the name of whichever MP Beech gave a copy, in the hope that they would 'report it to the Parliament'.[45]

This tendency for individual lobbyists to use printed texts in different ways, and to employ different kinds of texts for specialist tasks, reflected awareness that participation in parliamentary affairs might be a protracted and multi-stage process. Between 1641 and 1646, for example, the campaign for financial relief by Sir Thomas Dawes's creditors involved both a *True State* and a copy of *Mr Grenes Report*, even though it was recognized that 'the great affairs of the kingdom cannot admit of time for the report to be

---

[44] PA, MP 22 Nov. 1648: *Shadwell* (1648); *Glasse* (1641, M513A); *Elford's* (1649, E498A); *Axholm* (1653, B4638).

[45] *Auncient Tenants* (1650, C1012); *Harby* (1650, H680); *Crow's Case* (1648–1652, S3886A-7); BL, 190. g.13/103: *Brief Narrative* (1650); *Bendysh* (1650, B1867A); *Breviate* (1644, B4410); *Harby* (1658, H681); *Certaine Papers* (1649, C1720); *Hotham* (1653], H2899); Ball, *Narrative* (1656, B592); Webb, *Narrative* (1656, W1197); Beech, *Discovery* (1645?, B1679A).

made'. In the early 1650s, meanwhile, interloping merchants who lobbied against the Muscovy Company produced different texts to outline their 'case' and the 'heads' of their arguments, and in doing so they printed evidence from committee meetings and parliamentary reports, and recycled old breviates for 'every member' of the Commons. Likewise, when the Soapmakers agitated against the excise in 1650, the involvement of John Lilburne ensured that their proposals, arguments and counter-arguments were printed in a series of different pamphlets, which were either destined for the members of specific committees or else despatched to 'every individual member of Parliament ... against they come to pass their final determinations'.[46] And this variety is sometimes revealed during successive phases of particular campaigns. In July 1641, therefore, MPs were presented with a *Petition and Remonstrance* concerning the leather trade, and when this was referred to a committee, the petitioners circulated among its members a second short text containing *Certain Reasons why Tanned Leather Ought Not to be Bought and Sold*.[47]

The most striking example of this multiplication of lobbying texts, however, involves the 'poor almsmen of East Ham', many of whose texts only survive in the parliamentary archive. Their case centred on an almshouse that had been founded by Giles Bream, and on claims made by his trustees regarding mismanagement of the endowment, and like so many grievances it came to the attention of MPs after years in the law courts, and through a printed petition that was submitted in the opening months of the Long Parliament. This petition requested an official enquiry, but having been taken into consideration, the matter soon became lost in the parliamentary system, which prompted the trustees to experiment with new texts and new tactics. In October 1643 they produced not just a new petition for the Lords, but also an eight-page pamphlet for the committee that was appointed to consider their case. In other words, having used petitions to make themselves heard, the trustees then used a lobby document to provide a more substantial statement, and this set their petitions alongside a 'humble remonstrance' and the 'reasons and opinions' of several lawyers. To this they then added another short *Breviate* of their case, as well as a single-sheet account of *Lord Bramstones Report* from 1641. Indeed, when the Commons scheduled a hearing for 18 November 1643, the trustees prepared yet another

---

[46] *True State* (1645, T3104a); *Mr Grenes* (1646, E1662aA), pp. 1, 2, 6; PA, MP 1 Aug. 1646; Longleat, Whitelocke Parcel 7/81: *Proceedings* (1651); TNA, SP 18/65, fo. 139: *Every Member* (1654); SP 18/65, fos. 150–1: *Heads* (1654); *Soap-Makers* (1650, S4399); *Excise* (1650, T1742); *To Every* (1650, L2185); *Every Particular* (1650, T1340bA).

[47] Durham UL, MSP 30, fo. 72; *CJ*, ii. 224; *Petition* (1641, H3439); *Certain* (1641, W48).

printed sheet to outline their desired decision, and then presented a copy to the clerk with a handwritten endorsement, asking him to 'look upon these particulars' when preparing his parliamentary order.[48] As was so often the case, however, this hearing was delayed by more pressing business (the small matter of Archbishop Laud's trial), but rather than giving up hope, the trustees produced another petition and secured another hearing (9 December), for which they prepared by deploying yet more printed lobby documents. Indeed, similar lobbying continued even after peers dismissed the case in August 1644, in what was an increasingly desperate attempt to revive the business. This involved not just a summary of a fourteen-year campaign, but also a pitiful account of almsmen that had 'starved' along the way, and of others who were 'like to starve this winter'. One of these texts – a four-page history of the case from December 1644 – reminded peers that the full story was 'at large in print', and involved both flattery and frustration. The trustees exclaimed that 'no age' could demonstrate a case that was so 'honest, just and lawful', that had been 'so many years heard, read, debated, and approved', and that had been 'dismissed ... without relief', but although their incessant lobbying secured one final hearing, the case was finally buried in April 1646.[49]

This protracted and rather sad story illustrates perfectly the ways in which print could be appropriated to participate in parliament. It highlights the many forms that printed lobby documents took, the multiple uses to which they could be put and the potential for print to become a tool for ordinary citizens. It reveals, in other words, how print facilitated lobbying by those who had exhausted other legal and political channels, and who sought to do more than merely engage in petitioning. Nevertheless, even this startling demonstration of the exploitation of print represents only part of the story of the development of lobbying, and attention now needs to turn to different goals and different kinds of text.

iv Lobbying, projecting and legislation

Lobbying did not just involve the resolution of personal grievances and local problems, but also saw pressure being placed on parliament in relation to issues that had broader significance, and in the hope of influencing the

---

[48] *LJ*, vi. 271; PA, MP 3 Mar. 1641, 24 Oct. 1643: *Almesmen* (1643) and *Breviate* (1643); 2 Aug. 1641: *Bramstones* (1643); 18 Nov. 1643: *For our Particular* (1643).

[49] *LJ*, vi. 306, 333–5, 665–6; PA, MP 18 Nov. 1643, 19 Aug. 1644; 28 Oct. 1644: *Humble Certificate* (1643), p. 3; *Poore Alms-men* (1644, T1662); and *Poore almesmen* (1644?); PA, MP 8 Apr. 1646; *LJ*, viii. 259.

legislative process. Here, too, print was used as a flexible tool for submitting proposals, and here, too, interventions by ordinary citizens could be made in a discrete rather than a public fashion. This reflected the wisdom of an accomplished campaigner like Samuel Hartlib, who recommended that the lobbyist should undertake such projecting 'politickly', in such a way as to make councillors and grandees 'his conduit pipe, and himself the fountain'. The importance of doing so 'in secret' was so that MPs 'may have the sole credit and glory of the design in public', and Hartlib recognized that the 'best designs' would not otherwise be 'favoured effectually by statesmen, who laugh and slight rather than promote when anything of consequence is proposed nakedly to the public view'.[50] What Hartlib knew, and what can occasionally be documented, is that discrete lobbying could be more effective than public campaigning.

In some cases printed projecting involved little more than brief commentaries submitted alongside petitions, but much more interesting are those texts that contained detailed proposals, which began to emerge in the 1620s, and which subsequently involved fairly substantial pamphlets, including Hartlib's own *Memoriall*. The latter represented not just a petition, which encouraged his 'friends . . . in the Houses' to honour earlier promises to provide him with financial assistance, but also contained a detailed proposal for an 'agency' for the advancement of universal learning'.[51] On this occasion, MPs were presented with a free-standing lobby document, but other discretely circulated texts merely summarized proposals that could be found in more substantial works, to which readers were explicitly referred. This tactic was employed by Samuel Chidley in the 1650s, in relation to his ideas about church reform and the abolition of the death penalty, and by Peter Chamberlen in pursuit of his scheme to provide work for the poor in 1649. On this occasion Chamberlen not only relied on his 'chief agent' in the Commons, Sir James Harington, and on a brief lobby document called *Plus Ultra to the Parliament*, but also recommended that the latter should be read in tandem with a more substantial published work, *The Poore Mans Advocate*.[52]

With projecting, as with other forms of lobbying, printed texts could be devised for a series of different tasks and deployed in different ways. In many cases the aim was to secure the consideration of proposals by a parliamentary

[50] *Poor mans* (1649, B6231A); SUL, Hartlib 57/4/11/1–14; 28/1/16–17.
[51] *Distressed* (1641, I106); BL: Sloane 1467, fos. 37–40v; Harl. 7608, fos. 212v–3; Harl. 7617, fo. 87; *Proposal* (1659, P3715aA); SUL, Hartlib 29/6/19; *Memoriall* (1648, M1693A).
[52] Chidley, *To his Highness* (1656–7, C3843A-44), p. 4; Chidley, *Thunder* (1653, C3843); *CJ*, vii. 442, 446; SUL, Hartlib 28/1/19; *Plus Ultra* (1651, C1900A); *Poore Mans* (1649, C1901).

committee. This was attempted successfully by Andrews Burrell, whose *Remonstrance* regarding navy reform was distributed to MPs, and then referred to a committee, the members of which were instructed 'to hear Mr Burrell' and his ideas (January 1647). Some represented targeted interventions on issues that were due to be discussed on the floor of either House. In the case of Chidley, for example, this meant directing a short pamphlet to 'the chosen and betrusted princes' who were discussing Cromwellian kingship in March 1657. Others were submitted at the next stage of the parliamentary process, once matters had been referred to committees, either in relation to public bills or private proposals. Surviving evidence suggests that it would have cost only a few shillings to print 'reasons' either for or against a specific piece of legislation, and this was precisely what Katherine Pettus did in 1654, by using the experience of her own unhappy Chancery case to influence a committee that was preparing a bill for the relief of creditors and poor prisoners. Samuel Lambe's *Representation*, on the other hand, provided a brief text for the committee that had been appointed to consider his proposals, in response to earlier petitions and carefully circulated books.[53] What Lambe also demonstrates, of course, is that particular lobbyists not only devised different kinds of text, but also used more than one kind of printed work, either in tandem or sequentially. Dr Nicholas Gibbon, for example, an ejected clergyman who had been reduced to working as a manual labourer, submitted a *Tender* regarding his plans for religious accommodation at the same time as he offered another book – *The Reconciler* – to 'men of judgment'. Subsequently, he made another intervention in parliamentary proceedings by lobbying the Committee for the Propagation of the Gospel (March 1652), and then responded to their interest in his ideas by submitting *Humble Proposals*, as well as a diagramatic broadside entitled *A Summe or Body of Divinitie*. This last tactic was also employed by the lawyer William Leach, whose *Several Proposalls* were 'tendered to the consideration of the honourable committee for regulating of courts of justice' in 1650, with the promise to 'inform them at large' with more detailed proposals.[54]

Ultimately, the affordability of print made it possible for lobbying to involve not just projecting – in relation to novel ideas and idealistic schemes – but also fully developed proposals for legislation. This is another

---

[53] Burrell, *Remonstrance* (1646, B5973); *CJ*, v. 47; Chidley, *Parliament* (1657, C3846), p. 1; GL, MS 6440/2, fo. 322; Parkhurst, *Whereas* (1656, P488b); *Pettus* (1654, P1913); Lambe, *Humble* (1658, L228).

[54] Gibbon, *Tender* (1645, G657A); *Reconciler* (1646; G654); SUL, Hartlib 60/14/16, 22, 24; *CJ*, iv. 721; v. 55, 83; *LJ*, ix. 94; *Walker Revised*, 216; BL, Stowe 361, fo. 101: *Humble Proposals* (1652); *Summe* (1651?, G656); *Several Proposalls* (1650, S2802).

area where care is needed, since printed versions of draft bills did not always represent discrete pressure on MPs from outside Westminster. Some were circulated through official channels, as governments lobbied parliaments, and some were promulgated publicly rather than promoted discretely.[55] Public campaigning was occasionally undertaken, for example, by the law reformer, William Leach, but what makes him particularly interesting is that many of his printed texts were circulated to highly circumscribed audiences. As such he serves to highlight yet another neglected print genre, where texts often lurk in official archives, or survive only in references to people paying for the printing of draft bills.[56] And it is also another area where the rationale for appropriating print was complex but clear. Printing made it feasible to disperse copies of bills to every MP, something that was occasionally justified by the failure to find sponsors through personal approaches and targeted lobbying. It also made it possible to lobby committee members once bills had been taken into consideration, and on one occasion a printed bill was re-circulated with a scribal annotation encouraging its recipient to attend a forthcoming committee hearing.[57] Beyond this, however, a range of other genres can be detected. From the 1620s onwards, therefore, some breviates provided summary accounts of proposed legislation, for the attention of those committee members who were considering particular bills, but others offered reasons why bills should be passed, reminded MPs about the existence of bills that were in danger of becoming buried and grumbled about delays.[58]

Indeed, close scrutiny of specific campaigns reveals not just the motivation for lobbying, and the practices involved, but also the difficulties that were encountered and the results that could be achieved. Victors included the disgruntled legal clerks whose response to a draft ordinance for regulating Chancery involved a printed lobby document for a committee to 'take into their consideration'. This contained a 'fit expedient' for improving the bill, and claims that the proposed fees for copying legal documents – 2d per sheet and ten words *per* line – were 'very moderate'. They claimed that such rates were scarcely sufficient for 'the meanest scrivener's boy', or for 'one that sat close at his writing . . . all the day', let alone for those who also

---

[55] *Several Draughts* (1653, E2289A); *Court Merchant* (1659, E1262);

[56] *Proposalls* (1649–50, L777–9); *Abatement* (1652, L770); *Bills* (1651, L771); *Bribe-takers* (1652, L772); *Continuance* (1654, C5956); *Preservative* (1650, L776); Longleat, Whitelocke Parcel 7/90; CHC, BA/H/3/20/2, pp. 452, 461.

[57] *Bill* (1659, N495aA), sigs. A2–v; *Ordinance* (1646, B356); BL, Harl. 7617, fo. 16.

[58] BL, Harl. 7607, fos. 393–9, 404; Harl. 7608, fo. 41; Harl. 7614, fo. 116; *Reasons* (1649, R570F); TNA, SP 16/408, fo. 293: *Reasons*; Longleat, Whitelocke Parcel 7/89: *Hitcham*; Whitelocke Parcel 7/111: *Gooche*; PA, MP 1 Aug. 1646: *Creditors*.

advised clients and oversaw cases. Their suggestion was 'that 4*d*. per folio may be allowed . . . for all copies', and although their claims were challenged in other printed submissions to the committee, their lobbying paid off and their amendment was incorporated into the final ordinance.[59] Not everyone found lobbying so productive, however, and the experience of Thomas Duckett indicates how frustrating the process could be, while also demonstrating that print provided a means of plugging away over a protracted period. Duckett began his campaign in 1646, with a pamphlet that drew MPs' attention to his proposals for improving agricultural productivity, and that was produced after targeted approaches to MPs had proved fruitless, despite backing from the Monmouthshire committee. When this pamphlet also failed to attract sponsors, Duckett took his campaign to another level with a quasi-public pamphlet, *The Messenger of Profit* (1649), which reprinted unsuccessful petitions and certificates, rehearsed his proposals and reflected on the failure to secure an audience. Duckett bemoaned the fact that constant and costly attendance in the lobbies had been undermined by the pressing in of a 'multiplicity of affairs', and his aim was to secure meetings with individual MPs and the appointment of a committee to consider his ideas. When backers could still not be found, Duckett felt compelled to produce a third pamphlet in May 1651, which reflected on how 'emergent and indispensable occasions' had 'retarded' his expected hearing, and which expressed the hope that his proposals were 'still retained in your honours' memories'. Eventually, such persistence seemed to pay off. Duckett managed to secure hearings at the Committee of Trade in 1656, and his proposals found favour with MPs and looked set to generate reforming legislation, only for his hopes to be dashed when Cromwell dissolved the parliament. Only then did Duckett express his frustration by taking his ideas into the public domain, providing readers with a detailed account of his long and painful lobbying campaign.[60]

The contrasting fortunes of Duckett and the Chancery clerks thus offer a salutary reminder that the rationale for exploiting print was distinct from its demonstrable power, that it was perceived to be useful even if it did not achieve clear and direct results, and that it is sometimes necessary to analyse public discourse in the context of more restrained forms of participation. It is to the significance of *failed* lobbying that attention must now turn.

[59] *Reasons* (1654, R585A), pp. 1–4; *Ordinance* (1654, BL, E1064/31), pp. 525–6; *Printed Paper* (1654, P3503); *Reply* (1655, R1053).

[60] *Duckett* (1646, D2431), sigs. Av–B3; Duckett, *Messenger* (1649, D2430b), sig. B, pp. 2–3, 18–19; SUL, Hartlib 26/60: *Petition and Propositions* (1651), pp. 1, 2, 6–7; *Proceedings* (1657, D2430C), sigs. A–A3, B2, B4, C2–4); *Burton Diary*, i. 227–8.

v Frustration and radicalization

In May 1649 *Perfect Occurrences* published the text of a document that had just been delivered to MPs by Thomas Bushell. This reflected on an earlier paper that had 'remained in the clerk's hands' since mid March, and on how this delay had prompted Bushell to 'present my petition and case in print unto every individual member'. In other words, having circulated his *Case*, Bushell published a statement in a leading newspaper out of desperation.[61] Many other lobbyists faced similar frustrations, as a result of vested interests, business overload and political apathy, not to mention the periodic dissolution of parliament. Many of them followed Bushell's example, and many breviates that had been devised for discrete circulation found their way into the press as commentaries on parliamentary culture.[62] This section will explore the kinds of texts that emerged in response to frustrated lobbying, and the complex and dynamic nature of the relationship between tracts that were privately circulated and those that were publicly available. It will show that lobbying sometimes fostered debates that proved difficult to contain, and that in the face of intractable problems lobbyists sometimes reflected on the parliamentary process and changed their tactics and rhetoric. This will involve demonstrating how discrete participation could give way to public discourse, and how some lobbyists underwent a process of radicalization.[63]

First, the circulation and submission of printed texts often provoked counter-lobbying in print, whether collectively or individually. John Giffard's *Case* regarding his Forest of Dean iron works, which was distributed among MPs in 1649, provoked *Certaine Reasons* by the 'preservators' of the forest, which in turn led to Giffard's *Modest Vindication*, which was 'submitted to the wisdom and judgment of the parliament, and every member thereof'. Francis Swaine's *Considerations* regarding the legal system represented a direct response to another lobby document, entitled *Proposalls Concerning the Chancery* (1650), while William Beech's ideas about Milford Haven lighthouse were printed in response to a 'loose and lying pamphlet' by a rival, and Jeremiah Wattes's *Answer* regarding the excise was printed after he saw opponents 'at the Parliament door, setting forth self in print'.[64]

---

[61] *Occurrences*, 465.5125, p. 1054; *Thomas Bushell* (1649, B6242).
[62] *Proceedings*: 599.274, p. 4338; 599.148, pp. 2325–6; 599.215, pp. 3395–8; *Diurnall*, 503.126, pp. 1849–51.
[63] Brayne, *Once* (1651, B4332A), pp. 1–2; Vaughan, *Plea* (1651, V135).
[64] *Sope-makers* (1650, W391B); *Brief Relation* (1654, B4631); *John Giffard* (1649, C930B); *Certaine Reasons* (1650, C1749); *Modest* (1650, G692); *CJ*, vi. 342; BJL, DD/HO/2/73: Swaine,

A particularly vivid example of this phenomenon involves the fallout from a bill submitted by the Norwich weavers. This was presented in December 1648, but after making fairly rapid progress it subsequently became stalled, despite the best efforts of the town's MP, Thomas Atkin. It eventually became clear that this delay was caused by the local wool-combers, who used 'extraordinary means ... to retard it' and who provided the incentive for deploying print, in the form of the weavers' *Answer* to their rivals. This in turn provoked the wool-combers to print a *Modest Reply*, which set out their objection to the bill, and to what they considered 'a printed rayling paper', as well as to what they called 'the violent tide of unlimited and polefaced envy', and the 'filthy slime of obloquy and contempt'.[65] In other words, printed lobbying not only involved tactical escalation in response to frustration but also made it more likely that others would respond in kind, in ways that were likely to sour relations and inflame rhetoric.

Secondly, when lobbying generated print, and when printed lobbying provoked replies, the number of texts could quickly multiply. This risk of protracted exchanges is clear from the repeated interventions over fen drainage, as claims were met with counter-claims regarding both substantive issues and aggressive lobbying.[66] It is also clear from the complex campaign over the Post Office, where printed petitioning in the early 1640s led to committees being bombarded with numerous competing texts. Indeed, such exchanges continued for many years, as assiduous lobbyists like Henry Robinson became involved during the mid 1640s, and by 1654 at least three rival claimants were producing lobby documents to support petitions and influence decision-making, in both the Council of State and various committees. The so-called 'new undertakers' produced a four-page folio entitled *The Case of the Undertakers*, which prompted their rivals to produce *The Case of the First Undertakers*, while the claims of yet another group were submitted in yet another *Case*. Robinson, meanwhile, provided 'information' to MPs in a text that had first been printed 'in the beginning of the late Long Parliament'.[67]

Considerations; Proposalls (P3718); Beech, *Light-House* (1650, B1681) pp. 1–6; Beech, *Eliot* (1650, B1682A); Wattes, *Answer* (1653, W1153a), pp. 1–2.

[65] *CJ*, vi. 105–7, 120, 122, 127, 136, 142, 148, 161, 181, 259, 308, 311, 314, 322, 353, 358–9, 389, 416, 424, 456, 460, 463, 465, 471, 488, 496; BL, Add. 22620, fos. 119, 121, 125, 137, 139, 182; *Answer* (1650, T1705aA); *Modest Reply* (1650, T1735aA), pp. 1–2, 4, 7, 17, 19.

[66] *Peterborow* (1650, H3524a); TNA, SP 46/96, fos. 241v–4v: *The State* (1650); *Reply* (1650, R1054); *Paper Delivered* (1651, K465); *Reply to Sir William* (1655, R1062); *As it is* (1651, A51).

[67] *Humble* (1640, 25930.5); PA, MP 24 Dec. 1642; *Full and Cleare* (1642, F2276); *True Reply* (1641, T3085A); *Arguments* (1640, 22142.3); TNA, SP 16/514, fos. 103–10v: *Discourse* (1646); *CSPD 1653–4*, pp. 372–3; *CSPD 1654*, p. 21; TNA, SP 18/65, fos. 110, 115; SP 18/65, fos. 111–14v: *Case* (1654); SP 18/67, fos. 155–6: *Case of the First* (1654); SP 18/67, fo 146: *David Watkins* (1654); SP 18/65, fo. 117; SP 18/67, fos. 147–51.

Moreover, while such printed exchanges tended to involve circumscribed audiences, lobbying and counter-lobbying could easily spill over into public campaigning. Here again the process of escalation can be observed clearly from the fen drainage disputes, when lobby documents were targeted not just at MPs but also at wider audiences, as arguments between competing interest groups were played out in the public domain. But it is also evident in many less well-known cases, involving projectors, private individuals and local communities, as citizens became frustrated by the failure to secure hearings, and by the way in which allegations were sometimes broadcast 'upon the Exchange'. Following a lengthy Chancery dispute that stretched back to 1629, therefore, as well as petitions to the Long Parliament that had been neglected, the indebted and imprisoned London merchant, John Day, not only reprinted a petition in the hope of nudging peers to revive his case, and supplemented it with a lengthy remonstrance for discrete circulation at Westminster, but also produced a more widely available *Vindication*. The latter represented a response to an 'invective, false and scandalous remonstrance' by one of his enemies, and a frustrated reaction to the fact that his discrete response had been overlooked by the upper House, as a result of 'the multiplicity of their great affairs and their seldom sitting'.[68] Moreover, this process of escalation can certainly be observed in relation to disputed parliamentary elections, as with a pamphlet concerning underhand tactics at Reading (1654) and a tract by Henry Neville's disgruntled supporters in Berkshire (1656).[69] But it can be seen even more clearly from three small case studies. The first involves a dispute over the right to print Bibles, where a bill to grant a monopoly to Henry Hills and John Field provoked a printed *Case* by their rival, William Bentley, *A Short Answer* by Hills and Field, and *Proposals* by William Kilburne. When Hills and Field responded with *A True State of the Case*, however, their fiery rhetoric incited Kilburne's public response, entitled *Dangerous Errors*.[70] A second case related to complaints against the executors of John Pym, and involved a printed petition by Captain John Harris, and then a *Humble Remonstrance* with which to lobby committee members, as well as a printed response and finally Harris's public statement, entitled

---

[68] *Killigrew* (1649, K453), pp. 3–13; *Picklock* (1650, E594/4); *Drayner* (1647, D2121a); *News* (1654, N1007B); Durham UL, MSP 30, fo. 73v; Bodl. MS Tanner 66, fo. 119; *Walter Roberts* (1641, R1605a); Berks. RO, R/ACI/1/6, fos. 30–v; *Case* (1656, T1367A); Fowler, *Daemonium* (1656, F1693); *Alarum* (1659, A827), pp. 2, 5–7; Day, *Petition* (1646, D468C); Day, *Remonstrance* (1647, D468B), p. 51; Day, *Modest* (1646, D468A), pp. 1–4, 36, 39.

[69] *Admirable* (1654, F2200), pp. 2–3, 5–6; *True* (1656, T2560); *Nevill* (1659, N508A).

[70] *Bentley* (1656, B1944); *Short Answer* (1656, S3560); CUA, CUR 33.6(24); *True State* (1659, T3111A), p. 3; Kilburne, *Dangerous* (1659, K435).

The Second Humble Representation.[71] Perhaps the most striking case, however, involves the dispute between Thomas Violet and Peter Blondeau, over new schemes for coining. Blondeau's proposals were submitted to the Council of State in 1649, but while he initially found favour, he also encountered vigorous opposition from Violet and the Moniers Company, which resulted in further investigations and a great deal more lobbying. Moreover, as the tide of official opinion swung against him, Blondeau responded with a printed sheet of *Propositions*, as well as with new proposals, and he lobbied the hearing that he was granted with *An Answer to Severall Objections.* Thereafter he sought to revive his case by producing a potted history of his lobbying campaign and by criticizing officers of the Mint and their 'friends', who 'did so prevail with the committee that the business was deferred above a whole year', until his hopes were finally dashed by the dissolution of the Rump Parliament. As his frustration mounted, however, Blondeau was said to have ensured that such texts were also 'dispersed into the hands of the ignorant multitude', thereby convincing the Moniers that they 'must have a reply', which Violet made public as *The Answer of the Corporation of Moniers.*[72]

Thirdly, some lobbying campaigns spilled over into public discourse as a result of official involvement. For example, following months of hearings in response to a petition by clothworkers, Francis Thorpe's committee decided to set up something resembling a public enquiry, and ordered that copies of the petition should be printed and circulated, 'in respect all sorts of wool growers, wool sellers, [and] wool buyers ... are concerned in it' (March 1647). Sheriffs were instructed to 'disperse and publish' copies at the assizes and in 'public places', so that 'the people may have notice of it' and so that interested parties could attend a hearing that was scheduled for 12 May. The result was a flurry of petitions, pamphlets and lobby documents that responded to the clothworkers' claims, and that were directed to the 'worthy gentlemen of the committee for this business'. These were intended to be 'read by those concerned', and the aim was to ensure that 'as many members of the House as possible would be pleased to meet about this business so often as the committee appoints to meet'.[73] Similar texts continued to

---

[71] Beds. RO, X/171/57: *John Harris* (1651) and *Representation* (1651); *Second* (1651, H856A); *CJ*, vi. 589.

[72] *CSPD 1649–50*, pp. 295, 305, 352, 503–4; *CSPD 1650*, pp. 14, 35; *CSPD 1651*, pp. 174–5, 231–4, 280, 284, 487–9; *CSPD 1651–2*, pp. 152–7, 212, 214; *CSPD 1652–3*, pp. 280, 311, 349; TNA, SP 18/15, fo. 93: *Proposition* (1651, B3219B); SP 18/23, fos. 95–8: *Answer* (1652, B3219bA); *Humble* (1653, B3219cA); *Remonstrance* (1653, B3219A), pp. 11–12, 19–20, 22; Violet, *Answer* (1653, V579), sigs. A2–v, p. 3.

[73] *CJ*, iv. 722; Leics. RO, DE730/3, fo. 61; *Many Thousands* (1647, T1417); TNA, SP 16/515ii, fo. 136: *Unmasking* (1647, U85A); SP 16/515ii, fos. 124–33v: *Short View* (1647, S3638AC); *Briefe Answer* (1647, B4540A), pp. 1, 2; *These Things* (1647, T882B).

appear during the course of the parliamentary inquiry, not least through the efforts of the clothworkers' agents, Edmund Rozer and William Talbott, who 'did constantly attend with printed arguments'. They publicized at least one breviate in *Perfect Occurrences*, and provided MPs with longer memorials to narrate the history of the case and reiterate key arguments, and they also detailed their 'trouble, diligence and cost' as a result of the 'unwearied labours' of their opponents, and catalogued the 'uncivil and tumultuous carriage' of their rivals 'before this honourable committee'.[74]

What also seems clear, however, is that official involvement could also fuel the development of sophisticated lobbying through overt support for particular campaigns. Thus, when Sir John Gell produced a discrete lobby document containing the *True State* of his case, it was criticized by the editor of *Mercurius Politicus* as well as by the author of a pamphlet that was produced on a government press.[75] A much more obvious example, however, involves Lord Craven, a hugely wealthy royalist who used print in innovative ways as part of a campaign to repeal a 1652 act for the sale of his estate. During the trial of one of his accusers in 1653, therefore, Craven issued what amounted to press releases, which appeared in a number of leading newspapers, and printed a *True and Perfect Narrative* of his case. However, as a high-profile delinquent, Craven faced serious opposition from within the republican regime, and this ensured the appearance of a different version of *Lord Craven's Case*, which was published officially, and which exposed his exploitation of journalists. What makes the case important, however, is not merely the fact that Craven chose to respond, with *A Reply to a Certain Pamphlet*, but also that what began as a discrete lobbying campaign turned into a propaganda battle between rival political factions. This was because Craven's sympathizers, including Cromwell, ordered the business to be reconsidered in September 1654, thereby prompting another wave of lobbying through rival newspapers. Craven's opponents (including those who had purchased part of the estate) used *Severall Proceedings*, while Craven encouraged readers to attend forthcoming hearings by inserting notices into the government paper, *Politicus*, and also secured help from a government printer to produce yet another version of his *Case*.[76]

---

[74] *Breviate* (1648, B4416), p. 8; Rozer, *Reasons* (1649, R2165); *Occurrences*, 465.5125, pp. 1052–3; Talbott, *Generall* (1648, T127A), pp. 1–6; Rozer, *Narrative* (1651, R2164A), pp. 1–4; sigs. B–C4.

[75] DRO, D258/32/1/4–5: *True State* (1650, G467) and Bernard, *Confutation* (1650, B2005); *Politicus*, 361.016, p. 276.

[76] CCC, pp. 1616–26; *Proceedings*, 599.191, pp. 3014–6; *Diurnall*, 503.180, pp. 2723–4; *Perfect Account*, 496.124, pp. 983–5; *Weekly Intelligencer*, 688.120, pp. 855–6; *True and Perfect* (1653, T2536); *Lord Cravens* (1653, L3044); *Reply* (1653, R1050); *Proceedings*, 599.267, pp. 4229, 4239; 599.268, sig. 23H2v; *Purchasers* (1654, T1593); *Diurnall*, 503.257, pp. 3945–6; 503.260, p. 3987; 503.264, pp. 4053–4;

Fourthly, and finally, printed lobbying reveals not just the possibility of tactical and rhetorical escalation but also the potential for radical political thinking. This tended to mean low-level grumbling about months spent waiting patiently on committees, and about the delays caused by 'great and weighty affairs', but it could easily become much more serious. In 1648, for example, the clothiers openly criticized the behaviour of MPs, by claiming that parliament was too susceptible to the tactics of the wool staplers, so that business was hampered by 'adjournments, demurrs, [and] prejudice'. Lobbyists also pointed out when due process had not been followed and when legislative and 'jurisdictive' functions had been illegally combined, and they repeatedly reminded MPs about the need to respect earlier parliamentary declarations and 'the known laws of the land'.[77] Much more troubling, however, were accusations about political corruption. When Clement Walker complained about the loss of his Exchequer office in 1650, he not only challenged parliamentary authority but also made specific allegations against the MP, Humphrey Edwards, who was described as a 'half-faced cavalier', and as 'a parliament man upon an undue election', and who was said to have 'prevailed' upon the committee in his own interest. Other targets included James Temple, Edmund Prideaux, Miles Corbet and Francis Allen. Temple was accused of having reneged on promises to help William Beech, while Prideaux was said to have been responsible for 'great oppressions and injuries', not least by ensuring that petitions were overlooked and that official orders were ignored. Corbet, meanwhile, was alleged to have secured an office in Chancery in a corrupt and peremptory fashion, and to have penned a 'false report' regarding Thomas Coningsby, a former sheriff of Hertfordshire who had been arrested for distributing royalist proclamations. Having spent months waiting 'slavishly' on the Committee of Indemnity, moreover, Coningsby also criticized Allen, whom he described as 'a fierce stickler', and as someone who had turned 'moderate' MPs against him.[78]

Claims about corruption emerged most explosively, however, over fen drainage projects, amid perceptions that the 'adventurers' were supported by a 'faction' of 'active' MPs. Attention focused on men like Robert Scawen, whose position in the House was thought to be inconsistent with his role as 'solicitor' to one of the leading drainers, the Earl of Bedford, but it also

503.266, pp. 4090–2; 503.267, pp. 4103–6; *Politicus*, 361.231, pp. 4013–4; 361.232, p. 4038; 361.233, p. 4053; 361.239, pp. 5038–9; 361.240, pp. 5056–9, 5066; 361.241, pp. 5073–4; *Craven's Case* (1654, L3045).

[77] *Picklock* (1650, M1457), p. 15; *Narrative* (1651, R2164A), pp. 1–2; *Considerations* (1654, L1825A); Talbott, *Generall* (1648, T127A), pp. 1–3, 5.

[78] *Clement Walker* (1650, W323); *Mary Walker* (1650, W395); Beech, *Discovery* (1645, B1679A); Vaughan, *Breviate* (1653, V120); *True State* (1655, J681bA); *Sufferings* (1648, C5878A), pp. 2, 14.

addressed the issue of 'biased' committees. It was alleged that 'no witnesses were fairly examined' and that committee hearings were held 'in one corner or another', adjourned 'on purpose to vex and tire the people', and then reconvened once opponents had left London. It was also said that key pieces of legislation were brought to a vote when the Commons was 'thin', and Daniell Noddell, one of the most vociferous critics of the drainers, repeatedly attacked reports that had been 'cunningly and privately drawn'. His most bitter comments, however, were reserved for the MPs William Say and Henry Darley, who had personal interests in fenland projects, and who were said to have been 'coached' and 'feasted' by the drainers.[79] Ultimately, the willingness of men like Noddell to make their accusations public forced the adventurers to defend such MPs in an equally forthright fashion, but it also ensured that the tone of the debate became much more aggressive. Opponents of the drainers thus began to echo radical demands for committee hearings to be held with the doors 'freely open', and they also forged links with radical agitators like Lilburne and Wildman, who were enlisted as 'agents' and as electoral candidates who would 'call this parliament to account'. Although these ex-Levellers were clearly exploiting local agitation for their own political ends, Noddell's zeal is beyond question. Indeed, as someone who promised to print the freeholders' 'case', to nail it to parliament's door and to pull MPs 'out by the ears', it seems clear that his radicalism emerged out of his lobbying, rather than as a result of his association with such men.[80]

vi Conclusion

The goal of this chapter has been to recover the original purpose of a substantial range of printed texts, to explore the practices of their authors and to suggest that this offers revealing insights into contemporary political culture. The aim, in other words, has been to suggest that Cornelius Burges's *Case Concerning the Buying of Bishops Lands* (1659) was something other than an appeal to 'public opinion'; that Edward King's *Discovery* (1646) was not simply a 'public' exposé of the 'tyrannical' actions of the Lincolnshire committee; and that *Mr William Wheelers Case* (1645) was something more than a minor polemic by Henry Parker.[81] Burges's work

---

[79] *Anti-Projector* (1646, A3504), p. 4; *Peterborow* (1650, H3524a), p. 2; *Brief* (1653, B4638); *Daniel Noddell* (1653, N1217A), p. 2; Noddell, *Great* (1654, N1217B), pp. 13, 19–22.

[80] *Honour* (1651, A51); *Answer* (1653, A3338), pp. 1, 3–4; TNA, SP 18/37, fos. 14–18.

[81] D. Underdown, 'A case concerning bishops' lands', *EHR*, 78 (1963), p. 42; C. Holmes, 'Colonel King and Lincolnshire politics', *HJ*, 16 (1973), pp. 479–80; Parker, *Wheelers Case* (1645, P408).

was delivered more or less discretely to MPs, to express frustration over his progress in a protracted legal and petitioning campaign. King's pamphlet contained texts that had earlier been submitted to a committee, and was printed in the face of hostility within parliament, and it was distributed to MPs ahead of one of his hearings and only later received more widespread distribution. And Wheeler's tract represented an attempt by a struggling inventor to enlist a skilled writer in the production of a text that could be distributed to MPs, in the hope of finding parliamentary patronage.[82] In each case, an attempt was being made to do something more than 'mere' petitioning, but something other than 'public' campaigning.

These examples indicate that the meaning of many printed texts has been misunderstood, that insufficient attention has been paid to the practices associated with lobbying, and that this reflects unsustainable assumptions about the link between printing and publicity, as well as an extremely narrow approach to 'popular' politics. The argument of this chapter has been that, by rethinking printed texts and participatory practices in tandem, it is possible to enhance our appreciation of the ways in which ordinary citizens coped with their grievances and promoted their ideas. Printing made it easier to produce lobby documents, and this made the lobbying process much less costly and time-consuming, by reducing the amount of effort involved in finding and 'seasoning' friends at Westminster. This facilitated interventions in parliamentary proceedings, even if it could not exactly guarantee political success, and it enhanced the potential for participation, especially for those who had the least time and money to spare and who had few contacts within the political elite. Indeed, from comments by lobbyists and complaints by MPs, it seems clear that there was a direct correlation between the development of printed lobbying and the unprecedented pressure that MPs found themselves under, to the point where some Westminster insiders became exasperated over the degree to which committees were 'solicited' by members of the public and even sought to restrict the possibility for lobbying parliament.[83]

The result of such analysis of lobbying is that it is possible to challenge the significance of public discourse while also emphasizing the importance of political participation. It becomes clear once again that interventions in the public sphere can often only be understood in the context of more restrained activities, in which print was used discretely and purposefully, not just to petition the authorities at Westminster but also to contribute to

---

[82] *Burton Diary*, iii. 201; Bodl. MS Nalson 14, fos. 434–5; SUL, Hartlib 34/3/3.
[83] *Burton Diary*, i. 269, ii. 159–62; *Diurnall*, 503.203, sig. 9T; Jansson, vi. 89.

substantive deliberations. Moreover, by probing lobbying practices in some depth, a fascinating picture emerges regarding increasingly sophisticated participatory skills. Central to these skills was the ability to engage in tactical escalation, and printed lobbying ought to be considered in the context of a broad range of skills, and as something that was deployed with great care. Some of those who had other options for promoting and protecting their interests – personal contacts and the capacity to wage law – turned to print only after these avenues had been exhausted, in what represented a logical tactical shift. For those who lacked wealth and connections, however, printed interventions might have been their point of entry into the partic- ipatory world, although to the extent that their lobby documents supple- mented petitions, they, too, were displaying tactical awareness and taking their campaigns to a new level. Beyond this, tactical escalation was also central to the ways in which printed lobby documents were employed. Printed texts were used on some occasions but not on others; they could also perform a range of specialized tasks at different stages of the parliamentary process; and subtly different genres could be deployed sequentially. This varied use of lobby documents reflected awareness that print could be useful but not always effective, and that new tactics might need to be adopted. Tactical escalation also involved blurring the distinction between discrete lobbying and public campaigning, and analysing problems with the parlia- mentary system, even to the point of exposing political corruption. That contemporaries were acutely aware of such escalations in rhetoric and tactics is clear. Christopher Packe's experience with lobbyists caused him to worry that MPs would struggle to avoid making enemies or being accused of partiality, while fen drainers argued that the most aggressive forms of printed lobbying might 'accompany and aggravate' the 'clamours' that were being 'stirred up' by their opponents.[84] Tactical escalation, in other words, might not stop when lobbying spilled over into public discourse, and as such it is necessary to analyse more aggressive forms of political participation.

[84] *Burton Diary*, ii. 160–2; *News* (1654, N1007B), pp. 2–3; *Paper Delivered*.

CHAPTER 10

Printing, mass mobilization and protesting

In May 1647, William Browne, the spokesman for a group of frustrated petitioners, landed himself in trouble by saying that 'they had waited many days, and would wait no longer', and that they planned to 'take another course'. When an MP demanded to know his name, Browne compounded his offence by suggesting that the 'time may come when I may ask you your name', implying that representatives might be called to account. Similar sentiments were expressed in 1649 by Derbyshire miners who had 'petitioned long' but found 'no redress', who had printed a petition in the name of 'many thousand persons' and who then 'resolved to make use of what nature teacheth them for their own preservation'. They thus threatened to 'undermine' the 'House of robbers at Westminster', just as Charles Chipperfield exclaimed that a 'considerable party' of angry petitioners would pull out MPs 'by the ears'.[1] Other citizens who uttered similar claims reflected on the utility of print as a tactical device. Major White responded to being court-martialled in 1647 by using a printed 'vindication' to appeal for support from fellow soldiers, while John Poyntz used a printed statement to urge other people to join a larger petitioning campaign 'for the speedy execution of justice'. And in 1652 an insubordinate soldier called Obadiah Andrew not only railed against the Rump Parliament, but also explained how mounting frustration would lead to tactical escalation. He claimed that 'the parliament must not sit long, but must give an account for the money they have received and the blood they have shed', and he explained that 'first they shall have our petition ... or that failing ... our remonstrance', and he warned that the failure of such polite pressure would ensure that 'they shall have our presence'. Indeed, he boasted that 'some thousands were ready for the work' and 'waiting for the time'.[2]

---

[1] *Diurnall*, 504.199, p. 1595; DRO, D258/7/20/9: *Thomas Robinson* (1649); *Moon*, 248.24, p. 196; BL, Add. 78258, fo. 32.
[2] *Elencticus*, 312.03, p. 19; *Case* (1648, P3131D), pp. 7–8; BL, Add. 78260, fo. 94.

In many ways, such comments merely highlight the kinds of popular activism and street politics with which historians have become familiar, but the aim of this chapter is to demonstrate that they also draw attention to aspects of mass mobilization that have been overlooked, not least the role of print as a tactical device. Mass politics – in the form of 'monster' petitions, crowds and riots – has too often been studied in isolation from the broader context of 'polite' participation, and scholarship has all too frequently become polarized over whether 'popular' politics involved manipulation of the lower orders by the elite or spontaneous expressions of consciousness and allegiance.[3] This certainly reflects contemporary concerns about the possibility that petitions were framed at Westminster before being dispersed into the localities, and that underhand tactics were used to create the illusion of mass support. And it also mirrors contemporary assumptions about crowds that involved the 'scum of all ranks' being organized by 'eminent persons in both Houses'.[4] Nevertheless, such comments and arguments fail to do justice to the complexity of public politics, and recent scholarship suggests that conventional wisdom needs to be modified in three key ways. First, episodes of disorder frequently reveal coherent political messages, as well as recognition of the connections between local and national issues. With celebratory crowds, threatening mobs and disorderly elections, in other words, street politics could involve spontaneous and committed expressions of political awareness, and the frequency with which troops were mobilized in response indicates that the authorities genuinely feared the political effects of popular unrest.[5] Secondly, political elites sometimes tolerated and accommodated popular agitation, such that

[3] A. Fletcher, *Outbreak of the English Civil War* (London, 1985), pp. 92, 173–4, 191–3, 196; D. Underdown, 'The chalk and the cheese', *P&P*, 85 (1979), 25–48; J. Morrill, 'Mutiny and discontent in English provincial armies', *P&P*, 56 (1972), 49–74; M. Kishlansky, 'What happened at Ware?', *HJ*, 25 (1982), 827–39; B. Sharp, *In Contempt of all Authority* (Berkeley, 1980); P. Clark, 'Popular protest and disturbance in Kent', *EcHR*, 29 (1976), 365–82; K. Lindley, 'London and popular freedom in the 1640s', in *Freedom and the English Revolution*, ed. R. Richardson and R. Ridden (Manchester, 1986), pp. 111–50; B. Manning, *English People and the English Revolution* (London, 1991); K. Lindley, *Fenland Riots and the English Revolution* (London, 1982).

[4] *Persecutio* (1648), pp. 21, 24, 62, 64; *Ejected* (1648, S26) p. 3; *Westminster Projects*, 710.5, p. 2; Williams, *Discovery* (1643, W2665), p. 21; Bodl. MS Clarendon 29, fos. 72–v; 'Twysden journal', i. 201; *Englands* (1659, A3167), p. 3; HEH, HM 951, unfol.; FSL, W.b.600, p. 163; Northants. RO, IC 4631; *Lord* (1643, H1726), pp. 6, 8, 10; *Considerations* (1648, S4498), pp. 3–4.

[5] M. Braddick, 'Popular politics and public policy', *HJ*, 34 (1991), 597–626; A. Bellany, 'The murder of John Lambe', *P&P*, 200 (2008), 37–76; J. Morrill and J. Walter, 'Order and disorder in the English Revolution', in *Order and Disorder in Early Modern England*, ed. A. Fletcher and J. Stevenson (Cambridge, 1985), pp. 137–65; T. Harris, 'The Bawdy House riots of 1668', *HJ*, 29 (1986), 537–56; *Salusbury Corr.*, pp. 115, 119–20; BL: Add. 78221, fos. 98–v; Add. 11045, fo. 129; Add. 64921, fo. 122, 125v; Add. 78198, fo. 67v; HEH, HM 951, unfol.; *Diurnall*, 504.246, p. 1977; CLRO, Rep.59, fo. 189v; *Narration* (1648, F2349).

collaboration took place between 'high' and 'low' politics and that attempts were made to *co-opt* and *co-ordinate* a politically conscious public. Mass activity thus attests to the vibrancy of debate and discussion within contemporary communities, and can be shown to have involved ringleaders and followers from different walks of life, and particular petitions and crowds thus represented 'points of contact' between the elite and the citizenry, and revealed the brokerage of 'constables, middling parishioners and clerical demagogues'.[6] Thirdly, it is possible to detect not just a perceived link between 'licentious pamphlets' and 'tumultuous events', but also clear evidence that pamphlets, newspapers and broadsides offered ordinary citizens a political education, and that they served to integrate people into the political life of parliament.[7]

This chapter builds on such ideas by locating mass agitation within a spectrum of participatory behaviour, by examining the role of print as an organizational device, and by exploring the mechanics and logistics of popular politics. It will focus on the power of print to *activate*, rather than merely to *inculcate*, and on its role as an everyday tool for *co-ordinating* political participation. This will mean scrutinizing the ways in which printed texts were used in precise and targeted ways as part of quotidian political practice, to orchestrate particular kinds of behaviour on the part of both specific and general sections of the population (section i). It will also mean exploring the value of print as a means of organizing mass petitions and subscription campaigns, as well as the kinds of mass lobbying of parliament that became a prominent feature of the age (section ii). Thereafter the chapter will examine the role that print played in crowds and street politics, and the novel kinds of protest that became possible in the 1640s (section iii), before assessing the spectre of popular organization and violence during the Commonwealth and Protectorate (section iv). By revealing new dimensions to familiar episodes – such as the massed gathering of 5,000 Buckinghamshire petitioners in January 1642, and the 'tumultuous' and 'uncivil' gathering of seamen in October 1653 – the chapter will sidestep questions of elite manipulation and popular consciousness in favour of heightened awareness regarding the nature and scope of popular

---

[6] Harris, *London Crowds*, pp. 17, 24, 160, 171, 180; C. Holmes, 'Drainers and fenmen', in *Order and Disorder*, pp. 181–3; J. Walter, 'Confessional politics in pre-Civil War Essex', *HJ*, 44 (2001), 677–701; HEH, HM 66707; *Kingdomes*, 214.224, p. 646; *Londons* (1642, L2952); *Apprentices* (1641, W87); BL, Add. 11045, fos. 117–v; Add. 4460, fo. 75.

[7] Northants. RO, IC4631; T. Harris, 'Understanding popular politics in Restoration Britain', in *A Nation Transformed*, ed. A. Houston and S. Pincus (Cambridge, 2001), pp. 125–53; J. Walter, *Understanding Popular Violence in the English Revolution* (Cambridge, 1999), pp. 290–306, 330; D. Cressy, 'The Protestation protested', *HJ*, 45 (2002), 251–79.

participation.[8] It will show how practices that were developed by political elites had an educative effect upon the public, and how the techniques for mobilizing public support that emerged in the circumstances of Civil War and revolution were *appropriated* and *adapted* by ordinary citizens. It will also emphasize that even humble contemporaries displayed tactical awareness regarding the relationship between different participatory practices and strategies. And it will demonstrate that the official response to new kinds of politics 'without doors' helped to influence the tactical calculations that were made by contemporary citizens, and even played a part in the development of radical political ideas.

i Print as an organizational tool

Before analysing the role that printed texts played in mass politics, it is necessary to analyse how print emerged as an organizational tool in other areas of public life. The aim of this section is to demonstrate that print offered a cheap and efficient means of conveying messages to multiple recipients simultaneously, and that this *simultaneity* had profound consequences for the everyday world of politics and administration.[9] This not only meant the widespread dispersal of proclamations – declaratory and prohibitory texts that required an entire population to observe fairly general instructions – but also the emergence of ephemeral texts that were used in more direct, precise and targeted ways, and the appropriation of such practices for non-official purposes.

This *organizational* role of print was first recognized by administrators and civil servants, not least with *pro formas* that could be personalized and directed towards specific individuals, most obviously to relay precise instructions about when, where and how to pay taxes.[10] In the circumstances of Civil War, however, this bureaucratization of print became more obvious and more sophisticated, and printed demands for money, men and supplies were quickly joined by printed texts that summoned individuals to appear before official bodies, at set times and places, and in connection with any number of tasks. The Committee of Accounts regularly used printed forms – four of which could fit on one side of a printed sheet – to summon those whose financial paperwork needed to be scrutinized, and similar texts

---

[8] HEH, HM 46431; BL: Add. 78315, fo. 8; Add. 26785, fo. 60; *Diurnall*, 503.203, sigs. 9T–3v.
[9] E. Eisenstein, 'On revolution and the printed word', in *Revolution in History*, ed. R. Porter and M. Teich (Cambridge, 1986), p. 200.
[10] BL: Harl. 4712, fos. 241, 421; Stowe 142, fo. 54; Leics. RO, DE730/3, fos. 3v, 7v, 25.

were also used during the parliamentary visitation of Oxford University, and in order to secure subscriptions to the Republic's Engagement.[11] Such forms could be created in the capital and despatched all over the country, but they could also be used by local authorities. This was obviously true in London, where citizens like George Thomason received numerous demands from the militia commissioners for horse and arms, but similar tactics are also evident further afield. By the late 1650s, indeed, a variety of *pro formas* were being produced commercially by stationers like John Bellinger and Thomas Broad, to service the administrative needs of officials across the land.[12] Much more intriguing, however, is evidence about how such tactics were gradually adapted to facilitate the process of organizing meetings that gathered together carefully selected individuals. This was pioneered by livery companies to save money and energy, on the basis that it was considerably cheaper to produce thousands of printed 'tickets' than to notify members orally. Indeed, since many small tickets could be squeezed onto a single printed sheet, it was possible to acquire such material at rates as low as twenty per penny by the 1640s, and even small organizations generated ephemeral texts in vast quantities every year. That so few such items survive reflects the fact that they were eminently disposable, and at best that they tended to be recycled as scrap paper and as improvised bookmarks.[13] What makes them particularly important, however, is that it was quickly recognized that the utility of 'tickets' was political as well as bureaucratic. On some occasions, therefore, they were used to arrange extraordinary meetings, such as those that prepared for elections and petitioning campaigns, and this explains why the organizational power of print came to be appropriated by civic authorities in London. During the revolutionary era, therefore, the City printers produced thousands of tickets every year, at rates of 2,000 for £1 (or 8 per penny), not least to arrange meetings with parliamentary committees. It also explains why tickets

---

[11] Cornwall RO, RP1/7; *You Are Hereby* (1645, Y52B); *These Are* (1644, T878A); *Sir, I Am* (S3878C); *These Are* (1648, E2355A); BL, Stowe 185, fo. 49; *HMC 11th Report VII*, p. 217; TNA: SP 28/294, fo. 239; SP 19/106, fo. 235; SP 28/294, fos. 237–8, 602, 724, 1174, 1278–9; SP 28/295, fos. 129, 1088–1124, 1131–8; DRO, D1232/O34: *By Vertue* (1644); *Nos Quorum* (1647; N1396; O903A); Worcs. RO, BA1054/1/A178, A206; BA7335/4/4/6; Leeds UL, MS 1946/1/57.

[12] Staffs. RO, D868/2/45; TNA, SP 28/295, fos. 321, 445; SP 28/296, unfol.; Northants. RO, IC 3429; CKS, U455/O4; *You are Desired* (1650, S5809, BL, E608/14); *At the Committee* (1650, L2851MB); *Politicus*, 361.416, sig. Uuu; Leeds UL, MS 1946/1/34.

[13] Goldsmiths, Court Book Y, fo. 206; GL: MS 2150/1, fos. 62v, 104v, 115v, 122v; MS 11571/12, fos. 305, 353, 395v, 450v; MS 11571/13–14, unfol.; MS 12065/3, fos. 195, 218; GL, MS 5606/3, fos. 410v, 423v, 466v; MS 5303/1, fos. 57v, 66v, 80v, 109, 120v, 150, 153, 171, 182v; MS 4597/1, pp. 27, 38, 40; MS 4326/7, fos. 285v, 288, 335v; MS 3054/2, unfol; Earwaker, p. 126; CHC, BA/A/1/26/3, pp. 74–369; BL: Add. 4476, fo. 149; Add. 12496, fo. 458: *Virginia* (1624, 24844.3); CKS, U234/B1: *You are Desired*.

became a valued tool for administrators within parliament, not least to summon MPs to the Commons and ministers to the Westminster Assembly.[14]

What such evidence reveals is the potential for influencing the behaviour of groups as well as individuals, and although this often involved corporate organizations and official bodies summoning their own members, similar tactics were also applied much more widely. Indeed, tickets were issued fairly regularly to more or less diffuse groups of officials, from humble constables upwards, to ensure compliance with instructions regarding the listing of apprentices, the collection of loans and assessments, and the repair of highways, as well as the search for illicit arms and the monitoring of dissidents. Beyond London, meanwhile, local commissioners frequently received printed instructions relating to specific tasks, many of which only survive as annotated office copies, and during the 1650s deputy postmasters were given similar orders in the hope of ensuring that the conversations and meetings of 'disaffected persons' could be effectively policed.[15] Much more significant, however, was the use of print to mobilize *general* bodies of interested citizens. This can be seen most obviously with the printed texts that were addressed to Irish 'adventurers', who were repeatedly invited to meetings in order to 'give their advice and best assistance' regarding 'the weighty affairs now in hand', and to elect committees that could liaise with MPs. The notices by which such meetings were called specified where and when hearings would be held, and they were 'set up in several places of the city' and inserted into newspapers, thereby ensuring that they reached their intended audience. However, similar tactics were also evident in other contexts, such as when soldiers whose accounts needed to be processed were invited to the Red Lion in New Palace Yard, so that they might 'make good their demands'.[16] Sometimes, indeed, gatherings that were promoted

---

[14] CLRO: CCA 1/1, fo. 65v; 1/4, fo. 223v; 1/5, fos. 65v, 162v–3, 264; 1/6, fos. 54v, 163, 265v–6; 1/7, fos. 65v, 66, 150v; *Occurrences*, 465.5022, sig. X2v; *You Are Desired* (1648, S3904; BL, E435/30*); *This Day* (1643, E1619); *List* (1649, L2470); *CSPD 1645–7*, pp. 567, 572; TNA: SP 16/515ii, fos. 45, 71–2; SP 18/1, fo. 3; *CSPD 1649–50*, p. 1.

[15] CLRO, CCA 1/6, fos. 54v, 163, 265v–6; *These* (1658, M1970); *Committee* (1648, C5566); *Whereas* (1644, L2851I); *Ordinance* (1648, E2008); *Constables* (1642, T1393B); TNA: SP 28/296, unfol.; SP 28/295, fos. 460, 828–9; Worcs. RO, BA1054/1/A90, A135, A184b, A211, A248, A250, A254, A290–1; Bodl. MS Carte 80, fo. 109; Tanner 64, fos. 62v–69v; *Whereas* (1643, W1617B); *Private* (1653, P3529b); *Whereas* (1642, L2878B); *Sub-Committee* (1644, L2851M); *Declaration* (1643, D534); TNA, SP 23/254, fos. 148, 150; SP 23/259, fo. 170; *Politicus*, 361.180, pp. 2878–9; *Directions* (1644, D1536A); TNA, SP 18/42, fo. 215: *Private* (1653, P3529B); *CSPD 1653–4*, p. 328.

[16] *Die Veneris* (1644, E2773); *Grocers* (1644, E2590aA); *Die Jovis* (1643, S4840); *Commons* (1644, E2580); *Vicessimo* (1645, B6361); *Diurnall*, 504.025, p. 199; *Civicus*, 298.067, p. 633; *Kingdomes*, 214.103, p. 829; *Proceedings*, 599.218, pp. 3449–50; *Politicus*, 361.182, pp. 3011–12.

by print were even less exclusive, including meetings to facilitate the sale of Crown lands and delinquents' property, and in some cases these were overtly political, as when Charles I used a printed announcement to summon Yorkshire freeholders to a loyalist rally at Heworth Moor on 5 June 1642.[17] On other occasions, however, a rather more active and constructive form of participation was envisaged. Newspaper notices issued on behalf of the Committee for Removing Obstructions and the Commissioners for Discoveries not only provided readers with information about the times and places of their meetings, but also explained that the hearings were open to any interested parties or aggrieved citizens. More general still were meetings like the one that was arranged to consider the relief of Ireland (1645), the venue for which was publicized in print so that people 'may know to whom and to what place to repair' with their ideas. On this occasion parliament effectively established a public enquiry, the meetings of which were promoted through extensive advertising.[18]

The importance of these hitherto neglected genres of print is threefold. First, they indicate once again how the circumstances of Civil War ensured that administrative and bureaucratic structures became overtly politicized. Secondly, they demonstrate that the use of print by the political authorities increased the chances of people becoming integrated into political processes. Thirdly, and most importantly, they indicate the speed with which official practices were appropriated by ordinary citizens. Very quickly, therefore, organizational notices began to be used by members of the public, not just to create invitations – to parties and private funerals – but also to engage in political activism.[19] Any number of incidents reveal the use of printed tickets as part of agitation within livery companies, not least to monitor the performance of superiors and call for new elections, and in June 1643 printed notices encouraged London's clerks to rally at the piazza in Covent Garden as a volunteer defence force for the capital. Before the Long Parliament was even a year old, moreover, such tactics were also being used to exert influence at Westminster. In the summer of 1641, for example, printed sheets were circulated to advertise a meeting – at Sadlers' Hall at 2pm on 21 July – that was designed to gather information about MPs who used parliamentary privilege to avoid being sued. In a similar case,

[17] *Contractors* (1650, C5975); *Proceedings*, 599.011, p. 138; *Civicus*: 298.119, p. 1054; 298.063, p. 602; 298.092, p. 835; Larkin and Hughes, ii. 769–70; *HMC Cowper II*, p. 318; Northants. RO, IC 243.

[18] *Politicus*: 361.363, p. 7708; 361.317, p. 7092; *CSPD 1645–7*, p. 1; *Proceedings*, 599.188, pp. 2965–6; *Diurnall*, 503.177, p. 2684.

[19] *To all Fathers* (1649, G573); *HMC 5th Report*, p. 299; Vaughan, *Protectorate*, ii. 341–2; Lancs. RO, DDHU/53/31.

Thomason received more than one 'ticket' (which also appeared in *Mercurius Civicus*) inviting him to meetings at Scriveners' Hall, which had been summoned to identify royalist debtors and to lobby parliament.[20] By the early months of the Republic, moreover, such meetings had begun to take on a radical air. In May 1649, therefore, Leveller sympathisers in London used printed sheets to gather together their associates and elect new agitators 'in your several and respective wards', and to arrange other meetings within the city's wards, 'for the better carrying on of this work'.[21]

In the conditions of Civil War, therefore, print became a means for influencing the behaviour of more or less specific groups within society, and for organizing geographically dispersed individuals who shared common interests. In the process, however, it became a tool for members of the public rather than merely for the political elite, and ephemeral genres like tickets, flyers and newspapers were quickly exploited as part of everyday participatory practices that required organizing and co-ordinating fellow citizens. Appreciating this fact makes it possible to explore in much greater detail the ways in which print became integral to mass politics, and the ways in which contemporaries understood the participatory options that were open to them.

ii Subscription campaigns

The transformation of mass politics in the mid seventeenth century can only be understood in the context of other participatory strategies and the print revolution. This means that the practices associated with 'popular mobilisation' emerged out of more discrete and polite forms of engagement with Westminster politics, in order to express frustration and place additional pressure on parliament, and that they replicated methods that were originally devised by the political elite. And in both respects they also involved exploiting the possibilities that print offered for reaching out to broader sections of the political nation. The aim of this section is to support such claims by analysing the role of print during *subscription campaigns*, in terms of the processes that were involved in testing allegiance, securing compliance and enlisting widespread public support for particular initiatives and political demands.

---

[20] *To all Printers* (1645, T1329); GL, MS 4329/5 (1643–4), fos. 9–v; *It is Desired* (1643, E1599); *All such Persons* (1641, A941); *You are Requested* (1644, S3906, BL, E6/11); *It is Thought* (1644, I1088, BL, E6/18); *Civicus*: 298.065, p. 618; 298.066, pp. 622–6.
[21] *Thankfull* (1649, T835); *Pragmaticus*, 374.1, p. 8.

In an English context, the use of print to enlist and rally *concrete* support began in the 1640s, in association with political initiatives at Westminster. During 1641 and 1642, for example, print provided a valuable tool for testing the public response to the Protestation, thousands of copies of which were printed – at less than 1d per copy – and then despatched all over the country to secure support.[22] By this stage, indeed, it was fairly widely understood that print not only offered the quickest and cheapest means of distributing the text of such oaths, but also an effective way of collecting subscriptions, by providing documents that could literally be signed. Such methods were pioneered in relation to Scottish bonds and covenants from the 1590s onwards, and were then adopted in England in the early 1640s, at the precise moment when print became a ubiquitous device for promoting and recording popular support for either political side in a more general fashion. In 1643, for example, printed versions of the royalist protestation were used to gather signatures across north-west England, from individuals like Lord Capel.[23] Although such examples remained fairly rare, printed notices were frequently used to promote donations of money and supplies, not least in relation to the military campaign against Irish rebels and the humanitarian support for their Protestant victims. On other occasions 'notes' and 'bills' encouraged citizens to provide logistical support for the Earl of Essex's army, and to raise money for public works like the repair of Gloucester Cathedral.[24]

What is intriguing about such practices is the speed with which they were appropriated for non-official purposes, and used to promote mass petitions to parliament. In other words, as large-scale petitioning became an increasingly important feature of political culture – based upon the legitimating power of popular support – so the importance of print as an organizational device became much more obvious. Of course, such subscription campaigns were very often orchestrated within powerful gentry networks, which meant that petitioning could take place on a massive scale *without* the use of print. In counties like Herefordshire, Kent and Cornwall, therefore, it proved possible to use other methods to 'get hands, no matter how foul', not least by creating and distributing scribal petitions for signature in

---

[22] *Die Mercurii* (1641, E2609); *Die Veneris* (1641, E2721); BL: Add. 70109, unfol.; Add. 70003, fo. 225, 227; Shrops. RO, 212/364/72–72a; Notts. RO, PR.5767; TNA, AO3/1276; *Loving* (1642, L1090).

[23] NLS, MS 1656/3: *Solemn League* (1648, S4451), pp. 6–14; NLS: Cowan 901(1); Gray 753(13–16); *Confession* (1590); *HMC 2nd Report*, p. 67; BL, Add. 46399A, fos. 78–9; Lancs. RO, DAR/F/6.

[24] *We Who* (1641, W1184A); PA, MP 1641; *Collectors* (1642, C5222); CLRO, CCA 1/4, fo. 223v; TNA, SP 28/294, fo. 1241; *Forasmuch* (1647, F1425); SUL, Hartlib 53/1/2A; *Order* (1648, E2658); *Common* (1656, G884A).

individual parishes. Indeed, some country ministers were said to have enlisted the support of 'mean men', and to have solicited 'hedgers at the hedges, plowmen at the plow, threshers in the barns'.[25] This began to change, however, during the 1640s, not least with the emergence of petitioning on a national scale. Campaigning in this fashion began with the demand for a new parliament by the 'twelve peers' (September 1640), but although this genuinely involved an attempt to gather subscriptions rather than merely to publicize a cause, its signatories were almost certainly restricted to the county gentry.[26] Much more interesting, therefore, are subsequent episodes in which the pursuit of common goals involved attempts to secure broad popular support. Here, the organizational tasks were much more significant, and the key difference was the use of *exemplary* petitions, *shared* petitions and *parallel* petitions. During 1640 and 1641, for example, Puritan agitators encouraged supporters across the country to produce petitions regarding church reform by offering an example of the kinds of demands that should be made, while also recommending that each petition should use different language to avoid 'the suspicion of conspiracy'. Much more common, however, were 'blank' or 'parrot' petitions, which shared a common text even if the identity of the petitioners could be changed, or petitions that were produced by adapting texts from other parts of the country, including those that had appeared in print.[27] Such practices reinforce the sense that local petitions need to be placed in the context of wider political debates and Westminster politics, rather than merely being seen as expressions of local opinion, and a particularly dramatic example involves Derbyshire's petition to the king in the spring of 1642. Here surviving documentation provides a vivid picture both of the organizational issues involved in mobilizing popular support, and of the way in which other petitions were deliberately used as models.[28] Very

---

[25] *To his Excellency* (1653, T1355, BL, 669.f.17/11); BL: Eg. 1048, fos. 24–7; Add. 26785, fos. 53, 55–6; Add. 28000, fo. 363; Add. 64923, fo. 2; Add. 70003, fos. 192–v, 204; Add. 70108, unfol.; Add. 70109, unfol.; PA, MP 26 July 1641, 20 Dec. 1641, 10 Feb. 1642, 26 Feb. 1642, 5 May 1642; Shrops. RO, 212/364/72–a; CKS: U47/47/Z2/231–3; U47/47/O1, pp. 19–21; U951/C261/19; 'Twysden narrative', i. 202–6, 210–11, ii. 181–90; LPL, MS 1390, pp. 155, 157–9; HEH, EL 6945; Staffs. RO, D868/2/32; Antony, BC/24/2, fos. 57, 63, 65, 69.

[26] *Hatton Corr.*, p. 4; BL, Add. 4460, fo. 74v; Lancs. RO, DD/HU/46/21; ERO, D/DBa/A2/59.

[27] *CSPD 1640*, p. 564; *CSPD 1640–1*, pp. 40, 73, 84, 210; *CSPD 1641–3*, pp. 193, 197; TNA: SP 16/467, fo. 16; SP 16/470, fo. 180; BL: Add 23146, fo. 91v; Add. 26785, fo. 23; Shrops. RO, 212/364/78; SBT, DR98/1652/14–17; CKS, Fa/CPz5.

[28] P. Lake, 'Puritans, popularity and petitions', in *Politics, Religion and Popularity in Early Stuart Britain*, ed. T. Cogswell (Cambridge, 2002), pp. 259–89; J. Maltby, *Prayer Book and People in Elizabethan and Early Stuart England* (Cambridge, 1998), pp. 83–113, 143–56; DRO, D258/10/9/39; D258/10/29/19; D258/10/32/18; D258/10/86/57–9; D258/20/50; D258/30/25/1–2; D258/34/62.

occasionally, however, it is also possible to demonstrate that printed copies of petitions were circulated as a means of gathering signatures. In 1641, therefore, a printed pro-episcopacy petition from Oxford dons was circulated around the university's colleges for subscription, and one surviving copy contains a number of signatures from fellows of Exeter College.[29]

A second development that incentivized new organizational methods was the emergence of 'popular' petitioning. For campaigns that lacked gentry sponsors, printing made it possible to overcome financial and logistical obstacles, and the use of printed texts to call for petitions, promote subscriptions and gather signatures made mass petitioning a much more viable proposition, and a much more widespread phenomenon.[30] With Presbyterian petitioning during the 1640s, for example, it can be demonstrated that printed broadsides sometimes left space for the addition of signatures, and that hundreds of copies of petitions could be printed for distribution to well-wishers to 'get hands'. Some even left a blank space into which the name of a specific parish could be inserted. Such tactics represented a logical extension of practices that were used to secure support at Westminster, and it seems likely that most 'mass' petitions that were printed before being presented to parliament were either given to MPs or used to gather subscriptions, or both. Indeed in some cases annotations make explicit reference to the collection of signatures.[31] More importantly, of course, these methods were particularly valuable to radical activists. When Baptists used printed sheets to promote a petition in 1643, in the hope of getting 'as many hands as they can', they indicated that copies could be found 'at Mr Barbers in Threadneedle Street ... one for every parish'. Similarly, the Levellers circulated as many as 3,000 copies of individual petitions in the hope of gathering thousands of signatures, and then used exactly the same tactics to promote their *Agreement of the People*, and during the Interregnum such tactics became fairly standard, even if they were frowned upon by the authorities as something 'never done before', and as 'an ill precedent'. In 1650, therefore, a petition to revive the officers' *Agreement* was 'printed only for the better gathering of subscriptions', while a printed blank petition was used to secure mass support for

[29] OUA, SEP/V/3-4: *Colledges* (1641, O987).
[30] Leics. RO, DE730/4, fo. 42v; *Chirk Accounts*, p. 38; D. Zaret, *Origins of Democratic Culture* (Princeton, 2000), pp. 238–48.
[31] *Protestation* (1642, P3868); *Well-affected* (1643, T1658A); *Divers* (1646, T1658, BL, 669.f.10/58); Worcester College, AA.2.4/48: *Declaration*; *Humble* (1645, T1673, BL, 669.f.10/37); *Profession* (1653, P3644); *Voyce* (1653, W2814); *Representation* (1653, T1340); *Burton Diary*, iv. 456; Bodl. MS Nalson 14, fo. 160; MS Clarendon 30, fos. 211–v; *CJ*, vi. 170; PA, MP 22 Apr. 1642; BL, Add. 33936, fo. 235; Herts. RO, D/Elw/Z2; *Attestation* (1657, S2608, BL, 669.f.20/52).

constitutional reform in 1659. In the same year, moreover, the army council used printed copies of its 'representation and petition' to enlist support within the ranks, while those who objected to the army's intervention in parliamentary affairs launched a nationwide campaign that provided details about who would be responsible for co-ordinating petitioning in each county.[32]

For those who were engaged in collective petitioning, however, the use of print involved more than just the efficient gathering of signatures, and such tactics were also intimately connected with wider strategies for mobilizing support and engaging in tactical escalation. First, mass petitions, like those that were produced by individual citizens, could be used to attract publicity following their submission to parliament, and exploited by the political authorities, and some of those who submitted petitions to Richard Cromwell considered themselves to have been snubbed when their addresses were omitted from the official newspaper.[33] What this meant, of course, was that printed texts sometimes became highly controversial. Many were decried as being 'false' or 'forged', even if genuinely fraudulent petitions – like William Chillingworth's London petition of 1643 – were fairly rare. Many more, especially county petitions, were printed illicitly and involved spurious claims about representing the views of particular communities, and such situations frequently led to the production of counterpetitions and to rival groups boasting about the quality or quantity of their supporters.[34] What is less widely appreciated, however, is that the decision to print petitions sometimes involved conscious attempts to create exemplary texts, which could be circulated 'the kingdom over' to stir up support, especially within the army. In 1642, for example, Thomas Stockdale proposed printing the Yorkshire petition so that 'all the kingdom may take notice' and so that 'it may encourage others to the like forwardness'. More obviously, the numerous regimental petitions that expressed support for the Army *Remonstrance* in 1648 reflected conscious campaigning by the army

[32] *Certain Christians* (1643, N1473); *Kingdomes*, 214.271, p. 1027; 214.244, pp. 813, 815; *Declaration* (1648, D536), p. 1; Masterson, *Triumph* (1647, M1074), pp. 9–10, 14, 20–24; BL: Add. 50200, p. 35; Stowe 189, fos. 39–40; Add. 4165, fos. 33–4; *CJ*, v. 359; *Diurnall*, 504.226, pp. 1815–16; *Burton Diary*, iv. 456; *Divers* (1650, T1430); *Free-borne* (1659, T1397A), p. 3; *Remonstrance* (1659, R972), sigs. C–2v; Staffs. RO, D593/V/4/8.

[33] TNA, AO3/1088/1, part 2, fos. 1–v, 10; *LJ*, iv. 651–2, v. 107–8, 118; *CJ*, ii. 514, 607–8, vi. 177–8; PA, MP 8 June 1642; *HMC Popham*, p. 9; GMRO, E17/89/26/1–2; *Thousands* (1648, L2188).

[34] BL, Add. 70003, fo. 127; Sloane 1467, fo. 26; PA, MP 26 Feb. 1642; Braye 2, fos. 121, 123; *CCSP*, iv. 543; *Substantiall* (1642, C3888B, BL, E244/39); *LJ*, iv. 210–11, v. 192; *PJ*, i. 160–1, 165–6; *CJ*, ii. 661–2, 679; *Speech* (1641, P4278); *Hertford* (1642, H3522); *Petitions* (1641, T3510); *Humble* (1641, H3512); *New Birth* (1646, N581, BL, E350/12); *True Copie* (1646, T1274), pp. 2–4.

council, as well as the contagious effects of print culture, and Sir Thomas Fairfax explicitly encouraged newspaper coverage of petitions that were presented to him, so that they could be 'offered to the consideration of other counties'.[35] Indeed, similar practices were probably used throughout the revolutionary decades, not least in the context of agitation for a 'free' parliament in 1660. Here an exemplary petition was described as 'a general thing intended throughout our country', and was then circulated with the express goal that it would be adapted and adopted, and it seems perfectly clear that the appearance of a printed version inspired at least some other petitioners to follow suit.[36]

Secondly, organizational print could be used in tandem with more traditional methods for agitating the public, such as announcements from the parish pulpit, in yet another example of the tendency for official practices to be appropriated for non-official purposes. Ministers, of course, had long been valued as a means of communicating with the public, and during the revolutionary decades they were repeatedly co-opted by the authorities in novel ways, as printed texts were circulated so that they could be read in church. This usually involved attempts to publicize days of prayer, as with a printed flyer by which the mayor of London required ministers to announce a forthcoming day of humiliation (April 1649). But similar notices were also used to announce public meetings involving parliamentary committees, and to solicit financial contributions to the parliamentary cause. Sometimes such methods were even used to raise money for individual armies, and in 1644 Sir Thomas Middleton was permitted to circulate a variety of printed texts to London ministers in the hope of securing financial 'subscriptions' for his Cheshire forces. Indeed, on this occasion each congregation was also given a printed broadside that left space for the name of the parish and a list of signatures, thereby enabling Middleton to generate a detailed record of donors.[37] Very quickly, however, such tactics were mimicked by other interest groups. In 1649, for example,

[35] Bodl. MS Tanner 66, fos. 298–v; MS Carte 73, fos. 250–v; *New Birth* (1646, N581), pp. 3–5; *TSP*, vi. 291, 310; *Ludlow Memoirs*, i. 406–7; BL, Add. 18979, fo. 117; Worcester College, Clarke CXIV, fo. 104; Clarke XVI, fo. 19v; *Kingdomes*, 214.284, p. 1137; *Moderate* (1648, M2320); *Declaration* (1648, D527); *Severall* (1648, S2796); *True Copie* (1648, T2639); *Representation* (1648, T1360); *Declaration* (1648, D803); *Three Deputy* (1648, D771); *Humble* (1648, T1425A); *Diurnall*, 504.294, p. 2346.

[36] Bodl. MS Clarendon 68, fo. 214; Birmingham City Archives, MS 631039, fo. 1; Bodl. MS Eng. Lett.c.210, pp. 33, 37–8, 41; BL, Add. 21425, fo. 204; Cornwall RO, T1762; HEH, STTM 5/13; TNA, SP 18/219, fos. 43–6, 54–60, 75–6.

[37] *Civicus*, 298.066, pp. 622–6, 298.067, p. 633; *Whereas* (1643, E2784A); *Committee* (1645, W1060a); SUL, Hartlib 57/4/5; *Militia* (1644, L2851J); *By Vertue* (1641, R1122); TNA: SP 28/294, fos. 6, 162; SP 16/501, fo. 110; *Londino-Batavae*, III. 1923, 1926, 1976, 2001, 2045, 2152.

the sponsors of a new system of poor relief not only circulated a *pro forma* printed petition across the country, but also produced another printed text 'to be read in the parish churches'. The aim was to facilitate fundraising by William Wallis, a hosier at the sign of the Gun in Aldgate, where further copies of the petition were made available. Similar methods were also adopted by the fen drainers, who devised printed notices to be read in local churches announcing forthcoming meetings in Wisbech and Peterborough.[38]

Thirdly, the print culture of mass petitioning provides further evidence of the ways in which political frustration could lead to tactical escalation, and indeed to the use of radical rhetoric. A good example involves the campaign to secure help for the 'poor creditors' of the republican regime in the early 1650s. This involved a familiar story whereby long and fruitless petitioning and lobbying led to the printing of a petition, to demands for regular committee meetings to deal with the issue, and to calls for the election of a new representative, but the episode also reveals the adoption of much more sophisticated tactics in the face of insurmountable obstacles. This involved Samuel Chidley acting as a rallying point for those who had financial claims against the regime, and organizing yet another petition that involved a *collective* effort (September 1652). Chidley thus arranged for one Mr Pearson to 'constantly attend' at the Bell Savage on Ludgate Hill, in order to collect signatures and create a register of claims, and he promoted this venture with a printed flyer, a newspaper advert and even a campaigning newsbook, which encouraged people to consult with him in person at the Chequer in Bow Lane. Such tactics paid off handsomely, not just in the sense that Pearson was inundated with information, but also in the sense that Chidley secured the passage of legislation that was intended to ensure that the regime satisfied its creditors.[39]

Chidley's tactics were dramatic, but they were neither unique nor restricted to 'radicals', and the tactical escalations that were facilitated by print involved much more pervasive changes in practices and rhetoric. In 1648, for example, a quasi-royalist petition that called for the disbandment of the army and negotiations with the king was printed and circulated using fiery language, not least with a plea for London's 'honest freemen' to 'underwrite' it and send it to their common-councillors. Indeed, the freemen were encouraged to place radical demands on their representatives in

---

[38] *Humble Petition* (1649, T1484); SUL, Hartlib 57/4/9; Cambs. RO, R.59.31/9/5, fo. 9v.

[39] *Well-affected* (1651, T1706b); *All Those* (1652, C3834A); *Prisoners for Debt* (1653, T1402); *Diurnall*, 503.143, p. 2141; BL, Add. 21427, fo. 187; *Flying Eagle*, 154.2, pp. 15–16; 154.4, p. 26.

the City, by reminding them that they were elected to preserve liberties and advance the public good, rather than to promote private interests, by insisting that they could be held to account as 'proxies' and by threatening that elections would be revoked if individuals were found to have breached their trust.[40] Moreover, when mass petitioning was accompanied by mass lobbying of parliament, radical sentiments frequently came to the fore. This was because the authorities often responded by dismissing and even imprisoning those involved, and by attempting to limit the number of people who could follow a petition to Westminster.[41] In doing so, however, they frequently provoked heightened rhetoric about the infringement of participatory rights, and a tendency to think about political processes in increasingly systematic ways. One outraged supporter of a mass petition thus called for 'a known and certain rule between the people and their representatives', and for a 'contract' between voters and MPs that could be 'sealed' at the moment of elections.[42]

Fourthly, when mass mobilization extended beyond petitioning and the raising of money, print could play an important role in the *physical* mobilization of ordinary citizens. During the 1640s, therefore, tickets and newspaper notices were frequently used to organize the construction of defensive fortifications in London, to recruit 'labourers' for fen drainage projects and to enlist armies, for the simple reason that the print medium permitted dramatic results to be achieved at very short notice. A perfect illustration of this efficiency involves attempts to raise recruits for the parliamentarian army in the winter of 1642. On 5 November, therefore, flyers were distributed by the Committee of Safety requiring ministers to rally volunteers *the following day*, and to present a list of their names to the militia committee within hours, all of which was intended to permit an 8am muster on 8 November, only three days later. Similar texts emerged in the weeks and months that followed, not least as the authorities in London asked ministers to 'stir up your people . . . to join with the army' and to 'stand up for religion and liberties'.[43] Moreover, since individual ministers might prove obstructive or dilatory, such texts could also be distributed much

---

[40] *Humble Desires* (1648, H3415).

[41] Worcester College, Clarke XIX, fo. 33v; *Diurnall*, 504.300, sigs. 14C2, 10c; *Pragmaticus*, 369.209, sig. Iv; *CSPD 1653–4*, pp. 65–6, 88; BL, Add. 78198, fo. 26; Add. 4106, fos. 220–23v; *Politicus*, 361.164, p. 2625; *A&O*, i. 1139; *Tumultuous* (1648, E1433).

[42] Worcester College, Clarke XVI, fos. 7–8; *Diurnall*, 504.227, p. 1825; *Occurrences*, 465.5048, pp. 331–3; *Faith* (1649, F259), sigs. A–v; *Free-born* (1647, T1726); *Armies* (1648, A3715), pp. 2–3, 4–6, 6; LPL, MS 1390, pp. 157–9.

[43] CLRO, CCA 1/4, fo. 223v; *Politicus*, 361.559, p. 316; *Appointment* (1642, B6357); *Give Notice* (1642, L2878A); *You are Required* (1643, L2878C); *Londino-Batavae*, III. 1901, 1907–8.

more widely. It was by means of a printed appeal, therefore, that Charles I summoned Yorkshire royalists to a rendezvous on 20 May 1642, and although parliamentarians grumbled that this was likely to provoke 'jealousies' and 'distractions', they too adopted similar methods. A flyer requested that volunteers for the Earl of Essex's army should meet at the New Artillery Ground on 28 July, while in June 1645 printed sheets offered 'entertainment' at a Westminster tavern to anyone who was willing to serve in the Western Association. Moreover, as the royalist threat mounted in the summer of 1648, broadsides that were produced in London and York for proclamation by ministers used lurid language about 'bloody plots' to 'stirr up and awaken all true-hearted Englishmen'. Citizens were thus encouraged to 'join together as one man', and times and places were appointed for the gathering of armed men, 'for the beating back of this incroaching enemie'.[44] Moreover, such flyers were also supplemented by other genres, and newspaper adverts eventually became the preferred means of raising troops across the country. Those who were 'desirous to see Ireland and serve the commonwealth', for example, were encouraged to enlist at the Bell Savage on Ludgate Hill, the Black Swan in Hereford, the Red Lion at Brecon or the Angel in Carmarthen, at each of which they were promised 'considerable advance, constant pay, and suitable encouragement' (May 1651).[45]

From evidence regarding the organization of both royalist and parliamentarian armies, therefore, it is clear that print was valued not merely as an administrative tool for dealing with individuals and self-selecting groups, but also as an efficient means for reaching a national and socially diverse audience simultaneously. It is also clear that print made it possible to organize participation by large groups of citizens, most obviously in order to engage in tactical escalation in the circumstances of Civil War. As a result it is finally possible to explore the relationship between the print revolution and the transformation of street politics.

iii Organizing crowds

In addressing crowds and protests in the English Revolution, the aim of this section will be to move beyond the issues on which historians have traditionally focused, such as the political influence of street politics, the mood of

---

[44] By the King (1642, C2881); TNA, SP 16/490, fos. 131, 133; NLS, MS 2688, p. 573; Having (1644, C2347); Bodl. MS Tanner 61, fo. 165; Britanicus, 286.056, pp. 442–4; Bad News (1642, R10); Gentlemen (1645, A934); Kingdomes, 214.103, p. 829; Worthy (1648, A950); Committee (1648, B6361aA).

[45] Diurnall, 503.075, p. 1034; Politicus, 361.557, p. 284.

Londoners and the tactics of MPs. Instead, what follows will explore how print could be used to orchestrate large and well-timed gatherings in order to place pressure on parliament, and what will emerge is further evidence that traditional practices were transformed in the 1640s; that the willingness of political elites to integrate ordinary citizens into the political process had an educative effect; and that this was another area where official tactics were appropriated by agitators and activists for non-official purposes. Indeed, this reassessment of street politics will reinforce the sense that aggressive forms of participation need to be placed in the context of less demonstrative activities, and that protesting crowds tended to represent *conscious* tactical escalations.

Print was obviously not the only means of rallying crowds, of course, and traditional methods continued to play an important if problematic part in public politics. Verbal transmission of news may have generated crowds outside parliament in December 1640, forcing the adjournment of debates on church reform, and it was obviously central to popular agitation in Cumbria in late 1642. This involved 'the commons' around Kirkby Stephen entering into 'a combination' against the local gentry, generating 'great companies' and organizing delegations to 'draw up articles to be subscribed to in manner of an association'. Likewise, the use of 'drum and trumpet' to rally citizens also persisted, and proved effective in places like Dover, Devizes and Canterbury. Such tactics could also be turned against the authorities, of course, and in May 1645 women in Derby protested against taxation by processing 'up and down the town, beating drums and making proclamation', in the hope of orchestrating a rout of local excise commissioners.[46] However, oral methods of organization made it difficult to agitate quickly, while aural methods lacked subtlety and were probably rather risky for those whose campaigns were politically sensitive, and this explains why the apprentices who called for a 'free Parliament' in 1660 only used drums to rally support in the dead of night, to not very good effect.[47] The other alternative, of course, was textual mobilization, which had long been a feature of popular unrest, and which had been made a capital offence in the mid sixteenth century. Nevertheless, while 'scrolls and papers' could be an effective means of mobilizing citizens in a covert fashion, they were also costly and cumbersome, which meant that they tended to be short and

---

[46] Durham UL, MSP 30, fo. 5; Cumbria RO, D/MUS/5/5/Box 89/Bundle1/2; EKRO, Do/Fca/5, fos. 301–2v, 382v, 467v; Wilts. RO, G20/1/17, fo. 165v; CCL, CC/F/A/25, fos. 241–v, 242v; DRO, D258/12/16, p. 3.

[47] *HMC Popham*, p. 144.

vague, and they were difficult to produce in ways that reached a large and scattered audience quickly and efficiently. This meant that scribal organization was effective only in localized settings, and in tandem with other methods, as demonstrated by the Gillingham rioters who supplemented libels on maypoles with 'drums and muskets'.[48] As such, the importance of the period after 1640 lies in gradual recognition that print solved all of the problems associated with oral, aural and scribal agitation, and that it provided an affordable means of reaching a wide audience rapidly and surreptitiously.

Analysing this process begins with events at Westminster in the spring of 1641, when thousands of Londoners repeatedly massed around parliament during proceedings against the Earl of Strafford, sending shockwaves across the country and providing important evidence about participatory politics before the Civil Wars. This is partly because the scenes on 3 May need to be set in the context of the king's speech two days earlier, news of which travelled rapidly around the City and provoked as many as 6,000 people to descend on parliament. But it is also because the nature of the crowd changed over the course of three days. On 3 May those involved were 'masters and freemen' and 'men of good fashion', rather than apprentices, and the protest was vociferous but essentially non-threatening. Participants cried out for justice, but they were unarmed and did not 'offer any abuse', and their aim was to deliver a petition calling for Strafford's execution and for a strengthening of security at the Tower. Nevertheless, citizens apparently intimated that while they 'came unarmed now', they would return in larger numbers 'with swords and clubs' if their demands were not met, and the composition and mood of subsequent crowds was notably different. Protesters on 4 May were 'not men of fashion, but . . . mechanic people', and 'divers of them had swords', and they made it clear that 'if they could not have justice, the lords should hear of them in another manner'. On 5 May, moreover, Westminster witnessed 'the greatest confusion of all', and amid wild stories about popish plots 'the people ran all thither as if they were mad, with swords and clubs'.[49] In other words, whether or not such protests were stage-managed by the political elite, they also indicate that humble Londoners were *encouraged* to participate, and that crowds might

---

[48] *CSPD 1547–53*, nos. 378–9, 400; *APC 1547–50*, pp. 330–1; *SR*, iv. 104–5, 377; *CSPD 1629–31*, p. 386; *CSPD 1631–3*, p. 221; JRL: NP72/9; NP73/4.

[49] Staffs. RO, D(W)1778/I/i/19, 21; D661/20/2, pp. 94–5; BL: Add. 64922, fo. 29; Harl. 6424, fo. 58; *HMC Cowper II*, p. 281; *HMC 4th Report*, p. 295; Clarendon, i. 337; Bate, *Elenchus* (1685, B1083), p. 27; HEH, HM 66707; Bodl. MS Tanner 66, fos. 83v–4; Durham UL, MSP 30, fos. 34v, 35v; Cornwall RO, RP1/11.

prove difficult to control, which is probably the pertinent point about the involvement of John Lilburne. The future Leveller apparently threatened that crowds would grow larger and more heavily armed, and he was quoted as insisting that the protesters would 'have the deputy or the king'.[50]

More importantly, the events of May 1641 reveal popular knowledge of, and attitudes towards, individual MPs and peers. Strafford's supporters were identified and intimidated with 'a wonderful hideous noise', and protesters were evidently careful to press up against the coaches of specific courtiers. These included the unnamed noble who pleaded for patience, and who only made it to parliament once the 'wisest and greatest' among the protesters decided that 'we will take his word for once'. It also proved possible to recognize the Earl of Bristol, who was berated as 'an apostate from the cause of Christ' and as 'our mortal enemy', and who was reportedly told that 'we do not crave justice *from you*, but shall God willing shortly crave justice *upon you*'. Eventually, of course, the protesters secured a list of the 'Straffordians' (or 'betrayers of their country'), which was publicly displayed and circulated around the country, thereby prompting complaints that those who were named 'went in fear of their lives', and that they no longer had liberty to speak and vote according to their consciences. However, the episode also reveals contemporary knowledge about MPs whose opinions could be *respected*, and it is intriguing to note Sir Edward Dering's claim that the citizens 'did regard my advice as much, perhaps more, than any of the rest', as well as his boast that 'many took me by the hand whom I knew not, many said . . . there goes Sir Edward Dering, that is Sir Edward Dering, and God bless your worship'.[51]

Subsequent episodes of street politics during the 1640s – not least surrounding the 'Grand Remonstrance' and the campaign against the bishops in late 1641 – reinforce such conclusions about the integrative role of protests, and about the knowledge that protesters displayed. More importantly, however, they also reveal novel developments. Once again, therefore, it proved possible to bring large armed crowds to parliament at particularly tense moments, and this new round of protests did much to develop the image of John Venn, Isaac Pennington and Cornelius Burges as manipulators of 'myrmidions' in the City.[52] However, the real interest of such events lies in their participatory implications, and in the way in which

---

[50] PA, Braye 2, fo. 138; *HMC 10th Report VI*, pp. 140–1; *LJ*, iv. 233; Staffs. RO, D661/20/2, pp. 95–6.
[51] Staffs. RO, D661/20/2, pp. 94–6; Durham UL, MSP 30, fos. 34, 46–v; BL: Harl. 4931, fo. 126; Sloane 1467, fos. 72–v; Clarendon, i. 337; BL, Add. 26785, fo. 38.
[52] Bodl. MS Nalson 13, fos. 81r–v; Nalson, ii. 191; *Wise* (1641, V191); Williams, *Discovery* (1643, W2665) p. 22; *Venn* (1679, V193); *Pennington* (1643, P1147); *CSPD 1641–3*, p. 188; Clarendon, i. 455.

citizens 'without doors' were *schooled* by the political elite, and encouraged
to believe that it was legitimate to exert influence at Westminster when 'the
best affected party was like to be overpowered', so long as they dispersed
peacefully once specific goals had been achieved. This *educative* effect is
important because it may have ensured that 'the rabble' felt empowered to
influence other votes with 'swords and staves', even when they lacked
explicit sanction or instruction. It is certainly noteworthy, therefore, that
subsequent crowds – like the one that filled Westminster Palace in late
November 1641, and that 'accosted' MPs with 'great rudeness' over the fate
of the bishops – reveal no clear evidence of elite orchestration. And it is also
striking that such protesters demonstrated remarkable knowledge about
parliamentary affairs, in terms of identifying the MPs who merited special
attention. These included Sir John Strangeways, 'one of the greatest enemies we have', who was told that 'they came to him for his vote for the
putting down of the bishops'.[53]

The real novelty of these events, however, lay in how difficult it was to
turn back the clock to a more decorous age. Thus, while considerable
attention has been paid to the constitutional impact of the ensuing clampdown – the question of parliamentary control over the militia – it is also
possible to explore the impact on protesters. This was partly about the risk
to life and limb from official brutality, not least because of the Earl of
Dorset's rash order to open fire on citizens; but more importantly it was
about divisions over the legitimacy of mass petitioning. Some MPs obviously longed for the re-imposition of order, and William Smith clearly
hated the idea that citizens could 'prescribe' which laws should be enacted
and which individuals should be prosecuted, but many Londoners were
determined to persist with protests. For example, they continued to gather
in large numbers into late December, despite the risk of being attacked by
Thomas Lunsford's troops.[54] Indeed, as mass lobbying continued after the
attempted arrest of the Five Members in January 1642, it became clear that
'apprentices and labourers' refused to drop their campaign against the
bishops and that they were willing to increase the pressure on parliament.
They were reported as 'crying out . . . that for one that is here now, there will

---

[53] Bodl. MS Nalson 13, fos. 81–v, 83; MS Clarendon 20, fos. 129, 132; *D'Ewes*, ed. Coates, pp. 183–7, 211,
213–16; *Heads*, 181.102, pp. 3–4; *CJ*, ii. 324, 327, 341, 343, 348, 351, 359; Clarendon, i. 451, 455; *CSPD
1641–3*, pp. 186, 188; *HMC Buccleuch I*, p. 287; BL: Add. 28000, fo. 140; Add. 64922, fo. 77; *Bloody*
(1641, B3258), pp. 3–6; Devon RO, 1700M/CP 20; *Petition* (1642, T1496C); Bodl. MS Tanner 60,
fo. 220.

[54] *D'Ewes*, ed. Coates, pp. 211–30; *LJ*, iv. 491–6, 498; BL: Sloane 3317, fo. 22v; Add. 28000, fo. 48; Add.
64922, fo. 77; Clarendon, i. 451; *CJ*, ii. 327, 329; *Smith's Speech* (1641, S4145), p. 3; CLRO, JOR 40,
fos. 10–v; *By the King* (1641, C2821); *CSPD 1641–3*, p. 217; *Bloody*, pp. 3–5.

be five times as many here tomorrow', and they were also prepared to make threats against what they regarded as an unresponsive parliament.[55]

Thus far, of course, there is no evidence that such demonstrations and protests involved or required printed stimuli, but other evidence from the tense months before the outbreak of war indicates that print began to emerge as a weapon in mass politics, as both an organizational tool and a talisman. This may have been apparent as early as the Southwark disturbances of May 1640, in which a 'furious multitude' targeted Archbishop Laud for his role in the dissolution of the Short Parliament. This episode has attracted attention due to the anxiety that it provoked at court, but it is also interesting because the crowd – perhaps 1,200 strong – assembled at Lambeth following the circulation of two 'pasquills' or 'libels'. These were 'affixed to the pillars of the Old Exchange' and 'set upon posts and other places in the City', and they both encouraged Londoners to 'come now and help us, that we may destroy this subtle fox and hunt this ravening wolf out of his den', and arranged for a gathering at St George's Fields.[56] Moreover, while it is certainly possible that these texts were produced scribally, it was not long before printed notices – 'devilish devices to stir up sedition' – were being used to ensure that crowds appeared in particular locations, on certain days and for specific purposes. Indeed, this soon fostered a new kind of street politics, and one that was difficult to control, in ways that first became apparent following the attempted arrest of the Five Members in January 1642. This episode has become well known because a 'multitude' surrounded the king's entourage demanding 'the gospel and liberty of Parliament', and because Henry Walker threw a printed flyer into the royal coach; but what has not been considered is the possibility that his text, *To Your Tents, O Israel*, was scattered about the streets in order to rally the crowd.[57] Indeed, another aspect of these demonstrations that has been overlooked involves the way in which printed texts provided *mascots* to be carried by protesters, and totemic devices around which a crowd could unite. Most obviously, parliament reprinted the Protestation alongside a statement justifying recent activity by London's citizens, and when the Five Members made their triumphant return to Westminster on 10 January, they were accompanied by 3,000 of the trained bands, as well as 500 sailors, all of whom carried the text 'on their spears'. On this occasion the practice was

[55] BL, Add. 64922, fo. 93; *PJ*, i. 247, 286–7; LMA, MJ/SR/903/55.
[56] CUL, Buxton 102/9; BL: Harl. 383, fos. 163–4; Harl. 385, fo. 240; Add. 28000, fo. 16; Add. 11045, fos. 117–v; Add. 35331, fo. 77; Harl. 4931, fo. 8; Laud, *Works*, iii. 235, 284; LPL, MS 943, p. 717; HEH, EL 7833–5.
[57] BL, Add. 78220, fos. 13–v; Taylor, *Whole* (1642, T530), sig. A2v; *VII Articles* (1642, S2736), p. 6.

almost certainly encouraged by MPs, but this was not always the case, and the same tactic was also employed later in the month, when a broadside on behalf of 'many thousand poore people' was printed 'for the use of the petitioners who are to meet this present day in Moorfields, and from thence to go to the house of Parliament with it in their hands'.[58] Indeed, this use of print to achieve more than one organizational goal quickly became commonplace. Thus, when 4,000 protesters from Kent descended on parliament in support of their expelled MP, Sir Edward Dering, it was noted that 'they all had papers in their hats', and when Dering organized a controversial petition in April 1642, it was suspected that print was used to gather thousands of supporters at Blackheath, in order to accompany the petition to Westminster.[59]

In the months leading up to Civil War, therefore, print was used occasionally but inventively in relation to street politics, but its significance only really became apparent after the summer of 1642, as part of increasingly sophisticated and acrimonious political campaigning. The last weeks of 1642, therefore, saw not just tense debates over peace negotiations, but also dramatic activity by rival groups of Londoners. Demonstrations by hawks, who wanted to 'decide the business by the sword', provoked agitation by doves, the circulation of whose petition by 'persons of inferior quality' generated 'hot words', 'many blows' and numerous arrests.[60] The response of the peaceniks, however, was to raise the stakes by implementing a much more aggressive petitioning campaign, and by using print in a much more strategic fashion. They circulated printed copies of their petition and scattered copies of a tract called *A Complaint to the House of Commons*, and on Sunday 1 January 1643 they 'set up' printed bills 'in several places about the city', inviting apprentices 'to meet at the Piazzi in Covent Garden' the following day, 'by seven of the clock in the morning, in complete civil habit, without swords or staves'. This 'apprentices summons' generated a crowd of 2,000 people, who proceeded to march on parliament, only to encounter hostility from peers who expressed 'dislike of petitioning with multitudes'. It was at this point that things threatened to get ugly, and some of the 'ruder sort' apprehended one of their most high profile opponents, Viscount Saye,

---

[58] *Die Mercurii* (1642, E2613); BL: Add. 64922, fo. 81; Add. 78315, fo. 8; HEH, HM 46431; *CSPV 1640–2*, p. 281; *Many Thousand* (1642, T1437).

[59] *HMC 2nd Report*, p. 47; BL, Add. 64923, fo. 2; *CJ*, ii. 514; NLS, MS 2687, p. 1117; *Knyvett*, p. 100; Bodl. MS Add.C.132, fo. 91.

[60] *Diurnall*: 511.24A, sigs. Z–Z3; 511.28A, sig. Dd4; PA, MP 22 Dec. 1642; *Continuation*, 54.23A, p. 5; *Speciall Passages*, 605.18, pp. 152–3; Bodl. MS Tanner 64, fo. 109; Leeds UL, ML, Misc. Political Papers Vol. I, fo. 39.

and used 'strange words' about what would happen if parliament failed to 'grant them a peace'. The situation was eventually defused 'after much importunity' when the Lords agreed to admit a smaller delegation the following day, but what makes the incident intriguing is the clear pattern of events by which this decision was preceded. This involved a shift from simple petitioning to mass lobbying; the use of print to facilitate more aggressive tactics; a hostile reaction to such pressure from within parliament; and finally an angry response from citizens, which threatened to cause disorder. Little wonder then that the apprentices' final move was to print a statement in which they denied allegations about their malign motives and scandalous behaviour, protested about the attitude of peers and justified mass lobbying. The latter, indeed, was done by quoting a speech in which *an MP*, Nathaniel Fiennes, had defended the right of all those who subscribed to petitions to accompany them to Westminster.[61]

It would be possible to cite any number of other episodes where printed notices were used in precisely the same way, but this picture of the relationship between print, mass petitioning and street politics can most obviously be enriched by analysing subsequent agitation over peace.[62] Indeed, events in the summer of 1643 reveal how different forms of organization were combined into a coherent campaign, how such campaigns capitalized upon detailed knowledge about parliamentary processes and personalities, and how such tactics let to heightened tension by prompting opponents to modify their behaviour, and by forcing the authorities to respond. This chain of events began with a mass petition that demanded vigorous prosecution of the war effort, and then continued with the scattering of leaflets on 18 July. These encouraged Londoners to meet at Merchant Taylors' Hall the following day – 'at any hour . . . from 4 of the clock in the morning till 8 in the evening' – so that they could 'hear and subscribe a petition . . . for raising the whole people of the land as one man'. A connected summons promoted another meeting at Grocers' Hall two days later – 'between the hours of eight in the morning and eight at night' – and the organizers not only identified a group of sympathetic MPs who ought to sit as a committee for the 'general rising', but also planned to lobby parliament *en masse*. They explicitly asked readers to 'Shew this paper to your friends', and they added

[61] *LJ*, v. 496; *Speciall Passages*, 605.21B, p. 178; *Kingdomes*, 214.001, p. 8; *Diurnall*, 511.30A, sigs. Ffv–Ff2, Ff3; *Humble* (1643, H3407), pp. 3–7; *Accidents*, 579.18, p. 137; *Continuation*, 638.26, pp. 4–5; *You that Were* (1643, Y57, BL, E83/46); *Malignants* (1643, W1204), pp. 2–3; Bodl. MS Nalson 2, fo. 265v; *True* (1643, T3084), pp. 3, 5.
[62] *Marriners* (1643, T1479); *Informations*, 36.02, pp. 14–16; *Diurnall*, 511.33A, sig. Kk4; *Kingdomes*, 214.005, pp. 34–5; *Discovery* (1643, P4265A), sigs. Bv–2.

that 'if it be stuck up, let none presume to pull it down'. The result was that they secured support from 'thousands of judicious well-minded men', and that the petition was presented with a large crowd on 20 July.[63] However, the campaign did not stop here, and the 'violent spirits' responded to subsequent parliamentary debates by producing a 'libellous and scandalous writing' (5 August), as well as printed 'tickets' that were 'read in some pulpits' the following day. These were said to have been aimed at 'the dregs and rascality of the people', and they not only suggested that 'the well-affected party had been over-voted' in the Commons, but also encouraged citizens to 'repair to Westminster' on 6 August, and the upshot was that a hostile and 'seditious multitude' appeared outside parliament. According to some reports, members of the crowd 'assaulted' the Earl of Holland, as one of the leaders of the peace party, 'gave him base and vile language' and 'thrust him up and down', thereby prompting him to retire from parliament in disgust.[64]

With the campaign for a 'general rising', therefore, it is possible to observe the sophisticated and multi-purpose deployment of print. Texts were used to organize a mass petition, to orchestrate the appearance of crowds at short notice and to respond to debates in parliament, as well as to exploit detailed knowledge about individual members. Such tactics are intriguing not just because they made it vital for others to respond in kind, but also because they represented a form of tactical escalation that could result in violent disorder. Merely a day after the anti-peace protest, therefore, a large counter-protest was organized involving a 'multitude of women' who 'came down in great confusion', and contemporaries clearly saw in such tactics – including threats towards the MPs who opposed them – a conscious attempt to follow the example that had been set by a rival faction. The fact that all of the protesters wore identical white ribbons suggests that the protest was co-ordinated at a fairly high level, but it is also worth noting that the women – 'whores, bawds, oyster-women, kitchen stuff women, beggar women, and the scum of the suburbs' – displayed remarkable knowledge about individual members. They identified Pym as their arch-enemy and the Earl of Holland as their key ally, and they deliberately avoided using violence against Sir Simonds D'Ewes, upon whom they bestowed 'some benedictions'. The result, however, was that

[63] *All Sorts* (1643, A940); *All that Wish* (1643, A942); *Declaration* (1643, E2570); *Scout*, 485.04, p. 29; *Civicus*, 298.008, p. 62; *Informations*, 36.28, pp. 221, 223; *Diurnall*, 504.004, p. 31; *Humble* (1643, T1649); *Letter from Mercurius* (1643, L1489B), p. 31.

[64] BL, Harl. 165, fos. 145v–7, 227v, 229; *CJ*, iii. 196–8; *LJ*, vi. 172–3; Rushworth, v. 357; *Civicus*, 298.011, pp. 85–6; *Knyvett*, p. 126; *Baillie*, ii. 99.

what began as a peace protest turned into a violent encounter, as the women grew frustrated about the platitudinous response to their petition. They eventually 'pressed upon the outer doors' of the Commons, shouting 'give us these traitors that are against peace, that we may tear them in pieces', and their refusal to retreat ensured the use of force by nearby guards, resulting in numerous injuries and at least one death.[65]

These events in the summer of 1643 changed the tone of street politics irrevocably. They provoked resolutions against 'unlawful' assemblies and orders against using printed notices to organize crowds, and they also made politicians fearful about the possibility that crowds would be used to influence votes. However, they also ensured that print became a permanent fixture of political campaigning, especially at moments of factional tension and mounting frustration. This can best be demonstrated through the episode known as the 'forcing of the Houses' (26 July 1647), a key moment in the Presbyterian 'counter-revolution' when apprentices invaded the Palace of Westminster and prompted the flight of Independent MPs to the army. This has attracted attention because of suspicions that it was orchestrated by political grandees, but it also provides further evidence that forceful action tended to reflect the failure of formal petitioning, and that the period witnessed significant new developments in participatory culture. Rather than merely using intimidation to lobby MPs, therefore, the apprentices actually interrupted proceedings and forced the repeal of recent votes regarding the London militia, thereby demonstrating heightened awareness about parliament, a honing of skills and a willingness to escalate tactics in the face of obstruction. Moreover, while there is no evidence that print was used to organize the riot, the invasion of parliament was clearly bound up with a broader participatory culture in which print was a powerful organizational tool, and it obviously represented an act of desperation following a long and frustrating political campaign. Indeed, the 'forcing of the Houses' represented merely the final act in a protracted drama, and one in which a blizzard of print ephemera had been used to organize precise political action and to ratchet up the pressure on parliament.[66]

---

[65] BL: Harl. 165, fos. 149v–50; Add. 31116, p. 137; Add. 22619, fos. 97–v, 99; Add. 18778, fo. 14; Add. 64923, fo. 78; *CJ*, iii. 199; Bodl. MS Rawl. D.141, pp. 129–31; *Kingdomes*, 214.030, pp. 228–30; *Informations*, 36.30, pp. 231–2; *Knyvett*, pp. 126–7; *Civicus*, 298.011, pp. 85–8.

[66] *LJ*, vii. 76; *CJ*, iii. 707, v. 290–1, 316, 324, 452; CUL, Buxton 59/90; CLRO, JOR 40, fo. 240v; *Diurnall*: 504.209, pp. 1678–9; 504.214, p. 1724; 504.217, p. 1748; *HMC 5th Report*, p. 197; *Occurrences*: 465.5034, sig. Ll3v; 465.5035, sig. Llv; *Kingdomes*: 214.224, pp. 645–6; 214.225, p. 658; 214.226, pp. 662–3; 214.228, p. 683; Bodl. MS Clarendon 30, fo. 120; PA, MP 25 Sept. 1647, fos. 21–

This print context for the 'forcing of the Houses' stretched back to at least Easter 1647, and it involved repeated attempts to organize mass petitions, many of which were rejected as seditious breaches of parliamentary privilege. In April 1647, for example, a paper was posted around the City calling for 'fellow apprentices' to meet in Covent Garden at 7am on 20 April, 'for the prosecution of our late presented petition for recreation'. In the days and weeks that followed, a number of other petitions and 'posted' notices responded to calls for the dissolution of the army by attacking specific Presbyterian grandees, and these were 'published' by ministers and distributed far beyond London. Libels on 2 June encouraged disbanded soldiers to 'meet the next morning in the Palace of Westminster', and these 'reformados' duly responded by massing around the Commons, using 'high and ill language' and threatening to padlock the door 'to keep them in, till they had satisfied them'. On 11 June libels were 'scattered upon and down the streets in the night', in the hope of mobilizing 'a great number of apprentices' to appear at Westminster the following day, thereby provoking a 'contrary party' to do the same thing a day later. And on 17 June it was reported that '1,000 bills are now a printing' to call a meeting of 'covenanted' apprentices on the day of the next fast (30 June).[67] This flurry of activity involved different groups and competing goals, and it not only alarmed the authorities but also fed into allegations against the behaviour of the 'eleven members' who were impeached by the army. Nevertheless, attempts to prevent mass agitation proved fruitless. Indeed, on the very day that parliament considered the fate of these controversial Presbyterian MPs, the palace was mobbed by protesters, to the 'disturbance' of many of those who were sitting in the two Houses (20 June). More importantly, London's counter-revolutionary citizens produced printed copies of their *Solemne Engagement*, 'with a space left to every sheet for the setting their hands', and then dispersed it 'all over the city' (21 July). This was clearly a frustrated response to a parliament that was perceived to be unresponsive to more polite petitions. Indeed, while protesters certainly 'pulled down' recent orders regarding the militia, and tore them 'in pieces', the subsequent storming of Westminster Palace also represented an angry reaction to an order that

---

4v; *Perfect Summary*, 528.02, pp. 11–12; Beinecke, Osborn fb.155, pp. 237–8; BL, Add. 34169, fo. 28; *Sydney Papers*, p. 25; 'Lewis Dyve', p. 72; Claydon, Verney reel 8; *Mdx County Records*, iii. 100; *Ludlow Memoirs*, i. 161; Walker, *Relations* (1648, W334), pp. 41–2.

[67] *Diurnall*: 504.196, p. 1574; 504.197, p. 1577; 504.199, p. 1595; 504.200, p. 1612; 504.207, pp. 1656–7; BL, E384/12: 'Fellow apprentices'; E390/14: 'Unanimous answer'; E392/7: 'Renowned apprentices'; *CJ*, v. 134; PA, MP 27 Apr. 1647; BL: Add. 70005, fos. 248–v; Add. 34169, fo. 26; Worcester College, BB 8.16/65: *All Worthy*; *Occurrences*, 465.5022, sig. X4; Bodl. MS Tanner 58, fo. 198.

directly responded to the *Solemn Engagement* by banning such inflammatory devices.[68]

The tumultuous events of July 1647 thus represented the culmination of tension that had been building for months, and they revealed anger that resulted from the content of political debates as well as from the official response to a new kind of mass politics. They also revealed how frustration with parliament could cause tactics to escalate, and how innovative participatory methods were facilitated by novel uses of print. As such, they also represented the culmination of developments that had been increasingly apparent since 1640. During the revolution, in other words, street politics was transformed not just by direct involvement on the part of the political elite, and by the educative and integrative effects of the encouragement that they offered to citizen participation, but also by growing familiarity with parliamentary affairs, by the appropriation of official tactics for non-official purposes and by the exploitation of print. The result was that crowds became part of the tactical armoury of politicized citizens, and a sophisticated participatory device that could genuinely be organized 'from below'.

iv The spectre of organized violence

Of course, the events of July 1647 did not represent the end of the story, and in the weeks that followed there emerged further evidence of 'tickets' being printed and displayed 'upon posts in and about the city'. Nevertheless, the 'forcing of the Houses' probably marked a watershed in the history of mass politics, by ensuring that crowds and protests became inextricably linked with the power of print, the potential for popular organization and the spectre of violence, and the aim of this final section is to explore the impact of such practices and such fears in the decade that followed. This will involve demonstrating that street politics was not restricted to soldiers and Levellers, but more importantly it will involve describing an *escalatory cycle* of mass politics. This involved a spiral of anger and aggression, in which the frustrations that caused citizens to resort to street politics became exacerbated by official hostility towards mass agitation, and in which attempts to restore decorum made aggressive tactics all the more likely.[69]

---

[68] *CJ*, v. 217, 252; *LJ*, ix. 244; *Diurnall*: 504.205, p. 1631; 504.208, pp. 1664–5; *Petition* (1647, T1659 and S4439); PA, MP 24 July 1647; Bodl. MS Tanner 58, fo. 399; *Araignment* (1647, A3745), p. 2; 'Lewis Dyve', p. 71; *Sydney Papers*, p. 25; *Die Sabbathi* (1647, E1636).

[69] *Declaration* (1647, D664), pp. 125, 135; *Comparatis* (1647, C5603), p. 21; *Diurnall*, 504.214, p. 1723; *Die Veneris* (1647, E2670A); TNA, SP 16/515 part ii, fo. 78; CLRO, JOR 41x, fo. 110.

This cycle of frustration, suspicion and escalation is fairly evident in the activity of both royalists and radicals in the months leading up to the Second Civil War. Indeed, when Levellers orchestrated a petition in support of Sir John Maynard in February 1648, print became a powerful tool for a grass-roots campaign that mapped onto the civic geography of London. Printed slips were circulated in the hope of encouraging citizens to use their 'best endeavours' to gather subscriptions from 'all the inhabitants of your ward, whether masters or men-servants', and a central collection point was created at Shoemakers' Hall. This enabled support to be mobilized within twenty-four hours, and once the signatures had been collected, other printed papers were 'dispersed up and down' urging subscribers to go 'as one man . . . with a petition to the House of Commons on Friday next, to demand our liberties'. Likewise, printed copies of the petition invited 'well-affected persons' to repair 'peaceably' to Westminster 'on Friday morning next . . . to assist in delivering of this petition'. At Westminster, of course, such efforts to 'stir up' the people generated considerable anxiety because they were perceived to involve 'disobedience' and 'force', and this same fear of violence was also apparent during royalist agitation, as 'tumultuous' petitioning was orchestrated at higher social levels in the spring of 1648.[70] With the Essex petition, for example, the grand jury dispersed information about when and where petitioners should assemble in order to deliver their signatures, and by printing 500 copies of their demands they were able to enlist the support of 20,000 people and to organize a mass lobby of parliament 3,000 strong. Similar tactics were also evident in Kent, where troops were mobilized in response to the 'violent' dispersal of printed instructions, which were used to ensure that a large crowd gathered at Blackheath before accompanying the county petition to Westminster. And they were also evident in Surrey, where 500 printed copies of the county petition announced a rallying point at Putney Heath (8am on 16 May), and generated an armed crowd of 6,000 people, including 'country men' with sticks. Here, however, the mood was much more obviously threatening, and the petitioners insisted that 'we will have an answer, or else we will pull out the parliament by the ears'. They also added that 'we will have a new parliament, for this parliament only sit for their own ends, we will have an account of all the monies that we have paid'. The result, perhaps

---

[70] *Englands* (1648, M1455); BL, 669.f.11/125*: *You are Requested*; TNA, SP 16/516, fos. 17v–18; *Kingdomes*, 214.246, p. 830; *Wel-Affected* (1648, T1618); *CSPD 1648–9*, pp. 14–17; *Diurnall*, 504.252, p. 2026; *CJ*, v. 567.

inevitably, was bloodshed, as soldiers 'fell on them, shot some, cut and slashed a great many'.[71]

What emerges very clearly from such episodes is that print made it possible to express political frustration in novel and dramatic ways; that new kinds of mass activity provoked unease within parliament; and that this hardening of attitudes within the elite made public politics even more fraught. Indeed, it occasionally ensured that peaceful protests gave way to violent confrontations and that print was used to foment disorder. Thus, on the day that parliament rejected the Agitators' proposal to use Dean and Chapter lands for the payment of soldiers' arrears (11 November 1647), Edward Sexby hurriedly produced a short tract calling for a general rendez-vous at Ware. This was 'scattered up and down the streets', and those who turned up were famously provided with printed copies of the *Agreement of the People*, to be worn as a talisman. The Levellers, meanwhile, 'pasted up' printed bills in churches and upon 'several gates and posts throughout the city', as a means of gathering 80,000 signatures to a petition that demanded deliverance from 'bloody taskmasters'. However, while their supporters considered such tactics to be a popular *right*, the authorities detected an attempt to incite a 'tumult' and decided to imprison those responsible. This provoked yet another angry petition from the Levellers, in which MPs were denounced for treating petitioners in a partial and inconsistent fashion, and what makes the episode particularly intriguing is that officials *assumed* that such frustration would result in violent protests, and so mobilized the trained bands 'to assist the Parliament in case of danger'.[72]

The insurrectionary potential of print culture became most apparent, however, after the establishment of the Republic. The fear that royalists would use print to 'debauch' the people and raise a military force persisted until the Battle of Worcester, and in the summer of 1649 printed notices were explicitly used to encourage the 'young men' of London to meet in Tothill Fields at 8am on St James's day (25 July). The intention was perfectly clear, and protesters were urged to 'provide themselves with stones or some other weapons', so that the regicides could be 'pulled out by the ears' and 'receive the reward due to such rebellious and unnatural

[71] *Grand Jury* (1648, T1606); BL: Add. 34170, fos. 14–v; Add. 78198, fo. 64v; *Pragmaticus*, 369.125, sig. A4; Bodl. MS Nalson 22, fos. 362–v; *Kingdomes*, 214.261, pp. 945–6; 214.262, p. 957; *True Relation* (1648, T3013), pp. 1–2; *CSPD 1648–9*, pp. 63, 67; TNA, SP 16/516, fos. 65, 72; Carter, *Most True* (1650, C662), p. 14; *Letter* (1648, B13), pp. 4–5.
[72] *Agents* (1647, C6134); *Kingdomes*, 214.235, p. 734; BL, Add. 78198, fos. 21, 26v; *Elencticus*, 312.03, pp. 20–1; *Diurnall*, 504.227, p. 1825; LJ, ix. 546; PA, MP 29 Nov. 1647.

monsters'.[73] Much more troubling, however, were the Levellers, whose activity reveals a similar willingness to contemplate the organization of violence. Papers posted in Hertfordshire in March 1649 incited a tax strike, while in the following month printed sheets were 'scatred about the streets' to provoke the election of new agitators, and Leveller women began a campaign of action that eventually led to a bloody confrontation. Their agitation began peacefully enough, albeit in a highly organized fashion, as printed petitions were used to collect signatures across a network of wards and congregations and to organize a mass lobby. Supporters were instructed to 'meet at Westminster the 23 of this instant April 1649 between 8 and 9 of clock in the forenoon', and although they refrained from using physical violence on that occasion, 'their tongues pelted hail shot against the members' who passed into and out of parliament. Eventually, however, tempers became frayed, and having experienced violence by soldiers and intransigence by MPs, and having failed to secure 'satisfaction' with two further protests, the Levellers organized a series of meetings to discuss the possibility of an armed uprising.[74] During the following summer, moreover, parliament's persistent refusal to honour petitioners' rights and the 'book of declarations' led to further agitation. Although this ostensibly involved the use of a printed *Outcry* to promote meetings across the country, and to generate support for the *Agreement of the People*, the authorities suspected that this would result in 'blows' rather than petitioning, and their response was both swift and severe.[75]

By 1653 this *perceived* connection between printed agitation and violent insurrection was shown to be entirely rational. Following another of Lilburne's trials, therefore, the Levellers openly used print to incite violence, and copies of *A Charge of High Treason* were 'scatred about the streets' on the night of 14 August, with the aim of effecting the downfall of the republican regime. The *Charge* urged 'all the people of England' – including 'servants' – to mobilize with 'weapons of war' in 'every county town', to 'elect and choose' new MPs and to escort them to London 'with such forces of the several counties as they shall appear'. In other words, the Levellers sought to *impose* a new representative by force, and this printed call to arms was meant to ensure that the revolution would be co-ordinated, and that

---

[73] BL, Add. 19399, fo. 75; *Moon*, 248.12, p. 103.

[74] *Kingdomes Faithful Scout*, 210.07, p. 48; *All Worthy* (1649, A951; BL, E551/21); *Militaris*, 348.1, pp. 13–16; *Wel-affected* (1649, T1736), p. 8; *Mod. Messenger*, 124.01, pp. 2–3; *Occurrences*, 465.5121, pp. 990, 993; *Pragmaticus*, 370.02, sig. Bv; *Kingdomes*, 214.310, p. 1351; *Brittanicus*, 285.3, p. 26.

[75] *Outcry* (1649, L2152), pp. 4, 9–10, 12; *Thankfull* (1649, T835); *Pragmaticus*, 370.04A, sig. D2v; *CSPD 1649–50*, pp. 314, 546–7.

simultaneous and precisely timed risings would occur across the country. In the end, of course, the revolution failed to materialize, despite localized disorder, but the episode nevertheless indicates the widespread *expectation* that print would be effective, and the vigour with which the regime investigated the Leveller threat certainly attested to their 'indescribable' fear.[76] Moreover, even the failure of the Leveller coup did not cause such anxiety to fade. In the years after 1653 the authorities repeatedly investigated the role that printing played in plots against the regime, even if this sometimes meant that they *caused* rather than *prevented* trouble. In December 1659, for example, the army's concern that a petitioning campaign by London apprentices represented the first stage of a well-organized uprising led to a heavy-handed response by soldiers and brutal retaliation by their victims. This was almost certainly an over-reaction, but it was one that reflected fairly widespread fear that, by spreading 'damnable' declarations 'up and down the city', 100 'fanatics' could cause 'a hundred thousand' to take up arms.[77]

v Conclusion

London's premeditated crowds during the 1640s and 1650s are obviously distinct from food riots, enclosure protests and fen drainage disputes, as well as from episodes of festive misrule and moral disorder. Larger in scale and carefully timed, they generally involved demonstrations rather than the violent settling of grievances. Nevertheless, such differences should not be overplayed, and it is possible to make both historical and conceptual connections between rural unrest and street politics at Westminster. Parliamentary crowds could be genuinely 'popular', in terms of the people and the issues involved, and they could certainly reflect concerns that originated in local communities. They also need to be analysed in the context of a spectrum of participatory tactics, as aggressive forms of petitioning and lobbying, and as frustrated responses to an unresponsive political system. Indeed, like other forms of mass activity, the crowds that gathered outside parliament revealed awareness of legitimate political processes and lawful political action, and a sense of the need to employ more

---

[76] *Charge* (1653, C2055, BL, 669.f.17/52); *CSPD 1653–4*, pp. 151, 156, 180, 187, 197, 200, 436; *CJ*, vii. 333; *CSPV 1653–4*, pp. 132, 139, 142.

[77] *Politicus*: 361.244, p. 5132; 361.245, p. 5147; 361.357, pp. 7726–7; 361.358, p. 7742; 361.363, p. 7812; *Proceedings*, 599.286, p. 4536; *TSP*, vi. 163–4; Vaughan, *Protectorate*, ii. 184–5; BL, Add. 4158, fos. 99–v; Bodl. MS Clarendon 67, fos. 119, 178, 180, 186, 200, 222–v, 225, 226, 229; MS Carte 73, fos. 329, 333; CLRO, JOR 41x, fo. 212; *Rugg*, pp. 13, 19–20; *CSPD 1659–60*, p. 280; NLW, MS 9065E/2207; Som. RO, DD/TB/18/18, unfol.

forceful and intimidatory tactics once other options had been exhausted. As such, the aim of this chapter has been to reconnect London crowds with other forms of political participation, both at Westminster and beyond, and to suggest that this can be done by means of four key observations regarding the role of print in contemporary political culture.

First, printed news helped to ensure that crowd dynamics involved something more complex than either elite manipulation or popular spontaneity. This involved its role in fostering a vibrant political culture within a society that was physically and socially integrated, and where different social groups responded to parliamentary affairs collaboratively. Thus, while elites sometimes played a central role in organizing political crowds, those who participated in such gatherings not only demonstrated political knowledge and understanding, but also gained a valuable political education, in ways that fostered genuine political agency. Secondly, print could be used to influence behaviour in precise ways. The warrant, the summons and the receipt could now be mass produced, and print could be used to advertise, agitate and organize, beyond the bookstalls and quite literally on the streets. By thus offering speedy and affordable ways of conveying messages to large audiences simultaneously, print facilitated not just administrative efficiency but also the co-ordination of meetings, petitions and crowds. This made it possible to place 'popular' pressure on parliament at precise moments, at short notice and with substantial numbers, and 'tickets' both drew people onto the streets and provided them with talismanic texts around which to rally. In other words, when speed was of the essence and co-ordination was crucial, print proved to be an extremely useful tool. Thirdly, these benefits were recognized across the political nation – ideologically, socially and geographically – and organizational print genres were appropriated for non-official purposes by ordinary citizens as part of everyday political participation, as well as in connection with extraordinary agitation by individuals, interest groups and popular movements.

Finally, evidence about the link between mass activism and print culture reinforces the suggestive comments with which this chapter began. It reveals a participatory culture in which protests, riots and revolts were regarded as legitimate ways of responding to the failure to achieve results through more formal methods, and in which different political tactics were understood to be connected. It indicates that 'popular' politics could involve petitioning and printed petitioning, as well as the use of print to orchestrate mass petitioning and mass lobbying, and ultimately that it could involve the deployment of handbills to organize protests and disorder. And it demonstrates that in the context of parliamentary politics, such tactics were often employed sequentially, with violent disorder being seen as a conscious last resort rather than as a reflex response. Events that were not directly *orchestrated* by print can be shown to have taken place in political contexts that were *saturated* by print, and episodes where print was central to mass politics reveal not just an escalation of tactics, but also a dynamic interplay between new ways of participating and official attempts to restore decorum. In other words, the print revolution played a crucial role in transforming both participatory practices and political ideas.

CHAPTER II

Holding representatives to account

In May 1640, as Sir Thomas Peyton struggled to predict the fallout from the dissolution of the Short Parliament, he was struck by the fact that ordinary citizens had grown 'so wise . . . having received a diffusive knowledge from the dispersed house'. Almost two decades later, during elections in January 1659, the impact of such 'diffusive knowledge' was brought home very powerfully to Major Robert Harley, sometime Presbyterian MP and one of the victims of Pride's Purge. Harley's troubles began at the house of Edward Whalley – regicide, major-general and Cromwellian peer – during a conversation with Robert Weaver. Harley was rather too free with his views about a book by Payne Fisher (which was 'lying by the window'), about the royalist turncoat, Edmund Waller, and about printed ballads concerning Oliver and Richard Cromwell. Weaver managed to obtain Harley's copy of at least one of these texts, and promptly showed it to Whalley (his father-in-law), who showed it in turn to the Protector. Meanwhile, William Goffe (Weaver's brother-in-law) interrogated one of Harley's servants, and by using a mixture of promises and threats was able to persuade him to incriminate his employer. The upshot of such machinations was that Weaver obtained damning political ammunition, which he used to dramatic electoral effect in order to win Harley's old seat at Radnor.[1]

Harley quickly complained about being made to 'suffer upon public pretence to satisfy a private design', and his experience provides vivid evidence of a novel culture in which MPs were held to account by members of the public. The aim of this chapter is to argue that, by facilitating the publication of information regarding the attitudes and behaviour of prominent individuals, the print revolution made it possible for citizens to capitalize on the potential for judging their representatives (as described in Chapter 6). In other words, having already demonstrated that members of the public could read about and comment upon public figures, what

[1] *Oxinden Letters*, p. 173; BL: Add. 28000, fo. 14; Add. 70007, fos. 106–7v.

follows will show how awareness about the activities of such individuals led to informed *encounters* with MPs, and to a tendency to pass judgment on their performance. Such *interactions* were sometimes informal, impolite and aggressive, albeit in ways that revealed intriguing attitudes about how to ensure probity at Westminster (section i). But they could also be formal, either in terms of polite and discrete exchanges between MPs and their constituents, or in terms of electoral campaigns that were informed by the evidence about individual candidates (section ii). And they could also involve public criticism of individual MPs, involving not just expressions of personal frustration, but also increasingly radical claims about privilege and the need to be able to investigate and remove those who had broken their trust (section iii). The argument of the chapter will be that in each of these areas, the accessibility of the parliamentary system and the availability of political information led to informed engagement with MPs, and to new kinds of behaviour, and that print media gave citizens and constituents the chance to monitor MPs' performance as well as the mechanisms with which to call them to account. And it will also be argued that the novel ways in which members of the public interacted with MPs had important consequences for the political system, not just by affecting the electoral fortunes of particular candidates, but also by prompting citizens and politicians to reflect on the nature of political representation, and to develop new and fairly radical ideas about political accountability.

i Informal interactions with MPs

In January 1660, unusual snowmen appeared in Fleet Street, Cheapside and St Paul's Churchyard. With one eye and surrounded by old shoes, they were immediately recognizable as effigies of John Hewson, an ex-cobbler and a controversial soldier, MP and regicide. The aim was to effect a mock execution, and while one effigy had 'a haulter, or rope, around his neck' another involved a makeshift gibbet. Those responsible were memorializing the events of 5 December 1659, when trouble had flared following the attempt to suppress a mass petition by crypto-royalist apprentices. The soldiers involved had faced hostility and derision – they were 'hooted at all along the streets', and boys 'flung stones, tiles, turnips' – but particular attention had been paid to Hewson, who was met with cries of 'a cobbler, a cobbler'. This caused tempers to fray and led to the firing of shots, apparently at Hewson's command, resulting in at least one fatality. Plans were subsequently made to indict Hewson, but these were scuppered by a parliamentary pardon, and the symbolic lynching of Hewson's effigies represented a protest about the failure to execute justice upon a hated enemy and about the partiality of parliament. Moreover, with its fusion of mockery, festive misrule and well-informed political comment, the incident suggests that analysing the link between the circulation of information and the treatment of MPs should begin with street politics, with seditious speech and with crowd behaviour.[2] Taking its lead from the curious incident of Hewson's effigies, therefore, this section will explore *informal* interactions between MPs and members of the general public who were not their constituents. It will draw attention to the fact that citizens displayed specific knowledge about a range of MPs; demonstrate that such knowledge sometimes came from printed sources; and highlight a willingness to confront individual politicians, not least with aggressive rhetoric about political accountability.

Informal interactions between the public and the political elite naturally involved grumbling about parliament and its members. Moreover, while such murmuring was often faceless, it is occasionally possible to identify the specific brickmakers, gardeners and butchers who were responsible for describing MPs as 'rogues and rascals' in 'invective and railing speeches'.[3] With surprising regularity, moreover, verbal outbursts were made about *specific* MPs, and by humble Londoners rather than just radical activists. Very often, of course, oral discourse focused on men like 'King Pym the rascal' and Viscount Saye the 'roundhead rogue', both of whom were identifiable as 'traitors to their king', but it is also noteworthy that such public vilification sometimes involved precise accusations. Pym was accused of having 'taken a bribe of £30', and of having used his position as an MP to amass a sizeable personal fortune, and although these particular claims probably represented nothing more than idle gossip, others had greater credibility. These included reports that Pym and Saye had been involved in the illegal transportation of money overseas, and that they led the opposition to a peace settlement with the king.[4] Moreover, such comments were not restricted to Londoners. When Norwich merchants were investigated for 'foul and scandalous words' against 'some members of the House of Commons' in August 1642, it emerged that one of them had described the

---

[2] *Rugg*, p. 14, 17; *CP*, iv. 165–9; *Intelligencer*, 575.206, p. 930; *Pepys Diary*, i. 28; Bodl. MS Clarendon 67, fos. 119, 178, 180, 186, 200, 222–v, 225, 226, 229, 246–v; MS Carte 73, fos. 325, 329, 333.

[3] BL, Add. 78194, fo. 66; *Moon*, 248.02, p. 11; *Mdx County Recs*, iii. 102; LMA: MJ/SR/927/3, 952/109, 947/43, 925/98.

[4] LMA: MJ/SR/926/121, 939/34, 914/105; *Civicus*, 298.113, p. 1001; *CJ*, ii. 478, iii. 246–7; *Mdx County Recs*, iii. 87, 90; Bodl. MS Tanner 63, fo. 83; *Diurnall*, 511.19A, sig. T2; BL: Harl. 165, fo. 193; Add. 31116, p. 137; NLS, MS 2687, p. 1115.

Earl of Holland as 'a knave', while another had called Pym 'a traitor'. And neither were they aimed merely at political grandees. In August 1641 Nicholas Tabor of Cambridge unwisely opined that his local MP, John Lowry, was a 'fool' and an 'ass' who ought to be hanged, and during 1642 Sir Robert Harley was repeatedly informed about the abusive speeches made against him and his family in Herefordshire. In July 1642 a Colchester weaver called Stephen Lewes not only complained that members 'sat for their own ends to enrich themselves', but also singled out his own MP, Harbottle Grimston, who was said to have been little more than penniless 'before the Parliament', but who had since 'purchased seven hundred pounds a year'.[5]

More importantly, such specificity in terms of individuals and allegations was not restricted to alehouse banter. It also involved dramatic *confrontations*, in which members of the public directly challenged MPs and peers over their political views and behaviour. This has already been noted in terms of encounters with friends and enemies during demonstrations outside parliament, but it also involved ridicule, jeering and mockery. John Desborough was greeted in public by cries of 'phanatique, phanatique', and a group of politicians were made to toast the health of Charles I during illicit street celebrations to mark his birthday in 1647. One of the MPs who voted against Strafford's attainder, William Taylor, was accosted in Windsor by a constituent, who asked him to explain his decision, and Taylor's response – that he would 'not do murder with the sword of justice' – led to his expulsion from the Commons. And in February 1647 it was reported that 'a whole gang' had waylaid Cromwell on his way to the Commons, and that they followed him 'railing to the very door of the House'.[6] Ultimately, such incidents also involved violence, whether real, perceived or threatened. Straffordians like Sir John Strangeways 'went in fear of their lives, great abuses being lately offered against them', and in December 1641 the Bishop of Ely faced 'difficulty and danger' getting back to his House in Holborn, even at 2am, because 'a great rout of disordered people' searched every coach as it passed Charing Cross.[7] Moreover, while such episodes are generally analysed in terms of their impact upon individual politicians – many of whom abandoned parliament in disgust – they also highlight a broader trend towards knowledgeable citizens behaving in less than deferential ways.

[5] Bodl. MS Nalson 2, fos. 86–8; MS Tanner 62, fo. 313; Cooper, *Annals*, p. 314; *CJ*, ii. 252; BL, Add. 70110, fos. 65, 74–v; ERO, D/5/Sb2/7, fo. 298.
[6] Staffs. RO, D868/3/31; BL: Add. 78198, fo. 26; Sloane 1467, fo. 70; Add. 28000, fo. 95; *Oxinden Letters*, p. 198; Bodl. MS Clarendon, 29, fos. 134–v.
[7] Durham UL, MSP 30, fos. 46–v; HEH, HM 66707; Bodl. MS Tanner 66, fo. 220.

In July 1642 the wife of a London cook was questioned for 'scolding and railing' at the MP for Appleby, Sir John Brooke, 'in a base and vile manner in the open street'. Edward Brace was seen chasing the Earl of Lincoln down Water Lane during the riots of July 1647, and the woman known as 'Parliament Joan' apparently 'showed great incivilities' to the MP Sir James Harrington as he made his way to parliament in July 1649. Such hostility became particularly severe following the dissolution of the Rump in April 1653, when many members faced 'scorn and public reproach'. One commentator noted 'the frequent affronts ... as they pass the streets', and such obloquy also followed MPs into the country, not least with the 'outrage' committed upon the House of John Ashe of Freshford in June 1650.[8]

What is striking about such evidence of anger and intimidation is that the targets were not always prominent 'frontbenchers', and the same is also true of those who encountered real violence. Cromwell nearly fell prey to the 'roaring boys' who 'layd weight for him' in April 1648, and only escaped because he was riding in Lord Lisle's coach rather than in his own, although shots were subsequently fired at the windows of his house. And a similar incident occurred in February 1660, when festive celebrations to mark the return of a 'free parliament' – with bonfires, health-drinking and the roasting of 'rumps' – spilled over into a violent attack on the former Speaker, William Lenthall. Lenthall 'escaped very narrowly being killed' when his coach was attacked and 'had some rapiers run into it', having apparently been saved by his driver, who 'swore that he was not in the coach'. This enabled Lenthall to escape, although this did not stop his guards from being 'beaten and disarmed', or prevent his house from being 'assaulted'.[9] However, similar stories could also be told about many other MPs. In September 1648, Miles Corbet was 'affronted, assaulted and wounded' in the street, by men whose 'malice' was driven by awareness of his political record, while another MP was 'affronted by three gentlemen, who very well knew the said member, calling him by his name'.[10]

The problem with such evidence, of course, is that it is easier to discern popular awareness about specific MPs than to establish how it was acquired. However, while it may sometimes have involved local knowledge and personal experience, as well as the influence of ringleaders and agitators, there are also grounds for linking such behaviour to the publication and

---

[8] *D'Ewes*, ed. Coates, p. 214; Bodl. MS Tanner 66, fo. 220; *CSPD 1641–3*, p. 276; CKS, U269/O257; *LJ*, v. 317; LMA, MJ/SR/911/15; *HMC 5th Report*, p. 197; *CJ*, v. 316; *Diurnall*, 504.310, p. 2635; BL, Add. 78221, fo. 61v; *CSPD 1650*, pp. 126, 206.

[9] BL: Add. 78198, fo. 65; Add. 78200, fo. 4v.

[10] *Diurnall*, 504.270, pp. 2175–6; *Kingdomes*, 214.279, p. 1103.

circulation of political information. John Evelyn connected popular animosity towards MPs in April 1653 with a black-letter ballad entitled *The
Parliament Routed*, with its inverted image of the House of Commons and
its analysis of self-interested 'caterpillars', who 'voted, unvoted as fancy did
guide'. Other commentators blamed 'ballad mongers' for widespread popular derision of Richard Cromwell in 1659. Indeed, it seems highly likely
that other violent outbursts were directly inspired and encouraged by
printed texts. Disturbances during the funeral of John Bradshaw may
have been fomented by 'jeering books' such as *Bradshaw's Ghost*, which
attacked his career and reputation, and which was timed to coincide with
the ceremony. Likewise, the assault on Lenthall in February 1660 coincided
with hostile libels that were circulated around London and posted on his
door.[11] Most dramatically of all Hewson was repeatedly targeted by the
authors of satirical pamphlets and ballads, which invariably drew attention
to his humble origins and his political career, and although many of these
are hard to date with precision, some were certainly published before his
effigies appeared. Indeed, *The Out-Cry of the London Apprentices* explicitly
justified mob violence as a substitute for official justice, and by invoking the
pillory and festive misrule, it arguably inspired the symbolic justice to which
Hewson's icy doppelganger was subjected.[12]

By 1660, in other words, it is sometimes possible to make direct connections between print culture and the interactions that took place between
MPs and members of the public. Nevertheless, this link between the
availability of information and the process of passing judgment on public
figures dated back to 1641, when 'fiddlers' apparently sang songs about MPs,
and when the names of Straffordians were circulated and posted, 'as if the
old democracy of Rome . . . were now renewed and revived'. The publicity
surrounding parliamentary affairs certainly seems to have informed incidents of street politics, such as the occasion when peace protesters 'laid hold
of viscount Saye' in his coach in January 1643. This is because he had been
singled out for criticism in an inflammatory tract – *A Complaint to the House
of Commons* – that was scattered about the streets and used to rally crowds.
Likewise, it seems probable that the 'reformado' soldiers who reproached
Lord 'saw pit' Wharton in January 1647, and who decried 'the liberal gifts of
the Parliament to their own members', were provoked by printed texts in
similar ways. This is because it was in pamphlets and newspapers that such

[11] BL, Add. 78221, fos. 61–2; *Routed* (1653, S148B); BL, Eg. 2536, fo. 431; Aberdeen UL, MS 2538/3, fos.
158, 161; *Rugg*, p. 13; Beinecke, Osborn b.52, Vol. 1, p. 149.
[12] *Rugg*, pp. 26, 60; *Out-Cry* (1659, O598), pp. 5–8.

caricatures first developed, and that authors and editors provided readers with the evidence upon which such accusations were based.[13]

The importance of the Hewson episode also lies in the fact that it represents the culmination of developments in the popular language of political accountability. This sometimes involved attempts to remind MPs about their duties, responsibilities and promises, not least by comparing recent orders and votes with former promises and policies. But it also involved the language of broken trust, not least during the campaign waged against Nathaniel Fiennes by Clement Walker and William Prynne (1643). This involved a legal case over his conduct as governor of Bristol, as well as pamphlets containing articles of impeachment and a denunciation of his cowardice, and although the incident did not revolve around *parliamentary* performance, the aim was clearly to secure his removal from the Commons. This explains why Sir Simonds D'Ewes described the accusations as 'scandalous', and why he feared the creation of a destabilizing precedent, whereby 'all the members of the House might be impeached one after another, by any that should be maliciously disposed against them'. And it was also why Walker discovered that anyone who became involved in such campaigns was likely to face concerted, and even malicious, retribution.[14] Nevertheless, while MPs continued to claim special privileges, the upshot was that a member's immunity from prosecution could be waived, even if only in extraordinary circumstances and even if only as a result of factional manoeuvres. Indeed, some contemporaries could already detect a broad and worrying shift in popular attitudes towards the 'recall' of particular individuals. They pointed, for example, to events in August 1643, when targeted and informed anger relating to parliamentary proceedings involved more or less overt claims regarding the legitimacy of punishing MPs for their parliamentary activity. Thus, when women peace protesters failed to receive a satisfactory answer to their petition, they apparently behaved 'very uncivilly' towards some of the members, and used 'horrid expressions' and blood-curdling threats against those who were conceived to be 'averse to peace'. Indeed, they even threatened to 'tear Master Pym in pieces, and to pull the House of Commons down about their ears'. According to D'Ewes, such boldness could only be understood in terms of the legitimizing effect of political precedents, and he noted that 'as the

---

[13] Jansson, vi. 195; Staffs. RO, D661/20/2, p. 95; *Kingdomes*, 214.001, p. 8; *Complaint* (1642, C5620), p. 18; Bodl. MS Clarendon 29, fos. 72–v.

[14] *Breif Collection* [sic] (1647, E2533B); Bodl. MS Carte 8, fo. 70v; BL, Add. 31116, pp. 165–6, 183; *LJ*, vi. 240, 247.

former wicked faction had pretended that they would pluck out certain members ... because they were too forward for peace, so these indiscreet women, following their example ... threatened to use violence to those in the House of Commons as were enemies to peace'.[15]

However, while this language of accountability generated palpable hostility within Westminster, it also became noticeably more common, and it both fed into and developed out of high-profile impeachments and purges. In 1646 Thomas Juxon noted that demands were being made for the removal of Independent MPs who had 'betrayed their trust', while others detected pressure within the City for the removal of MPs who had been 'illegally chosen'. And by the spring of 1647 contemporaries could not fail to notice the prevalence of 'discontented speeches' within the army, the 'bitter language' that was used regarding MPs like Stapleton and Holles, and the calls that were being made to bring such men to account for 'miscarriages' in parliament. Such demands reached a peak with the impeachment of the 'eleven members' (June 1647), but this was thought likely to represent the start rather than the end of the process of winnowing the Commons. One commentator thus noted that 'there is no member but may be liable to be accused', and thus no MP who could escape the risk of being 'suspended in the House'.[16] Indeed, this 'tender subject' did not go away, and the following months witnessed threats to MPs from different directions and different factions. Within the army, for example, the Agitators threatened to dissolve the Commons 'by revoking the trust which the people gave them', on the grounds that this trust had been 'forfeited and abused to the ruin of the whole kingdom'. The 'forcing of the Houses' in July 1647, meanwhile, inspired petitions that called for a 'further purging' of 'all that acted when the speakers and other members went away'. And in November 1647, some commentators expected the army to 'march towards London' once again, and 'to purge the Houses' of Presbyterians, in which case 'it would be very dangerous to look like a parliament man'. Others anticipated that disbanded and maligned 'reformado' soldiers would impeach dozens of Independent MPs, who had 'given the public treasure to themselves, being feoffees in trust for the public'.[17]

---

[15] Bodl. MS Tanner 62, fos. 362v–3; BL: Harl. 165, fo. 209; Add. 31116, pp. 169, 200; Add. 64923, fo. 78; *Civicus*, 298.011, p. 88; *Informations*, 36.30, p. 232; BL, Harl. 165, fo. 149.

[16] *Juxon*, pp. 104–5, 157–8; BL: Add. 78193, fo. 102; Add. 70005, fos. 248–v; *Kingdomes*, 214.214, p. 572.

[17] 'Lewis Dyve', p. 65; *Diurnall* 504.216, sig. 10K3v; 504.219, pp. 1759–60; *Kingdomes*, 214.227, p. 674; BL, Add. 78198, fos. 19–v; *Answer* (1647, A3283), pp. 3, 5.

Such rumours and threats regarding a wholesale purification of parliament obviously reached their peak either side of Pride's Purge (December 1648), during which period further expulsions were anticipated, even if it was hard to predict who would be responsible. Rumours initially focused on a plot to massacre Independents who opposed negotiations with the king, but these gradually gave way to confidence that the Presbyterians were a more likely target, and that the army would 'impeach divers members, expel most of them, and new mould this present junto'. Moreover, as contemporaries came to terms with the subsequent removal of 'honest men' by Colonel Pride, new stories began to emerge about further purges. In July 1649, attention had become focused on the possibility that radical MPs would be targeted by royalists. As has already been noted, attempts were made to incite London's 'young men' to target 'all the regicides and bloody hell-hounds', so that they might be 'pulled out by the ears, and receive the reward due to such rebellious and unnatural monsters'.[18] Indeed, similar fears surfaced periodically throughout the following decade, most obviously as the power of a standing army became much more evident. Viscount Falkland feared that the army – the 'fourth estate' – was planning to 'turn us all out of doors' (April 1659), because he had heard about them discussing parliamentary proceedings in meetings and in print. By December 1659, moreover, commentators suggested that the country had grown sufficiently cynical about the army as to expect a purge of 'whatever Parliament they had set up . . . if they had not danced after their pipe'.[19]

The importance of such fears and rumours lies not just in their prevalence, but also in the light that they shed on contemporary attempts to rethink representation. Indeed, it is possible to demonstrate that the tendency to accuse specific MPs was intimately linked to the process of devising mechanisms for ensuring that new MPs could be systematically 'called to an account'. Little noticed within the regimental petitions of November 1648, therefore, were demands that 'rules' should be 'set down between the people and their representatives', and that 'an account be called for from all persons that have been entrusted with anything for the state'. Such demands echoed radical literature from the second half of the 1640s, as well as the journalism of men like Gilbert Mabbott, and having bubbled to the surface in 1648, such ideas re-emerged after the dissolution of the Rump in April 1653. Thus, Jeremy Baynes, who would soon be elected to the first protectoral

---

[18] *Diurnall*, 504.270, pp. 2175–6; *Kingdomes*, 214.279, p. 1103; BL, Add. 78221, fos. 24–v; FSL, V.a.436, p. 177; *Moon*, 248.12, p. 103.
[19] *Burton Diary*, iv. 449; *Parl. Intelligencer*, 486.101, p. 3.

parliament, predicted that future MPs could expect to be punished if they were found to 'come short of their duty'.[20] Indeed, ideas like these also reflected a growing sense that MPs could be punished using legal means rather than merely by force. In May 1659, therefore, Bledry Morgan formulated impeachment articles against the MP, Philip Jones, who was accused of 'high breach of trust', and in February 1660 Mathew Alured and John Okey were indicted for forcibly excluding old purged MPs when parliament reassembled in December 1659. On this occasion, indeed, the charge against them was circulated in print, with the explicit intention of encouraging similar prosecutions. Although these cases did not relate to the performance of *parliamentary* duties, the case of another former member, Thomas Kelsey, indicates that activity in the Commons could indeed be materially relevant. The printed *Articles* to which Kelsey was subjected – only weeks after he left parliament in May 1659 – demanded that he should be held to account for 'high crimes and misdemeanours', not least for his record as a Cromwellian MP and 'kingling'. More importantly, such tactics had already been deployed against a *sitting* MP. In 1649, therefore, a printed broadside outlined the 'treason and misdemeanours' of John Pyne, whose faults included military cowardice, arbitrary and corrupt behaviour on the Somerset committee, and the contriving of 'scandalous and seditious petitions', as well as attempts to 'carry' elections for his 'favourites' and the refusal to produce financial accounts.[21]

With these printed impeachments we reach the end of a spectrum of methods for interacting with MPs that have been dubbed 'informal', because they involved neither institutional procedures nor clear ties of the kind that existed between representative and constituent. This spectrum – which encompassed dangerous talk, aggressive crowds and purges, as well as the language of impeachment – reveals a culture of fairly knowledgeable criticism. This was rooted in the example set by MPs, and it was nurtured in the circumstances of Civil War, but it was also facilitated by the circulation of information and comment and by print culture. The result was that political accountability became a live issue, as contemporaries expressed their views about MPs by means of verbal assaults and festive misrule, as well as by threats of legal action and physical force. That such developments are also suggestive of a willingness and ability to reconsider the nature of representation and accountability will become much clearer by pursuing

---

[20] *Moderate*: 413.2014, p. 113, sig. O2; 413.2018, sigs. S3–v; 413.2039, Qq2; *Kingdomes*, 214.285, pp. 1146–7; BL, Add. 21422, fo. 61.

[21] *Articles* (1659, M2729A); *Rugg*, p. 42; *High Crimes* (1659, A3842), pp. 1–6; *Treason* (1649, A3877).

two key elements that emerge from the 'impeachments' of men like Pyne and Kelsey: the use of print to criticize specific MPs and, firstly, formal interactions between members and their constituents.

ii Formal interactions with MPs

In December 1646 John Venn faced severe criticism in Common Council for his performance as one of London's MPs. He was decried as a 'rascal' for doing so little to deserve money that had been paid 'to make up his broken breaches', and he allegedly made a swift exit for fear that 'they had pulled him in pieces'. Venn's experience highlights the possibility of formal interaction taking place between MPs and constituents, in ways that involved assessing their performance on the basis of knowledge about their activity.[22] In Venn's case this meant a face-to-face meeting, but it highlights a broader culture that this section will address, and quite different ways in which print fostered political accountability. What will emerge is evidence that the circulation of information in print prompted scrutiny of MPs, correspondence in which constituents used their knowledge to offer praise and blame, and changes in the behaviour of both the public and its representatives. The argument here will be that transparency fostered a rhetoric of trust and accountability, that vigorous discussions regarding the nature of representation cut across 'party' lines, and that many MPs recognized the need to modify their behaviour and to publicize their activity, not least in response to changes in electoral practice.

Formal interactions between individual MPs and the public tended to be much more polite than Venn's experience suggests. They could involve observation at close quarters by constituency agents or even the use of instructions, the latter of which were sometimes circulated in printed form. Most commonly, however, they involved private correspondence, in which constituents discussed an MP's activity, encouraged certain courses of action and either expressed gratitude or made complaints, not least about poor attendance.[23] In this regard the papers of Sir Edward Dering and Robert Bennet are particularly illuminating. Dering's correspondents in the opening weeks of the Long Parliament included Richard Skeffington, who explained that 'your action there sounds your praise to all eternity', while also insisting that MPs should 'lay aside all your own affairs, and not break

---

[22] BL, Add. 78193, fo. 102.
[23] D. Hirst, *Representative of the People* (Cambridge, 1975), p. 183; *Laudable* (1659, I1080A); *Proposals* (1653, J22); BL: Add. 70007, fo. 95; Add. 21423, fo. 37; Bodl. MS Tanner 58, fo. 777.

up until businesses be thoroughly settled'. Others were more specific, giving thanks for Dering's 'zeal and labours', noting what he had already done 'so worthily for the House of the Lord' and encouraging him to support the Kent petition concerning church government. Dering was not able to please everyone, of course, and some letters chided him for things that he had or had not done, and demonstrated concern that he was less Puritanical than had been hoped.[24] Bennet's correspondents, meanwhile, included Captain Cloke, whose letters spanned the period 1653 to 1659. During Barebone's Parliament, therefore, one letter encouraged Bennet to remain true to 'just principles' regarding the church, while another from May 1659 warned that excessive taxation would be the 'one great thing which will be apt to render you unlovely in the eyes of the nation'. Cloke added, however, that anger over financial 'miscarriages' would be 'much lessened' if MPs took 'a just course of calling in of men's accounts', and if they ensured that places of trust were given to men 'who hate covetousness'. In other words, while recognizing that Bennet had the opportunity to 'appear for and in the cause of God', Cloke pointed out that 'you have been something faulty heretofore in not improving your parts and gift to the utmost'. Subsequent letters expressed fears that Bennet had 'gotten some of that old craft, which will make a little danger swell great for your own end', and Cloke gave an explicit warning about the risks involved in reneging on former promises to abolish tithes. By November 1659, indeed, Cloke noted that 'men are very much dissatisfied with your transactions on divers accounts'.[25]

Such comments merely *hint* at awareness of what people like Dering and Bennet were doing at Westminster, but similar correspondence could sometimes be provoked by detailed awareness regarding an MP's political activity. The papers of Edward Harley reveal not just that parliamentary speeches were being read and discussed at Oxford University, but also that his father, Sir Robert Harley, was being criticized by constituents in Herefordshire for 'a late speech' which had impugned local commanders (June 1646). And in 1659 Adam Baynes received letters in response to reports of his 'unadvised and passionate expression' against the 'Other House', which were apparently being circulated 'to blot your reputation'.[26] These cases may merely have involved the restrained circulation of evidence within sociable networks, but Dering's papers indicate that MPs faced

---

[24] BL: Stowe 184, fos. 19, 23, 43–4; Add. 26785, fos. 23, 28, 84; CKS, U350/C2/88; J. Peacey, 'Sir Edward Dering, popularity and the public', *HJ*, 54 (2011), 955–83.

[25] FSL: X.d.483/108, 111; Add. 666.

[26] BL: Add. 70122, unfol.; Add. 70058, unfol.; Add. 21425, fos. 21, 26.

particularly serious scrutiny once their speeches became more widely available. As early as 1 December 1640, therefore, he was informed about 'the common rejoicing of all well affected people hereabouts for your worthy speaking and doing in this present parliament'; such letters reveal the penetration of manuscript separates, but also the much greater impact of printed versions. A correspondent in March 1641 who noted that locals were 'happy in our choice' explained that Dering's support grew noticeably as the circulation of his printed speeches fostered the opinion that he was one of the 'good patriots of the church and commonwealth'. Of course, print did not guarantee a favourable response, and the circulation of information probably served to polarize opinion rather than simply to strengthen the bonds of affection between Dering and his constituents. Indeed, he quickly discovered that radical reformers 'catched' at some passages in his recent speeches, and he was regularly taken to task for his activity. One correspondent in January 1642 explained that 'perusal of your last speech in parliament' had provoked 'some animadversions and notes'. He expressed sorrow that 'the bias of your judgment . . . should seem to sway so much to that side, which will certainly expose your late honourable esteem . . . to a great . . . diminution and distemper'. Such disillusionment was also echoed by Augustine Skinner, a prominent local Puritan, who would soon become an MP. He explained that 'in your election you were the sum of our county's delight, desires and hopes', and that onlookers had initially been heartened by Dering's willingness to 'give the first assault . . . on the Goliah of hierarchical episcopacy', but he also expressed fear that 'a recidination should be in the son of so many tears and prayers'.[27]

Dering's experience suggests that MPs came under mounting scrutiny from constituents, and similar evidence from the 1640s reveals the force with which expectations and anxieties could be expressed, by royalists and parliamentarians alike. Representatives could be told what services they were supposed to perform, for example, even if only in respectful terms. In 1654 Adam Baynes's constituents displayed satisfaction at his election, and expressed 'confidence' in his 'candid affection' to their interests, although a subsequent letter was rather more stern. This offered advice and assistance while also insisting that their grievances should be 'represented in the House'. Equally polite were Richard Lobb's letters to Robert Bennet from Plymouth during the restored Rump in 1659. These involved requests for action on issues such as the local tin industry, and even offered

[27] CKS, U350/C2/86; BL: Stowe 744, fos. 1, 13–v; Add. 26785, fos. 25, 63; Stowe 184, fos. 27–8; Peacey, 'Dering'.

advice about which MPs were likely to lend support, but they employed a tone of friendly expectation, and were accompanied by promises of considerable gratitude.[28] At other times, however, relations between MPs and their constituents became much more strained, leading to fascinating tussles like the one between the royalist gentry of Herefordshire (led by Wallop Brabazon) and their Puritan MP Sir Robert Harley in the spring of 1642. This dispute began when Brabazon and his colleagues raised a series of doubts about the Protestation, in terms of how subscriptions were to be taken, whether it was compulsory and whether it even remained relevant so long after it had first been introduced. It became acrimonious, however, when Harley was informed that he was expected to make local support for the king known to the Commons, as one 'whom we have trusted'. To Harley such comments were 'liable to exceptions'. He intimated that such behaviour might be taken as a sign of 'disaffection to Parliament's proceedings', and he expressed confidence that a more representative picture of the local mood would emerge in a county petition that would 'avow the Protestation which your letter seems so warily to decline'. The response from Brabazon and his friends, however, was to challenge the legitimacy of any petition that lacked the signatures of local grandees like themselves, and they also expressed suspicion that Harley was responsible for promoting the petition and that members of the lower orders were being courted in order to 'fill paper with names'. Such sentiments represented fairly predictable royalist fare, of course, but much more interesting were their claims about the nature of political representation. They insisted not just that it was their duty to convey such doubts about the Protestation, but also that it was Harley's role to relay such concerns to parliament, and they urged their MPs to pay closer attention to those who were in tune with 'the general desire of the shire'. More importantly, they added that 'we send you not with authority to govern us ... but with our consent for making and altering laws as to His Majesty, the Lords and Commons should seem good', and they even demanded electoral reform to ensure that MPs would serve 'diligently ... in discharge of the great trust reposed in them'.[29]

In other words, the straining of relations between MPs and constituents could lead to the use of forceful language and striking ideas. In August 1642 the gentry of Kent sought to 'instruct' their MP, Augustine Skinner, to express their loyalty to the king, in his capacity 'as our servant', and his refusal to comply provoked a published account of the incident. In late 1649

Edward Salmon announced that he had declined to sign the Engagement out of a desire to preserve his chances of holding MPs to account. He explained that he was 'unwilling to sign anything that should tend to the perpetuating of this parliament', and that he was 'altogether for elective statesmen and successive Parliaments'. And Robert Bennet's correspondence reveals that by August 1649 victims of Pride's Purge were prepared to sanction the recall of wayward MPs. John Moyle suggested that Cornish voters should 'intimate their desire unto our two knights of the shire, and all their unexcepted against burgesses, for their speedy repair to the Parliament', in order to perform the duties that constituents had 'reposed in them'. He also added, however, that their failure to comply would provoke a petition demanding 'new writs' and calling for the election of people to replace those who 'refuseth to serve and give their attendance'.[30] Ultimately, therefore, contemporaries began to employ the rhetoric of broken trust and threatened to revoke the authority that had been given to particular MPs. The logic of this position has already been observed in relation to a published critique of London's Common Council in 1648. This encouraged 'well-affected' freemen to explain to their representatives that 'we have elected you ... to preserve our liberties not inthrall them, to advance the public not your private interests', and insisted that they had the right to 'challenge' them to provide an 'account' of what they had done 'as our proxies'. The author also suggested that failure to produce a 'speedy account' would force citizens to conclude that 'you have broke the trust reposed in you by us'. However, such ideas also underpinned accusations against MPs. These included a complaint by the Kent committee in 1643, about the lack of support from MPs who had sought election 'ambitiously enough', as well as a petition from Sussex in 1644, about the inadequate services of the two county MPs.[31]

MPs, of course, did not take kindly to such criticism, but their comments are also indicative of growing realization that public sentiment regarding their performance needed to be taken into account. Sir Simonds D'Ewes considered this complaint from Kent to be 'insolent and impertinent', and to be the work of 'fiery spirits', and his colleagues frequently took refuge behind cherished parliamentary privileges.[32] Nevertheless, they were clearly worried that the spotlight of public scrutiny might generate informed

[30] *Humble Petition* (1642, H3497); BL, Add. 21418, fos. 97, 123, 145; FSL, X.d.483/44.
[31] *Humble Desires* (1648, H3415); BL: Harl. 164, fo. 356; Harl. 166, fo. 149; *Diurnall*, 504.064, p. 508; Bodl. MS Nalson 11, fos. 192–3.
[32] BL, Harl. 164, fo. 356; HEH, STT, Parliament Box 1/17; STT Parliament Box 2/27; BL, Add. 70081: *Die Lunae* (1641); Lincs. RO, MISC DON/914/3: *Die Lunae* (1641).

criticism of their behaviour, not least because of concerns about future electoral prospects. One MP in 1656 was troubled by reports that 'we are but a rag of a Parliament', made up of soldiers, courtiers and 'friends to my Lord Protector', and John Lambert admitted that free elections would merely return men who would 'sit as our judges for all we have done in this Parliament'. Moreover, while anxiety regarding the popular reaction to parliamentary proceedings was obviously not new – MPs in the 1620s had worried about how they would account to the electorate for voting subsidies without settling grievances – it certainly became much more common. In April 1657 Sir William Strickland denounced the idea of a land tax by saying that 'the people would never have chosen us if they had thought we would ever have moved that'. And in March 1659 Sir Henry Vane pointed out that the failure to deal with the nation's grievances would 'make the people that sent you think you came not to do their business'.[33] More importantly, MPs became apprehensive about being judged on their *individual* performance, rather than on their *collective* record. This was true of those who had been publicly identified as Straffordians, one of whom complained about being 'posted and much traduced', and demanded 'liberty ... to speak my conscience'. But it became much more obvious as time passed, not least in relation to the financial rewards that were available to MPs. In 1657 Thomas Bampfield moved that members should 'not give such large rewards to one another', reflecting that 'it was the blame of the Long Parliament', and he was supported by William Briscoe, who anticipated 'censure abroad', as well as by Robert Beake. The latter noted that 'we cannot cloister up this vote within these walls', that there was a danger of following the 'worst path ... that the Long Parliament trod in' and that 'the poor people's cries' made such gratuities 'ill-timed'. Other MPs shared this concern that 'there is nothing done or said here but [it] is told abroad', and were increasingly conscious about their public image. When Sir Thomas Widdrington complained about the public's ability to discuss 'what things pass in the House' – something he regarded as a 'high breach of privilege' – he did so in the knowledge that he lay under 'a great reproach' and that 'I bear all the blame in the business of the Vintners'.[34]

Widdrington obviously took account of popular sentiment very reluctantly, but there is clear evidence that the kinds of public scrutiny that became possible in the 1640s had a meaningful effect on the behaviour of MPs. Indeed, from cases like those of Thomas Atkin (MP for Norwich), it

[33] *Burton Diary*, i. 192–3, 281, ii. 24, iv. 313.
[34] BL, Sloane 1467, fos. 72–v; *Burton Diary*, ii. 197, 199, 237, iii. 29, iv. 213.

seems clear that it encouraged them to recognize their constituents' interests, to draw attention to their service and to compare their own behaviour
with that of others. Atkin's concern about how he was perceived by his
constituents prompted him to send them fairly frequent updates about his
activity at Westminster, in terms of the meetings he had attended and the
efforts he had made to get petitions considered. On one occasion, for
example, he reported on the progress of a proposal to unite two local
parishes by explaining that he and the town's other agents were 'daily
remembrancers at the Parliament door'. Drawing attention to such service
was clearly intended to ensure financial rewards. He complained about
being 'more neglected than any of my predecessors', and he pointed out
that in over four years he had received only £100, that he had incurred
significantly higher expenses and that 'what I suffer by your employment I
am sensible of, to my no small damage'.[35] His primary concern, however,
was to avoid the suspicion that he was an inactive MP. He asked his
constituents in 1646 to 'take it for no neglect in me' that their petition
and ordinance had not been considered, adding that 'I have done my
utmost and cannot yet prevail', and even that other MPs thought him
'too earnest'. Atkin was also more than willing to complain about the city's
other MP, Erasmus Earle. He insisted that his colleague should be 'fully
instructed' to 'mind the city business in Parliament', and he explained that
'as yet' Earle had 'not been in the House one hour', but instead pursued a
legal career in Westminster Hall, 'to his great advantage'. To Atkin such
behaviour represented a breach of the promises made by Earle at his
election, and he wondered what would become of the country 'if others
should do the like'.[36]

In the final analysis Atkin probably feared not just criticism but also
punishment at the polls, and it is possible to demonstrate that public
scrutiny also had an impact on electoral politics. Very often, of course,
contests and disputes involved grievances relating to the electoral *process* – as
with the marvellous story of Sir Henry Spiller 'charging' his opponents
'some with light horses' – but they can also be shown to have revolved
around the opinions and behaviour of individual candidates. In March 1640
it was alleged that one candidate, Mr Lyborne, 'did always oppose the king,
the Ship Money, and all monopolies', and attempts were also made to
'poison the good opinion' of voters in Kent with stories of Sir Edward
Dering's Puritanical refusal to 'go up to the rails to receive communion'. In

[35] BL, Add. 22620, fos. 113, 117, 131, 146.
[36] BL, Add. 22620, fos. 88, 115, 119, 121, 129, 137, 156, 162, 182.

1654, meanwhile, rumours about the Earl of Stamford's fondness for 'drinking and singing' were used to undermine his chance of securing election, and in 1656 Sir John Hobart was opposed because of 'his late relation to his highness'. More significantly, in the same year Robert Lilburne observed that 'meetings and councils' were held to orchestrate campaigns against 'friends of the government', and he added that in Durham and Northumberland voters were 'perfect in their lesson, saying they will have no swordsmen, no decimator . . . to serve in Parliament'.[37]

As time passed, moreover, electioneering betrayed much more detailed knowledge about the political record and parliamentary performance of particular candidates. Many voters in 1656 rejected anyone who received 'salary from the state', and candidates were also assessed in terms of their likely behaviour in the Commons. At Leeds in 1654, Presbyterians expressed opposition to Adam Baynes because he was insufficiently 'principled to religion', and as such they favoured Mr Allenson, 'in hopes [that] the zeal and rigid design of the Presbyter shall have the complacency in [the] next parliament'. Baynes's supporters insisted that such allegations revealed 'ignorance' – which is why George Gill took on 'the burden of a piece of Shakespeare' to write a narrative of the affair – but they were clearly grounded in hard evidence. In 1656, meanwhile, Edward Whalley believed that candidates were being vetted according to their attitude towards constitutional change, although he recognized that men like John Weaver might 'secure election upon false pretences' of loyalty to the Protectorate.[38] And at Hythe in 1659 a campaign was waged against Henry Oxinden of Barham because of his supposed involvement in the Kentish rising of 1648. Oxinden challenged such allegations by highlighting his solid parliamentarian record, only to encounter additional claims that he supported 'pulling down . . . the ministry' by withdrawing tithes from 'self-seeking ministers', and that he wanted to reform 'abuses . . . by the lawyers'.[39]

>The accuracy of such claims is arguably less important than their use in electioneering, and it seems clear that the political views of prospective MPs informed not just specific contests, but also the challenges that voters made to particular results. This was clear as early as 1646, when protests were made against the return of William Hudson at King's Lynn on the basis of his 'crimes and misdemeanours'. However, this is another phenomenon

---

[37] HEH, HM 951; BL: Add. 11045, fo. 97; Stowe 743, fo. 140; Stowe 184, fos. 10–11v; Bodl. MS North.c.4, fo. 91; *TSP*, v. 296–7.

[38] *TSP*, v. 296; BL: Add. 21422, fos. 384, 439, 410, 439; Add. 21427, fo. 211.

[39] BL, Add. 28004, fos. 31, 37, 43–4, 47, 49–50, 52; *Oxinden and Peyton Letters*, pp. 225–9.

that became much more obvious during the Protectorate, when observers were struck by the number of complaints made to the Commons.[40] These included cases in Leicestershire, Hereford and Kingston-upon-Thames, as well as a petition against George Courthop after the 1656 Sussex election, which portrayed him as a devotee of the prayer book and an active supporter of Charles Stuart. Courthop protested his innocence, and was able to overturn the council's decision to exclude him from the Commons, even though the allegations were, in fact, true. In this case the agitation against Courthop was probably organized by leading Cromwellians, but other protests were almost certainly spontaneous. These included elections involving Edmund Jones, Nathaniel Barton, Thomas Pury and George Glapthorne, which generated printed interventions and which have already been mentioned.[41] But they also included a great many other similar incidents, not least after the Restoration. Some commentators, for example, argued that Sir Walter St John would be unable to secure election anywhere in Wiltshire, as someone who was 'genuinely disliked' for serving in the parliamentarian army. Others expressed surprise that certain candidates achieved success by standing on a record of 'remarkable opposition to the bishops'.[42] What all of these cases share is that they drew upon new kinds of knowledge that circulated during the 1640s and 1650s and that they were facilitated by the print media. Indeed, there are occasionally grounds for thinking that the publicity given by newspapers to contested elections – like that involving Samuel Highland and Robert Warcupp at Southwark in 1654 – led to the submission of further relevant evidence. It seems perfectly clear, therefore, that the protest against John Wildman's return at Scarborough represented an explicit response to newspaper reports that had announced his election.[43]

Finally, and perhaps inevitably, the potential for being either held to account or misrepresented at the polls led some candidates to clarify their views and promote their records in a fairly public manner. Sir Edward Dering considered it perfectly appropriate for MPs to be lobbied by supporters and observed by constituents, and his awareness of being under scrutiny helps to explain his decision to circulate and publish his speeches and to explain his conduct. As a novice candidate in 1649,

---

[40] *Diurnall*: 504.134, p. 1075; 503.238, pp. 3644–5; *Proceedings*, 599.255, p. 4036.
[41] *Politicus*: 361.218, p. 3700; 361.219, pp. 3709–10; *Proceedings*, 599.256, p. 4055; *Diurnall*, 503.246, pp. 3771–2; *Memoirs of Sir George Courthop*, ed. S. Lomas (Cam. Soc. Miscellany 11, 1907), pp. 141–5; *TSP*, v. 382–3.
[42] Longleat, Thynne 9, fo. 196; Staffs. RO, D868/3/68a.
[43] *Politicus*: 361.218, p. 3700; 361.219, p. 3716; *Diurnall*, 503.246, pp. 3771–2; TNA, SP 18/74, fo. 166.

meanwhile, Robert Bennet circulated pamphlets containing his justification of the king's trial in order to attract support at West Looe, while those who had already sat in parliament occasionally advertised, explained and excused their earlier activity.[44] Some of the MPs who were prevented from taking their seats in 1656 apparently printed a statement explaining their situation, to 'acquaint those that sent them with the cause of their return', to indicate 'what a free parliament this is like to be' and to stir up opposition, and this was distributed across the country in large quantities. In 1660, meanwhile, Luke Robinson pre-empted a backlash against things that were 'said to be acted by me in the late differences', by explaining that he had 'not added one penny' to his estate as an MP, and indeed that he had been 'a great loser by the times'. Although he admitted to having done things by 'mistake' out of 'too much zeal', he protested that 'many thousands' had 'acted more than I, and some perhaps more to their own profit'. Even more revealing is a letter written by William Lenthall, in the hope of securing election at Oxford University in April 1660. Lenthall drew attention not just to the support he had received from General Monck, but also to the fact that 'you have enjoyed the benefit of my endeavours'. Indeed, he sought to counter 'the propositions made against me' by boasting that it would be hard to find anyone who could 'outstrip me in your service'. Similarly, when Phineas Andrews sought re-election at Hythe in 1661, he crowed about having given constituents a weekly account of parliamentary proceedings, and of having 'endeavoured their good with as much cost and pains as any that ever served them'. Once again, in other words, the nexus of print, politics and information produced situations in which political practices underwent change, and in which print not only underpinned changes in political culture but also made them manifest to voters.[45]

Formal interactions between MPs and constituents – involving correspondence, complaints and elections – thus shed revealing light on contemporary political culture. They demonstrate that voters became more assiduous in monitoring the performance of their representatives, more assertive in demanding zealous service and more aggressive in passing judgment on particular individuals, and they also shed further light on a fairly widespread process of rethinking the nature of representation and accountability. Moreover, they reveal that both participation and political

---

[44] Peacey, 'Dering', pp. 961–8; Hirst, *Representative*, pp. 184–5; FSL, X.d.483/37; Bennet, *King Charle's* (1649, B1886), p. 16.

[45] *TSP*, v. 456, 490–1; BL: Add. 78194, fo. 121; Add. 21425, fo. 222; Staffs. RO, D868/3/9a, 30; OUA, NEP/Supra/Reg.Ta, pp. 10–11; BL, Add. 28004, fo. 203.

thinking were predicated on developments in print culture, in terms of the exploitation of information provided by pamphlets and newspapers and the appropriation of print both by members of the public and their representatives. Ultimately, as the next section will demonstrate, this involved members of the public discussing MPs' performance in the public domain.

iii Printed criticism of representatives

In October 1653, John Ufflet produced a printed pamphlet entitled *A Caution to the Parliament*, in order to accuse members of the Committee of Accounts of financial wrongdoing. His targets were not MPs, even if a number of prominent members were shown to have behaved dishonourably, and none of his accusations were upheld by the authorities. Nevertheless, the incident is significant because Ufflet used print to shine a light into the heart of the political system, to make specific allegations against named individuals and to accuse officials of 'breach of trust'.[46] As such, he highlights a third kind of interaction between the public and the political elite, wherein individuals praised and blamed individual MPs and peers in print, in relation to their own experiences and grievances and in relation to their role as concerned constituents. The aim of this section is to demonstrate how ordinary citizens used print as a means of expressing frustration regarding the performance of specific members, of criticizing the efficiency of complaints mechanisms, and of challenging inappropriate uses of parliamentary privilege. It is also to show that these printed interventions tended to represent a conscious escalation of tactics, to involve heightened demands for political accountability and to display incipient 'radicalism'.

Printed reflections upon MPs could sometimes be very positive, although more often than not they were critical and hostile and involved little more than libelling. In October 1642 the citizens of Barnstaple used a newsbook to praise their MP, George Peard, and the corporation at Chipping Wycombe similarly used *Politicus* to justify their election of Thomas Scot in 1654. Even more striking is the open letter from the townsmen of Boston to their MP, Sir Anthony Irby. This represented a defiant vote of confidence following his seclusion at Pride's Purge, offered thanks for 'the several happinesses' that his service had brought to the town and responded to

---

[46] Ufflet, *Caution* (1653, U18); *Proceedings*: 599.211, pp. 3343–4; 600.014, pp. 181–8; *Diurnall*, 503.200, p. 3050; *Politicus*, 361.174, p. 2792.

'jealousies' about how he had executed his trust.[47] Such examples are fairly rare, however, and most public statements about MPs involved grievances and grumbling. As early as July 1641, Sir John Lenthall wrote to Sir Peter Temple (MP for Buckingham) about 'rogues in the common gaol' who 'so abuse us both ... every night they sing a scandalous libellous song of you and me, to which multitudes of people stand and hearken'. Such libelling thrived throughout the period, and in 1647 James Ramsey posted papers at the Exchange regarding debts owed by the Earl of Newport. Much more important, however, were the occasions when criticisms appeared in print, as with Lilburne's reproachful letter to Henry Marten in July 1647. Such episodes caused consternation for those who were being accused, but they also provoked more general annoyance, and at least some of the attempts that were made to enforce press controls involved direct responses to printed criticism of individual MPs.[48] However, what makes them particularly important is that they reveal contemporary attitudes to parliamentary privilege, political performance and the possibilities for securing redress, as well as to the ways in which citizens responded to their frustrations.

First, therefore, public criticism of MPs reveals a willingness to critique parliamentary privilege. Here a particularly valuable case involves Sir Peter Temple, who claimed privilege in order to avoid legal actions by his many creditors, and whose son, Sir Richard Temple, sought election to protect the family estate. Such tactics were scarcely new, of course, but they generated particularly severe grievances during a long parliament, and as such, leave was eventually given to raise the issue at the committee that was created to consider complaints against MPs. However, while Sir Peter was able to stay one step ahead of his creditors, this decision effectively legitimized allegations not merely about his finances but also about his crypto-royalism.[49] As a result he became one of a number of MPs against whom grievances were aired using similar mechanisms, in cases that exploited information circulating in the public domain and that sometimes found their way into print. This was not least because journalists like Gilbert Mabbott welcomed the chance to 'inform against members' like Edward Vaughan, whom he hoped would 'not be a phoenix'. Indeed, the case of Lord Howard of Escrick demonstrates how the appearance in print of corruption allegations fuelled the investigations that eventually resulted in his expulsion from the Commons.[50]

[47] *Speciall Passages*, 605.11, pp. 95–6; *Politicus*, 361.213, pp. 3615–18; *Letter* (1648, L1770).
[48] HEH, STT 1345; PA, MP 23 July 1647; *Copy* (1647, L2093); *CJ*, iii. 457–8, vii. 843.
[49] HEH, STT, Parliament Box 1/22, 43–44; STT, Parliament Box 2/8, 9, 14, 16, 18, 25.
[50] *Diurnall*, 504.200, pp. 1612; *Moderate*, 413.2041, sig. Ssv; *Aulicus*, 275.210B, p. 865; *Politicus*, 361.055, p. 894; DRO, D258/33/37/3–81.

Secondly, printed complaints about MPs focused on performance in parliament. Some such episodes are well known, not least because they involved agitators like John Lilburne and resulted in prosecution, and a particularly good example involves George Wither's pamphlet against Sir Richard Onslow, *Justitiarius Justificatus* (1646). This tract, which was written in response to Wither's removal from the county bench in Surrey, made sweeping allegations about Onslow's abuse of 'power and trust' for 'private ends', and described him as one of the 'false brethren' at Westminster who were prone to 'forget their duties'. Wither obviously recognized that this was a provocative act, but justified his conduct by claiming that the commonwealth was 'more endangered by . . . flatterers than free-thinkers', and that it was 'dishonoured' by MPs who were 'violently zealous for personal privileges'. He also argued that 'the disparagement of a particular member' was warranted if it exposed 'corruptions', and that 'it were better that one should suffer, than that all should be endangered by our silence'. Moreover, although the tract may have been intended for restricted circulation, it nevertheless represented a dramatic response to personal grievances. It was a reaction to the besmirching of Wither's character, to the failure to remedy Onslow's 'insolencies' and to the fact that Wither's 'losses and services' had not been 'represented' in parliament. Indeed, Wither chided MPs for not being able to 'discover some things by sitting in the House which we see, too often, by walking abroad'.[51]

Wither's case was obviously an extraordinary one, but it was echoed in less well-known episodes, which involved criticism of both specific individuals and of the parliamentary process. In May 1646 London Presbyterians got cold feet about using their remonstrance to criticize MPs like Henry Marten, and evidently deleted passages that described him as 'a man expelled from the House for spreading treason, and shuffled in again we know not how', and as 'one that never speaks in the House but when he is drunk, and yet speaks every day'. However, Thomas Coningsby of North Mimms showed no such restraint. In September 1647 he was sent to the Tower for a pamphlet that was addressed to 'all the world', that complained about Miles Corbet and the Committee of Examinations and that accused 'the commons' trustees' of not being 'protective to their trusters'.[52] Such anger was also evident in *The Mournfull-Cryes of Many Thousand Poore Tradesmen* (January 1648), a tract that commented on parliamentary

---

[51] *CJ*, iv. 235, 505, 639–40; Wither, *Justitiarius* (1646, W3165), pp. 1–3, 7, 13–15; BL, Add. 31116, pp. 528, 559; *Diary of John Harington*, pp. 18, 31.
[52] Cary, *Memorials*, i. 31–2; *To all the World* (1647, C5879), p. 14.

factions, demanded the translation of laws into English and complained about MPs who profited from the war while failing to declare their accounts. Its authors also added proposals for an elected committee of 'disengaged men' to hear complaints about MPs' financial impropriety, and made explicit reference to the likelihood of finding '£30,000 in Mr Richard Darley's hand, [and] £25,000 in Mr Thorpe's hands'. Indeed, such claims were then supplemented by an allegation regarding William Lenthall who, 'to cover his cozenage', was said to have given £22,000 to a servant 'to purchase land in his own name, though for his use'.[53]

Thirdly, as these cases make clear, the use of print to hold MPs like Lenthall to account often resulted from frustration over the failure to secure justice by other means. In May 1648, for example, Amon Wilbee provided a forensic account of Lenthall's failings and a detailed analysis of the cases in which he was involved. This involved allegations that he abused parliamentary processes to protect his brother, the notorious gaoler Sir John Lenthall, as well as claims that he had 'buried' petitions and complaints, to the point where he could be used to symbolize the 'company of ambitious, avaricious, factious men' at Westminster.[54] In Wilbee's case, of course, it is difficult to know whether such claims represented personal grievances against the Speaker, but other attacks on Lenthall clearly involved the use of print by individuals who considered themselves to be his victims. In June 1649 William Bray produced an open letter to Lenthall from his cell in Windsor Castle, following earlier appeals and petitions that had been delivered to parliament, including one that 'remains dead in your hands'. Bray professed to have been 'neglected' by Lenthall, who could apparently be moved by 'neither love to justice nor importunity', and he was unapologetic about making a public appeal for freedom from 'oppressive and illegal imprisonment'. Bray's attack was quickly followed by a broadside from Edward Jenkes, containing *Ten Articles . . . Against an Evil Member*, and although the printed text did not identify Lenthall, his name was added to each copy by hand. Like Bray, Jenkes resorted to print because of the way in which earlier complaints had been treated, and he made it clear that his allegations had already been submitted under oath to a parliamentary committee. His intention was to remind readers that the MPs who sat on this committee were obliged to consider the case, and to point out that Lenthall had endeavoured to 'corrupt many members of the Parliament' in order to 'conceal and smother the foregoing treacheries'. And it was also to give vent to his anger. Jenkes claimed that 'godly and honest' MPs would

[53] *Mournfull-Cryes* (1648, M2985).   [54] *Tertia Pars* (1648, W2115), pp. 1–9, 19–20, 26–34, 44.

become 'odious' if Lenthall was 'protected from a legal trial', and he urged 'free commonwealth-men' to 'join together' in order to urge Cromwell to prosecute Lenthall before a general council of the army.[55] Within a matter of weeks, moreover, Jenkes produced another denunciation of the Speaker, which included a much more detailed assault upon Westminster corruption. He complained that Lenthall had been exonerated of 'treachery against the state' by means of a 'false and scandalous' report from Lawrence Whitaker's Committee of Examinations, and he also claimed that by ignoring charges that had been 'proved against him' parliament had undermined the 'lives and liberties' of several of Lenthall's 'prosecutors'.[56]

This sense that the use of print reflected mounting frustration and anger, and that it was something to which individuals resorted only reluctantly, is also evident from other cases involving the Speaker. In 1657, for example, Captain John Bernard produced *Truths Triumph* after spending 'many years' and 'many hundred pounds' in 'finding out and laying open' plots and conspiracies by the regime's 'secret enemies'. He was particularly infuriated by the case of Lenthall, evidence of whose treason had apparently been suppressed by a 'false report', which whitewashed his 'wickedness'. What makes this intervention particularly intriguing is that the alleged crimes had taken place years earlier, and that Bernard had prepared 'a full answer to that false report' as long ago as 1649. He had resisted publishing it because of the perilous state of the new regime, and out of a concern that his accusations might cause the army to become 'divided and distracted'. By 1657, however, Bernard had grown desperate after years of imprisonment, and as a result of a 'scandalous pamphlet' that was designed to make him 'odious unto all posterity'. His response involved not just *Truths Triumph*, but also a broadside containing the texts of some of his petitions, which he hoped to circulate around London, 'to every minister of the gospel, and officer and soldier of the army'. The latter was explicitly seen as a last ditch effort to mobilize support before what he claimed was the appointed (and imminent) date of his execution.[57]

Fourthly, the kinds of frustration that led to the vilification of MPs in public statements can also be shown to have involved criticisms that were wide-ranging and radical. One such pamphlet was *The Prisoners Remonstrance*, which was addressed to 'every freeborn commoner of England' in August 1649. This referred to 'numberless petitions' that had

---

[55] Bray, *Heaven* (1649, B4303), pp. 1–2, 4; Jenkes, *Ten Articles* (1649, J624); BL, 669.f.14/57.
[56] *Edward Jenkes* (1649, J626).
[57] Bernard, *Truths* (1657, B2002), pp. 1–2; *John Bernard* (1657, B2004).

done little to alleviate the condition of debtors, and it blamed lawyers for the fact that the business had been 'imprisoned and recommitted . . . upon mere delusive objections, on purpose to protract the miseries of the afflicted'. More importantly, the author made specific allegations about how the matter had been 'tossed like a giddy ball from one hand to another', and about a litany of referrals, reports and re-commitments. These delays and obstructions were blamed on Lenthall, who was once again accused of protecting his brother, on Nicholas Lechmere – in whose hands it was 'like to have been buried in everlasting silence' – and on Robert Reynolds, by whom it was 'spun out' for a whole term 'in promises and repromises, protractions and rejoinders'. Indeed, certain parts of the narrative were decidedly Kafkaesque, with a cast of MPs that included Henry Marten, Bulstrode Whitelocke, Thomas Fell and Augustine Garland, and with twists and turns that involved repeated delays, unfulfilled orders and undelivered reports, as well as committees that 'never met at all'. The tract then concluded on a much more general note, by beseeching MPs to reflect on such 'disgraces', to 'abandon the society of self-interests and factions' and to 'purge yourselves from those jealousies the people have so wondrously conceived of your inclinations and proceedings'.[58]

Other incidents, moreover, indicate even more clearly how cases relating to individual citizens fed into and developed out of the period's radical movements. A case in point involves Thomas Elsliot, who emerged into print in 1652 with *The Lamb Taking of the Woolf.* Elsliot was clearly motivated by personal grievances, having apparently been arrested in the Commons lobby in 1649, and then incarcerated by the authorities, and his pamphlet evidently appeared in the wake of other printed texts that had been presented to MPs and the Committee of Indemnity in late 1651. What makes it intriguing, however, is that it involved a lengthy indictment of three prominent MPs – John Glyn, Edmund Prideaux and Thomas Twisden, who were described as 'traitors and enemies to this common-wealth', and as 'bribers, extortioners, ambidexters, cheaters, oppressors, and deluders'. These three were accused of working to 'destroy and subvert the fundamental and common laws', and of 'breaking the trust reposed in them', and such rhetorical flourishes were backed by detailed claims. Elsliot alleged that they had organized a parliamentary campaign to disband the army in 1647; that they had promoted a new army under Edward Massey and Sydenham Poyntz; and that they had been complicit in the 'forcing of the Houses'. More importantly, Elsliot also placed his own

---

[58] *Prisoners* (1649, H3602), pp. 3–7.

troubles in a broader context, associated himself with other victims of parliamentary authority, and used radical language and ideas. He accused these MPs of labouring to destroy Lilburne with 'false accusations and false aspersions', and he also alleged that they had rallied MPs to block the appointment of Cromwell as Captain General after his return from Ireland in 1649. Indeed, having described himself as a 'freeborn person of this nation' and likened his treatment to that of Lilburne, he also issued appeals to MPs who were known to have been sympathetic to the case of Josiah Primatt, reminded MPs about the need to prioritize 'salus populi' and repeatedly bemoaned the trampling of fundamental laws.[59]

With both Elsliot and the poor prisoners, therefore, private grievances fuelled printed accusations against MPs, and developed into radical critiques of parliament. This is a neglected phenomenon, and one which perhaps suggests that particular cases were taken up by campaigning activists, who saw an opportunity to make political capital out of genuine complaints. This certainly seems to have been the case with a remarkable series of pamphlets that were attributed to John Musgrave in the mid 1640s, and that emerged out of his bitter dispute with a local MP, John Barwis. In many ways this revealed a fairly typical picture of the connection between personal grievances and print culture. Musgrave's pamphlets expressed frustration that his complaints had been overlooked, that he had been 'wearied with attendance' and that he had been imprisoned for contempt. Equally typical was Musgrave's willingness to rehearse his case by reprinting old petitions and letters, and by complaining about those MPs – John Lisle, Sir Thomas Widdrington and John Blakiston – who had proved dilatory, obstructive and corrupt. What was less typical, however, was his allegation that Barwis had betrayed his trust and committed treason against the 'state', and his willingness to accuse his own MPs – Richard Tolson and James Bellingham – on the basis of their careers and parliamentary speeches. More extraordinary still was his challenge to MPs' parliamentary privilege and his radical critique of the Westminster system. Such behaviour inevitably angered parliament, and Musgrave was eventually indicted for treason, but what seems clear is that at least some of his pamphlets were produced by Lilburne and his friends, not least because Musgrave denied being responsible for them, and because explicit reference was made to Lilburne's own works.[60]

---

[59] Elsliot, *Lamb* (1652, E640), pp. 3–5, 8–11, 15, 17, 20, 22, 24; Elsliot, *Lambe Still* (1652, E639A).

[60] Musgrave, *Word* (1646, M3154), pp. 3, 7–10, 12–20; Musgrave, *Another* (1646, M3144), sigs. Av, A3–B3v; Musgrave, *Yet Another* (1646, M3155), pp. 1–12, 33–5, 39–43; Musgrave, *Fourth* (1647, M3148), pp. 8, 13, 17–18; Musgrave, *Declaration* (1647, M3147); *CJ*, iv. 322, 336, 682, v. 245, 316, 442–3, 584, vi. 69.

However, it is also possible that men like Elsliot were able to learn by reading about the experience of other plaintiffs like Josiah Primatt, and to be inspired by radical pamphleteers like John Harris, whose own pamphlets made much more specific criticisms of parliament than has often been recognized. In *The Antipodes*, for example, Harris not only decried parliament's resemblance to a 'close committee', and demanded mechanisms for holding MPs to account, but also made specific allegations against the 'wickedness' of 'trustees' like Sir John Clotworthy, Sir William Waller and Denzil Holles.[61] Moreover, it is also worth pointing out that this same blend of specific details and general analysis can also be detected in tracts like the *Remonstrance and Declaration of Severall Counties* (January 1649), which pursued an overtly royalist agenda. This pamphlet denied that MPs had 'authority, power, commission, instruction, or deputation' to prosecute Charles I, or to alter the constitution, and it produced a long list of the MPs who were guilty of usurping parliamentary power. It also demanded 'public justice against them', and insisted upon a revocation of 'all that trust, power and authority we formerly delegated and committed to them ... when we discern them palpably to abuse both it and us, from whom they are to receive their wages'.[62]

Cases like these betray relationships between the public and its representatives that were quite different from face-to-face confrontations, legal and forceful expulsions and the kinds of formal interaction that occurred before and after parliamentary elections. They demonstrate not just how awareness of parliament and its members was acquired, but also how frustrations developed during the participatory process, as well as how print could be deployed as a tactical means of expressing grievances regarding specific MPs, not least in relation to a radicalization of both thought and action.

iv Conclusion

This chapter has argued that the potential for holding individual MPs to account became a practical reality in the circumstances of Civil War and revolution. This involved more than merely the providentialism of Nehemiah Wallington, who argued that the death of the MP Sir Peter Leigh during a fight at a playhouse represented divine punishment for a speech defending public theatres. It involved more than merely the sending of plague sores into the House of Commons. And it involved more than

---

[61] Harris, *Antipodes* (1647, H42), sigs. A3, B–Bv.   [62] *Severall Counties* (1649, R961), pp. 4–8.

merely blunt talk about the desirability of parliament being 'blown up with gunpowder', for which Anne Hodson was prosecuted in the mid 1640s.[63] This is not to say that the period lacked abuse, intimidation and violence, and MPs and peers clearly had good cause to fear being ridiculed and assaulted in the streets. There was palpable fear in 1640, when a 'knave' was seen 'standing on top of a house in King Street', crying 'beware your heads', just as there was in 1647 when Leveller threats led to one MP becoming 'a little fearful of being killed or beaten'.[64] However, it is to suggest that such fear and aggression needs to be contextualized carefully, in order to appreciate the nature of contemporary beliefs and practices about political accountability, as well as the ways in which these underwent change during the 1640s and 1650s.

By exploring different kinds of interactions between the public and its politicians, this chapter has confirmed that the political nation was becoming broader and better informed, and that interventions in public life were becoming more complex and sophisticated. It has also confirmed that there existed a spectrum of political awareness, a spectrum of processes by which political understanding was achieved and a spectrum of methods for participating in national politics. And it has revealed four important conclusions. First, contemporaries exploited the openness of the political system to monitor the behaviour of MPs, to make judgments about their performance and to interact with them. Secondly, such interactions involved not just criticizing, challenging and confronting public figures, in more or less informed ways, but also the determination to call wayward and underperforming members to account, through seditious speech, crowd behaviour and festive misrule, as well as through private correspondence, elections and pamphleteering. Thirdly, such novel practices reflected a radicalization of political thought. They reflected the way in which the term 'representative' began to be used to refer to individual MPs, rather than to parliament as a whole, and the tendency for individual behaviour to be scrutinized as closely as collective performance. And they also reflected mounting concern about parts of the country that lacked sitting MPs and the 'murmuring' of citizens who felt that taxation was being imposed by people who did not 'represent them'.[65] Fourthly, print culture played an important part not just in enabling informed judgments to be made about individual politicians, but also in enabling these to be expressed in a more or less public fashion.

---

[63] FSL, V.a.436, p. 88; Bodl. MS Carte 80, fo. 123; BL, Sloane 1467, fo. 152; LMA, MJ/SR/925/98.
[64] BL, Add. 64921, fo.126; Claydon, Verney reel 8.
[65] *Kingdomes*, 214.290, pp. 1188–90; FSL, Add. 662.

Indeed, this connection between print, accessibility and accountability was perfectly clear to contemporary commentators like Lilburne, who expressly connected press freedom with political transparency, and who sought to ensure that 'all the treacherous and tyrannical designs may be the easier discovered, and so prevented'. Lilburne regarded this as 'a liberty of greatest concernment', and as something that only tyrants were 'engaged to prohibit', but what is interesting is that such comments could only be made by someone who had already witnessed the power of print. Lilburne, in other words, was seeking to preserve a revolution, and was demonstrating how far his dreams about political accountability had already become reality.[66]

---

[66] *Occurrences*, 465.5113, sig. Aaaaa.

Conclusion

The months surrounding the Restoration of the Stuart dynasty in 1660 reveal extraordinary evidence about print and political culture during the mid seventeenth century. Apart from the dramatic way in which readers were confronted by a plethora of newspapers and a flood of pamphlets, it was also evident that such material both fostered and reflected a participatory political culture, not least by offering precise evidence about members of the political elite. A particularly dramatic example is *The Mystery of the Good Old Cause* (July 1660), a detailed prosopographical analysis of former MPs that recycled evidence about their careers, political activity and financial profiteering, and that stigmatized 'recruiter' MPs, 'constant' Rumpers and king-killers. Thomas Boon was described as 'a cruel committee man', and one that 'got a vast estate' by having 'licked his fingers', a euphemism for financial peculation. Similar charges were levelled against any number of other individuals. William Ellis was described as a 'mighty thriving committee man' and Augustine Garland was called 'an indefatigable stickler in most committees'. Gilbert Millington was identified as chairman of the Committee for Plundered Ministers, while Giles Greene was linked with the chairmanship of the Navy Committee and Richard Salway was described as a 'main man in the Committee of Safety'. Others attracted comments for their famous and radical speeches (Thomas Chaloner), or for their nepotism (Giles Greene), and yet others were mocked by means of cruel nicknames. These made reference to power relationships within parliament, as with the description of Cornelius Holland as Sir Henry Vane's 'zany', as well as to political opportunism, as in case of Sir Henry 'Whimsey' Mildmay.[1]

Pamphlets like this not only held MPs up to public ridicule, but also served as electoral propaganda, and any number of texts provided information about the careers of individual MPs alongside explicit psephological

---

[1] *Mystery* (1660, M3191), pp. 1–3, 6, 10–11, 13, 18, 21–3, 26, 30.

394

advice. Lists appeared of known royalists, as well as of the recent Council of State, on the latter of which the 'ingenious and impartial reader' was invited to 'consider whether any person above named ought to have any share in the government of either Church or State'. Many such texts were produced in broadside format, doubtless for display. One offered poetic advice, suggesting that voters should 'have a care of your voices / make none had their hands / in church livings or lands', and then named over seventy Rumpers and regicides who ought to be rejected, and it explicitly argued for their identities to be *posted* in public. Another satirical text detailed the forty-one MPs who had taken a 'phanatique' oath in opposition to the Solemn League and Covenant, the ministry and the monarchy. *The Grand Memorandum*, meanwhile, identified those members who had been sitting when the Long Parliament had finally been dissolved, as well as the Rumpers who were present. It marked regicides with an accusing finger and used asterisks to indicate who had withdrawn from the Commons after the readmission of the secluded members. This information, too, was explicitly published so that people 'may see and know who have been their oppressors, and the fatal betrayers of their liberties', and so that they might be 'better guided in their future elections'. Once again it can be shown to have circulated across the country. The aim, in other words, was to ensure that old parliamentarians were held to account, and this could also mean influencing the fate of men whose lives and estates were in the hands of MPs. Not the least of these were the men who had been involved in the king's trial, whose activity was documented repeatedly in works like *Englands Black Tribunall* and *The Oglio of Traytors*.[2]

The pamphlets and broadsides of 1660 thus reflected a febrile political atmosphere, and they probably helped to ensure that certain individuals became the targets for popular criticism, while others stood up to be counted by exploiting various print genres. This *individualized* political culture was sometimes expressed in popular festivities, and many towns across the country – from Sherborne to Bury St Edmunds, Reading and Sandwich – witnessed extraordinary spectacles involving the identification and vilification of rogues and rebels. Indeed, this also involved ritualistic 'trials' and 'executions' of the effigies of both living and dead enemies, including Cromwell, Bradshaw and Hugh Peter. The copycat nature of

---

[2] *Declaration ... Oxon* (1660, D721); *Declaration ... Worcester* (1660, D715); BL, Eg. 2542, fo. 327: *A True List*; *Englands Directions* (1660, E2959); *Free-Parliament* (1660, F2117); *Phanatique* (1660, F395); *Grand* (1660, G1503); DRO, D258/15/2/12; *Black Tribunall* (1660, E2946); *Oglio* (1660, O188); *Catalogue* (1660, C1388).

such events reflected the speed with which news circulated, and the public burning of the Solemn League and Covenant in Bury St Edmunds was explicitly inspired by stories from other parts of the country. It involved the streets being 'strewed with rushes, and the windows hanged with garlands, and houses hung with the best pictures, and tapestry hangings', and the town was said to be 'full of flags and streamers', and as bonfires flared the locals engaged in 'merriment ... till midnight'.[3] And similar processes of news circulation and personalized politics can also be detected in the numerous loyal addresses that appeared in print from across the country, many of which involved conscious efforts to publicize the names of prominent royalists. As throughout the preceding decades, indeed, these texts and events made an impact across a fairly wide social spectrum. They were among the many newspapers and 'jeering' books that were read and commonplaced by Thomas Rugg, whose interest in current affairs during these months also extended to proceedings in parliament, analysis of political factions, and the names of the regicides, the latter of which were copied from a printed sheet. And of course Rugg was not alone in being obsessed with this torrent of 'printed sheets of paper'. He observed how Londoners took an interest in who was writing specific newspapers and he reflected on the consumption habits of fellow news addicts by noting that people 'bought up' such texts 'as fast as they could meet with any'. Indeed, this was not merely a London phenomenon, and John Martin of Rye reflected on how people were 'much accustomed to hear news' in 'this talkative age'.[4]

According to Rugg, moreover, the 'talkative' nature of political culture in 1660 was such that 'almost every man writ their minds and printed it'. This, too, was something that involved a personalized politics and a complex variety of print genres, rather than simply a public sphere of rational debate. Any number of individuals who were being attacked in print, and who had cause to fear for their safety, felt compelled to produce printed vindications, either for discrete circulation among MPs or for public consumption, as well as for insertion in newspapers. In November 1660, for example, Ignatius White printed a *Vindication* in response to 'the common reports raised by the malice of some and ignorance of others', which had 'done me great injuries from which I endeavour to vindicate myself by these leaves'. White added that this public statement was 'occasioned by a false relation' regarding the arrest of the regicide Thomas Scot, and he accused the author

---

[3] *Publicus*, 378.121, sigs. Tt–Tt2; BL, Add. 10116, fo. 212v; BL, Add. 10116, fo. 212v.
[4] *Gentry of Somerset-Shire* (1660, D678aA); *Rugg*, pp. 35–71; FSL, V.a.454, p. 69.

of *A True Narrative* of writing 'to the prejudice of truth and of my honour'. Such tactics were also employed by regicides, or by those accused of involvement in the king's trial, in texts that were sometimes targeted at MPs, but which could also be aimed at a much wider audience. These included a printed petition by John Lisle, a 'true and humble representation' by John Downes and *Thomas Waite's Case*, while Alderman Thomas Viner and John Gurdon attempted to persuade newspaper editors to correct untruths that had been peddled in print. Gurdon forced a publisher to correct a published list of those who had sat in judgment upon the king, having secured an official certificate to prove that he was 'never present at any meeting in the trial'. Viner, meanwhile, challenged a claim about his involvement in the High Court of Justice that had appeared in *The Mystery of the Good Old Cause*.[5]

The aim of this final chapter is to suggest that such evidence provides the perfect way of teasing out the significance of what has been discussed in the preceding pages. Most obviously it is valuable as a means of encapsulating many of the book's key findings (section i), but it is also useful as a reminder of the need to look beyond the Restoration and to explore the political legacies of the print revolution (section ii). The aim, in other words, is not just to reiterate that a new approach to the print revolution provides the key to recovering the participatory possibilities of the mid seventeenth century, but also to suggest that this provides a way of challenging conventional assumptions that the print revolution was transitory and epiphenomenal.

i Common politics in the English Revolution

What seems perfectly clear from the evidence about 1660 is that profound changes had occurred regarding the consumption of print, the provision of information and analysis concerning current affairs, and the utility of print as a means of participating in daily political life. First, this book has demonstrated the remarkable penetration of printed pamphlets and newspapers, the ways in which printed material was circulated, distributed, accessed and consumed, and the ways in which contemporaries responded to the flood of print. Secondly, evidence has revealed a democratization or vulgarization of knowledge. Pamphlets and newspapers made public and affordable what had once been secret, or at least privileged and expensive, in

---

[5] *Rugg*, p. 48; *NP*, iv. 261–2; *True Narrative* (1660, H17); Longleat, Whitelocke parcel 7/97: *Petition of John Lisle*; *John Downes* (1660, D2081); *Waites Case* (1660, W226A); *Exact Account*, 491.103, pp. 1005–6; *Publicus*, 378.121, p. 332.

terms of insights into the machinations of the parliamentary system, information regarding daily proceedings, and evidence about the activity of individual MPs. The regular appearance of such detailed material indicates the degree to which the political elite was willing to make parliament accessible and transparent, to tolerate popular participation and to sanction processes for holding individual MPs to account, either by making informed decisions at the polls or by submitting formal complaints to designated committees. And, thirdly, evidence has revealed the variety of ways in which members of the public appropriated print in order to participate in national political processes, as writers, petitioners, lobbyists or protesters, and as constituents and interested citizens. In other words, the combined effect of a physically accessible parliament and a steady flow of information regarding its processes, proceedings and personalities enabled members of the public to monitor events at Westminster, to make tactical interventions, and to make informed judgments about whether or not representatives were fulfilling their duties and putting the public service before private interests. Indeed, the frequency with which contemporaries undertook informed interactions with MPs reflected the legitimizing effect of their having been deliberately incorporated into a political system, and the educative effect of having observed political proceedings at close quarters.

Such evidence naturally prompts reflections on the 'impact' of print, and here great care is needed. This is partly a matter of calibrating assessments of how and why these developments occurred. It is important, in other words, to recognize structural factors like the development of the print industry and its distribution networks, as well as growing literacy, while also taking into account the importance of conjunctural forces. These included the circumstances of Civil War, the 'push' and 'pull' factors that promoted participation, and the transformation of parliament into a quasi-permanent 'institution' rather than an occasional 'event', not to mention the specific circumstances facing individual citizens. What this means is that print was not *responsible* for the emergence of a participatory political culture during the middle decades of the seventeenth century. Rather, it suggests that, in the structural and conjunctural conditions of the 1640s and 1650s, print became centrally important to the ways in which participatory culture developed, to the ways in which contemporaries experienced and responded to political developments and to political agency. Connected to this is a second conclusion: that print needs to be explored in ways that move beyond thinking about its role in generating popular awareness and consciousness. Meaningful popular politics was possible before the print revolution, and pamphlets and newspapers were not simply things to which members of the public reacted. As such the 'impact' of print needs to be assessed in terms of fostering and facilitating a more *intense* participatory culture, and one that developed through popular activity as much as through the conditions created by the political elite. The process by which print became central to a vibrant popular politics involved decisions and actions at Westminster and Whitehall as well as the activities of consumers and citizens.

This is why the central ambition of this book has been to concentrate on 'practices'. It explains why emphasis has been placed on how the practices of daily political life were adapted and developed in the light of contemporary pressures, circumstances and experiences, and in relation to specific problems, grievances and hopes. These practices involved coming to terms with, and coping with, print culture, and they also involved improvised methods of participation, at new political levels, and with new political tactics. They also involved expectations and frustrations that were bound up with the status of parliament and its evolution, and with aspirations about what could be achieved at Westminster. Parliament became, in other words, a much more important focus for political expectations. Such expectations may have been unrealistic, but they were nevertheless explicable given the prevalent official rhetoric about the institution's role in curing the country's ills, and given also the implicit and sometimes explicit encouragement that was given to public participation. The rhetoric and practices of MPs and peers, in other words, helped to promote ideas about the legitimacy of political participation, as well as informed interactions and interventions by constituents, petitioners and protesters. For members of the public, therefore, print provided information and insights that enhanced their understanding, as well as a means of expressing their views and taking action, and these processes involved something other than the generation of ideas and consciousness, and something other than the fostering of public debate. Instead, they involved the enhancement of political skills, the facilitation of detailed judgments regarding political events and the development of precise ways of using print, not least through genres that were 'private' as well as commercial, and useful for discrete as well as widespread 'publication'. The inescapable – if paradoxical – conclusion is that it is necessary to de-emphasize the public sphere while also placing much greater stress on the participatory nature of political culture.

Central to this enhanced participatory culture, and to the transformation of daily political practices, was the sophisticated use of print in response to frustrated expectations. Print was essential, in other words, to the ways in which parliamentary privilege was challenged, elections were influenced and grievances were settled, and to the ways in which contemporaries calibrated their responses and made tactical escalations. Indeed, the kinds of participatory experiences that prompted the exploitation of print also reveal how citizens became more likely to reflect on parliamentary procedures and personnel, and how the revolutionary conjuncture fostered a dynamic relationship between political practices and political thinking. In other words, increasingly assertive tactics for passing judgment on MPs mirrored attempts to establish better mechanisms for airing grievances and confronting poor performance, as well as attempts to justify new kinds of relationship between representatives and their constituents. These responses and arguments were not necessarily sophisticated or stable, let alone theoretically coherent, but they nevertheless indicate that contemporary ideas about representation and accountability were undergoing fundamental reconsideration. Indeed, this process of thinking about how the constitution *did*, *should* and *might* operate involved people on both sides of the parliamentary bar, and people with all sorts of political persuasions, and MPs of all kinds clearly recognized that they faced unprecedented scrutiny on the basis of their individual performances, and that this could lead to electoral repercussions and even mob violence. It was also a process that took place in more or less ephemeral print genres, rather than merely in substantial pamphlets and treatises, and it both fed into and emerged out of the arguments and the rhetoric of the people who are more conventionally thought of as being Civil War thinkers, from the Levellers to Henry Parker, John Milton and Marchamont Nedham. In short, as political relationships became strained, print became central to the ways in which frustrations were expressed, and to political thinking and theoretical innovation.

What was also central to the participatory and tactically sophisticated culture of the mid seventeenth century was a process of *integration*. Rather than thinking in terms of a polarized and stratified political culture, in other words, it is necessary to think about a spectrum of print genres, a spectrum of political awareness and a spectrum of practices and tactics, and about how these connected the elite with the popular, the national with the local and the traditional with the novel. First, these tactics and genres were common to royalists and parliamentarians, and people of all political persuasions developed new attitudes towards participation and participatory practices, albeit in ways that were not necessarily consistent or stable, and that involved pragmatism as well as principle. Secondly, different facets of popular politics became more obviously connected to each other and integrated with parliamentary business. In part this meant that the street politics of protests, crowds and even popular violence could be facilitated by print as an extension of formal processes, which were themselves changed as a result of new ways of utilizing print. But it also meant that it was more common for local issues – involving petitioning, protests and disorder – to generate printed interventions in Westminster affairs more readily. The combined effect was to increase the opportunities for making effective interventions in public life.

Third, integration involved bringing into the political nation people from across the social spectrum and across the country. This makes it hard to accept that parliament was a 'shadowy' entity, or that people were ignorant about the constitutional experiments of the revolutionary era, and it makes it possible to demonstrate that even humble individuals were eminently capable of becoming well informed about, and zealous followers of national affairs. In ways that have not always been fully appreciated, therefore, the ringleaders of the Gillingham riots can be shown to have boasted about how closely they followed parliamentary affairs, and their resistance can be shown to have been based on a clear (if not necessarily accurate) understanding of parliamentarian policies and proceedings, as well as on an appreciation of the importance of print culture. Likewise, the tactical armoury of the Derbyshire miners involved more than merely sophisticated local politics, based on ideas about rights and traditions, and something other than merely taking issues into the Westminster law courts and the domain of public debate. This is because attempts were also made to undertake mass petitioning, to use print tactically as a means of influencing parliamentary proceedings, and to appropriate newspapers as part of political campaigns. They even demanded better parliamentary representation, and then resorted to public appeals in the face of frustration and opposition. It would thus be an understatement to suggest that ordinary local people appropriated the *language* of parliamentarian and royalist politics in a 'grassroots version of national politics', even though 'their priorities were ultimately localist and traditional'.[6] Moreover, while the period almost certainly witnessed elements of conservatism and evidence of Puritan failure, this need not be viewed as a straightforward product of persistent localism or of loyalty to old ways. It may instead have resulted from purposeful engagement with and participation in national politics, and it seems probable that alienation from the regimes of the 1640s and 1650s

---

[6] DRO, D258/10/9/35; A. Wood, *Politics of Social Conflict* (Cambridge, 1999), pp. 256–91; Underdown, *Revel*, pp. 217–19.

reflected direct experience of parliamentary affairs and disappointed expectations of such institutions.

In thinking about the role of print in revolutionary England, therefore, it makes sense to conclude that, by virtue of becoming engaged with parliament and educated about its processes, proceedings and personalities, contemporaries from all walks of life developed the tools and skills with which to participate. They did so by reading and appropriating print, by becoming tactically, politically and constitutionally aware through personal experiences, and by attempting to resolve local grievances, defend reputations and promote causes. This increasingly sophisticated participatory culture – involving what Robert Putnam would call *doing* things rather than merely *spectating* and *commenting* – was common across the social spectrum, across the political divide and across the country. As such, what this book has been describing is the emergence of *common politics*, a term that involves the idea that political life became both *popular* and *shared*, even if it was not necessarily *equal*.[7] And by virtue of being shared, the participatory culture that this book has analysed seems to vindicate Hartlib's prediction that print technology would spread knowledge to ordinary citizens and make it harder to oppress the people. It makes it easier to agree with Sir Thomas Aston that the mid seventeenth century was 'a knowing age', in which 'old women without spectacles can discover popish plots; young men and apprentices assume to regulate the rebellion in Ireland; seamen and mariners reform the House of peers; poor men, porters and labourers spy out a malignant party and discipline them; the country clouted-shoe renew the decayed trade of the city, [and] the cobbler patch up religion'. It makes it plausible to argue that 'paper bullets' aimed at 'the inferior sort of people', and at the 'credulous vulgar', had 'invaded the sacred reins of government' and fomented civil war. And it seems to justify the contemporary sense that humble commoners had become 'statesmen', and that the period witnessed the 'kinging of the multitude'. For men like Sir Roger L'Estrange the press had made 'the multitude too familiar with the actions and counsels of their superiors, too pragmatical and censorious', and had given them 'not only an itch but a kind of colourable right and license to be meddling with the government'. Indeed, it was an understanding of Civil War print culture that prompted his insistence that 'the people neither have had, nor ever can have, nor ought to have, any right, power of faculty of government'; that 'the subject's part is resignation and obedience'; and

---

[7] R. Putnam, *Bowling Alone* (London, 2001), pp. 31–47, 341–2; R. Williams, *Culture and Society* (Harmondsworth, 1963), pp. 304–5.

that it was necessary to instil 'dutiful and honest principles into the common people'.[8]

However, such comments from men like L'Estrange do more than merely reinforce the impression that print culture helped to transform participatory politics during the revolutionary decades. They also make it necessary to assess whether the developments of the 1640s and 1650s made a lasting impact on political life. The final task, in other words, is to think beyond conventional periodization by considering the fate of the print revolution after 1660, and to nuance received wisdom regarding Restoration print culture. The aim, in other words, is to argue that, rather than being swept away by a tide of conservatism, many of the practices with which this book has been concerned survived, evolved and became even more significant.

ii Legacies of the print revolution

My aim in the space that remains is to challenge a fairly conventional piece of historiographical wisdom: that the return of Charles II heralded a turning back of the clock to an earlier age, through a combination of tighter press controls, overt official propaganda and the emasculation of the news industry. This story obviously contains much truth, and there is considerable evidence about the role and power of Sir Roger L'Estrange, the trials of libellers and pamphleteers, and the fact that papers like the *Gazette* were largely stripped of material relating to domestic affairs and parliamentary proceedings, at least until the lapse of licensing in 1679 and 1695. Nevertheless, by focusing on the issue of ideological consensus and division, on the 'public sphere' of commercial print, and on crowds and coffeehouses, as well as on the drama of the Popish Plot and the Exclusion Crisis, historians have unwittingly developed a misleading picture about the role of print during the Restoration. Indeed, by focusing on political participation, everyday political practices and the kinds of print genres that emerged in the preceding decades, it will be possible to emphasize that the period after 1660 witnessed both continuity and change, and both new developments as well as retrenchment, and to suggest that attempts to restrict public debate were not necessarily matched by efforts to curtail political

[8] Fuller, *Ephemeris* (1654, F2422), sig. ¶3; Spalding, *Memorialls*, i. 97; North, *Narrative* (1670, N1285), p. 29; Nalson, i. 665, ii. sig. Av, pp. 806–7, 809; *SR*, v. 308; *Borough of Leicester*, p. 488; *Ideology and Politics on the Eve of Restoration*, ed. T. Slaughter (Philadelphia, 1984), pp. 21, 56; J. Maltby, 'Petitions for episcopacy... 1641–1642', in *From Cranmer to Davidson*, ed. S. Taylor (London, 1999), p. 114; A. Marvell, *Rehearsal Transpos'd*, ed. D. Smith (Oxford, 1971), pp. 4–5; *Intelligencer*, 201.1001.

participation. What follows, in other words, represents an attempt to build on recent work that explores the impact of party upon public culture, and that identifies new developments in print culture, even if only in ways that tend to privilege public debate over discrete and practical participation. The aim, in other words, is to develop a broader perspective on the relationship between print, parliament and popular politics in the late seventeenth century.

There can be little doubt that, aside from the periods when licensing lapsed, Restoration print culture was very different from that which people experienced during the Civil Wars, and that the impact of censorship was considerable. Nevertheless, it would be a mistake to overestimate the degree to which the presses were silenced, not least because the government was determined to *police* but not *suppress* print culture, to propagandize as well as to censor, and to ensure that news was licensed and respectable rather than 'false' and 'licentious'.[9] It would also be a mistake to underestimate the possibilities for exploiting print for personal reasons and political causes, in ways that involved defending reputations and libelling public figures, and in ways that also involved the indiscriminate scattering of texts as well as the use of commercial publications. Such works continued to fascinate readers like Thomas Rugg, just as they continued to vex the authorities, whose fear of 'infamous libels' was fairly consistent for the remainder of the century. Authors continued to exploit the potential for producing scandalous texts extremely cheaply, and indeed there may have emerged something of a specialist trade in the production of more ephemeral printed texts. Pepys certainly noted that 'everybody is encouraged nowadays to speak and even print . . . as bad things . . . as ever'.[10] In addition, print may have continued to be used to organize protests, and evidence relating to riots and demonstrations by London's weavers certainly reveals the conscious connections that were made between petitioning, protesting and print, the uses of sophisticated organizational methods, and the escalation of tactics from formal and polite interventions in parliamentary processes to mass activity and violence.[11] Moreover, even tightly controlled Restoration newspapers remained an *interactive* medium that was susceptible to interventions by individuals. Indeed, the operating model of official newspapers involved

---

[9] *CSPD 1672*, p. 214.
[10] CUL, Sel.3.238/220: *Vindication of Sir Jonathan Raymond*; BL, Add. 10117, fos. 46v, 79, 82–v, 182v; CUL, Sel.3.238/252; GL, MS 11280A/2; Harris, *London Crowds*, p. 81.
[11] Harris, *London Crowds*, pp. 196, 203; Devon RO, Z19/40/6; *CSPD July–Sept. 1683*, p. 56.

systematic attempts to use local gentlemen as informers, in return for supplies of both printed and scribal news.[12]

What this attests to, in turn, is the remarkable appetite for news and pamphlets that persisted after 1660, across the country and across the social spectrum. This could be satisfied because of a permanent infrastructural change in the bookselling industry, and it generated ongoing concerns about the thirst for news among the lower orders, about the impact of such material on credulous readers, and about the threat posed by coffee-house culture.[13] Complaints about 'newsmongers', and about the 'itch of news', emerged from provincial England as well as from London, and contemporaries became acutely aware that hawkers and pedlars were responsible for distributing pamphlets, newspapers and seditious material across the country, and that regular supplies of newspapers could be purchased in most major towns.[14] Moreover, such concerns make perfect sense in the light of evidence regarding the consumption of newspapers and pamphlets. Occasionally this involves surviving pamphlet collections, such as the 1,400 pamphlets that the Verney family acquired during the late 1670s and early 1680s, or extant runs of newspapers such as the *Gazette* and the *Observator*. Indeed, while readers were clearly faced with a reduced range of newspaper titles, they nevertheless acquired them assiduously, and the *Gazette* circulated in unprecedented quantities and became highly profitable.[15] Furthermore, correspondence and financial accounts reveal a consistent demand for pamphlets and newspapers. Richard Coffin of Portledge in Devon employed a London agent, Richard Lapthorne, to deal with London booksellers and forward supplies of pamphlets, while Sir William Boothby of Ashbourne Hall in Derbyshire wrote directly to favoured booksellers in both London and Lichfield. He ordered 'all the printed pamphlets, sermons and discourses which come out', and he asked

[12] BL, Add. 78298, fo. 136; *CSPD 1671*, p. 448; *CSPD 1667–8*, p. 466; *Calendar of Wynn... Papers* (London, 1926), p. 380.

[13] Knights, *Representation*, pp. 225, 231, 250–2; I. Atherton, 'The itch grown a disease', in *News, Newspapers and Society in Early Modern Britain*, ed. J. Raymond (London, 1999), p. 56; J. Barry, 'The press and the politics of culture in Bristol, 1660–1775', in *Culture, Politics and Society in Britain* (Manchester, 1991), pp. 52, 57, 65–6; Harris, *London Crowds*, pp. 75, 93, 99, 107, 154.

[14] *CSPD 1667*, p. 415; M. Bell, 'Sturdy rogues and vagabonds', in *Mighty Engine*, ed. P. Isaac and M. McKay (Winchester, 2000), pp. 89–96; BL: Add. 71690, fos. 92–3, 108v; Add. 71691, fo. 20; Add. 71692, fos. 73v, 77, 86; FSL, L.c.1283, 1328.

[15] P. Hopkins, 'The Verney collection of popish plot pamphlets', *Bulletin of the Friends of Cambridge University Library*, 9 (1988), 5–15; Leeds UL, MS 1946/1, Box 7/4/1; CUL, Sel.3.238; *English Books of the Sixteenth and Seventeenth Centuries* (Christies, 26–27 Feb. 1969), p. 52; J. Childs, 'The sales of government Gazettes during the Exclusion Crisis', *EHR*, 102 (1987), 103–6; *HMC Ormonde New Series 3*, pp. 351–2.

to receive new supplies on a weekly basis. As with his predecessors in the 1640s, therefore, Boothby's claim to have been 'much in the dark' needs to be treated with considerable scepticism.[16] Similar strategies were also employed by John Locke and Sir John Wittewronge, both of whom were able to make informed purchases by virtue of having been supplied with the 'term catalogues', a new genre that alerted readers to recent publications. Those with more direct access to London booksellers, meanwhile, continued to record purchases of pamphlets and gazettes among incidental expenses. Such acquisitions were recorded alongside expenditure on beer and socks, tobacco and pipes, coffee and combs, and among payments for theatre-going and being touched for the king's evil, as well as with expenses for visiting the barber and the blacksmith, although in the case of the Earl of Leicester, they were also placed alongside purchases of paintings by Van Dyke and of a pet monkey. Bishop Cosin paid for newspapers on account between August and December 1665 (17s 4d), while Richard Moore had accounts with local carriers, which ensured that he received regular supplies of the *Gazette* throughout the 1660s and 1670s, at costs that rose from 8s per annum to 13s by 1679. A similar pattern is also evident higher up the social scale and across the county border in Kent. The Earl of Leicester's newspaper bills rose from 8s per year in 1677 to as much as £2 in 1679 and 1680, as he added other titles like *Mercurius Anglicus* and the *Domestick Intelligence*. Indeed, such was the penetration of newspapers during this period that, when letters were forwarded from Shillingham in Cornwall to Francis Buller in Welshpool (Powys) in October 1662, it was explained that they had been 'unburdened' of newsbooks, 'knowing you will see them in Wales before these can come by you'.[17]

Such evidence attests to a permanent shift in the appetite for and accessibility of cheap print, and evidence also suggests that members of the middling sort and lower orders were not just well informed, but also capable of reading critically and sceptically. Rugg certainly continued to be an astute observer of print culture in the 1660s. He not only commented favourably on the 'many incomparable books' by Sir Roger L'Estrange, but also noted the moment that this 'famous writer' took over the editing of newsbooks, when Henry Muddiman was 'put by as to that employment' (September 1663). He was also quick to spot the creation of the *Gazette* in

---

[16] Devon RO, Z19/40/3–6; BL, Add. 71689–92.
[17] Bodl. MS Locke b.2, fos. 35, 115–v; Herts. RO, D/Elw/F16; Antony, BA/20/12; FSL, V.a.419 (end-papers); FSL, A1792.8, fos. 2v–12v; Penshurst, MSS 344, 346; Bodl. MS MS Top.Essex.f.1, fos. 13v, 16, 21v, 28v, 29, 30, 46, 57, 65v, 67, 78, 79v; Durham Cathedral, Sharpe 163, p. 67; *Giles Moore*, pp. 306–12; Antony, BC/26/14/24.

1665.[18] News also filtered through to a humble seaman like Edward Barlow. His journal recorded thoughts on the fall of Clarendon in 1667, as well as knowledge about the Popish Plot, and it also reveals how parliamentary news reached below deck on ships as far away as the Indies. Similar material may also have made it into the hands of Roger Lowe, the village shopkeeper at Ashton-in-Makerfield (Lancashire), whose diary reveals his activity as a non-professional scrivener, his verbal re-delivery of sermons to groups of young women and his borrowing of books. It also records his frequent journeys to Warrington to buy and sell books from the shop of Mr Pickering, and his sometimes heated discussions about religion in local alehouses.[19]

With the consumption of printed news and pamphlets, therefore, it is vital to recognize the survival of practices that had developed during the revolutionary decades, and the same is also true in relation to methods for participating in parliamentary proceedings. This was partly a matter of the accessibility of Westminster Palace, and Samuel Pepys not only spent a great deal of time in the Great Hall – to hear news, buy books and meet MPs – but also frequented the lobbies and official chambers. There he delivered letters to members and waited for people 'at the Parliament door', and like other contemporaries, he was able to observe proceedings at conferences and committees, and even at debates. More than once he referred to having spent time 'up and down in the Hall and the Parliament house all the morning', and to the fact that great crowds could gather for high-profile hearings and royal speeches, and that 'many hundreds' could press into the lobbies.[20] This sense that the Palace of Westminster remained fairly accessible reflected official tolerance of the public that is perhaps surprising after the tumults of the 1640s and 1650s. However, it continued to be the case that rules were only tightened periodically in order to insure against 'disorder'; to prevent excessive crowds of 'footmen', 'lacqueys' and 'loose, idle and disorderly persons'; and to ensure that MPs could find seats in committees, as well as to preserve the secrecy of debates.[21]

---

[18] BL: Add. 10116, fos. 243, 269; Add. 10117, fos. 78v, 149.

[19] *Barlow's Journal*, ed. B. Lubbuck (2 vols, London, 1934), i. 148, ii. 318, 339, 341; *Diary of Roger Lowe*, ed. W. Sachse (London, 1938), pp. 15, 20, 25, 50–4, 66, 89, 99, 114.

[20] *Pepys Diary*, i. 4, 13, 19–20, 47, 50, 56, 58, 65, 75, 140, 225, 275, 301, ii. 4, 39, 130, 139, 170, iii. 5, 22, 33, 49, 52, 60–1, 83, 238, 253, 296, iv. 25, 111, 126, 135, 170, 207, 222, 232, 242, 303, 368, v. 139–40, 249, 338, vi. 8, 25, 39, 75, 151, 162, vii. 89, 129, 156, 186, 295, 304, 346, 359, 386, 414–15, viii. 2, 22, 34, 40, 86, 98, 151, 360, 422, 521, ix. 85, 169; *Diary of John Evelyn*, iv. 619.

[21] *Orders of the House of Commons* (London 1756), pp. 4, 6–9; *CJ*, x. 14, 15, 18–20; Petyt, *Lex* (1690, P2027aA), pp. 85, 90–91.

This openness also extended to information about parliament and its proceedings, and here, too, it is possible to observe continuity as well as retrenchment, not to mention developments that made participation even more intense. Evidence about committee membership seems to have returned to being privileged information, which could be acquired only scribally and at some cost, and debates, too, seem to have been less readily accessible, although there is a risk of exaggerating the degree of change and the extent of secrecy. It is certainly true that the only regularly available speeches were those of the monarch, the Speaker and the Lord Chancellor, although it is noteworthy that these attracted the attention of Londoners like Thomas Rugg as well as provincial newshounds like Giles Moore. And it is true that this was an area where change came only gradually, notably during periods of particular tension. Nevertheless, it also seems clear that a revived and increasingly vigorous scribal culture ensured that copies of parliamentary speeches became much more affordable.[22] The same was also true for other kinds of news – including evidence about votes – that enabled readers to follow proceedings in some detail. Here, too, there is evidence about opposition to the use of print to shed light on parliamentary business, and printing was certainly rare before the Exclusion Crisis. Nevertheless, evidence circulated fairly freely and affordably, not least in scribal newsletters, which were a great deal more affordable after 1660, which circulated widely across the country and which certainly became available in coffeehouses. The result was probably a surprisingly high level of awareness about parliamentary proceedings, something that is borne out by Rugg's 'diurnal', which frequently contained detailed notes about votes, bills, adjournments and prorogations.[23]

More importantly, it is also possible to detect a lively print culture regarding Westminster politics, which provided comment and analysis regarding membership, machinations and the performance of individual members. It remained possible to read pamphlets that explained parliamentary processes and scrutinized factionalism, and on the eve of a new session in 1669 a work called *The Alarm* was scattered in Westminster Hall to expose Lord Arlington's 'party' organization. It also remained possible to

---

[22] Bodl. MS J. Walker.c.4, fo. 298; Leeds UL, MS 1946/1, Vol. 146; DRO, D258/156/1/2; Penshurst, MS 346; BL: Add. 10116, fos. 202–3v, 204–8, 224, 226; Add. 10117, fos. 105–8, 133v, 178, 186v, 189v–91v, 207, 211, 213v, 218v; *Giles Moore*, p. 192.

[23] Leeds UL, MS 1946/1, Vol. 146; CUL, Sel.3.238; *CSPD 1667*, p. 415; *Letters... to Sir Joseph Williamson*, ed. W. Christie (Cam. Soc., 1874), pp. 164–5; Knights, *Opinion*, pp. 170–84; K. Maslen, 'The printing of the votes of the House of Commons', *The Library*, 5th series, 25 (1970), 120–35; BL, Add. 10117, *passim*.

purchase printed lists of MPs at affordable prices, many of which were scrutinized and annotated with care. Some readers noted changes in membership, while others recorded the dates of sessions and the names of clerks, and the use of dashes, manicules and codes indicates that some even analysed MPs in terms of their offices and parliamentary activity.[24] To such survivals of Civil War culture were added striking innovations, not least the fairly frequent publication of voting lists. These provided readers with evidence about the activity and opinions of individual members, and they were sometimes published alongside evidence regarding offices, salaries and pensions, as little more than blacklists and as weapons during parliamentary elections. This was apparent as early as 1677, when *A Seasonable Argument* exposed Danby's party organization and listed the 'principal labourers' in what was called 'the great design of popery and arbitrary power', as well as those who favoured maintaining a standing army. The upshot, however, was a detailed guide to the composition of parliament by county and constituency, complete with evidence about each MP's offices, pensions and personal connections. To such survivals and innovations, moreover, were added refinements of certain genres that had been introduced in the 1640s and 1650s. The calling of a new parliament in 1679, therefore, led to increasingly sophisticated electioneering. Voters were encouraged to 'choose your side', and the printed sheets that were posted and circulated sometimes supplemented general advice with rich evidence, with which to 'blacken and defame' specific candidates. What this amounts to is evidence that certain aspects of parliamentary print culture became a permanent fixture of political culture.[25] But it also indicates the persistence of debates regarding the nature of representation and accountability. This led to deliberations over the wisdom of publishing votes and debates and the benefits of introducing 'place bills', and the publication of pamphlets about political corruption, as well as the tendency to present MPs with 'instructions'. It also revealed competing visions regarding the role and duties of representatives, the desirability of keeping constituents informed about parliamentary performance and the feasibility of creating mechanisms whereby wrongdoing could be exposed and poor performance punished.

---

[24] *Letter* (1675, S2896); *CSPD 1668–9*, pp. 541–2; Leeds UL, MS 1946/1, Vol 146; CUL, Sel.3.238/223, 397; Penshurst, MS 346; BL, 1607/519: *Names of the Knights* (1661), pp. 10, 12; BL, 13/1(1): *Catalogue* (1665); BL, 13/1(2): *Exact* (1664/5).

[25] *Cobbett*, iv. appendix, cols. xxii–xxxiv ; BL, 1865.c.16; *CSPD 1680–1*,p. 675; Leeds UL, MS 1946/1, Vols. 143, 146; BL, Harl. 7020, fos. 33–48; HEH, STT Elections, Folders 6, 8; BL, Add. 70035, fo. 326; Add. 70012, fos. 312–13v; Stowe 180, fos. 96, 98–9; WYAS (Leeds), WYL150/5775; CUL, Sel.3.238/ 211–14, 218, 219, 222; Bodl. Wood 423/67; Knights, *Representation*, pp. 256–61; Knights, *Opinion*, pp. 208–11, 282–3; Harris, *London Crowds*, pp. 106–29, 153–5.

The result, indeed, was that during the final decades of the century it became *more* rather than *less* likely that MPs would be judged on their performance at the polls.[26]

Thus far, Restoration print culture has been shown to have involved innovations that were reversed, tendencies that survived and practices that were enhanced, but it is also possible to highlight certain ways in which the participatory culture of petitioning and lobbying became significantly *more intense* after 1660. This has largely been overlooked because of a preoccupation with public opinion, public debate and the public sphere, and because of a failure to recognize that printed texts were not always commercially available. With petitioning, for example, attention has focused rather understandably on 'monster' petitions, which resurfaced during the exclusion crisis, which attracted considerable popular support and which were sometimes organized through the deployment of printed texts. Such texts, many of which were published, have also been used to indicate the growing importance of public opinion, to signal a shift to less supplicatory 'addresses', and to highlight official nervousness about petitioning, protesting and street politics.[27] However, evidence from MPs' private papers also indicates that print played a highly significant role in more mundane petitioning, by mercantile interest groups as well as humble individuals and poor prisoners. Indeed, the printing of texts for discrete circulation at Westminster was undertaken on an unprecedented scale, and on matters as arcane as the repair of the road between Dunstable and Coventry or the licensing of alehouses. Indeed, while some MPs tried to ban the submission of printed petitions at the doors of either House in 1667, their proposal was voted down by MPs.[28]

These neglected texts are important for a number of reasons. They indicate that below the level of constitutional politics, the patterns and practices of daily political life went on largely uninterrupted. They provide a reminder that printed petitioning represented an escalatory step that could

---

[26] Hayton, *Commons*, iii. 1058, 1066; M. Knights, 'Parliament, print and corruption in later Stuart Britain', in *The Print Culture of Parliament, 1600–1800*, ed. J. Peacey (Edinburgh, 2007), pp. 49–61; Knights, *Representation*, pp. 131–2; D. Hayton, 'The country interest and the party system, c.1689–1720', in *Party and Party Management in Parliament, 1660–1784*, ed. C. Jones (Leicester, 1984), pp. 37–85; Knights, *Opinion*, pp. 179–80, 291–303; J. Miller, 'Representatives and represented in England', *PER*, 15 (1995), 125–32.

[27] Knights, *Opinion*, ch. 8; M. Knights, 'London petitions and parliamentary politics in 1679', *PH*, 12 (1993), 29–46; M. Knights, 'London's 'monster' petition of 1680', *HJ*, 36 (1993), 39–68; Knights, *Representation*, ch. 3; R. North, *Examen* (1740), pp. 542–3; *Life and Errors of John Dunton* (1705), 49–50; *SR*, v. 308.

[28] Leeds UL, MS 1946/1, Box 15/1, 5; CKS: U1015/O7/6–14; U1015/O39–41; DRO, D258/15/1/2; BL, 816. m.14/34; *CJ*, ix. 29; *Diary of John Milward*, ed. C. Robbins (Cambridge, 1938), p. 152.

heighten tension and provoke counter-petitioning in print. And they confirm that petitioning was intimately connected with other participatory practices like lobbying. In any number of cases, therefore, post-Restoration petitioners and lobbyists used print to re-apply tactics that had been developed and deployed in the 1640s and 1650s. These included Derbyshire miners, those involved in fen drainage disputes and rival groups of textile workers, some of whose interventions in the legislative process proved to be highly successful.[29] And they also included a sequestered royalist like Sir John Stawell. Here a campaign to overturn the sale of a personal estate that had begun in the early 1650s – with texts delivered to MPs 'at the Parliament door', as well as counter-lobbying that spiralled into published pamphlets – continued into the late 1650s and early 1660s, as Stawell reminded MPs about his troubles and expected a more favourable hearing.[30] Similar stories could be told about other seasoned petitioners and lobbyists, like Thomas Bushell, Henry Robinson and Thomas Violet. More importantly, however, archival evidence also indicates that such lobbying was in no way limited to cases involving personalities and issues that spilled over from the 1650s. Indeed, the use of print to petition and lobby became something that was adopted systematically, and by people from all walks of life and all parts of the country, rather than merely by groups like the East India Company. Lobbying, in other words, remained an everyday phenomenon, and one that has largely been neglected, with the result that scholars have singularly failed to appreciate how extensively print was used to influence decision-making, and how widely its utility was recognized.[31]

Here the problem is probably two-fold. In part, therefore, scholarship may have been hampered by conventional periodization, and historians who work exclusively with late seventeenth-century archives – which are

---

[29] BL, Add. 6677, fo. 103; Lincs. RO, MON7/17/31, 45, 51, 68, 74, 77; *Answer* (1690, A3402); *Case* (1690?, C1045); *Epworth* (1695?, C1113); Worcester College, AA.s.4/7: *Vindication*, p. 1; BL, 816.m.14/95: *Worsted Weavers*; *Reasons* (1663, R557bA); R. Dunn, 'The London weavers' riot', *Guildhall Studies in London History*, 1 (1973), p. 15.

[30] *Humble Petition* (1653, S5349); *Humble Remonstrance* (1653, S5351); *Diurnall*: 503 257, pp. 3945–6; 503.258, p. 3950; *Politicus*, 361.231, pp. 4013–4; *Reasons* (1654, R495); DRO, D258/53/42: *William Lawrence* (1654, L692), pp. 19–26; *Stawell* (1654, S5350); BL, RB.23.b.5145(1): *Sir John Stawell* (1654); *Answer* (1654, A3300); *Vindication* (1655, S5352); *Humble* (1659, S5350b); *Petition* (1659, S5350c); Worcester College, G.5.10/85: *Humble Petition* (1660); *Reasons* (1660, S5348b); Worcester College, CHF 1.5/16c: *Provided* (1660).

[31] *Bushell* (1660, B6243); BL, C.27.f.1/8: *Particular* (1660); BL: Add. 70035, fos. 26, 28–v, 30; Add. 70052, unfol.; Bodl. MS Tanner 91, fos. 182–v; *CSPD 1665–6*, p. 161; Robinson, *Case* (1663, R1666A); BL, Harl. 6034; Violet, *Appeal* (1660, V580); Violet, *Lords* (1660, V588A); Violet, *Case* (1662, C1190dA); *Petitions* (1661, V594A); Violet, *Petition* (1661, V584); *CSPD 1661–2*, p. 254; Violet, *King's* (1662, V586); A. Sherman, 'Pressure from Leadenhall', *Business History Review*, 50 (1976), 329–53.

awash with printed petitions and lobby documents – may have little sense
that they are observing genres that were unprecedentedly popular. They
may thus have taken such material for granted, and concluded that it was so
commonplace as not to warrant close scrutiny. For example, even the papers
of an obscure and fairly insignificant MP like Sir Michael Wentworth
contain dozens of texts that involved lobbying and counter-lobbying, on
all manner of topics relating to politics, religion and commerce, and that
offered reasons both for and against proposed bills.[32] In addition, however,
historians of the later Stuart age may also have suffered from a more general
tendency to assume that printed texts were generally intended for public
consumption, rather than for non-commercial and selective distribution
among MPs and officials. This would certainly be to misconstrue dozens of
printed texts that contained a *Case* or *Reasons* relating to disputed parliamentary elections, that were produced by defeated candidates, local constituents and those who claimed to have been 'duly returned', and that have
been noted as evidence of 'public' debate and discourse. And it would also
be to misrepresent the true nature of any number of other texts that were
sent to MPs, or indeed thrust into their hands, and then annotated and
preserved ahead of forthcoming debates and committee meetings, to which
they sometimes drew explicit attention. As in earlier periods, such uses of
print sometimes led to public debates, but they tended to begin in a more
discrete fashion, not least as parliamentary business dragged on, as opponents emerged and as frustrations grew.[33] Indeed, the prevalence of such
material quickly made it necessary to tweak the format, by adding printed
endorsements that enabled individual items to be filed and retrieved efficiently, and contemporary acceptance of such tactics eventually led to the
decision, in 1705, to *require* all breviates relating to private bills to be
submitted in a printed format.[34]

What seems clear, therefore, is not just that there is scope for rethinking
the print culture of Restoration England, but also that by doing so, new
light is shed on the revolutionary era. In other words, by shifting attention
away from commercial print and public discourse after 1660, and by
focusing instead on the participatory practices of daily political life, it
becomes clear that the return of Charles II did not represent a watershed
in English political culture. Whether in terms of the consumption of news

[32] Leeds UL, 1946/1, Box 15 and Vol. 146; Longleat, Thynne 62, fos. 16, 18; Thynne 33/167–8; HEH, EL
7970; BL, Add. 69956, fos. 83–93, 98–109.
[33] Leeds UL, 1946/1, Box 15 and Vol. 146; CKS, U1015/O23/26; TNA, SP 32/13, fo. 130; Knights,
'Corruption', pp. 49–61.
[34] *Liverpool Tractate*, ed. C. Strateman (New York, 1937), pp. 23–4; Knights, 'Corruption', p. 51.

and comment, the accessibility and transparency of the Westminster system, or the development of petitioning and lobbying, it seems clear that many of the experiments and improvizations of the mid seventeenth century became settled and standard practices thereafter, and even more important features of the parliamentary and public scene. Far from turning back the political clock, in other words, the Restoration regime sought to formalize the boundaries of acceptable participatory practice. In doing so it was continuing a process that had been ongoing since the mid 1640s, and more obviously since 1649, and it actually ensured that print culture became more fully embedded within political and parliamentary life, in ways that only a handful of historians of the eighteenth century have fully acknowledged.[35] As such, it can be suggested that, at the level of daily political life, the Civil Wars and Interregnum generated not merely short-lived experimentation but also permanent change. Indeed, it is even plausible to argue that, in combination with debates about the proper role of the press and print, about the legitimate role of popular politics, and about the relationships between MPs and the public, developments in everyday participatory practices represented one of the most powerful legacies of the English Revolution.

[35] J. Brewer, *Party Ideology and Popular Politics at the Accession of George III* (Cambridge, 1976); H. Dickinson, *The Politics of the People in Eighteenth Century Britain* (Basingstoke, 1995).

Manuscript sources

Aberdeen University Library

MS 2538 James Fraser travel diary

All Souls, Oxford

MS 167   State papers
MS 181   State papers

Alnwick Castle, Northumberland

Letters and Papers 18 Northumberland Papers, 1657–63
MS 548–52   John Fitzjames letterbooks
O.I.2f   Hugh Potter letterbook, 1644–6
U.I.6   Northumberland Accounts, 1641–9

Anthony House, Cornwall

Carew-Pole papers
Buller papers

Arundel Castle, Sussex

Howard papers

Badminton House, Gloucestershire

Sir Thomas Roe papers

Bedfordshire Record Office

St John of Bletso papers
Trevor-Wingfield papers
Bagshaw collection
Orlebar papers

Beinecke Library, Yale University

Osborn papers
Boswell papers
Edward S. Harkness pamphlets

Belvoir Castle, Leicestershire

Tollemache papers

Berkshire Record office

Lenthall papers
Reading borough

Berwick Record Office

Berwick borough

Bethlem Royal Hospital

Court Books

Birmingham City Archives

Knight papers
Fetherston correspondence

Bodleian Library, Oxford

MS Add.C.132   Parliamentary proceedings
MS Bankes   Bankes papers
MS Carte   Carte papers
MS Clarendon   Clarendon papers

MS Eng.Lett.b.1	Symon Archer papers
MS Eng.Lett.c.210	John Palmer correspondence
MS Eng.Hist.e.184	Gerbier papers
MS Eng.Hist.e.308	Roger Whitley papers
MS Eng.Misc.c.338	William Freke accounts
MS Eng.Misc.e.6	John Smyth of Nibley accounts
MS Eng.Misc.e.118	George Starkey diary
MS Eng.Misc.e.479	Henry Townshend papers
MS Locke b.2	Locke papers
MS Nalson	Lenthall papers
MS North.c.4	North papers
MS Rawl.A	Thurloe papers
MS Rawl.D.141	'England's Memorable Accidents'
MS Selden Supra 108	John Selden papers
MS Tanner	Tanner papers
MS Top.Essex.f.1	Personal account book
MS Top.Oxon.c.154	Oxford stationers
MS Top.Oxon.c.378	Thomas Wyatt diary
MS Walker.c.4	Royalist ministers
MS Wood 423	Anthony Wood papers

Bristol Record Office

Bristol borough

British Library

Add. 4106	Birch papers
Add. 4149	Ralph Starkey papers
Add. 4155–9	Thurloe papers
Add. 4165	Charles Fleetwood papers
Add. 4180	Sir Edward Nicholas papers
Add. 4191	Naval papers
Add. 4232	Thoresby papers
Add. 4377	Thomas Dalgarno papers
Add. 4460	Thoresby papers
Add. 4476	Birch papers
Add. 5494	Sequestration papers
Add. 5497	Ordinances, 1642–9
Add. 5756	Parliamentary papers

Add. 6521	'Diurnall occurrences'
Add. 6677, 6682	Derbyshire collections
Add. 8128	Sir Thomas Cotton accounts
Add. 9327	John Branthwaite papers
Add. 10116–7	Thomas Rugg diurnall
Add. 11043–5, 11047	Scudamore papers
Add. 15750, 15858	Sir Richard Browne papers
Add. 15903	Norwich borough papers
Add. 18778	Walter Yonge diary
Add. 18979	Fairfax papers
Add. 18982	Rupert correspondence
Add. 19399	Dawson Turner papers
Add. 19863	Payne Fisher papers
Add. 20065	Whitehall sermons, 1631–53
Add. 21066	Miscellaneous letters
Add. 21417–27	Adam Baynes papers
Add. 21935	Nehemiah Wallington papers
Add. 22466	Sir Edward Dering papers
Add. 22591	Miscellaneous tracts
Add. 22619–20	Norwich borough papers
Add. 22916	Sir Simonds D'Ewes papers
Add. 22919	Sir George Downing papers
Add. 23146	Thomas Dugard diary
Add. 24667	'The Scoute Generall'
Add. 24861	Richard Maijor papers
Add. 24863	Miscellaneous papers
Add. 26785	Sir Edward Dering papers
Add. 27395	Gawdy papers
Add. 27411	Calverley papers
Add. 28000–2, 28004, 28011	Oxinden papers
Add. 28191	Royalist inventories
Add. 28640	John Rous papers
Add. 28716	Committee of Privileges
Add. 28930	Ellis family papers
Add. 29623–4	Dover borough papers
Add. 31116	Lawrence Whitaker diary
Add. 31954	Sir Edward Nicholas papers
Add. 32093	Malet papers
Add. 32471	Revenue papers

Add. 32477	Jeremiah Baines papers
Add. 33058, 33145, 33148	Pelham papers
Add. 33374	John Jones papers
Add. 33936	Moreton papers
Add. 34161, 34169–72	Twysden papers
Add. 35297	John Syms journal
Add. 35331	Walter Yonge diary
Add. 37343	Bulstrode Whitelocke annals
Add. 37719	Sir John Gibson papers
Add. 38139	Sir Peter Manwood papers
Add. 38847, 38855	Hodgkin papers
Add. 39922	Miscellaneous papers
Add. 40883	Nehemiah Wallington diary
Add. 41202A	Sir Edward Nicholas papers
Add. 41844A	Middleton papers
Add. 42063	Clanricarde memoirs
Add. 43377	Miscellaneous papers
Add. 43724	Henry Cromwell correspondence
Add. 44846	Sir Thomas Peyton letterbook
Add. 44848	Capel-Cure papers
Add. 46189	William Jessop papers
Add. 46376A	John Harington papers
Add. 46500	Roger Hill letters
Add. 46931B	Egmont papers
Add. 47787	Dering papers
Add. 50200	John Boys papers
Add. 57929	Scottish commissioners papers
Add. 59785	Hammond papers
Add. 61481	Blenheim papers
Add. 62083	Pythouse papers
Add. 63465	Wentworth papers
Add. 64921–3, 69871, 69880, 69885, 69917, 69919, 69222–3, 69956	Coke papers
Add. 70002–7, 70012, 70035, 70052, 70058, 70066–8, 70081–2, 70087, 70091, 70105–13, 70122–3	Harley papers

Add. 70887	Dering papers
Add. 71448	Chaloner papers
Add. 71534	Marten papers
Add. 71689–92	Boothby papers
Add. 72275–6	John Castle letters
Add. 72439	Trumbull papers
Add. 72877	Petty papers
Add. 78191, 78193–8, 78220–3, 78225, 78231, 78233, 78258–60, 78262, 78298, 78303, 78315–6	Evelyn papers
Cotton Charter xvi.13	Sir Simonds D'Ewes accounts
Eg. 1048	Parliamentary papers
Eg. 1533	Silus Titus papers
Eg. 2096	Dover borough papers
Eg. 2194	Extracts from newspapers and pamphlets
Eg. 2534–6, 2542	Sir Edward Nicholas papers
Eg. 2618	William Clarke papers
Eg. 2646, 2648, 2651	Barrington papers
Eg. 2654	'A true relation' (1642)
Eg. 2715–6	Gawdy papers
Eg. 2983–4	Heath-Verney papers
Harl. 158, 160–66, 287, 374, 378–9, 382–3, 385	Sir Simonds D'Ewes papers
Harl. 389–90	Mead-Stuteville papers
Harl. 454	Sir Humphrey Mildmay diary
Harl. 478	John Moore diary
Harl. 813	Miscellaneous papers
Harl. 980	Gibbons collection
Harl. 1929	Cheshire papers
Harl. 2111, 2125, 2127	Randle Holme papers
Harl. 2135	Chester collections
Harl. 4262	'Diurnall Occurrences'
Harl. 4394, 4618	Catalogues of books
Harl. 4638	Library catalogue
Harl. 4712	Le Neve papers
Harl. 4931	Ussher papers
Harl. 6034	Thomas Violet papers
Harl. 6424	Bishop Warner papers

Harl. 6806, 6810	Parliamentary proceedings
Harl. 6865	Wanley papers
Harl. 7000	State papers
Harl. 7020	Miscellaneous political lists
Harl. 7607–8, 7614, 7617	Miscellaneous parliamentary papers
Harl. 7660	Sir Simonds D'Ewes papers
Lans. 213	Miscellaneous papers
Lans. 823	Henry Cromwell papers
Lans. 1232	Parliamentary speeches
RP 678	Ridout commonplace book
Sloane 203	Dr John Downes papers
Sloane 555	Prince Rupert's library
Sloane 771	Richard Smith library
Sloane 1346	Henry Power library
Sloane 1457	Nehemiah Wallington papers
Sloane 1467	Speeches and petitions
Sloane 1780	Library catalogue
Sloane 1983B	Miscellaneous papers
Sloane 3317	Parliamentary proceedings
Stowe 142, 180	Miscellaneous papers
Stowe 184–5	Sir Edward Dering papers
Stowe 189	Essex papers
Stowe 354	Parliamentary speeches
Stowe 743–4	Sir Edward Dering papers
E.362/2	George Wither, 'Humble Memorandum'
E.384/12	'Fellow apprentices' (1647)
E.390/14	'An unanimous answer' (1647)
E.392/7	'For the renowned apprentices' (1647)

Brotherton Library, Leeds University

Marten-Loder papers
Wentworth of Woolley Hall papers

Brymor Jones Library, University of Hull

Hotham papers

Buckinghamshire Record Office

Henry Croke papers
Hill papers
Way papers

Cambridge University Library

Add. 89   Parliamentary proceedings
Dd.viii.33   William Collins accounts
Dd.xi.73   William Whiteway papers
Buxton papers
Pell papers

Cambridgeshire Record Office

Bedford level papers

Canterbury Cathedral Archives

Canterbury borough
Elham Parish Records
Hale papers
Gardner papers

Centre for Kentish Studies, Maidstone

Boys papers
Cranfield papers
Dering papers
Faversham borough
Knatchbull papers
Maidstone borough
Oxinden papers
Papillon papers
Sackville papers
Sidney papers
Thanet papers
Twysden papers

Chatsworth House, Derbyshire

Bolton Abbey papers

Chequers, Buckinghamshire

MS 782   Army accounts, 1647–52

Chester Record Office

Chester borough
Cowper papers
Crewe papers
Wills and inventories

Chetham Library, Manchester

Ralph Assheton letters
Townley family library catalogue

Claydon House, Buckinghamshire

Verney papers

Cornwall Record Office

Bodmin borough
Carlyon of Tregrehan papers
Launceston borough
Liskeard borough
Miscellaneous Papers
Rashleigh papers
Rogers of Penrose papers
St Ives borough
Tremayne of St Ewe papers
Vyvyan papers

Corporation of London Record Office

City Cash Accounts
Journals of the Common Council
Repertories of the Court of Aldermen

Coventry History Centre

Coventry borough

Cumbria Record Office (Carlisle)

Bishop of Carlisle's registers
Carlisle borough
Lowther papers
Musgrave papers

Cumbria Record Office (Kendal)

Fleming papers

Derbyshire Record Office

Chandos Pole papers
Gell papers
Sanders papers

Devon Record Office

73/15   James and Bartholomew White chronicle
1148M Add/18/3   Hampton and Claverton petition, 1650

Drake of Colyton papers
Exeter borough
John Hayne accounts
Seymour of Berry Pomeroy papers
Tremayne papers

Dorset Record Office

Dorchester borough

Durham Cathedral Library

Hunter papers
Sharpe papers

Durham University Library

Cosin papers
Lawrence Womock letterbook
Mickelton-Spearman manuscripts
Wills and Inventories

East Kent Record Office, Dover

Cinque Ports brotherhood
Dover borough
Hythe borough
New Romney borough
Sandwich borough

East Sussex Record Office, Lewes

Frewen papers

Essex Record Office, Chelmsford

Barrington papers
Quarter sessions papers
D/DQs18   John Clopton diary
D/DRg3/4   Sir Simonds D'Ewes commonplace book

Flintshire Record Office

D/DE271   David Pennant notebook

Folger Shakespeare Library, Washington DC

Bacon-Townshend papers	
Newdigate newsletters	
150–373q	Newsbooks
222477q	Annotated almanack
A1792.8	Annotated almanack
Add. 959	Edmund Watson papers
Add. 984	Book catalogue
Add.1086	Sir James Hope petition
Add.662, 666	Robert Bennet papers
E.a.6	Commonplace book
F.c.7	Booth papers
G.b.2	Miscellaneous papers
G.b.6	Twysden papers
L.b.685	More papers
V.a.192	Parliamentary speeches
V.a.262	Commonplace book
V.a.275	George Turner papers
V.a.419	Annotated almanac
V.a.436	Nehemiah Wallington papers
V.a.454	John Martin letterbook
V.a.95	Christopher Parkes papers
V.b.161	Townshend family accounts
V.b.297	Sir Edward Dering papers
V.b.303	Political papers
W.b.600	Sir Humphrey Mildmay diary
X.c.23	Sir Gyles Mompesson letter
X.d.441	Henry Booth letters
X.d.443	Committee for Plundered Ministers
X.d.483	Robert Bennet papers
X.d.95	Books and stationery supplied to Prince of Wales, 1641

Gloucestershire Record Office

Crewe papers
Nathaniel Clutterbuck papers
Sherborne papers
Smyth of Nibley papers

Goldsmiths Company, London

Court Books

Greater Manchester Record Office

Legh of Lyme papers

Guildhall Library, London

MS 204	Nehemiah Wallington notebook
MS 11571	Grocers' Company
MS 12065	Armourers and Brasiers' Company
MS 16988	Ironmongers' Company
MS 2150	Poulters' Company
MS 2883	Blacksmiths' Company
MS 30032	Trinity House
MS 3054	Tylers and Bricklayers' Company
MSS 4326–9	Carpenters' Company
MS 4597	Shipwrights' Company
MS 5198	Brown Bakers' Company
MS 5303	Masons' Company
MS 5606	Coopers' Company
MS 6122	Plaisterers' Company
MS 6440	Butchers' Company
MSS 7396, 7428	Dutch Congregation
MSS 7911–52	New England Company

Hampshire Record Office

Winchester borough

Hatfield House, Hertfordshire

Earl of Salisbury bills

Henry E. Huntington Library, San Marino, California

Ellesmere papers
Hastings papers

Huntington Manuscripts
Stowe papers

Hertfordshire Record Office

Cowper papers
Grimston papers
Quarter sessions papers
Wittewronge papers

Houghton Library, Harvard University

Sir Henry Belasyse papers

Isle of Wight Record office

Oglander papers

John Rylands Library, Manchester

Legh of Lyme papers
Nicholas papers

King's Lynn Record office

King's Lynn borough

Lambeth Palace Library

Bramston papers
Gibson papers
Laud papers
Twysden papers

Lancashire Record Office

Bradshaw letters
Farington papers
Fazakerly papers
Jessop papers

Parker of Browsholme papers
Sir Gilbert Hoghton papers
Wills and inventories

Leicestershire Record Office

Bramston parish constables accounts
Finch papers
Hesilrige papers
Waltham on the Wolds parish constables accounts
Wills and inventories

Lincolnshire Record Office

Ancaster papers
Brownlow papers
Hatcher family accounts
Hill papers
Lincoln borough
Massingbeard-Mundy papers
Monson papers
Sir John Archer diary
Wills and inventories

Liverpool Record Office

Moore of Bankhall papers

Liverpool University Library

Moore of Bankhall papers

London Metropolitan Archives

Middlesex sessions papers

Longleat House

Portland papers
Thynne papers
Whitelocke papers

National Archives of Scotland

PA15/2   Evan Tyler accounts

National Library of Scotland

Adv.33.1.1/13   Denmilne papers
MS 20774   Fleming of Wigtown papers
MS 1656/3   Solemn League and Covenant (1648, S4451)
MS 2687–8   Parliamentary proceedings

Wodrow papers

National Library of Wales

11440D   John Jones letterbook

Wynn papers

Norfolk Record Office

Jerningham papers
Knyvett papers
L'Estrange papers
Norwich borough
Wodehouse papers
Yarmouth borough

Northamptonshire Record Office

Finch-Hatton papers
Isham papers
Papillon papers

Nottingham University Library

Clifton papers
Garway papers
Holles papers
Portland papers

Nottinghamshire Record Office

Hutchinson papers
Savile of Rufford papers
Thorpe parish accounts
Upton parish accounts
Wills and inventories

Oxford University Archives

NEP/supra/Reg.S-T	Convocation registers
SP/E/1	Miscellaneous papers
SEP.P.17b	Printing accounts
Wbα/10/11	Gerard Langbaine expenses, 1649
WPβ/21/4	Vice Chancellor's Accounts
WPγ/28/8	Miscellaneous papers

Parliamentary Archives, Westminster

Braye MSS
Main Papers

Penshurst

Sidney papers

Plymouth Record Office

Plymouth borough

Senate House Library, London

MS 26	Sir Thomas Reade papers
MS 201	Samuel Lambe, 'Seasonable Observations'

Shakespeare Birthplace Trust, Stratford-upon-Avon

Heath papers

Sheffield University Library

Hartlib Papers

Shropshire Record Office

Bridgewater papers
Ludlow borough

Somerset Record Office

Carew papers
Hippisley papers
Mildmay papers
Phelips papers

Staffordshire Record Office

Dyott papers
Langley papers
Legge papers
Leveson papers
Persehouse papers

Stationers Company, London

Court Book C
Liber A

Surrey History Centre, Woking

Guildford borough
Nicholas Papers

Tatton Park, Knutsford, Cheshire

MS 68.20   Nehemiah Wallington notebook

The National Archives, Kew

AO 3	Audit Office accounts
C115/N3	Scudamore papers
CHES	Palatinate of Chester Court papers
E 101	King's Remembrancer Accounts
PC 2	Privy Council registers
PRO 31/17/33	Council of State order book, 1658–9
PROB 11	Prerogative Court of Canterbury Wills
SO 3	Signet Office Docquet books
SP 14	State Papers Domestic, James I
SP 16	State Papers Domestic, Charles I
SP 18	State Papers Domestic, Interregnum
SP 19	Committee for the Advance of Money
SP 20	Sequestration Committee
SP 21	Committee of Both Kingdoms
SP 23	Committee for Compounding
SP 24	Committee for Indemnity
SP 28	Committee of Accounts
SP 32	State Papers Domestic, William and Mary
SP 46	State Papers Domestic: Supplementary
SP 77	State Papers Foreign: Flanders
SP 105	Levant Company

Trinity College Dublin

MS 805   Samuel Winter notebook

Tyne and Wear Archive Service

Newcastle borough

University College London

Ogden papers

University College Oxford

MS 83   Political commonplace book

Warwickshire Record Office

Feilding papers
Newdigate papers
Warwick Castle papers

West Yorkshire Archive Service (Leeds)

Ingilby papers
Vyner papers

William Salt Library, Stafford

Swinfen papers

Wiltshire Record Office

MS 2057   Civil War pamphlets

Devizes borough
New Sarum borough
Quarter sessions papers

Worcester College Oxford

Clarke papers

Worcestershire Record Office

Salwarpe parish records
Henry Townshend papers
Vernon papers
Worcester borough

Index

434

Lightning Source UK Ltd.
Milton Keynes UK
UKOW04n1811280914

239326UK00003B/26/P